Michèle Fitoussi was born in Tunisia to French parents, and has lived in Paris since the age of five. She has worked for the past twenty-five years at *Elle* magazine and has interviewed many influential decision makers and world leaders in areas as varied as politics, human sciences, sport, literature and the media.

Kate Bignold read French and German at Manchester University. She began her career in the art and design world before becoming a French to English translator in 2000. She lives in southwest England with her two children.

Lakshmi Ramakrishnan Iyer has been a translator from French and Italian into English since 2004, following a ten-year career in journalism, publishing and public relations in India and Italy. She lives in southwest France.

HELENA
RUBINSTEIN

THE WOMAN WHO INVENTED BEAUTY

Michèle Fitoussi

HELENA
RUBINSTEIN

THE WOMAN WHO INVENTED BEAUTY

Michèle Fitoussi

Translated from the French by Kate Bignold
and Lakshmi Ramakrishnan Iyer

Gallic Books
London

A Gallic Book

First published in France as *Helena Rubinstein: La femme qui inventa la beauté* by
Bernard Grasset, Paris, 2010

Translated by Kate Bignold and Lakshmi Ramakrishnan Iyer

All internal photographs: Archives Helena Rubinstein

First published in Great Britain in 2013 by Gallic Books,
59 Ebury Street, London, SW1W 0NZ

A CIP record for this book is available from the British Library
ISBN 978-1-908313-46-1

Typeset in Fournier MT Std by Gallic Books
Printed in the UK by CPI (UK) Ltd, Croydon, CR0 4YY

2 4 6 8 10 9 7 5 3 1

CONTENTS

PREFACE

'My life seems to have contained enough events, great and small, enough stress and strain to fill a half-dozen normal lives.'

Helena Rubinstein

People often ask me why I became interested in Helena Rubinstein. There is something mysterious about first encounters. So while we can never say exactly how things happen – most of the time, it is a question of chance – we do know the ways in which a person's story has marked us.

In this case, I knew nothing about her other than her name on beauty products that I didn't use, but the opening lines of her life story were enough: she was born in 1872 in Kazimierz, the Jewish quarter of Kraków; she had seven younger sisters – Pauline, Rosa, Regina, Stella, Ceska, Manka and Erna; and at the age of twenty-four she set off on a journey to Australia, armed with a parasol, twelve jars of cream, and an inexhaustible supply of *chutzpah*.

My imagination immediately began to run away with me. I saw her taking the train, her forehead pressed thoughtfully against the window, reciting her sisters' names like a mantra. I saw her four-foot-ten frame walking up the gangplank to board the ship that would sail halfway round the globe, taking two months to reach Australia. I saw this tiny pioneer disembarking in Melbourne, in this foreign land; I saw how she struggled, how she nearly gave up, then triumphed.

Even though I didn't know a great deal about her, Helena Rubinstein became for me a romantic heroine, a sort of Polish Scarlett O'Hara, a conqueror with a character forged of steel. As she stood there in her high heels, her motto – for she was someone who despised the past – could have been 'Onwards!' As the saying goes, 'Give a girl the right shoes, and she can conquer the world.'

A quick look at her tumultuous life confirmed my suspicions. She was little known and has been virtually forgotten, but her extraordinary life spanned nearly a century (she died in 1965 at the age of ninety-three) and four continents.

Driven by courage, intelligence and a will to succeed that would make her neglect her husbands, children and family, she built an empire that was both industrial and financial. More impressive still, she as good as invented modern cosmetics and ways to make them accessible to all. This was no easy task for a woman in those days – and it still isn't, whatever one might think; a woman who was poor, foreign and Jewish, to boot. But she loftily disregarded all four of these disadvantages – and it's anyone's guess which one was the greatest – and often turned them into strengths. She opened her first beauty institute in Melbourne in 1902, the same year Australian women were among the first in the world to obtain the right to vote. Helena would always be a firm supporter of women in their movement for equality, which throughout the twentieth century, meant not only fighting for their most basic rights, but also for the liberation of their bodies – first by freeing them from the shackles of the corset, then from the taboo of wearing make-up (until the early 1920s cosmetics were only worn by prostitutes and actresses).

As Helena would like to say, beauty is anything but frivolous. For her it was a 'new power', a means through which women could assert their independence. To want to charm or look your best are not signs of subservience if you know how to use them to your advantage. Helena believed that women must use the assets placed at their disposal if they are to conquer the world, or at least to make their place in it.

Cosmetics existed before Helena Rubinstein – they have existed since antiquity! – but she was the visionary who created modern beauty: scientific, rigorous and demanding, with an emphasis on moisturising, protecting against the harmful rays of the sun, massage, electricity, hydrotherapy, hygiene, diet, nutrition, physical exercise and surgery.

Her passion for art and aesthetics of every kind – painting, sculpture, architecture, furniture, decoration, haute couture, jewellery – drove her to become an obsessive collector (she was nicknamed 'a female Hearst') and inspired the colours of her make-up collections.

It was her innate sense of marketing that led her not only to promote her products successfully, but also to constantly invent sales techniques at her salons and retail outlets, to set professional standards for beauticians, and to use advertising as early as 1904.

She worked tirelessly and claimed that work was the best beauty treatment: 'Work has been indeed my best beauty treatment. I believe in hard work. It keeps the wrinkles out of the mind and the spirit. It helps to keep a woman young.'[2] She amassed a fortune almost single-handedly. She was known to be one of the richest women in the world: only a handful of peers had succeeded as well as her in the domain of beauty and fashion. Coco Chanel, Elizabeth Arden, and Estée Lauder were the few women who shared Helena Rubinstein's gift for putting themselves on stage and promoting their image.

She started out as Helena (or 'He-LAY-na', as she would pronounce it in America with her Yiddish-tinged Polish accent) then, as she became more successful, she would be known as Madame. That was what everyone called her, even members of her own family. Indeed, inside her there were two people: Helena the rebel, adventurer, lover; and Madame the businesswoman, billionaire and princess late in life.

My preference lies towards the younger woman, with her rebellious, reckless streak; but the older one continues to fascinate me. The portraits of her at this time tell us a great deal about her. Despite her expensive clothes and jewellery and lavish surroundings, she has the face of a Jewish grandmother, hard and frail at the same time. And that is what she was despite appearances, that is who she had never stopped being: the 'little lady from Kraków'[3] who all her life had struggled to master the proper etiquette.

During the long months I spent in the company of this visionary woman, I learned something new every day about her anticipation of trends and fashions, her gift for coming up with new ideas, her incredible ability to live through different eras, countries, wars, fashions, mores, always in the thick of things: the emancipation of Australian women; the belle époque in Europe; London of the 1910s as it shook off Victorian puritanism; the artistic and literary Montparnasse of the roaring twenties; the pre-war years in Paris and New York; the reconstruction of the 1950s and the democratisation of beauty; the 1960s and the advent of consumerism. And through it all lies the recurrent theme of women on their long march towards freedom.

Her life, which was stranger than fiction, reads like a historical and geographical compendium – she couldn't sit still, so she travelled by boat, train or plane, from one continent to the next, the way other people take the bus. It also featured, as does any saga, its share of drama, heartbreak, personal tragedy and great solitude.

She had her faults, and they were countless: she could be authoritarian, demanding, tyrannical, despotic, cruel, miserly, selfish, deceitful and even downright insensitive, but by the same token she could be generous, kind, attentive, charming, shy, open, tolerant, and wickedly funny. Like many people of her ilk, she was a living paradox, excessive, larger-than-life, even 'over the top', as Suzanne Slesin, her son Roy's daughter-in-law titled a book about her a few years ago.[4]

Her principal vanity, when late in life she took only a few minutes to do her hair and make-up, ever mindful not to waste time, was mendacity. She lied about everything, starting with her own age – she felt this was the best way to stay young and was more effective than any anti-wrinkle cream.

Like other celebrities eager to forge their own legend, she was constantly rewriting her own life, transforming it to suit her – hiding, veiling, misrepresenting, embellishing, exaggerating, preparing a dream for posterity. Rumours abound, as do inventions, contradictions, fables. Unto those that have shall more be given, and Helena was no exception to the rule. But at the same time, grey areas remain, although the documents, autobiographies, biographies, newspaper articles, administrative documents and testimonies of both the dead and living who knew her – and there are not many of this last category left – can shed some light on her life as a whole.

'She won't hold it against you if you re-create the legend yet again,' exclaimed her cousin Litka Goldberg-Fasse, during our first interview. 'Madame always lied about her life.' She added, after a moment of silence, 'What mattered most to her was to be talked about.'

Madame often said, 'If I hadn't done it, someone else would have.' Perhaps true. But she came first.

Michèle Fitoussi
June 2010

1

EXILE

From the moment she boarded the *Prinz Regent Luitpold*, a German liner that travelled back and forth between Europe and Australia, Helena Rubinstein felt as if she were in a state of weightlessness. She was free.

And while she might have sensed that a trying adventure lay ahead, she savoured every second of her miraculous journey, even if she didn't really know what to expect at the other end. She had hardly had time to realise that by leaving her country, she would at last be able to change her life and be who she wanted to be. She had no idea how she would go about it. And yet she hadn't hesitated when her family suggested emigration to her. In spite of all the real or imagined dangers that might lie ahead – shipwreck, accidents, and fatal diseases, not to mention encounters with the wrong crowd – she had agreed to set off on her own, to go thousands of miles from her native Poland to join three uncles she had never met before.

It was May 1896. Helena was twenty-four years old, with all her worldly belongings in an old trunk. There were days when her chest seemed to swell with all the desires she kept pent up inside until it felt like her heart might explode. She wanted to open her arms wide and embrace the world.

Despite the anxiety that had occasionally gripped her since she embarked in Genoa, she marvelled at what was going on around her. For the first time in her life, she actually felt something approaching happiness. When the weather was fine she went on deck and stared out at the ocean, fascinated by the changing light on the shifting waves: how she wished she could capture every nuance!

When it was too windy on deck, she would explore the gangways in cabin class, stopping at the music room or at the door to the smoking room, browsing through the books in the library. At the bar she would order a cup of tea and some fruitcake, savouring the pleasure of drinking out of china and using real silverware. Afterwards she would luxuriate in a plush sofa to read or embroider. Not once did she think about her family who had stayed behind in Kazimierz, the neighbourhood in Kraków where she grew up. She was not prone to nostalgia, at least not yet.

Fortunately she did not suffer from the seasickness that had consigned so many of her fellow passengers to their berths. In her thirst for discovery, she would even go down into steerage, evading the watchful eyes of the grumpy stewards who forbade passengers from going from one class to another. The sight of these scores of immigrants was wrenching: men and women all crowded together on the deck, lying next to each other moaning or shouting, vomiting their guts up on the floor. The stench of fuel, greasy food and unwashed bodies made her ill. She would hurry away again, fearful she might forfeit her spot on the upper deck were she to be discovered down below, as if she might somehow be forced to stay down there as punishment for trespassing. But that was the reaction of a poor person, and in a shot she was angry with herself for having felt that way.

One morning, leaning against the railing, with a parasol to protect her delicate skin (the sun, woman's mortal enemy!) she looked out, fascinated by the port of Bombay where the steamer had just docked. In the foreign crowd swarming on the quay below her she saw poverty, even more stark there in the harsh sunlight than in the hardships of a

16

Polish winter. She avoided looking at the crippled beggars, the coolies dressed in their cotton loincloths, the ragged children running after the Europeans; instead her gaze lingered on the Indian women in their brightly coloured saris, or the English ladies buttoned up to their chins despite the heat as they scolded the porters struggling with their luggage.

Before Bombay, the ship had stopped at Naples, Alexandria, Aden, and Port Said. On each occasion, Helena would study the crowds of people, then allow herself a short stroll along the port, weaving unsteadily as if she were still on board the rocking ship. Surrounded by itinerant pedlars, she stopped eagerly to rummage through their trinkets. With a serious expression and a frown on her brow, as if her entire life depended on it, she haggled with ease, counting on her fingers to make herself understood, then, at a price she had set herself, she bought glass jewellery, betel, pigments, ointments and powder, musk, amber, essences, tea, sequins and a few lengths of shimmering fabric.

Everywhere she went she would look at the women, fascinated by their exotic, changing beauty. The blonde, pale Italians of Liguria; the plump Neapolitans; the Egyptians and Yemenites, who were invisible save for eyes that burned beneath the veil; the Ethiopians with their fine features; the Asians with their gentle faces. All of them – old, young, ugly and even the little girls clinging to their mothers – had their own particular charm, a way about them, with kohl-rimmed eyes, sparkling teeth that made their olive skin darker still, heavy jewellery around their necks, arms or ankles, bright clothing, and perfume so rich and pungent it made her head spin.

Helena was more used to the fogs of Eastern Europe, and would shield her eyes. There was too much light, too much noise, too much of a crowd and too many dazzling colours; and yet she was absorbing it all, avidly, to keep for later.

*

Helena had a long line of admirers on board. Two young Italians, to begin with, who didn't understand a word of either Polish or Yiddish, and who invited her to dance every night with an ingenious display of mime. Her scant knowledge of German helped to establish closer ties. Then there was the Englishman with the moustache who spoke as if he had a red-hot potato in his mouth. Whenever he turned to Helena, his ruddy face seemed to catch fire. 'Oh, Miss Helena, you're so pretty.'

Miss Helena wasn't a real beauty, but her charm had an immediate effect. Her tiny size made her look like a little girl wearing heels that were too high. But her legs were slim, her bust shapely, and her figure had not yet filled out with age. She wore her black hair in a chignon low on her neck, pulled back from her ears and brow. Her features were regular, with high cheekbones, straight lips and skin so pale it was translucent. The first thing you noticed about her was her large, widespread eyes, with their velvety darkness, at times pensive, at times enquiring. 'A gaze of precision and observation, the kind of look you can tell excels at counting, examining files and numbers, studying formulas, or dreaming endlessly about beautiful things.'[1] At times, too, they could shoot daggers. Her seven sisters nicknamed her 'the Eagle'.[2]

From the start, she intrigued her admirers. She was a young woman travelling alone, and seemingly not at all frightened: this was virtually unheard of at the time. Only loose women dared to travel without chaperones. But her silence and restraint, along with a certain hardness in her eyes, soon made them realise she wasn't that kind of woman.

And while Helena enjoyed having a good time, she quickly set her limits. Her shyness kept her from going too far. Besides, what would her mother think? The strict principles of Gitel Rubinstein, known as Gitte, her prudishness and sense of virtue, were too well embedded in Helena. 'Every kiss seemed immoral to me, and the mysteries of sex remained ... mysteries.'[3] It would take time for her to let her guard down. She received no fewer than three marriage proposals in the course of the journey, and three times she turned her suitors down with a smile, as if each proposal was some boyish prank. She did not envisage a future tied to a man.

Every evening, after a few polkas in the ballroom, the young men gathered around her. The fifty or so passengers in cabin class had very quickly become acquainted. Shipboard romances blossomed. Attachments formed, seemingly indestructible, then dissolved when the journey ended. The men on board were brokers, explorers, gold prospectors, French officers, British diplomats, missionaries; the women were mistresses, dowagers, the wives of high-ranking officials. There was even a theatre troupe on tour. Helena befriended two Englishwomen who, like her, were on their way to Australia. The first, Lady Susanna, was travelling with her husband, the aide-de-camp to Lord Lamington, Governor of Queensland. The other, Helen MacDonald, lived in Melbourne and was about to be married. Before leaving the ship, Helena wrote down their addresses. She already had a knack for networking.

In the cabin class salon, the heat was stifling despite the ceiling fans. Helena sipped an iced tea to cool down. Her gaze glided over the wood panelling, the rosewood tables, the silverware and china dinner services, the crystal chandeliers, the tall sparkling mirror reflecting her face. All this refinement enchanted her. Then she went to join the little groups who were chattering gaily. Her hawk-like eyes recorded every detail – the clothes the women were wearing, their deportment, their hairstyles, the way they held their fans, the way they laughed or remained silent.

During the day she watched them play tennis or whist, and tried to memorise the rules. She knew so little about this world where everything seemed easy that she took in every detail and stored it all up for future use. She was completely ignorant when it came to social codes, manners, and even the art of conversation, which explained her stubborn silence. Another reason was – and always would be, no matter what she did – the fear of being judged because of her background. Even if she learned as she went along – and she was a quick learner – there would always be gaps she could not fill. Neither her fortune, nor her good taste, nor the lies she told to embellish her life would ever fill those gaps.

In the course of her very long life she would make other journeys from one continent to another. The sun would never set on her empire – the empire of beauty. But this first voyage was a seminal one and would leave its imprint: a taste for adventure, luxury, and beauty. To get what she wanted, Helena was prepared to work relentlessly; she had been brought up the hard way and was not afraid of work. And although she didn't yet know which way she was headed, she was already using everything in her power to overcome the limited existence to which her station in life might otherwise have condemned her.

Nature had given her every asset for success: boldness, energy, obstinacy, and intelligence. All she needed now was luck, and she promised herself she would push that luck. She knew there would be obstacles to overcome, but she believed in her destiny and refused to let herself down.

2

KAZIMIERZ

She was born Chaja Rubinstein, the eldest daughter of Hertzel Naftaly Rubinstein and Augusta Gitel Silberfeld, on 25 December 1872, under the sign of Capricorn.[1] She so despised her first name that she changed it as soon as she left the country: on the passenger list of the *Prinz Regent Luitpold* she was registered as Helena Juliet Rubinstein, aged twenty.

Four years younger than she really was: that was her way of thumbing her nose at the passage of time. She would always lie about her age and tell untruths about other details of her life with equal aplomb. Her earliest passports stated 1880 as the year of her birth.[2] Administrative bodies were not very particular at the time, and besides, she did look ten years younger. 'I've always thought a woman owed it to herself to treat the subject of her age with ambiguity,' she dictated for the opening pages of her autobiography at the ripe old age of ninety-three.[3]

Her place of birth, Kazimierz, was founded in 1335 by the Polish King Kazimir III as a separate fortified city next to Kraków, the capital. One hundred and fifty years later, all Kraków's Jews were ordered to live inside its walls. Over the centuries, the Jewish town of Kazimierz expanded alongside the Christian capital of Kraków, and benefited from varying degrees of protection from Polish sovereigns. Hertzel Rubinstein often told his daughter that in those days there was a fair amount of cultural cross-fertilisation with the rest of Europe. Jews came to the city from France, England, Italy, Spain and Bohemia, fleeing persecution.

The political situation, however, was unstable. Coveted by its neighbours, Poland was constantly invaded. In 1772, a first partition divided Poland (then part of the Polish-Lithuanian Commonwealth) into three territories: Austria annexed an area containing the two major cities Kraków and Lemberg and called it Galicia, while the rest of the union was divided between Russia to the east and Prussia to the west and north. A second partition took place in 1793. A third, two years later, destroyed the Polish-Lithuanian Commonwealth once and for all. In 1815, the Congress of Vienna created a fourth division, the Congress Kingdom of Poland, while Kraków, of which Kazimierz was now a suburb, was made an autonomous republic until the middle of the century. The city preserved its Polish heritage but, as with all of Galicia, remained a dependency of the Austro-Hungarian Empire.

Torn apart, Poland still refused to submit. Successive revolts for independence were met with bloody repression, which only served to intensify the nationalist movement. At the same time, waves of political emigrants left Poland, most of them headed for France – a brilliant community of painters, writers, musicians, and aristocrats for whom nostalgia served as artistic inspiration. Among them were Frédéric Chopin and poet Adam Mickiewicz. Many of the country's great masterpieces were created outside Poland.

Austria-Hungary claimed to be a civilised nation that allowed its subjects to live in peace. The fate of the Jews was somewhat more tolerable there than elsewhere. In 1822, when the walls of Kazimierz were demolished, the richest and most determined Jews settled in the Christian district. In 1867, Emperor Franz Josef finally granted them full rights. When Helena was born, Galicia, and all of Poland along with it, was in the feverish throes of modernisation. Railways, factories, and apartment buildings were being built, cities were expanding and streets were being widened, paved with stones and fitted with streetlamps and gutters.

With 26,000 Jews, a quarter of its population, Kraków became an important centre for Judaism. Synagogues and religious schools – *yeshivot* and *cheders* – were built. Increasing numbers of young people attended secondary school and university, breaking down social barriers. Jewish officials were elected. Galicia's Jewish doctors, lawyers, dentists, writers, poets, actors and musicians outnumbered Poles and Ukrainians in their respective professions.

Well-to-do families lived in the centre of town, in vast townhouses like those of the Catholics, filled with books, paintings, mirrors, tapestries and expensive furniture. The Orthodox community and poor Jews – who were often one and the same – stayed behind in Kazimierz. This was the case for Hertzel Rubinstein and his family. In spite of the economic boom, the vast majority of Jews still lived in poverty in Galicia, particularly in the countryside. In town, the artisans, tailors, carpenters, milliners, jewellers, and opticians fared somewhat better. But most importantly, assimilation was under way. The Jewish elite was becoming Polish.

However, anti-Semitism was by no means a thing of the past. As a child, Helena lay in bed and heard the adults talk in hushed voices about the pogroms. They described everything in detail: *shtetls* burned to the ground, synagogues desecrated, houses destroyed, mothers and daughters raped, babies thrown alive into the flames, old men forced to whip their peers, fathers massacred with pitchforks by Polish peasants, impaled by Ukrainian bayonets, scythed by Cossack sabres. Bloody nightmares haunted the sleep of the Rubinstein sisters: men hanging from their hands, shreds of flesh torn off, eyes gouged and tongues ripped out, heads cut off for soldiers to kick around.

Those Jews who could left in waves for less hostile countries. Between 1881 and 1914, 300,000 fled slaughter, war and poverty, emigrating to America or to Australia. Among them were Gitel's three brothers – John, Bernhard, and Louis Silberfeld – to whom Helena would eventually be sent.

Kraków was also an intellectual centre with theatres, publishing houses, literary salons, concert halls, and secret societies. There was the Jagiellonian University, the second oldest in Central Europe; Helena liked to tell a story of how she studied medicine there for a few months, before being forced to drop out because she couldn't stand the sight of blood.

In reality, she didn't even finish secondary school.[4] She attended the Jewish school in Kazimierz but at the age of sixteen, as was customary for girls of her social class, she had to end her studies. She did so reluctantly because she liked learning.

She had a quick intellect and a thirst for knowledge. Her favourite subjects were mathematics, literature, and history, particularly that of her country. She felt Polish to the depths of her soul.

And Jewish too. It couldn't be any other way with such a pious, well-respected family. Both branches of her family, the Rubinsteins and the Silberfelds, boasted several rabbis, wise men, scholars, and men of the Book. Her father's side could trace their lineage back to the famous Rashi of Troyes, one of the most famous authors of commentary on the Bible and the Talmud.[5] Salomon Rubinstein, Helena's great-grandfather, had been a rabbi. His son Aryeh, a cattle dealer, had three children, of which Hertzel Naftaly Rubinstein, Helena's father, was the eldest.

The family came from Dukla, a little town in the Carpathians. That's where Hertzel was born in 1840, and where he married Augusta Gitel Silberfeld, his cousin on his mother's side. Gitel was born in 1844, and was the ninth child of nineteen, of whom over half died before the age of twenty. Her father, Salomon Zale Silberfeld, had been a moneylender; Helena's eagerness for social promotion transformed him into a 'banker'.

The year before Helena's birth, Hertzel and Gitel Rubinstein settled in Kraków at 14 Szeroka Street, a narrow red stone building. As the family expanded – of the couple's fifteen children, only eight daughters would survive – they moved house frequently, but always stayed in the vicinity of Joszefa Street. That's where Hertzel Rubinstein ran a sort of bazaar, selling a bit of everything: eggs and preserves, huge barrels filled with herring, jars of pickles, candles, wheat and barley in bulk, kerosene. Walking in, the smell of brine and oil was overwhelming. Hertzel did not make a good living from his store but he did his best to feed his family. 'Jews didn't have an easy time of it in those days, we were people of very modest means, with virtually no money,' Helena would confess, much later on, in a rare moment of candour about her early years.[6]

The house where she was born stood close to five of Kazimierz's seven synagogues: the High synagogue, the Old synagogue, Popper's, Remuh, and Kupa. It was also near the mikveh, a ritual bathhouse where women went to cleanse themselves at the end of the week. The days were governed by the times for worship, the seasons and the holy days. Every morning and evening, Helena would hear the prayers and chants as they rose towards the heavens.

Her district was a labyrinth of paved streets, flanked on either side by large, balconied houses of wood or stone. It was home to all manner of shops, printing presses, newspapers, banks, cafés, markets, wedding houses, schools, cemeteries, and a hospital. On the shopfronts, names were written in Polish and Yiddish. Between the Miodowa, Dajwor, Wawrzynca, Bartosza and Joszefa streets and Nowy Square, prosperity and poverty lived side by side, as did culture and ignorance, religion and profanity.

Rabbis with *payot* in long black coats walked past pious Jews in fur hats and bearded *Hasidim* wearing belted caftans over trousers tucked into boots. Notables in their top hats ceremoniously greeted old men in velvet skullcaps as they scurried past with their sacred leather-bound tomes beneath their arms. Women in wigs, their heads covered with a stole or an embroidered bonnet, shooed away little boys with caps pulled down over their curls. Gaunt students clustered outside their *yeshivot*, endlessly debating a paragraph from the Talmud.

In the summer everyone lived outdoors in the street, or kept their windows wide open. From her bedroom, Helena could hear weeping, arguments, matrons shouting to each other from balconies where laundry was hung out to dry and the cries of waterbearers calling to their customers. Carts filled with bricks or hay, drawn by skeletal horses, regularly blocked the road, forcing everyone to make a detour.

Yentas, or busybodies, sprawled on tiny folding chairs, gossiped malevolently about their neighbours and scolded the small children chasing each other along the passageways between the courtyards. Pedlars displayed their wares on trestles piled high with precariously balanced treasures – old clothes, worn shoes, umbrellas, prayer shawls, books, phylacteries, and menorahs. Craftsmen repaired broken furniture in the street, while young girls went to fill their buckets at the fountain. From early morning, the neighbourhood buzzed with people at work, from cobblers, fishmongers and pawnbrokers to an old woman on her balcony embroidering trousseaus for the rich.

In the poorest areas, there were cries and insults, people shouting out in Yiddish, Polish, and German; crates were unloaded in the dust, and the streets ran ankle deep with refuse while buckets of dirty water were poured out onto the pavement. The stench of rotting fruit, cat's urine, smoked meat, onions, cumin, salted cucumbers and offal wafted on the thick air. In winter, the temperature could drop to thirty below, and icy gusts heaped snowdrifts along the pavements. The pitiless cold gripped you body and soul, walls rotted from the damp, and a leaden

26

grey sky hung over the city. When the snow melted, the streets filled with a muddy slush that ruined shoes and skirt hems.

Helena Rubinstein always preferred to keep silent about that chapter of her life, as if she were ashamed of it. She preferred to talk about Planty botanical gardens or St Anne's Church. She would rather chat away about the aristocrats' stately homes where she dreamed of being a guest and would later claim she had been. Depending on her mood, she might describe Kraków as a cultured, elegant city, or merely dreary and provincial. The reality lies somewhere in between, although the city boasts an abundance of medieval and gothic monuments – the royal castle of Wawel; the tomb of the Polish kings, which overlooks the city; the ramparts of the old town surrounded by the Botanical Gardens; St Mary's Basilica; St Catherine's Church; and the observatory. And the grandiose central marketplace, the Rynek, common to all Polish cities, with its famous Cloth Hall.

Whenever she could, Helena would leave Kazimierz behind to head down Stradom Street, then Grodska Street, to stroll past the stalls beneath the arcades. Here there were no Jews in greatcoats, or gossiping housewives, or wretched street urchins. The men sported top hats and bowlers; the women wore fine milliners' creations.

Young Helena admired the displays on the stalls as if she wanted to learn them by heart. She hadn't a single zloty in her purse, but she dreamed of being able, someday, to buy lace and silk and fur, diamonds and pearls and crystal. When she was rich she would strut about like these distinguished Polish women strolling around the square wrapped in their pelisses, or travel like the ladies she glimpsed in fine carriages pulled by elegant horses – instead of going everywhere on foot, through the mud, dragging her sisters behind her, as she had to do now.

Very early on, Helena mastered the art of transforming the episodes of her life, embellishing or blurring facts as she saw fit. Her imagination knew no bounds, so much so that it is difficult to know where the truth lies. She was more of a fabricator than a liar. She would spend her entire life painstakingly stitching together her personal legend, indifferent to any contradictions in her story.

And yet the reality is infinitely more interesting than the story she stubbornly enhanced. She may have wanted to deny it, but the fact remains that she came from these dark streets, these impoverished alleyways, these poorly paved courtyards with their prayer houses and *cheders* – an entire Jewish world that seemed immutable, rooted in the *shtetls* and ghettos of Galicia, Poland, or Ukraine, and which has vanished forever.

The harsh environment where she spent the first twenty-four years of her life inspired her with the passion to leave it behind. It was where she found her strength of character, her courage, and her adaptability, like any emigrant who makes a new life elsewhere.

But she was an impoverished Jewish woman, born in Poland at the end of the nineteenth century.

This meant that she was a nobody.

3

THE RUBINSTEIN FAMILY

Helena, Pauline, Rosa, Regina, Stella, Ceska, Manka and Erna Rubinstein: the litany of their names sounds like a nursery rhyme. They were all pretty dark-haired young women with milky white skin. The eldest and youngest were ten years apart. The atmosphere was always lively in their huge, gas-lit house: they would fight over a ribbon, a scarf; they would prance in front of the mirror. The centre of this den of females was Gitel Rubinstein: model mother and housewife, who performed miracles to make sure her family had everything they needed. Given her husband's erratic temperament, she was often lacking housekeeping money. Gitel sighed at the thought of her brothers and sisters who lived comfortably in Kraków, Vienna, Antwerp and beyond.

There were the things they had inherited: finely carved furniture, mirrors, silver chandeliers, linen in the wardrobes and an abundance of books. But they had to skimp on everything else – soap, bread, candles, servants. So many mouths to feed were a burden on their meagre income.

Eight daughters. Eight treasures. But also eight dowries.

Each one would have to be married, to a good match, if possible. This occupied Gitel's thoughts as soon as each was born. She was a good woman, plump with childbirth, and she wore a wig styled in the chignon customary for Orthodox Jewish wives. She scrupulously observed all the commandments of her faith, but that did not mean neglecting appearances, which counted as much as the purity of one's soul. She taught the little girls to sew their shirts and to knit and embroider, all things Gitel excelled at, and she made the patterns for their dresses and coats herself. Above all, she taught them the art of good grooming. She showed them how to take care of their hair, which they were very proud of. One hundred strokes of the brush every night before bedtime. That way the girls could practise their counting while brushing their hair. In the Rubinstein family, not even time was squandered.

Gitel was convinced that charm and inner beauty would enable her girls to win the love of the men who would marry them. It was out of the question for her to allow her girls to wear make-up. Only low women, or actresses like the great Helena Modjeska, were allowed to wear cosmetics. But it was still possible to protect one's face from the redness caused by the wind and frost, and remain respectable at the same time. So Gitel brought out her secret weapon.

Face cream.

Gitel's was made from plants, spermaceti, lanolin, essence of almond and extracts of Carpathian conifer bark. Every night, especially if it had been a bitingly cold day, her daughters would line up in their nightdresses according to height and impatiently lift their little faces like baby chicks seeking their food.

'Mama, Mama! On me! And me! No, Pauline, get out of the way, it's my turn!'

They liked to tell stories at home, and Gitel's story was that the cream had been made originally for Helena Modjeska by the Lykusky brothers, two Hungarian chemists who were customers of Hertzel's. Modjeska was the most famous actress in Poland. It was highly doubtful she ever visited the Rubinstein family, despite Helena's claims to the contrary, but the elder Lykusky brother, Jacob, probably came to dinner quite often. And he brought with him a big jar containing the precious mixture, wrapped in newspaper.

Gitel would transfer it into little ceramic pots that she stored in a cool spot in the pantry with the jars of pickles and onions. Her sense of thrift ensured the cream would last until the next delivery. The handful of beauty principles she passed on to her daughters would change the life of the eldest. Before Helena left for Australia, Gitel gave her twelve little jars, like twelve little talismans, to protect her.

Helena's position among her siblings shaped her personality significantly. 'When I was very young I already had to help my mother control the rebellious little troop. When you're the eldest of eight girls, you get into the habit of running things.'[1] She didn't altogether mind this, given her domineering character. She was both a tomboy and an accomplished young lady. A steamroller full of grace.

Control and charm – you could sum Helena up in those two words. At the age of twelve she was in charge of running the household. She became the 'department head', buying the food and linen 'with a spontaneous taste for what was finest and sturdiest'. In all likelihood these precocious duties shaped her talents as an organiser. 'I was the one who had to intervene and mediate between my younger sisters and our parents, which is the best training I could have had for managing my future employees.'[2] But she also had to carry out the other household tasks that their solitary servant could not handle on her own: making the beds, putting the water on to boil, fetching wood for the stove, helping the little girls to wash, overseeing their homework and separating them when they began to fight.

'Shh, shh, silence! Papa will punish you. And if he doesn't, I swear that I will!'

And then there was the table to set and clear, and the dishes to put away, keeping the ones for meat and dairy separate. And there were the preparations for the Sabbath and all the religious festivals – Rosh Hashanah, Yom Kippur, Hanukkah, Passover, Sukkot, Purim,

Shavuot. She had to get out the tablecloths, iron them, polish the silverware, light the candles, lay out the prayer books, keep an eye on the dinner in the kitchen – the chicken broth where the *kneidels* or the *gefilte* fish were cooking – then knead the *challah* bread with her mother. Gitel's sole ambition was for her daughters to become good *balaboostas*, accomplished homemakers. Because it wasn't enough just to catch a man: you had to know how to keep him.

That was clearly not Helena's ambition: she hated being stuck at home. From early adolescence she would hurry to join her father in the store to evade the chores her mother sought to burden her with. When she left school, she quickly found her place behind the counter. She would have preferred to continue her studies, but that was not an option.

Besides, she liked going to the store. She managed much better with the customers than her father did, she could count faster than he could, and she knew the inventory, orders and amounts owed or due down to the last zloty. Hertzel was better suited for reading holy texts than for commerce, so he appreciated her energy and skill with the bookkeeping. But he also got annoyed with her natural authoritarianism. They would have to marry her off quickly, but to do that they needed a dowry, and Hertzel never managed to put aside even the tiniest amount – not for Helena or any of the other sisters. The mere thought of it made him sigh. Then he would return his attention to his old books, submitting to the will of the Almighty, who was bound to help him sooner or later.

Helena was frequently irritated by her father's feebleness. Books, nothing but books … what was the point of all that studying if he couldn't feed his family? On two occasions she got him out of a tight spot. The first time, she went to bargain over the purchase of 20 litres of kerosene from a supplier who lived in Lemberg, the capital of Galicia. Her father had been stuck in bed with a bad back since the day before, and Gitel had far too much to do at home to go in his place.

Hertzel could not afford to lose the contract. The shipment had been resold at twice the price to a cattle merchant who had already paid a deposit. For once they would be able to finish the month without any debts. All evening long Helena heard her parents quarrelling, her father lamenting, her mother sighing. Always the same reproaches – Gitel bemoaning their poverty, and Hertzel berating her because he was ashamed. The young girl was fed up with their arguing.

As soon as she got up in the morning she announced that she would go to Lemberg on her father's behalf. He told her she was crazy and that the merchants would laugh in her face. Helena was so adamant that finally, with his wife's consent, he let her take the train, although he did send the shop boy to escort her. Just before she left for the central station on Lubicz Street, Gitel looked her daughter straight in the eyes.

'If you really want to be smart, above all you must listen. And don't say a word more than you have to.'

Helena managed to close the deal as they had hoped, for the price Hertzel had requested. All she'd had to do was stay firm. And no one had made fun of her.

Some time later, Hertzel ordered a huge quantity of eggs from Hungary that would have to be sold off again as quickly as possible. The shipment was running late and was due to arrive at the station in Kraków the day before the feast of the Assumption, which, in devoutly Catholic Poland, meant four days of public holidays with no workers available to unload it.

The city was baking in an August heat wave. No one ventured out into the hot streets until late afternoon. The railway carriages were turning into incubators and several chicks had already hatched. Fearful of his imminent ruin, Hertzel was trying in vain to obtain a special dispensation. Gitel was moaning and wailing. Without consulting her parents, Helena decided to go straight to the stationmaster on her own: she would persuade him to unload the shipment. After half an hour of

33

back and forth discussion, in which he did not have the last word, the stationmaster sent Helena to see the director of the railways, who was shut inside his furnace of an office sweating like a lump of lard.

The moment she came into the room, the director looked this tiny Jewish woman up and down with all the scorn she inspired in him. But Helena was so determined to get her way that she didn't give a damn what he thought. She sniffed and hiccupped and a stream of words flowed from her lips: eggs, my father, bankrupt. Then she started all over again, until the man became dizzy.

Exhausted, the director gave the order to unload the eggs onto the platform and waved her away. Helena ran all the way across Kraków as if she had a *dybbuk* on her heels and arrived home dishevelled, breathless, and flushed. Without pausing to catch her breath she gave the good news to her parents, who cursed her audacity but also thanked her for it. Hertzel was saved.

Much later, she would say that she owed her early accomplishments to her youth, her inexperience and the wise advice she received from her mother. 'My sense of triumph was a foretaste of what achievement in business could mean to me.'[3]

None of her efforts to change the course of their monotonous life found favour with Hertzel. Among other youthful scandals, there was an incident in which she sold the furniture from the bedroom she shared with Pauline, who was a year younger. Helena hated their huge rosewood bed: it reminded her of a catafalque and gave her nightmares. In the small hours she thought she could see ghosts, and she would grab Pauline's hand to calm her terror. In her opinion the termite-infested bedside tables were hopelessly old-fashioned. Her parents had inherited the furniture from their parents. As children were born and the family moved from house to house they added beds, wardrobes or dressers rescued from family attics or bought for a few zloty at the flea market. And everything was arranged haphazardly, without rhyme or reason, to Helena's despair.

She knew nearly every shop window in Stradom Street by heart, and a new furniture store had just opened. At first she just glimpsed inside, then she grew bolder and went in. There she saw a big, sober, modern bed with two matching bedside tables. 'This is the Biedermeier style,' the salesman told her. 'You need look no further, miss, this is as good as any you'll find in Vienna,' he added, in an affected tone.

Helena ran her hand over the polished wood. She liked the texture. She knew instinctively, without ever having been taught, how to distinguish the beautiful from the ugly, the refined from the vulgar. Throughout her life she would demonstrate this taste for beauty that seemed to have come out of nowhere. But she did not have the means to pay for the furniture; the price was exorbitant. To persuade her, the salesman suggested she pay on credit and even offered to take her old furniture. 'And since you seem to be in the know, I'll sell you this armchair half price. And I'll throw in that big standing mirror as a bonus.'

It was far too tempting. Helena haggled, something she was very good at, and managed to get an even better price. She would find a way to pay back the instalments. She picked a moment when her parents would be absent to have the furniture delivered. That way the surprise would be even greater. Luckily, Helena's maternal grandparents, Salomon and Rebecca, had invited the entire family to spend the Sabbath in their old house on the outskirts of Kazimierz. To avoid having to go along, Helena pleaded a headache, an ailment she frequently suffered from.

Gitel was worried. Normally her daughter never missed these visits. She was Rebecca's favourite granddaughter and the old woman always showered her with presents, such as embroidered handkerchiefs or lace collars. When Helena turned fifteen, her grandmother even gave her a string of pearls. Her sisters thought they would die of jealousy. Helena kept that necklace her entire life, and that precious gift was the beginning of her passion for jewellery. At her grandparents' there was also Stass, the handyman. He was very gifted with his hands, and he made miniature furniture for the little girls that were perfect imitations of the real thing. Helena never tired of discovering what new treasures he had created and this fascination would lead Helena to collect doll's houses all her life.

'Are you sure?' asked Gitel.

'I'm sure,' replied Helena. She needed peace and quiet and she would be able to rest in her room. Hertzel was calling irritably to his wife to hurry up, as she rushed to and fro, unable to bring herself to leave. 'We're going to be late,' he shouted; if his daughter wanted to sulk that was her business. Gitel gave in and went to join the rest of the family already crowded into the carriage.

All these interruptions made them late. Helena went to the window several times, filled with anxiety. The cart with its load of furniture was due to arrive any minute. Luckily, her family turned the corner at the very moment the shopkeeper came to unload his delivery. Helena spent the entire day arranging everything to her taste, making the bed and covering it with the counterpane she had just embroidered. Like her mother, she was very good at needlework.

Then she sat down to wait for her parents, confident that they would be pleased.

She had underestimated her father: Hertzel stood stock still at the threshold to the room. There could no longer be any doubt: his daughter was *meshuggah*, stark, raving mad. A *dybbuk* must have turned her head. To go selling the family furniture! What sort of behaviour was that! Who did she deal with? A store on Stradom Street? Who did she think she was! It must have cost an arm and a leg! Hertzel ordered her to follow him and rushed off to the store to return the furniture before it was too late.

Once again she had to obey her father. How long would this last? 'Until you get married,' replied Gitel firmly. 'And after that, you will have to obey your husband.'

'Yes, but who's going to want her?' said Hertzel bitterly when Helena had her back turned. 'Everyone knows how rebellious she can be. She's already turned down four suitors. And she is well over twenty!'

'Without a substantial dowry, she won't find a good match,' retorted Gitel. 'At her age she'll only find other women's cast-offs. And don't forget there are seven more after her who are waiting their turn.'

Hertzel pretended he hadn't heard. Gitel went to see the matchmakers, appealed to friends of friends, alerted all of Kazimierz and the immediate surroundings, Podgorze and Dukla, where she had been born, and in her agitation wondered if she shouldn't send emissaries to Lemberg. Finally, someone found her the one. Schmuel, a well-to-do old widower who lived in Kraków, in the Christian neighbourhood, agreed to marry their daughter without a dowry. He had seen her several times at the synagogue and found her very much to his liking.

Hertzel was relieved when his wife told him the news. Schmuel seemed an excellent match. The man would take their daughter off their hands and give her two or three children to start with. Thanks to him the she-devil would calm down. Now all that remained was to convince her.

The young woman listened first to her father and then to her mother. She looked at the two of them; for once she was speechless. She wasn't saying anything; that was a good sign, thought Hertzel. Gitel was more circumspect. She knew her daughter: this stillness did not bode well. Besides, hadn't she just shaken her head? And what's that she was murmuring? It was out of the question? That she would never marry that … that what? Not him, nor anyone else for that matter?

'But what do you want?' asked Hertzel, exasperated.

'Stanislaw.'

Astonished, Hertzel turned to his wife, who shrugged, as much in the dark as he was.

Stanislaw was a medical student who Helena claimed to have met outside the university. She went there from time to time, to wander around and daydream that she belonged to these groups of laughing, talking students who never paid her the slightest attention. They all had presence, but none could compare with Stanislaw. Curly hair and eyes like the skies of a Kraków summer – if only they could see him, in his frock coat with gold buttons … a real prince.

She had probably never even spoken to him. How could she go near him, with a father who was so particular about who she met? But one of her girlfriends who knew the young man had pointed him out to Helena one day when they were walking together. So eager was Helena for romance that she was sure that it was love at first sight. But that was not something she was prepared to tell her parents. On the contrary, she made things up, implying there was already something quite serious between her and Stanislaw. Anything rather than marry Schmuel.

At that point Hertzel Naftaly Rubinstein got extremely angry. He paced back and forth in the living room, shouting, ranting and raving against his daughter.

'*Shoyn gening*, that's enough! You will obey me!'

Gitel sat on the worn taffeta sofa wringing her hands. Her round face bobbed up and down to the rhythm of her husband's steps. '*Oy gevald*, what are we going to do with you?' she said over and over again through her tears.

'She spends much too much time away from home, how many times do I have to tell you?' said Hertzel reproachfully, overlooking the fact that he was usually the one who kept his daughter out of the house.

Helena was silent, but her mind was racing. She couldn't bear the idea of a life trapped in Kraków, where she was in love with an unattainable young man but was threatened with the prospect of marrying another. She would be condemned to the same deathly boring fate as her mother, her aunts, her grandmothers, and all those generations of women before her: countless children, monotonously repetitive Sabbaths, endless prayers and nothing but submission.

Tradition could not be changed. Particularly not to please young women. 'She's the eldest, she must be the first to marry. Otherwise, how will we find husbands for the others?' shouted Hertzel. 'You have already turned down so many good matches! Who do you think you are? You're nothing but a pretentious nuisance!'

Helena could hear her sisters whispering behind the parlour door. Not one of them would come to her rescue, for they were all terrified by their father's shouting. Besides, Helena had gone too far. She wouldn't get out of it this time.

Helena lifted her chin and stood tall like a rooster preparing for battle. Maybe she couldn't have Stanislaw, but she wasn't about to have old, bald Schmuel, either. At the age of twenty-one she was no longer a little girl. No one else had the right to make up her mind for her. Helena ran out of the room, hurtled past her sisters, slammed the door and locked herself in her room. She collapsed on her bed, sobbing with rage. *I hate them. I want to leave. Everything here is old and ugly and poor, and nothing ever changes. If I stay here I'll die.*

So Helena left.

She was amazed she found the courage. She sought refuge in

Kraków with her aunt Rosa Silberfeld Beckman, one of Gitel's sisters, who agreed to take her in for a few months. Not more than that, she warned; just time enough for Helena to find her bearings.

Helena had no intention of living in Rosa's dreary little house, or sharing a bedroom with her cousin Lola, for long. She had other ambitions. One of her mother's sisters, Chaja Silberfeld, lived in Vienna, where she was married to Liebisch Splitter, a furrier who ran a huge store with his three brothers. The magnificent Chaja invited young Helena to come and stay with her.[4] Helena would help her aunt to look after the house and work at her uncle's business.

The Splitters lived more comfortably than her parents. Their house was more spacious, their furniture more modern. Liebisch had a keen business sense; he was not a dreamer like Hertzel, and didn't spend his days with his nose in a book. He was making his fortune. Her cousins were kind to her, and Vienna was a real capital, with a wealth of museums, theatres, cafés and concert halls. Kraków was provincial in comparison.

Helena improved her knowledge of German and learned the basics of the luxury retail trade. There was no one like her for latching on to a customer, keeping her there and selling her the most expensive fur. She liked wearing them too. There is a photograph from those early years showing Helena posing in a black astrakhan coat.

Two years sped by. Helena had no time for leisure. She was working.

Her only entertainment was a ritual stroll along the banks of the Danube or in the Prater Gardens on the Sabbath. In response to Gitel's pleas, her aunt had introduced her to a few young men, but Helena turned them all down. Chaja Splitter did not insist. Her niece had made herself indispensable at the shop.

Helena wouldn't speak to her father, but continued to write to her mother. In all her letters Gitel asked the same question: When do you plan to get married? Helena invariably evaded the question;

marriage wasn't a woman's only fate. Her sisters' letters brought some consolation, but what they told her gave her no desire to return to Kraków. Nothing ever seemed to change there.

Selling furs was no life either. Not for her in any case. It was time to move on. Her cousin Eva, the daughter of her uncle Bernhard Silberfeld, Gitel's brother, had begun to write to her on a regular basis. Eva's mother had died young, and she had lived for a long time with Helena's family, like a ninth sister. When they were children they had been very close.

Eva had joined her father in Australia and had married Louis Levy, a violent alcoholic who raped and beat her and on two occasions nearly killed her. Somehow Eva found the strength to file for divorce. In her letters she asked Helena for help in looking after her three small children. Theodore, the youngest, was still an infant.

Australia? Helena had thought about it from time to time without really dwelling on it. She knew very little about that huge colonial country, but it definitely seemed an attractive option. When Eva described the vast amounts of space, the unending wilderness, the modern cities, Helena dreamed of freedom.

She gave it some thought, then confided in her aunt, who in turn spoke to her husband about it. They considered it to be an excellent plan. The Splitters were going to move to Antwerp, and would have no room for Helena, which meant that before long they would be leaving their niece without a job or a roof over her head. She didn't want to go with them anyway.

So Chaja wrote to Gitel, and everyone agreed: Helena should emigrate. As usual, later in life she would embellish the reasons for her departure: 'For a long time, since I was a child, it had been one of my dreams to go to Australia. My uncles had settled there before and our imaginations had been fed on letters from this remote land.'[5] Her decision to go into exile so far away would allow her to shape the

41

legend of her adventurous life as she saw fit. If she was leaving, it was because she wanted to. She didn't want to owe anything to anyone.

It was out of the question to let anyone suspect that it was her family who wanted to get rid of her by sending her thousands of miles away. Everyone viewed the Australian solution as an honourable way out for an unmarriageable young rebel. *Alteh moid*, old maid: that was the fate in store for her. But perhaps in the outback she might still meet a *gvir*, a rich husband, who would be willing to take her on despite her age, as Gitel never stopped hoping.

Helena let them say what they liked for fear they might change their mind. Once she was in Australia she would be too far away for them to come pestering her with that marriage business.

Gitel sold a piece of jewellery, one of the few she had left, and sent Helena the money with twelve jars of her precious face cream. Helena packed them in her suitcase beneath her dresses of pleated silk. The Splitters and other members of her family contributed to her purse.

Helena was able to buy a ticket in cabin class without dipping into her savings. And one day, more alone and more determined than ever, she boarded the train for the port of Genoa in Italy.

4

A MERCILESS NEW WORLD

Helena snapped her parasol shut before entering the store on 107 Whyte Street, next to the brick house with the wide porch that was now her home.[1] It was a general store, somewhat more modern than her father's in Kazimierz, with high counters, shelves and wooden crates. Her uncle Bernhard, who was also a sheep farmer and boasted that he was an optician to boot (a rather fancy word for the four pairs of spectacles he had on sale), sold a bit of everything in his store. Castor oil, shovels, sieves, dried biscuits, sugar, potatoes, poultices, ointment for horses' joints, halters, ropes, flour, nails, tools, black soap, spectacles, even clothing – twill trousers, raw linen shirts and wide-brimmed hats.

Helena couldn't stand the way the farmers' wives dressed, in their rough calico frocks and frumpy lace-up shoes. Even if it wasn't practical, every morning she put on one of her pleated silk dresses that constantly needed mending and her high-heeled boots that were worn down from riding horseback. Just the sight of a horse made her tremble. What an idea, to climb on its back! She wasn't cut out to be a horsewoman. Her only concession to country life was the apron she put on over her dress in order not to spoil it when she was working in the store.

It was the first thing she did on arrival every morning, just before she went behind the counter. There weren't any customers around, but she didn't know how to sit still. She opened the ledger and took up the inkstand. Very soon she was busy at her bookkeeping.

'Is that you now?' asked a gruff voice from the room in the back. 'Sure took long enough. What were you up to this time?'

'My English lessons,' she replied curtly. 'I've been going to school every day since I arrived, you ought to know.'

And as soon as I know enough English to manage on my own, I'll get away from here, she thought to herself, before immersing herself again in her figures.

Bernhard's Yiddish accent exasperated her. As did his loud, coarse voice, not to mention his bad manners. He chewed tobacco, burped and picked his nose without the least compunction. Rebecca Silberfeld, Helena's grandmother, would be furious if she could see her son's rough ways. He had become a real yokel, with his muddy boots, sleeve covers, and a pencil behind his ear. He didn't look out of place among all the colonists, gold prospectors and stockmen, or the ex-convicts deported from Europe. Things were different in the city: people were educated, well dressed, refined. She had noticed it at once when she got off the ship in Melbourne. The little she managed to see during the half-day she spent there, because Bernhard had some shopping to do, had immediately enchanted her. But in Coleraine there was nothing to do. The human species hardly mattered at all; in these parts, the sheep was king. Farmers raised sheep, the women who married the farmers looked after the sheep and had lots of children who would follow in their parents' footsteps. Their sole topics of conversation were childhood illnesses and complaints about the weather, their Aboriginal servants, the drought, the floods, and, of course, the sheep.

Helena hurried along with her calculations. It was getting hotter and hotter, and she wiped her damp forehead on her sleeve. She couldn't stand the climate – sweltering in summer, freezing, damp cold in winter. In fact, she couldn't stand anything about the place. She'd spent nearly two years in this little pioneer town of two thousand souls that had sprouted up in the middle of nowhere in the southwest corner of Victoria, and she still hadn't got used to it.

Coleraine was surrounded by vast, monotonous plains, swept by the violent wind that churned clouds of yellow dust in its wake and gave her headaches. Roughly six miles to the south was the Wannon River, which had given its name to the district, and which often flooded during the rainy season, isolating Coleraine and its surroundings.

Coleraine had a post office, three general stores including Bernhard's, a saddler, a smithy, a local newspaper, a jeweller, a tailor, three hotels, one presbytery and a private school run by two old maids, Miss Crouch and her niece Miss Arrovoye, where Helena was learning English with students who were fifteen years younger than her. And there were two or three pubs where the farmers got drunk after the horse races, the only entertainment in the region.

Helena felt lonely and abandoned. She had no friends in Coleraine, nor did she try to make any.

People were kind, obliging and supportive – but Helena had little to say to them other than neighbourly pleasantries and the usual customer dealings. If only Eva had stayed with her. But after a year in Coleraine, her cousin, who didn't get along with her father, had decided to go back to Melbourne with her three children.

Helena would have followed her if she'd known what she could do in the city. But with no money, where could she go? Now she had to prepare the meals all by herself. And she was also in charge of the housekeeping. Bernhard's house had all the modern comforts, with a real bathroom – a claw-footed bathtub and a shower – four bedrooms, a kitchen, living room and dining room.[2] But cleaning it all took a huge amount of time.

Her uncle wasn't even grateful to her for it. When he wasn't making fun of her lady-like clothing, the ridiculously high heels that she insisted on wearing even on the dirt roads, her parasols to protect her face, her fear of lizards, spiders and night noises, her urban mannerisms, her hopeless inability to ride horseback, or the charred legs of lamb, he said nothing. He could go for days without saying a thing, expressing himself solely through grunts and other unappealing noises. It was not surprising that he had never managed to remarry after the death of his wife, poor Aunt Chana. No sensible woman would want anything to do with such a man.

In the beginning, pressured by his insistent siblings writing all the way from Kraków, Bernhard was resolved to marry off his niece. During the first few months she was there, he introduced her to suitors chosen from among the handful of Polish, Romanian, and German Jews who lived in Coleraine and the surrounding villages of the Wannon district. All were charmed: Helena was a rare find in those parts. A *shayna maidel*, a pretty girl, judging by the appreciative gazes that followed her hourglass figure. And she had real character on top of it, which could come in very useful in this harsh terrain. They could already imagine her running their household, warming their bed, and keeping a strict watch over the many children they would be sure to give her.

But these men were farmers, blacksmiths, cobblers, gold washers: *proster mensh*, vulgar individuals who she could never imagine knowing in Kraków. So the mere thought of marrying one of them ...

And because she rejected them out of hand, without even so much as a smile — *no, I don't want that Yankel, I couldn't care less that his pub is the most popular one in Digby, nor do I want Moishe with his limp, or Nathan, he may be a rich farmer, but he's still no better than an* ongentrinken, *a drunkard* — Bernhard then resorted to introducing her to the remaining bachelors — *goyim* — in the area.

Helena wouldn't get married. Over and over she had to explain — politely to begin with, then raising her voice in what turned into shouting matches after each of her rejections – she had no intention of shutting herself off in Coleraine. And so Bernhard gave up on the idea. From that point on he kept an eye on everything she ate as if calculating the cost of each mouthful. And yet Helena ate like a bird. When he had been drinking, he predicted she would dry up like an old sheepskin tanned by the brickfielder – the desert wind – since she didn't want a man by her side.

But there was worse than Bernhard.

Louis, his younger brother, raised sheep in Merino, a little town twelve miles south of Coleraine. Louis was a lecherous bushman who slept with his boots on and spoke with a thick sheepherder's accent. When Helena walked by he would run his tongue over his lips, as if she were a bowl full of cream. Whenever she came to visit, he insisted on teaching her how to ride a horse. After only a few minutes, Helena would complain of a backache and ask to go home. She couldn't have said which was more frightening: the horse or her uncle.

Louis did not give up easily. His niece's rejections even seemed to excite him. The last time he had got too close to her, in the stable, touching her breasts, she had clouted him with her parasol. Not wanting to see Gitel's daughter disfigured – it would create havoc in the family – Bernhard had managed to calm his brother down, but only just. Louis had chased her, hurling insults.

Helena had run as fast as she could and sought refuge in the school where the pupils stared at her, their mouths agape.

'What's a "bugger"?' she had asked the teachers, Miss Crouch and Miss Arrovoye, when she had caught her breath.

The two old maids turned as crimson as the worn plush curtains in Helena's bedroom.

'Well, I suppose it's a lowlife person or some such thing,' murmured Miss Crouch, while Miss Arrovoye lowered her eyes.

Nothing was going to plan. Not that she had any real plans. Every night she went to bed in tears, exhausted, after working harder than any beast, except for the few hours when she went to the school.

She was overwhelmed by homesickness. She hated everything here: the climate, the people, the sheep, her uncles. It was too hard. God knows, life in Poland was anything but easy, but Australia ... She would never get used to it. Gitel would have cried for a whole week if she had even the faintest idea how her eldest daughter was living.

'Don't worry, Mama,' Helena would say over and over, looking at herself in the little mirror above the toilet. 'I cleanse my skin when I get up in the morning, I moisturise it with your cream, and I brush my hair for one hundred strokes before I go to bed, just the way you taught me.'

Gitel's ritual was one of the few memories that still tied Helena to the past. She had forgotten how often she used to rail against the confinement of her life back there, and how she had prayed to the heavens to help her find a way out.

Helena could almost feel the warmth of her family nest. The few letters she got from Kraków, which she read over and over until she knew them by heart, plunged her into a nostalgia that left her devastated long after she had read them. She was suffering from an oppressive, unshakeable despondency.

She was nearly twenty-seven, and her life was a complete and utter failure. She hadn't studied or got married, she worked like a brute and didn't earn a shilling. Her life was going nowhere in this hostile land, with her equally hostile uncles. And yet it was out of the question to return. To what? The same difficult life with no chance of escape? To see her family's pitying gazes? She could hear them from here: still not a penny to her name, our poor Chaja, and completely unmarriable. They would call her a *shlimazel*, an unlucky woman. Or worse yet, a *lebish*, a loser.

She had come this far, and had managed to avoid the pitfalls in her path. But one day she might fall off one of those damned horses and find herself with a broken back. Or she'd get bitten by one of those vicious little bush snakes that sneak into your sheets or your shoes and she would die after terrible suffering. Or that brute Louis would get what he wanted. He'd rape her in a dark alley and she'd damage her eyesight with weeping. If by chance she managed to survive, they were bound to force her to marry one of those yokels. And she wouldn't be able to get out of it.

Then she'd be stuck between the herds of children and sheep, her face ravaged by sun and wind; she'd grow old before her time, she'd be sun-wizened and wrinkled like the customers at the store or like those English ladies she had seen in Melbourne with their skin like parchment. Fortunately her mother had given her those jars of cream. Gitel's caring gesture along with Helena's fear of the sun's rays had kept her complexion like porcelain, earning her the appreciative gazes of men and the envious remarks of women.

'My dear, how do you manage to keep your skin so white?'

Helena replied in her bad English, compounded by the impossible Polish accent that she would never manage to lose: 'A family secret.'

And then, as if she were sharing a mysterious, precious treasure, she would reach under the counter for a little jar of cream, and rub some of it into her customer's skin. The women loved being looked after. Helena gave them advice, too: don't go out in the sun, it's a disaster for your skin; use a parasol and wear a hat. The women would leave Bernhard's general store enchanted.

Even though Helena had been parsimonious with her creams since her arrival, she was beginning to run out. No matter how often she told the farmers' wives that the cream was very expensive because it came from so far away, they still asked for more. Perhaps she could sell a few jars in the general store: Bernhard wouldn't say no. But to do that she would have to order some from Gitel.

One night when she couldn't get to sleep – in Coleraine, the night time was even more terrifying than the day – Helena went over her calculations for the hundredth time. If all went well, it would take two months for her mother to receive her letter, and two months for the parcel to travel from Kraków to Melbourne, then another two weeks to get the goods through customs and delivered.

It was far too long and far too complicated as well. It would be quicker for Helena to make the cream herself. It couldn't be that difficult. All she had to do was ask Jacob Lykusky for the formula. Uncle Jacob. The memory suddenly became very vivid: she felt homesick thinking about her mother's smile when she opened the large jars of cream the chemist had brought. He could not refuse her this favour.

Helena sat up in bed, her mind racing. Why hadn't she thought of this earlier? The Australian women were envious of her perfect complexion: she could offer them the means to obtain it. Or rather, sell it to them. She would make the cream and put it on sale in pretty little jars. If she knew how to go about it, before long she would be able to earn a living. But to invest in her research, she would need a little bit of money and, unfortunately, her savings had vanished long ago.

Bernhard was so tight with his money that Helena was sure he wouldn't even lend her a shilling. No one in Coleraine would lend her anything. She would have to find a way on her own. As the night progressed, Helena began to outline a plan that she would perfect as the weeks went by. She would leave Coleraine and go to Melbourne where she would open a beauty salon in a smart neighbourhood. She could picture it down to the last detail, imagining the colour on the walls and the shape of the furniture. Women would feel at home in her salon, and they would be able to leave their domestic worries and unruly children behind for a few hours.

Helena would teach them to look after their skin and to protect it with Gitel's cream. They might also need massages. Helena recalled how good it felt when her mother, in a rare moment of tenderness, would knead her back.

It did her good to dream, it helped her forget her wretched life. But every time she came up against the same problem: she had no money. How could she pay for the move to Melbourne? And to make her cream? These nagging questions wouldn't go away.

Then she remembered the old pharmacist who had a small dispensary in Sandford, the next town over. On her weekly trips to the market in her uncle's cart she always stopped in to see him. His tiny shop was dusty and old-fashioned, cluttered with jars of herbs, bark, oils, potions, salves, and ointments. Helena loved their medicinal smell.

Why hadn't she thought of this before? He would be her salvation. When the next market day came around, she left Bernhard with his cattle breeders and headed towards the pharmacy with a pounding heart.

At first she pretended to be nosing around the shop, removing stoppers from flasks, rearranging the jars of cream. Then she took a deep breath for courage and walked straight over to the old pharmacist.

'Say, Mr Henderson. Would you hire me to give you a hand?'

5

A TOUGH APPRENTICESHIP

Uncle Bernhard refused to let Helena go to Sandford. He would not hear of her working for the old pharmacist, who had immediately agreed to Helena's suggestion.

But the young woman stood her ground. She wouldn't stay on in Coleraine another minute, not for all the gold in the world. 'You're more stubborn than a bloody sheep!' shouted Bernhard, changing his whining tone for insults in Yiddish.

Helena glared at him icily and, without another word, she went back to her room to finish packing her things. Bernhard followed her and stood in the doorway, continuing to proffer insults but not daring to actually step in. Without saying a word, Helena went out into the street, dragging her heavy trunk behind her. He didn't lift a finger to help her.

A neighbour was waiting outside in his cart, a kind farmer who had agreed to drive her to Sandford. She climbed up on the seat and adjusted her hat, while the good man put her trunk in the back along with all the sheep.

'Good riddance,' was Bernhard's blessing, as the horses pulled away.

The pharmacist set her salary at twenty-two shillings a month to work all day long without interruption. It wasn't much, but it was a first taste of independence. Besides, Helena enjoyed meeting the customers. The women sought her out, just as they had done in her uncle's store. She listened to them with a mixture of curiosity and empathy, asking questions about their children, their husbands, their health. She did everything she could to help them, went to fetch the potions they needed from the back of the shop, filled their prescriptions. Working in the pharmacy gave her a heady feeling: she never tired of the infinitesimal sense of power her customers gave her by blindly following her advice.

Old Henderson taught her what he knew. Learning as she went, she mixed spermaceti and lily bulbs, paraffin and almond peel, wax and herbs, lavender and honey. She read the scientific treatises he recommended and more than once she rued the fact that she had not been allowed to study medicine. And she thought about handsome Stanislaw, the boy she had loved in Kraków, but less and less often now. His features had faded long ago. He must be married by now, she mused, with a horde of children. Helena was not the sort of woman to pine for a lost love, whether real or imaginary.

Helena took the last remaining jar of Lykusky's cream and examined it under the microscope, trying to identify its ingredients. She stayed up late night after night, straining her eyes and nearly falling asleep on her feet as she climbed the staircase leading up to her attic bedroom. In the morning she would get up before sunrise to clean the pharmacy, mop the floors and wipe the jars with a dust rag. In the evening she had to count up the day's takings after exhausting hours on her feet where she hadn't a moment to catch her breath. She didn't complain. She had always been a hard worker and now she was driven by her plan.

Gitel eventually wrote to her. She sent a few jars of cream with her letter. 'I can't send you more than that, my girl, everything is expensive here. Money doesn't grow on trees in Szeroka Street.'

Helena quickly read the two pages filled with news, but that was not what interested her. Gitel had no end of complaints: '*Oy gevelt*, your sisters are growing up, it's hard to marry them off without a dowry, your father is bankrupt again.'

She was beginning to feel discouraged when she came to the postscript: here was what she had been waiting for so impatiently. The magic formula. Or at least what her mother had gleaned of it. Herbs, pine bark, sesame, almond essence, oil, wax … With the letter in one hand and a pestle in the other, Helena scurried back to her research. It couldn't be as complicated as all that. And yet it was. She could not get the texture right. It was too liquid, or not liquid enough; too dry or too sticky.

Helena became her own guinea pig. Every night before going to bed she would try some of the day's mixture on her face. There were times she panicked: what if she woke up with her face covered in pimples? No, there could be no danger of that, at least not with these ingredients. But there was still something missing if she was to make her haphazard concoctions resemble a beauty cream worthy of the name.

Until one night a flash of inspiration came to her. It happened by chance, just as she was about to drift off. This often occurred between wakefulness and sleep, in that strange in-between state where thoughts and dreams collide and great revelations appear out of nowhere. Just when she least expected it, Helena started thinking about sheep. She had read in one of Mr Henderson's old books, hardly paying attention at the time, that their wool secreted a substance that was indispensable for the manufacture of cold cream (as the English ladies would say, carefully rounding their lips). That ingredient was lanolin. And suddenly she remembered what she had read. It all became crystal clear; it was as if the last piece of a jigsaw had fallen into place. Lanolin was exactly what she needed to add in order to obtain a cream that would be both soft and moisturising.

In one of the pharmacist's old tomes on cosmetology she found everything she needed to know about the softening properties of lanolin and also how to extract it from the fleece and purify it, because in its raw state suint – sheep sweat – gives off an unbearable stench.

She remembered how she used to wrinkle her nose whenever she went along certain narrow streets in Kazimierz where the tanners dried animal hides before transforming them into leather. To get rid of the smell, she would have to add rosewater or lavender and then water, too, which was essential for moisturising.

Lanolin was the missing link that would change lead into gold. Or more precisely, the lumpy mixture in her kettle into a finished product. Just a bit more patience and she would be rich. She was already savouring her revenge. But it would require a lot more hard work if she was to afford all the costly ingredients she needed, particularly with the pittance that Mr Henderson paid her. Helena was in a hurry. The years were flying by.

Then she recalled the pleasant face of Lady Susanna, the wife of the aide-de-camp to the Governor of Queensland who she had met on the *Prinz Regent Luitpold* on her crossing to Australia. Helena had her address in the little white silk purse in which she put her most precious documents for safekeeping. She wrote to Lady Susanna straight away and received a reply by return of post. Of course Susanna remembered Helena very well. How could one forget such a charming person? She finished her letter with an invitation to Brisbane. 'Stay as long as you like, my dear. You'll see, you'll love the town. Of course it's a bit provincial, it's not London or Melbourne, but you can find everything here.'

By now Helena was a master at packing her trunk, and she put together a few reasonably presentable outfits. Then she said farewell to her benefactor and boarded the train that would take her to a new life. It was a long journey, particularly for a young woman travelling on her own, but Helena was starting to get used to it. To reach Brisbane she would have to travel 1,200 miles through three colonies: Victoria, New South Wales and Queensland.

At last, after an endless week spent sleeping and staring at the landscape, Helena arrived, exhausted and dusty, at the central station in Brisbane.

But she was free, once again.

As she looked out from the hackney carriage taking her to her friend's house, Helena was mesmerised by all there was to discover around her. Brisbane, the capital of Queensland, was a pleasant, modern city, with wide avenues flanked by low buildings, restaurants, theatres, clothing stores and a brand-new electric tramway. English and German colonists had built the city fifty years earlier on the banks of the river of the same name, notorious for its repeated flooding. The last and most terrible flood had been in 1893, and everyone had a vivid memory of it. Every time the Brisbane flooded they had to rebuild all the houses along the river banks.

Helena took in all the sights of the city like a person starved of beauty for too long. She gazed in awe at the monuments in the classical style: the cathedral, the parliament, and the old mill that had been built by convicts; the entire country had been created by the sweat of their brows. The first convicts had arrived in Sydney in 1788, transported from England on the eleven ships of the First Fleet. At a time when British prisons were overflowing, Australia had become the ideal place to get rid of the surplus criminals. For nearly a century, convicts had been put to work building the country, often in terrible conditions. Transportation finally ended in 1868. Altogether, 160,000 souls – men, women, and children – had been transported, many of them younger than fifteen.

Helena had felt like a prisoner for so long that she couldn't help but sympathise with their story. In Coleraine if you went alone into a pub you were immediately taken for a loose woman. She wondered how she had managed to last there for so long.

On arrival at Susanna's, after their initial effusive greetings, followed by a good cup of tea, she shared with her friend her sanitised version of the years spent in Victoria. Her motto might well have been, 'Never complain, never explain'. Helena refused to be pitied. In her memoirs, she always gave the most basic outline of the more painful episodes in her life. She claimed her uncle was a big landowner, that she had had everything she needed but she refused to marry his brother, who had been making overtures to her. Helena must have smiled to herself whenever she delivered this particular lie, lowering her eyes like a terrified virgin. So it would have been awkward to stay on any longer, she explained. Besides, she was bored to death living the life of an idle young woman.

She said nothing about Bernhard's general store, or Louis's brutality, or Mr Henderson's pharmacy and the hours of relentless labour, washing, drying, preparing, selling ... The only time Helena told the truth was when she asked her friend to help her find a respectable job, because she had to earn a living. Touched by Helena's story and guessing at the sordid truth she had left unspoken, Susanna promised she would help.

The few weeks Helena spent in Brisbane were like a dream. Torn between her admiration for Susanna and her friends and her awareness of her own humble background, Helena no longer knew what to think. Her makeshift outfits seemed wretched in comparison to the latest London fashions the Brisbane ladies wore. But the sun and wind had wrought irreparable damage to their fair complexions, and they went into raptures over Helena's flawless skin, with its velvety texture and lack of wrinkles. These compliments restored her confidence in herself and, above all, her project. Soon she would be as wealthy as all these inaccessible women.

True to her promise, Susanna set about finding her friend a job and a place to live. By chance she heard that Lady Lamington, the wife of the Governor of Queensland, who was very popular for championing the cause of the Aboriginals, was looking for a reliable person to assist their nanny. The couple lived in Brisbane, but they had settled their two young children at their estate in Toowoomba, a hill resort located 80 miles from the town.

In Brisbane, the Lamingtons lived in the governor's residence, an imposing colonial manor set in vast gardens. As the wife of the aide-de-camp, Susanna had no difficulty in obtaining an interview for her friend. The couple seemed quite taken with Helena. They found her pretty, well mannered and reserved. As for Helena, she was more intimidated than she would have liked by the luxury of the house and its many servants. As was her wont, she revealed the bare minimum about her past. But the Lamingtons were curious, and plied her with questions.

'Seven sisters!' exclaimed Lady Lamington, amused. 'How can one have seven sisters?'

'Do you speak German?' asked Lord Lamington. 'That's very important. Oh really, you lived in Vienna? And French?'

'In Poland, where my father has a vast estate, I had a governess from Paris,' replied Helena without batting an eyelid. As the conversation progressed, touched by her hosts' interest, she began to feel more at ease.

The Lamingtons would never check up on what she told them. Helena lied with such unflinching candour that she could not fail to inspire trust. Moreover, the young woman was instantly at ease with the two small children, who in no time would be following her everywhere, seeking refuge in her arms. Her vivacity and intelligence made her more than an ordinary nanny. In a matter of days the family had adopted her, and she was promoted from household servant to lady's companion. To Helena this was every bit as humiliating, but the new position now gave her access to their world, and it opened a door to the aristocracy – even if it was by taking the back staircase.

Whenever the Lamingtons came to Toowoomba, Helena was invited to all the dinners and garden parties. Her initiation into the ways of high society began at the manor house. She learned the customs of the English aristocracy, something which would serve her well later in life in London, when she would keep company with the upper classes. For the time being she was observing, imitating, storing up impressions. How to behave at table, how to use an oyster fork, how to sip wine and smile when she had nothing to say, how to listen patiently while the gentlemen talked about hunting or the ladies about their household concerns.

Seen as a sort of charming, exotic creature in a country which had no lack of them, the young lady from Kraków was beginning to lose her rough edges. At the same time, she was able to continue her research on her cream.

All the states in Australia are richly endowed by nature, but Queensland's flora is perhaps the most diverse. Its treasure trove of plants could be used as ingredients in ointments and beauty creams. When she had time away from the nursery, Helena would go gathering plants. In Coleraine, the bush had never called to her, but here, when she went exploring around the estate, a basket on her arm to collect her treasures, she felt inspired.

Back in her room she carefully examined each of her finds, looking up the plant's properties and how it could be mixed with others to obtain the best effect. The library in the house was overflowing with books about botany, ancient tomes with plates, and encyclopedias, all of which added to her rudimentary knowledge of medicinal herbs.

The hours she spent poring over the old treatises were moments of pure happiness. She absorbed everything she read, memorising formulas. She learned that cosmetology was considered an art in its own right during antiquity, and formulas were recorded in the treatises of Galen, physician to the court of Marcus Aurelius, in those of Heraclitus of Taranto, and in those of Criton, who treated the wife of the emperor Trajan. The word came from the Greek *cosmos*, which means both adornment and order. Plato dismissed face paints and ointments because he was of the opinion that they created a foreign beauty, something unnatural, that he opposed to the beauty of the body, which could be shaped by gymnastics.

Another etymological theory suggests that the word comes from *kemet*, the black earth on the banks of the Nile which women used to protect themselves against the dry air and desert winds. The Egyptians were genuine chemists where beauty was concerned, capable of creating synthetic products that both embellished and healed the body. They made their favourite powders with ground gypsum perfumed with myrrh and frankincense. Other pomades included ochre to lighten the skin, olive oil, beeswax or rosewater. The use of toilet articles was common: ancient tweezers, combs, hairpins and mirrors have all been found, nestled inside pretty boxes.

In Athens and Rome, elegant women would soak in baths perfumed with aromatic oils obtained from pressed olives or bitter almonds and mixed with spices like cardamom and ginger, or essences of lily or iris. They applied white lead to their skins, unaware that it was poisonous, and made face masks with clay, starch, honey and asses' milk.

In the Middle Ages, barley beer was prescribed to give colour to the face, and belladonna to add sparkle to the eyes. Broad bean flour and chickpeas were added to the composition of beauty masks. A woman would remove all the hair from her face and body with strips of hot wax, and combat her wrinkles with the help of pomades made of wax, almond oil, crocodile fat, and the blood of hedgehogs, bats, or snakes. But the Church was opposed to any sort of embellishment, which it viewed as an attempt to alter the work of the Creator, leading women to indulge in futile occupations rather than working for the salvation of their souls. For clerics, the pursuit of beauty was the work of the Devil.

Helena never wearied of learning and writing things down. She couldn't get enough of the Marquise de Pompadour's natural recipes, like honey beaten with fresh cream and tonic chervil water to refresh the face. In the seventeenth century the skin's alabaster qualities were highly valued but difficult to preserve. One had to avoid the sun and the elements, but also the excesses of life at court, staying up late and eating rich food, all of which were devastating for the complexion. Ointments made from slug secretions and aromatic plants were applied at night to restore pallor and treat pimples.

This recently acquired knowledge merely confirmed what Helena had always suspected: the sun is bad for the skin and moisturising can repair many ill effects. She waited impatiently for the parcels of cream that her mother sent from Kraków every two or three months. The number of jars would vary depending on how much money Gitel had at her disposal. Helena would then invite all the women in the Lamington circle to test it, and her cream always met with the same success.

On 1 January 1901, a year after Helena's arrival in Toowoomba, the Australian Commonwealth was proclaimed, a federation of the country's six major colonies. On the twenty-second of that month, Queen Victoria died at the age of eighty. Her son Edward VII succeeded her, and several months later the first Australian Parliament in Melbourne was inaugurated.

The Lamingtons moved their children and servants back to Brisbane and were very busy with the coronation celebrations. In spite of herself, Helena was caught up in the whirlwind that would mark her real debut in society. Lady Lamington introduced her to all her friends as a beauty specialist. For shy Helena, who was still not at ease among the scornful, exclusive aristocracy, the only way to arouse people's interest was to talk about her cream and her plans to manufacture it.

They all found this terribly amusing and encouraged her as if it were some charming eccentricity. The English adored people like Helena. She played at being light-hearted, but her mind remained alert. She must not allow herself to become intoxicated by a world she knew she could never belong to, no matter what she did.

The interlude came to a sudden end when Lady Lamington informed her of the family's departure for Bombay. Over time the two women had developed a real respect for each other. But there was no room in Helena's heart for regret. She had never seen her stint as a domestic servant – albeit a privileged one – as anything other than temporary. It was time for her to start teaching Australian women how to be beautiful.

6

243 COLLINS STREET

A thirty-year-old woman who was determined to succeed in a city like Melbourne could do only one thing: work. Just like the thousands of other single young women who, in those days, made up more than a third of the workforce.

Melbourne was a new city of over 500,000 inhabitants. Founded in 1834 at the mouth of the River Yarra by two of Her Majesty's subjects, the city was named after the prime minister, Lord Melbourne. Twenty years later the land of convicts had become a promised land. And the rumour was spreading like wildfire: gold had been found in a river near Ballarat, just 65 miles north-west of Melbourne.

Eastern Australia experienced a gold rush frenzy comparable to that in California and Alaska. From all over the world men armed with picks and shovels disembarked in Port Phillip Bay and headed off to settle in the gold-mining towns that were spreading like weeds. The dream didn't last long – four years at most – but that didn't matter. Melbourne had begun to grow exponentially. There may have been little gold but the colonists were raking in money from real estate and finance. They were building churches, offices, cafés, restaurants, hotels and shopping galleries left, right and centre. Wide boulevards were laid out and parks were landscaped. In less than forty years Melbourne became one of the most important cities in the Empire and was known as the richest city in the world. Its stock exchange was as important as that of the financial hubs of New York and London, if not more so.

The economic crisis of 1891 brought a halt to the boundless expansion. Melbourne continued to develop but no longer with the frenzy of its early years. Before long, Sydney, the capital of New South Wales, had overtaken it. At the time of Helena's arrival, the city inhabited by over thirty nationalities was still known as Marvellous Melbourne, or Smellbourne, after the sophisticated sewer system the city had just installed. Helena marvelled at how modern it all was, far surpassing anything she had ever seen. In comparison, Kraków, Vienna and even Brisbane seemed dreary.

The only cloud on the horizon was the poverty that crippled her. Her savings from the salary she had received from the Lamingtons would be just enough to cover the rent of a furnished room and basic daily necessities while she looked for a job. Without the means to pay for them, she could only daydream about concerts, shows and restaurants.

During the hot summers the people of Melbourne lived outdoors. The women were healthy and muscular from playing tennis, pedalling merrily on their bicycles, and swimming in the sea, modestly clad from head to toe. An Australian swimmer, Annette Kellerman, would soon invent a more revealing swimsuit.

However, despite the protection offered by hats and parasols, the sun still damaged women's skin, and the winter wind chapped it, leaving premature lines around lips and eyelids. And, like the inhabitants of Coleraine and Brisbane, these city women did little to protect their skin.

As in all the major cities in Australia, novelty was more than welcome. The social system was far more advanced than in Europe. Workers' rights were respected – the hard-won eight-hour working day had just been introduced. Suffragettes were particularly active. In Sydney, Louisa Lawson, a writer, publisher and journalist, campaigned for women's rights. Ten years earlier she had founded *The Dawn*, a monthly journal with an all-female editorial team. Distributed throughout Australia and even overseas, the magazine discussed politics, domestic violence, and girls' education.

Thanks to the activism of these feminists, most Australian women were given the vote in 1902, four years after the women of New Zealand. Only the Aborigines were left out. They would wait another sixty-five years to be granted full citizenship, even though they had lived in Australia for over 50,000 years.

The role of women in this pioneer country, where life was tough for everyone, was almost as important as that of men. No one found it surprising to see so many young saleswomen, secretaries, journalists, barmaids, chambermaids, waitresses or telephone operators at the brand-new exchange. They earned half as much as their male colleagues, but they were intoxicated by their new independence. Besides, once they had paid the rent, bills and food, they still had a little bit left over to spend on trinkets, silk stockings or cosmetics. And they didn't refrain from spending.

Helena Rubinstein's spectacular rise in Australia could also be explained by her innate sense of timing, which, in business, as in love, is essential for success. She was in the right place at the right time, in a country where women were beginning to shake off the fetters that had been imposed on them for so long. In later years in London, Paris and New York, the scenario would be the same: her beauty expertise would keep step with women's progress. There was nothing frivolous about wanting to be beautiful, and besides, political rights, work, and financial autonomy went hand in hand with an improved appearance. This last point even became an act of resistance. Helena fully understood as much: to succeed in life, a modern woman owed it to herself to have not only a good mind, but also the good looks to go with it.

But for the time being Helena had not given this too much thought. What she wanted above all was to earn money, and quickly. After so many years of hardship, nothing and no one could frighten her, except poverty.

She found a room in a family guesthouse in the suburb of St Kilda, and had no choice but to take up two waitressing jobs, which would just about keep her head above water. She worked at La Maison Dorée in the mornings, and in the afternoon and evening at the Winter Gardens Tea Room, a café frequented by writers, musicians and artists. Up at dawn, she worked like a dog, until her legs were swollen and her feet sore. When at last she returned to her tiny lodgings, well after midnight, she hardly had the strength left to lie down on her bed, where she would drift off the minute her head hit the pillow.

There were evenings when she was so tired that she neglected Gitel's sacrosanct precepts: brush your hair, clean your face, apply your cream. But no matter how discouraged she became in such moments of extreme solitude and exhaustion, she had no intention of giving up. At dawn she would grit her teeth and head valiantly into the day.

She may have been down and out, but she had chosen her jobs wisely. La Maison Dorée and the Winter Gardens Tea Room were two strategic venues for meeting people. The salary was negligible, even if you counted the tips, but both were places where a clever young woman could easily hook a rich man and set herself up in a fine marriage. In Melbourne, as in Coleraine, men were easily swayed by Helena's charm. But she wasn't interested. She nimbly sidestepped any physical overtures.

Among her admirers were four friends who often came to drink a few pints together: Cyril Dillon was just starting out as a painter; Abel Isaacson had made his fortune selling wine, and always wore a fedora and a white silk tie with a pearl tie-pin; Herbert Farrow owned one of the most successful printing presses in the city; and finally there was Mr Thompson, manager of the Robur Tea Company, a firm that imported tea from India and China and manufactured porcelain and silver utensils.

Good-looking and something of a ladies' man, Thompson showered Helena with flowers. He was married, but she no longer worried about principles. Was he her first lover? She must have got over her prudishness after three years in Coleraine and one in Toowoomba, but Helena remained unerringly discreet on the topic. All four gentlemen served as stepping stones to her extraordinary success in Australia, but she erased them from her own official version: her legend was hers and hers alone.

In the mid 1950s, Helena returned to Australia for the last time with her secretary Patrick O'Higgins; Abel Isaacson, who was still alive, told the young man about the role the four of them had played in Helena's life. In 1971, when O'Higgins published his book about his employer,[1] Cyril Dillon, whose paintings now hung in various museums throughout Australia and the United States, confirmed Isaacson's story to an Australian journalist. In an interview with the *Melbourne Herald*,[2] he spoke at length about the roles he and the other three had played.

Because she saw them every day, either as a group or on their own, Helena ended up befriending them. The young men were intrigued by her, and questioned her relentlessly until she revealed her ambitions to them. She would start working on her cream the minute her shift ended. She had used part of her wages to buy lanolin and added water-lily essence to give the cream a more pleasant fragrance.

When she talked to them in her broken English sprinkled with Yiddish and Polish, her face lit up and her eyes sparkled. Suddenly she became a determined, confident young woman, who was convinced that life owed her something. They took her seriously and decided to help her, each in his own way. Thompson explained the importance

67

of marketing – a new word to describe the way one could influence the consumer if the product was presented in an attractive manner. The Robur Tea Company regularly bought space in the newspapers to run advertisements, and these had a real impact on sales. Once Helena had manufactured her cream she would have to do the same. Without advertising, you can't get anywhere, he concluded. Helena would remember his advice.

Cyril Dillon drew her a logo with an Egyptian motif that she used to illustrate her packaging. Dillon was charged with the layout of the first brochures, which were printed by Herbert Farrow. They would hand them out on the trams and in the train stations. Abel Isaacson would help her with the logistics.

A fifth man also entered the scene, Frederick Sheppard Grimwade, the president of a well-known pharmaceutical company. Was he too her lover? Once again, it remains a mystery. But thanks to Grimwade, Helena obtained Australian citizenship in May 1907.[3] Acting as a sponsor for his protégée, he signed the document. Better still, his laboratory provided the young woman with sophisticated tools that were indispensable for the manufacture of her cream – receptacles for mixing the ingredients, and cauldrons for high-temperature boiling.

Now known as Valaze, Helena's childhood cream was at last reborn, almost identical to what she remembered.

The origins of the name Valaze, which rang as sharp as that of a French aristocrat and meant 'gift from heaven' in Hungarian, are unknown, but it had instant appeal.

The cream didn't cost much to make, scarcely tenpence per jar. Thompson, who was also helping with the accounts, thought it should be sold for two shillings and threepence. 'Women won't buy anything that cheap,' declared Helena. 'When it comes to improving their appearance, they need to have the impression they're treating themselves to something exceptional. Let's see ... let's sell it to them for seven shillings and sevenpence.'

She had a perfect grasp of the psychology of her future customers. Not a single one would ever raise an eyebrow at the price tag; they all knew that beauty had a price. Before she had even found the premises for her shop, Helena put her jars on sale at local markets. She also went door to door to pharmacies, and left them with stock to sell. They took six jars the first week, then eight the next ... And on it went.

Women bought directly from Helena, too. They enjoyed her banter and the way she wasn't afraid to cheerfully scold them. The little jars sold like hot cakes. Every penny she took went into a cardboard box hidden under her mattress.

The Winter Gardens Tea Room was located in the Block Arcade shopping gallery which connected Elizabeth Street to Collins Street and Little Collins Street, three of the most elegant streets in town. Built in true Victorian style, the gallery filtered direct sunlight through its glass ceiling. As she came to know the neighbourhood, Helena found a tiny three-room apartment next to the restaurant at 138 Elizabeth Street. In all likelihood, Thompson and Grimwade lent her the money for her security deposit.

Helena also claimed to have borrowed $250 from Helen McDonald, whom she had met on the ship on her way to Australia. Whatever the case may be, she reimbursed her debts as soon as she could, as she hated owing money. One fine morning Helena handed in her waitress's apron and moved her meagre belongings and jars of cream to her new apartment, which would also be her company headquarters and factory. She immediately had her name engraved on a plaque and put it up at the entrance to the building: *Helena Rubinstein & Company*.

Shortly before her death, Helena – who had always been evasive about the composition of this initial cream – showed Patrick O'Higgins a slip of paper she had found while sorting through some old files. It was Jacob Lykusky's famous magic formula. She insisted the young man read it, maintaining it was a page of history.

On the torn, yellowed, time-worn paper were all the ingredients, written down in her large, old-fashioned handwriting, with its carefully executed upstrokes and downstrokes. O'Higgins, who had expected to find a list of exotic ingredients such as oriental almond essence and extract of Carpathian conifer bark, was disappointed. 'Vegetable wax, mineral oil and sesame.' That was it, although no doubt half the ingredients were missing from the recipe, and most importantly, so were the proportions in which they were to be mixed.

Right up to the end, Helena Rubinstein would keep the composition of that first Valaze cream a secret, and one can imagine that it had neither the fluidity nor the lightness of the products that came later. But it was full of promise, and had got off to a brilliant start. Thanks to the combined effects of marketing – Thompson's lessons – and the initial articles devoted to her in the press, sales continued to rise.

After only a few months, Helena was able to move from Elizabeth Street and in 1902 she opened her first beauty salon at 243 Collins Street.

7

BEAUTY IS POWER

Eugenia Stone was nibbling on the end of her pencil, a sure sign that she was extremely agitated.[1] There was certainly no lack of beauty salons in the country. Melbourne, Brisbane, Adelaide and Sydney had an abundance of hairdressers and massage parlours, manicure and pedicure salons, often run by Chinese immigrants. She herself had tested a number of them for her articles. But the three rooms of this sun-filled apartment on the third floor of a fine building in the centre of Melbourne were like nothing she had ever seen.

The unconventional decor was austere yet feminine, a far cry from the imposing Victorian taste. The white walls, pleated silk curtains, wicker dressers and chairs all gave the Valaze Maison de Beauté a European, even Parisian, feel. Eugenia shivered with excitement. It was so very chic and, above all, exactly what the modern woman required.

Miss Stone had come all the way from Sydney to see for herself the phenomenon that everyone was talking about. Despite searching for a flaw, she couldn't find anything negative to say about the cleanliness and charm of the premises, or the way the beauty products were displayed. The pretty black, white, and gold jars of cream filling the shelves made her want to snatch up every last one.

But the most incredible thing was the proprietor herself, a tiny woman with a tight chignon, and skin so pale it was almost transparent. Over her dark blue dress with moiré highlights she wore a white chemist's coat. When she spoke, the R's rolled off her tongue like a rush of pebbles. She massacred half the English words, mixing in two or three other languages. Eugenia Stone pricked up her ears but couldn't determine the origins of her accent. Rumour had it that she was Viennese.

The journalist had come at closing time. Miss Rubinstein was giving a beauty class to some of her clients and when she saw Eugenia Stone, she greeted her then suggested quite simply that she join their little group. Miss Stone had never heard anyone talk about skin in such a scientific way, the way a doctor or a biologist would.

Everything this young woman said bore the seal of common sense. Her clients were more than willing to believe her, and went away enchanted, carrying little black and beige bags bearing the name Helena Rubinstein. Each of them had bought at least three jars of cream.

It was long past closing time, but the shop was still full of people. Finally Helena decided it was time to quit for the day. She lowered the metal shutter herself and invited the journalist to take a seat. She gave the interview like a true professional and never stopped talking. Miss Stone's wrist was sore from taking notes. The readers of the women's section of the *Sydney Morning Herald* were going to love this article.[2] Even Miss Stone, who considered herself one of the leading female journalists in Sydney, was bowled over by Helena. In these early years of the twentieth century, in a country where women had made great strides, it was still not always easy to succeed in a man's world. But this young lady with the tight chignon was proof that determination could lead to success.

Everything she told Miss Stone – about her Polish origins, her interrupted medical studies in Kraków, her classes with the great chemists in Vienna, her years in Coleraine among the pioneers, and her friendship with the Lamingtons and their circle when she had known no one on her arrival in Australia – was remarkable. And then there was her salon. Helena explained simply that she did not have a great deal of money, so she had bought some bamboo furniture for a few pounds, set up a little laboratory that she referred to as her kitchen, and sewn curtains from one of her dresses. She had hand-painted the letters of her shop sign all by herself with pride and an unfaltering hand.

Her story had the ring of truth and Miss Stone was certain of her judgement. There had never been a lack of courageous women in this country, from the first pioneer women in the bush – Amazons who rode astride and killed ferocious animals with their shotguns – to the suffragettes whose cause Miss Stone had so often defended. This tiny little brunette was no exception. Before long she would do Australian women proud. And Australian men, too, for that matter.

Helena continued her explanations. Once she began, nothing could stop her.

'So you see, my dear,' she said, rolling her R's more emphatically than ever, 'as I was saying, my early research led me to a fundamental discovery – revolutionary, even. Women's skin can be classified in three categories: dry, oily, and normal. Just as there are three types of complexion: redhead, blonde, and brunette. No one noticed this before I did. But I've been observing women. That's my job. And I can assure you, moisturising is not the same for all women. Nor is protection. Each woman must learn to identify her skin type before she chooses her skincare. For the time being my range of products is still limited, but I am working night and day to expand it.'

Helena had used her intuition with regard to skin types very early on. Later she would be able to verify it with the help of the most advanced specialists. For the time being she was still experimenting, basing her conclusions on empirical observations. Yet her intuition was so sound that she rarely made a mistake. Female beauty was, for her, a vast domain just waiting to be exploited, and it was up to her to make it prosper – a notion that was even more intoxicating to her than the prospect of making money.

She understood one vital thing: 'Beauty is power. The greatest power of all.' So she asserted in one of the first advertisements, which appeared in *Table Talk* in 1904. In a world run by men, women had to compromise and be clever. Intelligence was a considerable asset but without charm it would not get you far. Together, the two were a fatal weapon.

It was the early twentieth century, and Helena had already anticipated the future of her fellow women, opting resolutely for modernity. Her faith in the power of beauty and a healthy lifestyle in order to 'win' was a real revolution. It would be adopted by feminists all over the world who were struggling, among other things, against the slavery to the corset.

Eugenia Stone went away from Collins Street with a few jars of Valaze wrapped in a pretty paper bag. 'It's a present,' insisted Helena. 'Yes, yes, I assure you, I like you very much.' How could she refuse? The journalist was delighted with the wrapping and the label printed in her new friend's handwriting. It would all look wonderful on her dressing table. In Australia no one had ever seen anything so refined.

Miss Stone had also tested the cream on her face. The sensation was smooth, the perfume delicate. She swore she would follow the expert's advice to the letter. Helena nodded with a smile. She knew how important the opinion of the press could be. Journalists were women like any others, and they liked to be spoiled – perhaps even more so than other women, given the impact of their articles, which could make or break a person's reputation. So they had to be pampered even more than ordinary people. Helena would always make sure she did: even when her success was established, not only would she give her products to journalists, but also dresses from her wardrobe and even jewellery from her own jewellery box.

Success came the moment the salon opened. The address circulated at dinner parties, at whist tables, at picnics along the banks of the Yarra. Scrupulously following her friend Thompson's advice, in 1904 Helena began to run advertisements in *Table Talk* in Melbourne, and in *The Advertiser* in Adelaide.

'Valaze cream by Dr Lykusky, the most famous European skin specialist, is the best moisturising cream. Valaze will improve even the worst skin problems in less than a month.'

She also began promoting mail order sales. But it was Eugenia Stone's article that gave her the boost she needed. 'Madame Rubinstein's cream is the answer to every Australian woman's prayers,' wrote the journalist in the conclusion of her much-read article.

Fifteen thousand letters and almost as many orders followed the publication of the article. Helena was taken by surprise. She opened the letters one after the other, and nearly all said the same thing.

'Dear Miss Rubinstein, I have very white skin with a lot of freckles, do you think it would be possible to …'

'Dear Madam, I live on a farm near Sydney. For some time now I've noticed dark spots on my face …'

Most of the envelopes contained banknotes or cheques. Helena's supplies alone would never be enough to fill all the orders. She set to work at once. Early in the morning, before opening her salon, she prepared her mixtures in her 'kitchen'. Then she filled the porcelain jars, applied the labels, placed them on the shelves, and stored the surplus in her bamboo dressers.

All day long she looked after her clientele on her own. In the evening, once she had written down the day's takings and expenses in a large ledger she had bought for that purpose, she answered her correspondence. In her letters she begged her future customers to be patient, because the cream would take 'eight weeks to arrive by boat'. More than anything, she wanted to maintain the legend that justified the high cost of the product: 'due to transportation and customs fees'. Besides, 'Carpathian pine' or 'essence of Hungarian rose' sounded more likely to inspire her customers' dreams than lanolin from Victorian sheep or water lilies from Queensland. This gave her a considerable advantage over the competition.

Helena offered to reimburse any clients who did not want to wait. Only one asked for her money back. The others agreed to be patient until the orders could be filled. But the problem remained: the task was a superhuman one, even for a force of nature like Helena. She didn't know how she would manage all on her own.

Many times she drifted off to sleep at her worktable in the early hours. When she awoke, the sun was already high in the sky and she just barely had time to wash and change and drink a quick cup of tea. The first clients were knocking on the door. Things couldn't go on this way. She really needed help this time. So she picked up her pen and a sheet of her new letterhead writing paper.

'Dear Dr Lykusky, Did you know that everyone is crazy about your cream in Australia? Women are fighting over it and I'm having trouble keeping up with the supplies. Would you like to come and work with me? I will draw up a contract in due form for you to sign, and I will buy your formula from you legally. I beg you, please accept, you won't regret it. I will send you the cost of your fare. Sincerely yours, et cetera.'

Three months later, Jacob Lykusky disembarked in Melbourne, but only for a short stay, as he had stipulated in his reply. Helena had said yes to his every request. Let him come, and then she'd see. Following Eugenia Stone's example, the journalists who came all published articles full of praise. Together with the advertisements in the newspapers these articles had a considerable impact on her clients. Now Helena could inform her followers that Dr Jacob Lykusky, a renowned Polish physician, was coming to give her a hand. This attracted a new category of women who were impressed by this scientific seal of approval.

Helena knew she needed staff, but she did not have the means to pay them, so she got in the habit of putting the men who asked her out to work. There were a number of newcomers to her usual group of admirers. Such a pretty young woman, all alone in Melbourne: they flocked around her like bees to honey.

When they came into the salon, one after the other, turning their hats in their damp hands, their hearts beating wildly with hope, they were sorely disappointed. Helena was far too busy experimenting with her concoctions in her 'kitchen' to drop everything and go out with them to the theatre or a concert. She would flutter her eyelashes and coquettishly say: 'John, you have such lovely handwriting, will you answer my mail for me? And you, Robert, with your broad shoulders, could you carry these boxes upstairs? Oh, and when you've finished, don't run off … there are some more in the courtyard … and in the shed …'

'And me, Miss Helena?'

She gave a sceptical look at the young man's skinny biceps and scrawny thighs, then she shook her head while her face lit up with a malicious smile.

'With your ready tongue, my dear, I'm sure you would do an excellent job of sticking on labels.'

That was how they spent their Sunday afternoons. There were rarely any young men brave enough to come back. Too busy to think about flirting, Helena did not even notice.

She eventually finished filling the first batch of orders. Lykusky helped her to reformulate the cream, which she had registered under the name Valaze. He also helped her to expand their range of products: together they manufactured a soap, an astringent lotion, and a cleansing cream. She launched a beauty ritual for which her clients paid top dollar. At the salon, she combined her know-how with the mix of gentleness and authority she had shown her sisters throughout her youth in Kraków.

'Above all, you must cover your whole face with the cleansing cream,' she explained, demonstrating as she spoke. 'It must penetrate every pore in your skin to dissolve the dirt accumulated during the day. Then you must use the astringent lotion to remove the residue. Just look at this towel! It's disgusting.'

Melbourne was not yet polluted by automobile exhaust fumes, but a day spent in town could leave one's skin horribly dirty. The fine white towel had turned completely grey. The clients were dismayed.

'Wait,' continued Helena, about to deal the killing blow. 'Now we have reached the third stage. You must apply Valaze cream to moisturise, protect and whiten your skin. I'll massage it slowly in order to allow the active ingredients to penetrate. You'll see, it's a real miracle.'

Above all, it was an economic miracle.

Her clients told their friends and sent them to the salon, or returned with them. Everyone bought cream. Astringent lotion as well, at the price of ten shillings and threepence. Prices had gone up yet again because of the 'customs duties'.

The money was pouring in.

After several months had gone by, Helena had a tidy sum sitting in her bank account. The cardboard box under her bed was a thing of the past. She paid back her debts, hired and trained a saleswoman and invested half of her earnings in advertising. From Melbourne to Brisbane, from Sydney to Perth, from Adelaide to Hobart, Helena's name was everywhere. Advertisements continued to sing the praises of the famous Dr Lykusky, the properties of Valaze cream, and its composition and origin, but Helena always made sure to include the address of her Salon de Beauté on Collins Street, because she also accepted mail order purchases.

Helena wrote her *Beauty in the Making* handbook, which explained both the skincare ritual and the properties of the cream, and had hundreds of copies printed. Clients could write to request a copy, including in their letter the coupon from the bottom of the advertisement. Helena also made the guide available at her salon.

For years, the text hardly differed, even though the language became more and more sophisticated. 'Explain everything clearly then add some blah blah,' she often said.[3] She was no fool. At a later point, she would ask actresses to endorse her products. Nellie Stewart, one of the biggest theatre stars in Australia, was playing in Melbourne for a few months. After the success of her play *Sweet Nell of Old Drury* everyone was talking about her, and spectators had memorised her most famous lines. It would not be long before she heard about Helena.

On first returning to her native country, the actress drove for miles in an open car without any thought of protecting herself from the sun. Her skin dried out and ugly spots covered her nose and cheeks.

Helena gave her diagnosis after examining her: 'My dear, you will recover your natural complexion. Do as I tell you, and don't leave anything out.'

Nellie kissed her as if they were the best of friends, which they did eventually become. Nellie Stewart agreed to be the first spokesperson for Valaze. 'It is the most marvellous blend I've ever used,' she declared on the advertising panels.

It is possible that Helena heard about the way in which Sarah Bernhardt had become a spokesperson for creams, soaps, perfumes and lotions when she stayed in New York in 1880.[4] Or perhaps she had come up with the strategy on her own. In any case, Helena had grasped the importance of using celebrities to endorse her products, and she would often turn to them in the future, since influential women, actresses, and socialites all became her icons.

Nellie Stewart often dropped in unannounced at the salon. One day she arrived with another Nellie: Nellie Melba. The buxom opera singer had also come home for a triumphant tour. Wearing a long embroidered coat and an extravagant hat covered in ostrich plumes, she sang the great aria from *Aida* by way of introduction. Then she turned her enormous body towards Helena, who was transfixed.

'Since you restored a peaches and cream complexion to my little Nellie, I'm sure you can come up with a cream that can improve my voice …'

'Dear lady, please be seated.'

The fragile wicker chairs looked as if they might collapse under the diva's weight so, wisely, she insisted on standing. Helena, who later said she felt 'like a dwarf' next to Melba's imposing frame, had to climb onto a chair to reach her height.

There were days when the queue of customers went all the way down the stairs and out into the street. The salon was getting too small and she could hardly push back the walls. Helena had spotted a new building at 274 Collins Street. She rented an apartment of seven small rooms that she was able to transform into three big ones by knocking down the walls.

The layout stayed the same: an office, the salon, a 'kitchen'. The walls were redone in a lovely pale green and the furniture was upgraded. Everything was decorated with the same 'artistic' good taste, as one of the Sydney dailies put it. It was still just as modern, carefully conceived for women's well-being. New items were added to the range of products, the team was expanded, and the money kept coming in.

In 1905, nine years after her arrival in Australia, Helena was thirty-three years old and had £100,000 in the bank. She owed her fortune to her phenomenal capacity for hard work – she never wasted a moment, nor did she skimp on the work required to manufacture her little jars by the thousands.

She earned twelve pence on each jar after she'd deducted various expenses, taxes, salaries, rent, and advertising, which, no matter how costly, always multiplied her income a hundredfold, as Mr Thompson had said it would. She still lived above the shop, spent very little on herself, other than what she thought was required to get people to talk about her brand, and saved every penny to put back into her company.

There were a few simple rules she learned during this period. Sixty years later she would still apply them. Never leave any correspondence unanswered. Listen attentively to everyone. Sleep on any important decisions. When in doubt, ask for advice and listen to it, before saying anything. She also learned, with experience, how to run a team and delegate tasks. She kept each branch of the business separate – the making of the cream, packaging, sales and advertising – but she always made sure that everything ran smoothly as a whole. 'I was passionate about every detail in those days, and have remained so.'[5]

She was aware that the situation was a fragile one: everything was going her way, but her luck could still turn. She could take pride in her success in Australia, and consolidate that success by opening a few additional salons in Sydney and Brisbane, as well as in Wellington in New Zealand, and that would be more than enough to ensure a good standard of living. But her success was driving her ever harder, and she wanted more and more from life. She had an entrepreneur's ambitious nature. And since she had succeeded just when everything had been conspiring to make her fail, she owed it to herself to continue to surpass her own expectations.

Convinced that the only true path to beauty was through science, she regretted more than ever that she had not been able to study medicine. Now that she had the means, she decided to fill in the gaps in her knowledge. She would use the knowledge to enhance her practical skills. She would return to the old continent, where she would find the best scientists, experts, universities, and libraries. She could assuage her thirst for learning, and refresh her knowledge.

In June 1905, she set sail once again. This time she was heading back to Europe.

8

BACK TO HER ROOTS

Kazimierz was the mandatory first stop of her trip, and it seemed poor, dirty, and cramped. Helena had grown accustomed to a comfortable life in Australia. She had travelled, and met people from all walks of life – settlers, ladies, businessmen, bankers. She had learned a great deal in their company, and her horizons had expanded. In Melbourne, perpetual movement seemed to be the norm, and the city never slept. Here, in Kazimierz, everything was the opposite. A heavy immobility reigned over everything and everyone. Nothing had changed since her departure: not the ageless rabbis, with their beards and worn black frock coats, nor the housewives gossiping on their doorsteps, nor the students with their skin grown pale from studying and standing outside the *yeshivot* debating a commentary on the Torah.

Even the streets seemed to have shrunk in her absence. The smell of greasy food wafting from the open windows made her feel nauseous. She noticed the peeling facades, the walls black with smoke, the garbage scattered along the grimy sidewalks as if she had never seen any of it before. In the carriage that took her from the station to her house – no mud-covered pavements for her on this trip – her childhood came back to her in flashes. She could never live here again, among people who now felt like foreigners to her.

Everything about Kraków disappointed her. It was all so provincial, even the shops around the Rynek. Helena's tastes had become more refined, and she had begun to wear clothing made by renowned dressmakers who copied the latest Paris fashions. The nostalgia she had felt from afar was preferable to such a disappointing reality.

But it was the reception her family gave her that upset her the most.

'Why are you wearing such a tight chignon?' asked Gitel in that reproachful voice Helena so disliked. 'You are ruining your hair. And if you continue dressing yourself up like that you'll never find a husband, my girl. Your sisters Pauline, Rosa and Regina are already married. As for you …!'

Gitel had aged. Her hands trembled, her face seemed set in a sneer, and too much hardship had accentuated her bitterness. Perhaps there was a touch of pique or envy in her reproaches as well. Her eldest daughter had succeeded, despite all their predictions. Helena was on the verge of raising her voice the way she used to, but then she merely shook her head. Her mother would never change. She was still obsessed with the marriage of her offspring, making lists of hoped-for or potential prospects like a miser counting his gold. Meanwhile, although three of Helena's sisters had found a husband, the others continued to mope about the house.

Hertzel was off in his corner, studying in silence. He, too, seemed to have shrunk: he was stooped and his beard completely white. With his velvet skullcap and shiny jacket, he looked more and more like his grandfather, the rabbi Salomon Rubinstein, whose stern face looked down from a painting on the living-room wall. He still refused to forgive his daughter and hardly spoke to her. After greeting her coldly, he returned to his books.

Fortunately Stella, Manka, Ceska and Erna were a lot more welcoming. They admired their older sister's elegance and were fascinated by her jewellery; they touched the fabric of her dress, commented on the lace, the price of her hat, and plied her with questions about her new life. They jabbered, giggled and criticised in their shrill schoolgirl voices.

Helena found ways to defuse their jealousy, joking and setting them dreaming with her stories about Australia. In their wide-eyed gazes she could see their desire to flee to a life elsewhere, the same desire that she herself had once felt. From her bag she took some Valaze cream and lotion, and she covered their faces with cream and massaged their skin the way their mother used to, while she explained her beauty principles and everything she had learned over the past ten years.

For a few hours she enjoyed the illusion that she had returned to the girly camaraderie of her childhood. But the spell was quickly broken. She was bored, and fled as soon as she could, on the pretext that she had important meetings. She would never see her parents again. This largely unsuccessful visit confirmed her belief that she had been right to choose the hard way out, for it had proved infinitely preferable to any forced marriage.

And yet her family members were still dear to her. Her sisters, cousins, uncles, and aunts were the only people she could trust. She wanted to make them her business associates, and she swore to herself that she would do so as soon as she had the chance. Before her departure she persuaded her younger sister Ceska, who was twenty-two at the time, and her cousin Lola, the daughter of her aunt Rosalie Beckman, to come and give her a hand in Melbourne. To give them the time to prepare their belongings, she arranged to meet them in Vienna.

There, Helena made the acquaintance of Dr Emmie List, who was renowned for her peeling treatments to eliminate acne and persistent blemishes. After six months of regular exfoliation, scars faded and the skin looked youthful again. The doctor became Helena's friend. When the time came for Helena to open her salon in London, she would have Dr List come and work with her.

Lola and Ceska joined her in Vienna. They took the train together to Germany, where surgeons were inventing new beauty techniques. In Berlin in 1901, Dr Eugene Hollander had been the first to perform a facelift on a Polish aristocrat. A few years later, Dr Jacques Joseph performed the first nose surgery. Of all these innovations the injection of paraffin into the face to make wrinkles disappear was the most spectacular.

But the consequences could also be disastrous, because when the paraffin moved beneath the skin it created undesirable hollows and lumps or even, on occasion, blindness or necrosis. Cosmetic surgery, which claimed to 'remedy ugliness and deformity', was still in its infancy.[1] The results obtained did not meet people's expectations. It was only after the First World War that surgeons would learn to repair the severe facial injuries suffered by soldiers in the trenches. For the time being, everyone agreed that these operations were bound to leave traces, and a new way would have to be found to reduce scarring.[2]

As they continued their journey, the three young women discovered spas. For Helena, they were a revelation. Her enthusiasm was so great that all through her life she would visit spas regularly to lose weight, rest, or treat a temporary depression, which often happened after she opened a new salon.

For European aristocrats, taking the waters was a rite of passage proving they had attained a certain social status. They would go to Brides-les-Bains or Eugénie-les-Bains, two hot thermal springs patronised by Napoléon III and his family. They also favoured Budapest, Baden-Baden and Marienbad, which became fashionable thanks to King Edward VII, who was a connoisseur of natural healing. Every spa had its own speciality and star physician who prescribed hydrotherapy, body wraps or chemical peels. 'There were many Hungarians and Romanians who were very good at skincare, and they taught me a great deal,' Helena would recall.[3]

In Wiesbaden, on the right bank of the Rhine, Helena befriended Dr Joseph Kapp, the director of the thermal baths, who prescribed a venous treatment for the circulatory ailments she was suffering from.

She observed his methods with every intention of copying them. The physician became one of her role models. Whenever she needed to update her medical knowledge, Helena, whose thirst for knowledge would never wane, would turn to Dr Kapp.

In Paris, the belle époque was synonymous with an insatiable appetite for life. Helena fell instantly in love with Paris, and it would remain one of her favourite cities. During her short stay she did some frenetic shopping: vases by Gallé, flasks by Lalique, jewellery, clothing, her first paintings.

She was only too happy to spend the money she had rightfully earned, and ordered her first haute couture garments from Doucet and Worth on the Rue de la Paix. She appreciated the discreet comfort of the salons and fitting rooms, and the shop girls waltzing to and fro in a whirlwind of ribbons, lace, satin, and velvet. When her outfits were delivered to the hotel, she spread them out on the big bed: jackets and tight-waisted dresses with long, gored skirts. She would have liked to wear them all at once.

All her life, Helena would go to the great couturiers for her wardrobe, initially because she liked their work, and subsequently as part of her quest to be her own best brand ambassador. Anything Helena spent was good for Helena Rubinstein. Besides, as she often said, 'couture and beauty go hand in hand'.

But she had not come all this way to be an idle tourist. In France, medicine and hygiene had evolved considerably. Since Pasteur's discovery of microbiology in 1860, the use of aseptic techniques had become compulsory in hospitals. Helena began her series of visits to Marcellin Berthelot, who invented disinfection through the use of bleach in 1875. The chemist was already very old – he would die two years later – and agreed to see her without a reference.

He gave her a masterclass on the principles governing the health of the skin and Helena sounded him out about her theory that skin could be classified into several types, which would enable her to expand her range of products. She consulted dermatologists, who taught her how to regenerate tissue, make it firmer, and delay the appearance of wrinkles. She would learn how electrical techniques were being applied to skincare barely a quarter of a century after their invention.

Some physicians did not take her seriously. A woman's place is in the home, they informed her. Why was she insisting on cluttering up her charming little head with complicated information that would be of no use to her?

Helena did not try to win them over. There were any number of well-known scholars who were only too eager to help her. But she had learned her lesson. To get what she wants, a pretty woman must never seem too smart. She wasn't used to subtle manoeuvring – she tended to mow down obstacles like a tank – but she was prepared to do whatever was necessary to get her way.

She was convinced that body care was an essential part of beauty, and took a keen interest in massage techniques using rollers to knead the flesh, which were said to eliminate jowls, double chins, and fat. Some rollers used electric current to massage the face, body and breasts more efficiently than by hand.[4] Healthy eating had not yet become the obsession of the century, but beauty-conscious women already knew how to improve their figures through treatments and diets that changed with the fashion and the season.

Helena's attentive visits to Parisian salons also enabled her to observe the treatments that were similar to those offered in spas: hydrotherapy to invigorate and shape the body, a variety of electrical treatments, light therapy, gymnastics and massages.[5] She would introduce these new treatments in her salon in Melbourne and subsequently in Europe and the United States, improving upon them as time went by. Where skincare was concerned, her imagination knew no bounds.

From everything she learned during her journey, she retained two or three significant ideas that would form the basis of her regimes. To increase the efficiency of her products and maintain a glowing complexion, it was vital to lead a healthy lifestyle, involving physical exercise, proper breathing techniques and a low-fat, low-toxin diet based on water, fruit juice and vegetables. Her future clients must realise it was not enough just to buy her cream, they must also apply her principles.

Her last stop was England. From there she would sail for Australia. In London, beauty was the preserve of the elite. Privilege was more sharply delineated here than elsewhere. A few English perfumers such as Atkinsons and Yardley dominated the market. Imported French brands, such as Coty, Bourjois and Rimmel remained expensive. Helena discovered them at Harrods on Brompton Road, a department store every bit as wonderful as the ones in Paris. She was accompanied by Ceska and Lola. The three young women were fascinated by the escalator in Harrods but were afraid to use it for fear of getting their long skirts caught.

They went on to inspect the beauty institutes on Bond Street, which didn't live up to expectations despite their luxurious interiors. *I'll have my work cut out for me here*, thought Helena, who had every intention of visiting England again. Everything she had seen, observed, and remembered had shown her, yet again, that beauty was something one must strive for and earn. The effort would be worth it; she firmly believed that there were no ugly women, only lazy ones.

She overlooked – or chose to overlook – the fact that all women are not equal when it comes to beauty, that the world was divided between those who had the time and the money to improve their physical condition and those who poverty condemned to premature ageing.

On the return voyage her trunks were crammed with new outfits and work supplies — slimming tablets, formulas to cure acne or the ill effects of the sun, and electric rollers to knead, massage and firm the legs, buttocks and breasts. She also brought back vases, particularly opaline ones, to add to her growing collection, paintings, knick-knacks, fabrics and ideas to redecorate her two salons.

A display advertisement in the Australian daily *The Talk* in 1906 announced that 'Mlle. Helena Rubinstein' had just returned from Europe. Her consultations with the most eminent skin specialists had enabled her to improve the treatment she offered at her 274 Collins Street salon. The text made special mention of her newly hired 'Viennese' assistants. The two young ladies took their role very seriously.

Ceska, however, found it difficult to get used to Australia and suffered from homesickness. And Helena was far too demanding. She made them work from dawn to dusk like slaves in a coal mine. Surely there were other things in life than beauty salons?

'No!' Helena replied categorically. 'Do you think I go around having fun? How do you expect to make a living otherwise?'

Ceska made a face and kept up her complaints, but eventually got used to her new life and spent hours in the 'kitchen' watching her sister concoct her new preparations, L'Eau Verte and L'Eau qui Pique. In the evening, Ceska was invited everywhere. Like all the Rubinstein daughters, she had inherited her mother's flawless complexion and looked younger than her age. And like Helena, she cheated, saying she was eighteen when in fact she was four years older, although being unmarried at twenty-two did not seem to bother her. Besides, no one in Australia seemed to mind whether you were married or not. A charming Englishman called Edward Cooper had begun to court her, and Ceska was not indifferent to his advances.

What of Helena? She was rich, pretty and still youthful despite being the wrong side of thirty-four. Her salon in Melbourne was virtually running itself, her beauty line perfect and her reputation firmly established. She, too, could give some thought to getting married.

But Miss Rubinstein was cut from a different cloth than most of the young women around her. It was not her ambition to start a family or raise children who would be just like her. In her dreams, there was no room for love letters, for wooing by moonlight, or languorous embraces. Her well-ordered brain buzzed with serious words like balance sheets, ledgers, turnover, or expansion. She was one of the few self-made women of her time and had every intention of continuing along that path. Her future was mapped out for her and she was determined to succeed – on her own. She had no need for men. She could not see what purpose they would serve.

Melbourne was beginning to seem too small for her.

She had set her sights on London, which was her kind of city – modern, elegant, bustling with activity. There was so much she could do there. During her brief stay in the capital, Helena had had ample time to observe Englishwomen: their cheeks, like Australian women's, were dry and blotchy. Many of them suffered from persistent acne which they did not know how to treat and so hid beneath thick layers of powder.

Helena could hardly contain her impatience. She already knew what she wanted to do. She would move to England at the beginning of the following year. Before that, she would oversee the opening of her salon in Sydney – work had already begun. Ceska would keep an eye on things. Helena was also still thinking of expanding to Wellington, New Zealand.

It was closing time. All alone in the salon, Helena could not bring herself to go home and take a rest. Her two employees had left half an hour earlier than usual, and Lola and Ceska had done the same. It had been a difficult week, with more clients than usual, and the young women were exhausted and had asked for some time off. Helena had agreed, almost in spite of herself, to let them go.

Once she had finished the books she would mop the floor and lower the heavy metal shutter. No task was too shameful or lowly for her. She stood behind the counter, busily adding up the day's receipts.

May could sometimes be as hot as the summer months in Melbourne. Heat was still radiating off the asphalt on this particular May evening, with little hope of cooler temperatures at night. Helena unbuttoned her bodice slightly more than was appropriate. Her cheeks had turned crimson and her forehead was damp with sweat. A few rebellious strands of hair escaped from her chignon. This unruly touch softened her habitually severe appearance and made her particularly charming.

'Do I have the honour of addressing Miss Helena Rubinstein?'

Surprised to hear a man's voice, she looked up and turned her hawk-eyed gaze on the man who had just raised his hat. He was a tall, elegant, dark-haired fellow wearing a starched shirt and a suit cut from the best fabric. He was carrying a few books and newspapers tucked under one arm. His bright eyes were surveying her closely from behind his round glasses. She had the impression he was taking note of her untidy appearance and open bodice, and hastily began buttoning it up.

'Yes?' she enquired.

'I met two of your sisters in Kraków a few months ago, when I went to visit my family,' the man said. 'They told me about you. I'm a journalist. I was born in Poland like you, but I'm an American citizen.'

A compatriot? He was charming and easy-going with a warm voice. Perhaps a bit too sure of himself. She relaxed a bit, wiped her forehead, tucked her hair back.

He had still not told her his name.

'Forgive me. I wasn't thinking straight. My name is Titus. Edward William Titus.'

Helena nibbled on her pen, and looked down at her ledger. Her heart was pounding and she could not understand why.

9

EDWARD WILLIAM TITUS

She had never met a man like Edward William Titus. He knew everything there was to know about painting, literature, music and politics, and was only too pleased to play Pygmalion. Helena could listen to him for hours on end – he was never pedantic or boring. He was a marvellous teacher: clear, precise and entertaining.

She thought she knew Melbourne well, but he took her to parts of the city she had never seen. Her long working days hadn't given her much opportunity for outings. Practically every evening, Edward took her to the theatre, the most popular form of entertainment in turn-of-the-century Australia. Companies from all over the world toured the cities and people flocked to each show eagerly. Audiences were very mixed and the atmosphere friendly – quite unlike the polite restraint of the European theatrical scene.

Helena was charmed by Edward's regular features and silver-tinged dark hair, which gave him the air of a distinguished English gentleman. He was always close shaven and smelt pleasantly of lavender cologne; his suits were tailor-made in London, his bootmaker was Italian, and his shirts came from Charvet of Paris.

He was also a fine connoisseur of women's fashions and approved of Helena's Parisian outfits. He noticed the tiniest details – the hang of a skirt, the ruffle on a blouse, or the trimming on a hat. When she returned home after an evening out with him, she would find herself humming a Grace Fletcher or Dorothy Brunton tune as she undressed in front of the mirror. They would have dinner after the show in Melbourne's most fashionable restaurants. 'The food's awful here,' Edward would complain, 'a far cry from in France. When we go to Paris, I'll take you out and you'll see what I mean.'

Helena felt like a country bumpkin. Edward had only just arrived in Melbourne and was already at home everywhere he went! He was on first-name terms with all the maîtres d', always got the best tables, and introduced her to French wine and Chinese food. 'He opened a whole new world to me,' she wrote.[1] His conversation was peppered with famous names, including many that Helena had never heard of: artists, writers, painters and intellectuals; the powerful, the titled, English noblewomen, Parisian countesses, and New York socialites. But although he was a snob and name-dropper, he wasn't remotely in awe of the wealthy and the privileged – to Helena's great surprise, for she had imagined them to be superior. 'It isn't who you are that's important, my dear, it's what you do,' he would tell her.

We don't know who Edward William Titus really was. His life before he met Helena Rubinstein in Australia remains shrouded in mystery. Just like her, he was deliberately vague about it. He is often described in biographies as 'a Polish-born American journalist', although little is known about the articles he wrote and the newspapers he worked for before he came to Australia.

According to Edward's nephew Emmanuel Ameisen, the representative of the French branch of Helena Rubinstein at the end of the 1930s and its managing director after the Second World War, Titus changed his name from Ameisen before leaving for Australia in 1904 or 1905.[2] It was a strange choice of name for a Jew, as Emmanuel's son Olivier points out: 'Titus was the Roman emperor who destroyed the

Temple of Jerusalem. But then Edward was a genuine nonconformist.'[3]

So, like Helena Rubinstein, Edward Titus had more than one life. In his first, he was born Arthur Ameisen on 25 July 1870 in Podgorze, a Kraków suburb. His father, Leo Ameisen, was married to Emilie Mandel and owned a small soda factory. The eldest of nine siblings, the youngest of whom was Emmanuel Ameisen's father Yakov, Arthur went to the state primary school in Kraków and continued his education at St Anne's gymnasium.[4]

He got a job at a newspaper owned by his uncle and worked as a journalist in Poland for three years. It was undoubtedly during this period that he learned English and French, which he spoke fluently, together with Polish, Italian, Yiddish and Hebrew. In 1891, aged twenty-one, he emigrated to the United States, sailing from Liverpool aboard the *Campania*. He lived in Pittsburgh, Pennsylvania, where a large Austro-Hungarian community had settled. He applied for American citizenship in 1893 and was granted it three years later.[5]

Soon after his arrival in Pittsburgh, Arthur Ameisen took a job at the Austrian consulate, where he worked for the consul Max Schamberg until 1895.[6] He studied law at the same time and, after graduating in 1897, set up the law firm Ameisen and Kramer, drawing his clientele chiefly from among his compatriots in Pittsburgh. He had been married once before meeting Helena Rubinstein and probably had two children, who refused to see him again after he had left their mother.[7,8] He never referred to them; only his family knew this great secret. Helena undoubtedly did too, but would never speak of it either.

His trail vanishes after Pittsburgh, and is picked up again a few years later, first in New York and then in Australia. Edward William Titus – aka Arthur Ameisen – may have kept some of his life secret, but this only added to his charm.

*

And now here he was living in Melbourne and very subtly courting Helena. He would often turn up at the Valaze beauty salon in the middle of the afternoon. Brushing aside the owner's protests, he would bear her off for a walk in Fitzroy or Queen Victoria Gardens, inaugurated the previous year in memory of the deceased monarch.

A blushing Helena would leave Ceska in charge of the parlour. Her sister and Lola would shoot her affectionate, teasing glances as she tied the ribbons on her hat, snatched up her umbrella, and disappeared on Edward's arm. She made an attempt at self-preservation by placing their relationship on a business footing: she hired Edward as her marketing and advertising manager. The man was devilishly talented. Words seemed to line up on the paper all by themselves as his pen flew across the page. Edward soon realised just how ambitious Helena was, and offered to help her expand her business.

She listened to his advice and accepted his innovative propositions. He was bursting with ideas and often set her head spinning, but he had a way of instantly grasping her suggestions. She only had to start a sentence and he would finish it for her. He was invaluable, and having such help was a totally new experience. Edward was the only person Helena knew who could think faster than she did, and he always managed to surprise her.

He could turn his hand to any task and do it well. He enhanced the design and packaging of her products and wrote the copy for her advertisements, adding a lyrical touch with quotations and poems. He had no lack of imagination, and suggested that Helena advertise her salon as a Viennese beauty institute that English and Australian salons simply couldn't compare with. His advertising copy, which appeared in newspapers such as *The Talk*, *The Mercury*, the *Sydney Morning Herald* and *The Australian Home Journal*, always followed the same pattern. He would start by giving future customers a specific reason for using the cosmetics, such as the adverse effects of the harsh Australian climate. Then he would extol Helena's experience and scientific knowledge and make women feel they were being singled out for special attention. In an advertisement headed 'What Women Want', he claimed Helena's creams imparted '*je ne sais quoi* ...'

To publicise Helena's *Beauty in the Making* handbook, he wrote: 'There is no other book in the world like it, no other so concise and luminous, so dependable and so thoroughly up-to-date.'[9] He also explained the importance of maintaining a youthful appearance: 'There is a saying that a woman is as old as she looks. Which means she is as old as her skin looks. Keep your skin young, and the years need have no terrors for you.'[10]

He also offered wives knowledgeable snippets of advice like: 'The man who, day after day, has to face across the breakfast table a wife, clever, well-read, possessing numerous accomplishments, but whose complexion is dreary and colourless – whose skin is coarse and unpleasing – this man will grin and bear it – sometimes.'[11]

He claimed Helena was 'one of the most famous benefactresses of her sex today'. He was bent on making her name synonymous with beauty care, writing: 'With Valaze she has introduced all sorts of delightful and efficacious things to keep healthy women beautiful.'[12]

It didn't take Edward long to build Helena's image and portray her as a brilliant and wealthy high priestess of beauty renowned throughout Europe, who was graciously putting her scientific skills at the service of fashionable Australian women. It was also Edward who hit upon her nickname.

'Helena, what would you say to being called "Madame"? Not Madame Helena Rubinstein, just Madame. It sounds good, don't you think?'

She was delighted, and said 'Madame' out loud to herself several times. That was the name she would come to be known by. In later years her employees, her customers, journalists, her family and even her children would all call her by that name. As for Edward, he preferred the affectionate moniker 'Petite Madame'.

With Edward backing her, Helena felt as if she could fly. In 1907 she opened her second salon in Sydney, at 158 Pitt Street. In 1908, she opened an equally successful salon in Wellington, New Zealand.

Edward was constantly at her side to advise her. In less than two years, he had become as vital to her as the air she breathed. Not a day went by without her asking for his opinion on any subject under the sun. He was not merely her employee; he was her guide, friend and partner. He worked alongside her by day and was seen everywhere with her by night.

She began to feel frightened. This wasn't the way she had intended to live her life. But she couldn't ignore the signs that she was falling in love. Edward was attractive and charismatic. He was obviously a ladies' man. He would make her suffer. Yet he seemed to take genuine pleasure in her company, and appeared to be fascinated by her success, drive, ambition and courage. She had told him the unvarnished truth about her departure from Kazimierz and the years of hardship that had followed.

One summer evening as they sat on the terrace of a French restaurant, she remained silent throughout dinner. She barely tasted the glass of Bordeaux that Edward had ordered as part of his plan to teach her about great vintages. For once, she heard not a word of his conversation as she sat lost in thought.

She tore a piece of bread into tiny morsels and rolled them into balls. Her nervousness hadn't escaped Edward's notice. He leaned towards her and took her hand in his. Trembling, she tried to pull her hand away, but he tightened his grip. They remained silent for a few moments. Helena's throat felt dry. She was afraid to hear what he was going to say. The wait seemed interminable.

'Helena,' he said slowly, 'I can see you are determined to build an empire. Marry me and we'll do it together.'

10

MAYFAIR LADY

It was raining in London – a sad, insistent drizzle that fell on her wide-brimmed velvet hat. It had rained the day before. And the day before that. And for the previous two weeks. When it wasn't raining, it was foggy – dense, icy cold, and clinging. Spring was a long time coming that April 1908. And, of course, there wasn't a hackney cab in sight.

Drenched and shivering, Helena gave in and took shelter on a porch. 'I mustn't lose heart,' she repeated to herself until it became a kind of obsession. Since Coleraine, she knew that the more ambitious one's goal, the greater the sacrifice. She chanted the phrase like a mantra on waking every morning in the small third-floor furnished flat she was renting in Arlington Street with a young Australian woman.

Madame didn't exist here. Her success and money – she had nearly half a million pounds stored safely in an Australian bank and had just opened a bank account in London – didn't stop her feeling like a stranger. In this impenetrable world governed by complicated codes that she was unable to decipher, she was alone once again. She would learn what to do, of course, as she had done before. But the early days were tough.

Helena wondered at least once a day if she had made a mistake in refusing to marry Edward. She missed him so much that just thinking about him sometimes made it hard to breathe. She was nostalgic for their conversations, their evenings out and their strong bond. She was still under his spell – that was the only way she could describe the overpowering feeling. She thought often about their last evening together in Melbourne, dissecting every word that had been said.

When, after what had seemed like an age, she had eventually replied 'no', his emotions had seemed genuine. 'No, Edward, I don't want to marry you. I'm sorry, but the answer's no.' She had had to muster all her courage to say those words and then assume an air of indifference when she saw the look of astonishment, sorrow and hurt pride on her companion's face as he registered the blow. Wrong-footed, Helena had felt obliged to soften her rejection: 'Give me some time; I need to prove myself in Europe.'

At first Edward hadn't replied, just looked her straight in the eye. She had braced herself again but he appeared to have understood. Then, being the kind of man who liked to have the last word, he had immediately said: 'Very well. But I'll join you there in a few months.'

Helena had never lacked the courage of her convictions. turning down old Schmuel, whom her parents had chosen as her intended; setting off for Australia on her own; confronting her uncles in Coleraine; living in the bush; working to survive; and opening her own salon. But none of these acts, driven by necessity or ambition, had seemed as difficult as turning Edward down. Like many capable women, her weak point was love. 'The truth is that my heart has always been divided between the people I have loved and the ambition that would not let me rest.'[1]

So once again she fled. It had become almost routine behaviour when she met an obstacle she couldn't otherwise overcome. Regret was rarely an issue – Helena didn't have time to mull over the past. Now she was here, London was the focus of all her attention. Edward had told her in great detail about the idiosyncrasies of its very closed aristocracy; of how London, with its two and a half million inhabitants, had the reputation of being the most enjoyable capital in the world, but where, depending on the area, glittering wealth existed alongside abject poverty.

Now that she was in the city as an immigrant and no longer a tourist, Helena wanted to see the shameful places that had been carefully hidden from sight the first time she had visited London, the way a beautiful woman might conceal a blemish on her face: the labourers in the docks; the prostitutes of Whitechapel; the urchins sleeping rough in St Giles; and her fellow Polish and Russian Jews crammed like livestock in East End slums. She had been hit by the foul stench of squalor, far worse than in the poorest corners of Kazimierz or the seedy parts of Melbourne, and hastily turned back.

Political battles didn't interest Helena, yet trouble was brewing. On 21 June 1908, a few weeks after her arrival, 200,000 angry women led by Emmeline Pankhurst and her daughter Christabel, the founders of the Women's Social and Political Union, rallied in Hyde Park to demand the right to vote. The intensification of the suffragette movement's actions led to dozens of its members being imprisoned. They held prolonged hunger strikes to protest against their arbitrary incarceration. It meant very little to Helena; she was only interested in liberating women's appearance, and she intended to make Englishwomen bolder by showing them how. In fact, steps had already been taken in that direction. Since the stylish King Edward VII's ascension to the throne, life in England had become less austere and attitudes more modern than under his mother, Queen Victoria.

Massage parlours and beauty salons had opened all over the place. In *The Queen*, the magazine read by aristocratic ladies of leisure, an advice column entitled 'Toilette' invited women with problem skin to write in under a pseudonym for strictly confidential, practical help. Women's publications dished out recipes, but there was no guarantee of the results. Applying these products to the skin was done at the readers' own risk and peril.

When Helena first arrived in London, ladies didn't dare be seen entering salons such as Mrs Henning's in South Molton Street by the light of day. It would have been almost as badly regarded as being caught out at a brothel. The salon owner had created a concealed entrance at the back of the shop so her wealthy clients could slip in unnoticed.

Success was by no means guaranteed. But no one else boasted as much expertise as Helena Rubinstein, or had her sales and marketing savvy, or a cream as miraculous as Valaze. She was the first person to successfully capitalise on women's desire for beauty and on men's enthusiasm for that desire.[2] She would reassure herself that she was the only person to have this talent coveted by women – the skill of creating and enhancing beauty

Alone, with Edward so far away, Helena could only look to herself for encouragement and strength, as she had done during that hateful period in Coleraine. Now, though, she had different advantages: money, salons and qualifications. She had been successful in Australia. *But in London you're a nobody*, a voice whispered to her, followed quickly by another that declared: *You will succeed – it's only a matter of time*. She adopted her tried-and-tested procedure for staying positive: running through all her exciting plans in her head.

The tiniest details of her new beauty salon were already etched in her mind. The choice of area was settled – Mayfair, Belgravia or Park Lane. Money attracts money, so one of London's smartest districts was a must. She had already decided the salon should occupy one of those elegant white neo-Palladian houses with pillars on the facade. The estate agent had taken her to view dozens of them, but there was always something not quite right.

In the evenings, to keep her loneliness at bay, she would go to the theatre. At the Duke of York's, she discovered Isadora Duncan, who was shocking polite society by dancing naked under veils. Helena marvelled at 'how she managed to combine the grace of a jungle cat with the manners of a great lady'.[3] With her completely new body shape, à la Klimt – slim thighs, long, willowy legs and narrow upper body – the dancer was, to Helena, the model emancipated woman.

A few years later, they met at a reception given by Margot Asquith, the then prime minister's wife. Isadora was wearing one of the voluminous trailing scarves she was famous for.

'Wouldn't it be safer and just as lovely if it were shorter?' asked Helena, surprised.

'My dear child, what about the effect?' answered Isadora, amused by her naivety.[4]

The scarf that intrigued Helena so much entered the history books twenty years later when one like it became entangled around the open-spoked wheel of a sports car the dancer was a passenger in, breaking her slender neck.

Helena was on the verge of giving up that cold, wet April when the estate agent showed her the gem of a property she had been waiting for: 24 Grafton Street, Mayfair. The perfect address. The elegant Georgian building had belonged to the recently deceased Robert Arthur Talbot Gascoyne-Cecil, third Marquess of Salisbury and prime minister under Queen Victoria, and had just been put up for rent by his heirs at £2,000 a year. The sum was more than Helena had hoped to pay, but once again she gambled on her good fortune. She knew that a Mayfair address for her salon was worth more than its weight in gold. Bordered by Oxford Street, Park Lane, Regent Street and Piccadilly, the area is named after an annual fair that was held there until 1706. Some years later, the site was developed by local architect Edward Shepherd into a large market surrounded by small houses, before becoming a fashionable address for London's high society in the twentieth century.

Mayfair was home to the privileged of the world. Attitudes and customs were set in stone. From April to May, in town from their country manors, the gentry threw balls, parties and private concerts, and thronged to the races and regattas. The lifestyle was traditional, elegant, arrogant and corseted.

Lord Salisbury's former property comprised twenty-six rooms over four floors. The first two floors would be given over to the shop and salon, while Helena would live on the third floor and set up her 'kitchen' in the attic. She hired architects for the interior renovation but relied on her own instincts for the decoration. There would be no wicker furniture or calico-covered chairs here, only white, cream, pink and other neutral pastel shades to create a luxurious yet understated feminine atmosphere. She demanded the best of everything.

Work was scheduled to take a few weeks. Helena knew she was taking an enormous risk and that London could reject her at the drop of a hat. *Or praise me to the skies*, she decided. Helena clearly relished a challenge.

As she could never stay put, she left the work under the supervision of her architects and headed to the continent again. In Paris she acquainted herself with the latest findings in dermatology and new electricity-based treatments, as well as updating her wardrobe. In Vienna, she persuaded Dr Emmie List, who had taught her the art of skin peeling, to come and join her staff.

On her return to London, Helena was brimming with energy and ideas for inventing new products, such as acne creams, toners and astringents. She visited Grafton Street every day to see how the refurbishments were progressing and was satisfied to find everything going according to plan.

'It's very beautiful, my dear friend. Well done!' said a familiar voice one day. She interrupted her conversation with the carpenter and turned around to find Edward standing there. She threw herself excitedly into his arms, dying to tell him how she had been feeling all those long, lonely weeks. How everything she had undertaken or discovered had had less charm when he wasn't around. But she was much too self-conscious and tongue-tied. So she just buried her face in his jacket and inhaled his pungent male smell: a mixture of lavender, tobacco and leather. Edward remained silent for once too, kissing her hair and stroking the back of her neck.

So this is love, she thought to herself. Thirty-six-year-old Helena had the courage of a man, the authority of a boss and the naivety of a virgin. They stayed in each other's arms for a moment, oblivious to the outside world, but were soon interrupted by a polite cough – they had forgotten the carpenter. Helena accepted Edward's suggestion that her cupboards would go best at the back of the room, then took him by the hand and showed him proudly around the house.

'What do you think?' she asked enthusiastically as they glimpsed the stunning view over the London rooftops from the third-floor window.

'Magnificent. You will never fail to impress me, my dear.'

Hearing these words made all the effort seem worthwhile.

Helena wondered how she had managed without Edward for so long. In some ways they were each other's opposite: she was reserved and lacked confidence – except where work was concerned – while he was impulsive and an extrovert. But they also had a great deal in common: both were nonconformists, endlessly curious about people and things, enthusiastic and visionary. Edward was the only person who could make her forget her business for a moment. He took her out every evening, as he had done in Melbourne.

London was buzzing with innovations, talent and culture. In the wake of the Entente Cordiale, the aristocracy flocked to the Franco-British Exhibition. Edward introduced Helena to a monocled Somerset Maugham sporting a pristine, close-fitting dinner jacket; to George Bernard Shaw, recognisable by his red beard and sumptuous hand-spun Jaeger clothes; and to dandy and theatre critic Max Beerbohm. Edward knew everyone here too and seemed so comfortable in their company. Helena felt positively provincial beside him. Although he was amused by her complexes, Edward was better than anyone else at reassuring her. 'You can hold your head high. You will be a queen here soon.'

They crossed paths with Rudyard Kipling, who had just won the Nobel Prize for Literature; James Barrie, whose play *Peter Pan* had received fantastic acclaim at its premiere four years earlier; Jerome K. Jerome; Virginia Stephen, Leonard Woolf's soon-to-be wife, and her sister Vanessa Bell and the rest of the Bloomsbury Group. The intellectual and political elite frequented the Café Royal, which had become the couple's hangout. After having lunch together, as they often did, Edward would linger, reading the papers or chatting to a friend, while Helena would dash off to the salon. The renovations were a little behind schedule, but she wanted it all to be perfect. And anyway, Edward's being there was all that mattered.

One stormy evening they took shelter on a restaurant porch while waiting for their cab to arrive. Huddled in his arms, Helena prayed that the rain wouldn't stop. Edward William Titus chose this moment to ask her once again to marry him.

They wed on 28 July 1908 in London with two close friends as witnesses.[5] It was a tender, very private ceremony. King Edward VII had just opened the Olympic Games and visitors from all over Europe thronged to the capital's purpose-built White City Stadium to watch the events. Consumed by their happiness, the newlyweds paid it little attention. At their lunchtime wedding reception at the Savoy Grill, Helena floated on a cloud, hardly touching her food.

Mr and Mrs Edward Titus chose to spend their honeymoon in the fashionable French resort of Nice, staying in the Riviera Palace, where Queen Victoria had been a regular guest. With its rococo buildings and extravagant millionaires' residences, the city remains the symbol of the belle époque. Rich foreigners holidayed there: the English in Cimiez and the Russians in the area around the Parc Impérial.

The couple visited Cannes, Grasse and Monte Carlo, and dined by candlelight at the Negresco Hotel and Le Ruhl Casino. After a dance or two, Edward would sit down at the card table while Helena looked on, enjoying the spectacle of it all. Playing for money didn't tempt her – she was only too aware of the price you had to pay to earn it. But the excesses of the Russian nobility amused her. Her husband told her countless anecdotes about their extravagant behaviour, their taste for partying and their crazy habit of betting their fortunes – and losing.

Every morning when they awoke, they felt like the world belonged to them. 'All this beauty has been created for us, my darling,' Edward would declare.

He showed her the silver-fringed sea lapping the jagged coastline, ornate cliff-top villas, gardens filled with rambling bougainvilleas and palm trees caressed by the mistral. Once night fell, she was intoxicated by his kisses, the smell of his cigar and the scent of honeysuckle hanging in the air. When she later recalled snuggling up beside him in their hotel bed, skin to skin, locked in embrace, she felt a wave of warmth flooding her chest. Edward was a good lover, tender and kind, and showed patience even when Helena's modesty stopped her from abandoning herself completely. He was the first to show her pleasure.

After making love, Helena felt like the queen of the whole world. She vowed to do everything in her power to keep such happiness intact. But she hadn't reckoned on their demons.

One morning she went out earlier than her husband. He was late in joining her so she returned to the hotel in the car to hurry him along as they had planned to visit the countryside inland of Nice for the last day of their honeymoon. She found Edward in the hotel lobby, locked in conversation with a very pretty redhead who Helena had spotted the evening before on account of her wonderful skin.

'She's ravishing, don't you think?' she had asked her husband at dinner.

'Who is? Oh, yes. She's a demi-mondaine. There are a lot of them around here hunting for prey.'

Edward had absent-mindedly watched the young woman, who was wearing a feather and diamond aigrette that fluttered like a flag above her flaming red locks, cross the restaurant dining room. Everyone had noticed her: the men darted her appreciative looks and the women rather more suspicious ones. Edward had turned back to his wife and planted a light kiss on the inside of her wrist.

'I only have eyes for you, my darling.' He had smiled.

But that morning, not only was he letting his eyes wander all over the redhead's assets, he had taken her small, gloved hand in his and, like a peacock fanning its tail, was performing the charm act that Helena knew so well. The woman was throwing her head back in laughter, her aigrette flicking to and fro. Edward was smiling with satisfaction.

Consumed with jealousy and rage, Helena rushed out of the hotel into the car and ordered the chauffeur to keep driving. After a few minutes she signalled to him to pull over and got out. The day before she had caught sight of a single-row pearl necklace in a jeweller's window. She headed straight to the shop to buy it, despite its exorbitant price.

Helena took the banknotes from her bag with a trembling hand, then asked the salesperson to help her put on the necklace. She returned to the car, asked to be dropped off at Nice station, and took the first train to Paris without even giving Edward the chance to explain himself. As soon as she arrived, luggage-less and in tears, at the Hôtel de Crillon, she put a call through to the Riviera Palace.

Edward was chain-smoking in the lobby, sick with worry about his wife's absence and on the verge of telephoning the police. He was relieved to hear her voice, but baffled by the drama that had been playing out in his wife's head.

He eventually said sorry. She said she regretted her foolish behaviour. There were apologies, promises and words of love. He jumped on the next train to Paris, joined her at the Crillon and the saga finished with champagne on their hotel room's terrace overlooking the Place de la Concorde.

Helena kept the necklace. It was the first piece in her 'quarrel jewel' collection. Each time her husband was unfaithful, it was her habit to buy jewellery – very expensive and preferably very big. Money didn't cure or console, just helped anaesthetise the wounds.

Her collection grew rather too quickly, from purchases that followed a chain of events: betrayal by Edward; tears and anger; compulsive shopping at Harry Winston or Cartier. Helena had always loved jewels: diamonds, sapphires, topazes, emeralds, carnelians, moonstones and especially pearls, for which she had developed a passion when her grandmother gave her the little pearl necklace, her first treasure, in Poland. She had spent the first pounds she earned in Collins Street on Australian pearls – 'my good pearls', as she called them, meaning they weren't associated with infidelity. She mixed them with other saltwater pearls, black and grey, wearing them like armour whenever she needed to feel good.

In the same way Helena couldn't resist a fine gemstone, Edward couldn't resist a pretty face. He had a penchant for cultivated socialites – the opposite of his wife, who was obsessed to distraction with her work, and not very cultured. Although she was quick to learn, she owed her urbane veneer largely to her husband. Edward did feel real affection towards her and admiration for her intelligence, energy, and audacity. She often impressed him and always surprised him. He was also happy to start a family with her. But his physical desire for her quickly faded. No doubt his financial dependence on her was a contributing factor.

His loss of interest in the marital bed caused her great suffering. Yet even during her most intense moments of distress, when jealousy tormented her to such a degree that she thought she might die, Helena never seriously contemplated leaving him. She forgave him because she believed – and he swore – that he would change. And after all, he always came back to her, so she was the winner. Or the loser, depending.

She learned to swallow her pride and transcend her frustration by purchasing jewellery, paintings, furniture and other rare and precious objects. Their marriage would bring highs and lows, arguments and reconciliations, calm periods and storms, reunions and long separations. Legally, it lasted thirty years.

11

24 GRAFTON STREET

Mr and Mrs Edward Titus returned to London to open Helena's Maison de Beauté Valaze. This time she commissioned a professional signwriter for the shopfront rather than painting the salon name herself. She also had a telephone line installed: Mayfair 4611. She repeated the number over and over again, proud of such a modern acquisition, and had it printed on business cards with her address.

The couple moved into the third floor, above the beauty salon. The flat was vast, bright, tastefully furnished, and pleasant to live in – perfect for a young couple starting out. Edward turned one room into an office to have somewhere quiet to write. He continued to produce advertising copy and got involved in all aspects of the company. To show her gratitude, when his wife officially established her English company, Helena Rubinstein Ltd, the following April, she granted him a 46 per cent share and herself the same. The rest went to her sister Ceska, who became the managing director, and to two of her managers.[1]

As soon as the salon opened, Edward urged her to buy advertising space in the newspapers. 'That isn't the right strategy,' she retorted. 'Clients will come. We must simply be patient and let word of mouth do its work. Let's wait a little.'

Sure enough, one by one, the London smart set began to arrive, driven by an overwhelming curiosity about Helena – who she was, where her strange accent came from, her sophisticated Paris fashions, and her ostentatious jewellery. They longed to find style errors she had committed in her renovation of Lord Salisbury's refined mansion. For Helena fell into three categories they mistrusted: foreigner, commoner, and Jew.

Yet rumour had it that her treatments worked wonders on the skin. So the lure of the new proved stronger than their snobbery for many. They still took the same precautions as when visiting Mrs Henning's salon, alighting from their carriages in Bruton Lane on the corner of Grafton Street – veiled to hide their faces – then hurrying up the front steps looking left and right to ensure no one was watching them. The sheer elegance of the place left critics speechless. The salon was simple yet sophisticated. The white and cream colour scheme, with pale pink accents here and there, gave this peaceful, feminine haven an almost medical feel.

Helena would appear instantly, as if by magic, through a door hidden behind a curtain, wearing a white chemist's coat over her taffeta dress. She greeted them formally, knowing that the gentry didn't care for familiarity, but immediately created a warm atmosphere by offering them a chair, a cup of tea and biscuits, handing them her business card, explaining how she worked, opening pots of cream and bottles of lotion, and mentioning Lady Lamington and the other high-society ladies who had been in her circle in Australia. She also made a point of highlighting her collaborations with doctors and dermatologists, and her experience of spas.

Clients were impressed by her confidence and connections, and intrigued by her accent. Most important to her were the set prices she charged. Ten guineas for twelve facials – the equivalent of US$2,000 in 1962 – for one monthly visit for an entire year, to include body massages and physical exercise. These upper-class women worth millions would raise their eyebrows and gasp, 'That's extremely expensive!' Helena would tell them that on the contrary it was a bargain – she had gone to the most remote corners of Europe to find the rare ingredients for her creams!

She would lean closer to her client and whisper confidentially that she had torn Dr Emmie List away from her Viennese patients to come and treat the skin of London ladies. 'Over there,' she explained, 'Dr List is such a renowned physician that even the wife of psychoanalyst Mr Freud used to go to her.' Helena was prepared to say anything to attract her clientele.

To complement her banter, she offered free treatment sessions and pots of Valaze, especially to the most titled and influential ladies. This elite should be her most important target group, her husband advised, who knew these snooty circles well. They were quickly won over, and began paying. At the end of her first year, Helena had a thousand good clients on her books and no longer needed to worry about her rent.

Cases of spectacular healing rapidly established her reputation. Among her first triumphs was a young aristocrat so disfigured by acne that she didn't dare step out of the house without a veil. The anxious lady visited the salon every week for six months. But the skin peels developed by Dr List and the Blackhead and Open Pore Cure formulated by Helena to combat greasy skin performed miracles: the spots disappeared and freshness was restored to her face. The grateful lady's friends soon flocked to the salon, impressed by the success of the treatment. Not long after, the client went to live in India with her husband and recommended that her new family-in-law visit Helena while on a trip to England. A group of maharanis accompanied by their mothers, daughters, aunts, cousins and servants descended on the salon, filling the rooms with heady perfumes, colourful silks, jangling bracelets, and sing-song voices. The appreciative Indian princesses offered Helena expensive jewels – rubies, emeralds, pearls, and topazes – every time Madame achieved results on their sun-damaged skin. She was thrilled.

The Irish Viceroy's wife, a cantankerous old biddy whose imposing chin was dotted with several unsightly hairs, asked Helena if her personal physician could come and inspect the establishment for hygiene purposes. 'Why, of course,' Helena answered politely. The doctor's glowing report proved more effective than any advertisement.

The Queen wrote: 'She has only been with us for a few weeks, in Lord Salisbury's fine old house [at] 24 Grafton Street, and has already made her mark – Mlle Rubinstein has the very valuable quality of inspiring you with confidence. She studied medically everything pertaining to the skin. She hails from the Austrian capital and she has also spent time in Russia.'[2]

Her clients needed informing and educating. Madame repeated over and over that beauty owed everything to science. On their first visit to the salon, each was offered a personalised consultation from a doctor and a beautician, which resulted in a tailor-made beauty care regime complete with diet and exercise recommendations. Each treatment was based on a very precise ritual.

Now that her reputation was growing, it was time to buy advertising space. Edward wrote the copy in the form of articles and interviews, and had the printer add photographs of satisfied clients to the final layout. In keeping with the tradition started by Helena, most were actresses. Kate Cutler, who had played in *Bellamy the Magnificent*, had sent her a glowing letter that Edward quoted from: 'I have used the Valaze preparations with best results.' Rising and established stars of the English stage Lily Elsie, May de Souza and Alice Crawford, along with Fanny Ward and Edna May, American actresses on tour in London, were also part of Helena's 'dream team'.

Their clever strategy paid off handsomely and Madame began to think about a make-up range. As cosmetics were used only by prostitutes and actresses at that time, this was a ground-breaking decision. Helena took advantage of her new allies in the theatre to learn their art. Gabrielle Ray, another champion of the Rubinstein brand, was an expert in the use of tinted face powders. Before each performance she would rub rouge onto her cheeks and shade black onto her eyelids. Ray was happy to share her know-how with Helena, who could already foresee the time when aristocratic and well-to-do ladies would consider make-up part of their daily beauty routine. But she also knew that change would be slow and that it wouldn't pay to rush things. In the meantime, she observed with interest the bolder of the prim Englishwomen trading their long skirts for loose-fitting, knee-length trousers designed for cycling, horse riding and golf, made popular by, and named after, a certain Amelia Bloomer. Others dared to rub a subtle colour on their cheekbones. Queen Alexandra was said to apply rouge to her face, but only at bedtime.

Margot Asquith, the prime minister's wife and 'one of the most alive and vivid personalities in the life of London',[3] had become a regular client at the Grafton Street salon and agreed to have her face made up. Helena showed her how to use pigments to highlight her bone structure and unusual beauty – 'very elegant, long nose, sharp profile … close-lipped but always in movement … that lofty bearing, those rapid and capricious gestures'.[4] The audacious Asquith dared to be seen about town wearing make-up, and was admired by all. It was yet more excellent publicity for the Maison de Beauté Valaze.

The two women became friends. Margot Asquith insisted on inviting the Tituses to her receptions attended by a smart, unconventional crowd. There Helena met the eccentric Baroness Catherine d'Erlanger, nicknamed 'Flame' because of her electric red hair, who became her client, then friend. The baroness, who lived in Byron's old house in Piccadilly, acted as Helena's guide through the complicated ins and outs of the gentry. They went treasure hunting together in flea markets and antique shops. Flame d'Erlanger was keen on over-the-top decorative styles but her unerring aristocratic eye kept her choices within the realms of good taste. She taught Helena to love the baroque, rococo and Venetian mirrors, and helped hone her talent for collecting tableware, furniture, linen and works of art. Helena's husband Edward, meanwhile, an insatiable bibliophile, amassed rare books and precious manuscripts.

Entertainment was a serious pastime for the English and Helena could have some fun at last. She soon found herself at the centre of London's social life, rubbing shoulders with the fashionable bohemians of the day, from artists to aristocrats. It filled her with joy and apprehension to be part of a world she had never imagined belonging to in Kraków. But in her wisdom she harboured no illusions. She knew they were invited to parties by hostesses who prided themselves on welcoming a wide variety of guests, including tradespeople. They would never have been accepted into those closed Mayfair and Belgravia circles, where social conventions had built impenetrable barriers and old English anti-Semitism was rife, through connections alone. A lot of money was needed, too, so when Helena was asked to dinner she would occasionally pay caterers', wine merchants' or florists' bills. Such word-of-mouth publicity from genuine aristocrats was invaluable, and she was happy to indulge them. Feeling indebted to her, they had no choice but to accept her invitations in return.[5] In the social columns, newspapers wrote complimentary or mocking anecdotes about the exotic Madame Rubinstein's salon, style and parties.

Helena had discovered she loved entertaining. Bohemian luxury was all the rage, so she created an informal atmosphere and decorated her tables imaginatively, carefully combining colours and styles. She arranged yellow and orange opalines on lime green tablecloths and mixed Japanese lacquerware with red Bohemian crystal glasses. She was the only hostess who dared to try such bold combinations and be so successful at it. She often hired a Polish chef to cook borscht, piroshki, vegetable soups and other dishes from her country. Her guests were amused by her original, rustic menu – it made a welcome change from quail and ortolan.

Edward, at ease with any subject, held brilliant conversations during which his wit and erudition shone. Guests were enchanted by his extensive knowledge. Helena stayed in the background during tableside debates; beneath her sophisticated hostess exterior hid the self-conscious little Jewish lady who still hadn't completely mastered the language or codes. But in her silence, she took it all in.

At a reception organised by the Polish Embassy, she was introduced to pianist Artur Rubinstein. Helena was on familiar territory: a fellow countryman at last. They discovered they had a lot in common beyond their language and surname (although searching far back in their respective family trees revealed no trace of a blood relationship). She invited him to play at her home and the two Rubinsteins became friends. She adopted Artur's philosophy on life as her own: 'The most important thing in life is to realise why one is alive. It is not only to build bridges and tall buildings or to make money, but to do something truly important, to do something for humanity.'[6] She couldn't agree more.

Helena's London years were a time of innovation: she invented several new preparations there, including Valaze Snow Lotion, a liquid powder; Novena Cerate face cream; Valaze Lip Lustre to protect lips from the wind and cold; Valaze Complexion Soap to cleanse the skin; and Valaze Blackhead and Open Pore Cure to combat blackheads. No doubt relying on her trusted team of chemist colleagues to help give concrete expression to her intuitions, she was involved in every stage of a product's life, from conception to packaging to processing mail orders from all over the world.

She sent for her sister Manka to come and work in Grafton Street. Helena taught her the trade, as she had done with Ceska in Melbourne and would do with Pauline in Paris.

Helena's work routine often included returning to the salon after an evening reception. Needing little sleep, she would work there until dawn, then slip into bed without a sound so as not to wake Edward. In business, the couple worked as a team, but in their private life they were less in tune. Edward went out too much and succumbed too readily to the temptation of pretty, available women. Helena found his adulterous behaviour intolerable. They would argue, then make up, only to begin quarrelling all over again. He would take refuge in his books. She would slam the door and go on trips abroad.

In December 1908, she returned to Australia and visited her sister Ceska, who was running the Sydney and Melbourne salons. These long crossings – time stolen from work, to her mind – were second nature to her by now. At the Grand Hotel Melbourne, she was swamped by journalists in the same way today's stars would be. 'How She Conquered the World's Metropolis' was the title of an article in *The Mercury*, one of many such press pieces to appear.[7] She had become a national heroine whom the Australians were proud to call their own. Helena took the opportunity to indulge her predilection for inventing her life story. According to the article, she had studied philosophy, history and literature to learn 'the annals of the world', as well as chemistry and anatomy under the greatest medical authorities in Europe.[8] It wasn't wholly untrue, but an exaggeration nonetheless. And yet she feigned modesty: 'There is nothing more distasteful to me,' Helena is quoted as saying, 'than speaking of myself. I would much rather tell you how glad I am to revisit Australia, the place of my first real success.'[9] This article penned by Dorothy C is representative of many others in its singing of Helena's praises: 'But most interesting indeed were the autograph letters … from women in Christiania, Rio de Janeiro, Constantinople,

Paris, and every nook and corner of Great Britain, from all over the world, in fact, letters with coronets, betraying the royal origin of the writer, asking for appointments, ordering preparations, and expressing thanks for results which have, till then, been impossible. One is indeed compelled to exclaim … "Oh, wonderful, most wonderful, and most wonderful! And yet again wonderful!"'[10]

Back in Europe, Helena stopped off in Paris, a city she had become addicted to. During her time in London, she would cross the Channel once or twice a month, often accompanied by Edward on the hunt for rare manuscripts and editions in the French capital's bookshops. She was seriously considering moving there.

She spent a great deal of time searching for the ideal location for a salon, and took advantage of her Paris trips to order outfits from the fashionable couturiers. Dressing in haute couture had become her passion. She would wear suits during the day and keep eccentric embroidered silk dresses with lace detailing for the evening. She left Charles Frederick Worth for his former assistant Paul Poiret, who had opened his own couture salon in 1903 and was the talk of the town. Influenced by the vogue for Orientalism, his collections featured kimonos, Ukrainian folk blouses and Greek tunics.

Poiret was a short man with a pointed beard and the rounded belly of a bon vivant. He was an eccentric but unfailingly elegant dresser. He is credited with freeing women from corsets. 'It was in the name of Liberty that I proclaimed the fall of the corset and the adoption of the brassiere, which, since then, has won the day.'[11] He also invented flesh-coloured stockings and suspenders to hold them up. More significantly, Poiret revolutionised the use of colour in fashion. He described throwing into the 'sheepcote' of washed-out shades and pastels 'a few rough wolves: reds, greens, violets, royal blues, that made all the rest sing aloud'.[12] Under Poiret's influence, fashion became an art form. The designer himself moved in artistic circles, and counted Picabia,

Derain, Vlaminck, Dufy and Paul Iribe among his friends. He designed theatrical scenery, founded a school of decorative arts named after one of his daughters, Martine, and dressed Mistinguett, Isadora Duncan and the great actresses of the day.

The couturier's salons initially occupied a mansion on the Avenue d'Antin. As soon as they opened, his catwalk shows proved so popular with the Paris in-crowd that he had to limit the spectators to buying clients. Poiret loved being at the epicentre of Parisian style and was notorious for throwing extravagant parties in his apartment overlooking the salon gardens.

Helena fell for Poiret as a couturier and a friend, and remained loyal to him for a long time, even after he was dethroned by Chanel. She made a point of visiting him on every trip to Paris, asking to see his newest collection, choosing a few dresses, then catching up on the latest gossip. With him, she could discuss all the subjects that fascinated her: beauty, fashion, art, furniture and painting. He had something intelligent to say about everything. Like her, he was self-taught, curious, conscientious and a go-getter. They shared a love of beautiful things, both thrived in the world around them and loved progress and excitement. They understood and admired each other. Poiret went on to be an important influence on Helena's choices in art and interior decoration, as well as designing some of her most beautiful outfits. They caused a sensation in London and earned her a long-term place on the list of the world's top ten best-dressed women.

In early 1909, on her return to the British capital after one of her flying trips to Paris, Helena learned some news that would disrupt all her plans: at thirty-seven, she was expecting her first child.

12

RICH AND FAMOUS

Helena hadn't expected Edward's reaction. When he met her off the train and she nervously told him the news, he couldn't conceal his joy. He hugged her tight and showered her with kisses in a display of ardour she had forgotten he was capable of. We don't know if she was aware he already had children in the United States, but on that day he acted as if it was the first time he was going to be a father.

The first few months were an ordeal. Morning sickness, dizziness and uncharacteristic tiredness left her almost chair bound when all she wanted to do was dash about, but she couldn't admit to feeling weak for fear of her damned doctors, who were in collusion with Edward in forcing her to take bed rest. So she gritted her teeth and made herself get up and go to work, even though chaos reigned inside her.

Helena hadn't wanted a child. Not immediately at least. For a start, their relationship wasn't working as well as it should. Arguments began without her always understanding why. A simple word or a tone of voice could spark them off. Or the way he smiled at a pretty woman.

The word 'separation' had even been mentioned, probably by Edward, which had an immediate calming effect on Helena. She couldn't imagine living apart from him so would make an effort and they would make up in bed that night, only to start quarrelling all over again the next day. Her jewellery collection had grown as a result, but it hadn't erased the memories of those stormy scenes.

The imminent arrival of their baby seemed to be changing all this, however. Edward was now attending to her every need. Yet she found it hard to feign happiness. The reality was that the birth was hampering Helena's professional plans. On her last trip to Paris she had met up with Madame Chambaron, a Russian beautician married to a Frenchman, whose beauty salon at 255 Rue du Faubourg Saint-Honoré was for sale.

She had liked the shop very much, despite its small size. The business was healthy and the account books well kept. The decor left a lot to be desired, but the potential was huge and the location one of the best in Paris: the Faubourg Saint-Honoré was an address to rival Grafton Street.

Helena had been intrigued to know why the middle-aged Russian was selling: 'You have an established clientele and your products are a success.'

'My husband doesn't like me working,' Madame Chambaron had answered. 'He has given me an ultimatum: my salon or him.'

Fortunately for Helena, Edward didn't force her to make that kind of choice. When they had married, he had promised never to stand in the way of her ambition. On the contrary, he had vowed to do all he could to help her succeed. She could still hear him pronouncing the words in the solemn tone he took when he wanted to be persuasive.

Edward did tell the truth on occasion, and that had been one of them. At that time, it was rare to come across men who were determined to support their wives and work alongside them. Helena certainly knew no one else like him in their circle and recognised that she was very lucky in that respect.

The shop at 255 Rue du Faubourg Saint-Honoré seemed an excellent opportunity and one she shouldn't pass up. Helena wrote to her sister Pauline in Kazimierz, nearly her twin in age and the most appearance-conscious of the eight Rubinstein girls, asking her to come and work for her in Paris. With Manka, 'a born manager and enthusiastic teacher', running the London shop and Ceska looking after her interests in Australia, Helena would be able to give birth with peace of mind.[1] But her proviso was that she would return to work as quickly as possible. Edward didn't agree – he wanted her to stop for the first few months at least. Helena didn't give a damn what he thought.

A few weeks before her due date, a heavily pregnant Helena returned to Paris to sign the sale contract with the Russian beautician. Included in the price were all the formulas for Madame Chambaron's own plant-based preparations, some of which were pasteurised to increase shelf life and improve hygiene. Helena was not familiar with the process but wasted no time in adopting it herself.

As soon as Pauline arrived in Paris, Helena took a few short days to train her up then handed over the management of the salon. Before heading back to London, she ordered a few tunic dresses from her friend Paul Poiret, certain their loose-fitting shape would suit her misshapen body.

The Tituses viewed a large Victorian house with twenty rooms in Roehampton Lane, next to Putney Heath, in a leafy London suburb. It was set in a huge, lush, landscaped garden with glasshouses, flower beds, a sweeping lawn and shade-giving trees. The house had belonged to banker J. P. Morgan, who had christened it Solna. They fell instantly in love and decided to move there. Helena had a library put in, a billiard room and an office where Edward could work peacefully, and had a telephone line installed: Putney 2285.[2] The house comprised various reception rooms, two enormous dressing rooms – one for her and the other for her husband's equally well-stocked wardrobe – as well as plenty of rooms for their private apartments.

At last Helena was able to give free rein to her passion for interior decoration. She adorned the house in an exuberant mix of styles: Louis XII paired with chinoiseries; Chippendale furniture with Empire; and so on. She turned the glasshouses into drawing rooms. One, christened the Scheherazade room and inspired by the craze for Orientalism on both sides of the Channel, had a fountain of crystal-clear water at its centre, sofas along the walls and cushions scattered over the floor, like in Paul Poiret's house. The nursery was styled to resemble a boat cabin and painted white and blue. Helena was sure she was expecting a boy.

Roy Valentine Titus came into the world on 12 December 1909. His mother had worked like a maniac right up to the delivery, stopping only when the doctors had confined her to her room. For nine months – which seemed like a century – she had cursed, sighed and counted the days. But, like every other woman in the world, she had been forced to obey nature.

Edward was overjoyed. 'He looks just like me,' he would say as he leaned over the cradle. Helena found the baby ugly, red-faced and wrinkled, her maternal instinct dampened by her keen sense of aesthetics. But her husband's happiness proved contagious. In spite of herself, she began to feel moved by this little scrap whose crying and gurgling filled the house. Edward reiterated his wish for her to stay at home and look after Roy herself, for the first few months at least. In a moment of weakness, she agreed. Since the baby had come into their life, her husband had become very loving again and she didn't want to disappoint him.

But she was unable to keep her promise, and returned to the Grafton Street salon almost immediately. Helena was an expert in the art of doublespeak and presented herself as an accomplished, modern woman who was capable of managing everything at once: business, relationship and motherhood. That was what she often told journalists and wrote on several occasions in her autobiography.[3] Nothing was further from the truth. Her thirst for success was stronger than everything else, so her career, or rather her ambition, took precedence.

So, as in all well-to-do families, Madame left Roy in the care of nurses, remembering to kiss him as she left in the morning and sparing the sleeping baby half a glance when she came home in the evening. To Edward's great displeasure, she made numerous trips to France. It was like trying to stop a shooting star.

Helena was furious to have missed the Faubourg Saint-Honoré opening. The salon wasn't attracting the rich, upper-class clients she had been hoping for. No doubt the Great Flood of January 1910, which had disrupted Parisian life, was to blame for their absence. People were forced to travel around the French capital in boats, so skincare was probably the least of their worries.

But the flood water wasn't the only reason. The salon was too small, the rushed decoration unsatisfactory and she hadn't put out any advertising. So she came up with other battle plans, including having a small factory built in the Paris suburb of Saint-Cloud to manufacture her beauty products. The premises opened in 1911 and, although not industrial in scale, marked a first step away from home-made production.

That year, Helena returned to Australia, once again against Edward's wishes. He thought the baby was too young to be deprived of his mother for so long. But she dug her heels in and won. She was looking forward to leading her own life for a few weeks and leaving the obligations of motherhood behind. Once again the Australian press honoured the country's heroine with headlines heralding her return. Helena inspected her Melbourne and Sydney salons and was very satisfied to find that they were being extremely well run in her absence. She returned to Europe with peace of mind, buzzing with ideas for her next goal: conquering France.

Back in Europe, the electrifying Ballets Russes had been causing a sensation from Brussels to Monte Carlo. Formed by Sergei Diaghilev in St Petersburg in 1907, the dance company had quickly severed ties with the Imperial Ballet from which it had grown, and, following two years of success in Russia, had embarked on an international tour amid great fanfare. In May 1909 the company's vibrant premiere of *Polovtsian Dances* from *Prince Igor* at the Théâtre du Châtelet in Paris had met with vociferous public acclaim. The Ballets attracted an ardent following among the intelligentsia and aristocracy.

On the invitation of the Marchioness of Ripon, the Ballets Russes travelled to London in 1911 for King George V's coronation celebrations. Once again, they set audiences ablaze. Edward wanted to be among the first to applaud the dancers and bought two tickets for *Petrushka*. Nijinsky's gravity-defying leaps and Stravinsky's music captivated Helena. But what excited her most were the set and costumes by Léon Bakst and Alexandre Benois. The combinations of purple and magenta, orange and yellow, and black and gold mesmerised the entire audience. Most gave a standing ovation and cried out for an encore, while a minority, very shocked by the free expression of the 'nude' bodies, shouted their indignation.

The Ballets Russes' lavish sets and electric colour combinations made an impression on all who saw them. They inspired Paul Poiret in his dress designs and Flame d'Erlanger in her interior decoration choices, so Helena decided she would use them too. After seeing the ballet one evening, she went straight to the Grafton Street salon and tore down the white brocade curtains at the windows. Edward found this very amusing and joined in. He loved his unpredictable wife the most during these moments. The next day, Helena ordered new, brightly coloured, Bakst- and Benois-inspired fabrics to replace the old virginal ones. From then on, flamboyance would be her trademark: her salons and homes all over the world would be decorated in bold colour schemes that clashed and dazzled.

It was a time of happiness in Helena's personal life. Roy's arrival had brought her and Edward closer together and they hardly quarrelled any more. Her husband's adoration of their son had rubbed off on her, prompting her to learn to love him too. In this calm and loving atmosphere, she fell pregnant again. Horace Gustave Titus was born in London on 3 May 1912. The Polish version of Horace is Hertzel and despite only having indirect news about her father from her sisters and Gitel's letters, Helena was keen to pay him this tribute.

Horace, unlike his brother, was a child born from love. Helena fell for him instantly. He would always be her favourite, the son she gave almost everything to. He was a gorgeous baby: cheerful, placid and easy to make a fuss over. Through him Helena discovered the joys of motherhood and took every opportunity to experience them.

Horace grew into a brilliant child, while Roy remained shy and reserved. Their mother often compared them: the good one and the bad one, the intelligent one and the difficult one. In public she embarrassed Roy by asking why he wasn't as clever as his younger brother – a question that terrified both children. Divide and rule: Helena found that this Machiavellian policy always paid off. She adopted it in her business too, playing her employees off against each other. No one warned her of the damage such tactics could do to the children's education; she probably wouldn't have followed their advice anyway.

At the age of six months, her beloved Horace was dropped on his head by a nurse. No physical trace of the accident would remain, but each time he made a scene – even in adulthood – Helena would explain her son's temperamental character by shrugging and saying: 'Horace is cuckoo.'[4]

The boys were both pampered and neglected by their mother. Edward granted them his presence when he could. Throughout their lives they would seek the warmth, attention and affection that Helena had not consistently given. She had no idea about child psychology and carted them from one new home to the next, from London to Paris to New York. During their childhood, she surrounded them with a horde of babysitters and private tutors, called them to her side when it suited her to spend time with them, then sent them back off to play as soon as they began to bore her. But children are adaptable creatures and the boys became used to having a part-time mother.

After Horace's birth, Edward once again begged Helena to slow down and take time off work. She took advantage of those few weeks to redecorate Solna. She had recently developed a passion for the work of Elie Nadelman, a very promising Polish sculptor she had met by chance at an exhibition of his work in a Bond Street gallery. Warsaw-born Nadelman lived in Paris, following a brief period in Munich.

Nadelman was a handsome, pleasant man, and a very talented artist. But his exhibition in London hadn't met with success – until Helena anonymously purchased all the sculptures on show. Nadelman wouldn't discover this until many years later. Buying in large quantities was a habit of Helena's – 'I'm a business woman, I'm used to buying in bulk,' she once explained[5] – although it was sometimes at the expense of quality. On this occasion, however, her instincts were right: Nadelman went on to be considered a pioneer of modern sculpture, although this recognition only came after his death in 1946. The pair struck up a friendship and Helena commissioned him to produce some marble bas-reliefs for the reception room walls at Solna. She went on to showcase many of his sculptures in her Paris and New York salons, and their patron–artist collaboration lasted for years.

Madame's love of art that was ahead of its time was an extension of her love of beauty. 'My avid desire to make women beautiful has always blended well with my insatiable thirst for all art forms,' she wrote.[6] Money enabled her to indulge this passion.

Her taste for the avant-garde developed to a large extent thanks to Edward's enlightened recommendations. But she acquired it on her own too, by visiting museums, exhibitions and artists' studios, listening to conversations, reading the newspapers and inquisitively observing the houses she was invited to. She also regularly befriended people who opened her eyes to new things.

On every trip to Paris she visited the studios of famous painters and never missed the Salon d'Automne to see the work of the artists she liked: Matisse, Derain, Picabia and Modigliani. In 1908, she asked high-society painter Paul César Helleu to produce her portrait. It was her way of becoming established in a milieu she wanted to be part of, and proclaiming it to the women who visited her beauty salons, where she would exhibit her most famous paintings. This portrait signalled that she belonged to their world. It was the first in a collection of portraits of Madame painted by Salvador Dalí, Marie Laurencin, Raoul Dufy, Christian Bérard and a dozen other great artists.

With art, she was always open-minded. Even bad taste interested her, on the condition that 'it is done with flair and a belief that it is right'.[7] She often showed a preference for pieces that were funny, strange or downright ugly (compared with accepted criteria) as long as they were powerful. She applied the same concept to beauty: any face could be beautiful on condition it had character. What she despised above all were sentimentality, conventionality and banality.

One of her 'teachers' was painter and sculptor Jacob Epstein, a close friend of Edward's. He introduced her to new trends and trained her eye to appreciate primitive art. At the time, primitive art's few followers included Matisse, Derain and Vlaminck. Helena's appreciation of new forms of beauty made her a pioneer once again. Her long stay in Australia, where she may have had the opportunity of seeing Aboriginal art, had possibly contributed to educating her eye.

Most primitive-art sales took place in Paris. Epstein, who visited the French capital less frequently than Helena, often asked her to bid for him. One day he dropped by Solna with an Hôtel Drouot auction catalogue that featured a wonderful Baoulé mask and Bambara statuette. She quickly became an expert in the sculptures of the different ethnic groups of Mali, the Congo and Senegal. When the pieces exceeded the price that Jacob Epstein was prepared to pay, Helena bought them for herself. And so her remarkable art collection began, and would grow over the years. Her friends were surprised by her choices: 'How strange,' they would say, 'to think of someone who has dedicated her life to beauty, buying such ugly things.'[8] But she was right to persist – primitive art soon became fashionable, inspiring artists like Gris, Modigliani and Picasso.

Some twenty years later, when Epstein saw the extensive collection that his 'pupil' had amassed, he exclaimed proudly: 'I made it for her – at a distance.'[9]

Since Edward VII's death in May 1910 and George V's accession to the throne, Paris had replaced London as the party capital. Helena brimmed with plans for conquering France and had no trouble persuading Edward to move there: he dreamed of setting up a publishing house and Paris was the place to be for literature as well as art. Helena was only too pleased to help finance his project as he had agreed to follow her. Like her, Edward was a nomad, a citizen of the world, used to moving and living wherever circumstances took him. She appreciated this quality in her husband. With him, everything seemed possible. In 1912, the Rubinstein-Titus caravan of children, nurses, books, works of art and clothing trunks crossed the Channel once and for all.

Helena Rubinstein was forty years old, looked thirty-five and told people she was thirty, at most. In barely a decade, she had become rich and famous. Her trajectory had been unique: in Melbourne and London, through willpower and intelligence alone, she had successfully penetrated circles that were normally closed to outsiders of lower birth and fortune.

This unconventional woman – judged by her century's standards – went from being pretty to beautiful, although her physique was far from fashionable. Beneath her languorous, Mediterranean-looking features lay a character of steel. It is well known, since Nero and Napoleon, that despots come in small sizes, and Helena was no exception to the rule. Four feet ten inches in height, she could be hard, tyrannical and demanding of both others and herself. She never looked back; to her, memories seemed a waste of time. She was barely interested in the present either. All that counted was the future.

Helena expressed herself little in public, preferring to follow the advice her mother had given her in Kazimierz, and listen. She remained shy all her life. When she did speak, her deep voice, thick Polish accent and mixing of languages, none of which she mastered fluently, added to her charm. Madame created her own unique style. Her hair, in which she never allowed a single grey strand, was always pulled tightly back from her large forehead in a severe chignon. Even when the use of make-up had become routine, she would wear little – just bright red lipstick to enhance her pale complexion. As for fashion, she wore only the best.

Her trademark hairstyle was complemented by accessories, consisting predominantly of large, showy jewellery. 'Because I'm small, I find that these accessories mixed with my clothes help forge my identity. This is very important for a woman who, like me, works hard in a world governed by men.'[10] Jewellery is a woman's best friend, she concluded.

Helena never left the house without a designer bag, matching shoes, silk stockings and polished nails. She didn't tolerate scruffiness in anyone else either and was quick to lecture even her most titled clients if she found that their appearance looked neglected.

Always ahead of her time, she understood that to become an icon it was necessary to present an eternal image of oneself and propagate it as widely as possible. So she constantly had herself photographed – in every place and every outfit – to immortalise herself for eternity.

Edward Titus helped her emerge, but Helena invented herself. In 1912, having brought her two children into the world, Madame was finally born.

13

PARIS, HERE I COME!

'Compared with the women of France the average American woman is still in kindergarten,' Edith Wharton wrote in an essay.[1] The American novelist, who spent every winter in her Faubourg Saint-Germain apartment in Paris, was a keen observer of the ways of French high society. 'As life is an art in France, so woman is an artist,' she commented.[2] Frenchwomen of the day were achieving greater social freedom but remained largely dependent on their husbands. Among the upper classes, the distribution of roles was nothing if not traditional: men provided the family income while their wives focused on the household and childcare. Adultery was considered a criminal offence, and prostitution a necessary evil.

However, there were various signs of gradual emancipation. Women had begun to escape the confines of home to host salons where they made social, political, artistic and literary contacts that would benefit their husbands. Feminists encouraged baccalauréat graduates to shoulder their way into university, then take up jobs as lawyers, lecturers, stenographers, typographers and coach drivers.

Women had begun to make a name for themselves in various fields. Camille Claudel was a renowned sculptor. Helena's fellow Pole Marie Curie, a scientist and the first woman to teach at the Sorbonne, was awarded the Nobel Prize for Physics in 1903 and received a second Nobel Prize, for Chemistry, in 1911. And this was only the beginning.

Parisian women were also one step ahead when it came to using their feminine charms. On moving to Paris, Helena realised that the city was a 'laboratory for beauty'.[3] During her frequent trips to the French capital, she had often admired the inimitable style of French noblewomen, who bought their clothes from fashion designers such as Paul Poiret and Jacques Doucet and wore plumed hats made by Caroline Reboux, known as the 'Queen of the Milliners'.

Middle-class women were not far behind. Sales of cosmetics had spread beyond beauty salons in the space of only a few years, and the opening of department stores had stoked the new craze. Some 15 million women regularly purchased fragrances, creams, clothes and accessories at these shops. By the turn of the century, women were estimated to have spent 90 million francs on perfumes by Coty, Guerlain, Houbigant, Roger et Gallet, Bourjois and Caron.[4] Dressmakers' apprentices, shop girls, telephone operators and teachers read about skin- and haircare products and perfumes in fashion journals and bought as many products as they could afford.[5]

Parisian women had Baron Haussmann to thank for their smart appearance. His underground sewer network had brought running water to bathrooms – the new temples of personal hygiene. Good hygiene was far from being the norm – Frenchwomen still 'don't smell like roses', as Eugène Schueller, a young chemist who had invented a synthetic hair dye and would go on to set up L'Oréal, put it.[6] But things were definitely improving.

Two different concepts of physical beauty existed at the time. The first kind reflected the traditional ideal of beauty – a tightly constricted waist, full breasts, a generous bottom and fleshy thighs. The other kind, which Helena preferred, was elegant and slender, chest thrust forward, back held straight and long, slim thighs.

Only a narrow strip of sea separated England from France, but aesthetic standards in the two countries were diametrically opposed. Englishwomen were primarily concerned with their delicate complexions, which wrinkled and reddened easily. During her London years, Helena had created and perfected products that wouldn't irritate their skin: all-day moisturising creams, astringent lotions and healing ointments. In Paris, on the other hand, women not only wanted to look good, they also wanted to break taboos. 'Nothing could be more opposed to the innocent desire to please than the use of make-up and cosmetics,' reads an extract from the 1827 *Encyclopédie Roret*, a layman's guide to technical subjects, good manners and the art of living.[7] Things had changed a lot since then. Nearly a century later, women were increasingly keen on using make-up. They were no longer afraid of looking like prostitutes or actresses. Wearing make-up had gradually become a right and a way for women to assert their independence.[8] Some women were even daring enough to go out with make-up on in the daytime.

Madame, who abhorred the French fad for pallid faces, sooty eyes and blood-red lips, found these attempts at self-assertion pathetic. She decided that teaching Parisian women moderation and putting a stop to what she described as a 'massacre' would be her priority.

The Tituses moved into the first floor of 255 Rue du Faubourg Saint-Honoré while waiting to find a more suitable home, which Edward would soon unearth in the heart of Montparnasse. Helena toiled late into the night in the back of the shop with the chemists from her Saint-Cloud factory, making lighter-textured foundation and adding colouring agents and pigments to her face powders. She was forever dissatisfied and incapable of settling for approximations; she would tirelessly start over and drive the people working with her to exhaustion. In the end she produced a creamy blush made out of Persian wax, natural oils and Bulgarian rose petals and her first tinted, delicately perfumed, mattifying face powder.

She owed a number of her breakthroughs to Paul Poiret. The two of them had long conversations in a mixture of English and French, which Madame had picked up on the job, although she couldn't speak it fluently. They obsessively discussed their favourite subject: feminine beauty and how to enhance it. The master designer had just launched Les Parfums de Rosine, a line of luxury perfumes he had named after one of his daughters.

In her Maison de Beauté (she had dropped the Valaze and renamed her salon Rubinstein), Helena taught Parisian women to fake a healthy look by applying a touch of red to their cheekbones and spreading it with their fingertips. She advised them to dust their noses, necks and shoulders with pastel powder. Their mouths needed a stronger colour such as raspberry or blueberry. She spread mauve shadow on their eyelids and darkened their lashes and eyebrows with antimony, the forerunner of mascara.

This American invention would appear in 1913. The tale of its creation involves chemistry and a brother's love. A New York chemist named T. L. Williams wanted to help his sister Maybel seduce the man she had fallen in love with, and concocted a mixture of coal dust and Vaseline in his laboratory to make her lashes darker and fuller. History does not recount whether she won the gentleman's heart, but the loving brother's invention made his fortune. Maybelline mascara – the name was a contraction of Maybel and Vaseline – was initially sold by mail order and went on to become the success it still is today. Helena would improve the technique a few years later.

Even as she developed her cosmetics line, Madame worked on the packaging of her products, which had to be as refined as their content if she was going to target the kind of upscale clients she had had in London. She spent hours in flea markets and antique dealers' shops looking for prettily decorated powder compacts and boxes, and had them copied. In later years, she would ask artists such as Marie

Laurencin, Raoul Dufy and Salvador Dalí to design them for her. She also took infinite care over choosing the paper her creams and lotions were wrapped in and the bags used to carry them.

She undertook a methodical conquest of Paris, leaving nothing to chance. She spent a considerable amount of time perfecting her scientific knowledge in the dermatology department of the Hôpital Saint-Louis, considered one of the best hospitals in France and possibly the world. Plastic surgery had emerged at the beginning of the century and was now starting to take off. However, surgeons still caused a fair amount of damage and didn't really conceive of surgery as a way to enhance the female body.

At the Hôpital Saint-Louis, Helena met Suzanne Noël, a gynaecologist who had retrained in plastic surgery after meeting an American actress whose forehead had been rebuilt after a car accident. Noël came up with an outpatient surgery technique that made it possible for the women she operated on to take up their everyday occupations almost immediately afterwards. 'They have their operations and they don't talk about it,'[9] she told Helena, who instantly grasped the possibilities that plastic surgery opened up for female beauty.

'My very first patients were desperate women,' continued the surgeon, who shared Helena's optimism about cosmetic surgery. 'Then I started getting other clients who came to see me because they loved art and beauty, and wanted to be beautiful too.'

Women no longer merely wanted to be attractive to men. They wanted to like themselves too.

With the help of her sister Pauline, who was now well versed in the beauty trade, Madame created new skincare products and trained young working women to apply them. She was ready for the aristocratic clientele she aspired to. A few of the duchesses and countesses who attended the lavish parties Paul Poiret regularly threw would look good in her appointment book.

One of Poiret's most unforgettable events was a 'Thousand and Two Nights' theme party at his townhouse in the Faubourg Saint-Honoré on 24 June 1911. On another occasion, he recreated a fête at the court of Versailles.

Helena had met the legendary socialite Misia Sert in London at a party at Lady Ripon's in honour of the Ballets Russes, and got on famously with her. 'Come and see me when you move to Paris,' the young woman had whispered to her in Polish. 'I receive friends every Thursday.'

Like all expatriate networks, the Polish community in Paris was very active and Misia, who, despite her Polish origins, was more Parisian than the Parisians themselves, was its queen bee. Married three times, she had taken her husband's name each time and been successively called Misia Natanson, Misia Edwards and Misia Sert, although accomplished snobs were only known by their first names in Paris.

The two women met for the second time at Poiret's and immediately became friends. Both were pleased to encounter a fellow countrywoman, although they had little in common apart from their nationality: one came from a traditional Jewish family of modest means, while the other had a Catholic upper-middle-class background.

Misia's world had always been populated by stylish, intellectual and aristocratic bohemians, who she would receive at her salon. She was talented at everything she undertook. An accomplished pianist, she was one of Fauré's most brilliant pupils and had toyed with the idea of a career in music. To the master's great disappointment, she had married her stepmother Matylda's nephew Thadée Natanson when she was barely eighteen. Their circle of friends included some of the most brilliant minds of the time: Stéphane Mallarmé, Paul Verlaine, Jules Renard, Tristan Bernard, Alfred Jarry, Paul Valéry, Paul Claudel and Guillaume Apollinaire, who all wrote for *La Revue Blanche*, the literary magazine Thaddée had recently started.

Misia's contemporaries called her the 'primitive princess'; she was the quintessence of charm, gaiety and grace. She was both the mainstay and muse of her set and modelled hundreds of times for the painters who gravitated around her: Renoir, Bonnard, Vuillard and Toulouse-Lautrec, not to mention Félix Vallotton, who was madly in love with her.

In 1907, she divorced her bankrupt husband and married the billionaire industrialist Alfred Edwards, who had been courting her assiduously. Misia was kept in great style. She collected priceless jewels and mixed with artists and high society. She was passionate about fashion and got to know the upcoming designer Coco Chanel, who would become both a close friend and a rival.

When Edwards left her for an actress, the Catalan painter José Maria Sert became Misia's lover and subsequently her husband, although he too ended up leaving her. Through José Maria Sert, Misia had made the acquaintance of Sergei Diaghilev. They soon became inseparable. Misia's life began to revolve around the Ballets Russes. She was their muse, patron and most ardent fan.

She found it perfectly natural to take 'the wealthy Helena Rubinstein'[10] under her wing. The industrious Helena was rather more inclined to work than socialise, but she knew from experience that a good social network was the first rung on the ladder of success. She couldn't have asked for a better mentor than Misia, although her opinion of her new friend wasn't one of unqualified admiration: 'Misia was a *meshuggah*, but always busy,' she would confide to her secretary Patrick O'Higgins half a century later.[11] However, she also told him that Misia had guided the innocent young thing she had been at the time and taught her the niceties required to navigate the maze of Parisian society. Thanks to Misia, Helena met every artist in Paris: the Bateau

Lavoir group, Braque, Gris, Picasso, Modigliani, Henri Rousseau and Matisse, who would always remain her favourite painter.

'It was she who gave me the idea of being painted, of all the portraits,' she told O'Higgins. 'Good for publicity, good for investment, good for all the empty walls.'[12]

She browsed antiques shops, art galleries, and artists' workshops in Misia's company the way she had done in London with Flame d'Erlanger, and refined her tastes. She bought incessantly, driving a hard bargain each time. Misia encouraged her to receive guests on Sundays, explaining that it would be a good way to build up her clientele and improve her French so as to get over her shyness at social gatherings. Helena was sceptical. Would she be capable of steering her way through such an impenetrable society, with all its codes and prejudices and unfamiliar customs? An insistent Misia took it upon herself to organise all the details of the first reception, from the buffet to the guest list, to convince Helena she was right.

Helena felt certain that first Sunday evening had been a disaster. The guests had turned up all right, but they had behaved very strangely. The men hadn't exchanged a single word with any of the women, they had merely ogled them lasciviously. She had thought it quite improper. Edward didn't agree. He had felt immediately at ease among all those intellectuals and socialites. As for Misia, she burst out laughing when Helena revealed her astonishment. The only thing required of a brilliant society hostess in Paris was that she provide plenty of good food and wine and invite enough pretty women for the men to look at and speculate about, she told Helena.

Misia knew what she was talking about. Madame Rubinstein's guests all returned the next week. However dubious their reasons for coming, at least they were there. Helena soon got used to it and became as successful a hostess in Paris as she had been in London.

She began to receive invitations in return. In the drawing room of the apartment on Quai Voltaire that Edwards had given Misia when he left her, Helena met Marcel Proust, who had modelled his character Madame Verdurin on their hostess. Many years later, Helena would tell her secretary about her meeting with the great writer, describing Proust in characteristically vivid terms as 'That boy who slept in a cork-lined room and wrote that very famous book I've never managed to read'.[13] Her bad memory for names would get worse as she got older.

She grew impatient as she tried to remember his name, and kept saying: 'That Marcel something.' When O'Higgins suggested 'Proust?' Helena nodded, relieved. She would describe Proust in her autobiography as an insignificant-looking youth in a floor-length fur coat, who 'smelt of mothballs'. The author of *Remembrance of Times Past* asked Helena several questions about make-up. Did socialites apply kohl to their eyes? Did she think a duchess would wear blush? Overcome as usual by shyness, Helena found it hard to reply and cut the conversation short. Half a century later, she would regret it bitterly.

'How was I to know he would become so famous?' she snapped.

Misia's circle of friends included the Countess de Chevigné, the Countess Greffhule, who had also been immortalised in Proust's book, the Grand Duchess Maria Pavlovna, the Princess de Broglie, the Duchess de Gramont and Colette, all of whom became regular customers at Helena's salon. Only a few months after it had opened, her Paris salon was as successful as the one in London. Helena had asked André Groult to redecorate the salon in the newly fashionable Art Nouveau style. The result was elegant and modern, exactly as she had visualised it.

Under Poiret's flowing dresses and liberated from stiff, constricting corsets, womanly curves had begun to spread. Madame hired a Swedish masseuse called Tilla to eliminate her clients' excess pounds. She took the ever-inventive Edward's advice and began to offer the most prominent society women in Paris a free beauty consultation and massage.

The great writer Colette accepted immediately. She enjoyed body care treatments so much that she would open her own salon in Paris in 1932, albeit not as successfully as Madame. Edward suggested his wife invite a journalist to come to the salon to record the novelist's impressions. Scenting the whiff of scandal that always accompanied Colette, the French press waited eagerly to see what she would say. Had she been massaged in the nude? She was such an exhibitionist that anything was possible.

'I've never felt so good,' she declared. 'I'm ready for anything now … I'm even ready for my husband.' The libertine added in her gravelly voice: 'Massage is a sacred duty. Frenchwomen owe it to themselves. How can they hope to keep a lover otherwise?'

Word got around Paris so fast that Tilla's appointment book was filled up in a trice. Several years later, Helena would tell journalists what her famous client had meant to say. Swedish massages weren't ordinary massages. Colette had been given a few 'extras' – a 'special' treatment involving a vibrator.

The use of this device was far from unusual and had no sexual connotations at the time. Manually stimulating the clitoris was a technique dating back to antiquity, when Galen of Pergamon hypothesised that sexual deprivation led to disorders such as hysteria. The physician recommended masturbation as a way to fully satisfy sexual desire. For several centuries, it was quite common for doctors and midwives to bring patients to orgasm in a medical environment.

The advances in electrical devices in the late nineteenth century freed doctors from the tedious task of pelvic massage. Electric and battery-operated vibrators became so popular that there were a dozen models for both sexes on display at the 1900 Universal Exhibition. Newspapers and catalogues carried advertisements for vibrators for use in the home. American advertisements encouraged husbands to buy one of these devices so that their wives could feel 'relaxed'. The vibrator was as common a domestic appliance as the electric toaster.

Moral standards changed after Freud and other psychiatrists finally recognised the existence of female sexuality. Genital stimulation outside the bonds of marriage began to be frowned upon, even in the privacy of the home. The vibrator gradually disappeared from doctors' offices and mail-order catalogues and became a clandestine object.

Helena had often seen vibrators used at spas. If she ever used one herself, she was far too prudish to admit it. She certainly bought a few vibrators for her salon, claiming they were an essential element of a good body care treatment. Like Colette, clients came back for more.

She preferred to heal her own frustrations by collecting anything money could buy: jewellery, paintings and objets d'art. She derived a great deal of pleasure from browsing antique dealers' shops and artists' studios and discovering and launching unknown artists.

Helena had conquered Paris in less than two years, just as she had previously conquered London. One hundred people worked for Helena Rubinstein in her five salons and Saint-Cloud factory. She had given three of her sisters and a few of her cousins jobs, and financially supported her family in Poland. To her great despair, however, her relationship with Edward kept disintegrating – it was as grim and strife-ridden as the Europe they lived in, which was tearing itself apart at its borders. The more Edward neglected her, the more she threw herself into work. The gap between them got wider by the day.

The imminent war gave Helena a new opportunity to do the escape artist act at which she had become a past master. This time it was in the hope of resolving her marital woes. Starting all over again elsewhere – she had been thinking of going to the United States in any case – would perhaps give her relationship with Edward fresh impetus.

On 28 June 1914, Archduke Franz Ferdinand, the heir apparent to the Austro-Hungarian throne, was assassinated in Sarajevo. This tragic event officially sparked off World War I. Jean Jaurès, the French socialist and pacifist, was murdered in Paris on 31 July. The next day, the French government ordered full mobilisation. The French capital was swept up in an incredible frenzy. People celebrated the departure of soldiers for the front with a mixture of euphoria and suppressed fear.

On 3 August, Germany declared war on France after invading Luxembourg and sending Belgium an ultimatum demanding free passage to France for its troops. On 20 August, German troops marched into Brussels. An attack on Paris seemed imminent. In September the first German plane flew over the French capital and dropped three bombs.

Private cars and 600 Paris taxis were requisitioned to carry soldiers to the front to fight the Battle of the Marne. Horse-drawn carriages reappeared on the streets of Paris. A young designer named Gabrielle Chanel, who had just opened a boutique in Deauville, came up with a wartime outfit for aristocratic women who had 'lost everything'.[14] It consisted of a floor-length A-line skirt and a loose-fitting sailor blouse over a shirt, worn with stacked heels and a plain straw hat. She also fashioned nurses' uniforms for them out of the remaining bed linen in big hotels.

Helena wanted a safe refuge for herself and her family. She had become an American citizen when she married Edward, and their two children were also American nationals. The Tituses decided they had to get to New York as soon as possible, but spent many sleepless nights weighing the pros and cons of their decision. Going to America would mean leaving behind everything they had in Europe – the salons, the houses, their collections and friends. After a lot of talking and arguing, they finally decided that she would go on ahead by herself and scout the place out. Edward and the boys would join her later with their furniture and luggage.

In the autumn of 1914, Madame took a train to Calais and a ferry to

Dover. She reached London after spending the entire nerve-racking journey in a state of sheer terror about being bombed.

In Liverpool she boarded a ship to New York. She tried to boost her spirits by constantly reminding herself that her family would soon be joining her. What with modern telecommunications technology such as the telegraph and the telephone, she would surely find a way to manage her businesses in Europe and Australia and keep in touch with her parents, who had remained in Poland. She had had no news of Hertzel and Gitel since war had broken out, which affected her far more than she would admit. The family remained an unending source of worry for her.

14

BEAUTY ENLIGHTENING
THE WORLD

Standing on the deck of the *Baltic*, Helena Rubinstein buttoned her overcoat, adjusted her hat and shot a glance at her maid to make sure she was carrying her jewellery box. Like other travellers before her who had caught their first glimpse of New York from the sea, Helena had been awestruck on emerging from her cabin, and was still feeling slightly stunned. The sky high above her was such a pure, cloudless blue that it almost made her forget what a relentlessly stormy crossing it had been. The Wall Street skyscrapers rose out of a low mist like glass-and-steel fortresses guarding the tip of Manhattan that jutted into the water like a ship's prow.

Buoyed by the sea air and hope, Helena made herself a whispered promise that chilly October 1914 morning: she would conquer this unknown land. It would be the fourth time she was starting life anew in a foreign country. She knew it would be a huge undertaking, and was feeling both excited and nervous. This was not merely a new land; it was a burgeoning market with spending power a thousand times greater than Europe's. Edward had often told her that everything was possible in America, but that you couldn't take anything for granted. She would have no room for error. Even so, she was looking forward to the thrill and challenge of a fresh start.

As she turned to look at the Statue of Liberty, it occurred to her that she could adapt its full title to make the perfect slogan: 'Beauty enlightening the world'.

*

Most of the *Baltic*'s 1,000 passengers were Americans leaving war-torn Europe for the safety of home. The outbreak of war appeared to have slowed the flow of shiploads of immigrants from Liverpool, Southampton, Hamburg and Bremen. Nearly 16 million impoverished people of every nationality, including 3 million Jews, had disembarked at Ellis Island since 1870, hoping to make their fortune in the New World, or at least live a better life. It would take more than a generation for them to overcome the abject poverty they had lived in for so long.

In large cities, immigrants formed supportive communities. Although the various communities – Irish, Italian, German, and Chinese – lived cheek by jowl, they didn't mix with each other. The vast majority lived in extremely crowded and unsanitary conditions, and were subjected to racism by early Americans and first- and second-generation immigrants afraid of losing their hard-won privileges. They believed that the unchecked flow of immigrants – the very melting pot that would shape the soul of America – had become a serious problem, and called for measures to slow it down. In the mid 1920s, under pressure from lobbies concerned about the shaky post-war economy, the American government would establish quotas to restrict the number of immigrants.

Helena Rubinstein had no cause for worry. She was American by marriage and had arrived with a name, know-how and plenty of money. The US Customs officials barely glanced at her passport with its false date of birth. Her designer clothes, jewellery and luxury luggage provided ample evidence of her wealth, and money was all it took to open this particular door.

However, successful women were a rare and poorly regarded species in early-twentieth-century America, and being Jewish was an added disadvantage. Like high society in London and Paris, members of America's white Protestant elite were frequently and virulently anti-Semitic, as were other communities, especially the Irish. Edward had warned her about this too, but it was a brand of rejection she was familiar with. It would take more than anti-Semitism to discourage her. Unlike other famous Jewish immigrants to America, she refused to change her name. It hadn't stopped her achieving success and renown so far, and she saw no reason to betray her roots. As for her gender, she had turned it into a strong point. Only a woman could come up with the right beauty products for other women.

She had been sick with worry ever since she boarded the ship in England, but not because she was concerned about the reception she would be given in America. Waves as tall as five-storey buildings had lashed the *Baltic* some nights, reminding the anxious passengers of the sinking of the *Titanic* two years earlier on the voyage from Southampton to New York. As the elements raged outside, Helena sat brooding in her cabin. Her thoughts skittered off in every direction – the war, her exile, sales, orders, raw materials, balance sheets, products, clients, her family and her collections. What state would she find them all in when she returned? She had slept very badly. The incessant howling of the wind had only worsened her migraine.

When they had said goodbye, she and Edward had agreed to meet up again in six months' time. He would pack their furniture and art collection and look after the boys while she found them an apartment and premises for her salon in New York. This sharing out of tasks was unusual for the time, but then they were an unusual couple.

Her husband remained her most trusted adviser. She knew she could rely on him for invaluable help and well-thought-out opinions. His advertisements always hit the spot – he was almost as familiar with the brand as she was, and used all the right words. He was also a loving and affectionate father. But she was the one who ran the business and made the final decisions. And owned the fortune.

*

Edward was impossible with money. He spent far too much, especially on books and clothes. He knew perfectly well how hard she worked and how much she paid in charges, duties and income tax; how she had to wage an unremitting battle against wasteful spending and watch out for careless mistakes that could happen at any moment and cost her business dearly. And extravagance wasn't the worst of his faults. Women were drawn to him like bees to a pot of honey and he would seduce them all if Helena didn't watch him like a hawk. A leopard can't change its spots. She had lost count of the number of exhausting quarrels they had had, which always led to the same accusations.

You can't have it all, she had concluded one morning after a noisy fit of weeping. It was probably her fate to be unlucky in love. *Oy vey*. Men! What with her weak father and her womanising husband, she had never been able to count on them.

At the end of the day it didn't really matter that Edward wasn't the perfect husband. She had more than enough family members to back her. She would call her sisters to the rescue. She'd get Manka to join her in New York, and send Ceska and her new English husband to London. She was sure she could find another sister or cousin to whom she could entrust the salons in Australia. She certainly had no lack of Rubinstein relatives, even if she didn't get on very well with her younger sisters.

Despite their constant squabbling, though, it was always Edward she turned to when she needed advice or just wanted to vent.

'My dear, these American women are pitiful. If only you could see their purple noses and grey lips and their faces chalk white from terrible powder. The United States could be my life's work,' Helena told Edward on the phone from her New York hotel room.[1]

Although American women didn't strike Helena as being particularly well groomed, they did care about their looks, especially in New York. The Gibson Girl, a character portrayed in illustrations by Charles Dana Gibson, was the feminine ideal. American women all wanted to look like this wholesome, fashionable, high-spirited girl who was comfortable in her skin and around men, for whom she was both a partner and a pal. The Gibson Girl was the precursor of the pin-up girl. She was tall and slim and wore her hair piled up on top of her head. Her corset set her curvy figure off to advantage. American women were evidently a couple of fashion generations behind their European counterparts, who had long abandoned the restrictive garment.

Like her compatriots, the Gibson Girl didn't wear make-up. A New York etiquette guide of the time specified that it was acceptable for women to wear blush and face powder to lunch at a restaurant, but never at dinner. The natural look was the magic formula. *Eat healthily, take exercise, get a good night's sleep and you'll be beautiful*, was the gist of an 1899 article in the *Denver Post* by a journalist who claimed that dieting, exercising, steam baths and massages were the secret of eternal youth.[2] Advocated by several magazines, this avant garde programme had a large number of American women followers. 'If you want beauty, think beauty' was the message; every woman could be beautiful if she chose. That had always been Helena's credo too, but she thought the much-touted natural look could do with a touch of sophistication.

The suffragette movement was very active in America. The state of Wyoming had granted women the right to vote in 1869, followed soon after by Utah and Idaho. Alongside their political debates, leading women's rights advocates of the day, such as Lucretia Mott, Elizabeth Cady, Charlotte Perkins Gilman and Inez Milholland, discussed feminine issues like sexuality, pregnancy, abortion and contraception at their meetings. Married women of the time were confined to the home and often unhappy with their post-childbirth bodies.

The 6 May 1912 Suffrage Parade in New York was widely covered in the press. No fewer than 20,000 women and 500 men all dressed in white responded to a call for action from feminist unions and groups, and marched from 59th Avenue to Washington Square to once again demand the right to vote. For the first time, most of the women were proudly wearing lipstick, a brave political gesture to affirm their independence and their desire to break away from conventions.

Many observers were shocked by the sight of women casually wearing lipstick as a statement of intent. Edward Bok, the publisher of *Ladies Home Journal*, observed: 'Men continue to see rouge as a mark of sex and sin.'[3] Nevertheless, 'The mania for make-up has spread from the theatrical profession up and down the line from the aristocratic lady in her private car to the saleswoman and factory girl', as Elizabeth Reid, a beauty specialist of the time, noted.[4]

American women would veer from puritanism to liberation in the space of only a few years. Ever alert to current trends, Helena immediately capitalised on women's burgeoning independence and self-assurance. She would turn women's demands for equal rights into a marketing opportunity for her products. The market was ripe for it: a new-found affluence was turning America into a consumer society. Magazines such as *Woman's Home Companion* urged women to go to the movies and carried advertisements for a variety of products, from Jell-O and Kellogg's to cars and gas cookers, not to mention cosmetic products such as Hind's Honey and Almond Cream, Pond's Cold Cream and Woodbury Facial Soap.

Helena exaggerated, as she often did, when she later claimed to have been a pioneer in a beauty wilderness. It was true that women entrepreneurs were thin on the ground, and that most of them had made a name for themselves in fashion, not beauty. Lane Bryant designed plus-size clothing and maternity clothes. Hattie Carnegie was the first American designer to launch a ready-to-wear label, and Carrie Marcus had set up Neiman Marcus, the first luxury department store in America, with her brother Herbert and her husband Al. All three women were Jewish; the first two had changed their names.

But beauty had its fair share of high priestesses and followers. As early as 1893, a journalist with *Harper's Bazaar* observed that: 'the culture of beauty has grown immensely during the past few years'.[5] In America, as in Europe, medical practitioners had begun to take an interest in face and body enhancement. Dermatologists and surgeons opened institutes where they carried out face restructuring operations.

However, new techniques such as electric skin peeling, paraffin injections under the skin to fill out cheeks and smooth out under-eye wrinkles, nose jobs and facelifts weren't entirely risk free. Many of these practitioners had only a passing acquaintance with formal training, or had learned their trade on the job. Nevertheless, more and more actresses went to see them, especially for facelifts, which were very much in vogue on either side of the Atlantic: Frenchwoman Sarah Bernhardt was one of the first celebrities to have cosmetic repair work.

The growing market for cosmetics was a boon for a number of emerging female careers. By 1914 there were 36,000 hairdressing salons, 25,000 manicure salons, and 30,000 massage and skincare parlours throughout America, especially in big cities. The Risers Manicure Parlor, which occupied several floors of a building in New York, offered every imaginable scalp, face and body ritual, including electric treatments, manicures, pedicures and epilation.

Women started going into business for themselves: the investment required was minimal and the profits excellent. Dozens of beauty brands appeared on the market in the early twentieth century. The products were usually concocted in the owner's kitchen or the back of the shop, and sold locally – in a neighbourhood or town, or within a community. One of the most successful women entrepreneurs of the time was Madam C. J. Walker. She had pictures of her own beaming face printed on jars of her hair products for African-American women, which were initially sold door to door, and went on to become America's first self-made female millionaire.

Another pioneer of the fledgling cosmetics industry had been Harriet Hubbard Ayer, who manufactured and marketed a face cream called Luxuria. Ayer triumphed over fate's blows many times in the course of her life. Born Harriet Hubbard in Chicago in 1849, she married Herbert Crawford Ayer when she was only sixteen and had three children, one of whom tragically died in the fire that devastated Chicago in 1871. She led a comfortable but monotonous existence as a wealthy man's wife, society hostess and keen patron of the arts for several years until she finally decided to take her life into her own hands. Fed up with her husband's infidelity and penchant for heavy drinking, she asked for a divorce after eighteen years of marriage – a scandalous, unheard-of move at the time. Taking her children with her, she left for New York, where she had to earn her living selling furniture at an antique dealer's shop, since her husband had filed for bankruptcy and couldn't pay alimony.

Having finally obtained a divorce, the plucky Harriet borrowed some money and set up the Récamier Manufacturing Company to sell her cream. She went around telling people that Madame Récamier, a Parisian socialite famed for her beauty, had given her the recipe for the preparation. Whatever the truth behind the story, the cream caught on and Harriet Hubbard Ayer became one of the first American women to make a fortune in the cosmetics business. She was a fervent advocate of the natural look in vogue at the time and abhorred strong perfumes such as musk, patchouli and rose, preferring the delicate fragrance of lavender, which she considered the only suitable perfume for sophisticated women.

However, Harriet's main financial backer, James Seymour, had romantic designs on her. When she rejected his advances, he took revenge by having her committed to a mental asylum in 1883 with the help of her ex-husband and eldest daughter, who had married Seymour's son. Seymour also took over her business. When Harriet took him to court, Seymour claimed she was addicted to drugs and too unstable to run a business.

Fourteen months later, with the help of her lawyers, Harriet was finally allowed to leave the asylum, but her health had been destroyed.

She eventually managed to win the case and get her business back from Seymour, but her career in the cosmetics business was over. However, she was resilient enough to start a new career as a journalist with the *New York World*, writing an extremely popular beauty column and publishing the bestselling *Harriet Hubbard Ayer's Book of Health and Beauty*. Her daughter Margaret took over the column after she died from influenza in 1903.

Four years after Harriet's death, Vincent Benjamin Thomas, whose wife, a theatre actress, was a friend of Margaret Ayer's, set up the Harriet Hubbard Ayer Corporation. He bought the brand and the franchise and took over as general manager of the firm. Thomas clearly had a nose for business – the cosmetics industry was starting to flourish in the United States – and ensured that Harriet Hubbard Ayer's expertise was kept alive for many years to come.

Helena was not in the least afraid of Harriet's enduring influence. She wasn't afraid of anyone, except one person: the woman who would become her main rival in the United States. 'That woman', as Helena referred to her with a mixture of contempt and fury, was Elizabeth Arden.

The fear was mutual. Throughout her career, the only person Elizabeth Arden would dislike and distrust was the Polish upstart who had been brazen enough to arrive on *her* territory as a conquering heroine.

It would be hard to find two more outwardly different women. Born

Florence Nightingale Graham in the Ontario countryside in Canada, Elizabeth Arden was petite and feminine. Her favourite colours were pink and gold. She liked horses, golf and the outdoor life, and could pass for a WASP in country clubs where Jews were not admitted. For more than half a century she would cultivate her patrician image, which was as trumped-up as the upper-class ancestry Helena claimed to have. She was revered by New York society women, who saw her as a role model, and she had no intention of giving up an inch of her territory.

Yet the two women were very alike in many ways, starting with the faultless complexions that were their own best advertising. They both lied about their origins and routinely knocked a few years off their age. Both of them were born on the lower rungs of the social ladder (Arden's mother was a nurse and her father a farmer), but had an ingrained taste for luxury and for putting themselves in the spotlight, as well as formidable business sense. Both were bold, authoritarian, tyrannical and hard as nails. And each woman was a genius in her own way.[6]

Florence Graham had briefly undertaken nurse's training, then worked as a salesgirl. In New York, she had worked for beauty specialist Eleanor Adair, who had salons in the Rue Cambon in Paris and Bond Street in London. Adair offered a range of treatments including electrolysis and a muscle-strapping system to lift sagging facial muscles. Out-of-town customers could purchase a complete at-home beauty treatment by mail order.[7]

Having learned the tricks of the trade from Eleanor Adair, Florence decided to set up her own cosmetics business. She opened her first salon on Fifth Avenue in partnership with a beautician named Elizabeth Hubbard in 1909. The two women parted ways two years later and Florence became sole owner. She changed her name to Elizabeth Arden, keeping her former partner's first name and hitting upon her last name while reading the Tennyson poem 'Enoch Arden'. She borrowed $6,000 from relatives to refurbish the salon and worked with a chemist to create a face cream called Amoretta, which was followed by her Venetian line of cosmetics. The Italian name reflected her innate flair for marketing and packaging. Her products were beautifully packaged in pink and gold jars. Arden opened two more beauty salons, in Boston and Washington, and married a silk salesman named Thomas Lewis, who would be her sales manager for nearly twenty years.

That was something else she had in common with Helena: both women employed their husbands and had to deal with the problems a man's inferior status in a relationship can lead to. 'Dear, never forget one little point. It's my business. You just work here,' Elizabeth Arden once told her husband.[8]

Helena Rubinstein had toured Europe in 1905; Elizabeth Arden set off on her own reconnaissance trip to Paris and London in 1912 to investigate all the latest beauty treatments. She must have visited Helena's salons but was presumably unfazed by her rival's importance as she was still number one in America – for the moment, at any rate.

By the time Helena Rubinstein got to New York, Elizabeth Arden was the uncontested queen of the American beauty market. She owned three salons, whose trademark feature was a heavy red door. Stern Brothers and Bonwit Teller, two department stores with a fashion-conscious clientele, stocked her Venetian product line.

Advertisements for Elizabeth Arden products appeared in *Vogue* and other women's magazines. She had also written a pamphlet titled *The Quest of the Beautiful* in which she positioned herself as a seeker of eternal youth. She championed women's rights, not least because it was good for business. She marched alongside the suffragettes at the 6 May 1912 parade and adapted their militant discourse to her own ends, famously saying: 'Every woman has the right to be beautiful.'

There was more than enough room for two players on the American cosmetics market. The only problem was that they both wanted to be number one.

*

The railroad had crisscrossed America for the past half-century and was a safe means of travel. Well aware that any successful conquest required knowledge of the territory, Helena set out to visit the country by comfortable Pullman train. Everywhere she went she established contacts, left her business card and took stock of local beauty needs, buoyed rather than daunted by the thought that she would have to start from scratch.

But first she had to take New York. She turned her entire attention to this objective as soon as she returned to the city. Six months after her arrival in the United States, she opened her first salon between 15th Street and 49th Avenue in one of the charming two-storey brownstones with stone stoops so characteristic of New York architecture. She would have liked to set up on Fifth Avenue, like Elizabeth Arden, whose salon neighboured some of the swankiest New York residences, but the owners of the building she had had her eye on had turned her down because she was Jewish, and she did not as yet have the wherewithal to retaliate with style the way she would in 1939, when she responded to the 'no Jews' policy at the Park Avenue apartment she was attempting to purchase by buying up the whole building.

Helena wanted her salon to reflect her image as a wealthy, sophisticated European, and went to see Paul T. Frankl, an Austrian furniture designer who had studied architecture in Vienna and Berlin and recently immigrated to the United States from Japan to wait out the war. He had opened a small interior decoration firm on Park Avenue. Madame was introduced to him by her protégé Elie Nadelman, whose passage to America she had paid for.

Nadelman had his own reasons for introducing Helena to Frankl. He was incensed to think that Madame might prefer to use work by other artists to decorate her salon, so wanted Frankl to act in his interests. 'That's easy,' Frankl told Nadelman. 'We shall shape all important rooms round or oval and put niches in them – that will force her hand!'⁹

The budget wasn't as generous as either of them had thought and wouldn't stretch to designing oval rooms, but Frankl fashioned shelves and hollow spaces in which Madame could place the sculptures she ended up commissioning Nadelman to make.

With the help of Witold Gordon, an artist who had also recently arrived from Paris, Paul Frankl managed a satisfactory compromise between Helena's avant-garde tastes and the traditional mahogany and rosewood furniture with stylised floral patterns that appealed to an establishment clientele. Black and white chintz drapes hung in one of the five treatment rooms, while another one had a fashionable Orientalist theme and featured Chinese wallpaper, gold sofas and black lacquer tables.

'We did the first beauty parlour,' Frankl would reminisce many years later.¹⁰ The salon decor, which gave clients the feeling they were stepping into a 'chic bourgeois' apartment, was unlike any other in town.¹¹ Elizabeth Arden's salon was also done up like a domestic interior, but had a completely different style.

The New York salon was Helena's flagship and featured cutting-edge equipment for her health and beauty treatments. Her concept of salon decor reflected a fast-emerging European trend – a modern setting that blurred the boundaries between beauty, art, fashion, interior design and luxury. The beauty salon 'became a space that acted on the body, transforming clients in ways that exceeded a simple makeover'.¹² Helena Rubinstein was the first to offer American society women a complete sensory experience under one roof.

The new salon won her instant renown. American journalists were quick to fall under Madame's spell, and gushed about how 'exotic' and 'glamorous' she was. A *Vogue* article described the salon as 'the ideal combination of visual pleasure and physical comfort', and went on to say Madame was 'obviously as continental and as chic as her charming individuality and Poiret costumes can make her. She has a Russian father and a Viennese mother. Her life story reads like a fairy tale.'[13]

This was precisely the way Madame saw herself: as 'the accepted adviser in beauty matters to the Royalty, Aristocracy and the great Artistes of Europe',[14] graciously bringing American women a touch of Parisian elegance with her outfits, her taste for art and her avant-garde approach. Newspapers and magazines described her as the 'Queen of Beauty' and a 'woman specialist' who 'worked tirelessly'. She proclaimed herself 'the greatest living beauty exponent'.

Edward finally arrived in New York with the boys in April 1915, a month before the salon was to open. Helena had been so tied up with her travels and the work on the salon that she hadn't had time to feel lonely or suffer separation pangs, but as she hugged her family, she realised how much she had missed them. The boys had grown taller and looked far too serious for their age, no doubt because of their lengthy separation from their mother and six months of living in wartime Paris.

Edward seemed very happy to see her. As soon as their initial excitement at being reunited had worn off, he began to fill her in on all the terrible news from Europe. Helena was torn between concern for their friends who had remained there and the satisfaction of knowing that her dear ones were now safe with her.

'It's a rotten war, Helena,' he said. 'All the hospitals are overcrowded. All those aristocratic ladies of leisure you're friends with in London and Paris, including your darling Misia, have volunteered to be nurses, and are taking their duties very much to heart. The British government has requisitioned Solna. They've turned it into a hospital. I've brought most of your paintings and your African art collection with me, but I couldn't bring it all.'

Helena took the news on the chin. She sensed that Edward was deeply affected despite his light-hearted tone. 'Things are really grim in Paris, you know,' he told her. 'Most of the writers and painters we know have been called up – Braque, Derain and Léger. Kisling has joined the Foreign Legion. And Modigliani's furious at being discharged because he's got tuberculosis. Picasso and Brancusi are still living in Montparnasse.'

He also had anecdotes to recount. 'Remember that young designer? The shy brunette called Coco Chanel who we met several times at Misia's? The one who made those simple straw hats you all bought? Well, after her Paris and Deauville boutiques, she's opened a couture house in Biarritz. She's doing lots of minimalist stuff with jersey. It's very masculine, very "Europe at war". It's nothing like Poiret's flamboyant styles, but I think you'd really like it.'

Helena was living in an apartment above the salon – a practical solution, since she worked all hours. Her family stayed there with her while Edward went house hunting. A few weeks later, he found a huge apartment in the Upper West Side and they moved in. But Helena detested the neighbourhood, claiming it was 'too Jewish' for her liking.[15] A few years later they moved to another apartment overlooking Central Park, which was far better suited to her own idea of her new social status.

Edward had got it into his head to buy a house in the country. He drove around looking at houses until he found the place of his dreams: a Tudor manor in Greenwich, Connecticut, only an hour's drive from New York. Called Tall Trees, the house was located on the evocatively named Indian Chase Drive, at the end of a pretty lane lined with rows of golden forsythia bushes. Three shady paths led down to a lake at the bottom of the grounds.

The landscape in this verdant corner of Connecticut reminded Helena of the gentle rolling hills of Normandy, which she had liked because of its climate and peaceful atmosphere. It was the ideal place for the children, who lived there all week with their private tutor, John O'Neal, while their parents were at work in New York. Although Roy and Horace hadn't been asked whether they wanted to move to Greenwich, they took to it immediately. They went rowing on the lake, built sand castles on the beach at Long Island Sound, learned to swim in the ocean, went camping and played in the woods. They got on very well with John, who was assisted by a small army of nannies Helena referred to as the 'nice women'.[16]

A rare family photograph shows Helena and her sons on the beach in the summer of 1918. The two boys smile joyfully at the camera. Helena poses between her sons in a black sleeveless swimsuit with a bathing cap on her head. She seems pensive and detached from the children's laughter – thinking about her business, perhaps. There are hardly any photographs of the whole family, possibly because they were rarely all together.

The unpretentious comfort and charm of the manor suited Helena perfectly. She felt so at ease at the house that she never sold it, even though she hardly spent any time there until after the war. She decorated it in a country house style with her usual penchant for mixing styles and epochs, the kitsch and the genuine, the beautiful and the bizarre, displaying a collection of wooden ducks alongside opaline antiques and hanging masterpieces above rustic furniture.

Their first summer in the US had been so warm that it occurred to her that she should start making sun protection creams for the face and body. Edward would write the copy for the advertisements as usual, and hit on the trailblazing idea of using scientific claims to promote her products. 'Freckling and sunburn can be prevented,' his text would read. 'It is an established fact that sunlight is composed of different colours and amongst these [are] blue rays and violet rays. If you shut out these rays when you develop your film or plate, so you can debar them from staining and browning the skin and complexion.'[17]

She was pleased with the idea of being the first cosmetics manufacturer to call on the authority of science and wondered what her rival would think. The mere mention of her name could send Helena into a rage. Elizabeth Arden had added a series of astringent lotions and creams to her main line of cosmetics, which now included Ardena Orange Skin Food, Ardena Astringent Cream and Ardena Anti-Wrinkle Cream. In response, Helena had created make-up products, a make-up remover and a Pasteurised Face Cream as well as her top-selling Water Lily Cleansing Cream, described as a luxury rejuvenating cream. Her original Valaze cream was being marketed in the United States as a skin cell regenerator.

The two women used very similar marketing strategies. If Madame claimed to be 'the greatest living beauty exponent', her rival had 'given her life to the study of the subject in America, Paris, London and Berlin'. When Elizabeth Arden opened exercise rooms in her salons, Helena Rubinstein promptly followed suit.

'We never met,' Helena replied shortly when she was once asked what she thought of Elizabeth Arden.

Helena's personal life wasn't enjoying the same success. Edward and she were growing further apart with every passing day. She threw herself into her work while he mingled with artists and intellectuals in Greenwich Village, including Parisians such as Marcel Duchamp, Henri Matisse and Francis Picabia, who had fled the war in Europe. This New York neighbourhood had become the heartland of boho chic and the avant-garde, where poets, feminists, politically committed writers and anarchists congregated. Following in the footsteps of Mark Twain, Henry James and Edgar Allan Poe at the end of the previous century, the city's radical thinkers had all migrated downtown, away from the puritan attitudes of the skyscraper district. Greenwich Village habitués advocated free love and accepted homosexuality, scrapped taboos and sneered at middle-class morality. They lived in communes and had scant regard for the church.

Although beauty products were his bread and butter, it was in the company of intellectuals rather than in his wife's salons that Edward Titus was really in his element. He was usually to be found at the Lafayette, the Reggio, the Breevort and other fashionable cafés with friends such as Eugene O'Neill, Man Ray, Leo Stein, and e. e. cummings.

Their days began at four in the afternoon, and Edward occasionally didn't come back home until dawn. He often had his friends over. Helena couldn't say she took to all of them, but she followed their conversations as diligently as she had done in the past when socialising with Edward's highbrow circles in London and Paris. She viewed these dinner parties as excellent opportunities for self-promotion. She only had to add a few journalists to the guest list to be sure of a mention in the next day's papers, especially since, thanks to Edward, she could count on New York's most illustrious nabobs and starving artists turning up at her table.

The serially adulterous Edward couldn't stop himself cheating on her. He salved his conscience by claiming that it was because he suffered, like the children, from her absence. Things came to a head when he succumbed to the charms of one of the ravishing young 'nice women' they employed at their country house, a nubile Australian, and went on a jaunt to Chicago with her.

Helena, who was constantly on the lookout for signs of Edward's infidelity, became suspicious and hired a private detective to follow him. The detective's report contained irrefutable proof that the couple had checked into a hotel under a false name. Although she was deeply hurt, she clung to the hope that it was all a mistake. But when the detective produced photographs and bills, it was clear that Edward really had cheated on her with the employee.

It was a double blow. Only two months earlier, after a particularly violent quarrel, she and Edward had made up in the same Chicago hotel. It had been a long time since they had made love to each other the way they had done that night. She had fallen asleep in his arms, reassured, happy and naively believing that they were truly going to make a fresh start.

A fresh wave of anger flooded through her. Her knee-jerk purchase of a huge ruby necklace failed to console her. This time he had gone too far. She wouldn't let him humiliate her ever again. They would have to separate. She kept mum about the affair for a few days as she pondered the best way to go about it.

A letter from Edward informing her he wanted to spend Christmas with her and the boys sent her into a fury. She threw her tactical approach out of the window and sent him the detective's report by return of post. Mortified to learn that he had been followed and caught in the act, Edward refused to speak to her – which was fine by Helena, as she no longer had anything to say to him. She had their assets divided up, bought his share of the business in Australia, and made him a generous financial settlement.

But they didn't divorce – not immediately, at any rate. She couldn't bring herself to, and neither could he.

15

THE GREAT RUBINSTEIN
ROAD TOUR

The war still raging in Europe wasn't uppermost in Helena Rubinstein's mind. She was busy pursuing her American expansion, city by city. After New York, she opened salons in Boston, Philadelphia and San Francisco, hiring teams to run them but organising the business herself. The preparation, manufacture and packaging of her products now took place in her new factory on Long Island, while the marketing strategy was devised in her New York offices. Every phase, right up to the sale of the products in her salons, was carefully thought out. America had made her the president of an ever-growing multinational company.

No laws controlling advertising existed in the United States. To launch a product, all you needed was a formula, capital and imagination.[1] Madame had all the raw materials she used rigorously tested for non-toxicity, which obliged most of her competitors to follow suit. Science, whose authority she was the first cosmetics manufacturer to call on, was one of her main advantages. To promote her scientific image, she posed wearing a white coat alongside her chemists in her laboratories and drummed out her message: science at the service of beauty. All her competitors now tried to outdo each other with pseudo-scientific advertisements that gave evidence of their products' effectiveness. 'My principles stimulated the competition and forced them to revise their methods. It was due recognition for me, but unmasked those who were exploiting women's gullibility,' she wrote.[2]

Helena had sent for Manka and couldn't wait to see her. She had further plans for expansion. Opening salons in every city in America was too risky and too onerous a move, so she would adopt a different sales tactic. Her golden rule had been to never sell her products outside her beauty institutes, but perhaps the time had come to democratise her brand. Her main concern was that only the beauty consultants in her salons, trained by her, had the requisite skills to advise customers and make sure their purchases were right for their needs. None of her skincare, haircare, make-up or perfume ranges should be used randomly. Launching Helena Rubinstein on the mass market, even the upscale market, carried the risk of undermining the brand's prestige.

Then again, she couldn't ignore retailers' requests. Managers of department stores such as the City of Paris in San Francisco, Marshall Field's in Chicago and Bullock's in Los Angeles were clamouring for her to become one of their suppliers. Drugstores and beauty parlours across smaller towns and suburbs demanded her products too.

Conquering America no longer involved only the elite: Madame soon realised that a much larger group had to be targeted. So she accepted retailers' requests but imposed certain conditions. Teaching customers her personal care routines was of vital importance and would ensure the longevity of her brand; all sales staff would have to be trained in the art. So Helena opened a beauty school in New York where beauty consultants spent six months learning the Helena Rubinstein way. The training cost between $250 and $500, but the resulting diploma was invaluable for a significant number of girls who had their sights set on a career. The job of beautician existed before Helena Rubinstein, but she gave it a framework and credibility as a 'real' profession.

To make sure that every last detail was taken care of, perfectionist Helena wanted to check the premises, customers and reliability of all the outlets herself. She could have adopted normal retail practice and sold her products through a wholesaler, but she found this idea most unsatisfactory. She was keen to meet the retailers in person and keep in regular contact with them in order to monitor their relations with her target customers.

Helena asked Edward, whom she'd achieved a well-timed reconciliation with, to look after the children for the months she would be away. Manka arrived in New York from war-torn Europe at the beginning of 1917, and they took off on their great Rubinstein road tour, accompanied by maids, beauty consultants, assistants and luggage galore.

Travelling by rail, or by road if there was no railway, one day in Atlanta, the next in Kansas City, Helena and Manka felt like actresses on tour. Their working days lasted eighteen hours. They slept in a different hotel or Pullman carriage every night and lived out of their suitcases. 'I don't think I've ever worked as much in my life, not that I'm someone who ever just sits around,' Helena wrote.[3] Manka, who was visiting America for the first time, went into raptures about the scenery she saw rushing past the window. The journey brought arguments, laughter, anger, tantrums, tiredness and sisterly love, not to mention the feeling of being pioneers, which Helena loved.

Their trip was exciting, exhausting and, most importantly, highly productive. The Rubinsteins created a network across towns all over the country. Helena's most basic product range, Valaze, would be sold through sales representatives in drugstores in the more chic suburbs, while top-of-the-line creams such as Water Lily Cleansing Cream would be stocked exclusively by upmarket shops and department stores.

During the day, the Rubinstein sisters presented their beauty treatments and gave customers private consultations, then in the evening they trained salesgirls to become qualified beauty consultants. Helena insisted their bosses send them to her beauticians' school in New York and finance their classes. She supplied uniforms and shop display units in the brand's colours. These sales and marketing techniques were revolutionary for the day and Helena Rubinstein could justifiably claim to have created them. 'The job of beauty consultant, common throughout the world today, is really my invention. I'm particularly proud of it.'[4]

Manka and she made a point of dressing in their elegant Parisian fashions. They wanted to give their customers their money's worth and impress the journalists who were following their trip with keen interest. Boston's local paper commented: 'Madame Rubinstein wore a tomato-coloured dress and eight strands of black pearls. Eight hundred women were enraptured by her lecture on treating the skin and on make-up for formal occasions.'[5]

Her European accent and French elegance intrigued her audience as much as anything she said. Unlike at society soirées, where she rarely opened her mouth, Helena didn't stop talking. She dispensed her deep-rooted convictions about hygiene, skincare, moisturising, facial gymnastics, diets, massage and physical exercise like a preacher to her flock. She repeated like a mantra that beauty was nothing if the body wasn't maintained. Her charisma was captivating and her promises seemed convincing.

Some women were scornful or sceptical but went to her out of curiosity. Most of them still believed in the virtues of a basic cold cream. Others had never used a cream in their lives. But all listened to her carefully, were easily persuaded, and always left with a little bag full of products designed, she said, to help them preserve or recapture their youthful looks. In addition to real or alleged active ingredients, these precious potions contained a large dose of Madame Rubinstein's fervour. Her faith in them certainly contributed to their effectiveness.

On Friday evenings, if she wasn't too far from New York, Helena would take a train home to spend a short weekend with her family, leaving again late on the Sunday afternoon. 'Now I know a weekend mother is not enough for any family,' she admitted to English journalist Jean Lorimer at the end of her life. 'I gave them all the material things that anyone could possibly want. But did I give them enough of myself? ... I would have liked to live 300 years to put everything right.'[6]

Launched in Australia, improved in Europe and perfected in the United States, the Rubinstein technique was infallible. When Helena at last returned to New York a few months after their very fruitful tour had begun, Manka continued to travel the length and breadth of the country. For years she trained retailers and their staff. In the 1930s, their sister Regina's daughter Mala would replace her.

Elizabeth Arden had reason to worry. In two to three years, Madame would become a celebrity all over America. Her customers could now choose between obtaining her products by mail order or buying them in department stores and pharmacies. Women were wild about her eye kohl, used since the time of Cleopatra and brought up to date by Helena. They loved the subtle colours of the make-up range that she described using a metaphor related to art – her treasured subject – as 'cosmetic masterpieces'.[7]

Although Helena continued to be inspired by theatre actresses, the stars of silent film – a very popular form of entertainment in America – also provided her with an invaluable source of ideas for both marketing and creating new products. Fashion editors interviewed Mary Pickford, Lillian Gish and Gloria Swanson about the way they dressed and their beauty techniques. Actresses did more for the adoption of make-up by the middle classes than any feminist movement. Helena hired a string of them to promote her brand.

Theda Bara, one of cinema's earliest sex symbols, who acted and posed half naked, was a particular favourite with movie audiences. The star believed that the camera didn't do her eyes justice, so she turned to Helena to find a way to emphasise them. Inspired by her beauty, Madame created a make-up collection called 'Vamp' in tribute to the name of her vampire character in the 1915 silent film *A Fool There Was*. It made such an impact that the word 'vamp' soon became a popular term for the kind of sexually predatory woman Bara had portrayed. She was the talk of the town. All Helena's clients clamoured for the same make-up. 'The effect was tremendously dramatic,' Madame remembered with amusement. 'It was a sensation reported in every newspaper and magazine – only little less of a sensation than when Theda Bara first painted her toenails!'[8] Women still had a long way to go before they could do whatever they liked to their bodies.

In November 1918, the war finally ended. Helena was eager to return to Europe but had aspects of her American business to sort out first. At the start of the following spring, she went back to France on her own, leaving her salons, factory and the supervision of her stockist network in the hands of her managers.

Somewhat against his will, Edward spent the summer with the children in Greenwich. He too was in a hurry to get back to France: he missed Paris and many of his friends were already there. Most of all, he wanted to distance himself from the Rubinstein world to pursue his own passions, reading and writing. All he dreamed of was becoming a journalist again, and of opening a bookshop and perhaps a publishing house in Montparnasse.

Like the warring parties, the couple had signed their own armistice. Separated de facto, Helena and Edward remained together in the eyes of the world, especially the media. They would present a united family front until further notice.

16

PARIS IS A MOVEABLE FEAST

The Paris Peace Conference, organised by the Allied victors following the end of the First World War, had been taking place in the French capital since the start of 1919. While the four great powers were reshaping the map of Europe, Paris oscillated between sadness and euphoria. Helena found her city unrecognisable. Gaunt demobilised soldiers roamed the boulevards. Civilian amputees begged for change at busy street corners. The French capital bore the ugly scars of war. Yellow paper covered the shattered stained-glass windows of Notre Dame Cathedral, a bomb crater marked the Tuileries Gardens and chestnut trees had been felled from the pavements for firewood. The severe shortages brought by the war – wood, coal, milk, bread and fuel – were still being felt.[1] France wept as it counted its war casualties: one and a half million dead and 4 million wounded. Too high a price to pay.

On Bastille Day 1919, Paul Poiret revived his party tradition and threw a grand ball to celebrate victory. Many more followed during those post-war years when the focus shifted to having fun. From the Faubourg Saint-Germain, where mere mortals were beginning to catch a glimpse of how the gods lived, much to the displeasure of the city's snobs, to the blossoming Montparnasse, Paris led the dance.

Life was one big excuse for a party. Cabaret shows starred girls sporting feathers and sequins. Paris nightlife swayed to the swinging rhythm of jazz, freshly arrived from New Orleans. Drum beats and singing trumpets filled the air, replacing the sounds of cannons, bombs and air-raid sirens. Muted melancholy and a sense of guilt at being alive gave way to an unparalleled frenzy.

The intense excitement of the roaring twenties was particularly palpable in Paris. Helena was in heaven: anything new thrilled her. Paris was a breeding ground for ideas; a place where every new invention quickly caught on, from radio, first transmitted from the Eiffel Tower, cocktail shakers, roller skating rinks and dance halls to the gramophone, the 5CV – the first people's car made by Citroën – and moving film, silent at first, with its stars all the way from the USA.

America was all the rage. The Americans were landing for the second time: US soldiers who had fought in France were coming back to enjoy the relaxed rhythm of life, good food, pretty women and a carefree atmosphere untouched by taboos. The strong dollar and weak franc allowed them to live like kings. The wealthy soon followed, led by Scott and Zelda Fitzgerald. Alcohol flowed like water, whereas Prohibition had forced drinking underground in the States. For writer Samuel Putnam, a friend of Edward's, 'The story of this generation is not Europe's alone; it forms a part of America's annals, both social and cultural.'[2]

Artists, bohemians, art dealers and tourists flocked to the famous district of Montparnasse, bordered by legendary cafés and bars: La Coupole, La Rotonde, Le Dôme, La Closerie des Lilas, the Dingo Bar and Le Jockey. At night, painters, dressmaker's apprentices, aristocrats and whores danced the foxtrot, the Charleston and the one-step in dance halls. Le Bœuf sur le Toit was the place to be for night owls: a friendly, vibrant and exotic venue where a clientele of Ballets Russes audiences partied until dawn. Pretty women rubbed shoulders with writers, musicians, painters, advertising executives, businessmen and poets and everyone got drunk on glory as much as alcohol.

Soon after Helena returned to Paris, she looked up her friend Misia Sert, who filled her in on all the goings-on in this funny, socialite artistic circle and updated her on Dada, the surrealists, the latest love affairs and recent break-ups. New York electrified Helena, but there was no place like Paris for entertainment.

Yet work was still her motivation and her obsession. On the boat over to Europe she had seen a real-estate advertisement in an out-of-date French newspaper for a salon at 126 Rue du Faubourg Saint-Honoré, a stone's throw from her existing beauty parlour. As she had plans to extend the premises, she had cabled her sister Pauline to find out more. Shortly after arriving in Paris, she purchased the property.

She began work to modernise it immediately and asked her old friend Paul Poiret to be in charge of the interior decoration. Helena displayed paintings, sculptures and African statues from her collections. Her art had been scattered during her absence, but through stubborn determination she managed to recover most of it, sometimes by buying it back, and must have taken a perverse pleasure in doing so.

As in the United States, women in France had changed. During the war they had taken on traditionally male responsibilities: caring for the wounded, driving convoys, running companies and replacing absent factory and farm workers. After that experience, they couldn't simply return to the domestic sphere. They were becoming emancipated, gaining a little more ground every day. Competitive-entrance higher education establishments remained closed to women, while universities rarely admitted them. Yet it was no longer a surprise for a woman to hold a degree, or a dishonour for her to have a job. Even wives began earning a living – as typists, school teachers, sales assistants and telephone operators, as well as doctors, lawyers and university professors. They wanted everything: financial independence, equality, freedom and the demise of conventions and taboos.

Women went out, smoked, wore make-up, drove cars, flaunted their sexuality, dressed up as men or shortened their skirts, shimmied until dawn in nightclubs, discussed their sex lives and declared themselves followers of Sigmund Freud, whose *A General Introduction to Psychoanalysis*, published in Vienna in 1916, had left a lasting impression on them. Everything had been turned upside down: women got married for love; flirting and friendships with men were now permitted; divorcees were no longer ostracised by society; and courtesans disappeared into the background.

The new icon was the sexy, seductive flapper from America, who had replaced the Gibson Girl. The word 'flapper', defined as 'a fashionable young woman intent on enjoying herself and flouting conventional standards of behaviour', has several origins: literally making reference to the unstrapped buckles of their shoes, it was also once a term for a teenage girl, and for a young bird learning to fly. The look was tall, slim, straight-waisted and simple – the curves of the previous century were out.

Appearance was of paramount importance to the modern woman. Her physique was no longer shapely and she appeared to have grown taller.[3] According to France's newly launched monthly fashion and lifestyle magazines *Le Jardin des Modes* and *Vogue*, the ideal weight had dropped by 1 stone 8 pounds (10 kilograms). War was waged against spare tyres and cellulite. To stay thin, appearance-conscious girls resorted to all kinds of torture: appointments with dieticians, pills, massages, surgery and cocaine, which had become the fashionable drug of the day thanks to its two-in-one role of suppressing the appetite and keeping you going on the dance floor for hours on end.

Liberated young women adopted mascara, lipstick and blusher. Arden, Rubinstein and Guerlain designed reticules and handbags in the Art Deco style to carry them in, as well as magnificent powder compacts and tubes of rouge that resembled jewellery. Make-up became the trademark of these sassy women. They redid their eyes and lips in public – to be provocative and because they were driven by an intense feeling of freedom. Perfume was also the prerogative of emancipated women and Chanel triumphed with her No. 5.

Gabrielle 'Coco' Chanel was in the process of making Paul Poiret and his extravagant style look old-fashioned. She imposed the colour black, sleek straight lines, fluid shapes and jersey fabrics. She designed clothing for active women who needed to feel comfortable in their bodies. Slimness was for sale at her Rue Cambon store. Many women copied Coco Chanel's short haircut. She had sacrificed her longer hair on the altar of modernity in 1917 because she found it annoying.[4]

Short hair was furiously trendy on both sides of the Atlantic. F. Scott Fitzgerald, the quintessential flapper portraitist, wrote a short story about the phenomenon called 'Bernice Bobs her Hair'. One in three Frenchwomen demanded the adolescent style when they went to the hairdresser's. Poiret was incensed by the flood of boyish-looking girls and complained that they looked malnourished. The couturier was wrong: androgyny was a serious trend. Three years later, Victor Margueritte sold over a million copies of his novel *La Garçonne* (English title: *The Bachelor Girl*), establishing the word *garçonne* as the French translation of 'flapper' and an accepted everyday term meaning 'boyish'.

Helena had anticipated a trend for body worship long before. She had already launched an exercise class at her Paris salon and hired ballet master Mikhail Mordkin to teach 'Rubinstein Rhythmics' in New York.[5] Society was now obsessed with the body beautiful. Women devoted their time to sport – tennis, golf, cycling, swimming and outdoor games – and stripped off like Josephine Baker in *La Revue Nègre*. In films, plays and magazines and on beaches from Deauville to Nice, around France, they revealed their legs, breasts and bottoms. The first naturists appeared. Chanel proved to be a trendsetter once again:

she was photographed on the Duke of Wellington's yacht sporting a sun-kissed face and launched the fashion for suntans, which became a symbol of beauty and health.

Helena, who had an aversion to the sun throughout her life, added to her range of UV-protective products. Beauty treatments for the body, from scrubs and waxing to leg massages and pedicures, were developing widely. It was no surprise to Helena – they had already been available at her salons for ages.

But this progress had its flip side. Guilt, which has gnawed away at women since the dawn of time, was now directed to their faces and figures. 'Only you can make yourselves beautiful,' preached women's magazines. Fashion photography, which was gradually becoming professional and replacing illustrations, offered them images of women with perfect, smooth bodies – photographs that had been touched up to hide imperfections, with skin blemishes rubbed out.[6]

Helena Rubinstein was partly responsible for this quest for physical perfection. She constantly advised women to 'help nature' and recommended that they sculpt their stomachs and thighs, tone their arms, harden their muscles through massages and correct diet, and, of course, take care of their skin. As society stipulated they look young and attractive, women had an eternal duty to make an effort. Beauty was a combat sport – you had to suffer to achieve it.

Madame was convinced that all women wanted beauty. 'If you can show me a woman who doesn't want to look young and beautiful – well I'm afraid she isn't in her right mind,' she pronounced to Allison Grey, a journalist on *American Magazine*, in a lengthy interview in 1922.[7] The cult of eternal youth was here to stay, according to Helena. She said that the worst thing for a face is when the oval sags, as it is a clear indication that a woman has aged. She talked at length about cosmetic surgery, which she wholeheartedly supported. It isn't known whether she underwent it herself; she lacked courage and, above all, time when it came to caring for herself. But face alterations always fascinated her, regardless.

Techniques had advanced thanks to the war. To repair soldiers' severe facial injuries, surgeons had performed skin grafts on those with serious burns and replaced facial bones with bone from the hips or lower limbs. The procedures hadn't always been successful, but immense progress had been made.

In the United States, Dr Harold Gillies, who had operated on over 2,000 soldiers with facial injuries following the Battle of the Somme and had published a book on facial plastic surgery, was now working as a successful cosmetic surgeon, performing facelifts on fearless, broad-minded American women. Their pain-shy French counterparts remained hesitant about going under the knife – they preferred the gentle approach.

In New York and Paris, the talk of the town was the famous Dr Voronoff, who had invented a rejuvenating serum made with monkey glands. Helena's physician Dr Kapp had experimented with it in Vienna and Berlin and she boasted of having studied its properties with them.

Madame continued to maintain that beauty must remain the most important thing in every woman's life, whatever her age or situation. Even if they were happily married and thought their husbands loved them just the way they were, they were mistaken! Helena was always severe with these 'lazy' ones, as she was with those who spent a fortune on luxurious toiletries and neglected the basic steps in facial skincare. 'The unfortunate thing is that too many of them depend on make-up. I do not object to a little rouge and a discriminating use of powder. But some of the cream which so many girls and women apply as a base on which to put an elaborate make-up are ruinous to the natural beauty of the complexion.'

The Titus family didn't live together during this period. Roy and Horace had been sent to boarding school near New York and only saw their parents during the school holidays. Mainly just their father, Edward, though, as he was keen to keep an eye on their education. Most of the time, however, they stayed at their home in Greenwich in the care of their tutor and a tribe of aunts, uncles, cousins, nannies and babysitters. Hardly the ideal life for a twelve- and a nine-year-old. No doubt they suffered, but they had no choice.

A photo shows them with their mother in front of the Greenwich house that she had had renovated by the modernist architect Rudolph Schindler, who also designed the interior of her Los Angeles salon. Madame is posing in an embroidered tunic dress by Poiret, while the boys are wearing white shirts with the sleeves rolled up and white trousers, with their hair neatly combed back. Horace and Helena have their arms around each other, as is often the case when they are photographed together. Roy stands slightly apart, as he always did. The photograph speaks volumes about the relationship between the mother and her sons.

Edward had returned to France in the summer of 1919, a few months after his wife. He continued to work for the brand, but also began contributing to literary magazine *This Quarter*, published by American poet Ernest Walsh and his companion Ethel Moorhead, then, from 1922, to *The Transatlantic Review*, launched by Ford Madox Ford, whose assistant was a young Ernest Hemingway.

Relations between the Tituses were as chaotic as ever. Their arguments continued whichever side of the Atlantic they were on. Helena criticised her husband for his infidelities and the money she gave him, even though he was still her employee. Edward urged her to work less and take more care of her family. As usual, she went her own way and pursued her company's expansion in Europe and the States.

She now divided her life between the two continents. Following the opening of each European salon, she would stay for a few weeks at one of her favourite spas in Switzerland or Germany in an attempt to treat her migraines and circulation problems. Or she would indulge her passion for travelling and take a boat to a country she hadn't visited before. The East always held a particular fascination for her. In 1921, she went to Tunisia with painter Jean Lurçat, her mentor in art at the time. A photo shows her perched on a camel looking very apprehensive, just as she does astride a horse in the Australian outback, in a shot of her taken at the start of her career.

She was nevertheless still in love with her husband, and continued to be plagued by jealousy. Every woman who came near him was a potential rival. Her aggressiveness, nervousness and constant recriminations did nothing for peace between them. But despite the upsets that should have torn them apart, the couple remained united. Helena wanted to invest in property in Paris and bought a beautiful modern apartment block at 216 Boulevard Raspail with a geometric facade and huge bow windows that flooded the building with light. Edward found it, with his usual nose for a good thing. His infallible taste made him Helena's most invaluable adviser. She respected his gift for recognising quality in whatever shape or form.

Edward helped her set up a holding company to purchase various properties as the market was booming. As he spoke fluent French, it was his job to deal with the lawyers, and read through and approve the contracts. He suggested setting up a theatre and cinema on the ground floor of the Boulevard Raspail building with a view to staging poetry recitals and modern plays. He also had the idea of putting in studios to rent out to friends so that they could be surrounded by artists.

The couple took the duplex apartment on the fifth floor as their living quarters. Architect Bruno Elkuken and painter Louis Marcoussis, whom the Tituses commissioned to undertake the renovation and interior design, wanted it to be a model of Art Deco. Both men were Polish; this wasn't the first time Helena employed compatriots. Whatever she did, wherever she went, her native country always remained on her mind.

She also purchased Breuil Mill in Combs-la-Ville, Normandy, which became her French country home, like Greenwich was her American retreat. Not long after, she bought the building occupied by the Jockey Club, a nightclub on the corner of Rue Campagne-Première where artists and their models, and writers and their muses drank gin and absinthe until the small hours. The manager, American artist Hilaire Hiler, a friend of Edward's, was a prominent member of the 'Lost Generation', the artistic US expatriate crowd that congregated in Montparnasse.

Lastly, again on her husband's advice, Helena bought a building at 52 Rue du Faubourg Saint-Honoré, where she would later set up her third salon and her offices.

Edward finally found his own premises: a tiny property at 4 Rue Delambre in the heart of Montparnasse. He made it into a bookshop with the esoteric name At the Sign of the Black Manikin. The logo – designed by Witold Gordon, the Rubinstein brand's artistic director – depicted a black silhouette of an androgynous figure standing on a snake and brandishing a book in one hand and a sword in the other. The bookshop sold rare editions, original manuscripts, drawings and photos, and widely established Edward's name as a bibliophile. Edward had a reputation for only selling books to people who loved them even more than him; it was Helena who paid the mortgage.

The district had no lack of book lovers, bookshops and publishing houses. In 1919, Edward's fellow American Sylvia Beach had opened the English-language bookstore and lending library Shakespeare and Company in Rue Dupuytren. A couple of years later she moved it to 12 Rue de l'Odéon, where it became the hub of Anglo-American literary culture in Paris.

Following in the footsteps of Sylvia Beach, and Caresse and Harry Crosby, who founded the Black Sun Press in 1927 and published writers such as D. H. Lawrence, Ezra Pound and Kay Boyle, Edward Titus decided to become a publisher too, especially as his stock of antiquarian books was starting to run out. He established a small publishing house, Black Manikin Press, within his bookshop. The press was located a few doors down. He published works by a range of cult Anglo-American authors and poets, illustrated by Man Ray or Jean Cocteau. As a man of letters himself, he also brought out his own English translations of poetry by Paul Valéry and Charles Baudelaire. During its seven years of existence, Black Manikin Press published an eclectic, specialised and bold selection of twenty-five titles in limited editions.

Another of his publications was Ludwig Lewisohn's *The Case of Mr Crump*, which he sold by subscription. Every American publisher had rejected it for being provocative and scandalous. The book told the story of a failed marriage, a subject Edward was well versed in, and was hailed by Freud as 'an incomparable masterpiece'. Yet the business wasn't profitable and Helena turned a deaf ear to his requests for money.

In 1929, when Edward decided to buy up *This Quarter* from Ethel Moorhead, who had lost her co-editor Ernest Walsh to tuberculosis two years earlier, Helena refused to finance what she called his 'hare-brained idea', despite the fact that he had plans to publish such names as André Breton, Samuel Beckett, Hemingway and Lawrence.[8] 'All that interests you about me is my material resource,' she wrote to him.[9] But she ended up giving him the money. It must have been a bitter pill for him to swallow, yet again.

Around that time, Edward convinced his prestigious French contacts Colette, arts patron Marie-Laure de Noailles and poet and novelist Louise de Vilmorin to write texts for the Rubinstein brand. Helena was less dazzled by these icons than her husband. She invited them to lunch one after the other to ask them for 'good ideas'. Louise de Vilmorin suggested she call the fragrance she was planning to create Five O'Clock, influenced by France's craze for adopting English

182

words. 'I gave her a few hundred francs in exchange,' Helena later said. 'The poor little thing is so extravagant! Always broke.'[10]

Edward intended to employ the same marketing principles for his magazine that he used to promote Helena Rubinstein. He wrote a regular column, organised literary prizes that he awarded to young American and English poets, and encouraged the newspapers to write about them. He had Goethe, Rimbaud, Rilke and Hermann Hesse translated, and published Natalie Barney, Gertrude Stein, D. H. Lawrence, Aldous Huxley, Paul Valéry, Ernest Hemingway and Samuel Beckett. He went into partnership with Samuel Putnam, an American author and translator who worked with Sylvia Beach, but disagreements soon arose. Putnam found Edward pretentious and they couldn't reconcile their differences in taste.

Edward no doubt had his faults, but his love for literature was real and deep. He still couldn't manage to pay his writers, though, and continued to beg his wife for money. Helena didn't understand why he was so attracted to them. 'I never had a moment to read their books. To me they were *meshuggah* ... and I always had to pay for their meals!' she confided to her secretary Patrick O'Higgins.[11]

Yet she seemed to be proud of the small theatre Edward had set up in their Boulevard Raspail building. She explained with amusement that one evening the police had intervened, alleging that some of the plays were too subversive. 'This was my only encounter with the law as a "political revolutionary",' she remembered.[12] Years later, she still couldn't understand what the government had found dangerous about those innocent performances, and concluded that they had been 'overly impulsive about the whole thing'.[13] Their theatre was closed down. A cinema, Studio Raspail (still in existence today), took its place, and Edward screened films there by his friend Man Ray.

Like his wife, Edward wanted it all, even if they desired different things. He wanted to reconcile the contradictory: a bohemian lifestyle and a comfortable one; family and freedom; employment and risk; advertising copy and literary texts; the avant-garde and classical literature; individualism and the group. This hard-to-categorise man made quite a few enemies in Montparnasse, especially among the readers of *This Quarter*, who hated his luxurious book editions and he seemed to forget that nobody apart from them read their magazine. If he had had his own means, Edward would have probably been a patron.

Edward William Titus was a man of paradoxes. Far from being an accursed poet, he was a carefully cultivated dandy, always dressed up to the nines, complete with monocle, tie, cane and hat. He kept company with the cream of the aristocracy and consorted with all the genuine and phoney geniuses who hung out on the Left Bank. A virtuoso snob, he refused to mix with the rabble. Yet an easy-going lifestyle suited him. He could no longer bear luxury, chauffeurs and the grand style his wife lived in, even if he was happy to derive benefit from it. He aspired to a quiet life. He wanted to live like a local in Montparnasse, a regular in the area's cafés and bookshops.

In many people's eyes, however, he remained the husband of 'rich Madame Rubinstein', and was therefore suspect. Helena would embarrass him when she turned up in her chauffeur-driven car wearing make-up and priceless jewels, furs and hats to mingle with the masses on the Left Bank. She insisted on accompanying him to the Dôme and the Dingo, the Americans' stamping grounds. She would force him to pay for everyone even though the done thing was to split the bill. This made Edward feel uncomfortable, like an intruder, when he so wanted to be considered one of them.

As usual, Helena behaved like the wealthy, generous doyenne, convinced that that was what people expected of her. Despite the plumpness that was setting in, she looked younger than her fifty-five years. Yet she had reached that delicate age when a woman has to admit that her beauty is gradually fading, that men's desire is fleeting and that for love to last, it has to be based on a close partnership. Though wonderful shared memories with Edward were thin on the ground, she still lived in hope, but he refused to give her what she wanted. This waiting in vain drove Helena to despair and torment. From time to time they had physical relations, but increasingly rarely. Their arguments always struck up again the next day. They poured out their feelings to each other in letters. Helena never lost her habit of committing everything to paper. Her correspondence to Edward could be doleful, sarcastic or severe, depending on her mood. Frustrated and dissatisfied by their relationship but incapable of changing it, she kept score like the wounded wife and regularly got her own back with underhand tactics such as withholding her cheque book. She never failed to remind him of her financial power.

Edward was more moderate and lucid, and often melancholic. In depressed moments, he sent her poems expressing sadness about her absences, for his own and their sons' sakes. 'I dined at home alone this evening, the table was so cold and my heart so strange.'[14] Often he was devious, and sometimes even cruel. He responded to the humiliation of constantly having to ask her for money by making her feel guilty or by using emotional blackmail. But the sentiment never changed: can't live with you, can't live without you.

In Helena's sweetened version of events, their relationship and society life were filled with nothing but happiness and harmony. 'My husband and I see each other five or six times a year like all modern couples,' she explained to a journalist in *The New Yorker*.[15] Honesty later forced her to admit that her absences had indeed been the cause of their marital break-up.

17

FRIEND TO ARTISTS

'From being guests in the homes of people we didn't know, we found ourselves accepting invitations from shopkeepers – prominent ones but shopkeepers all the same; to think, we wouldn't so much as greet them before the war. Mademoiselle Chanel was the first couturière to be invited back.'[1] Whatever the snobs thought about it, Coco Chanel had been a society icon in Paris for a long time. Madame wasn't yet at that stage, but she certainly liked entertaining.

Thanks to the presence of Edward, the authors he published and the young artists whose paintings she bought, Helena's dinners and parties were always a great success. Her guests enjoyed her generous menus and her exquisite taste in table decoration.

Early on in their marriage, on a trip to Vienna, Edward and she ordered a silver service designed by Joseph Hoffman for Fledermaus and had every piece engraved with a T (for Titus) at the centre.[2] It was more than a simple dinner service: it was a work of art chosen by a couple in perfect harmony (he guided, she purchased). But the student soon learned to demonstrate her taste without needing her teacher.

D. H. Lawrence and his wife, Frieda, were members of the circle they regularly entertained. The bearded writer was terse, feverish and extremely reserved. 'In our home he would sit in a corner of the room refusing to mix with other guests,' Madame remembered. 'It was only when he noticed that I was as quiet and shy that he started talking to me.'[3]

Helena could be shy, but it depended on her mood. When she learned that the writer had published a short story called 'Sun' in her husband's magazine, she boldly told him that she didn't agree with its promotion of sun-worshipping. She explained at length why the sun was women's worst enemy: it dried out and discoloured the skin, and accelerated the appearance of wrinkles. 'If I'd known,' said Lawrence, very concerned, 'I would have scrapped the story or made it anti-sun.'[4]

Another frequent guest was American author William Faulkner, who was similar to Lawrence in temperament: 'quiet, aloof, and strangely removed from the life about him'.[5] The first time Helena welcomed him to her home, his silence alarmed her. It made an impression on everyone. She worried that he was ill. 'No, ma'am, just thinking of home.'[6]

The young Ernest Hemingway was voluble and opinionated. Helena found him handsome and virile with his deep, dark eyes, full lips and dark hair brushed back from a high forehead. He had a boyish way of talking about himself and his exploits with women, even though he was married at the time to Hadley Richardson, the first of his four wives. Despite this, 'it was impossible not to like him,' Helena said.[7] At least that was her official line in her autobiography. She described the writer in rather a different tone to her secretary Patrick O'Higgins: 'Women liked him, but I didn't. He was a loudmouth and a show-off.'[8]

James Joyce loved long conversations that revolved around literature. He even suggested writing his hostess's beauty advertisements, in the style of *Ulysses*. 'Women will be so puzzled,' he added, 'they will rush out and buy.'[9] As usual, Helena described him rather more candidly to O'Higgins: 'Joyce? He smelled bad … couldn't see … ate like a bird.'[10]

Coco Chanel, who could be so harsh, especially towards women, was often a guest at Helena's dinners too. Ladies all over Paris wore Chanel's ylang-ylang- and jasmine-based perfume, No. 5. Helena had met her at Misia Sert's before the war and loved wearing her fashions.

Photos show her in elegant yet practical black or grey Chanel suits – the perfect attire for a wealthy working woman.

One day, when the two women found themselves alone together for a dress fitting, Helena plucked up the courage to ask Coco why she had never married, given all the men who worshipped her, including the Duke of Westminster. 'What?' Chanel cried. 'And become the third duchess? No. I am Mademoiselle Chanel and I shall remain so, just as you will always be Madame Rubinstein. These are our rightful titles.'[11] The dress designer had shed many tears when her lover Boy Capel was killed in a car accident in December 1919. Since then, she had flaunted her affairs with Grand Duke Dimitri Pavlovich, eleven years her junior, followed by French poet Pierre Reverdy, the Duke of Westminster and a few others.

Years later, when both women had reached the age of memories and regrets, they met up again at Diana Vreeland's home before she became editor of American *Vogue*. Coco Chanel had stopped off in New York on her way back from Hawaii and Diana Vreeland had invited her to dinner. In the middle of the meal, the fashion designer asked her hostess to call the wonderful Helena, that 'splendour of a Polish Jewess'.[12] Vreeland carried out her wish and telephoned Madame to invite her along after dinner. It was summer. Chanel wore a white suit with the skirt just below the knee, a white lace shirt and a stylish gardenia in her short hair. Helena sported a long, bright pink Chinese silk coat with a high collar. They retired to a room alone and stood opposite each other talking for hours, oblivious to their surroundings, the time and their hostess. Now and again a worried Vreeland opened the door to check everything was all right ('I thought perhaps they had a suicide pact!'), then left quietly again. Each time, the women hadn't moved – two geniuses face to face. 'I had never been in the presence of such strength of personality. Both of them,' remembered Vreeland, who knew her fair share of big characters.

'Of course, there'd been men in their lives who had helped them, but they earned every cent they made by themselves,' Vreeland wrote when recounting the Chanel and Helena scene. She wondered if they had ever been happy, then concluded amusingly, 'To be contented – that's for the cows,' before adding: 'But I think that they *were*, at least when they were in power, at the wheel, and when they were running everything. And they did – these two women ruled empires.'[13]

Their conversation took an intimate turn as the women talked about the great loves of their lives. Chanel gave Helena one of the sharp, knowing looks she was famous for and asked her if she had ever had a lover. 'I [have] had neither the time nor the inclination,' Helena admitted.

'You may have been lucky,' retorted Chanel.[14]

It was impossible to know if she was joking or serious. Helena nodded her head and said nothing. Their discussion soon came to an end. The two women took leave of their hostess and thanked her for the excellent evening. Many years later, Helena thought back to the scene and that odd exchange. 'Lucky?' she muttered to herself. 'I wonder.'[15]

At the end of her life, Madame often asked herself if her relationship with Edward would have taken a different course if she had shown less inflexibility. Always faithful to him, she never accepted the slightest infidelity on his part. She wondered if she should have been more accommodating. 'Perhaps it would have been better if I'd had some affairs myself. I've always regretted this. I think it would have made me a nicer person. But actually at that time, Edward was the only man I'd ever kissed.'[16] But you can't change how you're made. She certainly couldn't.

Art was as important as ever in Madame's life. In Paris, she hunted for fine objects in flea markets and antique shops, including the one owned by Christian Dior in the Rue Boétie. He guided Madame in her purchases and they struck up a close friendship that lasted until her death. When Dior opened his couture house and at all his future catwalk shows, Helena was there, sitting in the front row.

She always bought a great deal, sometimes too much. Before the war, she had already purchased a striking number of paintings. Her collection included Sisleys, Degas, Monets and eight Renoirs. As soon as she returned to Paris, her compulsion took hold again. She had a predilection for the avant-garde, and after a few years owned works by all the leading painters and sculptors: Bonnard, Brancusi, Braque, Miró, Pascin, Kisling, Picasso, Helleu, Marie Laurencin, Modigliani, Maillol, Juan Gris, van Dongen, Dufy and Léger.

Helena formed friendships with the artists and invited them to her home. She also mixed with art dealers and patrons. As a guest at Gertrude Stein's, Helena recalled a house 'with so many paintings to the ceiling, hanging on the back of doors, in the kitchen, in the bathroom'.[17] Despite her very busy life, Madame always managed to find an hour or two to go and visit the artists' studios in Montparnasse and Montmartre. She also bought whatever took her fancy in galleries. She hung many of her purchases in her beauty salons, which was unheard of at the time.

In the early 1950s, a nineteen-year-old Pierre Bergé (who went on to become chairman of Yves Saint Laurent and is now president of the Pierre Bergé–Yves Saint Laurent Foundation) often visited his painter friend Bernard Buffet in his studio located in the courtyard of Helena Rubinstein's Faubourg Saint-Honoré beauty salon. One day he noticed a sculpture by Brancusi, *The White Negress*, in her salon window. It was a double revelation for the self-taught young man: 'I discovered Brancusi, whose name I hadn't even heard of, and learned at the same time that you could display a work of that quality in a beauty salon window. Later, when Yves Saint Laurent opened his first shop in the Rue du Faubourg Saint-Honoré, a few metres from Helena

Rubinstein's salon, we placed two huge Jean Dunant vases we had just purchased in the window. Unconsciously, I must have been influenced by her.'[18]

Helena was unable to resist a beautiful work of art, so much so that she often forgot what she had bought. 'I've got so many paintings,' she declared, 'that I don't know where to hang them anymore'[19] – though she certainly had no lack of houses to display them in. Sometimes she left them abandoned in cupboards. Patrick O'Higgins found many a priceless painting hoarded away, not indexed at all and insufficiently insured.

One afternoon in her Greenwich home, a large painting by Max Ernst hanging in a corridor caught O'Higgins's eye. 'It only cost me two hundred dollars,' Madame revealed. Another time, in her Park Avenue apartment in New York, they made some incredible discoveries in Helena's wardrobes. O'Higgins found seven drawings by Juan Gris stuffed into an old clothes box, a Picasso from his cubist period and a set of lithographs by Matisse, Helena's favourite artist, on top of a pile of old sheets. Completely taken aback, O'Higgins questioned her about them. She made a vague gesture with her hand, shrugged her shoulders and replied that they were fakes, examples of her 'little mistakes'.[20] For once she was wrong: they were originals.

Among the young artists Madame admired and invited to her home was Marc Chagall. He had sparkling eyes and a shock of blond hair. After a few glasses of wine, he would sing Russian songs or tell long, funny stories in Yiddish. He had such a lively mind and caustic sense of humour that Helena invited him on a regular basis. His presence assured the success of any party.

Chagall often came with Braque or other painter friends. He introduced Helena to Louis Marcoussis, who took her to visit artists' studios and became one of her best advisers. But she didn't always follow his recommendations and as a result missed several masterpieces or bought second-rate works and even fakes. But she remained fatalistic. Every piece she owned was bought from an artist she had fond memories of. Their sentimental value was even higher than their market value: 'I cherish them no less than my Picassos, my Modiglianis and my Rouaults,' she said.[21]

It upset Marcoussis when Helena ignored his advice. If she had listened to him more often, her collection would have been worth more. She once refused a Picasso selling for 6,000 francs whose value increased tenfold a few years later. She was the first to admit that she bought mainly on instinct. Speculation wasn't her aim. 'When I bought a picture because I thought I was getting a bargain, it most often turned out to be a mistake. But when I purchased what I knew gave me real inner joy, or because I wanted to encourage an artist whose talent I recognised, I usually chose well.'[22]

Among Helena's favourite works of art were *The Bathers* by Renoir, *Autumn* by Roger de la Fresnaye, *Portrait of a Woman* by Kees van Dongen and a study for *Les Demoiselles d'Avignon* by Picasso, given to her as a present by a client whose acne-pitted face she had healed. The young lady had left the drawing with the concierge with a note stapled to the newspaper it was wrapped in: 'Thank you for my beautiful skin.'[23] Helena never managed to find her again to thank her.

Her passion for collecting had become an obsession. Opaline glass, dolls' houses, crockery, silverware, jewellery, curios, furniture – everything interested her. Helped by fashion and speculation, her pieces of African art, purchased on Jacob Epstein's good advice, saw their prices rocket. Everyone wanted to own some. The more new statues she bought, the more she learned to love 'their expressive intensity'.[24]

Charles Ratton, a Parisian art dealer, sold Helena a statuette known as the 'Bangwa Queen', one of the most beautiful pieces in her

Born in 1872, Helena Rubinstein (centre) was the eldest of eight girls. In this portrait, taken before Helena left her birthplace in Poland, her mother, Gitel, is seated on the right, while Helena is flanked by three of her sisters.

Helena in 1905, during her first visit to Paris, in an evening dress by the English designer Worth. Helena continued to be dressed by great couturiers, including Doucet, Poiret, Chanel, Balenciaga, Schiaparelli and Yves Saint Laurent.

A rare portrait of Helena with her two sons, Roy (left) and Horace, taken at her country house in Greenwich, Connecticut. Helena wears an embroidered tunic dress by Poiret. The boys spent much of their time at Greenwich with their tutor, while their parents ran Helena's business from New York.

Three of the Rubinstein sisters in 1920: (from left) Manka, Helena and Stella. Manka arrived in the United States from war-torn Europe in 1917 and was soon responsible for training Helena's American sales force. Stella, acknowledged as the most beautiful of all the sisters, managed Helena's business in France for many years.

Helena's passion for travelling, especially by ocean liner, meant she sometimes spent half the year at sea. Here she poses with her son Roy, the artist and designer Ladislas Medgyes, and the composer Nicolas Nabokov. Medgyes designed the interiors of many of Helena's beauty salons and created the famous illuminated Lucite bed for her Park Avenue apartment.

Edward William Titus, Helena's first husband, was a charming Polish-born American journalist. His advertising and marketing acumen was instrumental in the early success and expansion of Helena's business. He loved the intellectual life of Paris's Left Bank and his small publishing house, Black Manikin, was an early publisher of Gertrude Stein, D. H. Lawrence, Aldous Huxley, Ernest Hemingway and Samuel Beckett.

Helena with her second husband, the Georgian prince Artchil Gourielli-Tchkonia, who was twenty-three years her junior. They married in 1938, the year of Helena's divorce from Edward.

Helena in one of her favourite outfits, designed by Edward Molyneux.

Helena with her niece, Mala Rubinstein Silson. Although Helena never made it official, the devoted Mala was the successor she had always wished for. Rigorously trained in all aspects of the business by Helena, Mala had no equal when it came to teaching women about beauty. Here, both women wear Chanel dresses and hold ceremonial masks from Helena's impressive collection of primitive art.

Helena was the first cosmetics manufacturer to call on the authority of science and liked to pose in her laboratories at Saint-Cloud and Long Island, often clad in a white lab coat and surrounded by chemical apparatus. She regularly travelled to European spas to study the latest developments in skincare and beauty treatments.

Valaze, Helena's original product, was developed in Poland by a Hungarian chemist and made its commercial debut in 1902, the year Helena opened her first shop in Melbourne. Right up to the end, Helena kept the composition of that first Valaze cream a secret, but presumably it had neither the fluidity nor the lightness of products that came later.

In the summer of 1959, aged eighty-seven, Helena flew to Moscow to represent the US cosmetic industry at the American National Exhibition. She immediately grasped the opportunities the mammoth Russian market offered.

Helena's salons in Paris, London and New York were decorated by internationally acclaimed artists and designers. The architect Harold Sterner oversaw the fit-out of her third New York salon, which opened at 715 Fifth Avenue in 1936. He commissioned de Chirico to paint the mural, while the stool was designed by Jean Michel Frank (both above). On the second floor (below), the marble reliefs were sculpted by Elie Nadelman, the drawings were by Modigliani and the rug was designed by Fernand Léger.

In 1934, Helena bought the Hôtel de Vesselin at 24 Quai de Béthune on the Ile Saint-Louis and used its penthouse as her Paris home. This photo, taken in 1938 on the majestic terrace, followed the awarding of the Helena Rubinstein prize for modern art to the sculptor Henri Laurens. Among the judges of the award were Henri Matisse (standing back left, beside Helena), Marie Cuttoli, Georges Braque, Paul Éluard, Fernand Léger and Louis Marcoussis.

Salvador Dalí and Helena met in 1941 and in 1943 he painted her portrait, depicting her chained by her jewels to a rocky cliff overlooking an emerald-green sea. Dalí would later say the portrait of Helena had relaunched his career. She hung it in her new apartment at 625 Park Avenue, New York.

Helena with Eleanor Roosevelt, a woman Helena greatly admired and whose charity work she supported. During World War II, Helena was invited to the White House where Eleanor's husband, President Roosevelt, told her the story of an Englishwoman who had been carried out of a bombed building on a stretcher. Even before she was given pain relief, she begged the ambulance officers to pass her a lipstick from her handbag. 'Your war effort is to keep up the morale of our women. And you are doing it splendidly,' concluded the President. Unbeknown to Helena, he told the same story to her hated rival, Elizabeth Arden.

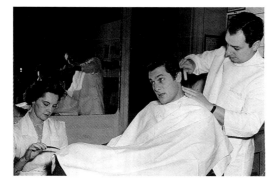

Tony Curtis was one of the most loyal clients of the House of Gourielli, the men's salon named after Helena's second husband, but the concept was perhaps too far ahead of its time. The salon closed in 1955 and Helena repackaged its products under the Rubinstein brand, because a 'good cook can prepare a meal using a few leftovers'.

Helena in 1955 with Pablo Picasso. He refused to paint her portrait, but made at least forty sketches of Madame. According to John Richardson, Picasso's biographer, the artist was convinced he would die before Helena if he finished her portrait.

Helena with Kees van Dongen in 1958. Madame purchased many works directly from artists' studios. Her love of art was an extension of her love of beauty. 'My avid desire to make women beautiful has always blended well with my insatiable thirst for all art forms,' she wrote. Money enabled her to indulge this passion.

Helena with Elizabeth Taylor. From her earliest days in business in Australia, Helena grasped the importance of using celebrities to endorse her products.

Helena's collection of portraits of herself included works by Raoul Dufy, Edward Lintott, Marie Laurencin, Christian Bérard, Graham Sutherland, Dora Maar, Paul Tchelitchew, Jacques Helleu and Salvador Dalí. The Graham Sutherland portrait (centre top) is perhaps the most striking; the Marie Laurencin (below the Sutherland) is the gentlest.

Helena was such a noted collector of primitive art – *Life* magazine dubbed her 'a female small-scale Hearst' – that in 1935 MoMA displayed seventeen of her African sculptures alongside pieces belonging to Henri Matisse and Paul Guillaume. In 1990, a statuette known as the 'Bangwa Queen', once the pride of Helena's collection, sold for just over US$3.5 million.

collection and her personal favourite. The Cameroonian figure dating from the mid nineteenth century represents a princess or a priestess. Edward once lent the piece to Man Ray because he was mad about it, and he photographed it with one of Paul Poiret's former models, Ady. Madame's collection was so famous that the director of the Metropolitan Museum of Art in New York wanted to buy it from her. She refused but was flattered nonetheless.

For Helena, interior decoration was inextricably linked to art. From very early on, she knew what she liked, and hired only the best to work on her salons and homes. In 1913, at the Salon des Artistes Décorateurs, she had admired lacquer screens by Irish architect and designer Eileen Grey who by now had a shop at 140 Rue du Faubourg Saint-Honoré a few doors along from her salon. Madame stopped by to browse for a rug or a piece of furniture. Grey's work was controversial but Helena liked her, as she did the diminutive, doe-eyed French interior designer Jean-Michel Frank, who had been put on a pedestal by Charles and Marie-Laure de Noailles ever since he had decorated, or rather 'defurnished', their mansion in the Place des États-Unis. Frank was known for his pared-down design style. He also worked with cabinetmakers from the Ateliers de la Ruche who made furniture designed by French Art Deco masters Pierre Chareau, Émile-Jacques Ruhlmann and André Groult, which Helena bought or had copied for her apartments and salons.

Just as impressive as her works of art was Madame's wardrobe, which included outfits by Caroline Reboux, Elsa Schiaparelli (Helena was one of her first clients), Edward Molyneux, Paul Poiret, Lanvin and Lucien Lelong. She also accumulated accessories: hats, stoles, furs, belts and, of course, jewellery, both fine and costume. She nevertheless committed the odd fashion faux pas from time to time. Like wearing Chanel pyjamas and wide-legged trousers – wonderful on a tall, slender figure, but rather unflattering on Helena. And although she tirelessly advocated diets, exercise and massages, she didn't practise what she preached. 'Considering how hard I work,' she said to justify herself, 'I can't afford not to eat well.'[25]

She still wore little make-up, except her trademark dark lipstick, and dyed her white hair jet black, often unevenly. At nearly sixty, she refused to grow old. Her energy wouldn't allow it anyway.

18

BEAUTY BECOMES BIG BUSINESS

'Travel', a *New York Post* writer remarked, was 'Madame Rubinstein's middle name.'[1] It was certainly one of Helena's favourite hobbies. She often said the weeks she spent at sea on floating palaces were the only time she could relax. She would allow herself a few on-board distractions: cocktails, dinners and bridge, which she had originally taken up in Australia and which had since become a fashionable game. Or she would shut herself up in her luxurious cabin to indulge in her letter-writing mania, posting her missives to relatives and company managers the minute she got off the ship. Best of all, she could treat herself to lie-ins and long naps. The opportunity to catch up on her sleep was one of the main attractions of the journey. She rarely slept more than five hours a night as a rule.

Transatlantic cruises were her favourite. Each time she saw the Statue of Liberty appear on the horizon from the deck of a ship, she felt the adrenalin rush she had experienced on her first trip to America. New York suited her go-getting personality. She approved of New Yorkers, who took work seriously and didn't waste their time on pointless chatter. In fact the entire country was extremely business oriented. The early 1920s had ushered in an economic boom, and consumer society had arrived with a bang. Anything could be invented and bought, and disposed of and replaced just as easily – radios, plastic gadgets, synthetic fabrics, cigarette lighters, telephones, Kleenex,

Kotex, deodorants and depilatory creams. These affordable inventions made life easier and more fun.

Fun and frolic were the watchwords in the roaring twenties. Even Prohibition couldn't stop people enjoying themselves. Under pressure from religious leaders concerned with the morals of society and feminists campaigning against domestic violence, Congress had passed the 18th amendment forbidding the sale of alcohol. But it would take more than a law to make people stop drinking. Carefree revellers danced the Charleston and the foxtrot in nightclubs and jived to jazz tunes by Duke Ellington and Count Basie. Audiences flocked to Broadway to applaud performances of George Gershwin's *Rhapsody in Blue* and revues featuring the brother-and-sister dance duo Fred and Adele Astaire (Fred would go on to make several films with Ginger Rogers, his most famous dance partner). Radio stations played Dixieland music. Al Jolson starred in *The Jazz Singer*, the first full-length talking film. Clara Bow, the heroine of the film *It* – and the original It Girl – was idolised by young girls who copied her wavy bob, arched, pencilled eyebrows and heart-shaped mouth highlighted with bright red lipstick. Her vitality, exuberance and sheer animal magnetism undoubtedly fuelled people's fascination with her. Like other silent movie stars such as Theda Bara and Louise Brooks, Bow was better known for her sex appeal than her acting talent.

Advertising was progressing by leaps and bounds, generating staggering amounts of revenue and promoting the expansion of the print media. Cosmetics firms had the fifth highest advertising spend overall and were the second biggest advertisers in *Town and Country*, *Harper's Bazaar* and *Vogue*. Advertisements for beauty products made up twenty per cent of magazine pages in 1929. Brands such as Pond's, Elizabeth Arden and Helena Rubinstein had monthly advertising budgets ranging from $20,000 to $60,000. The return on investment was huge, as women's magazines had begun to set fashion trends and influence consumers' spending habits.[2]

The 1920s also marked the emergence of beauty contests: the first Miss America beauty pageant was held in 1921. With hundreds of creams, powders and lipsticks to choose from, the average American woman was buying $300 worth of cosmetics each year. By the late 1920s, women were spending an estimated $700 million a year on beauty products in department stores, going to the hairdresser's, and massages in beauty salons. Cosmetics were a personal indulgence as well as a seduction tool for modern women, who were free at last to wear as much make-up as they wanted. As one observer points out, 'Women linked cosmetics use to an emergent notion of their own modernity.'[3]

The financial implications of women's liberation were also becoming clear. Beauty had become a full-scale business, and mass production democratised access to beauty products. Helena Rubinstein contributed significantly to this sea change. Her Saint-Cloud and Long Island factories produced more than seventy lines of cosmetics, including her all-new 'reducing preparations', the body-slimming creams she launched in 1923. Her rival wasn't far behind. Elizabeth Arden had established her brand in America and Europe with the help of her husband and manager Thomas Lewis and her sister Gladys, who ran the French branch of the company and the Paris salon. Like Madame, Arden had her own factories. Her products were sold in her own salons, upmarket New York department stores such as Bonwit Teller, Macy's and Neiman Marcus and select outlets in Detroit, Washington, Philadelphia, San Francisco and Los Angeles. She could boast a range of seventy-five products, including the bestselling Orange Skin Food and Venetian Bleaching Cream.

Both women had to contend with competitors wanting their slice of the profitable pie: French brands such as René Coty, Guerlain, Roger and Gallet and Bourjois, which had appeared on the US market at the beginning of the century, and popular home-grown cosmetics giants such as Pond's, as well as smaller brands – both established and emerging – pulled along by a rapidly expanding market, such as Carl Weeks, Noxzema, Maybelline, Barbara Gould and Max Factor. But Helena Rubinstein and Elizabeth Arden were each other's main adversaries – the two of them were slugging it out for top place in the big leagues. Their dislike was mutual, and each woman kept a sharp eye out for the other's new ideas. They used similar marketing methods, such as inviting customers to write in about their skin problems and sending each one personalised advice. Madame would inspect every single letter she received and instantly assess the writer's financial situation. 'This is ordinary letter paper,' she would say. 'She doesn't have much money. I'll only recommend two products, not the entire treatment.' The only difference between the two women was their customer profile. While Elizabeth Arden kept her focus on wealthy women, Helena Rubinstein was increasingly targeting a middle-class clientele. There was certainly a market out there: one quarter of American women over the age of sixteen were working, with money to spend, in the 1920s.

However, Helena Rubinstein's and Elizabeth Arden's success was the exception to the rule in a business now predominantly run by men keenly aware that there was big money at stake. The days when beauty was a cottage industry were well and truly over. Department -store salons had taken over from independent beauty salons. Women such as Dorothy Grey, Peggy Sage and Kathleen Mary Quinlan had enjoyed their moment in the sun, then sold their small cosmetics labels. The conventional gender division of labour had become very much the norm in a business that had originally been invented by women for women. Men owned companies and put other men in managerial, supervisory and decision-making jobs. Women – generally white college graduates – found jobs in marketing, advertising, journalism, cosmetics and sales. A few top-flight female executives handled nationwide campaigns targeting women consumers at large agencies, while smaller fry held jobs at local branches, writing copy for department stores and small companies. Whatever their place in the pecking order, all these women acted as interlocutors between male manufacturers and female customers.[4]

Their copy aimed at women was written in a chatty tone, using 'the woman's viewpoint'. Although these copywriters – intelligent, cultured, politically active and pioneering women – had no illusions about the artificiality of their prose, they never challenged the established tradition of confining women to gender stereotypes. Their copy used tried-and-tested stock phrases any woman could understand, even the ones who couldn't afford visits to an upmarket Elizabeth Arden or Helena Rubinstein salon. Advertising was a leveller, keeping female readers of every stripe up to date with the latest fashion and beauty trends, even as the copy perpetuated the most ingrained clichés about women.

Madame, who cultivated her own image as a successful businesswoman, shared the advertisements' simplistic standpoint. She believed no one could understand and interpret a woman's desires better than another woman, and could imagine no greater ambition for any woman than a job in beauty. She made it a point of honour to hire almost exclusively female staff, and felt very close to her employees. At lunchtime, she would often invite the company's secretaries – her 'little girls', as she called them – to bring their lunchboxes to her office, where she would make them try out new products. Their opinion was important to her. She used their reactions and suggestions to expand the brand's range. She would ask them questions about the products they were testing and make a note of the ones they liked or vetoed.

Her unconditional support of women did not, however, extend to appointing a woman manager. There wasn't one single female factory supervisor or marketing or finance manager in her company. Salon manager was the highest position a woman could aspire to. Helena assigned the top jobs to men for the simple reason that she felt safer with a man at the helm. She was equally doubtful about her sisters' abilities and often had them work under the supervision of male employees, although she painted a picture of sisterly unity whenever she talked to the press. The saga of the pretty Polish sisters went down very well with journalists, and Madame never passed up an opportunity to tell it.

The Rubinstein family 'dream team' continued to grow: Ceska was in London; Manka was courageously crisscrossing the United States training beauty consultants; Stella was in Chicago being prepared to take over from Pauline in Paris; and Erna had joined her sisters in the US. Regina was the only one of Helena's sisters to have remained in Kraków, but three of her four children would soon be working for their famous aunt. Helena sponsored any of her Polish relatives who wanted to come to America. She paid their passage, put them up, encouraged and trained them, supported them financially and hired them to work in one or other of her salons. But she remained sole mistress on board and exercised sovereign power. Jean Cocteau dubbed her the 'Empress of Beauty'.

In 1928, she moved her New York salon to a stately building formerly owned by railroad magnate Collis P. Huntington at 8 East 57th Street, at the intersection with Fifth Avenue. She had visited dozens of places, but hadn't liked any of them. As soon as she clapped eyes on this one she was ready to sign on the dotted line. When the surprised estate agent asked her why she had come to such a quick decision after turning down so many other properties, she simply said: 'I like the staircase.'

She kept the staircase and had the rest of the building entirely renovated. The architect Benjamin Whinston renovated the facade while Paul T. Frankl revamped the interior. He designed most of the furniture together with Donald Deskey, the most sought-after interior designer in town. The linoleum floors – an innovation at the time – were covered in carpets from Maison Myrbor in Paris, some of them designed by painter Louis Marcoussis. Émile-Jacques Ruhlmann designed the wall lights, and sketches by Fernand Léger adorned the walls. The press also lauded the renovation of her Chicago salon. *Good Furniture* magazine described it as 'the most extensive example in Chicago of modern interior decoration adapted to a commercial establishment'.[5] Madame had a minor nervous collapse after it opened, as she so often did after a salon opening, and had to go to a sanatorium for a 'post-salon' rest. She always looked forward to these breaks and factored them into her busy schedule.

Her honeymoon with the press continued. 'To the skeptical she offers a tour of inspection at the Long Island factory,' a *Time* magazine article said, going on to describe the rows of half-opened water lilies in the factory, kept fresh until their essence could be collected and used to make creams, powders and lipsticks.[6] Tubes of chopped cucumber were stacked alongside bunches of Italian parsley, boxes of eggs, butter and cream and crates of grapefruit and a variety of other fruit and vegetables. 'Madame Rubinstein is justly proud of her products, noted for their active qualities, making the skin tingle,' the article continued.[7]

In 1928 *The New Yorker* published a four-page profile by Jo Swerling of 'the woman without a country'.[8] Helena had decked herself out in her finest jewellery for the interview, explaining in her idiosyncratic mix of English, Polish, French and Yiddish that it was 'gude' for publicity. The article described her success story: 'On her payroll in all parts of the world are nearly 3,000 people, in addition to those who are employed by the 5,000 selling agents who handle her products. There are remote cities which have Rubinstein agencies where there are not even Ford agencies.'

Swerling went into detail about Helena's funny little habits: the long letters she swamped her employees with each day, which she wrote on the back of menus to avoid waste, and her odd amnesia when it came to remembering people's surnames. Some of her employees had been working for her for years, but she still referred to them as 'the fat man' or 'the deaf woman' or 'hook nose'. People sometimes wondered whether these lapses were a ploy to destabilise the person Helena was talking to, as she generally had an exceptionally precise memory for the tiniest details; for instance, she would immediately notice if a piece of salon furniture had been moved.

The *New Yorker* writer described Madame as a walking paradox, capable of extreme frugality as well as prodigious extravagance. 'She can go a whole year without buying anything at all and wearing the same hat, then suddenly spend vast amounts of money during a three-day shopping spree. There are several outfits she has never worn in her wardrobe of clothes from Paris and London.'

Helena placed her life in the spotlight with consummate flair for self-promotion. Her communication was calculated, her lies skilfully told and her image carefully honed. She always had herself photographed or painted at home, dressed in great style, wearing her best jewellery and surrounded by objects demonstrating her sophisticated taste. There is also the occasional portrait of her in a white lab coat in one of her salons or factories. She would urge the artist to make her look slimmer and younger, and had paintings and portraits retouched.

There are before and after versions of one particular photograph by Cecil Beaton in which she poses in front of a classical white marble statue by Elie Nadelman – her face as it appeared in the original photograph and the corrections she made in black ink: add more hair, reshape the shoulder, take off the face wrinkles and tighten up the saggy arm skin. The result was obviously spectacular – she looked ten years younger. Who needed cosmetic surgery, electrical massages or skin peelings when you could wave the magic wand of technology?

19

THE LITTLE LADY TAKES ON
WALL STREET

Like most other immigrants to America, the German Jewish Lehman brothers – Henry, Emanuel and Mayer – were self-made men.

Henry was twenty-one when he set off for the New World in 1844. The American south was full of flourishing cotton plantations, and there was plenty of money to be made from cotton trading. Several of Henry's relatives had settled in Alabama. A cousin sold him a wagonload of farming merchandise on credit and Henry became a travelling salesman. By the end of his first year in America, Henry Lehman opened a general store in Montgomery. When Emanuel arrived in 1847, the brothers opened a bigger shop and called it H. Lehman & Bros. The shop changed names again, to Lehman Brothers, when Mayer joined them in 1850. The local farmers were often short of ready cash, and got into the habit of paying for their purchases in bales of cotton. The Lehmans began to focus on cotton brokerage and set up a New York branch.

Henry died in 1855. Mayer and Emanuel moved their headquarters to New York after the American Civil War and listed the company on the stock exchange in 1887. By the early twentieth century, Lehman Brothers had expanded its commodity broking to sugar, grain, coffee and petroleum. After Mayer's and Emanuel's deaths, the second generation of Lehmans took over and moved the firm into investment banking. Practically all the businesses they invested in were Jewish owned; the Lehmans had come up against the anti-Semitism of the Protestant establishment when they moved to New York. Together with other wealthy Jewish families, they set up their own circles and country clubs rather than attempt to gain entry to places where they were not wanted.[1] Their children were given a modern education – the boys attended Ivy League universities – but every Lehman, male or female, married within the community.

Beauty was unknown territory for the Lehman men, who did business in an all-male corporate environment. They did, however, have a nose for new opportunities, and were keen to explore the profit-making possibilities of the burgeoning cosmetics market. Everything pointed to the Helena Rubinstein brand being a sound and profitable investment. The Lehmans pored over Helena's balance sheets. The previous year, she had raked in $2 million of gross earnings and a sizeable profit of $960,000.[2] What was more, the woman who owned the company was a Polish Jew. It ticked all their boxes. The Lehmans' decision was made – they would buy the company, list it on the stock exchange and flood the market with glamorous Rubinstein products. They made an offer and waited for Helena's response. It was well known that Madame was fond of money. How would she be able to resist such a windfall, especially as they were willing to pay cash? The Lehmans offered her a whopping $7.3 million – approximately $90 million at today's prices. Madame had already received buyout offers, but never such a tempting one. It was rumoured that a French company had offered her a tidy sum for her company three years earlier, and that she had found a trumped-up excuse to turn them down. 'We cannot get together – you think in francs, I in pounds,' she had told them.[3]

But the Lehmans had far more financial clout. She didn't have to think their offer over for long. She accepted. After all, she would only be selling 75 per cent of her shares in the American company. She would still own the factories and her businesses in Europe and Australia. The

Lehmans promised not to fire any of her staff and asked her to continue representing the brand. According to the terms of the contract, she would be honorary chairman, make appearances at charity galas and society evenings and continue to create her products, in exchange for letting them run the company the way they wanted.

She concluded the sale on 11 December 1928, having managed to keep it a secret. She was now officially a billionaire: 'I sold the American corporation for one reason only – to save my marriage. It was a sacrifice, for my business had always meant more to me than money ... I felt there was no alternative, however,' she says in her autobiography.[4] It was a touching confession, but was she telling the whole truth? Was Edward really the only reason for her decision? She hadn't said a word to him about the sale. Perhaps she was waiting for the right moment because she wasn't sure how he would take the news. She was certainly under very few illusions about their relationship by this time. The last time she had gone to Paris, they had had their separation made legal.

But they were still playing cat and mouse with each other. Edward would ask her for money for his publishing ventures and Helena would refuse to give it to him. The more insistent his demands, the more inflexible she became. Then, after she had managed to send him into a fury, she would dole out the money in dribs and drabs. They still wrote to each other, but their correspondence had turned bitter. If she backed his magazine, he told her, there 'would be enough glory for all'.

'What do I have to do with your glory?' she snapped in her reply. 'I have always been your instrument and through me you have achieved many things.'

'There was no need, Helena, to add insult when replying,' he answered. 'It takes two ... to share anything and you refuse to play. You don't have to sleep with one to share his or her life.'[5]

There was a fresh exchange of letters and new misunderstandings.

Each felt victimised by the other. Helena complained that she had always worked herself into the ground to ensure her family's well-being and never been given the consideration she thought she deserved. She had taken on all the responsibilities and the work while her husband had reserved the lion's share of the enjoyment for himself. 'You come to me for help and go elsewhere for fun,' she wrote.[6] In reply, he accused her of systematically humiliating him. Their mutual incomprehension gradually worsened.

Horace, then studying at Cambridge, had a car accident – the first of many. Edward and she agreed to call a truce to go and see their son and tell him they were worried about him. It was a short-lived respite. Edward was unaware that his wife had sold her American company. She still hadn't got up the courage to tell him the news. He heard rumours about the sale and then read about it in the papers – it hadn't taken long for the French press to get wind of the story. He felt wounded by her silence and reproached her bitterly. They had another quarrel. He spent Christmas on his own in Paris while she went to Australia with their sons.

Meanwhile, Edward's business was looking up. He earned himself money and recognition with a couple of back-to-back publishing coups. In 1929, the year he bought *This Quarter*, he published the second edition of the D. H. Lawrence novel *Lady Chatterley's Lover* (Lawrence had had the first edition printed in Florence the previous year). Edward knew he was taking a risk because the book had created a scandal. Sylvia Beach had refused to publish it, deeming it too sexually explicit. In any case, working with James Joyce gave her quite enough to do. So she put Lawrence in touch with Edward.

The success of the novel went some way towards mopping up Black Manikin's debts. Lawrence was suffering from increasingly severe tuberculosis and would have little opportunity to enjoy his new-found fortune. He died the following year in the south of France, where he had gone to rest in the company of his wife Frieda. Edward Titus was one of the few people to attend the funeral.

Edward had another runaway bestseller up his sleeve. He had hired Samuel Putnam to translate the memoirs of Kiki of Montparnasse. *Kiki's Memoirs* came out in 1930, a year after the release of the French edition. The book had a preface by Hemingway and photographs by Kiki's long-time lover Man Ray. Born Alice Prin, Kiki was an illegitimate child brought up in extreme poverty. She became Polish artist Maurice Mendjizky's live-in lover, and posed for his friends Moise Kisling and Tsuguharu Foujita. The latter's portrait of Kiki, *Reclining Nude with Toile de Jouy*, was a sensation at the Salon d'Automne art fair. Kiki also modelled for Modigliani and Derain. She was a neighbourhood icon.

Buoyed by his newly attained fame, Edward patched things up with Helena. She was truly happy to hear about her husband's success and wrote to him from New York to congratulate him.

Playing the stock market had become all the rage in the United States, and women traded shares as actively as men. When Lehman Brothers listed Helena Rubinstein, women bought 80 per cent of the shares. This led to a paradoxical situation similar to that of many small cosmetics firms that had sold their stock. Helena Rubinstein, a company set up and developed by a woman and staffed almost entirely by women, with an overwhelmingly female shareholder base to boot, was run by male bankers who knew absolutely nothing about the beauty business.

Lehman Brothers flooded the market with low-price products, not realising that turning Helena Rubinstein into a mass-market brand would tarnish its upscale image. Although Madame had always been wary of mass distribution, she initially thought their strategy might work. She soon realised it was impossible. Women didn't like paying next to nothing for products they perceived as being high value, and affluent women turned up their noses at a brand even low earners could afford. The Lehmans were at a loss when it came to marketing strategies. They could recite stock prices off the top of their heads, but had no knowledge of the subtle needs of women consumers.

Their other problem was Helena, who was a real thorn in their side. Although she had signed a contract full of clauses stipulating that she wouldn't interfere, she had no intention of keeping quiet and staying out of it. Selling her creams in grocery stores would ruin her brand, and that was something she simply couldn't accept. The company was her child, her creation. She had spent thirty years working her fingers to the bone – often to the detriment of her personal life – to make it a success. All that effort to stand by and watch those idiots dismantle her life's work by selling her precious products any old how – lined up on grocery-store shelves between the peas and the washing powder? She was so consumed with rage that she nearly made herself ill.

The indignant letters she received from managers of department stores fuelled her anger. They complained that the new owners were undermining the brand, and refused to continue carrying the Rubinstein product line. Helena bombarded the Lehmans with threatening missives. When they refused to answer, she got her stockbrokers to supply her with the addresses of all the company's female shareholders and wrote letters to every single one of them, criticising the new management and asking them to write to Lehman Brothers and express their displeasure. The Lehmans began to receive a flood of letters from all over the country. And their troubles were only starting. Madame was hell-bent on buying up the shares, one by one if it came to that, to get her company back. She wrote letters, made telephone calls and girded herself to travel the length and breadth of the country to buy back her stock.

The twenty-fourth of October 1929 would go down in history as 'Black Thursday', when a stock market bubble caused by the speculative fever and margin buying that had been going on since 1927 suddenly burst. The 1920s surge in industrial output had been slowing down, and capital was being invested in the stock market rather than the real economy. Share prices were rising faster than corporate profits, which in turn were growing faster than production and wages. Stock prices shot up by as much as 120 per cent from March to September 1929 and then started to fall. A sudden steep decline in share prices led to a wave of panic selling on 24 October. Wall Street collapsed and stock markets across the world fell like dominoes. US stocks lost $72 billion worth of market value. General Motors, US Steel, General Electric, and Goldman Sachs shares plummeted. So did Lehman Brothers' – including Helena Rubinstein stock, which dropped from $60 to $3 per share.[7]

It was not just a financial catastrophe as far as Madame was concerned. The business she had built from scratch was the thing she held most dear. She tried to put a brave face on things, but she began to spend sleepless nights worrying about all the things that were going wrong in her life: her business, her health and her relationship with Edward. As usual, however, adversity brought out the best in her. As she lay wide awake in bed one night she came up with a plan. She ordered her stockbrokers to buy up as many Helena Rubinstein shares as they could. Her shares had fallen further, and small shareholders were only too happy to recoup a bit of money by selling their shares before they became completely worthless. Ironically enough, Madame used a substantial chunk of Lehman cash to buy back her shares, and prepared to bargain with them from a position of strength once she had won back control of her business. She forced them to sell her the rest of the stock. The share buyback cost her $1.5 million – a trifle compared to the profit she would make. She pocketed a cool $5.8 million on the deal.

'Madame Rubinstein is financially illiterate,' the Lehmans muttered with bad grace.[8] On the contrary, Madame had clearly demonstrated her financial acumen. The Wall Street whizzes would have done better not to underestimate their diminutive female rival. It was the first time their strength and male superiority had been given a knock – and by a woman at that. Ninety years on, this David versus Goliath tussle remains a celebratory tale. Some observers have accused her of insider trading – perhaps the Lehmans spread the rumour to exact revenge – but Madame could hardly have had advance knowledge of a stock market crash that took the whole world by surprise. What she did have was intuition – and, as always, the luck of the devil. Gambling with fate has built many a fortune. In less than two years, Madame had become one of the richest women in America.

Throughout the long-drawn-out negotiations, she had struggled with the fear that she would fail to buy up enough shares to have the Lehmans with their backs to the wall. She couldn't stand the thought of losing. Since she had to keep her wheeling and dealing under wraps, she turned for reassurance to her usual confidant: Edward. Back in Paris, his reaction was totally unexpected. 'At worst it means a money tragedy,' he told her. '... Time and life slips by ... I wish you would win out. But if you do not win, you will gain something more valuable ... You have two fine boys, whom you do not enjoy possessing, you have a husband ... who loves you truly and sincerely, whatever his faults are ... These are the only things that substantially matter. The children's life, your life and mine, the combined life of the four of us.'[9]

It was time for her to choose once and for all between work and family. She had often complained in her letters to her husband that she was tired of living out of a suitcase and merely passing through all her magnificent, expensively decorated houses. She longed for the settled existence she needed to achieve balance and well-being; she'd had more than enough of 'pick-nicking', as she put it.[10] No one in her inner circle could understand what it was that made her so restless, least of all her sons. But there was really only one decision she could make. Her frequent assertion that she was 'born to work' was now truer than ever. She had to rebuild her business from scratch in the country where she had nearly lost it all. She prepared to go back to America, much to the displeasure of Edward, who had naively assumed she would give it all up to settle down with him in their Boulevard Raspail apartment.

Edward needed stability too. He was unable to put up any longer with their incessant quarrelling, the low blows, the humiliations and constant mutual sniping. He was fed up of having to ask her for money all the time. Although he no longer wanted to have sex with Helena, he thought they could offer each other easy, undemanding companionship. Helena couldn't accept the idea of a platonic relationship – not with Edward, the only man she had ever loved. She wanted it all; she refused to settle for crumbs. But the embers of their relationship were proving hard to rekindle. Madame swallowed her chagrin and left for New York, impatient to be back in business.

20

MOURNING FOR HAPPINESS

Helena could hear the mounting clamour of protest from the windows of her office above her beauty salon on 57th Street. The crowd of demonstrators protesting against hunger, unemployment and the high cost of living was growing larger by the minute. The angry shouts of the 35,000 protestors marching along the streets of New York could be heard inside the hushed atmosphere of the salon, which was usually an oasis of peace and pampering.

Even Helena's wealthiest customers were aware that America and the rest of the world were deep in the throes of the Great Depression. The financial maelstrom that had turned Helena into a billionaire overnight and allowed her to keep all her staff had burgeoned into an unprecedented economic crisis. Thousands of people had lost their jobs.

Helena was one of the lucky few – she had weathered the crisis with her wealth intact. She appeared to have everything: success, money and prestige. Everything except love. She missed Edward terribly. So she kept busy, doubling her own workload and urging her staff to work harder.

She set off on another tour of America to promote her first book, *The Art of Feminine Beauty*. She had entrusted the actual writing of it to a ghost writer, but the ideas in the book were all her own. The first two chapters told Helena's story. She had prettied it up considerably, especially her childhood in Poland and her early years in Australia.

The book's artful mix of fact and fiction would become the accepted version of her life story. However, the book was mainly about beauty – and here Madame had little need for untruths and embellishment. She was in her element when talking about the subject, and some of her insights were nothing short of visionary. 'I am certain,' she said, 'that a day will come when a fifty-year-old woman will easily be able to pass for thirty, and a seventy-year-old to claim she is at an age of vigorous maturity.'

Women needed frivolous pleasures more than ever in these tough times. They purchased the book for themselves and gave copies to friends. Helena gave interviews all over the country. In September 1930, she arrived in Boston with her secretaries and publicists in tow. Her trunks were filled with a two-year supply of clothes. She had always been incapable of travelling light and didn't see why she should. After all, she had to change outfits several times a day to impress the press.

One journalist, Grace Davidson, wrote a long article about her for the *Boston Post*. The accompanying photo showed Madame wearing a beautiful Poiret dress and several strands of black pearls around her chubby neck. When the journalist asked how large her fortune was, Helena promptly replied: 'Twenty million dollars.' She had said the first figure that came to mind. It hardly mattered whether it was true. The more she flaunted her fortune, the more people would respect her.

Helena told Davidson: 'Women have a duty to keep young. We should live adventurous lives, travel, work hard, earn money, spend it, love someone deeply, have children.'[1] She certainly practised what she preached, albeit not very successfully for the last two points. She had as little time as ever for her sons, who had grown into young men. As for love ...

Edward and she made one last reconciliation attempt in Paris some time after her book promotion tour. He came to meet her off the boat at Le Havre and was taken aback to see that she was accompanied not only by her maid but also by her new best friend, Grace Davidson. The journalist had been Helena's constant companion since the publication of her well-received *Boston Post* article. Although Helena wanted nothing so much as to get back with her husband, she had panicked just before leaving at the thought of finding herself alone with him. When Edward was around, she became incapable of the strategic thinking that was second nature to her when she was doing business. She would start out with the intention of recapturing his heart and always end up doing and saying things that had the opposite effect. So she had convinced shy young Grace to come to Europe with her, and paid her passage. Edward was too polite to say anything in front of the journalist. However, the unbroken silence he maintained for the entire duration of the drive to Paris spoke volumes.

Edward didn't want a divorce either. He was a flirt and a womaniser, and was capable of the odd cruel remark to assuage his male ego when his financial dependence on his wife became too hard to bear. Nevertheless, a part of him still nurtured dreams of a normal family life. And of course a separation from Helena would leave him near penniless, which would be even worse than having to beg his wife for the money she grudgingly gave him.

Miss Davidson dined with the Tituses at La Coupole and stayed on for a nightcap at the Select. She was with them again bright and early next morning. She wasn't entirely sure what she was meant to be doing in Paris and found these encounters 'strange' and 'tense', although she freely admitted to finding Edward thoroughly charming.[2] The only time Helena appeared to relax on the short trip was at a society evening to which the sculptor Constantin Brancusi had also been invited. Helena had just bought one of his masterpieces, *The White Negress*. They spent the better part of the evening chatting, and Brancusi's lavish compliments lifted her mood.

Madame had made Brancusi's acquaintance some time earlier.

Born in Romania in 1876, he had come to Paris at the beginning of the twentieth century to study at the École des Beaux-Arts. Helena liked his marble and bronze sculptures, which were simplified to the point of abstraction. She had already bought one of the sculptures in his *Birds in Space* series. They shared a passion for African art. 'Far better than all those tramps and *schnorrers* Edward likes to hang out with!'[3] Madame hissed afterwards to a mystified Grace.

Helena returned to Paris on her own several times after that visit. Each trip only made her feel more pessimistic about her relationship with Edward. Her despondency made her vulnerable, and she fell prey to the vicious rumours spread by the hangers-on and gossipmongers in her circle. 'Don't tell me you didn't know about your husband's latest mistress!' Polish artist Tamara de Lempicka exclaimed when Helena went to buy a painting from her. The alleged 'latest mistress' was a young woman named Anaïs Nin (later renowned as a memoirist and author), who had contacted Edward because she was looking for a publisher for the D. H. Lawrence biography she was writing. Edward had read a few pages of *An Unprofessional Study* and encouraged her to continue.

Helena had no proof they were having an affair, but once she had got the idea in her head she wouldn't let it go. Madame threatened to start divorce proceedings. Edward strenuously denied the accusation, but she refused to believe him. She didn't believe anything he said any more. She didn't want to believe him. And in addition to taking away the management of her properties in Paris and giving them to Stella's husband, she gave orders for the Jockey Club, his favourite Paris nightclub, to be razed to the ground and replaced with a block of rental flats.

Edward published Anaïs Nin's book in 1932. It would be the last book to come out of the Black Manikin Press. Helena filed for a divorce, which she obtained in 1938. She was tired of supporting Edward and subsidising his publishing ventures. She no longer wanted to live in the Boulevard Raspail apartment, even if it meant forgoing its beautiful Art Deco interior, and asked Stella and Paul to move in. Meanwhile, Madame decided to buy a property on the Ile Saint-Louis, which Misia Sert's ex-husband had put up for sale, the Hôtel de Vesselin at 24 Quai de Béthune. Helena's lawyers got to work on the lengthy process of evicting the tenants, which would drag on for nearly three years.

The Tituses were seeing hardly anything of each other by this point. 'Their marriage broke up only because of money,' Eugénie Metz, Helena's housekeeper at Quai de Béthune, told Patrick O'Higgins in the 1950s on his first trip to Paris. Metz and her husband Gaston had been working for Helena since the 1920s. As O'Higgins had only recently been appointed Madame's secretary and didn't know much about her life, Eugénie took it upon herself to fill him in on the complicated Titus–Rubinstein marriage. 'Madame will tell you otherwise,' Eugénie said to O'Higgins. 'She'll tell you he had mistresses. That's true. What else would he do? She never gave him a moment. God knows how she found the time to have two sons!'[4]

Helena took to travelling once more to shake off her despondency over the collapse of her marriage. She suffered acute appendicitis in Vienna and had to have her appendix removed, after which she underwent a hysterectomy. She spent a long time convalescing at Ceska's home in London. Halfway through 1931, the sisters received news of their father's death. Helena, who couldn't abide funerals, sent Manka to Kraków in her place. Worse was to come – one week later, her mother Gitel was dead, too. A remorse-stricken Helena fell into a deep depression and was confined to bed. In her loneliness, she became consumed with guilt and nostalgia as long-buried images came back to haunt her. She thought back to Kazimierz, Melbourne and London and wistfully recalled the good times with Edward. She berated herself for not having visited her parents more often. Overcome by sorrow, she forgot about the grievances she had nurtured against them.

Her heart and spirit were broken. It was so unlike her that everyone – her family, doctors and employees – became worried. Her doctors advised an extended convalescence in the Swiss Alps. Helena complied meekly. She knew herself and was well aware she was in need of rest. She gradually recovered her strength, and when she returned to Paris, she resumed her quarrels with Edward with renewed vigour – a sure sign that she was back on form. She went back to New York and immersed herself in work once more. She had heard good reports about a man named Harry Johnston and hired him to be her new sales director, offering him lavish pay to restructure her company.

Work had always been her panacea and she now threw herself into it more obsessively than ever to keep thoughts of Edward at bay. She undertook a full-scale renovation of the five-storey building at 52 Rue du Faubourg Saint-Honoré and decided the Grafton Street salon in London needed a makeover too. With her unerring eye for upcoming talent, she hired controversial architect Erno Goldfinger and his associate Andras Szivessy to do the job.

The result was hybrid but spectacular, with floor-to-ceiling black metal mirrors on the walls and carpets with grey stripes. Helena disliked it thoroughly. It was too modern and far too eccentric. She refused to pay Goldfinger's bill. Although they had heated arguments at the time, Goldfinger remembered her in a positive light. Despite Helena's misgivings, the salon was much admired when it reopened. It got Goldfinger noticed and enhanced Madame's reputation for outfitting her salons with avant-garde interior and exterior decoration.

In Paris the recession brought the heyday of Montparnasse to a close. Café society and the bohemian lifestyle became a thing of the past as cash-strapped American artists increasingly set sail for home.

Edward pulled down the shutters of the Rue Delambre bookshop, packed up his legendary book collection and moved to Cagnes-sur-Mer on the French Riviera, where many artists and intellectuals had settled. He continued to send his estranged wife appeals for money. Helena acquiesced or refused, depending on her mood. She could, of course, afford to satisfy all his demands, however unreasonable. It was in no small part thanks to Edward that Helena had amassed her fortune in the first place.

21

FAMILY LIFE

If Helena had hoped that either Roy or Horace would provide a shoulder to cry on after her break-up with Edward, she was in for a disappointment. She had neglected them for years and now found herself paying the price, although they must have been deeply affected by their parents' separation. Horace had always got on well with his father and often went to see him in Cagnes, while Roy distanced himself from Edward without, however, growing any closer to his mother.

Roy, the docile, self-effacing son, was ploughing his way through a degree course at the Harvard School of Business Administration after a year at Princeton and an undistinguished BA from Oxford. He had applied to these prestigious universities to please his parents, especially Helena, but would have much preferred a career in music. Like his younger brother Horace, he was a talented musician.

Ever since he was a little boy, Roy had constantly sought – and never obtained – a sign of approval from 'Mother', as the boys called her. Helena always seemed to be disappointed in him. She disapproved of nearly everything he did, and made him feel he would never measure up to her expectations. They had a tension-filled relationship. Although he longed for her appreciation, he tiptoed around her because he was terrified of her scornful remarks and sudden fits of temper.

It wasn't that she didn't love him – on the contrary. Her children meant a great deal to her, and she could be very affectionate towards them. Looking back and taking stock at the end of her life, she would regret not having spent enough time with them. Perhaps she simply wasn't capable of unconditional love. Her relationship with Edward had suffered because of her inability to put love before career, and her relationship with her sons would fare no better.

Roy had felt rejected ever since he was tiny. Helena overlooked him because he came in the way of her business at a crucial stage of her career. She would try to make it up to him as he got older by showering him with presents and money, arranging for him to live in comfortable, luxurious surroundings and giving him and Horace the finest education money could buy. He had never lacked for anything, except the most important thing of all: his mother's affection and encouragement. He had forged his identity with little help from Helena, and tried to come to terms with it even though it can't have been easy, feeling rejected by one's own mother.

Roy joined the business after coming out of university, like practically everyone else in Helena's family, but kept very much to himself. He had an unhappy personal life. He married four times and had one daughter, whom he named Helena, in 1958. After his first three marriages, he had resigned himself to being unlucky in love until he met Niuta Grodzius, a Lithuanian-born American widow with two teenage children, Louis and Suzanne. Niuta's first husband Benno Slesin and second husband Bernard Miller had both died. Niuta would become the mother Roy had never had. She would nurture and comfort him, heal his wounds and help him to get over his alcohol addiction. After their wedding he moved into Niuta's apartment on Park Avenue, bringing only two suitcases with him. 'He had no possessions,' Suzanne Slesin, Niuta's daughter, would recall many years later in *Over the Top*, her superb book on Helena Rubinstein's artistic vision. He no longer wanted to owe his mother anything.[1]

Horace, on the other hand, was rebellious and unstable. He had dropped out of Cambridge after his car accident. He wanted to be a writer or a painter, or both. 'Horace, like Edward and my own father, was the artistic one,' Helena said in her autobiography. 'Like them, he preferred books to bookkeeping.' He had also inherited his mother's stubborn temperament, and refused to bend to her will. When he was twenty, he had a short story published in a British magazine and was paid three guineas for it. Edward was proud of his nonconformist son, who was obviously a chip off the old block. Mother, however, was unimpressed. She was annoyed by her family's bookish tendencies and worried that Horace would turn out to be an impractical dreamer like Edward. She was very keen on getting him into the business alongside Roy, and insisted the boys work at the Long Island factory during their summer holidays. Roy also spent a couple of months learning the ropes at the Grafton Street salon after his first year at Oxford.

Horace would only give in to his mother's badgering when he had nothing better to do, or if he desperately needed money. He was a brilliant but destructive young man who got into trouble constantly, probably in order to get his mother to notice him: gambling debts, failed projects and car accidents. Each time she bailed him out he got into an even worse fix. He went off to Tahiti to become a painter, but came back a few months later. He then enrolled in an art school, only to drop out. In the early 1930s he married Evelyn Schmitka, a sweet, carefree girl who had grown up in Woodstock. Helena promptly nicknamed her 'the butcher's daughter' (Evelyn's father was indeed a butcher by trade). Horace had two children with Evelyn: a daughter, Toby, and a son, Barry. They divorced shortly after the birth of their son. Helena's grandchildren would only have vague memories of their grandmother, whom they saw very rarely, although she relates in her autobiography that Horace's children lived with her for a time.[2]

Deep down, Helena had always regretted not having a daughter she could pass her business on to. She had given nearly all her sisters a job but kept them at arm's length and often treated them harshly. They admired and feared their eldest sister, but their jealousy of her tainted the relationship between them. The passing of the years did nothing to improve matters. Helena had a huge fight with Manka when the latter decided to sell her shares in the company and leave because she was tired of her job as travelling representative of the Helena Rubinstein brand. Helena flew into a rage and accused Manka of ingratitude. But Manka refused to change her mind and began gradually withdrawing from the business. Madame mentally reviewed the list of her relatives, as she had always done, to find someone to replace her.

Regina, the only one of Helena's sisters to have remained in Poland, was still living in Kraków. She had four children: Jacques, Oscar, Rachel and Mala. The youngest, Mala, had been fascinated since she was a little girl by her wealthy aunt, who was a family legend. She had heard Helena's rags-to-riches story countless times throughout her childhood. When she was around twelve, Mala developed persistent acne and wrote to Helena, who sent her letters full of advice. Their correspondence continued after the young girl's acne had healed. Mala lived a carefree existence in Kraków with her parents and friends and when she was asked what she would like to be when she grew up, she would say she wanted to get married and have lots of children, or be a poet, or perhaps both. She wrote cheerful letters about school and her tennis lessons to Helena, who encouraged her to keep playing the game. On her frequent trips abroad, Helena never forgot to send a postcard to her niece. Mala dreamed of travelling to all the countries her aunt visited so often.

When Mala completed her education, Helena invited her to come to Paris. It was universally agreed that Mala Kolin was the prettiest, most stylish girl in the family. She had delicate features framed by a mass of thick dark hair. With her radiant smile and sparkling eyes, she charmed everyone she met. As if that weren't enough, she was sweet-natured, considerate and a good listener. Helena was proud of her young niece and made time for her – something she had rarely done with her sons. She took Mala to museums and art galleries, Braque's and van Dongen's studios, the Folies Bergère to applaud Josephine Baker, and the cinema to watch Raimu perform in the triumphant film adaptation of Marcel Pagnol's stage play *Marius*. She took her to dinner at the Ritz, the Café de la Paix and La Coupole on the Left Bank, where a few painters still congregated. Mala was dazzled by the style and splendour of her aunt's lifestyle, which she had so far only been able to guess at. When she returned home, Kraków seemed narrow and provincial. She began to feel bored and couldn't wait to leave. Madame had just hired Mala's two bothers: Oscar, the eldest, as head chemist at the Saint-Cloud factory, and Jacques as supervisor of the Toronto factory. She asked Mala if she would like to work for her too.

The young woman moved to Paris in the early 1930s, filled with joyful hope at the prospect of embarking on a new life close to the aunt she so admired. She certainly hadn't expected to be made to work so hard. Mala would write: 'The affectionate woman I knew as Aunt Helena in private was Madame Rubinstein in business and there was no overlap of roles.'[3] Helena immediately started training Mala, whose dreams of leading an exciting life in Paris were dashed when her aunt packed her off to Vienna and Berlin to learn about dermatology, facial treatments and massages. By the time she returned after her six-month training stint, she had acquired a firm grasp of beauty industry basics. She started out working at the Faubourg Saint-Honoré salon, moving on to jobs in the factory, the office and department store beauty counters selling Rubinstein products. Even her weekends were spent working. Madame was inflexible: Mala's priority was to learn the business inside out. 'The price of kinship was high, but the lessons I learnt were invaluable,' Mala said.[4]

Helena sent her to the most far-flung corners of France to continue her education as a Rubinstein sales representative, and passed on the advice Gitel had given her when she was a young girl: 'If you want to be smart, just listen and play dumb.' Mala took the advice. 'I'm still listening and still learning,' she later recalled.[5] Women in remote French towns and villages knew little about cosmetics – advertising hadn't yet reached the French provinces – and were sceptical of Mala's beauty advice. It was a real challenge to convince them to use Rubinstein products. Mala realised it was vital to use a personalised approach. She would listen to each woman to identify her particular needs, as Helena had taught her to do, and only then would she recommend suitable products.

Since the young woman spoke five languages fluently, Helena next sent her on a tour of Switzerland and Germany and all the European factories. Mala taught trainee beauty consultants about facial massage and muscle-kneading techniques, skincare treatment methods and the importance of healthy eating and physical exercise. Her hard work paid off when she was put in charge of running the Paris salon. She changed her name from Kolin to Rubinstein at her aunt's request.

Helena was very strict with her niece. She didn't allow her the slightest of lapses. One evening, Mala got into a lively discussion with a diplomat at a British Embassy reception. She was very good at making sparkling conversation, and the man seemed to have fallen thoroughly under her spell. Helena bore down on her niece like an assault tank and hissed into her ear: 'Act stupid!' Poor Mala found it very hard to pretend she was bird-brained.

When she left the salon after a long day's work, she liked to go swimming, play tennis, make sculptures, write poetry and read books by Colette and Virginia Woolf. She regularly accompanied her new circle of Parisian friends to museums and art galleries, or to the theatre to watch plays by Jean Giraudoux and Marcel Pagnol. She enjoyed her life in Paris; she couldn't imagine a happier existence, especially after she met and fell in love with her mother's cousin Victor. He was the son of John Silberfeld – one of Regina and Helena's three uncles in Australia, who had subsequently emigrated to Antwerp. Victor would later drop the surname Silberfeld and become known as Victor Silson.

Helena chose that moment to send her niece to the United States. Mala was heartbroken at the thought of leaving Victor and her life in Paris, but she didn't have a choice. How could she turn down her aunt? She put on a brave face and would gloss over the incident in her book, saying the move to a new continent had appealed to her sense of adventure. She arrived in New York in January 1934. Like Helena before her, she was dazzled by her first glimpse of the city, blanketed in snow like Kraków in winter. She marvelled afresh each morning at the white expanse of Central Park from her room at The Pierre. However, she didn't stay in New York for long – she had been sent to America to take over from Manka. Helena joined Mala shortly afterwards to keep her company on her first coast-to-coast tour of America.

People all over the country were working as hard as they could to get back on their feet following the stock market crash that had plunged the economy into a depression. Money was scarce and spending was rationed. Small-town women had only a sketchy idea of events in the outside world: often the radio and a few magazines were their only sources of information. Mala met a cross-section of women on her travels – farm women who had only ever used soap and water, housewives for whom skincare began and ended with cold cream, middle-class women who thought make-up was vulgar and young working girls eager to learn about new cosmetics. She had to find a way to teach all these women about beauty care in a language each one would understand. 'I felt like a rare bird watched through the binoculars of the most avid ornothologists,' Mala would recall.[6]

She quickly got used to life in America, despite her huge workload and irregular hours. Helena had meanwhile hired Victor and found him a job in the American company. Mala and Victor managed to see each other despite their hectic schedules, and even found time to get married. The honeymoon would have to wait, however: Mala set off on a demonstration tour immediately after the wedding. Although she added her husband's surname to her own, she would always be known as Mala Rubinstein.

After two interminable years of travelling around the country to learn everything there was to know about the American cosmetics market, Mala was put in charge of the New York salon. Madame's protégée had turned into as much of a perfectionist as her mentor. 'Make up your mind now and forever that where your appearance is concerned "good" isn't good enough – "better" must be your aim.'[7] The two women had become extremely close. Although Helena never made it official, the devoted Mala was the successor she had always wished for in her heart. Mala had no equal when it came to teaching women about beauty.

Madame clucked over Mala like a mother hen. 'You work too hard,' she would often tell her. 'Come to Greenwich with me and get some rest.' Mala would abandon her life, her friends and her husband on Saturday evenings to go to Connecticut with her aunt. She didn't get much rest, though – Helena would bang on her door at seven on the Sunday morning, calling: 'Mala, you're not still in bed, are you? Wake up! I've just had an idea.'

Fond though she was of Mala, Madame rarely paid her a compliment. Helena wasn't in the habit of flattering people, and she didn't make an exception even for Mala. The highest praise Mala ever earned from her aunt was the comment: 'Mala, I'm never bored when you're around.' Another time, after a demonstration, Helena went up to her and said abruptly: 'You teach me a lot, you know.' It was only towards the end of her life that Madame lowered her guard. When a journalist asked her a question during an interview two days before she died, she whispered: 'Ask Mala. She knows more about everything than I do.' Mala, who was sitting in on the interview, became worried. When she got home that evening, she told her husband she had a bad feeling. 'Something's wrong with her,' she said. 'It's the first time she's ever paid me a compliment.'[8]

22

STAY YOUNG!

Women went star crazy with the advent of the 'talkies', dyeing their hair platinum blonde like Jean Harlow, copying Marlene Dietrich's finger wave hairstyle and Greta Garbo's straight bob and adopting Katharine Hepburn's androgynous style. There were two main looks in the 1930s – all-out glamour and girl next door – and sales-focused manufacturers provided women with a plethora of beauty products to achieve these styles. However, cosmetics firms were badly hit when the Roosevelt administration introduced excise duties on luxury goods – including cosmetics – in an attempt to balance the budget. The millions of women consumers who bought beauty products were furious. The modern lipstick theory – which holds that sales of beauty products increase during an economic crisis because women who can't afford to buy a new dress transfer their desire to splurge to a new tube of lipstick – proved to be extremely plausible in recession-hit America. Gaggles of young women crowded around the beauty and make-up counters at Macy's and Saks during their lunch hour. They would grab a quick sandwich or salad, then spend the rest of their break trying out lipsticks and mascara. Their choices were often influenced by beauty etiquette tips in women's magazines, such as: 'Coloring the eyeline and beading the lashes were fun for the evening but bad tastes in daylight; acceptable for adults but not for girls under eighteen.'[1] Advertising drew heavily on newly fashionable psychobabble, using terms such as 'neurosis', 'self-esteem', 'inferiority complex' and 'subconscious' to sell the humblest of creams and tiniest tubes of rouge. A facial massage no longer merely improved skin tone – it gave 'a whole new point of view on life'.[2]

Helena was still trying to take her mind off her failed marriage, and began to ponder new strategies for her business. She was convinced of the need to invest in serious research into anti-ageing creams. There were no beauty products specifically targeted at women going through menopause, which was mentioned in hushed tones, as if it were a disease. Elizabeth Arden, who was also experimenting with anti-ageing formulas, was brave enough to be her own guinea pig. The immediate effect was to make her face break out in pimples. Madame chuckled when she heard the news. The product she herself launched was a day and night cream combo called Hormone Twin Youthifiers, which claimed to rejuvenate mature skin.

Launching a new cream in America was starting to become a far trickier affair than in the past. A federal law regulating cosmetics was in the making in response to concerns about false advertising and cosmetic safety. A coal tar-based eyelash dye had caused serious injuries, and one woman had actually gone blind after using it. Helena Rubinstein and Elizabeth Arden, who had initially paid little heed to the call for regulation, soon realised it was inevitable. Women's organisations demanding new, more stringent legislation had a powerful champion in Eleanor Roosevelt. The Food, Drug and Cosmetics Act was finally passed in 1938. Although lobbying by cosmetics manufacturers ensured that products would not be subject to pre-market approval, new labelling requirements were introduced for cosmetic products. The American Medical Association set up a commission to identify inflated advertising claims such as 'allergy free', which could no longer be used unless the manufacturer could back it up with scientific proof. Cosmetics firms were also required to list all ingredients on product labels or provide the list if a customer asked for it.

Brands such as Chanel, Yardley, Bourjois, Elizabeth Arden and Helena Rubinstein all fell foul of the new advertising law. The FDA was sceptical about the Youthifier's ability to reverse the signs of ageing. Helena's original cream, Valaze Skin Food, had to be renamed after the FDA issued a statement warning manufacturers against using names implying beauty creams had food value. 'What to do?' a discouraged Helena asked Sara Fox, a bright university graduate she had recently hired to handle marketing strategy, after the FDA statement. Sara suggested renaming the product 'Wake Up Cream'. Helena communicated her approval of Sara's brainwave with a laconic: 'Clever!'

Helena continued her whirlwind tours of all the countries in her cosmetics empire. Although she spent only brief periods of time in each of her many homes, they were all run as if she would be arriving at any minute. When she was in residence, she would have fresh flowers delivered each day, go through the housekeeping accounts with a fine-tooth comb and plan the menus for her frequent supper parties. She had a well-established reputation as a formidable hostess in Paris, London and New York, and went out of her way to create a welcoming atmosphere at her sought-after parties, which she also used as opportunities to introduce a new product. 'I used my imagination,' she said in her autobiography. 'She hovers over her hundreds of guests with all the pleasant fuss and excitement usually exhibited by any little hausfrau passing around her own gingerbread,' a *Mademoiselle* writer gushed. 'It's really rather cute when she bears down upon you with a canapé or watercress sandwiches, you can hardly help feeling flattered.'[3]

Mademoiselle was one of a long list of magazines to publish detailed descriptions of Madame's lifestyle. Women around the world never seemed to tire of reading about Helena. 'She must cross the Atlantic at least eight times a year to supervise the thousands of people she employs,' the article went on. 'She is highly conscious that a great many people depend on her for their livelihood, and therefore works ceaselessly. Some of her employees have been with her since the beginning.' The article made no reference to the failings – her harshness, the impossible demands she made, the lies she frequently told – that could make her such a tyrant to work for. The writer merely presented her as a woman who hadn't let success and money go to her head, which was quite true. Helena claimed she was far too busy to indulge in the beauty treatments her salons offered. Although she advised other women to, she never exercised or played sport herself, and hated being massaged. But she was scrupulous about her skincare routine. Before going out, she always applied her creams and foundation, and did her own make-up in natural light.

She was extremely adept at courting the press. Journalists loved being on the receiving end of what she described as her 'little gifts'. They found her abrupt manner endearing and made much of her 'victory' over Lehman Brothers. She was reliably good copy – apart from her amazing success story, they knew she could be depended on for an entertaining story or innovative product they could unveil to their readers. Madame was good friends with Janet Flanner, the Paris correspondent for *The New Yorker* who wrote a wonderful 'Letter from Paris' column for nearly half a century, but her favourite magazines were *Vogue* and *Harper's Bazaar*.

Madame's best friend in glossy magazine circles was Carmel Snow, who had started out at *Vogue*, then joined *Harper's Bazaar*. She had the latest fashion trends at her fingertips and could analyse them in a New York minute. When she arrived in the French capital for the collections, she put all the other fashion journalists in the shade. She prided herself on having made *Harper's Bazaar* a magazine for 'well-dressed women with well-dressed minds', and worked with some of the major artistic names of the time, boosting the careers of the likes of Jean Cocteau, Truman Capote, Cecil Beaton, Christian Bérard and Man Ray, as well as Cristóbal Balenciaga and Christian Dior when they were unknowns.[4] She was the first to do an outdoor swimwear shoot with a model running along a beach – until then, models wearing swimsuits were photographed in studios with artificial decor. With her talent-spotting genius, she discovered future stars in many spheres, including dance and literature.

Helena was also very close to Marie-Louise Bousquet, the Paris correspondent for *Harper's Bazaar*. Lively, quick with a biting wit, Bousquet was a permanent fixture in the Paris smart set. For several years she held a salon in her apartment overlooking the Palais Bourbon where artists, writers, actors and musicians mingled with the glitterati.

The Depression had hit middle-class women hard, but high-society life in Paris was still an endless whirl of parties. The beau monde looked up to arts patron Marie-Laure de Noailles, the trendsetting 'Baba' de Faucigny Lucigne, and Princess Natalie Paley, the second wife of fashion designer Lucien Lelong and later Cocteau's lover. The three women were inseparable friends, and could be seen at all the chicest society evenings. They were among the era's '*Vogue* women', photographed by the magazine in the striking costumes they wore to fabulous 1930s masquerade parties such as Count Étienne de Beaumont's Spring Ball, Daisy Fellowes's Oriental Ball, Nicky de Gunzburg's 'Bal des Valses' and the Alice in Wonderland Ball, which gossip columnist Elsa Maxwell and Christian Bérard attended together, dressed as Tweedledum and Tweedledee.

Madame remained one of Chanel's and Poiret's most faithful customers, and started wearing Schiaparelli as soon as the flamboyant Italian-born couturière appeared on the fashion scene. 'Schiap', as she was known, was influenced by the surrealist movement and worked closely with Christian Bérard and Salvador Dalí. Jean Cocteau designed embroidery motifs interspersed with poetic phrases for her to use on evening dresses, while Louis Aragon and Elsa Triolet designed a necklace with beads that looked like aspirins. Along with Helena, film actresses such as Katharine Hepburn, Merle Oberon, Michèle Morgan, and Simone Simon were regular customers. Herself a *jolie laide*, Schiaparelli created designs suited to women with irregular features and attitude. Helena too thought any woman could be attractive, if she made an effort. 'There are no ugly women,' she said in her autobiography, 'only lazy ones.'[5]

Madame also bought outfits from English couturier Edward Molyneux and French designer Madeleine Vionnet. She loved wearing Vionnet's beautiful dresses, conceived in three dimensions by draping fabric over a mannequin rather than sketching designs. She was introduced to the work of Balenciaga, who would become one of her firm favourites.

She was more enamoured than ever of Parisian fashions. The corset had made a comeback in the form of a stomach-flattening girdle. By the mid 1930s, skirts had dropped below the knee in accordance with the hemline theory, which states that when hemlines rise so do stock prices, while longer skirts are a sure sign of a depressed economy. Women wore calf-length suits or dresses by day and long, figure-hugging numbers, often cut low in the back, at night. Curvaceous femininity and classic styles were back in fashion; the frivolous, boyish look of the 1920s was out. In the second half of the decade, the rising number of sportswomen such as tennis champion Suzanne Lenglen and the advent in 1936 of the first paid holidays for French workers helped to lighten up these conservative fashions. Women on seaside holidays started wearing shorts and showing off their legs once more. Open-air pursuits, nudism and physical exercise were becoming popular, and fashionable women sported a healthy look and a year-round tan. As early as 1932, Helena Rubinstein (somewhat paradoxically) launched tanning lamps to stimulate melanin production. In 1936, she launched Cote d'Azur, the first water-resistant self-tanning lotion.

Women's fashions began making a feature of accessories, including fine and costume jewellery and especially headwear: toques, bonnets and cloche hats. Helena owned a huge collection. Her vast wardrobe was meticulously organised. She kept all her pre-1914 dresses, furs and low-heeled shoes – her wardrobe basics – in her New York apartment. She had hundreds of pairs of shoes made to measure for her tiny feet, and bought an equally large number of ready-made pairs for everyday use. She had more than a million dollars' worth of jewellery, which she threw pell-mell into old Bergdorf Goodman boxes that she stored in drawers, under piles of clothes and under her bed. Having observed Helena's careless attitude to her jewellery and the way she would rummage through the boxes to pull out the diamond, topaz or ruby piece she was after, Sara Fox told her it wasn't a safe way to store her jewels. Helena shrugged helplessly. Roy had bought her a safe, but she could never remember the combination. Sara Fox went out and bought Helena a filing cabinet, and neatly arranged all the jewels in the drawers in alphabetical order: D for diamonds, R for rubies and so on. Madame was delighted with Sara's system and adopted it from then on. 'This is what I call a *klug* solution,' she recalled approvingly in her autobiography. '*Klug* is a useful German word meaning clever.'[6]

23

WHO IS THE FAIREST OF THEM ALL?

Madame was furious. The large red door of Elizabeth Arden's swanky new beauty institute on Fifth Avenue and 55th Street seemed to be silently mocking her. It was like a red rag to a bull. A uniformed doorman guarded the entrance, just as at every other residential building on the Upper East Side.

Each time Helena drove past the salon, she flew into a rage. She had never been inside, of course, but a few charitable souls had given her blow-by-blow descriptions. Since the press covered Miss Arden's activities as widely as they did Madame's, the salon opening had received extensive coverage in several publications. Helena had seen photos of it in *Vogue* and *Fortune* and could recite every detail of the decor from memory: the huge painting by Georgia O'Keeffe, Arden's favourite American painter, that hung in the lobby; the exercise room's pink and green satin curtains and chairs; jade-green glass walls and crystal lights; and the furnishings on all five floors. 'Chic ... pervades the rarefied atmosphere and the pastel corners of her salon,' *Fortune* magazine wrote.[1] Helena's own salon didn't stand up well in comparison.

Madame was all the more enraged because the article pitted her against her rival and she came off worst. Arden was described as having a clientele of wealthy arbiters of taste, debutantes and heiresses. As for Helena, *Fortune* disdainfully noted that although her salons had been on the market longest, they 'have passed their days of chic, [though] the Rubinstein business is still most probably the biggest of its kind'.[2]

Life made things worse by stating: 'In the high-price field, Arden is Rubinstein's great competitor.'[3] The two women detested each other, though they were fated to live at close quarters. They attended the same gala evenings and previews and dined at the same restaurants. They launched similar products made with the same ingredients within days of each other, were friends with the same beauty editors and haughtily looked past each other when their paths crossed, though each would steal glances at the other out of the corner of her eye.

As *Fortune* had pointed out, however, Arden had a more 'chic' image, which she cultivated carefully. Her products were famed for their sophisticated packaging. Her precious horses – 'my little darlings', she called them – contributed to the making of one of her top-selling products, the miraculous Eight Hour Cream, which she had initially created to soothe her thoroughbreds' strained joints. In 1934 she opened a beauty spa she named Maine Chance after her favourite horse, where she taught women who could afford the steep admission fee about diet and fitness.

Madame had noticed that women tended to buy Rubinstein products for their own use and Arden products as gifts. She wasn't sure whether this was cause for concern or rejoicing. She chose to be upbeat about it. After all, her profits were certainly larger. Unlike Arden, she didn't waste money on expensive packaging. 'With her packaging and my product, we could have ruled the world,' she later said.[4]

Their rivalry was common knowledge and press descriptions of it were occasionally in dubious taste. Some of the *Fortune* writer's comments were questionable to say the least. He called Helena 'buxom' and 'swarthy', and sneeringly said she was 'addicted to smartly exotic dress'. Edward was dismissively referred to as 'a husband' who 'sells books in a stall by the Seine'.[5] The writer's comments were emblematic of the anti-Semitism that continued to lurk under the polished veneer of New York high society.

Madame shrugged off the slurs. It was the red door that really got to her, even though she knew the beauty salon concept had had its day. Salons were now reserved for the elite few. Most of her customers were middle-class women who preferred to buy beauty products at retail stores. Beauty salons throughout America were losing money. But she needed a prestigious address to keep her brand image intact, and she owed it to herself to outdo the woman she referred to as 'the other one'.[6]

Helena had to do something to top Elizabeth Arden. So she too bought a building on Fifth Avenue, at number 715. She put architect Harold Sterner in charge of designing the facade and had him engrave her name on it in lower case in the style of Edward's friend e. e. cummings, who wrote many of his poems completely in lower case. It was a tribute of sorts to her husband.

The new salon allowed her to stage a triumphal comeback to the American beauty scene. Decorated by Ladislas Medgyes and Martine Kane, the salon was primarily a formidable publicity machine. But it was also a triumph of modern architecture and interior design. Spread over four floors, it surpassed all her other salons for sheer splendour and refinement. Paintings by Giorgio de Chirico, sketches by Modigliani and murals by Petar Pallavicini adorned walls sheathed in metallic blue wallpaper. Pieces by Nadelman and young American sculptor Malvina Hoffman sat atop furniture by Jean-Michel Frank and carpets designed by Miró. Madame displayed some of her finest African pieces in the window of her salon. Elsewhere, customers could admire her collection of dolls' houses, a sequin-covered portrait of her by Pavel Tchelitchew and another portrait by Marie Laurencin, which drew rave reviews from art critics. The second-floor library had a collection of rare books about beauty, and the corporate offices were located on the top floor. It was the most opulent and masterfully executed of Helena's salons – the most American one too, with works by popular New York artists. The word 'swanky' inevitably cropped up when the salon was mentioned in the press.

Best of all, it was the perfect setting in which to launch Helena's new 'Day of Beauty' concept. 'Come for a Day of Beauty', the advertisements read. 'Slimming ... low calorie lunches ... massage ... relaxing facials.'[7] Women arrived at eight in the morning and were given a complete makeover by a small army of well-being specialists: physicians, physical therapists, masseurs, dieticians, hairdressers, make-up artists, beauticians and manicurists. By the end of the day, even the plainest of women left the salon looking and feeling fantastic.

The experience began with a full consultation – height, weight, medical history, eating habits and existing beauty routine – so as to draw up a personalised programme for the customer's Day of Beauty. The treatments included facial gymnastics under the supervision of a Viennese specialist, followed by a facial massage; a milk or herbal bath; a body polish and massage with Helena's new Body Firming Lotion; an electrotonic treatment including the use of warm paraffin wax to improve circulation and reduce cellulite; a shower with firming oil; and the use of tanning lamps to give the skin a sun-kissed look. And then, of course, there was the famous San O Thermo table – Madame's pièce de résistance – to melt away excess fat and rejuvenate the skin cells.

After a low-calorie lunch of vegetables, grilled fish and fresh fruit, the customer would be back on the beauty trail in the afternoon with facial treatments, a scalp massage, a haircut in the latest Paris style and a manicure and pedicure in the boudoir treatment room decorated with marble bas-reliefs by Malvina Hoffman. The last step was a make-up lesson in a room with simulated natural light.

The pampering came at a price – from $35 to $150. But customers went away fully satisfied they had been given their money's worth. Some would angle for a little extra something. Leaning closer to the elegant hostess accompanying them to the cash register with their purchases, they would whisper: 'I've heard Madame Rubinstein has a cream made up exclusively for her own use.' The young woman would nod gravely and reply: 'It's quite true. But Madame Rubinstein doesn't want to sell it because it's very expensive to make. She would feel uncomfortable selling a cream at such an exorbitant price.' The customer would immediately say: 'I don't mind! I'd be happy to pay whatever it costs. I've been told it's a wonderful product.'

'Well, if you're sure,' the hostess would reply. And she would slip the cream into the delighted customer's bag for an extra $50.

No sooner had the new salon become a paying proposition, thanks to lavish advertising, than rivals besides Arden began to emerge on the beauty market, each determined to rake in their share of the profits. One such competitor was Charles Revson, the founder of Revlon, whose insatiable appetite for power was outweighed only by his boorishness. Madame treated him with withering scorn, calling him 'that nail man'.

Revson's story was similar to that of the thousands of European and Jewish immigrants who built America. He was born in Montreal in 1906, although he would always claim Boston as his birthplace because he thought it sounded classier. He was raised in Manchester, New Hampshire, where his family – of Russian, Lithuanian, Austro-Hungarian and German Jewish descent – had moved a short time after his birth. His working-class parents struggled to bring up their three sons. His mother died young, and his uncles and aunts took over the task of raising the boys. Charles Revson started working as soon as he left secondary school. He got a job as a clothes salesman and then began working his way up the career ladder at a small cosmetics firm. He quit the job when he was refused a promotion, and decided to strike out on his own. He teamed up with his brother and a chemist named Charles Lachman to start a small beauty business in New York with a mere $300 in capital. He came onto the market with much fanfare, launching a range of long-lasting nail polishes that proved extremely popular with customers.

Diana Vreeland had unwittingly provided him with the nail polish formula.[8] The future editor of *Vogue* had been invited to Flame d'Erlanger's house in Venice along with socialites and artists such as Christian Bérard, who was there with a manicurist friend. The friend, known simply as Perrera, was mad about beautiful female hands like other men are foot fetishists, and had turned his passion into a trade. He used a gold manicure set Queen Ena of Spain had given him, and polish that dried instantly to make nails as strong and hard as stone. Christian Bérard liked nothing better than to sit and watch Perrera lacquering women's nails, like an artist wielding his brush over a painting.

Perrera gave two bottles of his magic lacquer to Diana Vreeland, who took them back to New York with her. When the polish ran out, Vreeland was so downcast that her young manicurist offered to have her boyfriend study its composition and copy it for her. Only too happy to take the manicurist up on the offer, Vreeland idly enquired what the boyfriend's name was. 'Charles Revson,' the young woman replied innocently.

Revson had already created a wide palette of colours, but his polishes took a long time to dry and started flaking too soon. He copied Perrera's miracle polish and went on to become 'the nail polish king'.[9] His first advertisement appeared in *The New Yorker* in 1935 and featured a young New York socialite wearing bright red Revlon polish on her perfectly manicured nails. The cost of the ad used up Revson's entire advertising budget for the year, but he knew it would be a sure-fire crowd puller.

Meanwhile, Max Factor and Germaine Monteil were becoming

established beauty brands. But sure of their superiority, Elizabeth Arden and Helena Rubinstein feared none of these newcomers. They were too busy pulling dirty tricks on each other to think about forging a common front against the enemy. However, the new entrants into the cosmetics fray were all extremely ambitious. The make-up war was shaping up to be cut-throat.

After Helena Rubinstein had opened her extravagant new salon, Elizabeth Arden counter-attacked by offering Madame's general manager Harry Johnston a colossal sum of money to change sides. Not content with leaving Madame's employ, the traitor took eleven members of her staff with him.

'What to do?' Helena wondered yet again. The latest assault had taken her unawares, and she was getting tired of the constant vigilance required to stay at the top. Her rival's attacks always undermined her and she found herself incapable of summoning the energy to retaliate. Fearing she would sink into depression once again, her doctors recommended a stay at the Bircher-Benner Clinic in Zurich. Unlike the run-of-the-mill sanatoriums, this one was reputed for Dr Bircher-Benner's pioneering theories on diet. He invented health food and was ahead of his time in making sure his patients ate only chemical- and pesticide-free organic produce. 'I saw hundreds of men and women who had been sent there by their own doctors eating raw fruits and vegetables, nuts and whole cereals under the watchful direction of Dr Bircher-Benner,' Helena would recall.[10]

For Helena, he prescribed a diet of 'living matter': muesli, raw fruits and vegetables, as well as plenty of rest. In the space of two months she lost ten pounds and recovered her strength – so much so that when she returned to New York, everyone admired her svelte figure and healthy complexion. All her friends exclaimed over how much younger she looked and begged her to let them in on her secret.

Most importantly, Madame was feeling revitalised and ready to go back into battle. She had the Swiss nutritionist's diet printed on the menu of the restaurant in her Fifth Avenue salon. But she had no experience of the restaurant business. Although she had a steady stream of customers, she had priced her menus too low to recoup the vast sums she had invested. She was forced to close the place down. Still, it wasn't a complete loss. Fresh from her Bircher-Benner experience, she published *Food for Beauty*, a diet book in which she provided recipes for low-fat dishes and sauces and low-calorie menus comprising raw vegetables, pulses, sprouted seeds and cereals. 'Now I have answered the question that at once comes to mind when you hear that a woman in my field writes a book on food and diet. The food you eat determines how great will be your beauty.'[11] Her substantial earnings from sales of the book made up to some extent for her restaurant loss.

She herself had soon lapsed back into eating her favourite foods – salmon, bagels and cream cheese, and chicken wings – and put on all the weight she had lost. She was too impatient, too highly strung and too fond of eating to follow the good advice she gave so freely to other people.

Helena was working tirelessly on several fronts. Now that the renovation of the 52 Rue du Faubourg Saint-Honoré salon in Paris was complete, she was free to turn her attention to the Quai de Béthune house, empty at long last of all its tenants. When neighbouring residents and the press protested against her plans to demolish the five-storey building constructed in 1641 by the Sun King's chief architect Louis Le Vau, she justified her decision by saying the foundations had been undermined by repeated flooding of the Seine. She knocked down everything, except for the wooden entrance with its beautiful sculptures by Étienne Le Hongre. 'I bought it for a song, but it cost me a whole opera to fix up,' she would say later.[12] She spent several years and a substantial chunk of the money she had received from Lehman Brothers on the renovation.

Misia Sert introduced Helena to French architect Louis Süe, who had redesigned Poiret's townhouse, originally the property of the aristocratic D'Aguesseau family. Madame gave Süe carte blanche. In a departure from the traditional layout of Paris townhouses, the architect placed Helena's apartments on the top floor. Her living space extended over the three main parts of the building, two of which were connected by an enclosed glass bridge. In the huge stairwell, one of Brancusi's bronze *Bird in Space* sculptures stood in front of a window giving on to the Church of Saint-Louis-en-l'Ile. It was the first modern building in an area of Paris where classical architecture still holds sway. Although it was – and remains – controversial, its style is sympathetic to the historical facades of the neighbouring buildings.

The rooftop terrace was filled with a profusion of flowers and evergreens and could comfortably host up to 300 people. Madame never tired of looking out over the Eiffel Tower, the dome of the Sacré Cœur Basilica and the spires of Notre Dame Cathedral. 'My terrace is one of the loveliest spots in the world,' she often said.[13] She certainly owned one of the most fabulous properties in the French capital. She had asked Süe and Louis Marcoussis to find and buy the furniture, but she supervised all the decorating work.

No two rooms were alike in this opulent chaos, and passing from one to another was like taking an accelerated tour of the world's art and furniture styles. It was undoubtedly excessive ('too much', to use Helena's favourite expression, which summed her up quite well, too) but the overall effect managed to be harmonious. Classical Greek sculptures abounded in the Napoleon III gallery, which also had a painting by Roger de la Fresnaye and a portrait of Helena by Christian Bérard. This was one of Helena's favourite paintings. It showed her wearing a simple white smock dress with a shawl thrown over her shoulders, cradling baby Horace in her arms. Bérard had captured a mother's love for her child in his touching portrait, which was a far cry from the subject's public image. Helena's collection of portraits of herself also included works by Raoul Dufy, Baron Kurt Ferdinand von Pantz and Edward Lintott.

The rooms flowed into each other to create the impression of one vast space. The large, circular drawing room with marble Doric columns along the walls, Louis XVI chairs and Regency-style tables and panoramic views of the Seine was truly spectacular. The dominant colour scheme was emerald green, and Louis Marcoussis had painted enormous murals in hues evocative of Picasso and Miró's tapestry designs.

The entrance, library and drawing room were filled with masterpieces of African and Oceanic art. In the dining room furnished with Biedermeier furniture, the walls were covered with hand-block-printed wallpaper from Lyon and hung with Picassos and Modiglianis. The Charles X furniture in Helena's bedroom, by far her favourite room, had originally belonged to the French princess Mathilde Bonaparte. Misia had sold Helena the bed and the armchairs, which were upholstered in gold satin and encrusted with mother-of-pearl. 'Of all my apartments, this one is my favourite,' she once said. 'I have worked on its decoration and I'm constantly making improvements and alterations.'[14]

Louis Süe won a coveted architecture award in 1937 for the building's technical innovations, such as the indoor lift and ceiling heating system, despite sardonic comments in the press about 'Madame Rubinstein's charming fifty-room pied-à-terre, which Mr Süe has filled with gold bathtubs, platinum telephones and innumerable Picassos of every period and size'.[15] The description wasn't that far off the mark: there were no gold bathtubs, but Helena had certainly not scrimped on the decor.

When the apartment was ready, Helena commissioned photographer Dora Maar, Pablo Picasso's muse and mistress, to do a series of photographs of the rooms and five portraits of herself. Madame spent years decorating the Quai de Béthune house, frequently changing things around and making improvements; her passion for collecting knew no limits.

Everyone who was anyone in Paris could be spotted in Madame's rooftop garden on summer evenings. In 1938, she set up a modern art prize. Cubist sculptor Henri Laurens won the prize the first year. Helena solemnly handed him a cheque for 25,000 francs – around €13,500 in today's money. A photograph of the event shows the jury, made up of Henri Matisse, Georges Braque, Fernand Léger, Louis Marcoussis, Paul Éluard and Jean Cassou, posing alongside Helena. The outbreak of the Second World War put paid to the ceremony the following year. But in those halcyon pre-war days, the rooftop terrace would host many of the glittering society parties Madame loved to throw.

24

PRINCESS GOURIELLI

Madame had reluctantly got accustomed to being single again. She resorted to her usual ploys to overcome her loneliness: burying herself in work more assiduously than ever, travelling and indulging her passion for bridge. When in Paris she went to bridge parties at the home of Countess Marie-Blanche de Polignac. Unlike her withdrawn mother, fashion designer Jeanne Lanvin, the countess was a keen socialite. She frequently hosted games at her Rue Barbey-de-Jouy residence in the 7th arrondissement, where celebrity guests mingled with Russian aristocrats who had emigrated to France after the October Revolution and now earned their living giving the Parisian elite bridge lessons.

One evening in 1935, Helena found herself sitting across the table from a big, handsome man in his forties whose high cheekbones and narrow eyes betrayed his Slavic ancestry. Prince Artchil Gourielli-Tchkonia was a warm, humorous and easy-going bon vivant. She had an excellent time in his company. Although he played to win, as she did, he kept up a stream of amusing patter that made her laugh all through their game. She couldn't remember the last time she had had such an enjoyable evening. She smiled even when he teased her about being a sore loser because she had got worked up about losing a few francs.

Was he a genuine aristocrat? Who could tell? There were any number of Russian émigrés claiming noble lineage in the French capital – almost as many as their taxi driver compatriots. The prince was a Francophile, having spent most of his childhood in France. He had then joined the military academy in Moscow, and fought in Riga during the revolution. His father was a well-known literary critic, and the Gourielli family could trace its history back to the thirteenth century. Helena was certainly impressed by his title, genuine or not. She was in no hurry to marry again, but if she did she wouldn't mind becoming a princess into the bargain.

'What do I need a husband for?' she replied gaily when her friends asked her why she didn't marry again (she was officially separated, but not divorced from Edward). She said nothing about her increasingly tender feelings for the prince. 'Oh, a husband always comes in handy, darling – to call you a taxi, if nothing else,' replied one of her group of close friends, who were always pressing Helena to start over with a new man.

Helena arranged to play bridge very often over the next few weeks. By some strange coincidence, she always had the prince as her partner. Then she organised a game at Quai de Béthune and invited Artchil along.

She gave him the grand tour of the apartment, showing him her art collections and antique furniture. She couldn't tell whether he was impressed or put off by the ostentatious display. His upbringing had taught him restraint, and his face was imperturbable. Helena led him to the terrace to admire the view of Paris. The moon shone placidly in the clear night sky, enveloping them in its kindly beam. She felt comfortable with this man. So what if he was twenty-three years younger than her? He was so much more reassuring than Edward, and far more entertaining. Artchil's ready laugh and incomparable sense of humour relaxed her. She didn't have to pretend to be cultured or rack her brains for an intelligent subject of conversation. Everything seemed to go so naturally and easily when they were together. He had a positive outlook on life and a bon vivant's appealing conviction that each new day is a fresh opportunity for enjoyment. Helena desperately needed such lightness in her life. She was far too burdened with obligations and responsibilities.

As one of their evenings together drew to a close, Artchil suddenly departed from his usual light-hearted banter. 'Helena, would you do me the honour of having dinner with me tomorrow evening?' he asked her solemnly.

'Tomorrow evening?' she echoed, dismayed. 'I can't – I'm leaving for New York!'

Artchil took her hand and held it gently in his. She felt no insistence in his grasp, just undemanding affection and friendship. She was grateful he wasn't coming on too strong. But the touch of his hand felt so warm and comforting. Perhaps she did need a husband after all – a man who would make her feel like a woman once again, even though she was getting on in years.

'What's your favourite restaurant in New York?' Artchil asked.

'The Colony,' she replied. The restaurant was the watering hole of the rich and famous, the place to see and be seen in the Big Apple. Helena was a regular and had her own table.

'Fine,' he said. 'Let's make a reservation for the next time I'm in New York.' There was a little smile playing on his lips, and Helena wondered fleetingly if he was making fun of her. But his face grew serious again as soon as he read the anxiety on hers. She was more than sixty years old, but her eyes were those of a little girl seeking reassurance. When they said goodbye, he brushed his fingers across her lips. She couldn't help trembling, even as she told herself not to be a silly fool.

She was swept up in the whirl of business and social life as soon as she arrived in New York but that didn't stop her heart beating faster when her secretary rang her one morning to say she had a prince on the line, and did Helena want to take the call?

'Helena?' said the familiar tones when she picked up the phone. 'It's

Artchil. You haven't forgotten our date, I hope? I'm in New York. I've booked us a table for tonight at the Colony.'

When he asked for her hand in marriage he did it by the book, the old-fashioned way, but Helena hedged, wanting to think his proposal over. She asked Artchil if he could prove he was of noble descent. He produced a copy of the *Almanach du Gotha*, the directory of European nobility, and showed her the page featuring the genealogy of his family. Helena was reassured. Impoverished though he might be, Artchil was a true aristocrat. And anyway it didn't matter if he had no money – she had more than enough for both of them.

They saw a lot of each other over the next three years, going out together, playing bridge and holidaying. Helena had plenty of time to observe Artchil at close quarters, and he never came up short. He was the ideal companion for a rich, successful woman like her. He knew everyone – the wealthy, the powerful, the titled, Hollywood stars – and was greeted warmly everywhere he went. Their combined address books read like a *Who's Who* of the time.

Helena's divorce from Edward Titus had been granted in February 1938, and she and Artchil were married in Baltimore in June 1938, three years after their first meeting. They held a fabulous wedding reception at Quai de Béthune on Bastille Day with the cream of Paris in attendance.

Helena was so thrilled to be married to a prince that she insisted on being called Princess Gourielli-Tchkonia. The title gave her a heady feeling; it added a touch of frivolity to her work-focused lifestyle, and impressed everyone she knew in Paris and New York. Best of all, it got right up snobbish Elizabeth Arden's nose. Helena crowed with delight.

Artchil was forty-three to Helena's sixty-six, but she had as much energy as any forty-year-old. Their relationship was based on mutual friendship and esteem, and they would turn out to be a happy couple. 'He was a simple man with the appetites, the manners, the rough humour of a peasant smiled upon by fortune,' Patrick O'Higgins wrote in his biography of Helena.[1]

The couple agreed from the outset that they would sleep in separate bedrooms. If Artchil had any extramarital affairs he was certainly very discreet about them, out of respect for his wife. 'My wife is a very rich, very clever Jewish hausfrau,' he would say proudly. In the course of her dinner parties she would often reprimand him affectionately but firmly: 'Artchie, don't drink too much! Oh, Artchie, don't say silly things!'

The Rubinstein family took the new arrival to their hearts. 'It was always so much more fun when he came along to a family meeting,' recalls Diane Moss, Oscar Kolin's daughter and Madame's great-niece.[2] 'He was so handsome with his silver hair and black cigarette holder. He wore a signet ring with his coat of arms engraved on it.'

Artchil was one of the rare points the family agreed on. The Rubinsteins were usually at loggerheads with each other. Horace couldn't stand his brother Roy and his cousin Oscar Kolin, Mala's brother. Roy didn't get on with his father, Edward. Helena doted on Oscar and Mala and played her sons off against her nephew within the business. She had little common ground with her sisters. Contrary to all expectations, Roy and Horace fell under Artchil's spell and approved of him marrying their mother, because her happiness had softened the rough edges of her character.

The newlyweds embarked on a round-the-world cruise. They were accompanied by Sara Fox, the Rubinstein press and publicity manager, as Madame didn't want to pass up any PR opportunities. She was particularly keen to take her new husband to Australia. She showed him around the Melbourne and Sydney salons and took him to some of her favourite haunts. But she kept quiet about the early Elizabeth Street days and her years of suffering in Coleraine.

Smith's Weekly published an in-depth profile of the couple titled 'The Prince and the Not-So-Pauperess'. Two writers had been specially commissioned to do the interview. 'When we went to visit them in their hotel suite,' the journalists wrote, 'they talked to us, not in a boudoir, but in a room filled with the clattering of a typewriter, the fluttering and scurrying of a secretary and a publicity man and the coming and going of telegraph messengers – the temporary workshop of the Big Business Woman.'[3]

Australians made much of their heroine and lauded Madame's financial success. She had started out with a simple cream costing a few pence and now headed an empire with a 3,000-strong, mainly female international workforce and annual sales of $2 million.

'I'm not interested in money,' she claimed. It wasn't the least of her paradoxes, the journalists noted. Helena Rubinstein Inc. made hundreds of products, but Madame herself used 'for the most part only one cream'. She described Artchil, whom the journalists found to be 'shy', as a 'man so particular about his appearance' he even used some of her products. 'Plenty of other men use it. Some use lipsticks and powder,' she explained. Artchil hastened to add that he only used her moisturising creams.

He was as laid-back as his wife was restless, and would have liked her to stop working. Artchil believed in taking life one day at a time and devoting himself to the pursuit of pleasure. He liked Australia, and suggested they buy a property there and raise horses. Helena refused outright. Her work took up all her time. 'I have worked 300 years and I'm fit for another 300 years,' she once said.[4]

Madame returned from her honeymoon a contented woman. When her employees bumped into her in the corridors of the New York office, she made none of her usual sarcastic quips about their outfit, posture, make-up or hairstyle. She didn't fly into rages any more. She smiled all the time. How had Artchil wrought such a change in her?

Her new-found tranquillity was not merely the Prince's doing, however. She was quietly plotting revenge. Elizabeth Arden had stolen Helena's manager along with eleven of her employees the previous year. After much thought, Madame had finally hit on a way to get her own back. In 1934 Elizabeth Arden had divorced her husband Tommy Lewis and fired him from his post as general manager of the company. She had written a clause into the divorce settlement preventing him from working in the cosmetics business for five years. Now the five years were up, Lewis no longer had any obligations towards his ex-wife. Madame, who had been waiting for this moment, hired him at an enormous salary of $50,000 – more than $800,000 in today's money. Arden's fury was worth every penny. The pill was all the more bitter to swallow because she had meanwhile fired Madame's former manager Harry Johnston for his less-than-satisfactory performance.

Four years later, she would cock a snook at Madame by netting a prince of her own – a Russian one. But Helena couldn't care less. Her business was flourishing. The chemists at her Viennese laboratory had come up with the world's first waterproof mascara and she had launched it at the 1939 New York World's Fair, where it was worn by swimmers performing a water ballet at the Aquacade. The mascara was put on the market the next year, and would go on to become one of the brand's bestselling products.

Oddly enough, Helena and Edward had remarried within weeks of each other. Edward had fallen in love with Erica de Meuronurech, a twenty-year-old Swiss girl forty-eight years his junior, who he had met at his friend Jacob Epstein's house in London. Erica was a ravishing blonde with blue eyes the colour of Delft china, and heiress to a Bernese banking family to boot. She had just arrived in the British capital to start university. Her parents had allowed her to go to London on her own on condition she stayed with the Swiss consul and his wife, who were to act as her chaperones.

On her second day in London, the diplomat took Erica along to Jacob Epstein's instead of his wife, who was feeling poorly. The painter had some illustrious guests that day, notably Winston Churchill, whose portrait he was painting and who arrived very late, after all the other guests were already at table.[5] Erica had been seated between Edward and Horace Titus. Horace, now twenty-six, was also divorced, with two young children. It might have been more appropriate for Erica to fall for him. But she had eyes and ears only for Edward, whose conversation and sheer erudition swept her off her feet. It was love at first sight for both of them.

Edward travelled to Berne to see the de Meuronurech family. According to Erica, her parents didn't make a fuss over their daughter's desire to marry a man old enough to be her grandfather. 'Edward Titus was a gentleman and he made an excellent impression on them,' she says.[6]

The de Meuronurechs must have helped the couple financially. Erica went to live with Edward in Cagnes-sur-Mer in the south of France. She got on well with his sons – who were both older than her – especially Horace, who was closer to his father than Roy. Edward and Erica didn't go on to have any children, probably because Edward thought he was too old to embark afresh on the adventure of fatherhood.

Two years before his death in 1951, nonconformist as ever, he persuaded Erica to get a divorce from him and marry George Friedman, a good friend of theirs who was closer to her own age. He must have wanted to ensure she would be taken care of. Erica would have a child late in life: an only daughter, Barbara, who was born in the mid 1950s.

In between socialising, travelling and working flat out, Helena managed to find the time to buy a superb apartment in New York at 895 Park Avenue, a short distance from her beauty salon. She hired designer Donald Deskey, who was a favourite with New York's beautiful people, to do the interiors. He used pared-down aesthetics and a predominance of yellow, green and white. Draperies of heavy cellophane covered the walls and windows of the second-floor drawing room to create a shimmering effect. Helena's Nadelman bronzes and École de Paris paintings fitted perfectly into this setting. However, she soon tired of Deskey's radically simplified style and asked Louis Süe to add a few flamboyant touches. The apartment took on a baroque feel better suited to her taste. Süe livened up Jean-Michel Frank's minimalist furniture with pink drapes, Venetian mirrors and African statues.

Helena had a private suite put in for Artchil. The prince rarely awoke before noon, and he would spend the afternoon organising bridge games and gourmet dinners. Helena generally worked late and preferred to spend the evening at home if she didn't have any social obligations. 'Doesn't it bother you that he goes out on his own?' a friend asked her once. 'Not at all!' she replied. 'Being with Artchil gives me all the benefits of marriage. He loves socialising, but he understands perfectly well that I don't always want to. And he tells me all the latest gossip when he comes home.'

She also said her husband was a great help with the business and gave her valuable advice, though she didn't always take it. His greatest quality, as far as she was concerned, was that he made her relax. If he noticed she was looking tired, he would casually mention an art dealer with an interesting collection of china or antiques he had heard about, or tell her about a promising young artist he had met. She could never resist going to see the dealer or artist for herself with Artchil.

These cherished moments out of her busy schedule strengthened their relationship.

They set about planning an enjoyable life together, deciding to spend six months of the year in New York and Greenwich and the other half in Paris, at the Quai de Béthune apartment and the mill Helena had bought and renovated a few years previously in Combs-la-Ville. Helena was still working far too much for Artchil's liking; he was all for a life of leisure and good living.

They were in Paris when Germany invaded Poland on 1 September 1939. On 3 September, France declared war on Germany. The French had spent the summer in a state of mounting tension, awaiting the German offensive with a mixture of anxiety and disbelief. They kept telling themselves the Germans wouldn't dare attack the French army – wasn't it the best in the world?

All the buses and taxis were requisitioned to carry troops to the front as soon as war was declared. The streets of Paris thronged with soldiers called up to fight, some sporting the uniforms they had worn in the last war.

Helena and Artchil left Paris at the last minute, in May 1940, when the Germans were at the gates of Paris after having successfully broken through the French lines. They booked two one-way tickets to New York on the USS *Manhattan*. Helena had refused to envisage the possibility of France and Germany going to war for the second time in her life and having to flee yet again. She had doggedly continued to believe it wouldn't happen, and only made up her mind to leave when it became obvious she had no other choice.

But she had prepared a back-up plan anyway. Over the past few years, an increasingly anxious Helena had observed Hitler's rise to power in Germany, the introduction of anti-Jewish laws and Kristallnacht: the night in November 1938 when Jewish homes, synagogues and businesses were looted and burned. Even before the Germans had invaded Poland, she had made sure her family were safe in Argentina, London and New York, although, sadly, some of them had refused to leave Kraków. She also had a lot of her artworks shipped to America, though the bulk of her collections were still in France.

The Gouriellis left behind the Quai de Béthune apartment, the Combs-la-Ville mill and Helena's other Paris properties, which she had asked her lawyers to move into to ensure they wouldn't be occupied. The Gestapo did requisition Quai de Béthune. Helena had rented it to Countess Johanna de Knecht, but the young woman, who had gone to New York with some friends, couldn't get passage back to Paris after war broke out. She met Charles Revson a short time later and fell in love with him. They were married within the year. Understandably enough, Madame didn't renew the lease.[7]

25

WATCHING THE WAR FROM
NEW YORK

Madame's days were filled with work and yet more work, and most of her evenings with engagements – a cocktail party, private view, society dinner or charity gala to raise funds for people in war-torn Europe and soldiers on the front line. She would supervise, scold and bully her employees, give press interviews and pose for photographs at home. *Life* magazine had just published a seven-page profile of her.

The news from Europe, and especially Poland, threw Helena into despair. Hertzel and Gitel Rubinstein had had the good fortune to die before Hitler's invasion of their country. Many of the other members of the Rubinstein and Silberfeld families had emigrated to Australia or the United States. Yet, week after week, Madame received letters from relatives, friends and acquaintances caught up in the upheaval in Poland and elsewhere in Europe, begging her to help them to get out.

Her younger sister Regina was still living in Kraków with her husband Mozsejz Kolin. It had been a long time since Helena had seen her, but they had always kept in touch by letter, and Mala often gave her aunt news from home. Helena knew she still had a few relatives in the old country. She didn't know all of them. Some had been young children when she'd left, and others hadn't even been born then. But her family was sacred to her, and she grew increasingly anxious as the news from Poland slowed to a trickle. She had long discussions with Mala, who couldn't sleep because she was worried sick about her parents.

At least Mala's older brother Henry was safe in Toronto with his family. Her other brother Oscar was still in France. After being taken prisoner by the Germans in Dunkirk, he had escaped, joined the French Resistance and gone into hiding. His wife, Berthe, and two daughters, Jacqueline and Diane, had fled to the south of France, where they found a passage to New York. Helena helped them to find an apartment, just as she helped any Polish Jew who managed to overcome the difficulty of obtaining a visa and made it to New York to find a job and a place to live.

The German army had occupied Kraków in the first week of September 1939. The persecution of Jewish people began almost immediately, and worsened after the Germans turned the city into the capital of the General Government of Poland. In May 1940, most of Kraków's 60,000 Jews were driven out into the surrounding villages. The following year, the Nazis herded the 20,000-odd Jews still living within the town into a cramped ghetto with barbed-wire fences and high stone walls in the suburb of Podgorze, Edward Titus's birthplace. They were forced to work in Nazi factories inside the ghetto and building sites elsewhere in Kraków.

In December 1940, Helena decided to take her mind off the war by going on a cruise with Artchil and Sara Fox to Central and South America, where she set off on one of her habitual art- buying sprees. In Mexico, Diego Rivera and Frida Kahlo got her interested in the country's folk art. She became friends with the couple and bought some of their paintings. She also started a collection of children's portraits. She became so enamoured of Mexico and Mexican painters that from then on she would rearrange her schedule to include a trip back there at least once a year.

From Mexico, they travelled to Argentina, where she purchased an entire building in Buenos Aires and opened a salon there a month later, then on to Brazil where she did exactly the same thing in Rio de Janeiro. In Argentina she bought jewellery, precious objets d'art and dozens of the silver gourds that gauchos drank from. When she returned to New York, she had the gourds copied, sold them in her salons and gave the money to the Polish Red Cross, one of many charities she supported.

She used the opening of the House of Gourielli, her ground-breaking boutique selling products for men, to stage a two-week exhibition of American and Mexican paintings for the benefit of China's war effort, and held a reception to honour Madame Chiang Kai-shek.

In the spring of 1942, she transformed the entire second floor of the Fifth Avenue salon into an art gallery, the Helena Rubinstein New Art Centre, with proceeds going to the Red Cross. For the 25-cent admission fee, visitors could admire a historic survey of modernist paintings and sculpture, some owned by Madame and many on loan from Peggy Guggenheim's gallery. 'Of course, holding an art show for charity within the salon space had the added advantage of luring potential customers into the establishment,' one modern-day observer points out.[1] No opportunity for promotion was ever missed.

Erica and Edward Titus arrived in New York in July 1940, not long after Helena and Artchil's return from Paris. Edward immediately took up with the many European intellectuals and artists who had booked passage to America when war broke out.

Ships carrying refugees continued to cross the Atlantic. On 3 March 1942, the Artists in Exile exhibition displayed works by fourteen artists, among them Breton, Chagall, Ernst, Léger, Mondrian, Zadkine, André Masson, Matta Echaurren, Yves Tanguy and Amédée Ozenfant. Marcel Duchamp joined his friends in New York later that year, and in October Peggy Guggenheim showcased his work at the inaugural exhibition of her new gallery on the top floor of a 57th Street building.

Admission proceeds went to the American Red Cross. The Gourielli-Tchkonias may well have run into the Tituses at the event, but Helena and Edward would have had little to say to each other by this time.

Madame had just made the acquaintance of Salvador Dalí, another leading light of New York's wartime bohemia, who had been a friend of Edward's in Paris. Dalí had been introduced to America by art dealer Julian Levy, who had organised an exhibition of surrealist works, including Dalí's *The Persistence of Memory* with its now-iconic melting watches, in 1932. In 1941, like many other European artists, the Spanish surrealist painter had fled to America. Helena commissioned him to paint a portrait of her in 1943. He titled it *Princess Arthchild Gourielli-Helena Rubinstein* and depicted Helena chained by her jewels to a rocky cliff overlooking an emerald green sea. Dalí would later say the portrait of Helena had launched his career. She hung it in her new apartment at 625 Park Avenue and 69th Street.

Helena had been on the lookout for a new apartment for quite some time, and finally found one that suited her flamboyant style – a thirty-six-room triplex penthouse a few blocks from the Rubinstein building. 'I've fallen in love with a castle in the sky,' she wrote in a letter to her son Roy.[2]

But a profusely apologetic estate agent rang her shortly before she was to sign the lease. 'I'm terribly sorry, Madame Rubinstein,' he said. 'The co-owners say they don't want Jews in the building.'

Helena was far from naive. She had known ever since she first arrived in the country in 1915 that anti-Semitism was rife in America, especially in upper-crust white society. She hadn't been able to open her first salon on Fifth Avenue because the owners of the building hadn't wanted a Jew occupying the premises. And she hadn't been wealthy enough at the time to oppose them – she'd had to locate her salon elsewhere.

Madame was well aware that some residential neighbourhoods were either tacitly or overtly off limits to Jews. She also knew Jews were refused admittance into some private schools and universities, and several posh country clubs. Atlantic City had separate beaches for whites, blacks and Jews. Some Americans openly aired their right-wing views, such as aviator Charles Lindbergh, who had spent time in Germany before the war and was suspected of being a Nazi sympathiser. He spoke out against the danger of Jewish influence in the American motion picture industry, press, radio and government.

Automobile tycoon Henry Ford, a fanatical anti-Semite, received the Grand Cross of the German Eagle, a Nazi decoration for distinguished foreigners, in 1938. Ford had attacked and demonised Jews since the end of the First World War. Although he was forced to recant his views in 1927 after a libel suit and a boycott of Ford products by Jewish consumers, he continued to express his anti-Semitic beliefs in private. He wasn't the only one. Anti-Semitism had been growing at all levels of American society since the start of the Second World War.[3]

Madame generally steered clear of the controversy. Although her surname, which she had always refused to change, was a dead giveaway, she had never felt particularly Jewish. She had despised Orthodox Jews since her childhood days in Kazimierz, and was prone to reject anything she thought 'too Jewish'. Religion bored her. She never set foot in a synagogue unless she had to, for a wedding or bar mitzvah. She didn't keep kosher or go out of her way to mix with the Jewish community, and gave with equal generosity to gentile and Jewish charities. Apart from her family members, her lawyer and a few managers, hardly any of her 3,000 employees were Jewish.

But this particular refusal felt like a slap in the face, and Helena flew into a temper. She wasn't about to put up with anything as totally absurd as this at her age. 'No Jews?' she spat. 'Make them an offer. I'm buying up the entire building.'

Madame became the owner of 625 Park Avenue, one of the chicest addresses in New York. There was a breathtaking view of Manhattan from the terrace running around the entire apartment. She hired Max Weschler, an architect she got on with extremely well because he was always willing to carry out her craziest ideas, and had the triplex decorated in her trademark bold style: a combination of opulence, refinement and unconventionality.

The apartment entrance was on the middle floor and led straight into a vast hallway the size of a gallery with a black and white marble tiled floor. It housed the majority of her Elie Nadelman sculptures alongside some of her collection of paintings by modern masters, most of which she had had sent over from France.

Like 24 Quai de Béthune, the apartment was a cornucopia of different styles. The modern French living room was furnished with silk- and velvet-upholstered sofas and armchairs in shades ranging from purple to magenta. The white and gold baroque dining room contained a host of priceless objects, including part of her African art collection. She took coffee in the card room, made for playing bridge. Although smaller in size than the others, it was Madame's favourite room: the Venetian furniture and three dream-like murals painted by Salvador Dalí made it a work of art in its own right.

Also on the entrance floor were six bedrooms. Madame's was decked out with stunning transparent acrylic furniture designed by her friend Ladislas Medgyes that was often photographed, especially the illuminated Lucite bed. Tapestries by Rouault and elaborate mirrors hung everywhere, alongside tall tribal statues from Oceania and opaline vases. Dozens of paintings – by Braque, Picasso, Miró, Chagall, Derain, Modigliani and Matisse – decorated the walls. A critic once referred to them as 'unimportant paintings by every important painter of the nineteenth and twentieth centuries'.[4] On the top floor of the apartment were a ballroom and a large room for her collection of dolls' houses.

To support the war effort, Helena grew vegetables on the terrace and christened it the 'farm in the sky'.[5] In 1943, she gave a memorable garden party in aid of the US Crop Corps, an organisation of voluntary auxiliary farm workers, and the event was covered by *The New Yorker*. 'A great many international-looking fellows were standing about talking in French and drinking Scotch and soda, although a dark green vegetable juice of Madame Rubinstein's own concoction was also available. One of the guests was Salvador Dalí, whom we've seen quite a lot of lately.'

As the *New Yorker* journalists were leaving, they caught their first glimpse of their hostess, 'who was standing all by herself near a table which had on it a plate containing four raw potatoes under a glass cover. She looked inscrutable and we couldn't tell what kind of time she was having.'[6]

Whether she was having a good time or not didn't enter into it. Society receptions were part and parcel of her obligations. The Gouriellis threw very popular parties attended by New York high society. A few days before the date, Madame would send the newspapers her guest list. Even in New York, Helena prided herself on being able to come up with a decent smattering of the aristocrats she loved to hobnob with, whom she mixed, as at every good party, with artists, writers, journalists and socialites. Her guests were very flattered to be received at the 'Rubinstein Hilton' and her receptions were the talk of the town in Manhattan.[7]

As part of Operation Torch in North Africa, the US Government ordered Helena Rubinstein products for soldiers fighting in the deserts. Their sunburned skin needed moisturising and treating, and their faces had to be covered in camouflage paint. Helena and Mala designed special kits and Washington bought 60,000 of them. Each one had *HR Inc.* written on the packaging. The order came just at the right time for the company's coffers, which had taken a bashing under the wartime economy.

Helena Rubinstein was invited to the White House and President Roosevelt told her about a story he had read and been impressed by. It concerned an English woman who had been carried out of a blitzed building on a stretcher. Even before she had been given pain relief, she begged the ambulance men to pass her her lipstick from her handbag. 'Your war effort is to help keep up the morale of our women. And you are doing it splendidly,' concluded the President.[8]

He said the same thing to Elizabeth Arden, in the same place but not at the same time. Each woman felt like the guardian of Roosevelt's wishes and stepped up her efforts to invent and produce. It was said that in Germany, when Hitler had wanted to ban make-up, women simply refused to work.

The metal shortage didn't make their task any easier. Only Charles Revson had had the forethought to stockpile metal. That man! Women adored him but Helena hated him as much as she did Arden. However, she had to accept that she was now locked into a continuous battle with him. The two women were as coy as he was provocative. They put the accent on romanticism, he emphasised sexuality: *You can be a sex bomb!* his posters proclaimed.

Revson flooded the market with brash colours. His palette was infinite and he invented new ones every day. *The market is an insatiable monster*, thought Madame, who had been forced to cut expenditure in certain areas – particularly advertising. She hadn't given her employees a pay rise either, which led to a strike by her Long Island factory workers at the end of 1941. She wouldn't have even imagined it possible: the word 'strike' wasn't in her vocabulary. To begin with, she had refused to meet with the unions, but her employees' determination forced her to give in and resign herself to increasing 200 salaries.

She had to analyse the market, innovate and ask herself the question 'What do women want?' every single day. It was the same key question on the lips of advertising executives, fashion designers, perfumers, milliners, designers, shoemakers, furriers, beauticians and everyone else in the gigantic beauty-serving industry. The answer was simple: in these hard times, women were hungry for simple pleasures, distractions and seduction. Despite their limited means, they were spending $517 million a year on beauty products.[9]

Helena decided to create a new fragrance. One fine spring day, 500 little wicker baskets with blue and pink balloons attached to their handles were released into the sky from the top of Bonwit Teller department store. Inside each was a bottle of Heaven Sent perfume, whose design was inspired by a bottle Madame had bought in Mexico. A small card was attached that read 'Out of the blue for you'. American women went wild for it.

Greta Garbo and Jean Harlow continued to be Hollywood's hottest stars. But for the women workers who had replaced their husbands, sons and brothers who were away at war, the new idols were Katharine Hepburn with her rolled-up sleeves, wide-legged trousers and flat shoes, and Rosalind Russell with her men's suits and deep voice.

A popular song called 'Rosie the Riveter' portrayed a woman worker in the weapons industry. With her hair neatly tied up under her red headscarf with white polka dots and her painted lips and nails, Rosie embodied the preservation of femininity within a male activity. 'We Can Do It' proclaimed the posters showing her parading in dungarees with puffed-up, Popeye-style biceps.

American women were no longer 'job stealers'. In the space of four years, six million of them were working, driven by patriotic duty. The US Government had decided that their salaries should be equal to men's, and the unions supported the principle. It wasn't feminism though – people simply feared that if women's pay stayed lower, bosses would favour them over men once the war had ended. At the start of the conflict, 95 per cent of women said they would stop working once their husbands came home from the front, but by the time the hostilities stopped, 80 per cent of them wanted to remain in employment. This led to a conflict of interest between male and female aspirations. Instead of encouraging women to become emancipated, society kept pushing them back into the home.

As soon as America joined the war, Roy wanted to enlist. His perfect knowledge of several European languages, including French, influenced his appointment to the Office of Strategic Services (the US secret services). From his post in Washington, he wrote long, plaintive letters to his mother. Jealous of everything and everyone, he badgered her with requests: for money; to borrow her car when he was on leave; and for her to buy him a house. Most of all, he complained about the bad atmosphere in the company.

Oscar Kolin finally managed to embark for the United States, where his family had already taken shelter, and resumed his position as company director. Roy didn't understand why his cousin was being paid such an inflated salary. All his letters were written in the same tone and childlike scrawl, addressed to 'Mother dear'. 'Keep your sense of humour,' he would conclude though, no doubt in an attempt to soften the effect of his recriminations.

In her replies, Helena chose to stir up the latent tension between the members of her family. She praised Oscar's qualities and once more compared her two sons. 'Horace never asks me for anything,' she wrote. 'He bought a house for $30,000 and will be paying a monthly rental.' Having lectured Roy and highlighted his younger brother's good points, she would enclose a cheque with her letter.[10] Humiliated yet again, Roy would drown his anger in alcohol – something he was making rather a habit of.

Unlike his cousin and his brother, Horace hadn't been able to enlist. Of fragile health since childhood, he had been declared unfit for service. Like Roy, Horace hated Oscar and accused his mother of favouritism. In truth, Oscar Kolin was a charmer. He preferred long one-to-one meetings with Madame to discuss sales and marketing to all the notes, letters and memos his cousins bombarded her with.

Horace felt very lonely at the office without Roy – all the more so because Helena often travelled to Mexico and left him on his own with the hated Oscar. In a letter to his mother, Horace compared their family to the one in the Lillian Hellman play *Little Foxes*, which had triumphed on Broadway and become a successful film. 'Both tear each other apart through greed,' he declared.

A psychiatrist would have had a field day with this tense mother–son relationship. Both brothers did in fact have their fair share of time on the analyst's couch, but never successfully overcame their childhood demons. Hovering over their heads were Hertzel's ghost and the image of Edward as a jack-of-all-trades and master of none, as Helena liked to describe him – and Horace. She was glad she hadn't had a son with Artchil.

But other, much deeper grief struck the family. Helena's sister Regina Kolin and her husband Mozsejz were exterminated at Auschwitz in 1942. One year later, the Nazi-created Jewish Ghetto in Kraków was liquidated and thousands of men, women and children were deported to the nearby Auschwitz and Plaszow concentration camps and Belzec extermination camp.

In January 1945, the last prisoners left in Plaszow were sent to Auschwitz to be evacuated to the west. The Germans attempted to clear all traces of the crimes committed in the camp by Amon Goeth and his henchmen, and ordered the communal graves to be re-opened in order to exhume and burn the corpses.

The war came to an end. The Americans, British and Soviets discovered the appalling truth about the mass graves and inhuman detention conditions. Thousands of extermination camp survivors, the vast majority of them Jews, wandered the streets of eastern Europe like emaciated ghosts. Millions of families tried to find their missing ones and grieved for their dead, Helena included; she had lost her sister, brother-in-law, uncles, aunts and cousins. The Kazimierz of her childhood had died, emptied of its Jewish inhabitants, who were gone forever.

Giza Goldberg, the daughter of one of Helena's paternal uncles, had also lost her husband and son. Her daughter Lilith, known as Litka, aged just sixteen, had managed to live out the war in hiding in Poland and Hungary. The teenager owed her survival to her intelligence and innate adaptability. Thanks to forged identity papers her mother had acquired, she passed for a Polish Catholic throughout the war, managing to keep her cool even during the worst moments. Mother and daughter met up again at the end of the conflict.

Giza wrote to Helena from Kraków to ask her for help. They had absolutely nothing left: no house, no money and no family. Madame paid their air tickets to Paris, where she put them up in a small apartment she owned. Litka, who liked school, said she was keen to study for her baccalauréat. 'Why should she do her bac? I didn't!' Madame exclaimed. With that slip of the tongue, Madame put paid to the self-created legend that had her briefly studying medicine at Kraków University. Education wasn't part of her plans for these cousins – working in her Paris salon was.

In her apartment in the 15th arrondissement of Paris, eighty-five-year-old Litka Goldberg-Fasse nostalgically remembers her past, surrounded by period furniture and paintings originally from Quai de Béthune that she bought when Helena died. She has only good memories of the thirty years she worked in the Faubourg Saint-Honoré salon. It is an experience she is truly proud of.

Litka's skin is magnificent and almost wrinkle-free. Faithful to the Rubinstein beauty precepts, she has looked after it all her life. She recalls with admiration and tenderness the woman who saved her life. 'My mother used to tell me that her own father, my grandfather, had put money into the family kitty to pay for Madame's passage to Australia. It's true that she was authoritarian. Nobody dared contradict her, and she often frightened us. Her work came before anything else. But she was generous and attentive to others. She had a particular fondness for my mother and me. Thanks to her, we never wanted for anything.'[11]

26

REBUILDING ONCE AGAIN

Helena arrived back in Paris on a September morning in 1945, absolutely exhausted from her chaotic journey. Crossing the Atlantic on a Liberty ship built for transporting troops bore no resemblance to her luxurious pre-war sea voyages. The ticket she had only just managed to snap up by paying a fortune entitled her to a minute cabin that she reluctantly had to share with five other women. Artchil had been unable to accompany her as it was too difficult to obtain another ticket, even though they had been prepared to pay. But he had promised to join her as soon as he could.

As well as being worn out, Helena was filled with anxiety. She could have done with the prince's reassuring presence, his smile, his warmth and his humour. Everything she had seen since Le Havre through the windows of the car she had hired – at great expense, as petrol was a rarity – broke her heart, she wrote.[1] The France she had left five years earlier was nothing but ruins and devastation. The state of her Quai de Béthune apartment, which she went straight to, deepened her sorrow and shocked her to the core. It was worse than she had been told in New York. 'What an extraordinary thing for grown men to do,' she muttered to herself as she dashed from one room to the other to assess the damage.[2]

The apartment had been methodically pillaged and abused, as if the occupiers had taken painstaking, perverse pleasure in ransacking it. Many pieces of furniture and decorative objects were missing, including a mother-of-pearl chest of drawers, Napoleon III armchairs, vases and pieces of porcelain. There were dark marks on the wallpaper where paintings had once hung. The furniture that was left was damaged: broken chair backs; cigarette burns on a marquetry sideboard; delicate velvet armchairs slashed until the horsehair stuffing and springs had come out. Her Louis XVI card table had been moved to the terrace and left out in all weather for several seasons. The Aubusson carpet was riddled with bullet holes, the hall walls too, and an antique statue of Aphrodite had served as target practice for the soldiers. What shocked Helena the most was to discover that the Nazis had thrown furniture out of the windows just before vacating the building, 'in one final, senseless act of destruction'.[3]

Later, once Paris life had returned to normal, she would ask Louis Süe, who was in charge of the penthouse renovation, to keep the damage in the hall 'as a reminder of the senseless destruction of war'.[4] In the meantime, they were able to camp there in reasonable comfort. The Germans had left the sheets, blankets and pillows. After getting some rest, Madame assessed her French losses.

The Saint-Cloud factory was wrecked and all the cream and lotion formulas had been stolen. The mill at Combs-la-Ville had been ransacked and every last basin and bathtub smashed to smithereens. Her bank accounts had been confiscated, her money had disappeared and her files been disposed of. But material possessions didn't count in comparison with the heavy human losses being mourned all around her: hundreds of thousands of soldiers dead, prisoners deported and civilians killed during the bombings.

For her first few weeks, Helena set out on a daily search for lost friends, relations and staff. She made regular visits to the police station to obtain information and addresses, and tried to piece together what had happened to them all. She discovered that some, like Louis Marcoussis, had died; his death grieved her deeply. Others had lost everything. Her sales director, Emmanuel Ameisen (Edward Titus's nephew), had just returned home exhausted and gaunt, but at least he was still alive. In 1940, he had been taken prisoner by the Germans and sent off to a camp in Pomerania where he stayed until the arrival of General Patton right at the end of the war.

Helena was thrilled to see her old Quai de Béthune staff, Gaston, Eugénie and Marguerite, and took them back on. The penthouse became a meeting place and a canteen. Madame scrounged provisions to the best of her ability to feed the steady stream of friends who dropped by in search of warmth and comfort.

A year after the Liberation of Paris, the situation in the French capital remained unstable. Ration tickets were still common currency for food and clothes. People spent hours and hours queuing – except the rich, who continued to shop on the black market. In most districts, the electricity, gas and water were cut off at certain times of the day. There was no charcoal for heating or to run trains on, and no petrol for cars and taxis. Parisians walked or cycled everywhere, or took the metro when it was working.

The small miracle in all this was that the telephone still worked. Helena was able to converse with Artchil who was living his happy, jet-set life in Hollywood, and with her son Horace in New York. She sent for him to join her in Paris as soon as transatlantic crossings became regular again, in an attempt to get closer to him and because she nevertheless felt a little alone.

She could have left for the United States again right away to find the comfort that her wealth and age – she was seventy-two at the time – made completely legitimate. No one would have held it against her. Members of her senior staff, most of all Oscar Kolin, were in a better position than her to save what there still was to be saved. But she hated delegating. And her pioneer's soul told her to stay. She intended to rebuild it all again herself, as she had done before. The idea didn't frighten her, it excited her. She wanted to show everyone the battle was worth winning. Action made her feel alive, like Paris, whose pulse still beat despite the restrictions and shortages, despite the shops and restaurants being closed.

Her priority was to take back possession of what was rightfully hers. With no files to show, she had to prove her identity and ownership during interminable interviews with the authorities that put her patience to the test. As soon as she got back her beauty salon, which had been run by the Germans then closed for lack of merchandise, she got to work putting it to rights and re-employing her staff – those who were still alive and happy to come back, at any rate.

Every morning, she left the Quai de Béthune and walked to the Rue du Faubourg Saint-Honoré accompanied by Horace. Even wounded, slow-moving and lacking everything, the city gave her a sense of well-being that New York couldn't. She and Horace chatted the length of the route. Mother and son walking along together made a touching family scene. She small and stocky, wrapped in her furs, wearing a bowler hat and adjusting her determined pace to the strides of the strapping, bearded man next to her; he trying to take her arm, then giving up when he felt her stiffen slightly. She could never stand being touched. But by his side, she seemed to soften – for a few minutes at least. It was perhaps a combination of the Paris air, the winter sun that turned the dark water of the Seine iridescent with a thousand coloured pearls, and her acute awareness that she was lucky to be alive and have her son with her when so many others had perished.

Although sorrow, unspoken resentment, anger, pain and lack of understanding had and always would plague their relationship, that time spent rebuilding the exterior world was warm and harmonious. There was no time for regrets; Helena hated them as much as she disliked outbursts of grief or tenderness. Like everyone else, she had a heart, and like everyone else she suffered, more often than people might have thought. Yet she was incapable of showing her feelings or expressing what she felt. Intimate words never crossed her lips.

As the factory no longer existed, Madame began the search for perfumes, lanolin and everything else she needed to make her products. The few available raw materials were rationed. On the black market, sweet almond oil traded for up to 800 francs a litre. So she told Artchil, who was still in Hollywood, what she wanted and had him send it over. The first deliveries didn't start arriving until weeks and even months later.

Parisians were suffering from chilblains. High-society women asked transatlantic travellers to bring Vaseline back from New York. All were in need of moisturisers for their hands and faces, as well as make-up. Lipstick was better than any antidepressant. So Madame donned her chemist's coat once more, rolled up her sleeves and got busy in her 'kitchen'. She blended anything she had to hand to make creams, which she packaged and sold herself like in the good old days in Melbourne and London. She had no need of artifice to look young, just hard work. Indefatigable Helena. She was always the first to arrive and the last to leave. Her dogged determination paid off and the Faubourg Saint-Honoré salon was soon back in business. With renovations by Louis Süe, it would be as, if not more, stunning than before.

The fashion press slowly resurfaced and began cobbling together beauty advice for women. In November 1945, on her return from the United States, Hélène Lazareff launched *Elle* magazine.

A young woman called Edmonde Charles-Roux, an ambassador's daughter who had been a nurse then a Resistance fighter in the war, was hired as the magazine's editor. Two years later she joined *Vogue*, where she worked as a columnist before becoming editor-in-chief and imposing her style.

Helena and Edmonde met in the office of Michel de Brunhoff, the magazine's director. Their half-century age gap didn't stop them forming a close friendship that remained strong for twenty years. Edmonde Charles-Roux remembers with a combination of affection and admiration 'this blockish little lady, very Polish and very Jewish, brave, tolerant, open-minded, with a unique vision of people and things, whose two favourite expressions were "alright" and "too much"'.[5]

'Helena Rubinstein persuaded me to write,' she continued. 'She had detected a talent for writing in me and gave me the keys to a little house that adjoined her mill at Combs-la-Ville so I had somewhere quiet to work. I went there every weekend for two years. While I was there I started writing my first novel, *To Forget Palermo*. She used to gather all her family there: Mala, Horace and her sisters. We saw each other regularly, every time she came to stay in Paris. We'd have lunch together and I'd go with her to the studios of the artists she liked and to art galleries. I had no money back then. She used to give me presents all the time: things like a pearl necklace and a mink scarf. Her constant attentions helped me a lot.'

A generous soul and quick to recognise and encourage talent, Helena could nevertheless be contradictory. She cursed Oscar, who had got it into his head to give money to every refugee of his acquaintance who dropped by the shop. Yet she herself encouraged family members who had survived the Holocaust to move to Paris and gave them shelter, food, work and money for studying. She decided who to help and who to love.

Post-war society was still disorientated. Demobilised soldiers found it impossible to live in harmony with their wives again after all those years of separation. Many filed for divorce. Yet the couple and the family seemed to represent the safest nest. General de Gaulle issued an emotional plea for France to rebuild herself, and the resulting baby boom saw the birth of 860,000 children in the country between 1946 and 1950 and as many again during the following decade.

Men returned to their jobs, which had a disastrous seesaw effect on work opportunities for women, a situation that continued until the mid 1960s. Housewives, who became key targets for advertising men, dedicated seventy-four hours a week to scrubbing, washing, ironing and polishing.

Women's magazines urged women to combine domestic chores and elegance, and gave advice on how to be a good wife and mother and still remain stylish. Young female school-leavers wanted to be secretaries, nurses and teachers. They were heartily encouraged to take up these professions, which posed no threat to male power. But Frenchwomen at last had the right to vote. A government ordinance in April 1944 allowed them to be citizens in their own right.

The parties and fancy-dress balls started again. But style-conscious women had to make do with their pre-war wardrobes. During the Occupation, fashion had become a form of DIY: women cut new clothes from curtains, sheets, old dresses and men's jackets. The shortage years following the Liberation demanded just as much imagination. Only the nouveau riche, who had made their fortune on the black market, could afford to wear clothes from the couture houses that hadn't closed.

Helena's protégé Christian Dior, who had guided her in her purchases from the art gallery he ran before the war, had had to change profession when the family firm collapsed as a result of the 1929 crash. Encouraged by high-society clairvoyant Madame Delahaye, who had predicted he would make his fortune through women, Dior sold a few fashion illustrations to *Vogue* and then turned his hand to couture.

His February 1947 catwalk show financed by 'King of Cotton' Marcel Boussac launched the New Look, which featured longer hemlines and full skirts, despite the fabric rationing still in force. After the understated pre-war Chanel years, his feminine, billowing, sophisticated look was revolutionary. And the entire world fell for it.

Madame sat in the front row at his Avenue Montaigne show alongside her fashion-press friends Carmel Snow and Marie-Louise Bousquet, as well as Lady Diana Cooper, the wife of the British Ambassador to France. They had met for the first time in London in the 1910s when Diana Manners, as she was called before she married Duff Cooper, was an active member of Margot Asquith's clique. 'My dear,' asked the curious and no doubt rather jealous Helena, 'what have you been doing to stay so slim for the thirty-five years I have known you?'

'Sliced grapefruit. I put it on my face and eat it.'

Helena nodded, puzzled. She was aware that the acid from citrus fruit was an excellent skin tonic, but didn't dare ask if the very same grapefruit that started out as a compress on Lady Cooper's face actually ended up on her plate.

Helena at last met up again with Artchil in London. They scoured the capital looking for the best location for her new salon because 24 Grafton Street had been destroyed by the bombing. She thought back nostalgically to the first time she had searched for a property there all those years ago, and shared the story with Artchil. The prince had heard it many times before, and read about it in the papers – it was part of the Rubinstein legend. But each time Helena added new details. She suddenly interrupted herself and signalled to the taxi driver to pull over. She took a wad of pound notes out of her crocodile bag, paid and asked for a receipt, then hurried out of the taxi, dragging Artchil with her. She pointed to a lovely eighteenth-century house that had escaped the bombings. This was where she wanted to open her new salon. It belonged to Mrs Willie James, a famous Edwardian hostess who had even entertained the King there, and was up for rent. The address was 3 Grafton Street, a stone's throw from her old premises.

Helena had the interior refurbished but didn't touch the facade with its lovely old-fashioned porch and front steps. Ceska, who had just come back from New York, would run it with Boris Forter, whom Helena had hired to manage the first London salon in 1937.

Madame's European tour took her to Switzerland ('only good for banking'),[6] Italy, Spain and even Germany, as she wanted to bury the past. In each place, she opened or renovated salons, built factories and strengthened distribution networks. European clients wanted new Rubinstein products imported from the United States, and she pandered to them by proclaiming that each new preparation launched in Europe came from America. And vice versa. *If only they knew that the formulas, ingredients and packaging are all exactly the same*, she said to herself.

Five years later, it was mission accomplished. Thanks to her relentless hard work and the skill of the brand's director Emmanuel Ameisen, her business had become the most prosperous in France again, even bigger than Elizabeth Arden. For Helena, there always seemed to be forty-eight hours in a day.

27

THE PINK JUNGLE

With her business in Europe back on track, Madame returned to America. The country was in mourning for the 300,000 soldiers killed liberating Europe. The wartime economy had been reoriented to the production of consumer goods targeted at a new, very promising market – the urban middle classes. Congress had passed a law authorising the construction of new homes on the outskirts of towns and cities. Cheery suburbs sprang up everywhere, with rows of carbon-copy houses and tiny yards, each with a basketball hoop, barbecue and kids playing baseball as if they were Joe DiMaggio.

All the interiors were based on the same design. The ground floor comprised a kitchen equipped with the latest food processor and household appliances plus a living-cum-dining room, while the first floor contained the bedrooms. This model of modern living, which went on to be exported all over the world, glorified the newly reinstated housewife. Rosie the Riveter was a distant memory. It was as if she had never existed. As soon as the war ended, 4 million women lost their jobs, 2 million of them in heavy industry. Those who hung on to their jobs were secretaries or salesgirls and had no hope of entering positions of responsibility.

Female employment figures gradually rose, but this progress was met by a backlash encouraged by analysts, advertising executives and the media, who all proclaimed somewhat triumphantly that – to everyone's delight – women had returned to the home. As in France, the flappers had disappeared and been replaced as if by magic by loving wives and fulfilled mothers.

Home sweet home became the bastion against communism and evil. More and more people married, and at a younger age. They went on to have two to three children per family. Middle-class girls went to university with the aim of finding a good husband with good prospects. Once they had the ring on their finger they tidied their degrees or diplomas away in the cupboard along with their wedding dresses and stayed at home. On the face of it, they seemed perfectly happy to accept this Victorian model being imposed on them once again. But psychiatrists' couches were always occupied and alcohol and tranquilliser consumption increased. In their model suburbs with their well-fed children and their breadwinning husbands who caught the 5 p.m. train home from the city every evening, they were slowly being bored to death. It was 'the problem that has no name', described ten years later by Betty Friedan in her feminist book *The Feminine Mystique*, which sent shock waves through society.

The good health of the economy rested on women's shoulders. They were counted on to spend money. All of them bought cosmetics. In 1948, nine out of ten American women owned at least one tube of lipstick, and a quarter of them some mascara and an eyeshadow palette.

These products were now available to buy in gigantic supermarkets and shopping malls – modern America's new temples of consumerism. At the same time, home sales were growing: Avon multiplied its turnover by eight in fifteen years. Ad men at the big Madison Avenue agencies segmented the market into more and more specific sectors to target consumers better: housewives, female students, secretaries, saleswomen, African-Americans, Asians, etc.

As it had been at the start of the century, the general rule for make-up was invisibility (wear it, but don't let it show), but a new concept was now all the rage too: indelibility (lipstick that 'stays on you, not on him').[1]

In 1949, Madame launched Silk Powder, a new face powder using real silk, which became a bestseller in Europe. In the United States, the Food and Drug Administration vetoed it at first, but Helena's marketing department found another way to present it and the powder was allowed onto the American market. But Madame never lost sight of the fact that make-up was just one of many sides of her business. Over the decade that followed the war, she created two creams: her first firming product, Contour Lift Firm; and her first oil-in-water emulsion, Lanolin Vitamin Formula, which contained derivatives of purified lanolin. It was an innovation. Until then, creams were composed of a water-in-oil emulsion, in which water droplets were dispersed in an oil phase and gave a moisturising and protective but oily texture. The oil-in-water emulsion, in which oil droplets are dispersed in a water phase, produced a lighter substance.

A new Helena Rubinstein salon beauty programme was launched, with Mala in charge. The Five-Day Life of Beauty was a basic beauty care course for young working women delivered through salon sessions in the evenings after work and all day on Saturdays. The programme revolved around skin analyses and treatments, make-up advice, dietary recommendations and physical exercise. The brand also spread the good word in hospitals by devising beauty therapy programmes to lift the spirits and improve the health of the physically ill. At the same time, Mala created beauty courses for the blind.

The battle with Madame's competitors continued to rage, to such an extent that *Time* magazine nicknamed the cosmetics market 'the pink jungle'.[2] To Helena's immense displeasure, Elizabeth Arden hired her own best director, George Carol. Six months later, the defector had dinner with Horace and asked for his old job back. Carol's version of the story went that he had resigned because he could no longer bear Arden. In return, Arden spread rumours that she had fired him because he was useless. Whatever had really gone on, Madame took Carol back and paid him a sizeable salary, firstly to make Horace happy and secondly because she hoped he would give her first-hand information about her rival. The two women constantly spied on each other and often invented the same concepts at the same time. Because the market was always crying out for innovations, they even recycled old products and rechristened them in line with current tastes.

One particular Arden success exasperated Madame: her perfume My Love, whose advertising campaign and packaging were illustrated by Jean Cocteau. For Helena, who knew and liked the writer, it was a stab in the back. She took it like a betrayal. A short time after, she heard that Miss Arden had had an accident: one of her horses had bitten one of her fingertips off. 'Oh dear. Such a shame. Do tell me, how is the horse?' Madame enquired.[3]

Charles Revson, who was still very much engaged in the battle, had become another of Helena's bêtes noires. So much so that it kept her awake at night. In 1947, he had opened a salon and set up his offices in a huge building on Fifth Avenue, boosted by a survey that left his competitors far behind: 95 per cent of women who used nail varnish owned at least one bottle by his brand, Revlon. He had also conquered the cream market by launching Eterna 27. The name had been carefully chosen by his marketing department: twenty-five sounded too young and thirty too old.[4]

Revson didn't stop there. When Madame launched Ultra Feminine, he responded with Ultima. She was livid, but Revson continued his compelling rise. The quality of his products may at times have left something to be desired, but their names were pure genius. In an age when teenagers ruled, you had to serve up dreams and humour and cater to their colourful tastes. So he came up with shades like Pink Coconut, Frosted Champagne Taffy and Pineapple Yum Yum, which hit their target straight away.

He was reputed to be a very tough businessman. He had marketing in his blood. To launch one of his new lipsticks, he placed a full-page ad in *The New York Times* depicting a hole surrounded by smoke. The only words on the page read: 'Where's the fire?' A week later, the flamboyant lipstick Where's the Fire was on everyone's lips. In 1952, Revson launched Fire & Ice lip and nail colour accompanied by a revolutionary advertising campaign. It featured a photograph by Richard Avedon of top model Dorian Leigh oozing sex appeal in a skin-tight silver gown with long, claw-like scarlet nails and her lips parted, ready to kiss. She appears to float in the air. On the right-hand page, eleven very intimate questions set out like a test asked readers, 'Are you made for Fire & Ice?' They included: 'Have you ever danced with your shoes off?', 'Do you secretly hope the next man you meet will be a psychiatrist?' and 'If tourist flights were running, would you take a trip to Mars?'[5] Women answered with a resounding 'yes' and felt as if they had been given a free therapy session. The campaign was unusually intelligent. Miss Fire & Ice was a blend of the two stereotypes imposed on women: sexy and nice. The message was clear: spending your money for pleasure was no longer a sin. Fire & Ice was the talk of the town and shares in Revlon rose to such an extent that even Helena bought some.

But the unexpected outsider, the woman who would overshadow them all in time, was already on the starting blocks and champing at the bit for her hour to come.

Josephine Esther Mentzer, better known by the name Estée Lauder, was born in 1908 in Queens, New York, into a family of Hungarian and Czech Jews. Her father, Abraham, ran a hardware shop. As a young girl working for him, she learned the art of selling and the importance of packaging. Her paternal uncle John made beauty creams. She would watch attentively as he heated them on the kitchen stove. Uncle John gradually taught her all he knew.

In the early 1930s, Josephine Mentzer married Joseph Lauter, an Austrian-born Jew who worked as a textile salesman. Their married life was unconventional: they had a son, Leonard, in 1932; divorced; then remarried ten years later and had another son, Ronald. Esther Mentzer Lauter, who had changed her name to Estée Lauder, continued to sell her creams under her name. In 1946, she established her small family business.

The venture had begun with four products: two creams, a cleansing oil and a lotion. For a long time she sold to a limited customer base. The only people who worked for the business were Estée, her husband, their sons, one of her daughters-in-law and a secretary who doubled as a telephone operator. Then the business had expanded. Estée was younger than her two rivals and, by observing them, she became aware of the power of image and decided to fashion her own. So she visited beauty salons and department stores in person, won over shoppers and enthused clients with her charming patter. The new kid on the beauty block had arrived.

For every purchase, Estée Lauder offered customers free samples; the bonus miniatures went down a storm.

As creative with the truth as Helena and Arden and just as wilful, Lauder invented a rich Catholic pedigree for herself (her mother was half Catholic) and said she had been brought up in a luxury house on Long Island with stables, a chauffeur and an Italian nanny. Her father's hardware store soon became a thing of the past.

When Lauder launched her first perfume, Youth Dew, in 1953, after Helena had already named one of her creams Skin Dew, her adversaries realised that she was now playing in the major league. The strong, enveloping fragrance was, and is to this day, either loved or hated.

Arden found Estée Lauder terribly common. Madame loathed her too. But Lauder was a serious rival – one most definitely to be reckoned with.

Madame didn't want to take any chances, so she called on the services of David Ogilvy, a British man who had emigrated to New York and set up an advertising agency on Madison Avenue in 1948.[6] In the space of just a few years, by inventing and setting the rules of modern advertising, he had become the undisputed king of the ad men who now called the shots in the advertising world and the media. Ogilvy had flaming red hair and piercing blue eyes; he spoke, acted and looked like an aristocratic English gentleman with his tweed suits, bow ties and good manners. A young lady served him tea in his office at five o'clock every afternoon. He smoked like a chimney: pipes, cigarettes and fat cigars. He was sexy, charming, eccentric and a snob, and travelled around in a chauffeur-driven Rolls. Men and women alike were won over by his movie-star charisma. To him, his job was like a permanent show.

When Ogilvy opened his agency, Helena Rubinstein was one of his first clients. He had the greatest respect and admiration for her, and was appalled by the anti-Semitism that was rife in the advertising world in New York.

It was only natural that two people working in the image business and so addicted to showmanship should meet and get along. Madame hired Ogilvy to support Horace, whose small agency looked after the brand's advertising with in-house assistance from Sara Fox. Ogilvy immediately got much more involved than he would have liked in the family's complicated relationships, and found himself the arbiter between mother and son. Poor Horace. In Madame's entourage, he was the one who suffered most at the hands of her fiery character. His position in the business was always unclear too because he depended on his mother's goodwill. Sometimes, as soon as she gave him a task, a job or privilege, she took them away from him again. Or else she would ask his opinion, then show his ideas to her managers and not do anything he had suggested. Other times, she would let him run his projects his own way, but go behind his back and tell her directors to put a stop to his ideas or set them aside until someone else took them over. He submitted brilliant campaigns to her, but she considered them extravagant because she had no confidence in him. She found him eccentric, idealistic and not pragmatic enough.

At well over forty, Horace was an intelligent man and, like Madame, often visionary. But he could also be all over the place, like an unstable, hot-headed teenager. Brought up by his mother only intermittently and oppressed by her domineering character, he felt forever misunderstood. Helena was more possessive, demanding, versatile and cruel towards him than ever. When she spoke of him, it was often with sadness but also much love.[7] 'Horace is brilliant!' she would say. Yet she couldn't stop herself adding, 'Horace is gaga!' and that his business sense was next to zero. Meanwhile Horace complained that his mother only respected those who took her money. She still hoped he would change and become more reasonable, but their conversations inevitably turned into confrontations. When Horace started having therapy, Madame went behind his back and sent the psychiatrist the anxious notes he had written her at work.

Horace did have a habit of getting involved in disastrous situations. In the early 1950s he had an affair with a young dancer who was the girlfriend of a gangster. The boyfriend blackmailed Horace, who responded by abducting and illegally confining the couple. He was arrested and sent to prison for a few days. It caused quite a scandal in New York. 'Only Horace would have the ridiculous idea of kidnapping a gangster!' Helena seethed.

And only Artchil knew how to calm his fiery wife. He rarely lost his composure in the face of her anger. He took advantage of his gilded life with panache, frequently went to Hollywood, where he had even more friends than in New York, and accompanied Madame on her travels around Europe and South America.

On a trip to Grasse where Helena was visiting the perfume factories and fields, the prince fell in love with a white stone building inland and persuaded his wife to purchase it. Like all White Russians, Artchil was mad about the French Riviera, especially Cannes, where a large community of his compatriots always stayed. Helena, who could never refuse him anything, bought the house. She also bought him a yacht, but sold it again fairly soon.

Louis Süe was once again commissioned to carry out the renovations. Unlike her other homes, Helena wanted to make Maison Blanche, as they had named it, a simple, bucolic place with a green and white colour scheme. The house oozed charm, nestled in a small olive grove surrounded by wild lavender. Just below the grove, they had an Olympic-size swimming pool dug out.

This little piece of paradise was immortalised in a series of photographs by Brassaï, who was more familiar with Paris by night than second homes. The photographer frequented the same artistic circles as Helena, contributed to *Harper's Bazaar* and lived nearby, so she had probably commissioned him to take the pictures. They show Madame posing in the middle of a field of flowers and looking rather ill at ease between the branches of an olive tree.

As charming as the house was, it remained uninhabited most of the time, which made it sad and austere. 'A luxury hotel,' remarked Patrick O'Higgins when he visited for the first time. It lacked Madame's usual muddle, her signature warm colours, stacks of objects and overflowing collections.

Artchil soon tired of his whim. He preferred to sun himself in Palm Beach, Florida, or at movie stars' homes in Los Angeles. Helena never had time to go there and, besides, lying on a deck chair and napping in the shade lulled by the song of the cicadas had never been her idea of a leisure activity.

Much to her chagrin, the couple only stayed at Maison Blanche five or six times. 'I should have named it "Éléphant Blanc"!' she moaned. 'Cost a fortune. Useless.'[8]

28

THE LAST MAN IN HER LIFE

He was tall and red-haired, with the trim build and upright bearing of a former army man. Irishman Patrick O'Higgins was born in Paris between the wars, and would later recall a childhood spent in an 'atmosphere of obedience'.[1] His wealthy, well-travelled, cosmopolitan parents sent him off to boarding school, first in the UK and then in Switzerland, when he was a young boy. After joining the Canadian Army at eighteen, he was sent to England and transferred to the Irish Guards. He was severely wounded when serving as an infantry officer in the Rhineland campaign in 1945, and had to spend two years in hospital.

After being discharged from the army, Patrick O'Higgins went to New York, where a small legacy from an American grandmother allowed him to hang out at the city's nightspots, mingle with Greenwich Village artists and make friends in high-society circles, in which he was perfectly at ease. He had no trouble at all landing a job as a journalist with *Flair*, a magazine launched in 1950 by New York socialite Fleur Cowles.

Fate had him cross paths with Madame. He was walking briskly along Madison Avenue one morning on his way to work when he caught sight of a tiny woman enveloped in a mink coat with a black bowler hat jammed tightly on her head, scuttling along the wide pavement. O'Higgins was a naturally curious man, and he was so amused and intrigued by his first glimpse of Madame that he couldn't resist tailing her.

As she hastened along, Madame bumped into Count Federico Pallavicini, an Italian painter and decorator much in vogue among the jet set, whose signature style could be seen in some of her own apartments. Pallavicini, who also happened to be art director for *Flair*, greeted O'Higgins, and introduced him to Madame. Helena surveyed the young man's studied casual style – well-worn tweed jacket, tailored shirt and finely crafted leather shoes – and liked what she saw. Then, without having said a single word to him, she turned on her heel and trotted off in the direction of her office.

A disconcerted O'Higgins asked his colleague who she was. 'She's the Sarah Bernhardt of beauty,' Pallavicini replied, astonished that a man about town such as O'Higgins should have to ask.[2] But O'Higgins genuinely had no idea who Helena Rubinstein was and knew absolutely nothing about the beauty business.

Some time after that first meeting, they saw each other again at one of Fleur Cowles's cocktail parties. Madame beckoned him to join her, and proceeded to give him a thorough grilling. Her insatiable curiosity about other people's lives hadn't diminished with age, and the company of young people in particular always made her feel reinvigorated. When O'Higgins told her he worked at *Flair*, she gave a sceptical shrug. The magazine was far too extravagant, she told him, and it wouldn't last.

Although Helena Rubinstein was half a century older than Patrick O'Higgins, the two of them became inseparable over the next fifteen years. It was an entirely platonic bond – O'Higgins made no secret of his homosexuality. Their strange relationship would go through highs and quite a few lows. Although his eccentric employer could often be gratuitously nasty, O'Higgins would be an attentive and faithful companion throughout. She hired him to be her assistant, but over the years he would also become her head of marketing, nanny, Man Friday and spiritual heir.

People who knew him say O'Higgins had a wry British sense of humour, with a touch of insolent familiarity.[3] His attitude to Madame was witty and irreverent; like a kitten, he alternated between affectionate purring and playful smacks. Their relationship was a permanent tug of war in which neither side ever won. She would bark out orders and he would obey. When he rebelled, she cajoled – only to start bullying him all over again.

He was frequently annoyed by her dictatorial ways and her idiosyncrasies, which got worse as she got older. But he managed to keep things in perspective even as he fulfilled her slightest whim. He did his job with professional integrity as well as a sense of profound empathy with his employer. Helena appreciated his tact, his devotion, his sense of humour and ear for languages. As time went by she increasingly thought of him as a third son.

Some years after she died, he told the story of their uncommon life together in a memoir full of wonderful anecdotes.[4] The tone is often caustic but he is never hurtful or cruel, although the portrait he paints of Madame occasionally borders on caricature, possibly because their relationship turned bitter towards the end. Helena became increasingly selfish in her old age, and O'Higgins found it hard to forgive her for it. Yet he was inconsolable when she died.

Madame was nearly eighty when she hired him. She still didn't need glasses, walked up stairs without any help and worked seven days a week. She had turned the top floor of her New York triplex into an art gallery open to the public. The first exhibition showcased work by young American painters. As usual, it was a ploy to get her brand talked about and, as usual, it worked. The press wrote enthusiastic reviews of the paintings on display and art magazines asked to photograph Helena's own collections.

Madame's bankers were obviously thrilled with the publicity such events generated, and the accompanying rise in the company's profits. Readers were fascinated by their peek into Madame's world and identified with her, even though she was rich beyond their wildest dreams. They couldn't afford to collect art, so they bought a tube of Rubinstein lipstick instead. Women enjoyed reading how she had built up her art collection with the money she had earned from her hard work. Because Helena Rubinstein had gained her financial independence all by herself, she had become a model for American women.

Madame had a wide range of interests. She didn't go to the theatre as often as she used to because she had turned into a film buff. She went to the movies every Tuesday evening, as often as not with Sara Fox. She would give her butler Albert the evening off and pick a good Western. She liked John Ford movies best, especially the ones starring John Wayne. When the film was over, she would insist on staying on to see it a second time. Although she liked nothing so much as a quiet evening at home playing bridge with Artchil and a few family members, she quite enjoyed going to society evenings, especially if she was likely to be interviewed by a journalist from *Vogue*, *Harper's*, or *Glamour*. She often threw lunch and dinner parties, and would invite her carefully chosen guests to visit her art gallery and admire her collection of paintings.

When *Flair* folded, O'Higgins, who was freelancing for *Harper's Bazaar*, wrote and told Helena she had been right. She wrote back from Paris, promising him a job when she returned to New York. She was as good as her word: she took him on as her secretary, bargaining his salary pretensions down to what O'Higgins later described as a 'miserly' $7,000 a year.

He started out in the mailroom, a strategic launching pad for an ambitious young employee, as long as they didn't stay there too long. His tiny office next to Madame's was little bigger than a broom cupboard, but 'Madame's new protégé', as the rest of her jealous staff scornfully called him, was hardly in a position to complain.

Ruth Hopkins, the head secretary, gave O'Higgins the lowdown on who was who in the company. She described all the Rubinstein family members one by one, starting with the prince, who was universally considered to be a 'sweetie pie'.[5] Oscar Kolin, who looked like David Niven, was 'vice president, Lord Pooh Bah and chief executioner'. Roy, the president of the board, hardly ever set foot in the office, unlike his brother, Horace, who had a finger in every pie. Finally, there was clever, pretty Mala, who ran the Fifth Avenue salon and was well liked by everyone.

The list of non-family employees included Harold Weill, who handled Madame's legal affairs from his own law firm. Chief accountant Jerome Levande was Madame's scapegoat. She heaped abuse on him in Yiddish – *nudnik* (bore) was the most flattering term she used. Then there was sales manager George Carol, public relations manager Amy Blaisdel, publicity and in-house marketing manager Sara Fox and export manager Richard Augenblick, a favourite of Helena's, who she referred to as 'the gentleman'.

Rubinstein employees around the world distrusted and routinely spied on each other, whatever their position in the hierarchy or the family. In the Paris office, Helena's sister Stella and the French branch manager Emmanuel Ameisen couldn't stand each other. In London, Ceska Cooper and Boris Forter were at loggerheads. In New York, Horace loathed Oscar, especially after he was made executive vice president. The promotion made Horace mad with jealousy. Sara Fox didn't like Richard Augenblick, and Jerome Levande wouldn't give George Carol the time of day. Madame always did her best to divide and rule, manipulating her employees and playing them off against each other the way she did with her sons and her nephew.

Her fits of temper and forgetfulness were legendary. Everyone was required to instantly guess who she was talking about when she started spewing her anger, since she was rarely capable of remembering her unwitting victim's name. One day she got into such a paroxysm of rage that she actually forgot her nephew was called Oscar.

Patrick O'Higgins unravelled the tangled web of Madame's relationships as he went along. Her employees and family were performers in a pageant directed by the visionary and tyrannical old lady. And he soon realised that his employer lived to work. Business came before pleasure, love and family in her book.

Helena kept telling him money was a curse. But she used her vast fortune to control the lives of her sisters, her husband, her sons, her nephews and nieces and her employees. She scrutinised their expenses and ensured they couldn't make a move without her approval. Anyone who tried to stand up to her soon regretted it.

She got bored when things were going too smoothly, so she would contrive to sow discord among the ranks, then sit back and enjoy the resulting kerfuffle. She stirred things up in the lower echelons too. Her favourite strategy was to get newly hired secretaries to tell her what was happening in various departments. She would fix the hapless young woman with a steely gaze, patting her hand reassuringly all the while, and the secretary would tell all. No sooner had she left than Helena would ring the unsuspecting department head and tear a strip off him.

Madame was always up at dawn and would charge into the office bright and early, announcing her arrival with a bellowed 'What's new?' She got cracking as soon as she was at her desk, summoning her secretaries (she never bothered to learn their names, calling each one 'my little girl'), reading outgoing mail, making changes and having everything redone. She would bustle around checking everyone was hard at work, urge them to work harder, give orders she would cancel a couple of hours later and interrogate every single employee, from the sales director to the doorman.

Helena's mornings were invariably taken up with meetings with the various department heads. She would inspect a new packaging idea and insult whoever had come up with it if she didn't like it, or thought it too costly. She railed ever more energetically against wastage as she got older. She rarely set a foot wrong when it came to choosing the name of a new product. Everyone was allowed to make suggestions, but she always had the last word.

When she was feeling stressed she would pop a mint drop or toffee into her mouth. She always had handfuls of them in her bags and desk drawers. If she took her rings off, it was a sure sign she was going to get angry. The culprit sitting across the desk from her would lower their head and prepare to weather the storm. Her secretaries swapped tips on the latest tranquillisers in their lunch hour.

But she wasn't only feared. Helena Rubinstein was looked up to and respected in New York, Paris, London and a host of other capitals. She had literally changed the face of America and the world, journalists enthused. She was variously described as a pioneer, an enlightened being and a creator. She fascinated every woman in the world.

Helena could also be extremely generous. She sweetened up the press by offering them little gifts. She would occasionally wear a piece of jewellery she could do without during an interview and give it to the journalist, who would be all the more appreciative because it was such a personalised present.

She also lavished little attentions on her employees, especially the rank and file. Anna, one of her young salon hostesses, once invited Helena to her birthday party. It happened to be an extremely cold and snowy winter's evening, and the company's top brass had declined

Anna's invitation – she wasn't important enough for them to make the effort. Although Madame was feeling ill, she pulled herself out of bed, put on her best jewellery and made an appearance at the party just as Anna was blowing out the twenty-five candles on her cake.

Although her business was now a global corporation, she continued to run it like her own personal empire, with herself as queen lording it over her subjects. But she had become so successful and famous that no one dared challenge her authority. By the mid 1950s, American women were spending $4 billion a year on beauty products and treatments. Helena Rubinstein Inc. had 26,000 employees and annual international sales amounting to $22 million. Rubinstein salons and outlets abroad sold $12 million worth of products.[6]

Since she was increasingly obsessed with her tax bills, Horace suggested she set up a philanthropic foundation to reduce them. For once she took his advice, starting charitable organisations in the UK and the Far East, and setting up the Helena Rubinstein Foundation in New York. Horace wanted the American foundation to fund innovative scientific research whose results could benefit the brand, but Helena was mainly interested in the tax relief aspect. However, she also wanted to help disadvantaged women and children – a goal that remains the foundation's main focus today.

She opened a new factory in Canada and replaced her now-obsolete Long Island factory with a new one in Roslyn. The $4.5-million factory spread over an area of nearly 2 miles. Helena had automated assembly lines installed to triple her production, as well as machines to fill a million bottles and jars a day and huge mixing vats to churn up cream and cologne.[7]

She also moved her headquarters to larger premises at 655 Fifth Avenue, and hired several new vice presidents and managers. The top-heavy hierarchy was counter-productive, which made her furious. Yet she wouldn't let go of the reins, and still refused to delegate.

Managing the huge, many-headed hydra the Rubinstein empire had turned into on a daily basis was anything but easy or restful. The 'Empress' was travelling more than ever. She began to feel increasingly tired. She supervised everything and everyone the way she had done when she was thirty, but at eighty her failing health wasn't up to it any more.

Although she was always surrounded by people, Helena was a lonely woman who had few genuine friends. In 1951, the news that Edward Titus had died in Cagnes-sur-Mer swept her back to that long-ago time of passionate love, angry recriminations, fits of jealousy and suffering. She bottled up her own pain, and proved incapable, once again, of consoling her sons.

She asked O'Higgins to keep an eye on Horace, who had been staying with his ailing father in the south of France, and get him out of the house to 'keep him busy, to cheer him up'.[8] She herself was more deeply affected than she could have imagined by Edward's death. He had been the great love of her life, the father of her sons. But when she heard the sad news she reacted stoically the way she always did, plunging back into her hectic lifestyle to keep her sorrow at bay.

Madame didn't want to brood over this bad news – all she wanted to do was go back to Europe. She asked O'Higgins if he would accompany her. But when the young man enthusiastically agreed, she tried to dissuade him from coming. One of her major faults – being contradictory – had become even worse with old age. She couldn't bear people either opposing her or giving in to her too easily.

Her secretary had quickly twigged how she worked and kept his chin up despite the staff's part mocking, part serious comments. They all knew Madame's funny little ways and made fun of them behind her back. One colleague advised O'Higgins to make sure he always switched off his bedroom lights and not to use the lift too much because wasting electricity ('electric', as she called it) made her hysterical. Another warned him to keep an eye on the zips of his boss's dresses: 'If they're open, a storm's brewing.'[9]

Helena, who moved with the times, now travelled everywhere by aeroplane despite her penchant for ocean liners. In the early 1950s, transatlantic flights took fourteen hours and included a compulsory stop at Shannon airport in Ireland. As soon as she landed, Madame was surrounded by a merry group of nuns and signed autographs left, right and centre. In exchange, she took their addresses and promised to send them samples of her products. She kept her word. *That's the way to improve customer loyalty to my brand*, she thought. *A few little samples won't ruin me.*

Madame visited France religiously two to three times a year. The country was taking a long time to recover after the war. Frenchwomen oscillated between two styles: mother and seductress, housewife and sex object, influenced by the sensual, well-endowed actresses who were gracing the world's screens, women like Gina Lollobrigida, Sophia Loren, Silvana Mangano and Marilyn Monroe. But from Calais to Cannes, it was Brigitte Bardot's sex appeal that was setting the crowds on fire.

In interviews, Helena Rubinstein somewhat disingenuously stated that a woman could take care of herself 'with just two creams and ten minutes of her time each day'.[10] Fortunately for her company, her customers were more inclined to spend than save. It was in the zeitgeist. Even though times were still tough and purchasing power still low, people had a boundless thirst for novelty. Like America, France was caught up in consumer fever, and the rise of youth culture – music, jeans, T-shirts and films – would spread US influence still further. Protesting against anything from across the Atlantic immediately relegated you to the category of an old fool.

Which was far from the case for Madame. In Paris, Emmanuel Ameisen, the managing director of her French firm – 'the most competent man in the business, a lazy bum but clever, shrewd', to use Helena's own words – came to pick Madame and O'Higgins up at Orly airport.[11] Gaston the chauffeur dropped them off at Quai de Béthune, where they were welcomed by her housekeepers Eugénie and Marguerite. O'Higgins was immediately shown his bedroom: a spartan, wood-clad affair that stood in stark contrast to the rest of the apartment. It was Artchil's room when he was there. The prince had his own entrance so nobody could check his comings and goings.

Marguerite told him about the Edward Titus days. She had known him well, having entered the family's service in the 1920s to look after the house and the two boys. 'Madame was very jealous and that torment hardened her. When they separated, she no longer thought of anything but work, and the prince has been unable to change that, despite all his efforts.'[12]

Marguerite, who had witnessed intimate revelations, secret arguments, infidelities and resentments, judged her employer affectionately but sternly, as did Gaston and Eugénie. All three complained of her stinginess: she would settle only half of any bills they brought her because she was convinced they were stealing from her. They took their revenge by serving her scant portions of revolting food while they feasted in the kitchen (as O'Higgins, still starving after a particularly frugal dinner, would go on to discover).

Madame also allotted her domestic staff a miserable housekeeping budget, just as she paid waiters derisory tips, kept switching the lights off, and moaned when her employees left the office at 6 p.m. 'Too much' was her mantra when told the price of anything and everything – her 'international bon mot', as journalists called it. Yet she could spend $10,000 during a single afternoon's shopping at Dior and Hermès, where she was a loyal customer. She bought pairs of shoes by the dozen and four or five Kelly bags at a time.

But she also helped many people around her survive. She often gave jobs, sometimes unnecessary ones, to 'poor women' as she called them: widows, retirees and war survivors. She still employed four of her sisters. Stella Osostowicz, the chairman of her French business, had always been the most beautiful according to Emmanuel Ameisen. He thought she possessed, more than any of the other Rubinstein sisters, 'a sort of magic'.[13] She undoubtedly had her physique to thank for her collection of husbands.

Stella wanted to get married for the third time, to Count de Bruchard, and asked her oldest sister for a substantial dowry. Helena baulked, ranted and raved, but eventually gave in. The bond between the two sisters was as stormy and complicated as those between the rest of the family.

Before they had left for Paris, Horace had described in detail to O'Higgins what to expect there, no doubt hoping to scare him. He said that Stella had recently threatened to commit suicide and that his mother's comment had been merciless: 'She won't kill herself – she's just ordered four dresses.'

In line with Horace's predictions, Madame ruled her secretary with an iron hand. She telephoned him in his bedroom each morning at six o'clock sharp. The young man, who was out every night sampling the pleasures of the French capital's gay scene, was exhausted. As soon as they finished breakfast, she dragged him along to the Rue du Faubourg Saint-Honoré where she charged around like a fury, scolding her staff, her sister Stella, and most of all, Emmanuel Ameisen.

O'Higgins was surprised by the beauty salon: he thought it small, outmoded and grubby, in contrast to the luxury and refinement of the New York premises. As in New York, Helena's office door was always open and staff could be summoned at any moment of the day. The pace of work was as furious too. O'Higgins typed letters, acted as an interpreter or spokesman and attended marketing meetings. At one such gathering about Deep Cleanser, the make-up remover Madame was developing, he thought up her new slogan: 'Helena Rubinstein, the first lady of beauty science'.

One of O'Higgins's tasks was to organise lunches with the journalists and editors of the biggest women's magazines. Irène Brin, the *Harper's Bazaar* representative in Rome and Paris correspondent for eight Italian newspapers, was invited to one such occasion at the Hôtel de Castiglione in the Rue du Faubourg Saint-Honoré. Throughout the meal, Signora Brin tried to persuade Madame to take a trip to Rome, where her husband Gasparo del Corso owned an art gallery.

The pair met up again the next day at Marie-Louise Bousquet's apartment. Bousquet had been the undisputed queen of Parisian life since the 1930s. She held her salon, 'my corridor' as she called it, every Thursday from 6 to 9 p.m. in her home on the Place du Palais Bourbon. It was *the* social event for *le tout Paris*.

Marie-Louise Bousquet got around with the aid of a gold-headed cane that she pounded like an auctioneer's hammer. Helena often used to give her 'little' presents, like a car and cash. 'The magazine doesn't pay her much. She needs money,' she explained.[14]

Bousquet nicknamed O'Higgins Helena Rubinstein's 'lovair'. She wasn't the only one to embroider on such an unlikely relationship. Because they saw the couple together so often, many in the small, incestuous fashion, beauty and media world had their doubts. Although O'Higgins's lifestyle left no room for ambiguity, Madame worried that her husband would be jealous. But she ended up shrugging her shoulders and claiming she couldn't care less about what people said and hoped that her secretary felt the same. Deep down, and despite her sense of propriety, she was probably thrilled to be the subject of such rumours.

Signora Brin wouldn't leave them alone and introduced them to her husband, Gasparo del Corso. He explained that art in Italy was undergoing a renaissance and filled Madame in on a project of his. He invited her to fund twenty young Italian artists to produce paintings of imaginary scenes of life in the United States, a country they had never visited. He planned to organise a touring exhibition of their work, first in Europe, then America. Helena promised to give serious consideration to his request.

Life in Paris continued as normal for Madame, including an endless round of society lunches, often thrown at her Quai de Béthune apartment. On one such occasion she invited Edmonde Charles-Roux from *Vogue*, who came along with a lanky young friend of hers called Hubert de Givenchy, as well as Janet Flanner from *The New Yorker*, Baron Elie de Rothschild, André Malraux and a dozen other guests. Helena served them caviar on gold crockery she normally kept hidden away in a safe in the bathroom.

'Madame,' observed O'Higgins, 'was one of those women who due to their own lack of small talk somehow managed to relax the shy.'[15] Malraux, who had started off inhibited, eventually loosened up and delivered a brilliant half-hour monologue addressing every possible topic, from archaeology to make-up, and the mortuary art of Black Africa to the Dogon and Senoufo tribes of Mali, whose statues Madame owned by the dozen and had on display around the place. After coffee, she took them on a tour of the apartment and out onto her legendary terrace with its incredible view of the city's key monuments. She showed them the Greek statue of Aphrodite, which she considered one of her most important treasures and which had been riddled with bullet holes by the Nazi occupiers. Malraux asked her if she had resumed her business in Germany. 'Business is business! German money is good money!'[16] she answered. Even though members of her family had died in extermination camps, the past was the past for Madame. Only the living counted.

As he took his leave, André Malraux leaned over to Baron de Rothschild and whispered, 'What a phenomenon!'

'Yes, but she's also just like my great-grandmother,' de Rothschild replied. 'A *groisser fardiner* – a big breadwinner in the family.'[17]

Patrick O'Higgins also accompanied his boss to artists' studios. His very first visit was to Kees van Dongen's. Van Dongen was the same age as Madame and they had known each other since the golden Montparnasse years. Adorning the walls were numerous portraits he had painted, of people like Mistinguett, the Dolly Sisters and Josephine Baker, whose make-up Helena remembered having done when she was starting out at the Casino de Paris. Van Dongen bettered that, recalling he had once painted Baker's breasts.

Helena bought one of the artist's paintings for 8 million francs (it tripled in value when he died), but not without furiously haggling with his very young wife, who intended to use the money to buy a house in the south of France. When they left, Helena, who was jubilant about her successful bargaining, asked her secretary to remind her to send Madame van Dongen some products, as she thought she had dry skin. It was her habitual diagnosis.

Helena loved buying things wherever she was, and dragged O'Higgins into department stores, supermarkets (they were the future, she predicted) and antique shops. Once, at Cartier, she bought a gold fluted box containing two sapphire- and ruby-encrusted gold tubes of rouge. She had it copied the following year for a new lipstick, Nite 'n Day, that she was launching in New York. No one, least of all Cartier, had any idea she had borrowed the design.

Madame also did the rounds of the couture houses, accompanied by a little woman who followed her like her shadow, memorised all the new details, then reproduced the models at more reasonable prices. Balenciaga remained her favourite, but Dior, Lanvin, Jacques Fath, Givenchy, Jean Dessès and the very young Guy Laroche also had the honour of her presence at their catwalk shows. Later on, she also became a client of Pierre Cardin, André Courrèges and Yves Saint Laurent, who would be the last of her preferred couturiers.

When Chanel reopened her fashion house in 1954 following fifteen years of purgatory, Madame went to see her first collection in the Rue Cambon. Chanel's suits no longer flattered her plump figure, but she adopted the accessories in a flash.

After their prolonged French stay, Madame and O'Higgins travelled to Vienna where she was expected for a press conference. The trip proved fruitful. Madame met up with her Austrian countess friend who had invented the waterproof mascara launched during the Aquacade water ballet at the 1939 New York World's Fair.

The countess was working with Victor Silson, Mala's husband, and a few technicians, on a very ingenious new system. Mascara-Matic, a name Sara Fox came up with, was brought out a few years later, in 1958. It was revolutionary: the case women normally had to spit into to moisten the mascara was replaced by a steel tube containing a fluid formula which you dipped a brush into. Goodbye compact mascara cakes and stuck-together lashes.

They continued to Italy. But Madame's age was catching up with her. She felt tired. No sooner did they arrive in Rome than she contracted a bout of pneumonia that nearly killed her. An Italian doctor saved her life by putting her on oxygen and antibiotics. She made a spectacularly speedy recovery. Helena was so impressed by the results of the new penicillin-based treatment that she bought 5 million shares in the laboratory that manufactured it.

Panicked by his employer's condition before her miraculous revival, Patrick O'Higgins had called Horace in the south of France, near Cannes, where he had taken refuge to write and paint after his attempt at kidnapping the gangster. O'Higgins told him his mother was dying and asked him to come immediately. But when he arrived, Horace found Helena on top form, grumbling and telling him off as usual. Although she didn't say so, deep down she was very pleased her son had come running to her bedside. He was well over forty, but she still treated him like a child, ruffling his hair as she listed his talents to all those who passed by. 'He's artistic and literary,' she said, as if praising the qualities of a school-leaver wondering about his future.

Horace stayed in Rome for the duration of his mother's convalescence. He went out a great deal, mixed with the city's celebrities and artists, treated whole tables of guests at restaurants and charged it to his mother's account.

O'Higgins and he grew to like each other and forged a sincere friendship. They convinced Helena to get involved in the art sponsorship project. The exhibition *Twenty Imaginary Views of the American Scene by Twenty Young Italian Artists* showcased some of Italy's best painters of the 1950s, including Enrico d'Assia, Alberto Burri, Mirko, Ivan Mosca and Pericle Fazzini. Horace and O'Higgins selected them together. The show started out in Rome in 1953, before travelling to New York, to Helena's private art gallery on the top floor of her triplex. The proceeds went to charitable associations. The exhibition then toured for two years around the United States, where it attracted the same high visitor figures as in New York and Rome.

Madame was in heaven. The return on her $8,000 investment was estimated at half a million dollars' worth of free advertising. When she died, the twenty paintings were valued at over $100,000.

*

After Rome, Madame wanted to visit Maison Blanche, her property near Grasse. The doctor had ordered a long convalescence and she also decided she 'needed some air'. Horace drove them there in a hired Pontiac convertible and Madame sat in the front seat next to him all wrapped up in her furs. O'Higgins sat in the back squashed between suitcases. On the way, the trio stopped for dinner at the Hôtel Welcome in Villefranche. Jean Cocteau and Jean Marais were eating there, accompanied by the Duchess of Gramont and by Cocteau's latest muse, the extremely wealthy Francine Weisweiller, who owned the Villa Santo Sospir in Saint Jean Cap Ferrat.

On that particular evening, Jean Cocteau greeted Helena with great pomp as the 'Empress of Byzantium'. Madame milked his attention. 'Such a poet,' she simpered, before suggesting they all have lunch together the following day. Cocteau accepted and invited them to Madame Weisweiller's villa. He then continued to shower Helena with compliments. Cocteau was nevertheless one of the few people to properly see through her ways. He said to O'Higgins a year later: 'Madame Rubinstein feeds off human differences, especially those of her own invention. But beware of her silences! When they occur, she's planning an attack!'[18]

Horace hadn't just been painting and writing in his south of France retreat: he had taken it into his head to make perfume. With a couple of American friends he had created a jasmine farm and opened a refinery near Grasse. Oscar Kolin had written to his aunt to inform her that his cousin had spent a huge sum of money on the project, which of course threw Madame into a fit of rage. Everybody – Chanel, Rochas, Lanvin, Guerlain and herself included – sourced supplies from a perfume specialist called Monsieur Amic, who grew jasmine in industrial quantities to reduce manufacturing costs.

Nevertheless, Horace managed to convince his mother to come

and see his fields, which lay just a few miles from Maison Blanche. But the visit was a fiasco. Madame spent barely ten minutes there, racing around the house, the plantations and the laboratory. She found the whole setup pathetic, denigrated everything she was shown and was rude, if not downright contemptuous, towards her son's friends. Horace was shocked into silence by the affront. He continued not to say a word as they drove away. But his ashen face spoke volumes.

The trio was early for their lunch at Madame Weisweiller's. Horace came out of his sulk and suggested going to have a drink at La Réserve, the most expensive restaurant in Beaulieu. 'Are you mad?' protested his mother.

Horace threw on the brakes and turned to her, his face now crimson. O'Higgins thought he would pass out from anger. The word 'mad' had been the catalyst. Horace was wild with fury. He called his mother 'cruel', 'wicked' and 'a miser' and criticised her for thinking only of money – her 'God'.[19] Then he threw the keys onto O'Higgins's lap, got out of the car and slammed the door, leaving Patrick stunned and Helena trembling.

29

THE SHOW MUST GO ON

There was no denying her impossible character. Her mood swings, short-temperedness, authoritarianism and tyrannical behaviour had only got worse with age. Everyone was frightened of her, everyone avoided her when she was in a rage, and everyone complained about her as soon as the storm had passed, dreading a fresh outburst of anger at any moment. But everyone also knew that deep down the Helena who terrorised them could also be tender, generous and as helpless as a child when dealing with her emotions. It wasn't always clear which of her multiple personalities was the real her, perhaps not even to herself.

The quarrel with her son caused her more suffering than she cared to admit. After the altercation in the car, O'Higgins and she returned to Maison Blanche without saying a word. Horace now refused point-blank to talk to her and had sought refuge with some friends, so Madame cut short her Grasse trip and returned to New York with her secretary a month earlier than planned.

She walked down the corridors at work in silence, her face so sombre that everyone wondered what on earth had happened. She was preoccupied, absent even. She locked herself away in her office, ate lunch alone and hoped in vain that Horace would write or telephone to apologise. But he did nothing of the kind. He was sulking in the south of France. And she was suffering.

O'Higgins had a hard job of it too. Madame had made him swear not to breathe a word of what had happened, but how could he keep his promise when Oscar Kolin and Artchil Gourielli were inviting him to lunch to find out more? Loyal to the pact he had made with his boss, the young man refused to fill them in. He had become a master in the art of sidestepping: he remained vague, avoided precise answers and pretended he knew nothing. Only Roy, misjudged by his mother as 'nice but ordinary', had seen through her.[1] He realised right away that she had fallen out with his brother. And the rumour quickly spread around the offices.

But, as usual, her bout of low spirits didn't last long. She created for herself a much-needed diversion: refurbishing her men's salon, the House of Gourielli, which was falling apart at the seams. Ironically, it had long been a bee in Horace's bonnet. It made him furious to see such a beautiful project neglected. But as with everything else, she had chosen not to listen to him.

She had since realised for herself that revamping the shop was crucial if she wanted to keep her lead in the men's beauty market. In the mid 1950s, the industry generated sales of $150 million a year. The possibilities were endless. But it wasn't a one-horse race. Not long after the first Gourielli products came out, Elizabeth Arden launched her own men's range: an aftershave, an eau de toilette, a talc, a dusting powder and a moisturising lotion just for her London clients. Helena couldn't let her have the advantage.

But the balance sheet was a disaster: the House of Gourielli was losing vast sums of money. With nobody to look after it but the 'poor women' Helena employed wherever she could, the shop had quickly started looking dated and was overrun with inferior odds and ends. After much thought, Madame hired Elinor McVickar, a former beauty editor of *Harper's Bazaar*. She decided that her secretary should help her get the business back on its feet and be a guinea pig for all the different products she planned to create. O'Higgins was to become the Gourielli man, the image of this house that had fallen into disrepair.

Artchil, who was just back from a winter holiday in Palm Beach, was up in arms about Mrs McVickar's idea to put a barber's shop on the second floor. He protested with all his might: a Russian prince could not put his name to such a project. But McVickar took no notice and decided to renovate the salon. She ordered all the necessary furniture and equipment, along with shampoos and hair dyes, lotions and face creams for men made using formulas for women's beauty products. As the guinea pig, O'Higgins had to try and test so many products that he ended up dreaming about them at night. Sometimes the lotions had a miraculous, beautifying effect on his skin, but other times the experiment was a woeful failure and left him with spots all over his face.

Right in the middle of the refurbishment work, Madame was rushed to hospital. They had discovered cancer in her neck and she required emergency surgery. News rarely crossed the cordon sanitaire her family had created around her. Horace was notified immediately and flew over from France to see his mother, who immediately forgave him. It was touching to see them make their peace with each other. Madame instantly felt a little better.

She then asked for Patrick O'Higgins to come and see her. He found her looking much older and very frail. He went to see her every day after work and spent the weekends with her. She confided in him that although the members of her family surrounded her with love, they had nothing interesting to tell her. She was bored and watched television for distraction. David Ogilvy insisted that she should sponsor a TV programme, like Charles Revson had done with a series called *The $64,000 Question*. The channel had approached her before the 'nail man' but she hadn't believed in it and had emphatically refused. The programme's success now made her think it over.

She made a gradual recovery and slowly started working again. She asked for additional telephone lines to be installed in her hospital room, along with typewriters and telexes. Her secretaries took turns to be by her bedside every morning so she could dictate her mail. Every day, Patrick O'Higgins informed her about progress at the House of Gourielli. She appointed him advertising director: 'People like you,' she said. 'To be successful in publicity, people have to like you.'[2]

From her hospital bed, Madame supervised all the finer details of the launch party. She had chosen a Thursday evening, the night elegant people socialised.

On the evening of the opening, the shop was soon bursting at the seams with celebrities, from the Gabor sisters and Gore Vidal to Truman Capote and Salvador Dalí. Madame, who everyone thought was on her sick bed, made a surprise appearance wearing a new dress styled like a Russian peasant's blouse and dripping in her finest jewels. Although supported on each side by a doctor and a nurse, she held herself erect, as straight as a classical statue and very steady on her feet. She pushed her way through the crowd and greeted guests left and right like an empress, acknowledging their respects with a nod. She kissed her relations, who couldn't believe she was there and criticised the doctor for letting her go out. She gestured to them to be quiet and flashed O'Higgins the mischievous smile of a young girl thrilled with the good trick she has just played. Despite her haughty appearance, she was suffering too much to stay longer than ten minutes. As she left, she asked for a plate of smoked salmon: the hospital food was horrible, she said.

Madame recovered but her legendary energy seemed to have left her. The new House of Gourielli could have been a success but Helena couldn't keep up the pace. She grew tired of resisting and finally gave in to the prince's refusal to see his name associated with a barber's shop. She loosened her grip. The House of Gourielli, which was losing over $200,000 a year, eventually closed. It was no doubt ahead of its time.

O'Higgins took up his position with her again. He found himself back in his minuscule office right next to hers, the two of them working on projects together and travelling as a two-man band. In November 1955, while they were staying in Quai de Béthune in Paris, a telephone call woke the young man before dawn. Artchil Gourielli had just suffered a heart attack and died.

Patrick O'Higgins went to give Madame the news. In spite of the very early hour, she was already awake and sitting upright in her bed with a breakfast tray on her lap. The room was barely lit by the bedside lights and the grey November sky added to the atmosphere of gloom. Before her secretary had even opened his mouth, she knew.

For what seemed like forever to the young man, Madame moaned and sobbed while everyone fussed around trying to console her. Artchil's death was an unimaginable loss for Helena. Throughout their eighteen years as a couple, she had truly loved the prince, possessively to begin with, then with more equanimity. They had had a happy relationship, almost without ups and downs – the complete opposite of her marriage with Edward Titus.

Artchil had been a dear, amusing and attentive companion. He was a born joker and compliment payer. He knew how to have a good time and lived life to the full – leisure pursuits, gambling, holidays, bridge games, the social whirl – unostentatiously but unapologetically, as if it were his due. Although he often went out on his own, having given up any attempt to involve his wife, who was always too caught up in her business, he had infinite respect for her. 'Besides Helena, every woman is uninteresting,' he told anyone who would listen.[3] His many pleasures required money, but Helena was always generous towards him and he never took advantage of her.

When he died, Madame became the prince's sole heir as he had no family. When they had married, she had had stipulated in the contract that everything she gave Artchil would come back to her if he died first.

313

It was a rather strange arrangement given that he was twenty years her junior. But as usual, it had been an intuitive move on Madame's part: on his death, Artchil paid his widow back half a million dollars.

For what seemed like weeks, Madame lay prostrate in her bed, unable to get up and not wanting to see anyone. Telegrams, letters and telephone calls came in from Paris, London, New York and the rest of the world. People sent her flowers and left business cards, but she answered nothing. She didn't even want to go to Artchil's funeral. She hated burials as they made her think of her own death. By refusing to bury her husband, she was defying fate: no coffin, no mourning, no grief. But as childish as this denial was, it didn't stop her pain. She missed Artchil constantly.

But she had to get over it somehow. Her old instinct for survival was kicking in.

After a long period of bed rest, she decided to accomplish a long-nurtured project that meant a lot to her: having her portrait painted by Pablo Picasso. Madame had known the artist since the end of the First World War and often used to visit him in his Rue de la Boétie studio. The first painting of his she bought was a portrait of Pablo, Picasso's son with Russian ballerina Olga Koklova. She purchased many more of his works over the following years, including his *Women* tapestry, which hung on a wall in her New York triplex. Their paths had crossed on many occasions, but Picasso was never part of the circle of artists who gravitated around the Tituses during the 1920s.

Helena had dreamed for a long time of adding a portrait of herself by Picasso to her collection. But he had turned a deaf ear to her letters and telegrams. Some thought he didn't trust Helena. Others wondered if he disliked her authoritarian character. One version of the story was that she had simply forgotten to offer to pay him. Whatever the truth, he had never responded to her pleas – until the summer before, when after dozens of phone calls and letters she had finally got what she wanted and posed twice for him. But obligations had forced her to return to New York. Artchil's death gave her an excuse to pose for him again – it could distract her from her sorrow. Perhaps she thought that the artist's brush would make her immortal, record her for posterity. Whatever her reasons, she wanted this painting.

Helena flew to Nice, accompanied by O'Higgins, and went to stay with her sister Stella in Cannes. Picasso didn't want to receive Madame. Since her arrival at the Côte d'Azur, she had been inundating him with phone calls, which had no effect on him. He got a maid to answer and say he was out or else took the call himself and disguised his voice. This game lasted until she eventually discovered his ruse. It would take more than that to discourage her, so she decided to visit him unannounced, accompanied by her sister and her secretary.

Picasso, who at seventy-five showed the same inexhaustible energy as Madame, lived in the Cannes district of La Californie, a residential area of small apartment blocks and pretty villas built at the start of the century, with Jacqueline Roque, who was forty-five years younger than him. The couple were having drinks with art dealer Daniel Kahnweiler and actor Gary Cooper when Madame charged into the garden with her retinue. Picasso and Helena fell into each other's arms.

Picasso suggested Helena, Stella and O'Higgins share the picnic of cold meats washed down with a good red wine, which the trio willingly accepted. Later that evening, he drove them home in his dilapidated old Citroën without having mentioned the famous portrait. When he dropped them off, Helena brought the subject up, absolutely insisting that he do one of her. Reluctantly, Picasso told her to come back at six o'clock the following evening.

She turned up with O'Higgins the next day on the dot of six. Picasso asked her to take a seat in the dining room. Through the window, she could see the garden. A solid bronze sculpture stood under nearly every tree and the view stretched as far as the Mediterranean.

Helena wore a brightly coloured Mexican blouse the artist had selected for her from all the clothes she had brought along. He positioned himself at a table in front of her and drew on large sheets of paper. Nobody in the house was allowed to disturb the private meeting between the two legends. O'Higgins sat down on the terrace with Jacqueline and leafed through cinema magazines in silence. Inside, Picasso and Madame chatted away like two old chums.

'First, how old are you?' the painter asked brusquely.

'Older than you,' she replied in the same tone.

He smiled, then looked at his model at length, as if examining a fragile piece of china. 'You have large ears,' he said at last. 'They are as large as mine. Elephants also have large ears. They live forever. We will too!'

He put down his pencil, went up to her and peered some more. 'The distance between your ears and your eyes is exactly the same as mine. That means you are a genius – just like me!'[4]

Picasso did forty sketches of Helena in all. He drew her face, her hands and her jewellery, undoubtedly with a view to starting a proper portrait of her one day. Some of the drawings are hard, cruel even, and depict the authoritarian old woman and tyrant she had become. Others are more mischievous or more complex. He often lingered on her hands, as if they were more expressive than her face, and emphasised with lines alone the contrast between her simple attire and the extravagance of her rings and bracelets. But he never went beyond sketches.

For years afterwards, Madame asked him over and over again to finish his work and turn the sketches into a painting. She sent him letters, photos of herself and presents for him and for Jacqueline, including an African charm she had owned since she was a girl and was extremely attached to. She flattered him, begged him and threatened him, but to no avail. One day, he asked her what the hurry was. 'You and I have many years yet. There is plenty of time.'[5] By now well into her eighties, she was only too aware of what life held in store.

She would never see him again. According to art historian John Richardson, Picasso's biographer, the artist was convinced he would die before her if he finished her portrait. He refused to give his model his sketches, but showed them to Richardson, who thought they were 'brilliant'. Richardson omitted to state what he really thought about her 'ring-covered claws' and her face that made her look 'as bald [and] rapacious as an eagle'.[6] Instead he lied that Picasso had 'ennobled' Helena, adding, this time with an element of truth, that he had made her 'his eagle'.

Back in New York after the Cannes interlude, Madame threw herself headlong into work once more. It took her mind off Artchil's death. But more importantly, Arden, Revlon and Lauder, her direct competitors, weren't giving her the slightest respite. The battle to stay on top of a market that showed no signs of slowing down was getting tougher by the day.

Mid-1950s American women were spending $4 billion a year on beauty products. Looking good was more of a priority than ever for the 20 million working women in the country. Smoky eyes were the latest make-up trend, and women used eyeliner to create the look. Beauty icons such as Ingrid Bergman, Elizabeth Taylor, Cyd Charisse, Grace Kelly, Rita Hayworth, Kim Novak and Marilyn Monroe all had a doe-eyed gaze. Women copied their looks down to the last detail, from their lacquered hairstyles to their vertiginous heels.

There were colossal sums of money at stake, which offered rich pickings for other sectors too, especially advertising. Ad agencies created campaigns and bought space in the print media, on the radio and, of course, their latest favourite, television. Madame couldn't understand what all the fuss over the idiot box was about, but David Ogilvy ended up convincing her to give it a try. She was livid because Charles Revson had made a hugely successful foray into television by sponsoring *The $64,000 Question*. The show had given his sales such a boost that Revlon's turnover now outstripped Helena Rubinstein's. So she agreed to sponsor a mediocre but very popular show featuring Imogene Coca and Sid Caesar.

A sixty-second spot glorifying Madame aired just before the show's opening credits. Perched on an ornate chair, wearing a sable-trimmed white satin Dior dress and a few strings of pearls around her neck, she rattled off her spiel in her inimitable accent. 'I'm Helena Rubinstein. Give me just ten minutes of your time and I'll make you look ten years younger.'[7]

Television audiences loved her appearance. And they loved hearing her say her lines in her captivating voice – except that the voice they heard wasn't Helena's. A Russian actress had been hired to record the text. The agency had resorted to this subterfuge because Madame would have been incapable of reading the text without stumbling over every word. The hands covered in rings that viewers saw weren't hers either: they were her niece Mala's, because Helena could be terribly clumsy. It was definitely Helena sitting in the chair, though.

Much to her displeasure, the ad did nothing for her sales. But she acquired a kind of personal aura she had never previously had, despite her brand being so renowned. People were very familiar with her products, but they knew nothing about the woman behind them. The legendary billionaire in her ivory tower, so remote from their lives that she almost seemed a fictional character, had suddenly turned into this little woman steeped in humanity who had devoted her life to beauty.

At nearly eighty-five, Helena had become popular. Cabaret singers imitated her in nightclubs and *The New Yorker* published a cartoon of her. Taxi drivers began to recognise her and say 'Hi, Helena!' when she got into their cab. They would ask about her family. Some would even be so bold as to address her affectionately in Yiddish. Leonard Lyons, the country's best-known columnist, whose *New York Post* column titled 'The Lyons Den' was eagerly awaited by readers six times a week, nicknamed her 'the Jewish Queen Victoria'.

Television had turned her into a national celebrity. She kept on buying ad time even after the Sid Caesar show was pulled off the air, brushing aside the misgivings of her family, who couldn't understand this new fixation of hers. But Madame had figured out how advertising worked. When she launched a new deodorant, her spots aired before the wrestling matches she loved to watch – in fact, she thoroughly enjoyed any violent combat sport on TV. 'Sweat. That's the best way to sell this kind of product,' she said, cutting short any protests.[8] She was proved right when drugstores throughout the country sold over a million of her deodorants.

She rubbed her hands in glee when Revlon's image took a beating after it was discovered that *The $64,000 Question* was rigged: some contestants were fed the answers before the show to make sure they would win. No one could actually prove anything, however, and in the end the result of the quiz show scandal was that Revlon shares soared to their highest point ever. Some time later it emerged that Charles Revson was suspected of having bugs installed at his competitors' premises to spy on them. Helena would never have thought of such a thing.

Helena had made yet another abortive attempt at a rapprochement with her sons after Artchil's death. Roy, who was running the Long Island factory, had married for the third time. Although he had named his baby daughter born in 1958 after his mother, he still avoided Helena as much as possible. Horace was losing interest in the business. The previous year, he had crashed into another car and injured its four passengers, all members of the same family. He had been getting into car accidents ever since he had been old enough to drive.

Madame was in Paris with Patrick O'Higgins on the fateful day in April 1958 when they heard the terrible news. Forty-six-year-old Horace had been in yet another car crash – his last. He had been driving too fast, as usual, along a Long Island bridge when his car smashed into a pylon. He was taken to hospital, where his condition didn't appear to be cause for concern. But he died of a heart attack two days later. One way or another, Horace Titus's fragile heart had always been his weak point.

Patrick O'Higgins was once again the bearer of bad tidings, and watched as the same distressing scenario he had witnessed when he told Helena about Artchil's death played out once again. It was like a curse repeating itself. Madame, who had been diagnosed with diabetes a few years earlier and was prone to fainting fits, passed out cold, overcome with emotion. For the next ten days, she was incapable of getting out of bed and refused to see anyone except for a few close friends. Telephone calls, telegrams of condolence and huge bouquets of flowers flooded into Quai de Béthune from all over the world. But Madame lay in bed as motionless as a stone. She found this second blow even harder to bear. And this time sedatives were of no help.

Horace had been a lot like his mother, probably too like her for them to get along. They were both impulsive and enthusiastic, and sometimes too trusting. 'Horace was Madame's favourite because he was always in trouble,' one of her friends said. 'If there's anything Madame likes as much as work, it's people with problems.'[9]

Helena's books reveal the occasional moment of introspection tinged with the guilt she otherwise rarely felt. 'I do sometimes blame myself for making so much money and sweeping my sons up into the maelstrom of my business,' she once wrote, musing that it might have been more personally enriching for Horace to pursue his inner need to paint and write, even if it meant living in poverty.[10]

She hinted at the depth of her grief in the autobiography she dictated a few years later: 'If it had not been for my family and the many members of my staff who, I suspect, deliberately tried to keep my mind occupied with the day-to-day problems of the business, I know that I could not have continued,' she recalled.[11] That was probably the most she was capable of saying – and by her standards it was a lot.

She returned to New York, retreated behind a wall of silence and deadened her pain with work, her only remedy against suffering. A dear friend of hers, a younger woman who had once had an affair with Horace, came to see her at the office to offer her sympathy. Helena greeted her calmly, shut the door behind her and sat down again. 'Now I can cry,' she said, her voice breaking as she burst into tears.

But this was America. And in America, whatever happens, the show must go on. Her friend had told her that on the afternoon when Helena had finally been able to cry. 'You're a matriarch,' she had said. 'It's up to you to show us how to behave.'[12] So, like a punch-drunk boxer heaving himself up off the floor seconds before the fatal bell sounds, Helena straightened up yet again, ready to overcome fate's latest blow and focus on her objectives.

Cecil Beaton had sent a sympathy note to Patrick O'Higgins, who was an old friend of his. The scribbled PS informed O'Higgins that Graham Sutherland wanted to paint Madame Rubinstein. Sutherland was one of the most famous painters in England. His portraits of Somerset Maugham and Winston Churchill were widely agreed to be absolute masterpieces. 'It's a chance in a lifetime,' the photographer wrote. 'She'll be the first woman he's painted.'[13]

Madame accepted the proposal unhesitatingly. She thought the portrait would be an excellent distraction, like her sittings for Picasso after Artchil's death three years earlier. Besides, she loved London. Being in the city brought back happy memories of her rare moments of married bliss with Edward and the birth of her sons, born, as she would recall in her autobiography, 'like true Cockneys, "within the sound of Bow Bells"'. She liked London's ambience.

The city never failed to lift Helena's spirits. There was a palpable energy in the air, an enthusiasm she found nowhere else, which put a spring in her step. She felt young again when she was in London. 'If I had the youthful proportions of today I would most certainly buy most of my clothes in London,' she wrote. 'They are contemporary. It may be that I am a little tired of the endless Paris showings, the exhausting fittings and the high prices.'[14] Swinging London was just around the corner, its arrival heralded by the opening of I Was Lord Kitchener's Valet and Biba, the first of the quirky Carnaby Street shops. It wouldn't be long before the Who and the Rolling Stones were playing gigs at the Marquee Club. Madame – who was extremely sensitive to atmosphere, loved everything about London, and was even toying with the idea of starting up a Pop Art collection – instantly grasped that it was here in the heart of old England that Europe would quench its creative thirst. And that, for once, America would follow, not lead.

For now, though, all she could think of was the portrait. She had Graham Sutherland come to Claridge's, as she had decided she would sit for him there.

The first round of sittings took a week to complete. Graham Sutherland and his wife Cathy lived in a renovated old farm an hour out of London, so the painter had a long daily commute to go and see Madame at her hotel. After eight days, when he had sketched Madame from every possible angle, he decided he needed a break. All that to-ing and fro-ing had tired him out. Madame left for Paris, inviting him to join her there with his wife when he was ready. In Paris, she went back to working twelve hours a day to make up for lost time.

On the morning of her appointment with Sutherland, Madame took a long look at herself in the bathroom mirror and was filled with distaste at the image of the haggard old lady staring back at her. She thought she looked fat and ugly. She hated the sight of herself and began to worry Sutherland might not want to paint her any more. In a desperate gambit to lose a few pounds fast, the woman who had preached the virtues of physical exercise and dieting all her life, and built a whole business around those virtues, hastily downed a few laxatives.

And she didn't do it in half measures. In the space of a few minutes she had swallowed half a bottle of castor oil, a handful of senna tablets, a large glass of warm grapefruit juice and two cups of very strong black coffee. The mixture sloshed around in her empty stomach, making her feel nauseous. Her chronic diabetes made her sicker. Madame fainted. As she fell, her face hit one of her bed's solid bronze legs.

When she came to, she didn't call for help. She returned to the bathroom and ran herself a bath. The warm water revived her spirits. Feeling better now, she applied a thick layer of make-up in garish shades of red and green to conceal the dark circles under her eyes, and slipped into an embroidered red Balenciaga evening gown. With her oversize jewellery, tight chignon and face painted like an old-time battle-ready Indian chief, she looked like 'Theda Bara cast as Count Dracula'.[15] It was hardly the image she wanted to give the world of the great Madame Rubinstein.

But Sutherland was fascinated. He thought her make-up was 'sensational' and wanted to paint her exactly as she was. In fact he decided to put away all the sketches he had done and start from scratch. Helena sat for him every day for a week.

Then Madame returned to New York and Sutherland went back to his studio to finish the portrait, later exhibited at a frame-maker's in the King's Road. Graham Sutherland had done not one but two life-size portraits of her, one sitting and one standing, and was also showing several of his sketches of her face.

The first portrait – the best-known one – depicted her as an austere, tyrannical old woman, a 'vengeful autocrat'.[16] 'Is that really what I look like?' she asked her secretary. O'Higgins dodged the question, thinking all the while that it was a most striking resemblance. The painter had glimpsed her inner nature and captured the severe, imperious side to her personality. Madame thoroughly disliked this portrayal of her character. She thought the portraits made her look like a witch and that they would be bad for her image as the Empress of Beauty.

The portraits were displayed at the Tate Gallery some time later. Madame refused to go to the private view, but the exhibition attracted more than 100,000 Londoners. Art critics unanimously praised the artist's talent and the model who had courageously posed for 'such daring and harsh brush strokes'.[17] The Queen and the Queen Mother were among the visitors to the Tate, which impressed Helena far more than all the praise.

Television had brought her to the public's notice in New York, and the portrait made her famous in London. Helena became flavour of the month. The press rediscovered her and published several articles telling the story of 'the little lady from Kraków'. The *Sunday Times* even offered to publish her memoirs.

When the exhibition was over, Madame hung the portrait in the entrance hallway of her Park Avenue apartment since everyone in her circle seemed to like it, though she didn't. Press baron Lord Beaverbrook bought the second portrait for his art gallery in New Brunswick, Canada. Sutherland's early sketches went to the São Paulo Museum of Art and the presidential palace in Brasilia. All of which made Helena change her mind – perhaps it wasn't such a bad portrait after all. She refused to admit she had had a change of heart though.

'Why have you hung it in your house then?' a friend asked her.

'There was an empty space on the wall!' she replied.

Madame knew from past experience that travel was a bulwark against suffering. She would undertake several long-distance trips in the company of Patrick O'Higgins until her death seven years later. Her compulsive travelling kept her alive. 'At an age when most women take to rocking chairs, Madame Rubinstein takes to plane, boat, car and rickshaw,'[18] one journalist wrote.

Being abroad took the edge off Helena's difficult temperament, which had got worse in old age. Under foreign skies, she became placid, fatalistic and friendly – almost likeable. Little wonder she never had any trouble persuading O'Higgins to accompany her. They set off on a four-month trip, which included Helena's first trip to Japan.

The Japanese beauty industry went as far back as Europe's or America's. Madame was aware that conquering a market dominated by established brands like Shiseido, launched in 1872 by a Japanese Navy pharmacist, and Kanebo, set up in 1887, would be no easy task. Both brands boasted cutting-edge research labs and had started exporting to the West, while newcomer Shu Uemura was also making a name for itself. But since the Japanese nurtured a fascination with all things Western, Helena decided it was worth it to try and break into the market.

She waded into the fray with her old vigour, holding conferences and meetings with possible associates, investors and bankers – all of them male. Japanese men weren't accustomed to dealing with women, even powerful ones. Fortunately, their respect for elderly people proved stronger than their male chauvinism. Although it would take four years for the Helena Rubinstein line of cosmetics to be launched in Japan, her products would go on to be very successful there.

The Far Eastern journey continued. Madame adored Hong Kong, where she stuffed herself with Chinese food and went on a hectic shopping spree, buying tons of pearls and miles of silk. She found the cheongsam – the long, sleeveless Chinese tunic dress – so becoming that she had several made up by a street tailor and later often wore them at her New York parties.

In Australia, O'Higgins was surprised to discover that his employer was still considered a national heroine. In Melbourne, Sydney, Adelaide and Perth, she received a rousing welcome. But she refused to set foot in Coleraine. 'I was hungry, lonely, poor in that awful place. I worked twenty hours every day including Sunday. I swear, if I had to do it all over again, I'd sooner kill myself.'[19]

From Australia they went to Europe. In Paris, Coco Chanel offered to accompany Madame to Switzerland and said she would teach her to relax. 'But I don't *want* to relax!' Madame protested.

No sooner had she returned to New York than she was off again, to Israel this time. Three years earlier she had visited her niece Rachel, Mala and Oscar's sister, in the Neveih Etan kibbutz in the Beit Shean Valley facing the Jordanian frontier.

Mala, who had often been to see her sister with her husband Victor Silson, was extremely enthusiastic about Israel and had encouraged Madame to visit. Helena was full of admiration for the hard-working, courageous Israeli people. She identified with their pioneering spirit and drew renewed strength from her niece's unflagging energy and zeal.

When she left Israel, Helena promised herself she would return. She sought appointments with government representatives on her next trip to the country. Vera Weizmann, the widow of Israel's first president, asked her for some beauty tips when they lunched together. 'You have dry skin!' Helena replied. It was the stock phrase she trotted out for any woman, and once they had reached a certain age she wasn't likely to be proved wrong.

At a luncheon given in her honour by Prime Minister David Ben-Gurion, she met Golda Meir, then Israel's Foreign Minister. Helena was on her guard, unsure how to react to a woman she clearly thought superior to her. She promised to build a factory in Israel if the government opened a museum in her name. But when the Helena Rubinstein Pavilion for Contemporary Art was inaugurated in Tel Aviv in January 1959, it was a disappointment. She didn't like the architecture and thought the building wasn't imposing enough. And it wasn't even entirely devoted to her: the pavilion was part of a museum complex. Then again, she had only given Israel half a million dollars – a far cry from the sum required to build the museum of her dreams.

She'd had her nose put out of joint, so donated only a few of her paintings. But she did bequeath to the pavilion the collection of dolls' houses she had painstakingly added to for over half a century. It included some 20,000 pieces of exquisite antique miniature furniture and hundreds of tiny dolls in vintage clothing. Her Israeli factory was completed three years later, in 1962.

In the summer of 1959, Helena flew to Moscow with Mala, Ceska, Patrick and the nurse who now accompanied her everywhere she went. At eighty-seven, her increasingly fragile health required constant surveillance. The West had cautiously begun to establish trade relations with Soviet Russia, and the American State Department had invited Helena to help represent the US cosmetic industry at the American National Exhibition in Moscow. Madame had never been interested in politics (apart from a soft spot for General de Gaulle), but she immediately grasped the opportunities the mammoth Russian market offered. Above all, she was thrilled to be getting first dibs on a territory her competitors would soon be squabbling over. She spent $100,000 setting up the Helena Rubinstein pavilion and having thousands of brochures printed in Russian. Held at Park Sokilniki, the fair was so important it was officially opened by US Vice-President Richard Nixon and Russian Prime Minister Nikita Khrushchev in person.

Each time she had a problem getting served at the hotel or a restaurant, she slipped the employee a tube of lipstick. The universal language of beauty – and the few words of Russian Artchil had taught

327

her – helped her to get over the linguistic hurdle. She arrived at the fair at opening time each morning. Rather than sit in one of the official stands with the dignitaries, she chose to demonstrate products in her pavilion with Mala, like in the good old days when she was a young woman in Australia.

The fair officials disapproved, but Russian women crowded around her. The stand was never empty. These women – young, old, pretty, plain – had been deprived of beauty products for years and were eager for beauty advice and product samples. No one could have understood their need better than Madame, and she worked as hard as she could to satisfy them.

When she returned from Moscow she was on top form, even though she had been on the go the whole time. Patrick O'Higgins, on the other hand, was exhausted. Intrigued and a bit put out by her superior stamina, he asked her why she was always in a flurry of activity. What exactly was she chasing after?

'Does all this travel really mean anything?'

'It helps me,' she replied. 'I *am* the business.' In a murmur, she added: 'Besides, it helps me to survive.'[20]

30

NOBODY LIVES FOREVER

So she survived. She went to Europe twice a year with a nurse, a doctor and the indispensable O'Higgins in tow. She never missed the Paris haute couture collections in January and July. Her passion for fashion hadn't diminished with the years. Helena was front and centre when Yves Saint Laurent presented his first catwalk show in the Rue Spontini in January 1962, as she had been when Poiret, Chanel, Schiaparelli, Balenciaga and Dior and all the other fashion designers she had discovered or encouraged made their debuts. She bought a shantung suit, a chiffon dress, an embroidered tunic and a coat. She would change her mind about the last item a few days later and order a dress instead.

The Yves Saint Laurent Foundation archive preserves every single order placed with the couture house starting from that maiden show. Madame's is one of the very first names in the very first order book. Pierre Bergé remembers that Helena Rubinstein supplied the make-up for the first show. Madame wanted to make perfumes for Yves Saint Laurent, but for reasons Bergé can no longer recall, her staff thwarted her plans.

He met Helena at Marie-Louise Bousquet's a few years before Saint Laurent opened his couture house, and remembers her with admiration. 'She had an unusually intelligent gaze and an aristocratic bearing,' he says. 'She was a lady. She never flaunted her fortune. Art always came first with her.'[1]

Patrick O'Higgins arranged for her to be photographed everywhere she went. Cameras flashed and mikes were pushed under her nose as soon as she arrived at a catwalk show, preview, inauguration or cocktail party. At nearly ninety – though of course she would never admit her real age – she still enjoyed basking in the spotlight.

Madame rented out the first floor of Quai de Béthune to Georges Pompidou, who held a postgraduate literature degree from the highly selective École Normale Supérieure, and had been a member of the French Council of State and chairman of Rothschild Bank before being appointed President Charles de Gaulle's chief of staff. In April 1962 de Gaulle named him prime minister. Pompidou's circle had always known he was destined for great things.

The Pompidous were exemplary tenants. They were a refined, well-mannered couple, though a bit too serious for Madame's liking. She could see into their rooms when she looked down from the dining room of her apartment and took childish pleasure in spying on them. She fluffed up with pride when Georges Pompidou remained at Quai de Béthune instead of moving to Hôtel Matignon, the official residence of the French prime minister.

An official state car left Quai de Béthune at 8.50 a.m. on the dot every morning to whisk the new Prime Minister to his office. A police car and two motorcycles drove ahead to clear the route. Madame gave orders for her taxi to arrive at the same hour each morning, and instructed the driver to tail the motorcade so she could sail through the red lights on her way to the Rue du Faubourg Saint-Honoré and save on the taxi fare.

Starting new projects was another way to survive. She was all fired up about her new London flat. She had tracked down a large two-storey Edwardian building in Knightsbridge. It was poorly laid out and the consulting architects discouraged her from buying it, but as usual Madame went her own sweet way.

Promising thirty-year-old interior designer David Hicks was the name on everyone's lips. Madame had met him at a reception in Fleur Cowles's flat and thought him very talented. Hicks had all the right credentials: he had studied art at the Central School in London and was married to Prince Philip's cousin Lady Pamela Mountbatten. But the commission to decorate Helena's flat was just the nudge he needed to get himself noticed by the movers and shakers of the time.

She had him come to the site, where the builders were already hard at work demolishing walls. They sat on a crate in a corner of the kitchen to chat. Hicks asked Madame a lot of very specific questions, including what colour she had in mind for the walls. She called her secretary and asked him to bring her a pair of scissors, whereupon she snipped a piece of fabric off her purple silk Balenciaga dress and handed it to the astonished Hicks. 'That's what I want,' she informed him.

Small and compact, the flat had three bedrooms and a living room-cum-dining room. Hicks had designed the living room with purple wool tweed wallpaper that matched the colour swatch Helena had given him. She moved in her cherished Nadelman sculptures, African statuettes and Victorian chairs. Paintings by Picasso, Jean-Michel Atlan, Antoni Clavé and Chagall hung on the walls. There was a small portrait of her friend Poiret by Roger de la Fresnaye in her bedroom. The press raved about the decorator's work. True to form, Hicks had eschewed any hint of ostentatious luxury and brought his rigorous aesthetic to bear on the tiniest detail. Madame loved everything about the flat except for the poky, impractical kitchen.

She didn't stay there often because she was always short of time, but when she did she liked to sit on the terrace, looking out over Hyde Park and thinking about her eventful past and uncertain future.

Patrick O'Higgins's mother died of an embolism in 1962. He had been extremely attached to her. He was grief-stricken and plagued by guilt.

He blamed himself for putting his employer first and seeing so little of his mother towards the end of her life. Madame swept aside his sorrow and took him to Europe with her after the funeral. She gave him the same treatment she had so successfully applied to herself after Artchil's and Horace's deaths: she overworked him.

An exhausted O'Higgins caught a bad cold in Paris, where there was a nasty bug going around, and was bedridden for a few days. When his fever had gone down, Madame summoned him and shouted abuse at him for having left her all alone. Spitting with rage, she called him a 'good-for-nothing'.

It wasn't the first time she'd spoken out of turn. She had become increasingly foul-tempered and unfair to him and the rest of her circle as she aged. But the 'good-for-nothing' was one word too many. He felt as if he had been slapped. He was terribly hurt, and felt he didn't want to see her ever again. He had a relapse. He was so weak he could barely stand, and had to be taken to hospital. But it wasn't a recurrence of the flu. He was diagnosed with depression.

Madame didn't bother telephoning to see how he was doing or sending him flowers. She maintained an obstinate silence, as if it was all his fault. O'Higgins felt even worse. He decided he wasn't going to forgive her this time. French couturier Jean Dessès, who was so fond of Madame he teasingly called her 'my fiancée', stepped into the breach. Since O'Higgins didn't have a penny to his name, Dessès paid for him to go to La Mamounia in Marrakech to convalesce after the month he had spent in hospital. O'Higgins sent a note to Madame to tell her he would be away, but he didn't tell her where he was going.

Madame was starting to feel twinges of remorse. The stubborn old woman had always masked her emotions. She had been unwilling to admit that O'Higgins meant a great deal to her and that she missed him. It was only after her friends and family repeatedly urged her to make it up with him that she changed her mind. She began to think about the incident and gradually realised that her harsh words had genuinely hurt his feelings. Once she had decided she wanted him back, after learning his whereabouts from a friend she started inundating him with letters and messages.

O'Higgins, who had been seriously thinking about quitting his ungrateful employer, began to waver. He weighed up his options. He could either earn a living being at Madame's beck and call or embrace freedom – and financial insecurity. He was moved when he read her letters. Madame had had a nervous breakdown too and was taking bed rest at Stella's in Cannes.

She wrote him affectionate letters every single day. 'I love you like a mother – the mother you've lost,' she always told him.

When O'Higgins felt fully recovered, he returned to Paris and went to Quai de Béthune. Madame was still in Cannes; she wasn't expected back until the next day. Gaston, Eugénie and Marguerite, the three household employees, were overjoyed to see him. 'Madame was in a terrible state,' they told him. 'She really loves you. What else does she have to love? But you're young and she is old. It's for you to make peace.'[2]

The next day O'Higgins went to the airport to meet his employer, his arms filled with his peace offering – one of the huge, expensive bouquets Helena liked. Her face lit up when she saw him. She smiled for the first time in months. But she raised her little gloved hand in a warning gesture, as if to say: 'Let's not overdo the sentiment.'

They talked about this and that – Morocco, Cannes. The seemingly inconsequential chit-chat was their way of burying the hatchet.

Madame would be gentler and more loving with O'Higgins from then on, though she would be no less demanding. She often asked about his health and kept an eye out for him. He in turn looked after her like a devoted son. Their temporary separation had only enhanced their mutual affection.

*

Helena was more than ninety years old by this time. Her mind was as sharp as ever, but her body could no longer keep up. She had fainting fits more and more often because of her diabetes. A suite was always kept in readiness for her at New York Hospital. She was rushed there on a regular basis as soon as she showed signs of weakness, and put on oxygen for a few days until she was breathing normally again. Although she still wanted to be involved in everything, she was forced to slow the pace.

She popped a plethora of pills each day: tranquillisers, anti-diabetics, blood pressure pills, diuretics and sleeping tablets. She suffered from insomnia despite her clockwork sleep schedule: she was in bed by 10 p.m. each night and awoke at 6 a.m. on the dot. In the last few years of her life, she stayed in bed all morning and read her mail – 'even the circulars!'[3] Her lawyer came to see her at 8.30 a.m. each morning, and then she would meet her stockbrokers.

From her bed she would also telephone friends and business associates throughout the world and dictate letters to her secretaries. O'Higgins would arrive, followed by Roy, Oscar or Mala. When she rose towards the end of the morning she took a hot bath, moisturised her face and body, did some stretching exercises and put on her make-up. Her maid helped her put her hair into her perennial chignon. 'There were times when I would have liked a more frilly hair-do, but I have always been a bit short on patience where my appearance was concerned, and besides, the day awaits me … decisions, people, and time slipping by.'[4]

Madame was a great favourite with the world's press. They marvelled at her wealth and down-to-earth manner, her courage, energy, dedication to work and caustic humour. Stories about Helena invariably had titles such as 'Princess of the Beauty Business', 'The Richest Woman in the

World' and 'The Most Fascinating Woman in the Beauty Business'. She was an icon.

The press were complimentary about her extraordinary business acumen and intrigued by her total indifference towards the past – an unusual trait in an elderly woman. She confessed that she lost interest in a product as soon as it had been launched. 'I prefer to look ahead to twenty years from now. But of course I've also got to think about the next two, three or five years,' she would say.[5] When she was asked if she planned to retire, her answer was always the same: 'No! Absolutely not!'

Helena carted her will around with her everywhere. She even slept with it under her pillow. She had drafted it in the late 1950s in a big black leather-covered 200-page notebook resembling a small bible. She kept writing codicils, adding beneficiaries and writing others out each time she became disenchanted with one person or took a fancy to another.

One morning in 1964, Helena's lawyer Harold Weill decided not to keep their 8.30 a.m. appointment. He had quarrelled with her the previous day and was still sulking. Madame, who had been up at the crack of dawn as usual, was venting about his lateness when three burglars posing as flower delivery men rang the doorbell. They tied up her butler, Albert, and the two housekeepers and burst into Madame's bedroom.

She was sitting straight up in her Lucite bed reading *The New York Times* and chewing on a piece of toast. The burglars demanded the keys to her safe. Anyone who read the newspapers was well aware she had more than a million dollars' worth of jewellery in her apartment.

'I may be an old woman, but I'm not scared of you,' she told them. 'You can shoot me if you like, but you're getting nothing from me. Now get out!'

The keys to the safe were in her purse, buried under some newspapers on the bed next to her. As the burglars ransacked the room, looking under furniture, opening drawers and throwing clothes out of the closet, she sneaked the keys out of her purse and slipped them into the only place she could think of – her ample cleavage.

She was just in time. One of the men had spotted the purse and came over to empty its contents on the bed. He was so busy scrabbling for the five $20 bills it contained that he didn't see Madame covering up the pair of diamond earrings that had also fallen out with a used tissue. The earrings were worth at least $40,000.

She sat there cool as a cucumber, watching the thieves frenziedly searching for the keys. They couldn't open the safe in the bathroom without it. She even started to find the situation funny. She pointed to the man who had taken the money from her purse. 'Your friend's taken a hundred dollars,' she told the other two. 'You'd better make sure he shares it with you.'

They stormed over to the bed, hauled her off it, tore her satin sheets into strips and tied her up on a chair with them. Madame began to scream loudly, and the thieves fled. Her butler had managed to untie himself and came to free her, after which he made calls to the police and Madame's immediate circle.

Weill arrived first. Mala and Roy's wife, Niuta, got there shortly after the police. Now quaking with delayed fright, Madame kept describing the thieves as 'nice boys': decent-looking fellows with clean, manicured hands. She was sure they knew her. Perhaps they had worked for her at some point, as maintenance men, or waiters at one of her receptions.

'They were amateurs,' she said scornfully a little later.

The news got around and journalists and television crews lined up on her doorstep. Harold Weill, who was feeling guilty about staying away that morning, offered to drive her to Greenwich so she could rest.

'You must be worn out, Madame,' he said. She categorically refused to do anything of the kind.

'Rest?' she snapped. 'Are you crazy? Hand me that lipstick and let those journalists in. This is great publicity for the business.'

Madame dressed and carefully made up her face, put on the diamond earrings the burglars had overlooked and described the whole incident for the flock of journalists eagerly proffering their mikes. New Yorkers talked about it for quite some time. It did wonders for her popularity.

But the burglary affected her in other ways. She had always had a suspicious nature and now she turned paranoid, thinking everyone was out to either steal from her or betray her. She had the locks to her apartment changed and a new alarm installed. She worried she wouldn't be as lucky if there was another burglary. For the first time in her life, Madame suddenly felt very old.

She got on a plane to Paris, wanting to visit the city one last time and meet all her old friends there, especially the group of women she had nicknamed 'the intellectuals'. Her faithful friend Edmonde Charles-Roux wrote a flattering piece about her for *Vogue*, describing her as 'an elegant woman with a calm but authoritative voice'.[6]

With O'Higgins at her side, Madame visited her favourite French haunts: the Saint-Ouen flea market, Honfleur and her Saint-Cloud factory. She had sold Maison Blanche several years before to a member of former French President René Coty's family. 'I hope they'll like it better than I did,' she had said. But she had kept the mill at Combs-la-Ville, and that summer she gave the last of her famous parties there for 200 guests.

It was such perfect weather that she had all the furniture moved out of the house and into the garden, where a buffet was laid out. The bar was set up in the stables to keep the drinks cool. As a finishing touch, she had her staff hang all the paintings that adorned her country house

– the Monets, Renoirs, Chagalls and Modiglianis – from the trees. There was a little stream lined with weeping willows a short distance from the house. 'We'll put the Picassos in the shade of the willows,' she decided. 'He's always hated parties.' Relating the anecdote later, *Daily Express* writer Jean Lorimer wrote: 'Helena Rubinstein was probably the greatest, craziest and most generous party giver of the century, Elsa Maxwell excepted.'[7]

Madame's thoughts were turning inexorably towards death even as she tried to live life to the fullest. Little by little, she had allowed Revlon, Max Factor, Estée Lauder and Avon to outstrip her. Her only consolation was that she was still way ahead of Elizabeth Arden. In 1963, David Ogilvy brought his thirteen-year collaboration with Helena Rubinstein to an end. When he had started up his agency on Madison Avenue, the company had been one of his first clients. But times had changed and he had bigger fish to fry: Revlon's ad budget was ten times the size of hers.

Meanwhile, a British publisher wanted her to write her autobiography. Although Madame had never been much of a one for looking back, she accepted the proposal and got to work, hiring journalist Jean Lorimer to be her ghost writer. Patrick O'Higgins, who later revised the text, encouraged her to be truthful. He told her people would want to read her real life story, warts and all, not a watered-down version, but Helena refused. If her life was being recorded for posterity, she wanted to make sure she looked good. But she did let a few genuine confidences slip. At her last meeting with Jean Lorimer in December 1964, Madame had a rare fit of nostalgia. She admitted to feeling a failure – with her father, her first husband and her two sons. She had caused her father great grief by refusing to marry the man he had chosen for her and leaving for Australia instead. She should have been more considerate of Edward's feelings. She had been so obsessed by her business that she had spent only a month or two of the year with him. Of course he had

had flings, but she had known they weren't serious.[8]

The minutes ticked by. Madame remained lost in thought. The journalist held her breath for fear of shattering the fragile moment. Then Helena spoke again, almost in a whisper: 'I can say this now but at the time I was far too young and inexperienced to understand. Perhaps it would have been better if I'd had some affairs myself. I've always regretted this. I think it would have made me a nicer person. But actually at that time Edward was the only man I'd ever kissed.'[9]

On 31 March 1965, she started feeling poorly. She had spent the whole of the previous afternoon at the Long Island factory. That morning, she had summoned her staff to her bedroom for a meeting. She had criticised the layout of a new advertising campaign. She found the letters too small and the text too skimpy. Then she nearly bit Mala's head off for having made the instructions for using a new make-up product too complicated. 'You've got to keep it simple so everyone can understand what to do,' she admonished.[10]

Work over, she settled back against her pillows and asked them to give her the latest gossip. Was Givenchy still designing Audrey Hepburn's clothes, she wanted to know. 'He's a gentleman and she's a lady – they understand one another.' Someone asked if she had enjoyed *Goldfinger*, which she had gone to see the previous evening with Sara Fox. 'Too brutal!' she exclaimed. 'It sets a bad example. But I saw it only once!'[11]

Her doctors took her to New York Hospital that afternoon. She had a heart attack and then an embolism. She died the next morning in her hospital room. Alone. She was ninety-three.

Her death made the front pages of all the major American newspapers and was written up in the international press. Journalists around the world recalled her legendary status and described her sprawling empire. The *New York Herald Tribune* scrapped Eugenia Sheppard's popular column to make space for a tribute to Helena by Patrick O'Higgins. He summed up the feelings of her family and staff with these words: 'We thought she was immortal.'

At the time of her death, the Helena Rubinstein brand was established in more than thirty countries, owned fourteen factories and had a staff of 32,000 in salons, factories and laboratories in fifteen different countries. Madame's personal fortune amounted to $100 million in property, stocks and bonds, jewellery, artworks, furniture and money stashed in bank accounts on three continents.

The wake was held at a funeral parlour. A taxi strike had paralysed traffic, but New York's A-list still managed to find their way to the funeral parlour to offer their last respects. Madame seemed even tinier in her coffin than she had been in real life. She looked like 'a small doll – one that was Mexican in its opulence and beauty'.[12] 'I'll never forget the nobility of her features,' O'Higgins wrote in his tribute.[13]

Madame was laid to rest with her husband Prince Artchil Gourielli.

31

THE EMPIRE WITHOUT ITS EMPRESS

The will Madame had jealously guarded until she breathed her last was forty-four pages long, including twenty-seven pages of codicils, and allocated varying amounts of money to several hundred beneficiaries. Not everyone was happy with her bequests. Many of them felt they had been short-changed, such as Madame's Filipino butler, Albert, who was furious when he discovered she had rewarded him for years of loyal service with a measly $500 annual pension.

Mala got Madame's black and white pearl sets, a Derain, a Nadelman, a Kandinsky and a $5,000 annuity, and kept her senior post with the company. O'Higgins philosophically interpreted this to mean that Helena had wanted her niece to keep the business going. 'Had she left her a princely sum, who knows? Mala might have retired.'[1] But she didn't. Roy headed the empire in the ruling triumvirate that took over after Madame's death. The other two were Mala, who remained in charge of the creative side of things, and her brother Oscar, who was appointed vice-president of the company.

Patrick O'Higgins hadn't been particularly well rewarded for his loyalty either. Madame had left him $5,000 in cash and an annual pension of $2,000 to be paid out until his death (he died in June 1980, aged fifty-eight). According to Madame's lawyer Harold Weill, she had scornfully said, 'So he doesn't starve to death!' when adding that particular codicil. Amazingly, Patrick O'Higgins not only backed her decision, he even justified it. After all, he said, he wasn't part of the family, and he had worked for his immensely rich employer for only fourteen years. The cash and the annuity worked out to a total of $45,000, assuming he lived for another twenty years (he didn't know he'd be dead in fifteen years' time). Madame probably hadn't wanted to leave him all that money in one go. She knew what a spendthrift he was. He was sure she had wanted to protect him from himself.

A few months after Madame's death, the Parke-Bernet Galleries in New York auctioned her jewellery collection. Although the event received extensive media coverage and created a major buzz, the results were disappointing. Practically all the pieces were snapped up in a mere three hours, but the pearls she had bought on the French Riviera after discovering Edward's first fling, her rings, pear-shaped diamond earrings, sapphires, topazes and her emeralds the size of bottle stoppers brought only half a million dollars – less than half the amount the auctioneers had expected them to sell for.

Parke-Bernet put her art collection up for sale shortly afterwards. The two-day auction brought a total of $5 million, half of which was swallowed up by inheritance tax. The annotated five-volume catalogue listed Madame's paintings, sculptures, drawings, engravings, antique furniture and African and Oceanic statues and objets d'art. More than 10,000 visitors seized the unprecedented opportunity to admire her collection of masterpieces.

The fakes – Madame's 'little mistakes', like the Picasso portrait of Guillaume Apollinaire – were taken off the catalogue. But the rest of the collection went under the hammer for sums that were astronomical compared to the pittance Madame had paid for them. One of her Senuofo masks sold for $90,000, while Brancusi's *Bird in Flight* statue went for $140,000.

In 1990, the collectors who had paid $29,000 at the Parke-Bernet auction for the 'Bangwa Queen' statuette, the pride of Madame's African art collection, sold it for just over $3.5 million. The same year,

Sotheby's resold Brancusi's *The White Negress* for $8 million.

Madame's closest relatives – her sons, grandchildren, nephews and nieces – were the main beneficiaries of her will. But she had stipulated that after payment of inheritance tax, the bulk of her fortune was to be invested in a family-owned trust that would pay out dividends to her family members. It was her way of making it clear she wanted them to continue working for a living.

The remaining money went to the Helena Rubinstein Foundation, which still occupies its original Madison Avenue premises. When the company was sold some years later, the family's shares in the American business, foreign subsidiaries and properties were also made over to the foundation, whose board is largely made up of Rubinstein family members. Oscar Kolin's daughter Diane Moss took over from her father as president and chief executive officer of the board. When Roy died in April 1989, his stepchildren, Suzanne and Louis Slesin, were respectively appointed director and treasurer.

The walls of the foundation's workaday offices are hung with paintings worth a small fortune: the portraits of Madame by Dalí, Dufy, Marie Laurencin, Helleu, and Vertès. The Graham Sutherland portrait is undoubtedly the most striking, the Marie Laurencin one the gentlest. 'My fortune comes from women and should benefit them and their children, to better their quality of life,' Madame said when she set up her foundation in 1953. Until 2011, when it was wound up, the Helena Rubinstein Foundation allocated grants amounting to up to $2 million each year, mainly to support programmes in education, arts and health.

The Park Avenue triplex – Helena's 'castle in the sky' – was bought by a lawyer, who subsequently resold it to none other than Charles Revson. How the 'nail man' must have relished his posthumous pot shot at the Empress of Beauty! He spent more than two years getting the penthouse refurbished to suit his flashy taste. Invited to dinner at

Revson's a few years later, Patrick O'Higgins cast a sardonic eye over the decor reeking of new money and was unable to find anything to like about it. 'Madame would have laughed her chuckle with glee,' he commented. 'She used to say, "the Nail King had very ordinary taste … but then that's why he's so successful."'[2]

Quai de Béthune was sold to the Count of Chandon, then resold to a wealthy Lebanese gentleman before changing hands for the third time. Parisian interior designer François Joseph Graf, who recently revamped the entire place, says the only traces of Helena's original apartment are the majestic terrace with its sweeping view of Paris and the staircase banister.[3]

Stella spent the rest of her life in the 216 Boulevard Raspail apartment her sister had given her the use of. Ceska lived in the London pied-à-terre decorated by David Hicks until her death eighteen months after Helena's.

Perhaps ill at ease on the throne of her colossal business empire, Madame's heirs sold the company to Colgate-Palmolive in 1973 for $143 million and got out of the beauty industry. Colgate, too, floundered in its attempts to keep the business afloat. Despite blockbuster ad campaigns, the brand continued its free fall.

A small cosmetics firm called Albi Enterprises Inc. bought Helena Rubinstein in 1980 and tried equally unsuccessfully to restore it to its former glory. The real turnaround came when L'Oréal bought the company in 1988. Helena Rubinstein products are now distributed in around thirty countries, mainly in Europe and Asia, and sales are booming.

The brand that invented the first automatic mascara continues to transform scientific expertise into inventive make-up products. Lash Queen Feline Blacks mascara has been a consistent top-seller in recent years, while products such as the Collagenist and Prodigy line – the most recent creation being Prodigy Powercell, which stimulates skin cell regeneration – are the result of cutting-edge research. The brand has a constant focus on innovation and works closely with scientists the way Madame herself used to. Says Elisabeth Sandager, the brand's international general manager: 'If Helena Rubinstein were alive today, I'm sure she would have endorsed the partnership we signed in 2008 with internationally renowned plastic surgeon Dr Pfulg, founder of the Laclinic beauty clinic in Montreux, Switzerland, to develop a pioneering line of beauty products drawing from surgical techniques.'

According to L'Oréal France vice-president Béatrice Dautresme,[4] the Women in Science programme co-founded by L'Oréal and UNESCO to recognise the achievements of exceptional female scientists across the globe has been directly inspired by Madame's obsessive quest to put science at the service of beauty.

In 2007, actress Demi Moore – a woman as 'strong, determined, smart and seductive'[5] as Helena Rubinstein herself – was signed on as the face of the brand. Madame would have approved.

NOTES

PREFACE

1 Rubinstein, Helena, *The Art of Feminine Beauty*, Horace Liveright, 1930.
2 Rubinstein, Helena, *My Life for Beauty*, Simon & Schuster, 1965.
3 Brown Keifer, Elaine, 'Madame Rubinstein: The Little Lady from Kraków Has Made a Fabulous Success of Selling Beauty', *Life*, 21 July 1941.
4 Slesin, Suzanne, *Over the Top: Helena Rubinstein, Extraordinary Style, Beauty, Art, Fashion and Design*, Pointed Leaf Press, 2004.

1. EXILE

1 Charles-Roux, Edmonde, 1957.
2 Rubinstein, Helena, *My Life for Beauty*, op. cit.
3 ibid.

2. KAZIMIERZ

1 Helena's year of birth is controversial; it is found in different sources as both 1870 and 1872. The latter is given by Patrick O'Higgins in his book, *Madame: An Intimate Biography of Helena Rubinstein*, Viking Press, 1971.
2 Photocopies of Helena Rubinstein's 1922 passport (www.ancestry.com).
3 Rubinstein, Helena, *My Life for Beauty*, op. cit.
4 Author's interview with Litka Goldberg-Fasse, Helena Rubinstein's second cousin, June 2009.
5 Alfred Silberfeld, genealogist.
6 O'Higgins, *Madame*, op. cit.

3. THE RUBINSTEIN FAMILY

1 Rubinstein, Helena, *Je suis Esthéticienne*, Éditions du Conquistador, 1957.
2 Rubinstein, Helena, *My Life for Beauty*, op. cit.
3 ibid.
4 Woodhead, Lindy, *War Paint: Madame Helena Rubinstein and Miss Elizabeth Arden, Their Lives, Their Times, Their Rivalry*, John Wiley & Sons Inc., 2004.

5 Rubinstein, Helena, *The Art of Feminine Beauty*, op. cit.

4. A MERCILESS NEW WORLD
1 *The Age*, Melbourne, 25 August 1979.
2 ibid.

6. 243 COLLINS STREET
1 O'Higgins, *Madame*, op. cit.
2 *The Herald*, Melbourne, 1971.
3 Photocopies of Helena Rubinstein's application for naturalisation as an Australian citizen (source: Antoine Silberfeld).

7. BEAUTY IS POWER
1 Fabe, Maxene, *Beauty Millionaire: The Life of Helena Rubinstein*, Crowell, 1972.
2 Helena cited Eugenia Stone as a journalist from Sydney in *My Life for Beauty*, and the *Sydney Morning Herald* was one of the only papers to have a women's supplement, so I have deduced that that was the publication she was writing for. She also worked for *Table Talk* in Melbourne.
3 O'Higgins, *Madame*, op. cit.
4 Vigarello, Georges, *Histoire de la beauté: le corps et l'art d'embellir de la Renaissance à nos jours*, Points Seuil, 2007.
5 Rubinstein, Helena, *The Art of Feminine Beauty*, op. cit.

8. BACK TO HER ROOTS
1 Vigarello, *Histoire de la beauté*, op. cit.
2 Gilman, Sander, 'La chirurgie de la beauté', *100 000 ans de beauté*, Gallimard for L'Oréal, 2009.
3 O'Higgins, *Madame*, op. cit.
4 Vigarello, op. cit.
5 ibid.

9. EDWARD WILLIAM TITUS
1 Rubinstein, Helena, *My Life for Beauty*, op. cit.
2 O'Higgins, *Madame*, op. cit.
3 Ameisen, Dr Olivier, *Le Dernier Verre*, Denoël, 2008.

4 Email to the author from Eva Ameisen (the daughter of Edward Titus's nephew Emmanuel Ameisen) in May 2010. Emmanuel Ameisen's grandfather had nine children: Arthur (Edward Titus), David, Mala, Lisa, Sarah, Frida, Hanka, Oleg and Jacob (Emmanuel's father). When Emmanuel left Poland for France before the Second World War, his uncle Edward Titus, whom he admired immensely, got him a job with Helena Rubinstein and put him up at his flat in the Rue Delambre. (Author's telephone conversation with Emmanuel Ameisen's son Olivier in May 2010.)

5 Photocopies of Edward Titus's and Helena Rubinstein's passports in 1922 and 1923 respectively; Arthur Ameisen's application for naturalisation as an American citizen (www.ancestry.com).

6 Biography of Arthur Ameisen.
http://genealogytrails.com/penn/allegheny/allegpa_bios_a.html

7 www.ancestry.com

8 Author's email correspondence with Barry Titus and Eva Ameisen, 2010.

9 *The Mercury*, 29 December 1909.

10 *Brisbane Courier*, 18 March 1911.

11 *Sunday Times*, 14 March 1909.

12 'Care of the Skin', *Sydney Morning Herald*, 16 October 1909.

10. MAYFAIR LADY

1 Rubinstein, Helena, *My Life for Beauty*, op. cit.

2 Swerling, Jo, 'Profiles: Beauty in Jars and Vials', *The New Yorker*, 30 June 1928.

3 Rubinstein, Helena, *My Life for Beauty*, op. cit.

4 ibid.

5 London marriage index, June to September 1908 (www.ancestry.com).

11. 24 GRAFTON STREET

1 Woodhead, *War Paint*, op. cit.

2 *The Queen*, 3 February 1909.

3 Poiret, Paul, *My First Fifty Years*, Victor Gollancz, 1931.

4 ibid.

5 Woodhead, op. cit.

6 Rubinstein, Helena, *Je suis Esthéticienne*, op. cit.

7 'How She Conquered the World's Metropolis', *The Mercury*, 27 March 1909.

8 ibid.

9 ibid.

10 ibid.

11 Poiret, *My First Fifty Years*, op. cit.

12 ibid.

12. Rich and Famous

1 Rubinstein, Helena, *My Life for Beauty*, op. cit.

2 London telephone directory, page 754 (www.ancestry.com)

3 Rubinstein, Helena, *My Life for Beauty*, op. cit.

4 O'Higgins, *Madame*, op. cit.

5 James, T. F., 'Princess of the Beauty Business', *Cosmopolitan*, June 1959.

6 Rubinstein, Helena, *Je suis Esthéticienne*, op. cit.

7 Helena Rubinstein archives.

8 Tashjian, Dickran, *A Boatload of Madmen: Surrealism and the American Avant-Garde, 1920–1950*, Thames and Hudson, 1995.

9 Helena Rubinstein archives.

10 ibid.

13. Paris, Here I Come!

1 Wharton, Edith, *French Ways and Their Meaning*, D. Appleton and Company, 1919.

2 ibid.

3 Rubinstein, Helena, *Je suis Esthéticienne*, op. cit.

4 Vigarello, *Histoire de la beauté*, op. cit.

5 ibid.

6 Marseille, Jacques, *L'Oréal 1909–2009*, Librairie Académique Perrin, 2009.

7 Melchior-Bonnet, Sabine, 'La beauté veut se voir', *100 000 ans de beauté*, op. cit.

8 ibid.

9 Gilman, Sander, in *100 000 ans de beauté*, op. cit.

10 O'Higgins, *Madame*, op. cit.

11 ibid.

12 ibid.

13 ibid.

14 Charles-Roux, Edmonde, *Chanel and Her World*, Vendome Press, 2005.

14. Beauty Enlightening the World

1 Rubinstein, Helena, *My Life for Beauty*, op. cit.

2 Banner, Lois W., *American Beauty*, Knopf, 1983.

3 ibid., as quoted in Woodhead, *War Paint*, op. cit.

4 Banner, op. cit.

5 Peiss, Kathy, *Hope in a Jar: The Making of America's Beauty Culture*, Holt Paperbacks, 1998.

6 Woodhead, op. cit.

7 Vigarello, *Histoire de la beauté*, op. cit.

8 Grossman, Ann Carol and Reisman, Arnie (directors), *The Powder and the Glory*, PBS, 2009.

9 Slesin, *Over the Top*, op. cit.

10 ibid.

11 Clifford, Marie J., 'Helena Rubinstein's Beauty Salons, Fashion, and Modernist Display', *Winterthur Portfolio*, Vol. 38, No. 2/3 (Summer–Autumn 2003), University of Chicago Press.

12 ibid.

13 ibid.

14 ibid.

15 O'Higgins, *Madame*, op. cit.

16 ibid.

17 Rubinstein, Helena, *My Life for Beauty*, op. cit.

15. The Great Rubinstein Road Tour

1 Rubinstein, Helena, *Je suis Esthéticienne*, op. cit.

2 ibid.

3 ibid.

4 ibid.

5 *Daily Express*, 5 April 1965.

6 Rubinstein, Helena, *My Life for Beauty*, op. cit.

7 Helena Rubinstein archives.

8 Rubinstein, Helena, *My Life for Beauty*, op. cit.

16. Paris is a Moveable Feast

1 MacMillan, Margaret, *Paris 1919: Six Months that Changed the World*, Random House Trade Paperbacks, 2003.

2 Putnam, Samuel, *Paris was our Mistress: Memoirs of a Lost and Found Generation*, Southern Illinois University Press, 1970.

3 *Vogue*, 1934, quoted in Vigarello, *Histoire de la beauté*, op. cit.

4 Morand, Paul, *The Allure of Chanel*, Pushkin Press, 2009.

5 Woodhead, *War Paint*, op. cit.

6 Herschdorfer, Nathalie, 'Extension du domaine du rêve' in *100,000 ans de beauté*, op. cit.

7 Grey, Allison, 'People who want to look young and beautiful', *American Magazine*, December 1922.

8 Woodhead, op. cit.

9 O'Higgins, *Madame*, op. cit.

10 ibid.

11 ibid.

12 Rubinstein, Helena, *My Life for Beauty*, op. cit.

13 ibid.

14 Poem by Edward Titus to his wife, 1920.

15 Swerling, 'Profiles: Beauty in Jars and Vials', op. cit.

17. FRIEND TO ARTISTS

1 Sachs, *Au temps du Bœuf sur le Toit*, Les Cahiers Rouges, Grasset et Fasquelle, 1987

2 Slesin, *Over the Top*, op. cit.

3 Rubinstein, Helena, *My Life for Beauty*, op. cit.

4 ibid.

5 ibid.

6 ibid.

7 ibid.

8 O'Higgins, *Madame*, op. cit.

9 Rubinstein, Helena, *My Life for Beauty*, op. cit.

10 O'Higgins, op. cit.

11 Rubinstein, Helena, *My Life for Beauty*, op. cit.

12 Vreeland, Diana, *DV*, DaCapo Press, 2004.

13 ibid.

14 Rubinstein, Helena, *My Life for Beauty*, op. cit.

15 ibid.

16 *Daily Express*, 6 April 1965.

17 Helena Rubinstein archives.

18 Author's interview with Pierre Bergé, February 2010.

19 O'Higgins, op. cit.

20 ibid.

21 Rubinstein, Helena, *My Life for Beauty*, op. cit.

22 ibid.

23 Helena Rubinstein archives.

24 ibid.

25 O'Higgins, op. cit.

18. BEAUTY BECOMES BIG BUSINESS

1 *New York Post*, 9 February 1939.

2 Peiss, *Hope in a Jar*, op. cit.

3 ibid.

4 ibid.

5 Slesin, *Over the Top*, op. cit.

6 *Time* magazine, 30 June 1928.

7 ibid.

8 Swerling, 'Profiles: Beauty in Jars and Vials', op. cit.

19. THE LITTLE LADY TAKES ON WALL STREET

1 Dinnerstein, Leonard, *Antisemitism in America*, Oxford University Press, 1994.

2 Woodhead, *War Paint*, op. cit.

3 Swerling, 'Profiles: Beauty in Jars and Vials', op. cit.

4 Rubinstein, Helena, *My Life for Beauty*, op. cit.

5 Woodhead, op. cit.

6 ibid.

7 Rubinstein, Helena, *My Life for Beauty*, op. cit.

8 *Life*, July 1941, op. cit.

9 Woodhead, op. cit.

10 ibid.

20. MOURNING FOR HAPPINESS

1 Woodhead, *War Paint*, op. cit.

2 Rubinstein, Helena, *The Art of Feminine Beauty*, op. cit.

3 Woodhead, op. cit.

4 O'Higgins, *Madame*, op. cit.

21. Family Life

1 Slesin, *Over the Top*, op. cit.

2 Author's email correspondence with Barry Titus, January 2010.

3 Rubinstein, Mala, *The Mala Rubinstein Book of Beauty*, Doubleday, 1973.

4 ibid.

5 ibid.

6 ibid.

7 ibid.

8 ibid.

22. Stay Young!

1 Peiss, *Hope in a Jar*, op. cit.

2 ibid.

3 *Mademoiselle*, August 1937.

4 Rowlands, Penelope, *A Dash of Daring: Carmel Snow and her Life in Fashion, Art and Letters*, Simon & Schuster, 2005.

5 Rubinstein, Helena, *My Life for Beauty*, op. cit.

6 ibid.

23. Who is the Fairest of Them All?

1 'Elizabeth Arden: Queen', *Fortune*, August 1930.

2 ibid.

3 *Life*, July 1941, op. cit.

4 O'Higgins, *Madame*, op. cit.

5 'Elizabeth Arden: Queen', *Fortune*, op. cit.

6 O'Higgins, op. cit.

7 Rubinstein, Helena, *My Life for Beauty*, op. cit.

8 Vreeland, *DV*, op. cit.

9 ibid.

10 Rubinstein, Helena, *Food for Beauty*, David McKay, 1938.

11 ibid.

12 Slesin, *Over the Top*, op. cit.

13 Rubinstein, Helena, *My Life for Beauty*, op. cit.

14 Helena Rubinstein archives.

15 *Candide* (newspaper), 1939.

24. PRINCESS GOURIELLI

1 O'Higgins, *Madame*, op. cit.
2 Author's interview with Helena Rubinstein's great-niece Diane Moss, June 2009.
3 *Smith's Weekly*, November 1938.
4 *Life*, July 1941, op. cit.
5 Author's interview with Erica Titus Friedman in Cannes, May 2009.
6 ibid.
7 Tobias, Andrew, *Fire and Ice: The Story of Charles Revson, the Man who Built the Revlon Empire*, William Morrow & Company, 1976.

25. WATCHING THE WAR FROM NEW YORK

1 Clifford, 'Helena Rubinstein's Beauty Salons, Fashion, and Modernist Display', op. cit.
2 Rubinstein, Helena, *My Life for Beauty*, op. cit.
3 Dinnerstein, *Antisemitism in America*, op. cit.
4 O'Higgins, *Madame*, op. cit.
5 Rubinstein, Helena, *My Life for Beauty*, op. cit.
6 Lardner, David, 'The Talk of the Town: Up on the Farm', *The New Yorker*, 22 May 1943.
7 Rubinstein, Helena, *My Life for Beauty*, op. cit.
8 ibid.
9 Woodhead, *War Paint*, op. cit.
10 Letters written by Roy Titus to his mother, lent to the author by Suzanne Slesin.
11 Author's interview with Litka Goldberg-Fasse, Helena Rubinstein's second cousin, June 2009.

26. REBUILDING ONCE AGAIN

1 Rubinstein, Helena, *My Life for Beauty*, op. cit.
2 ibid.
3 ibid.
4 ibid.
5 Author's interview with Edmonde Charles-Roux, June 2009.
6 O'Higgins, *Madame*, op. cit.

27. THE PINK JUNGLE

1 Peiss, *Hope in a Jar*, op. cit.

2 'Modern Living: The Pink Jungle', *Time* magazine, 16 June 1958.

3 Woodhead, *War Paint*, op. cit.

4 Tobias, *Fire and Ice*, op. cit.

5 Peiss, *Hope in a Jar*, op. cit.

6 *Sunday Times*, January 1962.

7 O'Higgins, *Madame*, op. cit.

8 ibid.

28. THE LAST MAN IN HER LIFE

1 O'Higgins, *Madame*, op. cit.

2 ibid.

3 Author's interview with Bernard Minoret, February 2010.

4 O'Higgins, *Madame*, op. cit.

5 ibid.

6 'Cosmetics: Beauty's Handmaiden', *Time* magazine, 26 January 1953.

7 ibid.

8 Woodhead, *War Paint*, op. cit.

9 O'Higgins, *Madame*, op. cit.

10 *Life*, July 1941.

11 O'Higgins, *Madame*, op. cit.

12 ibid.

13 ibid.

14 ibid.

15 ibid.

16 ibid.

17 ibid.

18 ibid.

19 ibid.

29. THE SHOW MUST GO ON

1 O'Higgins, *Madame*, op. cit.

2 ibid.

3 ibid.

4 Rubinstein, Helena, *My Life for Beauty*, op. cit.

5 ibid.

6 Richardson, John, *The Sorcerer's Apprentice: Picasso, Provence and Douglas Cooper*, Chicago Press, 2001.

7 O'Higgins, *Madame*, op. cit.

8 ibid.

9 James, T. F., 'Princess of the Beauty Business', *Cosmopolitan*, op. cit.

10 Rubinstein, Helena, *Je suis Esthéticienne*, op. cit.

11 Rubinstein, Helena, *My Life for Beauty*, op. cit.

12 ibid.

13 O'Higgins, *Madame*, op. cit.

14 Rubinstein, Helena, *My Life for Beauty*, op. cit.

15 O'Higgins, op. cit.

16 ibid.

17 ibid.

18 James, op. cit.

19 ibid.

20 O'Higgins, op. cit.

30. NOBODY LIVES FOREVER

1 Author's interview with Pierre Bergé, February 2010.

2 O'Higgins, *Madame*, op. cit.

3 Rubinstein, Helena, *My Life for Beauty*, op. cit.

4 ibid.

5 James, 'Princess of the Beauty Business', *Cosmopolitan*, op. cit.

6 O'Higgins, op. cit.

7 *Daily Express*, 6 April 1965.

8 ibid.

9 ibid.

10 O'Higgins, *Madame*, op. cit.

11 ibid.

12 ibid.

13 O'Higgins, Patrick, 'A tribute', *New York Herald Tribune*, 11 April 1965.

31. THE EMPIRE WITHOUT ITS EMPRESS

1 O'Higgins, *Madame*, op. cit.

2 ibid.

3 Author's telephone interview with architect and interior decorator François

Joseph Graf, October 2009.

4 Author's interview with Béatrice Dautresme, vice-president of L'Oréal France.

5 Quote from the Helena Rubinstein section of the L'Oréal website.

BIBLIOGRAPHY

AUTOBIOGRAPHY AND OTHER BOOKS BY HELENA RUBINSTEIN
Rubinstein, Helena, *My Life for Beauty*, Simon & Schuster, 1965.
Rubinstein, Helena, *Je suis Esthéticienne*, Éditions du Conquistador, 1957.
Rubinstein Helena, *The Art of Feminine Beauty*, Horace Liveright, 1930.
Rubinstein, Helena, *Food for Beauty*, David McKay, 1938.

BIOGRAPHIES OF HELENA RUBINSTEIN
Fabe, Maxene, *Beauty Millionaire: The Life of Helena Rubinstein*, Thomas Y. Crowell Co., 1972.
Jazdzewksi, Catherine, *Helena Rubinstein*, Assouline, 2003.
Leveau-Fernandez, Madeleine, *Helena Rubinstein*, Flammarion, 2003.
O'Higgins, Patrick, *Madame: An Intimate Biography of Helena Rubinstein*, Viking Press, 1971.
Slesin, Suzanne, *Over the Top: Helena Rubinstein, Extraordinary Style, Beauty, Art, Fashion and Design*, Pointed Leaf Press, 2004.
Woodhead, Lindy, *War Paint: Madame Helena Rubinstein and Miss Elizabeth Arden, Their Lives, Their Times, Their Rivalry*, John Wiley & Sons Inc., 2004.

OTHER NON-FICTION – IN FRENCH
Ameisen, Dr Olivier, *Le Dernier Verre*, Denoël, 2008.
Arnaud, Claude, *Jean Cocteau*, NRF Gallimard, 2003.
Baudot, François, *Schiaparelli*, Assouline, 1997.
Benaim, Laurence, *Marie-Laure de Noailles: La Vicomtesse du Bizarre*, Grasset, 2001.
Bonal, Gérard and Maget, Frédéric (eds), *Colette journaliste*, Éditions du Seuil, 2010.
Chalmet, Véronique, *Peggy Guggenheim*, Payot, 2009.
Colombani, Marie-Françoise and Fitoussi, Michèle, *ELLE, une Histoire des Femmes 1945–2005*, Éditions Filippachi, 2005.
De Saint Pern, Dominique, *Les Amants du Soleil noir*, Grasset, 2005.
De Saint Pern, Dominique, *L'extravagante Dorothy Parker*, Grasset, 1994.

Dorleans, Francis, *Snob Society*, Flammarion, 2009.

Frank, Dan, *Bohèmes*, Calmann Lévy, 1998.

Fugier, Anne Martin, *Les Salons de la IIIᵉ République*, Perrin, 2003.

Londres, Albert, *Le Juif errant est arrivé*, Le Serpent à Plumes, 1998.

Loyer, Emmanuelle, *Paris à New York: Intellectuels et artistes français en exil (1940–1947)*, Grasset, 2005.

Monnier, Adrienne, *Éternelle libraire* (not for sale: distributed free of charge at an independent bookseller event in France in April 2010).

Mugnier (l'Abbé), *Journal*, Mercure de France, 1985.

Murat, Laure, *Passage de l'Odéon: Sylvia Beach, Adrienne Monnier et la vie littéraire à Paris dans l'entre-deux-guerres*, Fayard, 2003.

Peretz, Pauline (ed.), *New York, histoire, promenades, anthologie, dictionnaire*, Robert Laffont Bouquins, 2009.

Ripa, Yannick, *Les femmes en France de 1880 à nos jours*, Éditions du Chêne, 2007.

Sachs, Maurice, *Au temps du Bœuf sur le toit*, Les Cahiers Rouges, Grasset et Fasquelle, 1987.

Sarde, Michèle, *Colette, libre et entravée*, Points Seuil, 1984.

Vigarello, Georges, *Histoire de la beauté: le corps et l'art d'embellir de la Renaissance à nos jours*, Points Seuil, 2007.

Wagener, Françoise, *Je suis née inconsolable: Louise de Vilmorin*, Albin Michel, 2008.

Le goût de l'Australie (various authors), Mercure de France, 2009.

100 000 ans de beauté, Gallimard for L'Oréal, 2009.

OTHER NON-FICTION – IN ENGLISH

Allan, Tony, *Americans in Paris*, Bison Books, 1977.

Allen, Frederick Lewis, *Only Yesterday: An Informal History of the 1920s*, Harper & Row, 1931.

Ballard, Bettina, *In My Fashion*, David McKay Company Inc., 1960.

Banner, Lois W., *American Beauty*, Knopf, 1983.

Callaghan, Morley, *That Summer in Paris*, Exile Editions, 2007.

Charles-Roux, Edmonde, *Chanel and Her World*, Vendome Press, 2005.

Cowles, Fleur, *Friends & Memories*, Jonathan Cape, 1975.

Dinnerstein, Leonard, *Antisemitism in America*, Oxford University Press, 1994.

Dwight, Eleanor, *Diana Vreeland*, William Morrow, 2002.

Eco, Umberto (ed.), *On Beauty: A History of a Western Idea*, Secker & Warburg, 2004.

Fitch, Noël Riley, *Sylvia Beach and the Lost Generation: A History of Literary Paris in the Twenties and Thirties*, W.W. Norton & Company, 1985.

Flanner, Janet, *Paris Journal: 1944–1955*, HBJ Books, 1988.

Flanner, Janet, *Paris Journal: 1956–1964*, HBJ Books, 1988.

Glassco, John, *Memoirs of Montparnasse*, Oxford University Press, 1970.

Gold, Arthur and Fitzdale, Robert, *Misia: The Life of Misia Sert*, Knopf, 1980.

Klüver, Billy and Martin, Julie, *Kiki's Paris: Artists and Lovers 1900–1930*, Harry N. Abrams, 1989.

Lee, Hermione, *Edith Wharton*, Random House, 2007.

Libo, Kenneth (ed.), *Lots of Lehmans: The Family of Mayer Lehman of Lehman Brothers, Remembered by His Descendants*, Centre for Jewish History, Syracuse University Press, 2007.

Markowski, Stanislaw, *Kazimierz, The Jewish Quarter of Cracow, 1870–1988*, Wydawnictwo AA, 2006.

Morand, Paul, *The Allure of Chanel*, Pushkin Press, 2009.

Morand, Paul, *A Frenchman's London*, Cassell, 1934.

Peiss, Kathy, *Hope in a Jar: The Making of America's Beauty Culture*, Holt Paperbacks, 1998.

Poiret, Paul, *My First Fifty Years*, Victor Gollancz, 1931.

Putnam, Samuel, *Paris was our Mistress: Memoirs of a Lost and Found Generation*, Southern Illinois University Press, 1970.

Putnam, Samuel (translator), *Kiki's Memoirs*, At the Sign of the Black Manikin Press, 1930.

Richardson, John, *The Sorcerer's Apprentice: Picasso, Provence and Douglas Cooper*, Chicago Press, 2001.

Rowlands, Penelope, *A Dash of Daring: Carmel Snow and Her Life in Fashion, Art, and Letters*, Atria Books, Simon & Schuster, 2005.

Rubinstein, Mala, *The Mala Rubinstein Book of Beauty*, Doubleday, 1973.

Tashjian, Dickran, *A Boatload of Madmen: Surrealism and the American Avant-Garde, 1920–1950*, Thames and Hudson, 1995.

Tobias, Andrew, *Fire and Ice: The Story of Charles Revson, the Man Who Built the Revlon Empire*, William Morrow & Company, 1976

Vreeland, Diana, *DV*, DaCapo Press, 2004.

Wharton, Edith, *A Backward Glance: An Autobiography*, Simon & Schuster, 1998.

Wharton, Edith, *French Ways and Their Meaning*, D. Appleton and Company, 1919.

Zweig, Stefan, *The World of Yesterday*, Pushkin Press, 2009.

NOVELS

Hemingway, Ernest, *A Moveable Feast*, Jonathan Cape, 1964.

Lawrence, D. H., *Lady Chatterley's Lover*, Tipografia Giuntina, 1928.

Lewisohn, Ludwig, *The Case of Mr Crump*, Edward W. Titus, 1926.

Singer, Isaac Bashevis, *The Manor*, Farrar, Straus & Giroux, 1967.

Singer, Isaac Bashevis, *The Spinoza of Market Street*, Farrar, Straus & Cudahy, 1961.

Sulitzer, Paul-Loup, *The Empress*, Grafton, 1989.

Sulitzer, Paul-Loup, *Hannah*, Poseidon Press, 1989.

Verne, Jules, *Around the World in Eighty Days*, Collector's Library, 2005.

CATALOGUES

The Helena Rubinstein Collection Catalogs (Sales 20–29 April 1965), Parke-Bernet Galleries, New York, 1966.

ESSAYS

Clifford, Marie J., 'Helena Rubinstein's Beauty Salons, Fashion, and Modernist Display' in *Winterthur Portfolio*, Vol. 38, No. 2/3 (Summer–Autumn 2003), University of Chicago Press.

Karady, Victor, 'Les Juifs et les États-nations dans l'Europe contemporaine', *Actes de la recherche en sciences sociales*, 1997 (http://www.persee.fr).

Röskau-Rydel, Isabel, 'La société multiculturelle et multinationale de Galicie de 1772 à 1918 : Allemands, Polonais, Ukrainiens et Juifs', *Annuaire de l'École pratique des hautes études*, 2008. (http://ashp.revues.org/index469.html)

DVD

Grossman, Ann Carol and Reisman, Arnie (directors), *The Powder and the Glory*, PBS, documentary based on *War Paint* by Lindy Woodhead.

WEBSITES

www.ancestry.com

www.genealogy.com

www.onlinenewspapers.com/australi.htm
http://trove.nla.gov.au/newspaper
www.oldmagazinearticles.com
www.krakow-info.com/JewishQ.htm
www.circe.paris-sorbonne.fr/ ('Dix siècles de présence juive à Cracovie')
www.scrapbookpages.com/poland/kazimierz
www.lexilogos.com/english/yiddish_dictionary.htm
www.nytimes.com
www.time.com

Index of Names

Mountbatten, Lady Pamela, 331

Acknowledgements

I'd like to thank Jane Creech, Barbara Friedman, Diane Moss, Nicholas Pappas and Laurie Shapley in New York; Alfred Silberfeld and Barry Titus in Florida; Olivier Ameisen, Eva Ameisen, Pierre Bergé, Marie Chauveau, Edmonde Charles-Roux, Charles Dantzig, Béatrice Dautresme, Litka Fasse, François Joseph Graf, Bernard Minoret, Christine Mue, Elaine Sciolino, Antoine Silberfeld and Maougocha Smorag in Paris; Erica Friedman in Cannes and Christian Wolmar in London for their interest in the project, their kindness and their time. All of them enlightened and guided me one way or another.

A huge posthumous 'thank you' to Patrick O'Higgins. His amusing, affectionate and lively book about his employer Helena Rubinstein instantly made me fall for her. How I wish I could have met him.

I'm also indebted to Elisabeth Sandager, the international general manager for L'Oréal's luxury products division; Marie-Hélène Arwheiller, a former Helena Rubinstein communications and image manager; and her successor, Florence Lafragette, for giving me access to the invaluable Helena Rubinstein archives in Paris, and for their constant help and support with my research.

An equally big 'thank you' to Thierry Consigny.

My thanks also go to Suzanne Slesin, who so generously opened up her archives and publishing house in New York and shared her memories of and admiration for her step-grandmother Helena with me.

I'd like to thank my publisher and very dear friend Manuel Carcassonne, who came up with the idea for the book, believed in it from the start and forced me to dig deeper, go further and give better than my best.

Thanks to Charline Bourgeois-Taquet for being such an enthusiastic and amazingly sharp-eyed reader, and to the 'dream team' at Grasset, my publishers in Paris – Christophe Bataille, Antoine Boussin, Aline Gurdiel, Agnès Nivière, Muguette Vivian and Jean-François Paga (a truly inspired art director).

Thank you to Susanna Lea for her energy, her friendship and her 'Give a girl the right shoes and she can conquer the world' quote.

Thanks to my friend Marie-Françoise Colombani, who kept me going through the long winter of 2010 with her giggles and gossip. She knows all the whys and the wherefores better than anyone else. I hope she remembers our sleep-fuddled email exchanges at five o'clock in the morning on our first day of work. We'll laugh about it one day. Actually, we already do.

Last but not least, I am grateful to Guy Princ, who for the past sixteen years has uncomplainingly put up with me spending the weekends poring over books and the evenings writing, being up at dawn and coming to bed far too late, all those three's-a-crowd holidays (me, him and my laptop), my (temporary) fits of temper, my stress, fatigue, and unavailability. His support is more precious than I can say.

of moonlight on the water of the great lake. He limped down to the shore. He was walking in the curve of a bay. His feet crushed the wild mint and waves of it rose to his nostrils. He saw the wooded point out from him and he stumbled towards it. He couldn't be seen, but that did not make him safe. There was no inch safe now for him on this side.

When he reached the point and looked at the short stretch of water between him and the other shore he knew that he couldn't swim that far. It was only a few hundred yards, but he was too tired and he had never swum that far before. So wearily he went back into the wood. He searched it in the moonlight until he found a fallen tree that would suit him. Lying there for a year or more it was well rotted, the outer part had broken away, but its core was sound. He managed to raise it on his shoulder and stumbled with it to the shore. Much of it fell away, rotten, but enough remained. He waded with it into the deep water. He got it under his oxters, held the spade and the sodden sack free of the water and kicked out with his feet. The water was calm. There was little wind. In about ten minutes he was free of the path of moonlight and yard by yard the dark bulk of the far shore came nearer to him.

He thought of the giant pike of the lake about which the fishermen told such tales. He wondered if one of them would come up for a look and snap off one of his feet. This made him laugh weakly. It's just the proof of how unsafe land animals feel once they are on the deep water.

The shore came closer and closer until he felt stones under his feet when he let them down, so he freed himself from the almost sinking log and stumbled and fell and rose again until he felt the coarse sand, and then his heart sank as the bulk of a big man rose from the grey rocks where he had blended and came towards him. He had a big stick in his hand and he spoke in Irish and he said: 'Well, boy, it took you a long time to get here.'

Dualta just dropped the spade and sack and sat down drearily on the sand.

4

DUALTA SAID: 'Weren't they cunning to send you to wait for me here? I didn't grant them that much brains.'

'Who's this you talk about?' the man asked.

'Them, over there,' said Dualta, nodding his head at the opposite shore, looking innocent and pleasant under the subtle moonlight.

The man spat.

'The curse of the devil on them,' he said.

Dualta was surprised. 'You mean they didn't plant you?' he asked.

The man laughed. 'The only one who will plant me is the grave-digger,' he said. 'Stir yourself from that. You must be wet. You'll die of the fever.'

Dualta rose to his feet. Now he felt his whole body shivering. 'I don't understand. I thought you were one of them.'

'I was at the fair with a little pig,' the man said. 'I saw. It was a brave but foolish thing you did. When I came home I climbed the hill behind. It was good. It was like a story you can see. You on the Mount and the horses and the dogs. I could see it all until the sun went under. I saw the way you were moving. I would have crossed to you with my old thing of a boat, but I was afraid they would see that on the water and be guided to you. So I waited.'

'But how about your gentlemen? Won't they know?'

'Let them scratch their own skin. Come. The house is a piece away. The walk will warm you. I will carry your spade.' He took it from him and set off walking. Dualta followed him. The wet clothes were cold on him but his heart was warm. He felt like laughing. If this wasn't a trick! Could there be such deceit in such an open countenance? He stopped still. He could run away. The man had close ears. He turned and looked at the motionless figure. He seemed to divine the thoughts of Dualta.

'No, no, man,' he said. 'It won't do. You will have to take to people. Would I betray you? My name is Joyce.'

'It is a good name,' said Dualta.

'Our portion of it was never dirtied,' said the man.

'Over there nobody raised a hand or a voice for me,' said Dualta, 'only my uncle, the schoolmaster.'

'He was a good man,' said Joyce, 'and it was his duty. Why should the others pay a penalty for your spirit?'

'You are,' said Dualta.

'Not me,' the man laughed. 'I teach foxes their tricks. Your passing will leave no more on me than a soft summer wind on the water. Come with me, for God's sake, or you will perish with the dampness.'

He turned then and walked on.

Dualta followed him, calling out, 'Forgive it to me that I doubted you. I am not wise.'

'Who is?' the man asked, raising his voice. 'Máirtin is my name.'

'My deep thanks to you, Máirtin,' said Dualta.

'Save your wind,' said Máirtin. 'It's a stiff climb and you must by this time be weary.'

It was a stiff climb, through deep heather and fading thick sedge and soft places where he sank to his shins in brown slime and only with an effort plucked his feet free. He was tired, so the climb took it out of him, but at least it warmed his body and set his clothes steaming. The thick-set bare-footed man ahead of him walked casually as if he was on a level place with a fair surface.

Dualta was pleased when they came into a declivity where a house was built by a tumbling mountain stream. The moon shone on the whitewash of the house, and the spilled waters of the stream flashed like precious stones. Behind the hill was a cliff, deeply indented by the stream.

Máirtin waited for him at the door of the house. He saw that the house had no chimney, just a hole in the thatch through which smoke came and was flattened by the twirling currents of air.

'You are welcome,' Máirtin said when he reached him. 'Go

in and stand in front of the fire.'

Dualta ducked his head and entered. The place was lighted only by the flames of a roaring turf fire on the open hearth. His nose was assailed with smells, smoke and children and, yes, pigs. There was a sow lying on straw in a corner to his right, penned in by birch poles on short trestles. He looked around. He saw many eyes glinting at him. His eyes became accustomed to the light and he began to pick out the children. Very small, and up. They all seemed the same. He could only tell their sex if they had grown a little big for their tattered wool petticoats. A bigger girl with a dress and a barefooted woman standing near the fire lifting the lid off a steaming potato-pot.

'God bless all here,' Dualta said.

'You are welcome,' the woman said, straightening up.

Máirtin spoke from behind him.

'This is Dualta, the nephew of the schoolmaster,' he said. 'He is as wet as a trout. Pull the clothes off him, Máire, and let him stand in front of the fire.'

'God bless us,' the woman said, 'he looks drowned. Go away, children. Pull down, Dualta.'

Dualta was embarrassed. He heard Máirtin chuckling.

'Go back up in the room, girls,' he said then, 'and let the man dry out without your eyes on him.'

Four persons detached themselves from the shades. They disappeared behind an opening near the hearth. He heard murmured words and giggles as they vanished. He started to strip himself. It was wonderful to feel the warmth of the fire on his body. Máirtin took his wet clothes and hung them from the iron crooks in the hearth. They began to steam like himself. Then he felt the woman rubbing at his back with a coarse cloth. She was clucking with her tongue. 'How will you live?' she asked. 'You're destroyed with the dampness.' He relaxed.

'Here,' said Máirtin, 'will we empty the sack?'

'Do that,' said Dualta. 'The things in there must be destroyed too.' Máirtin loosed the neck of the wet sack from the spade and reached for the contents. Very pitiful. His extra clothes, his shoes and a pair of woollen stockings. Máirtin hung them all, shaking his head. Then he took out two books. They

30

were wet but one of them had a leather binding and it had saved them. Máirtin looked at them. 'This is the English writing, is it?'

Dualta looked. It was a copy of Goldsmith's *History of England, Rome and Greece*. 'It is,' he said.

'You read and write then?' Máirtin asked.

'I told you my uncle was the schoolmaster,' said Dualta.

'That's a wonderful thing, powerful,' said Máirtin. 'We have no teacher here yet. Some say the priest will get one soon. If you had time you could teach us all to write, or maybe just the little ones. We are ignorant. It is very sad. Maybe the young ones will be better off?'

'Maybe they are better off now without it,' said Dualta.

'No, you are wrong,' said Máirtin. 'This is an English book too?' He was holding up a wet book. The pages were stuck. He was gently releasing them.

'Yes,' said Dualta. 'That's one about the travels of Gulliver.'

'I've heard some of the stories of him,' said Máirtin. 'The old mother knew a lot of tales. She is dead now, God rest her.'

'You are well dry at the back,' said Máire, handing him the cloth. 'Now rub yourself. I will turn out the pot.'

He took the cloth and rubbed himself. He felt better.

Máirtin looked at him. He will make a fine man, he thought, not too big but big enough.

'You will be like this Gulliver yourself now, I'm afraid,' he said. 'You will have to travel farther than malice.'

'Wrap yourself in this and sit,' said Máire. She put a thin blanket around his shoulders and at his legs he felt the round cut from a tree. It was seasoned and worn smooth and was a good stool. He pulled the blanket around him and sat.

'You can come down now, girls,' Máirtin called. 'The man is visible.'

They came down from the room huddled close together, shyly as if he was going to murder them. The other small ones had come closer to him, sitting on the stone floor, their eyes glinting.

'How many have you?' he asked.

'Nine, thank God,' said Máirtin. 'Four girls and four boys

31

and big Paidi that's out visiting. He's tracking a girl but she'll have none of him. He has nothing and her father has six cattle.'

'Maybe the girl prefers Paidi to the cattle?'

'She does not,' said Máirtin. 'She has a head on her shoulders. Sell trout and eat salted herrings.'

Máire was turning the drained pot of potatoes onto a flat round kish. They steamed in their big pile. Some of the jackets were open invitingly.

'You must be weak with the hunger,' said Máirtin. ''Take up and eat.' He crossed himself. Some of the small children were already reaching. They had to pull back their hands reluctantly and cross themselves and listen to their father thanking God melodiously for the pot of potatoes. Then they grabbed.

The potatoes were red hot. They had to dance them from hand to hand as they skinned them. Máire put a tin of coarse salt beside the kish and handed Dualta a tin mug of buttermilk. He bit into the potato and supped the buttermilk. Bit and sup. Bit and sup and he was as hungry as an animal, but had to restrain himself from eating too fast.

'Paidi will miss his meal,' said Máire.

'Let the girl pay for his company,' said Máirtin.

The children laughed and the girls giggled, but nobody stopped from reducing the big pile of potatoes. The sow behind them woke from her snoozing and grunted hungrily as the smell of the fresh boiled potatoes reached into her subconscious.

Dualta felt warm, and safe, and the happenings of the day no longer seemed such a nightmare.

He woke with a start, frightened. Over his head in the loft a cock was crowing. It was a weird sound in the enclosed space of the kitchen. He heard a voice calling, and arms were reaching with a stick. There was an indignant fluttering of wings, a seeming waterfall of feathers as the cock and the chickens flew down from the loft and were chased, protesting like titled ladies, into the dawn. All this he could see without opening his eyes. He felt very tired still. He heard the sow protesting then and grunting like an old gentleman as she too was driven from the warm place and out of the door. The straw and its covering where he slept were warm. Beside him the four little boys were sleeping, head to toe like oat-sheaves in a cart. They looked very young and innocent, their hair tousled, their young faces and brows untroubled.

Then he saw Máirtín at the door. He came over to him.

'You are awake,' he said. 'Rise up fast. There are boats crossing the loch.' Dualta felt his heart sinking as he pushed aside the blanket. The little boys slept on. He put the blanket back over them. He was wearing his own dried shirt. It didn't take him long to get into his breeches. 'I have all ready for you,' Máirtín was saying. 'All packed away. Paidi is keeping an eye on them. We have some cold potatoes that will take the edge off your hunger as you go. I will call him. He will be with you.'

Dualta didn't answer him. Máirtín went out the door.

Máire, who had been listening to them, suddenly sat on the stool and dropped her head in her hands. He could see long streaks of grey in her brown hair. She wasn't an old woman. Her shoulders were heaving.

'Tell me what is wrong?' Dualta asked. 'Have I upset you?'

She shook her head.

'Paidi is going away,' she said.

'He will be back at Christmas,' said Dualta.

'He will be missed,' she said. 'He is very lively.'

'It's not as if he was going away for ever," said Dualta. 'You have eight others.'

'That makes no difference,' she said. 'Miss one, miss all. Each one is a new bit of your heart. When he goes it is taken away.'

Máirtín was at the door again.

'Are you all but ready?' Máirtín asked.

'Yes,' said Dualta. He looked at Máire. She had blue eyes. One time she must have been beautiful. She had regular features.

'I thank you,' he said to her, trying to express all that he felt in a few words. 'May you be blessed.' He went to the door and into the light. The sun was barely over the horizon. Here they were shut away from its light by the hills behind. He saw the young man running towards him. He was jumping wet places

33

like a goat. A big young man with thickly muscled bare legs, unruly brown hair, big white teeth in a generous mouth, and well-worn patched clothes.

He stopped in front of them.

'They are halfway across,' he said. 'You must be important, Dualta. They want very much to get close to you. Maybe they want you to marry one of their daughters. Did you injure her?'

He thought this was funny. He laughed, slapping his thigh.

'You better go if you are going,' said Máirtin. He spoke gruffly. He didn't meet his son's eyes, Dualta noticed.

'Yes,' said Paidi. 'I will get my things and say farewell to the family. Are the young ones awake?'

'They seem to be still sleeping,' said Dualta.

'That's as well,' said Paidi, 'otherwise they would be making noises like bonhams. Anyone would think I was going away for ever.'

'If he didn't go and earn a little at the digging,' said Máirtin, 'how would we pay our rent? Isn't it better for him to go for a little than for the lot of us to be tramping the roads for ever?'

'That's right,' said Dualta.

'When they grow up anyhow,' said Máirtin, 'it's cursed little of them you see. To eat is all. Other times they are chasing girls or playing cards or dancing at cross-roads. Isn't it very little of them you see anyhow? They might as well be away. Paidi will get you across the hills. He is to meet other diggers on the far side and you can travel south together.'

'That will be good,' said Dualta. 'They say down there that there are men who are not afraid of their landlords. They even kill them.'

Máirtin was silent.

'Take it easy,' he said then. 'You are too young to feel that way. There is great talk of a man called O Connell. He is only a Munsterman but there might be some good in him.'

'I have heard of him,' said Dualta. 'He talks. He doesn't do anything.'

'The gift of the talk might be better than a charge from a gun,' said Máirtin.

Paidi came running out of the house with a spade on his

34

shoulder and the bundle tied to it.

'Come on,' Paidi called. 'Are we to be here all day? Shouldn't we have miles of the road over us by now? Women and children! Listen, I leave you well, father. I will be back with the Christmas and some gold guineas in my pocket. You hear?'

'I do,' said Máirtin. 'Don't stand there talking about them. Be off with you and may the luck rise with the both of you. Here's your spade and things, Dualta. I nearly deprived you of them.'

There was a sound of soft wailing coming from the house.

'Come on! Come with me!' said Paidi, suddenly moving away. Dualta looked at Máirtin.

'Thank you from my heart, Máirtin,' he said and then followed after. Paidi set a murderous pace. He jumped the stream from rock to rock, his bare feet gripping the wet stones like suckers. Then he turned right and started climbing the hill. He looked back once. Máire was at the door and the girls were clustered around her like chickens. They were waving their hands.

'You'd think a man was going away for ever,' Paidi was saying. Then he said no more. The climbing took all of their breath and attention. Halfway, they rested. The sat in the heather. They could no longer see Máirtin's house. They could see the edge of the lake and the place where three boats were pulled up on the shore. Below them they saw groupings of houses clustered together in valley villages, up on the sides of hills, where they had been forced to carve fields from stony ground and boggy land.

'You needn't worry,' said Paidi. 'In a good cause, the biggest and most expert liars in Ireland live down there.'

'How did they know I crossed?' Dualta asked.

'Somebody the other side must have seen you,' said Paidi. 'We better get over the crest. The lads will be waiting on the road on the far side. You won't be alone any more, Dualta. We'll get through to the south, don't fear. I wouldn't mind if we had to spill a bit of blood doing it either.' He looked back once more and was sorry he had done so. Some of the young ones had climbed a shoulder of a hill and were standing there waving. You could see sadness in their waving.

Paidi turned away and began furiously to climb the hill.

When they topped the great hill and before they moved down they could see a thousand lakes stretched at their feet. Paidi searched the ground below with his eyes. Dualta could make out the winding ribbon of dirt road going in and out between the lakes like a snake. Paidi shouted. He professed to see a cluster of men moving on the road. Dualta couldn't make them out. Paidi said, laughing, 'You wouldn't do in the Revenue,' and set off running.

It took them nearly an hour to reach the rough road below where ten young men were gathered waiting for them. As they came in sight, they shouted and waved, calling, 'Run! Run, you devils!' and Paidi and Dualta looked at one another and smiled and started to run. It was hardly fair. Dualta was slender and less heavy. If you roll a light rock and a heavy rock down the side of a hill, which gets below first? I don't know, but Dualta was the first to reach the road.

'Oh, you are getting weak, Paidi,' one young man said. 'It must be all the courting.'

They laughed at this.

Paidi, almost breathless, said, 'This is Dualta. He is coming with us.'

They welcomed him. They were roughly dressed in homespun clothes. They carried spades, and some of them had their shoes tied around their necks. They were well burnt by the sun. One of them was sitting at the side of the road tying a rag on a bloody big toe.

'Were you dancing, Fursa?' Paidi asked him. They laughed.

'I hit me toe against a cursed rock,' said Furso. Tenderly he patted the brand-new shoes hanging around his neck. 'Wasn't it a damn good job I wasn't wearing my new shoes.'

They laughed hilariously at this old joke and then in a group they hefted their spades and their sparse possessions and set out for the distant town, the bottleneck leading to the south.

It was a fine day and the sun shone on them.

5

THEY WERE sitting on stones outside some of the thatched houses in the liberties, putting on their shoes, when they saw the long procession coming from behind them. They had been about five hours walking, but Dualta had felt the road short on him. All the diggers were young. The eldest of them wasn't yet twenty-one. They were light-hearted and they joked and they sang and they told stories about the odd people in their own places. They talked about how much they might earn in the south. Some held that they might get up to tenpence a day. Others were more pessimistic. They thought maybe five-pence with a meal of potatoes. Fursa said it was a pity they couldn't have made the trip in August when they could have gone to Dublin and crossed to Scotland. He said one of theirs who had to return because he had lost three fingers with a carelessly swung sickle had been making over a shilling a day, and after paying his way on the boat he had two pounds fifteen shillings when he got home. Wasn't this wealth in a short time?

'He had to walk and work for it,' said Paidi.

Tomás Mór was walking carefully on the road trying to get the feel of his shoes. He was hobbling.

'God, they are killing me!' he said. 'They are murder. I'll never abide them. Curse them! I'll take them off again.'

'You won't,' said Fursa. 'Do you want to make a disgrace of us walking the town in your bare hooves? Don't they think little enough of us as it is?'

Dualta tentatively walked himself. It had been many months since he had worn shoes. They were made big for him, but the woollen stockings and the pressure of the hard leather were compressing his feet so that they felt like hot coals.

'Watch what's coming up the road,' said Fursa. 'What's happening?'

They looked. The procession stretched in a long file. It was headed by a carriage drawn by two horses. Behind that were men on horseback, then people walking and a few common carts with people sitting up on them, more people walking, and the rear was brought up by further men on horseback.

'I declare it must be an election. There must be an election in town,' said Fursa. 'Hey,' he called to a man across the street leaning on the half-door of his house. 'What's up in town? Is there an election?' The man cupped his ear with his hand. Fursa went halfway across to him. 'Is there an election, I asked?' he shouted.

'Oh, yes, yes, yes,' said the man. 'Why don't you talk proper Irish?'

Paidi laughed. 'You hear that, Fursa,' he said. 'Take the turf out of your mouth.'

'I've a good mind to go over and break your mouth,' said Fursa to the man.

'What you say?' he asked.

'I hope it's an election,' said Tomás Mór. 'We might get a few free drinks by stealth.'

'I said I'd like to give you a kick in the belly,' said Fursa, whose face was red. The rest of them laughed, watching his rage.

'I don't understand a word you're saying,' the man said. He was genuinely exasperated.

'You ignorant bostoon!' Fursa shouted.

'Ah,' the man said. 'I know what that means. You can't come from the bog and talk like that to your betters. Get on about your business or I'll go over and chastise you.'

Fursa was dancing with rage in the middle of the rutted road.

The carriage was level with him. It slowly passed by. There was an upright gentleman sitting in it. His hands were resting on a stick. He had a tall grey hat on him. He kept his eyes strictly in front of him, never looked out of the window.

Then Paidi started calling sheep.

'Ma-a-a-a! Ma-a-a-a! Ma-a-a-a!' The rest of them took it up too. People came to the doors of houses grinning to see what it was about, and they too started calling sheep.

Dualta watched the leading horseman. You could recognise

the agent and behind him the bailiff, attended by satellite bailiffs with thick blackthorn sticks in their hands. They were walking. There were at least thirty people walking or riding the carts. These didn't like the calling. Some of them flushed. Some of them just looked straight ahead. Some of them dropped their eyes.

Dualta felt sorry for them. It wasn't their fault. They were the forty-shilling freeholders, who were neither free nor holding anything. They did look like sheep, gathered into the fold, tended by shepherds who told them there was an election and when and how they were to go and who they were to vote for. It was as simple as that. If they didn't do what they were told, their houses would be pulled down about their ears and they would be given the road. Dualta wondered what he would do if he was a forty-shilling freeholder. It didn't mean anything anyhow. It was just a device created by the landlords to make things look good. The more freeholders they had whom they could make vote in the right way, the greater their chances for patronage in a sea of corruption.

They weren't all meek. One big walking man shook his fist at them and would have come to them if his wife wasn't pulling at his elbow. Three of the bailiffs came out of the line and walked towards them, waving their sticks.

They contented themselves with saying, 'Hold your tongues, you!' because they were faced by twelve healthy young men with spades whose digging edges were sharpened by stones. Some day, Dualta thought, cynically, these same young men would be in the shoes of their fathers and they too, however full of bile, and whatever dignity and pride they had to swallow, would join in the landlord's procession to the polling booths.

'Leave them be,' Dualta suddenly said, loudly.

The others looked at him wonderingly. But they stopped.

But what they had started continued. The chorus of Ma-a-a's went with the procession all through the west liberties, by the collection of thatched houses, right up to the three-storey stone houses built this side of the bridge.

The diggers, walking carefully and painfully in their shoes, shouldered their spades and walked towards the bridge after the voters. From here in, the whole place was as packed with people as a potato pit with potatoes. There was hardly room to move. One or two dray-type carts with goods on them were having a hard time getting through the crowds. The drivers were standing lashing the patient horses and cursing at the people. Plodding horses with baskets on their panniers were everywhere, their owners shouting to let them through, let them through. You could distinguish the country people from the townspeople by their ruddy faces and heavy-type clothes. Many town children, badly clad, barefooted, dirty-faced, were eeling their way, shouting and begging with dirty little palms upturned, and even stealing, Dualta saw, as they grabbed a cake from a stall and ran. There was no order at all. It was all confusion. Somewhere up ahead of them, some brass instruments were blaring. Lots of men were drunk, singing to the sky with their heads back. His nostrils were brutally assailed with unaccustomed smells so that he had to pinch them. Not that that did any good. The road and pavements were badly pot-holed and had been filled with rubbish that was tramped down and exuded very unsavoury smells, particularly once they had passed the clean torrent of the river piling under the bridge.

Here there were many drunken men wearing coloured favours in their hats and waving black sticks. They started to shout at the carriage ahead and at those following the carriage. 'Go home! Go home, ye cowards! Ye traitors! Ye dirty vote-sellers!' Many worse things, and cabbage stalks and dirt, were flung from the side.

The bailiff came back on his horse to them. He looked at them.

'Do you want a free drink, some free food?' he asked.

'Ah,' said Fursa, 'you are talking to our bellies.'

'Go each side of the people then,' the bailiff said, 'as far as the booths and we'll fill them for ye.'

Fursa looked at Paidi. They grinned. They nodded. 'We're your men,' said Paidi. 'Hey, lads. Split up, each side of the freeholders, and guard them with your lives. We don't know who they are voting for but sure they came from the west side of the bridge.'

They laughed and split into two sides and using the handles of their spades freely they walked as a guard each side of the people. They were nearly all tall young men and strong men. When the others Maa-ed they meigled. When the others waved their black sticks they swung their gleaming spades which were longer and had a further reach. They drew on their deep knowledge of the language to return a double curse for a single one, a scorching obscenity for an insulting one. It was a wonderful bedlam of noise and counter-noise, with the citizens straining their necks to see and people leaning precariously out of the narrow windows of the tall-storied houses to cheer and counter-cheer and sometimes throw things on to the gathering below.

Dualta felt excited with it. The streets were so narrow and the houses so tall that the sound reverberated all over the sky. He got glimpses of the shop windows through the narrow panes. He got glimpses through the arches into the Spanish-type courtyards, men thronged and jammed into the tippling houses, the smell of spices and horse-dung and sweat and dirt and harness and oil and smoke. He had never been in the midst of so many people before. He felt choked, smothered, blocking the blow of a blackthorn stick with the handle of the spade, laughing into a suffused drunken countenance. When he was called 'You Connemara pig!' he would answer 'You Galway gurnet!' and whether his insulter came from Galway or not, it seemed to infuriate him. One of them appealed to God in heaven and then jammed his beaver hat down on his own face. But they were all sturdy and they kept the barrier, so that the freeholders they were protecting became bold and hurled back insults too, and rose in their carts and made speeches to the sky. And all the time Dualta knew that the gentleman in the carriage ahead of them was sitting with his face to the front and his hands on his stick and he might as well be anywhere but where he was for all the attention he was paying to the mob.

After some time they made their way into the open space where the booths were. Here it was not as noisy. Disdainful soldiers sat on horses and looked down from their eminence. Elegantly dressed ladies sat on seats on the steps of the Court-house and watched the confusion as if they were at a playhouse. Satins and curling hair and flashing teeth, and smooth men in expensive breeches with tall velvet collars and gleaming hats tilted over one eye. The soldiers held the opening into the square so that they left the main noise behind them, and the horsemen dismounted, and the men came down from their carts and they went into the booths and publicly and in a loud voice announced who was their man, and God help them if they forgot who he was, as some of them were inclined to do, never having met him and knowing nothing about him. Some of them had taken the time to have his name written on a piece of paper which they looked at before they called out his name confidently as if they were in the room the day his mother was delivered of him. Dualta saw little of this. He was eating cold beef, a thing he had not done for many a year, and mutton, and eating great chunks from a white loaf, and drinking flagons of Persse's porter and glasses of Joyce's whisky, he who had never drunk anything stronger than buttermilk. But his life was so changed, and he felt that it was changed for good here in an alien place smothered with people, where it was hard to breathe and impossible to think, where his heart was aching for the slow philosophical speech of his Uncle Marcus, the scholars chanting, the evening he had missed in the house of the father of Sorcha, the laughter and the sly humour and the fresh wind blowing on the Mount, and the sight of the sun on the waters of the lake – all that, all that behind him, hatred in him for what had made him leave it, fear in him of what was before him. Lost he was, like a feather on an outgoing tide, like a thistle on the wind, like a call in a valley deriding you as it receded, so sad that he sat and rested his back against a stall and cried, silently, the tears running down his face, inside he jeering at himself remembering that they said a man was soft in drink.

Paidi's face leering at him. 'Get up! Get up, Dualta! See what I have found for you!' Paidi not drunk. His eyes clear. Shaking his head. A girl with red hair and white skin looking

42

at him, a frown between her brows. He is only a child, what have ye done to him? Not a child. A man I am. We are slaves. You hear that? Look at those stupid people walking into those stupid booths and voting for men they never heard of. Is this the action of free men, or is it the action of slaves?

Paidi saying, 'I didn't know he knew books so well. Get up and we'll go to the dry lodgings. This is Ellen. She pities you. She will get us dry lodgings where they stay themselves in Crotty's of Gut Lane. Isn't she decent? Come, come, Dualta, my father would kill me if he saw I had done this to you. Come, let us help you.'

I need no help from anyone. I am on my own. I can rise to my own feet and walk. All the things I can weep for too, singing in my head.

Paidi calling, 'Come on, men, come on, we are going to the lodgings, gather yourselves and follow after us.'

Walking. Paidi's strong hand under his elbow, and a girl's hand holding his other arm. Sometimes his arm hit against her soft breast and it only made him want to cry, bringing back to his mind in a vague misty flash the time he had a mother, that he belonged to somebody.

There was the press of people again, the loud shouting. The cursing, forcing their way through throngs and multitudes. Shouting and cursing. What was the world coming to? Where was the place that there was only the cry of the curlew, the blackbird's frightened clack at the going down of the sun. Connemara cattle! Galway gurnets! Clashing of wood on wood and shouts and screams of laughter. This was what elections meant so, where simple people chose honest men who would represent them in Corporation or the faraway dreamland of London where their representatives would go in order to bring in more Coercion Acts, or something else that would bind them deeper to their chains. Where all these thoughts came from, liberated from a bottle, or from the austere style of the poets talking of long times ago when men were free and had access to the boards of their lords to argue and declare their freedom and their rights. He remembered no more.

6

THEY STOOD for sale in the market-place of the southern town.

It was an uneasy town.

They had seen the posted notice on a tree as they were coming in that morning. On top of the notice was a crude drawing of a coffin.

Underneath the coffin was written in the two tongues:

> This is waiting for any Digger
> who hires himself for less
> than ONE SHILLING per day.
>   signed
>   Captain White.

They were staring at it when one of the new police came from the town and tore it from the tree. He was a smart-looking man with his flat conical hat. There weren't a lot of these new police around. They were already beginning to be called Peelers on account of the man who had created them. They were sent to act as the leaven in the dough of the baronial police known as the rough-and-ready boys. This one had been a soldier, Dualta thought. He walked very straight.

He said to them: 'You know what this is?'

Of course they looked at him stupidly with their mouths half open. So to their surprise he broke into fluent Irish.

'You do not accept this,' he said. 'You will go in and hire yourselves at the prevailing rates and you will not allow yourselves to be intimidated by anyone. You will be protected.'

'We thank you,' said Dualta, so he marched away from them, before going, turning to point to a most official-looking notice further on. Instead of a coffin this had a crown on the top of it, but it more or less meant the same thing, that under the Insurrection Act of such a date and the Coercion Act of such another date, this district was under military law. You were to be at

44

home at such a time and not abroad at such another time, not to gather together in groups of more than two or three.

'Between the Whiteboys and the Kingsboys,' said Dualta, grinning, 'I can see we are going to have a hard time.'

Paidi was uneasy.

'Maybe we ought to pass this town by, Dualta,' he said. 'Why should we want trouble? I just want to make a few pounds in peace and go home.'

'There aren't a lot of towns left, Paidi,' said Dualta. 'And the season is getting late. I like the look of this town. Let us go in and see what happens.'

'I don't like police,' said Paidi. 'I don't like soldiers. I feel towards them as a fisherman feels towards a red-headed woman or the blacksmith feels towards the tailor.'

Dualta laughed.

'Come, Paidi,' he said. 'Don't you feel the blood quickening in your veins? Here we will have a combination of work and danger.'

'Maybe it's what you are looking for,' said Paidi, 'but I want none of it. I would like to make my own trouble, not to have it ready made like a suit of clothes.'

Dualta set off walking towards the old west gate of the town. Paidi caught up with him.

You noticed the silence in the market-place. That was unusual. Market-places are always full of sound, people calling and shouting, cursing or singing. But here sound was muted. They passed by long rows of thatched cottages, some of them very dirty-looking. There were many puddles in the badly paved road. They could hear the sound of their own shoes on the stones. You could trace the silence to the soldiers who sat on trained horses, unmoving, silent except for the noise the bit made when a horse occasionally shook his head, or to the armed rough-and-ready boys who moved in twos or fours, not erect figures like the Peeler but slouching, untidy, some of them fat, looking around them with suspicious eyes.

The silence reminded Dualta of the mountain. Mostly on account of the rain, mountains sing. There are always streams rushing down the sides of them, bubbling and gurgling their way, gouging out a bed. So it is a strange thing to walk a mountain in a drought, going after sheep or herding heifers to the new sedge, if there has been a drought and the mountain goes silent. The silence is almost shocking, like this market-place now.

They came to the hiring place. They could recognise it from the way the cold sun was reflecting from the brightened blades of the spades of the diggers.

They joined this group of men, who looked at them silently, with no animosity, and no friendliness either for that matter. Dualta tried to think of where they had come from. It was hard to tell. He knew there was no Connachtman among them, but that was as far as he could go. He marvelled at the antipathy to the Connachtmen they had met on their way. Near Galway it was fear of the Connemaramen; further south it was the Connachtmen. He supposed it was natural. Bands of men going and coming from the harvest were well behaved in places, but sometimes when they had money they got drunk in the dry lodgings, and they sang wild songs and they danced wild dances and they cried, and sometimes they made love with their wild magic to the girls, and when they departed, sometimes in the dark of night, without paying the twopence for the shelter, they left behind them curses and tears.

He thought of his companions. One by one or two by two they had dropped off. Most of them he had liked. One or two of them he had not liked. They were brutal, almost primitive, illiterate. These were the ones that would fight at the drop of a hat over nothing, their faces red, their eyes with red anger in them. Paidi was different. He had to be as the son of his father. Dualta was sure he could have hired himself before this, but that he wanted to be with Dualta. Did he promise his father some such? Did he think Dualta wasn't able to look after him-self? He felt older than Paidi, although he wasn't. But he liked his honesty, the purity of his joking, his deference towards women: he the man with the reputation he had among his fellows. Paidi was a good man. Dualta hoped that they would not be parted.

But they were, of course.

46

A large man with a roll of fat on his neck and very plump cheeks. It was somewhat like buying a bullock you were suspicious of. This man walked around the thinning group of diggers, in front of them and then around the back of them, sizing them up. The only thing he didn't do was to poke their buttocks with his stick. Paidi caught his eye. Paidi wasn't tall, but he was powerfully muscular-looking. How many baskets of potatoes could you dig in a day? They had boasted about their prowess on the road, claiming feats of digging that would shame Fionn Mac Cumhail. How much turf could they cut in a day? How much hay could they lay with the scythe? Paidi never boasted. Just he would say: 'Oh, a fair amount, a fair amount!'

'Come here to me,' the man beckoned Paidi. He went to him.

'You will dig for me?' the man asked.

'For how much?' asked Paidi.

'Eightpence,' said the man.

Paidi opened his blue eyes wide. 'Oh, I would be afraid,' he said. 'We read a notice on a tree. They said they would fill the coffins of men that worked for less than a shilling a day.'

'The curse of hell on them!' said the man. 'It's easy known that they don't have to hire anyone.'

'Maybe they wouldn't put their own people in coffins,' said Paidi. 'But I'm a stranger. They would plant me and sleep easy. I will give you value for your money.'

The man looked at him.

'A shilling less twopence for food,' he said. Paidi thought over that. He nodded. 'All right,' he said, 'if you will hire my friend.'

'Who is he?' he asked. Paidi pointed him out. 'He looks thin,' the man said. 'Would he have the staying power? He looks more like a clerk.'

'He's stronger than a dray-horse,' said Paidi.

'I don't want another digger,' the man said. 'I'm a poor man. Come with me,' he said in a loud voice. 'I will give you a shilling a day.' This for the benefit of the listeners. He walked up to Dualta. 'Your friend wants you,' he said. 'You only look like a boy to me, so I will give you boys' wages and food.'

Dualta smiled.

'Judging by the look of you,' he said, 'the food would be thin.'

Surprisingly the man laughed. His belly shook.

'Wit is a poor digger of potatoes,' he said. 'I don't want you but your friend wants you. I cannot pay two men's wages.'

'I will wait,' said Dualta. 'Go with the man, Paidi.'

A cloud passed over Paidi's open countenance.

'Who are you?' Dualta asked the man.

'I am Heffernan,' the man said. 'I live near the cross of the Hanging Tree, six miles to the north-east of the town.'

'See, Paidi,' said Dualta. 'I know where you are. On the Sunday sometime I will seek you.

Paidi didn't want to leave him. He thought how much he had enjoyed the company of Dualta, sharing the knowledge he possessed that he had plucked from his ability to read. Many things, true companionship. Paidi thought, This is fine, but how can the poor afford pleasures? He should have hired himself out days ago. Each day he didn't work was so much less to pay the rent at home. And they were so depending on his labour. He decided.

'I will be seeing you so. You will trace me?' he asked.

'I will,' said Dualta.

'I have a cart the other side of the town,' Heffernan said. He walked away, almost waddling. Paidi shouldered his spade. He looked quickly into Dualta's eyes, and then dropped his head.

'I will go,' he said. 'I will see you.'

'With the help of God,' said Dualta. He watched him as he turned away. Paidi walked slowly and then quickened his pace with determination. He didn't turn his head. Soon they were lost to sight. Dualta looked at the sky. It was coldly blue with flecks of fine-weather clouds traced all over it. It's as well to be without Paidi, he thought. Now I have no props at all. I am on my own. It is better to be this way. You cannot afford to become fond of people. Opposite him a hill rose high over the roofs of the thatched houses. It was a tall hill with the wide river at the foot of it. It could remind him of home if it wasn't a cultivated hill, right up to its peak, a verdant hill, fully clothed with green fields and tall timber.

The Bianconi car passed him, on its long trip to Limerick. It was a silent journey for this car. Normally there was great noise and confusion when the Bianconi cars passed, plagued with the shouts of about fifty beggar boys, nearly naked, pleading with their hands out and practised tears in their eyes, the driver cracking the whip and shouting, the people settling into their precarious perches, the ladies in the long seats holding on to their bonnets, the jingling of the harness. Now it passed in silence, and even the horses seemed to be trotting carefully and decorously.

There were many gentlemen in the town. They rode their horses and they were all heavily armed, pistols sticking out all over them, and behind them their bullyboys walked or rode carrying sticks or blunderbusses over their shoulders. Something is really stirring in this place, Dualta thought, if only I could get to the heart of it.

'You there, come here,' he heard a voice calling. He focussed his eyes. There was a horseman in the middle of the road pointing at him with a whip. He was a young man, well dressed, white breeches of broadcloth pushed into black polished boots with the tops turned down. Bile rose in Dualta at the sight of him. He could have been the Half-Sir. Dualta didn't move.

'Do you hear me talking to you? Come here!'

Dualta didn't move. He saw the anger rising in the young man's face. Very quickly he was off his horse, the reins trailing, and he was approaching Dualta with determination.

'When I call, come to me, do you hear?' he was saying as he came forward. He was not deterred by the sudden flashing of the eyes of the boy facing him nor by the way his knuckles had whitened on the handle of the spade. I will let him hit me, Dualta thought, and then I will split him with the spade.

The form of the policeman stepped between them.

'Is there anything wrong, sir?' this man asked. He was the one who had torn down the notice.

'I called this thick,' said the gentleman, 'and he spurned me. If you stand aside, Sergeant, I will teach him manners.'

'Sir, things are tense in this town today. It would be better for the peace if you decided to be reasonable.' He looked at

49

Dualta. 'I don't think this fellow understands English,' he said.

'Yes, I do,' said Dualta. 'You are mixing me up with my friend. He did not understand English. I do.'

'Why didn't you answer the gentleman?' the policeman asked.

'I am not a dog,' said Dualta. 'He beckoned as if he was calling his dog.'

'You are for hire, aren't you?' the young gentleman asked angrily.

'Yes,' said Dualta.

'Well, then,' he said, as if this was the end of the argument.

'I have to like the looks of the people I will hire myself to,' said Dualta. 'I don't like your looks.'

The young man's face became suffused with anger. Dualta's face was white under the sun-colour and his eyes were sparking. The young man suddenly looked around him and was upset by what he saw. They were deeply surrounded by a ring of countrymen. It seemed to have happened in a moment. Tall men and short men and young men, with impassive faces, just looking at him. They were completely hemmed in. The ring around them was at least five men deep. At the outer ring some of the rough-and-ready boys were trying to force their way into the centre, but were unable to make their way through the solid mass of bodies.

'If you desire to hit me with that whip, just do so,' said Dualta.

The policeman looked around him.

'Now, now,' he said. 'No need for that tone, I'm sure. The gentleman had no intention of hitting you.'

'Certainly not,' said the gentleman. 'Why should I soil my whip?' He was brave enough. He started to walk through the crowd of men as if they weren't there. They opened a lane for him. He reached his horse. He mounted. He sat looking down at them. They all stared back at him impassively. He was daunted, you could see that. He would like to make a gesture but he couldn't think of one. So he brought the whip down viciously on the flank of the horse. The horse whinnied and reared and then galloped.

The policeman said to Dualta, 'You are a lucky young man.'

Dualta said, 'Why do you say that?'

'Many reasons,' said the policeman. Then he turned to the crowd. 'Go on now! Go about your business. Break up this crowd. It's against the law.'

Gradually the mass moved, drifting away until Dualta was left with the policeman and the three or four rough-and-ready boys ruefully regarding the sergeant.

'You could be a dead young man now,' said the policeman. 'Watch yourself. Keep out of trouble. It's possible that the young gentleman will be back with friends. I would advise you to change your position.'

'I will stay where I am,' said Dualta.

'I told you,' said the policeman and walked away. The others followed him, looking like mongrels trailing a greyhound.

Dualta was looking after him when a voice said, 'Has no man hired you?'

Automatically, as if he had read it, Dualta said: 'No man, Lord.'

Then he turned to look at the voice. He was looking at a tall man with a deeply lined face. He wore no hat. He had white hair that looked too old for his face. It was a strong face, with two lines of bitterness cutting between his nose and his chin. His eyes were a very pale blue and his eyebrows were black. A strange interesting-looking countenance.

'You are a young man of learning,' he said.

'I have some,' said Dualta. He noticed they were talking Irish. Sometimes he found it hard to understand the Irish of the south. They put the emphasis on different parts of the words and almost sang some of the vowels, elided more, thinned others. But this man spoke very clearly.

'Do you seek trouble deliberately?' he asked. 'Do you wish to embrace it?'

'No,' said Dualta. 'He reminded me of somebody. My good sense deserted me.'

'You are not without courage,' said the man.

'What is courage?' Dualta asked.

'Facing your oppressors with a straight back,' said the man.

51

'That is courage. But it must be done at an opportune time. You are free to be hired. Will you hire yourself to me?'

'What is the rate?' Dualta asked.

The man laughed.

'I don't know,' he said. 'Whatever you are worth. Maybe nothing. You will get opportunities to fight oppression. You will be able to hit back. Does the thought of that please you?'

'It does,' said Dualta.

The man held out his hand. 'My name is Cuan McCarthy,' he said. 'You will have to trust me.'

Dualta felt the hard hand that firmly grasped his own. The look of the man was open and direct, and held promise. Of what? Dualta didn't know, but his pulse tingled.

'I am your man,' he said.

'Come with me,' said Cuan. 'I have a spare horse which I purchased today. That will be your first job, to ride it, without a saddle,' he added.

'My seat would not know the feel of a saddle,' said Dualta. 'It was educated to the bare back of a pony.'

The man smiled.

'We will go the back way,' he said. 'Because the policeman was right. Your antagonist will return. We will leave him to weep.'

He turned abruptly and walked away.

Dualta hefted his spade and followed him and his heart was beating faster than usual.

7

THE WOMAN said: 'Are you ready?'

'Yes,' said Dualta, dipping his quill in the inkhorn.

'The first one to Tooley,' she said. 'Write that he has only hours to withdraw his bid on the land of the Ryans. You know how to say it.'

Dualta wrote:

'Tooley: You have been warned.
You have only hours left.
Go now, and withdraw your bid.
You know the consequences.
Captain Right.'

Nothing disturbed the silence but the scratching of the quill on the paper. Dualta considered it. He decided to leave it bare without any flourishes. He rose from the table and carried it over to her. Before he handed it to her he held it in front of the fire to dry, careful that the thin ink didn't run. She took it. She was sitting beside the fire. Her head bent over the letter. Her hair was uncovered. She was an enormous fat woman. Her hair was still black. It was parted in the centre and pulled back. It gleamed. She had a good forehead. From below her forehead her face started to swell. Then her body, all the way down to her ankles. She had small feet. They were encased in boots that would barely fasten around her ankles. He watched her as she read. Her face didn't register anything.

'Now the other,' she said as she folded the letter carefully.

He went back to the table. He thought, tickling his lips with the goosequill. This one would have to be different.

He crossed a cross with a cross three times on the head of the paper. That looked spiky. Then he wrote:

'Hanley: This is the last warning.
Go, or you will sleep in the
Embrace of the Briars.
Captain Rock.'

He smiled as he read that. He thought of Hanley, Wilcocks' bailiff, a white-skinned man, with soft hands and a comfortable stomach. He thought of him being stripped naked, of the six-foot hole being dug in the earth, filled around with briars, and the soft body of Hanley being forced into this bed. He had a bald head. It would be gleaming whitely in the light of the torches. He would undoubtedly scream as the briars tore his soft flesh. He would be terrified at the thought of the briar-bed. Dualta thought he could afford to smile. Because it had never been done to anyone around here yet. The threat of it was sufficient as soon as the word of its having been done to someone somewhere else, sometime, percolated into the valley. He wondered if anyone had ever slept in the briar-bed. He was assured that they had done so in other places. But as far as Dualta was concerned it was a game. He loved writing these threatening letters.

He went and handed it to her. She read it and laughed.

'That will frighten Hanley,' she said. 'He is soft. It would do him no harm to get a few briar thorns into his softness. We will add to the letter with a bit of action. He is already afeard. I would say that he is ready to go.'

He was glad that she was pleased. She was a formidable woman. Perhaps it was the fatness of her that never allowed an expression to move the heaviness of her countenance. The small hands, the small feet looked innocuous, Missis Annie, widow woman who ran a small shop at the cross-roads in the valley. She had small even teeth and when she smiled she looked so jolly.

'How long have you been here now?' she asked.

'Say six months,' said Dualta.

'We will have to get another writer,' she said.

'Why so?' he asked. 'Am I not satisfactory?'

'Oh, yes, dear,' she said. 'But they get to know. You can tell a man from his hand. If it is too well known, some day you will write and somebody will see and recognise, and they will say, "Oh, that is the hand of the young Connachtman that works for Annie." You see?'

'Yes,' said Dualta.

'But you will advise,' she said. 'Some of your imaginations would chill the blood of an eel. Go see if there is any sign of McCarthy.'

Dualta went to the door.

It was a good sheltered valley, covered off by the Knockmealdown mountains, and if you were high enough you looked left and saw the Galtees away off, and when you looked right you could see the Monevalaghs, with the Comeraghs behind them. He supposed that was why the people were fighters. The

54

men all seemed to have long jaws that could clamp shut like the grip of a vice. The valley itself was rich and lush, cultivated almost to the peak of the hills, a thing Dualta could never get used to. But if you looked closely you realised that all the houses were pressed back up into the high ground. The river that bisected the valley had rich fields on either side of it, and these rich fields seemed as if they had inexorably pushed back the houses and the smaller fields, pressed them and forced them back up the hills, while on the far side of the river a three-storey stone house, with pillars at its great front door, lay snug in the middle of a park-field of thirty acres. The sun was shining on it now. The river was gleaming, the fresh leaves were peeping on the great trees in the parkland. Behind the house he could see the carriage-houses and the haybarns and the horse stalls. He thought: if the little houses and fields had been pushed back over the years, they were now reaching out and bit by bit trying to embrace part of what they had been deprived of, and the rich lands were shivering.

'You are looking at your future home,' said the voice behind him.

'What's that?' said Dualta. He turned and saw Cuan. 'I never saw you coming although I was on the watch for you. What do you mean, my future home?'

'You are going to live there,' said Cuan.

'I am?' asked Dualta. 'I suppose I'm going to marry Wilcock's daughter?'

McCarthy laughed.

'Don't be that ambitious,' he said. 'No, we have been gradually reducing his workmen as you know. So we are going to send you to work for him. He will be pleased to have you. He would be pleased to have a cripple, not to mind a strong man.'

'Do you wish to make me a Trojan horse?' Dualta asked.

'The very thing,' said McCarthy, 'the very thing. Come in and we will talk to Annie.'

They went towards the house. Then Cuan's eye was caught by the movement in the valley. 'Stop,' he said. They turned and looked. On the road behind the big house there was a cavalcade of men moving. The dark-clothed ones were on horseback. They were armed. There were other horsemen and walking men with implements on their shoulders. Cuan walked quickly to the door. 'Come out, Annie,' he called. 'They are going to knock Morogh Ryan.' He came back and stood beside Dualta. His fists were clenched, Dualta saw, and the jaw muscles were bulging on his face. His eyes were slitted as he watched. The bitter lines near his mouth were very deep.

'He is for eviction?' Dualta asked.

'He is,' said Cuan. 'He is for eviction.'

'He is a weak man,' said Dualta. 'He was bound to go to the wall some day.'

Cuan turned on him. 'Whose fault?' he asked. 'Whose fault? Because he is weak all the more reason that he should find true justice. A strong man can look after himself. Your day will come! You talk like that and your day will come too, then you will look around you and you will find no pity.'

Dualta remained silent. Morogh Ryan bid for land at a very high price. He had five acres. He paid a rent of five pounds an acre. That was twenty-five pounds. Even with his potatoes and his bit of oats and his cows and his pig, it was not enough to pay the rent. Because he was a lazy man anyhow, and he grew weeds. You didn't need to be a prophet to know that he would one day fall. It was part of life. He wasn't a good man with land. He should never have bid for what he couldn't afford.

'You can't understand,' said Cuan. 'You are young. You dismiss men like straws. It's not the men. It's the system. Morogh has five children. What will become of them? He will go into a town and at the outskirts he will build a wretched shelter. He will beg and look for odd jobs and he will scour rubbish-heaps. Unless God is better to him than now, he will have to sell the small bodies of his daughters for a stone of potatoes. Yes, he is a weak man, is Morogh.'

Annie was standing beside them. Her arms were folded. They watched it all enacted. The people converging on the house. There was no wall around it. Just a rough yard in front with the manure-heap piled high near the door. There was smoke rising from the thatch. The sun didn't glint off the windows because they held no glass. They saw the figure of

56

Morogh at the door, and then his wife, and the children emerging like rabbits out of a burrow. They saw the hands waving. It didn't take long. They saw the hooks tied to ropes thrown over the thatch and the men straining, like the rope-pulling teams at the harvest sports, and then there was a crack, audible even to them watching, and the roof collapsed. It was a one-roomed cottage. The supports of the thatch were gone, just one or two blackened beams crooked and exposed and the marks of the fire on the inside of one gable. That was all. Smoke started to rise from the ruins as the fallen thatch fell on the still burning turf fire. It smouldered and burst into flame. Dualta's heart stopped at the sight. It brought back to him the sight of the death of the house of his Uncle Marcus. But that was free. That was done by a free man. This was different.

They remained.

'We are not men,' Cuan was saying. 'We should be all over there, every man of us with pikes and pitchforks and sleans, all in one mass to prevent them from doing this.'

'What good would it do for everyone to die?' Annie asked. 'That would please them. They could clean out the valley at one stroke. No. It is better to repay.'

Then after a pause she said, 'Well, Tooley will pay for this. Tooley will pay!'

'Tonight, Dualta,' said Cuan. 'You will come. It's about time you saw the result of your letters. It might restore some of your pity for the poor.'

'I'm not wanting in pity,' said Dualta.

'We'll see,' said Cuan. 'We'll see!'

They took soot from the chimney of Cuan's house and they rubbed it on their faces. Then they took the prepared rush torches, unlighted, and went into the night. The horses were tied at the back of the house. They mounted them and gave them their heads, because it was the dark of the moon. The stars were obscured by clouds.

Dualta was excited. These were the sort of actions he had wanted. Mounted men in the night, soot, torches, the sound of a shod hoof hitting a stone. The horses seemed to know where they were going. They left the rough road and descended the hill. The bushes blocking the gaps into the fields had all been removed. The horses seemed to find their way to the gaps as if it was broad daylight.

There was a sheen on the river, hardly perceptible. You could hear the gentle rustling of the dead rushes, and the scamper of a frightened water-hen. The horses bent their heads, widened their nostrils and scented the water before they crossed. It was quite deep but the ford was hard underfoot. Dualta felt the water kissing his shoes. They laboured up the other bank and trotted to the fields on the far side. In about ten minutes they came to the grove of willow trees. They couldn't see but they heard the movement of horses pacing and being quietened; the slap of a hard palm on the neck of a horse; uneasy horses whinnying and being gently shushed.

They stopped there. Cuan spoke: 'Are we all here?'

'We are all here,' a voice answered him. 'Don't light the torches until we are about the house,' he said. 'Did men bring the kettles?' 'They will be at the place,' he was answered. 'The police are all gone,' said Cuan. 'They had to escort that dangerous criminal Morogh Ryan out of the valley.' There was a snort of laughter. 'When the flames go up, flee, and let the horses loose on the hills. Go to bed. We move. Now!'

Dualta felt the excitement now. The fact that you could not see added to it. Hearing voices out of the darkness. The smell of the horses. Being surrounded by men you knew but couldn't recognise. He thought: Maybe I should have stayed at home and organised something like this for the Half-Sir, but at least now I know. Now I know how it is done. It all gave you a feeling of power. That you were hitting back; that you were concealed and free from discovery. You were an anonymous freedom-fighter under the soft spring cloak of darkness.

First the horses walked and then when they had negotiated the fields and felt their hooves on the rough road they trotted, and then somebody shouted and they ran. The sound of twenty horsemen on the road was exhilarating. It was dangerous. Men and horses all around you. Tossing manes and squeals and shouts. One or two dogs started to bark.

Then they were there, just when his blood was being warmed. There were other horsemen waiting.

'Spread around,' said the voice of Cuan. Dualta stayed where he was, facing the house. He saw the horsemen moving out on either side. There was a faint reflection from the white-washed walls of Tooley's house. 'Light up!' said the voice of Cuan. On the left there was the splutter of an expensive match-stick and then a torch flared and from the one torch others were lighted until a ring of flaming torches lit up the house in an unnatural glow. Inside the kitchen of the house a dog started to bark.

Cuan called: 'Come out, Tooley! Tooley, come out!'

There was a silence then. Nothing but the dog barking and the hissing of the torches. Dualta imagined Tooley. Tooley would be frightened, he thought. It was a wonderful way to frighten a man.

Cuan didn't give him long. His voice was hard. 'Come out, Tooley!' he called. Dualta tried to imagine Tooley, waking up. His realisation. How his stomach would contract with fear. He would reach for his breeches, hurriedly pull them on, pull back the bolt on the door.

A baby started to cry in the house. Dualta's heart sank. A baby! But Tooley was a comparatively young man. He was bound to have a baby. It didn't matter. The door opened and Tooley came out. Shirt and breeches and bare feet, his brown curly hair tousled. He was a big man. His chest was stretching his shirt. He had a big jaw. He blinked in the light of the torches. He didn't seem very afraid. He didn't seem as afraid as he should be.

'What do you want?' he asked.

'You were warned, Tooley,' said Cuan. 'Many times. You were told not to bid for Ryan's land.'

'I need Ryan's land,' said Tooley. 'I have ten children. The five acres I possess are not enough. Ryan was lazy. I want that land to live.'

'You pay no attention to the wishes of the people?' Cuan asked.

'Who are the people?' asked Tooley, his big fists clenched.

'If they are men let them face me, not write letters behind closed doors like timorous women. I have a right to live. I have a right to feed my children. I have a right to better myself. And that I'll do, if all the cowards in Ireland were gathered out there, skulking behind torches.'

There was a movement to the right of him. A horse and rider came into the light. Dualta saw an arm raised. He saw the heavy stick fall on the side of Tooley's head. He heard the sound of the blow. Tooley shut his eyes. That was all. He opened them again. The horseman fell back. There was the sound of a scream as Tooley's wife came from behind him. She held his arm.

'Tom! Tom! Tom!' she said. He put a hand on her hand. The blood was flowing freely from his forehead down the side of his face. But he kept looking at them and his eyes were brave as ever. Dualta felt his stomach heaving.

'Bring the kettles!' Cuan called. 'Get your children out of the house!'

'What are you going to do?' Tooley asked.

'We are going to burn you out,' said Cuan. 'You were warned.'

Tooley was going to protest. Was he going to beseech?

'Brave men,' he said. 'Oh, the brave men of Ireland! Burn me? I'll build again. A hundred times. If you want to drive me out of this valley you will have to kill me.'

'Men like you have been killed before,' said Cuan.

'From the back of a bush,' said Tooley. 'From a drain, from a ditch, where rats lurk. Is there a man that will face me in the daylight among you?' Furiously he wiped the blood from his eye.

'Put the coals in the thatch,' Cuan called coldly.

Dualta saw the men with the swinging kettles. They were glowing from the live turf-sods they carried. He saw them being extracted glowing from the kettles and being stuck under the straw thatch. There were about ten of them. They started to burn, to smoke, to glow.

Tooley's shoulders slumped. Then he went back into the house. His wife followed him. She was sobbing. They brought.

out their children. One of them was a baby in arms. Two more were barely able to walk. They were frightened, the young ones, and crying. They made up for Tooley. Some of the bigger children started to bring out pieces of things from the house, hurrying them away. Tooley himself and his wife. The horsemen didn't help. Dualta wanted to get down and help, but he knew now that it was forbidden.

The horsemen waited there until the thatch was well alight. The Tooleys rushed in and out faster and faster as the flames caught hold. The horsemen waited there until they saw pieces of flaming stuff falling into the inside of the house, until there was no hope of it being saved, and then, on Cuan's one word, they turned away from there. The torches had sizzled to death, but there was plenty of light from the burning house.

Dualta kept his head down. There was plenty of light now to recognise people. But he didn't want to. He didn't want to know who they were. He looked back once. Tooley was standing up as straight as a good mountain-ash tree, looking after them. There was anger in his face and a touch of helplessness, but no fear at all, Dualta thought, no fear at all.

He followed after the silent horsemen.

8

DUALTA WAS lying on the thick branch of a chestnut tree that spread like the rafters of a roof over the muddy avenue. It was night. The light of the moon was filtering through the bare branches. The brown sticky leaves of the chestnut tree were at the bursting point. He could barely make out the shape of Cuan sitting behind the bole of a tree on the other side. He was cradling the pistol between his knees.

He heard a hiss from Cuan and stiffened on the branch and took a tight hold of the stick in his right hand. He listened. At the far end of the avenue the sound of the horseshoe hitting a stone. So Hanley was on the way.

Later he heard a tiny whistle that Cuan emitted.

61

Dualta waited for the shot from the pistol. When it came he leaned down and hit at Hanley's beaver hat with the stick. It was a good bit of timing. The horse shied, Hanley half fell off. He shouted. Then he got to the ground and, leaving his hat and his horse and everything else, he set off running up the avenue. He was shouting: 'Ah! Ah! Ah!' as if all the devils in hell were after him.

They found their horses where they had left them. They got safely through the woods and into the hills. The horses knew their way. They were sure-footed. The excitement died for Dualta. He ceased to chuckle over Hanley. Besides, Cuan was dour. He didn't want to talk about it. It was nearly dawn when they stood on the last hill that led down to the town. They could see the dark bulk of it below, and the gleam from the broad river.

'What is our real reason for coming here, Cuan?' Dualta asked.

'We are going to look at a hanging,' said Cuan.

'A hanging!' Dualta exclaimed, and his heart sank.

'That's right,' said Cuan. 'In case you think it is all for fun like games played on a corpse at a wake.'

'Do I need to be convinced?' Dualta asked.

'You do,' said Cuan. 'You are jibbing at going to Wilcocks, aren't you?'

'It's too much like being a spy,' said Dualta. 'I am a faulty person, I know, but I like to be in the open.'

'You'll see what happens to people who are in the open,' said Cuan angrily.

'I don't want to see men hanged,' said Dualta. 'You go and I will wait for you.'

'Why are you afraid?' Cuan asked him.

'Not fear,' said Dualta. 'It's not decent to watch men dying.'

'There has to be a purpose in the things we are doing,' said Cuan. 'It's not just ideas in a thinking head. There must be reason. This is a reason. It is the working of landlordism. They insisted on a Coercion Act. You have to see the fruits of this, if you want to know what we are fighting about. Have you ever watched people dying?'

'Yes,' said Dualta, tight-lipped.

'Well, this is no different,' said Cuan. 'You can even pray for them and for yourself that some day you too won't decorate a rope. This is a country where you can see innocent men dying with a look of bewilderment on their faces. No man minds dying for something he has done. It must be a terrible thing for a man to die when he has done nothing.'

'Who are they?' Dualta asked.

'They are the two men who are supposed to have shot Riddler the bailiff,' said Cuan.

'Did they shoot him?' asked Dualta.

'One of them did,' said Cuan, 'but the other knew nothing about it.'

'They wouldn't hang an innocent man,' said Dualta.

Cuan laughed. It wasn't free laughter. He jogged ahead. Dualta followed him reluctantly. They came down from the hill on to the long dirt road that wound its way to the town. It was a spring day. You could see the green grass shooting through the yellow-tipped frost-bitten grasses of the fields. The woodbine in the hedges was in leaf as it twined its deadly tentacles on everything within its reach.

I must see more young people, Dualta thought. I have been too long with older people. They will sap the youth in me. I will wake up one day and find that my youth is past and that I have not enjoyed it at all. Suddenly he thought of Paidi. That's it, next Sunday he would set out early and travel to the place where Paidi was working, at the village of the cross of the Hanging Tree. He thought of Paidi. Eat, sleep, joke, talk to the girls the language of understatement and flattery. Bailiffs, Coercion Acts, vengeance, freedom, all passed over Paidi's head. He thought of making money to bring home for his people. That was all. And laughing when the occasion arose, that was all. Dualta felt guilty that he hadn't gone across to see him. But he was so busy, and Paidi and what he was doing were as far apart as day and night, day and night.

There was silence in the town. It was like the silence that had enwrapped it when he and Paidi had come to the hiring fair.

There were not many people in the poorer parts of the town. The doors were closed. That was not usual. Some children playing in the dust, thin dogs barking at the two horses as they passed. They stopped at the big shop where Annie got her provisions and they walked the horses into the yard. The boy there took them and led them into a stall. 'Big day? Big day?' he asked. 'That's right, Murt,' said Cuan. He gave him a list. 'Get that filled,' he said, 'and load it on the horses.' 'Right, man, right,' said Murt, taking it. 'I'll see to that. Are ye going to look?' 'Yes,' said Cuan. 'I'd go meself,' said Murt, 'if I wasn't as busy as a flea on a dog. Funerals or hangings, you can't keep up with the custom.' 'Lucky for you,' said Cuan, and they walked towards the square.

When they turned into the better street and walked towards the square, they saw that it was crowded. Well-dressed people. In the square itself there were carriages drawn up. Dualta was sickened to see that there were some women in the carriages. There were some country people. Not many. There was a double line of soldiers facing out from the gallows. The only raucous sound was the call of the chapmen selling their penny broadsheets, *The Seven Champions of Christendom, Irish Rogues and Raparees, The Life and Adventures of Captain Freney, The Battle of Aughrim, Hibernian Tales,* and others about murderers, grave-robbers, the battle of Waterloo. They were appropriate tales for a hanging.

Anyhow, Dualta was thinking, I don't have to look. I can close my eyes. Every man is provided with curtains over his eyes if he wishes to use them.

'See,' Cuan was saying, 'how they conduct everything with panoply? Even the sordid business of hanging, they give it colour and form.'

'Why do you say that one man is innocent?' Dualta asked.

'I know,' said Cuan. 'I have talked with the people from the place. I know the other three men who were there. This young man happened to be in the wrong place at the wrong time. He was heard talking to the older man by an informer. He recognised him by his Connacht accent. Like yours. It could have been you. We didn't get the informer. They sent him out of the country, better guarded than the jewels of a king. We hope that some day somebody will catch up with him. Even if they do not, he will get a crick in his neck looking over his shoulder for the rest of his life. The innocent young man was coming home from courting a girl.'

The country women with the cloaks had gone on their knees. They took rosary beads from their pockets. There was a stirring among the soldiers, a stiffening of their backs. Their hands tightened on their guns.

Dualta felt his left leg trembling.

The two men mounted the gallows from behind. Their arms were bound. There was a priest out in front reading from a black book.

Then he could see them. It was to be a double hanging. The squat pleasant-faced hangman stood between them. He had his coat off. His arms were bared. The man on the right was a big-chested, grey-haired man with a determined face. His mouth was clamped shut. His thick neck was bare. He was a muscular man. He looked rocklike. The young man had curly brown hair falling over his forehead. His hair was being moved by the gentle wind. He was low-sized, powerful-looking, but his mouth was open and he was crying. Tears were pouring down his cheeks.

Dualta felt as if he had been kicked in the heart.

'Paidi!' he called. He felt a strong grip on his arm.

'Shush, Dualta,' said Cuan. There were heads turning.

'It's Paidi, Paidi,' said Dualta. The blood had drained from his face. He made a move to shove through the people. Cuan held on to him. 'Be easy, Dualta,' he said. 'Be easy.' 'But it's Paidi,' said Dualta.

Paidi hadn't heard him.

Dualta felt his whole body drained. He was shocked all over. He couldn't move now even if he wanted to. But it couldn't be Paidi. If you knew Paidi. This couldn't be Paidi. Paidi wouldn't even be bothered holding a gun. He wouldn't know what side the ball came from. Scream now about a miscarriage of justice. Who do you scream to, cold-faced indifferent officers of martial law, taking damn good care that somebody hangs to try and break a conspiracy of silence? But he's too young. He isn't twenty. Is he the first to go like that? What about his mother and father and all those kids waiting for him to come home in the glen in the hills near the great lake? Well, it's waiting they will be. They would have lost him anyhow to a woman sometime. They won't even know properly. Read the papers in the English tongue. He had read them himself. But you don't think of people's proper names when they are written in English and they are Irish in your head. You don't even recognise the words.

He stood there helpless, unbelieving, rooted, trembling, drained, what will I do, who will I go to, but these things don't take long. Before his horrified eyes, the living ones fell and the bodies swung, and there were still tears on Paidi's dead cheeks when Dualta turned away and groped his way free of the square and stumbled down the street. Free of the crowd, he leaned against a house and vomited. He wished to die. He groaned and went on holding his stomach with his arms.

I am the one, he thought. I betrayed him. I didn't go near him. This would not have happened if I had gone to see him, talked to him. He could never face his people. Paidi would not have come this far south if it wasn't for Dualta. Keep an eye on him, he could hear Paidi's father say. Stay with him until he is settled. And what had been Dualta's thanks for his kindness? Oh, great God, he groaned.

He blindly recognised the place they had left the horses. He went in there, and into the horse stall, and sat on hay in the corner and buried his face in his arms. The horse stirred and widened his nostrils and sniffed at his hair.

A long time, a long time before the blood came back to his body.

He knew Cuan was there. He knew he had been there for some time. He didn't talk. Somebody had to talk eventually.

'I didn't know you knew him, Dualta,' he said. 'I didn't know.'

'We came together from Connacht,' said Dualta.

'I'm sorry. I'm truly sorry,' said Cuan.

'The men that were there, they knew he had nothing to do

66

with it,' said Dualta. 'Cuan, why didn't they come forward and say so?'

'They would have hanged too,' said Cuan. 'They wouldn't have saved Paidi. Just five dead instead of two.'

'I would have come forward,' said Dualta. Cuan was silent.

'What will happen to his body?' Dualta asked.

'That will be taken care of,' said Cuan. 'The people over there will look after it. I'm truly sorry, Dualta. I didn't know. If I knew we would never have gone.'

'I might never have known if we hadn't gone,' said Dualta. 'There are so many hangings.'

'That's right,' said Cuan. 'There are so many hangings.' He was silent. 'I will see to the goods and we will go home,' he said then. 'I will tell you when all is ready.'

Dualta dropped his head in his arms again.

He heard Cuan's call, and rose and went stiffly into the yard. He had to shade his eyes from the light with his arm. The horses were heavily burdened. He had difficulty getting on his horse's back. Then they headed out of the town.

He knew none of the way they went. His horse just followed after Cuan's.

He thought, I was worrying about my youth. Paidi is gone out like a light, just like a light you quench, and not in fair time. So now you know what murder really is, whether it is by the hand of a civilian or by the hand of rulers with all the outward show of justice and impartiality. This was no law. It was law without reason or hope for the people who came under its shadow.

I have lost my youth well and truly now, he thought.

Only one sentence he spoke.

'I will go to Wilcocks, Cuan,' he said.

'Listen, Dualta,' said Cuan, 'I didn't mean . . .'

'I will go to Wilcocks,' he said.

Cuan was silent.

9

H E DISDAINED the back avenue into the house.
He went to the main wrought-iron gates. They were double gates, as tall as two men and a half, yet they opened easily. They were well hung. Inside the gate was the small squat house of Bullock, the English field bailiff. Dualta walked past. There was smoke from the chimney. The door was open.

It was a pleasant avenue. It was shaded by poplar trees. To his left the great open fields sloped to the river. Their vastness was broken in places by towering beech trees, some copper-coloured, some green. Red cattle grazed the fields or rested in the shade of the branches of the beeches. The whole valley was hazy in the June sun. From here you could see the whitewashed houses well up in the hills. He supposed they could look menacing enough if you were afraid of them.

The drive wound pleasantly. The trees ended and the drive opened into a large semicircle in front of the house where the carriages could turn if they were only visiting. The drive was well kept, hard ground-in gravel, that had been well scuffled of grass and weeds.

He stood there and looked at the house, a solid three-storey stone-built house with a pillared doorway with very tall eight-paned windows on each side of the doorway and slightly smaller windows on the top floors. He noticed that the bottom windows were ready to be barricaded, the heavy iron-bound shutters were there ready to be hung on the great spikes that had been driven into the stonework. Wilcocks' was the only place in the area that hadn't been barricaded, but apparently Hanley's leaving had made him feel cautious. Many big houses had been surprised. Arms had been stolen, servitors beaten. The front door was big and solid, the panels carved from the thick timber. It was oil-polished and gleamed dully in the sunshine.

He stood there for a little longer, and then hefting his bundle

68

on the spade handle he walked around the house towards the back-quarters. The house was as broad as it was long. At the back there was a great cobblestoned yard closed in on all sides by two-storey slated stables and carriage houses. The yard was empty. They were all in the fields, all but the turf-boy who was tending the fires under the two great pots of boiling potatoes. One was for the pigs and the other was for the workers. The boy stood and rubbed the turf-smoke out of his eyes. Dualta nodded at him and then went in the open back door into the kitchen.

It was a huge kitchen. Great copper pots and pans burnished bright hung on the walls facing him. There was a big rough table sitting in the middle of the flagged floor. Rough chairs and two enormous kitchen cupboards groaning with their weight of delf and jugs and plates and mugs. There were two girls cleaning vegetables at the table and a great big fat woman with big bare feet cutting into a joint of meat with a bloodied knife. The girls saw him first as he blocked the light. They looked up at him, their knives in mid-air. 'God bless the good work,' he said politely. Then the fat lady turned. She hadn't small eyes like Annie, he noticed. She had big eyes in a red face. She could be cranky, he thought, so he smiled at her and softened his eyes. He knew that he wasn't ugly and that his smile could be a useful weapon. Its effect on the girls was immediate, but it brought nothing from the fat lady but a grunt.

'It's a grand sight,' said Dualta, 'to see three beautiful maidens around a table.' The girls giggled. The fat lady was not amused. She looked him up and down from toe to crown. His shoes were polished, his hose were neatly darned by himself, his breeches were corduroy but new, and the belt that held them up was new. His shirt was clean, his jacket fairly respectable and his hair was shining. He was newly shaved. He knew all this. So he showed her his teeth again in a pleasant smile. They were good and white, from the application of a mixture of soot and salt rubbed on with his finger.

'We don't feed the beggars until night,' she said, and turned back to her meat cutting.

'Do you insult everyone that comes into the house?' he asked.

'It depends what they come for,' she said. 'What's under you?'

'I am looking for work,' said Dualta.

'We have enough maid-servants,' she said.

'You might be deceived by my delicate build,' said Dualta. He rolled his eyes at her significantly. She laughed freely. He was getting on with her, he thought. That was the password, charm Biddy, they said and the house is yours.

At this moment he was pushed from behind by a large hand. He staggered over to the table. The coarse voice had said, 'Out of my way.' He turned to look at the giant who came in. He was carrying a bale of cut logs on his shoulder. He went towards the huge fireplace and dropped the bale with a terrible clatter into the great chest.

'Christy,' said Dualta grimly, 'if you weren't as big as you are, and I didn't want to dirty this nice clean kitchen with you, I'd make you pay for that push.'

Christy looked at him. His big face disappeared into a thousand furrows as he looked at him. Then he scratched his curly hair and pointed a large finger at him and said, 'Dualta!'

'The light dawned,' said Dualta.

'You know this fellow, Christy,' Biddy said.

'That's Dualta,' said Christy, 'he's from Annie's.'

'I'd have told you, Biddy,' one of the girls said, 'if you gave me a chance.'

'What are you doing out of Annie's?' Biddy asked.

'She put me,' said Dualta sadly.

'Did she catch your hand in the money-box?' she asked rudely.

'No,' said Dualta. 'But I'm a Connachtman.'

'I can tell that from your speech,' she said.

'So people didn't like me,' said Dualta.

'I don't wonder,' said Biddy.

'I like Connachtmen,' said the tall girl. 'My name is Nora, Dualta.'

'Hello, Nora,' said Dualta.

'I liked you, Dualta,' said Christy after thought.

70

'Thanks, Christy,' said Dualta. 'I liked you too before you pushed me.'

'You were in the way of the door,' said Christy reasonably.

'Ah,' said Dualta.

'I heard about you,' said Biddy. 'You were good at sums, people said, and the writing. It's a wonder Annie let you go. She can't write her own name.'

'Reading and writing and arithmetic,' said Dualta. 'I can write love letters or begging letters, but I'm better at love letters. I can multiply, and divide and subtract. I can dig as many potatoes as any man. I can cut five carts of turf in a day. I can sow a meadow. I'm one of the best men that ever came into this district, and the poor creatures in the valley don't know it.'

'You have the gift of boasting anyhow,' said Biddy. 'What do you want here?'

'I don't know,' said Dualta. 'I was going home, and then thought I'd stop and see if you people would have any use for me. Would it be too much to ask if I could see himself, then?'

Biddy was wiping her hands on her apron. She was looking at him shrewdly.

'I'll see,' she said abruptly. 'Keep an eye on him, you, and don't let him steal anything.' She went out of a door.

'She likes you,' said Nora. 'Sit down, Dualta.'

'How do you know she likes me?' he asked.

'The way she talks to you,' said Nora. He sat near the table. He looked at Nora. She was a dark-haired girl with black eyes.

'I'd hate to hear her so if she loved somebody,' said Dualta.

'But why are you leaving Annie, Dualta?' asked Christy. Dualta looked at his puzzled face and thought it is only the really simple people who go to the heart of the matter.

'People up there don't like me,' he said patiently. 'Some of them are a queer lot. Very suspicious.' Silence descended on them for the moment. He broke it. 'Who is the little one?' he asked. She was a small fair girl. She blushed easily, as now. 'That's Teresa,' said Nora. 'You won't get a word out of her. I hope you work here, Dualta.'

'Is there room for me?' he asked.

71

'They've lost a lot of people,' she said. 'Even Teresa and myself got letters.'

'Oh,' said Dualta. He had written them himself. It was odd to see an anonymous Nora Criodan and Teresa Flannery becoming real in front of his eyes. 'They didn't frighten you?' he asked.

'Not me,' she said with determination, 'but Teresa was crying. She's soft.'

He looked at the blushing Teresa. What a nice manly occupation, he thought, writing letters to frighten girls!

'I got no letters at all,' said Christy.

'They were probably afraid of you,' said Dualta.

'I'm not afraid of them,' said Christy.

'Best of men,' said Dualta.

'All right,' said Biddy from the door. Dualta was startled. With her so silent bare feet, he hadn't heard her coming. 'Come with me now,' she said, 'and don't forget to keep your tongue in your mouth.'

He rose. 'I'll leave this,' he said about the spade and his bundle. Nora took them. 'They'll be in the corner for you,' she said. 'I hope you are lucky.'

'So do I,' he said. He followed Biddy. They came into a large hall that stretched from here to the front door. It was a big hall of polished wood and panelled walls. The staircase bisected the hall. It had slender railings and a polished mahogany handrail. There were rugs made of sheepskin on the floors. Dualta walked on the tips of his toes. This was the first time he had ever been in a house like this. Back in his own place, the nearest he had come to one was peeping in at it from the railings of the front gate. The coloured glass at the sides of the front door threw dancing coloured reflections on the floor. He thought those were pretty.

Biddy opened a door. 'Wait in here now,' she said.

'Thank you, ma'am,' he said and walked in.

There was a carpet on the floor. His feet made no sound.

'Don't touch anything,' she said, and closed the door after her.

He drew in his breath. It was a library. There were leather-

72

bound volumes with gold-leaf lettering. He swivelled his head as he read the titles. All the knowledge that a man could want was here: Dryden, Scott, Shakespeare, Encyclopædias, *Costtumes of the Nations*, *Wild Sports of the East*, Pinkerton's *Voyages*, Blagdon's *India*, Byron, Johnson, Swift, Paley, Goldsmith, Hume, Gibbon, Pope, Hogarth, books on travel, bound magazines, poetry, Greek books, Latin books, volume after volume. Enough to make you groan at the sight of them. So many you wanted that it would take a whole lifetime to get hold of, one by one, time by time, in cheap battered and bowdlerised editions, sold as waste by the chapmen.

There was a table used as a reading desk. There were account books open on this. There was a quill pen resting in an inkwell. It was as if a presence had been and gone. An elusive scent. He thought that Wilcocks would hardly use scent, or would he? What did he know about people like Wilcocks, just to see him from a distance riding his horse and spit in the dust as he passed?

There was an English magazine open under his eyes on the table. He looked at it. A whole page was taken up with a funny drawing. The blood rose in his face as he examined it. It was an Irish drawing, the man in the middle waving a shillelagh, a man in tattered clothes with the face of an ape, a small pug nose, red faced. Other people reeling drunk, waving kegs. All of them had apelike faces. The women had apelike faces. So had the children. The women were ugly, with dirty clothes, streeling hair. The children looked like the demons carved on old churches in France, in a drawing he once saw. Not one of them had a redeeming feature. He tried to read the caption. It was a strange mixture of English that the Irish were supposed to speak, like the hieroglyphics on an Egyptian tomb. He thought of all the people he knew. He tried to place them beside this crew of sub-humans displayed as typical. His resting hand on the desk clenched into a white fist.

That was the way the girl saw him as she came into the room. The white fist, the muscles bunched at the side of his jaw, a scar on his cheekbone that was standing out whitely against his suffused face. His nostrils flaring. She was surprised. She walked behind him and looked down at what was obviously moving him. He didn't know she was there.

'You don't approve of the cartoon?' she said.

'Are we apes?' he asked. 'We are not animals. We have souls. We are like other human beings. We can laugh and cry. We can love and hate. Do we speak with stones in our mouth like gobbling turkeys? Have we fallen so low that this is the way we are seen? Even by our enemies?'

Then he realised. The tension left him. He smelled again the scent that had been in the room with him before. He turned. A girl with calm brown eyes was regarding him. She was well dressed. Superior cloth. Her skin was very smooth. She was half laughing at him, watching his face composing itself. He had given himself away. She watched the life going out of his countenance, the secret look that she was so used to veiling his thoughts. She was Wilcocks' daughter of course. Not very often seen. Home this last year from being educated in Dublin and London and France. Not home long enough for people to get to assess her. They said she was all right. She was kind. She helped the really poor without ostentation, and without forcing tracts on them vilifying the Blessed Virgin.

'I'm sorry, Miss,' he said. 'You caught me when I wasn't looking.'

'I caught you when you *were* looking,' she said. She moved to the table. She sat down behind the account books.

'You haven't answered my question,' she said. He was trying to think of her name. He had overheard it. A strange name because it didn't fit her and who she was. An Irish name, of all things, tied on to such an Ascendancy name as Wilcocks.

'I cannot answer it, Miss Una,' he said. He thought of it in time. What do I do now, he wondered? Do I revert to being humble and ingratiating and secret? She was a very good-looking girl. She looked very Irish, dark, with the creamy white skin so many handsome Irish girls wore unconsciously. He could think of Irish girls in the hills better-looking than she, if they had the polish and attention of the toilette.

'Why?' she asked.

'I am on the wrong side of the road,' he said, recklessly.

74

'You are in a better position to answer it than me.'

She looked at him.

'All right,' she said. 'It's really very simple. It is induced by fear.'

'I don't understand that,' he said.

'You ridicule what you fear,' she said, 'in order by laughing at it to make it appear innocuous.' She watched him thinking over this. He looked at her with closer attention.

'Why?' he asked.

'Well,' she said, 'you are many, we are few. There are a few thousand people who own the whole country surrounded on all sides by millions and millions of people who do not wish them well. Is this true?'

'It could be,' he said cautiously.

'All you have to do now is look up at the houses on the hills looking down at us here to feel this. We are one against how many? Particularly now, with violence. So you see, we are afraid. It has always been the same. There is violence and savage repression, leading to horror and a guilty conscience, so you will always find that at times of acute violence, the ridicule becomes sharper and uglier and more depraved. It will continue. You will have to put up with it. It is part of life now.'

'Does a thing like that make you laugh, then?' he asked. 'Does it amuse you?'

'No,' she said. 'It makes me sad.'

What kind of a girl is this one at all? he wondered. She saw his wonder.

'I surprise you?' she asked.

'Yes,' he said.

'Not everybody is an enemy, you know,' she said. 'There are people on the other side who think, if they are educated. They don't at all feel that the Irish people are near apes. You don't look like an ape yourself. You are one of the people. What is your name?'

'My name is Duane,' he said. 'Dualta.'

'Your speech is not Tipperary,' she said.

'I am from Connacht,' he said. 'I am from the mountains.'

'I detect pride in your attitude,' she said.

'Every man is proud of his own place,' he said, 'if he is a man.'

'Why did you leave it then?' she asked.

'The young landlord hit me with a whip because I was in the way of his horse,' he said, putting his hand up to the scar, 'so I tumbled him from his horse and had to take off and run.' He was more than surprised, he was amazed at his own frankness.

She saw the flash of hate in his eyes at the remembrance.

'Do you consider then that all landlords are to be equated on the same level as the one you tumbled?'

This was shrewd. Actually he had never thought about it much. He had never tried to find out. What opportunities had he for finding out?

'I don't know,' he answered.

'You were right to tumble him,' she said. 'I would have done the same myself. All men are entitled to personal dignity.'

'You look young,' he said, 'and you talk with age, and I'm sure you would have given him a bad time if you were me.' He laughed. He had a picture of this girl with the determined chin punishing the Half-Sir most vigorously. She laughed too, as if the same picture had flashed into her mind. Dualta felt the sharpness of the whole thing easing away from him in the laughter.

They were laughing like this when the door opened again and Wilcocks came in. It could only be he. His eyebrows rose at the sight of his daughter laughing freely with the young countryman.

'Well,' he said loudly, 'what about him?' Dualta stopped laughing. The girl didn't stop abruptly. She allowed the laughter to taper away. Dualta saw a tall man with grey hair and a moustache. He had a strong face. The girl saw the curtain coming down on the face of the young man.

'He can read and write,' she said. 'Are you a good hand at accounts?' she asked.

'Yes,' said Dualta. 'I can do accounts.'

'Why did you leave Annie?' Wilcocks asked. He came into the room. He stood facing him, his hands behind his back. 'She is a decent woman. She gets a lot of custom from us. Why did

76

you leave her?'

'It was best,' said Dualta. 'The people did not take to me because I was a Connachtman.'

'A bunch of bloody scoundrels,' said Wilcocks. 'But we'll weed them out.' He went to the window. He looked up at the hills. 'We'll weed them out,' he said, 'if I have to knock every house in the valley.' He turned back. 'Can you use a gun?'

'No, sir,' said Dualta. 'I cannot. I never handled one. You know what would happen to one of us if we were found with a gun?'

'Quite right too,' said Wilcocks. 'They'd have us all shot in our beds. I suppose you are the wrong religion?'

'I am a Catholic,' said Dualta.

'Well, I hope you are a better one than some of them in the valley,' said Wilcocks. 'What do you think, Una, is he all right? Will he do?'

She didn't say so immediately. They waited.

'Yes, father,' she said. 'I think so.'

'Right,' said Wilcocks. 'You can help with the accounts. Since these scum drove off my bailiffs, we are short-handed there. Also you can look after my daughter when she is abroad. You will learn how to use a gun. And use it if you have to. You can help other ways too. We are short-handed. We'll give you fair wages, and you can sleep in the house. I have a feeling. I don't like the feeling I have. They are up to something out there, God damn them. But I'm able for them. They will be sorry people. Right, Una, I'm going out. Look after it. If you are satisfied, that's all right with me. Dammit, you are turning out better than if you were a son. What's his name, did you say?'

'Duane,' said Una.

'All right, Duane. Do right by me and I'll do right by you. And don't be afraid. That Hanley fellow was like a fainting girl. One shot at him and he's running like a rabbit with a thistle in his scutch.'

He went out abruptly. He left a bit of his heavy personality behind him.

She rose. 'I'll show you the house,' she said. 'You will have to see to it that the shutters go up on the windows. They are very slow.'

'Am I a guard of the body, then?' he asked.

'I can take care of myself,' she said. 'But it is as well to take precautions.' She went out of the room. He followed her. She showed him the main rooms below. She enjoyed at second-hand his scrutiny of each of them. They were furnished with many beautiful pieces. She noted the way he walked softly. Upstairs she showed him a room where he would sleep. It was in the attic. There was a skylight through which he could examine the stars. An iron bedstead and a few chests. It was full of June sun reflecting off the white walls.

He said, 'Why are you called with an Irish name?'

She answered, 'One time my father was very Irish. He read all the old legends and the sagas. He married a girl from Limerick. He met her at a hunt ball. She was a Catholic, but she changed for him. He had a very strong personality. He was a very good-looking man.' That accounts for it, he thought, the Irishness of her. What other grand lady like her would bother to go the rounds of the house with a new man?

'You do not come here to hurt us?' he heard her asking then. 'You have not come here with a different purpose?' He kept his muscles from stiffening. She was a very shrewd girl. It was a few seconds before he turned to face her, a look of puzzlement on his face.

'I would never hurt you, Miss Una,' he said.

'Not me,' she said, 'us. All of us.' She had a very direct look. Her eyes were deep-sunken ones, seeming to be looking at him from a long distance.

'I will never hurt you or yours,' he said.

She looked at him again for a time, trying to get behind the completely sincere-sounding voice of his.

'All right,' she said. 'You can get food in the kitchen. I'll send for you when I want you.'

Then she left him. He looked after her for a long time.

That night he lay on his bed and he looked at the stars with his hands under his head. He thought: Well, Cuan, I have done what you wanted, and I hope it will be as easy as you think. He thought of the crying Paidi with his broken neck, and his jaw tightened. He couldn't sleep. Eventually he rose and put the mattress on the floor. That was better. He slept then and before sleeping decided that he would have to be very wary of the girl with the direct eyes.

10

HE WENT to the carriage house. He grabbed the small light two-wheeled cart and pulled it into the yard. Torpey put his head out of the horse stable looking at him sourly. He was an ugly man, Torpey. He wasn't surprised that Una preferred to have himself with her instead of the dour man who seemed to be able to talk nothing but horse language.

'Harness up for Miss Una,' said Dualta. He went to help him. They went to the stall of the honey-coloured mare with the white tail and mane. Whatever else, Torpey kept the horses in great shape. Torpey put on the harness and led the horse outside.

'You go?' he asked Dualta.

'I go,' said Dualta. Torpey grunted. He didn't like Dualta.

'Careful,' said Torpey. 'Watch. You look out. Mind the mare.'

'I'll mind her,' said Dualta. 'It doesn't matter if I break my neck?'

'No,' said Torpey.

'That's what I thought,' said Dualta.

He got into the padded seat, held the reins, clucked his tongue at the mare and drove her sedately out of the yard and around to the front of the house. The mare waited patiently. The front door was open. Wilcocks appeared there. He shouted from the steps. 'What's up, Duane?'

'Miss Una is going out, sir,' said Dualta.

Wilcocks came down a few steps.

'This bloody O Connell,' he shouted. 'You see he is getting nearly a thousand pounds a week out of this Catholic rent?'

79

'It's a lot of money, sir,' said Dualta.

Wilcocks came down another few steps.

'The bloody demagogue'll buy the whole country,' he said.

'I didn't know the country could be bought, sir,' said Dualta.

Wilcocks peered at him under his heavy eyebrows. Then he hooted with laughter. But he sobered.

'Sometimes you might be too bright for your own good, Duane,' he said. 'What do the people see in him? They are flocking after him like dogs in heat. You watch that fellow, Duane. He hates us all. He'll drag the whole country into the mud.'

Dualta was about to say that most of the country was in the mud anyhow, but he held his peace. Wilcocks was using Dualta as if he was addressing the nation.

'They are even inviting him to London,' said Wilcocks. 'Imagine that. An ignoramus like that in London! What's the Government thinking of over there? They should clap him in irons. Imagine consulting O Connell. Are they gone mad?'

'He has become very powerful, sir,' said Dualta.

'A sorry day, dammit,' said Wilcocks. 'Before we know where we are we'll have men like Christy making maiden speeches in the House of Commons.'

A picture of Christy standing up in the House of Commons addressing the people there came into Dualta's mind. He had to laugh. Wilcocks watched him. He was pleased with his laughter. 'Well, it could happen,' he said. 'You mark my words. They should have confined that fellow to the Kerry bogs that spawned him. Ah, hello, dear, you are off again?'

This to Una who came into the doorway, pulling on long gloves over her bare arms.

'Yes, father,' she said. 'I won't be long.'

'Be careful, Duane,' said Wilcocks. 'I don't like things. Keep your eyes open. Things have been too quiet in the valley.'

'I'll be careful, sir,' said Dualta.

He could have told him that while his daughter was with him she was as safe as if she was in a vault in a bank.

'Right,' said Wilcocks. 'O Connell in London, by God! Catholic Relief. What's coming over them?' He turned back into the house again. Dualta helped Una into the cart and mounted himself.

'Where to, Miss?' he asked.

'The same place, Dualta,' she said.

He clucked at the mare and they clopped sedately down the drive into the avenue of the poplars.

He always felt very content with her. She had that effect on people. She was a calm girl. He had driven her to many balls and feasts. He had noticed the way she attracted the young bucks. She was a good-looking girl and when she was dressed up in special finery she attracted them. When they came to say good night to her, he might not have existed. They didn't even see him, no more than they saw the drivers of the other carriages. But she did. Enquired if he had enjoyed himself.

Sitting beside Una now, smelling the sweetness of her, his conscience troubled him. He told himself that in this he wasn't entitled to a conscience.

She said, 'Would you change your religion, Dualta?'

He was startled from his thoughts.

'That's a queer question,' he said.

'Why is it queer?' she asked. 'You would be considerably bettered if you became a Protestant, wouldn't you?'

'Yes,' he said. 'There are better jobs open, security. I would be favoured. Why do you ask this?'

'You don't seem on the surface,' she said, 'to be a very good Catholic, so why shouldn't you embrace something that would improve your life?'

He glanced at her. Her face was almost expressionless. She wasn't looking at him.

'How do you know I am not a good Catholic?' he asked.

'I don't,' she said. 'On the surface you don't appear so. You don't go to Confession, do you, very often?'

He didn't. But he wondered how she knew. He couldn't go to Confession. If he went to Confession he would have to tell about the depredations he took part in, and be asked how he was going to make material reparation for the injuries he had caused. He was very uneasy.

'I didn't notice you trying to proselytise before,' he said.

'Why do you start on me?'

'No,' she said. 'It's not that. I am just asking you. Would you change your religion from indifferent Catholicism to indifferent Protestantism?'

'No,' he said.

'Why?' she asked.

'I haven't thought about it much,' he said. 'Just that it's there.'

'I see,' she said. 'I just wanted to know.'

'Are you any wiser after my answer?' he asked.

She laughed.

'I don't think so,' she said, and then she grew silent again.

He clucked at the mare, slapped the reins on her rump. She was inclined to laze if she thought you had forgotten her.

Three miles from the house they came to the place of the assignation. This was the fourth time he had come here with her. She had been on her own too. There was a gateway that led into a small wood of pine trees, young ones planted about twelve years. There was a path that wound through it and ended up at the river where it tumbled over a fall of about twenty feet. He got down and opened the gate and led the mare inside, walked her about ten yards until she was hidden from the road and could graze the sparse grass that grew beside the rutted track.

He helped Una down.

'Thank you,' she said. She was thinking deeply, he thought. She didn't give him her courteous smile and admonition about waiting for her. He wondered if that released him from the implied promise of not following as he watched her slim figure going down the track, her hands holding up the skirt so that it wouldn't sweep the dust.

He sat down to think about it. He plucked a blade of grass and chewed it. He thought it had a pine taste, and wondered if the mare noticed this and if it made the grass tastier or not.

He thought she must be meeting a lover. This thought disappointed him. She didn't seem to be the sort of person to do things under cover. But perhaps if her lover was a young impoverished man? Most of the landlord parents set great store on who their daughters married. They had to have some money as well as class. It wouldn't do for Wilcocks' daughter to marry just any young man, he knew, but also he had thought that she was the kind of person who, if she fell in love, would just trot out the young man to her father and say: 'Here is your future son-in-law.' She had a determined chin. He knew so little about their lives. In their own way they secreted themselves from the watching eyes of the servants they possessed. Normally it would have been all one to him. Let them be born; let them marry; let them die, time, place or person, what was it to do with him? They were a strange race beyond his ken. But you couldn't be meeting a person like Una, doing things for her, laughing with her, joking, talking, and not permit a part of you to show, and also get to like her very much. He had to admit that. It was a dangerous thing to do. After all, these people were his enemies. Wasn't he fighting them? Didn't he wish to injure them? So it was a dangerous thing to permit yourself to begin to like them. Where would that leave warfare?

He got to his feet and set off through the woods.

It's part of your job, he told himself as he placed his feet cautiously on the pine needles, moved from tree to tree, drawing near the eternal booming of the waterfall. She might be seeing an Army man or even a policeman. She might be a sort of spy, a calm person outwardly who was undermining the conspiracy in the valley, getting ropes ready for the lot of them.

He knew this thinking was ridiculous, but it eased his conscience at the thought that he was going to spy on her. After all she hadn't said that he was to wait for her. He had kept his curiosity in check before. But she had told him to wait then. Today she had said nothing.

The nearer he came to the waterfall, the lower he got to the ground. Close to the river the trees were sparser and the ferns were thick and tall and beginning to turn golden. The atmosphere was very oppressive. The clouds were very low. The heavens were due to open.

He parted the ferns in front of his eyes and looked into the glade.

He saw the broad back of a man. He was sitting on a fallen

tree trunk, a black-clad back, with light-brown hair tied. She was standing up. She had her gloves off. She was kneading them and slapping them. She would walk away from him towards the brink of the fall, and she would seem to be outlined in the spray that was rising from the pool. She would spread her arms, and stamp her foot. She came back. She was appealing to him. She sat beside him on the log, half facing him. He shook his head. He now got up and walked to the edge of the fall, then he turned and walked back towards her. He was talking, expostulating, and as he turned and faced him Dualta saw that he was a priest. He didn't know him. He wasn't either of the two priests in the valley. It was no love scene he had come upon. He could hear no words, nor did he want to hear any, as he started to withdraw, just a word here and there over the sound of the water. The priest was urging her to be patient over something, not to press things to an issue. That's all he could make out as he withdrew, ashamed of himself, thinking that if she had made up her mind to something, even the priest had a poor chance of persuading her to the contrary.

But why a priest? he wondered. Why a priest? What was wrong with her? Meeting a priest in secret? It's none of my business, he thought. What business is it of mine? He thought what a low opinion he had of himself at the moment. Now he knew and he would do well to forget it as quickly as possible. But he wondered how the priest had come, so when he reached the mare he cut off right into the woods, and smelled the brown horse before he saw him, a light horse saddled and tied to a tree. The horse saw him. He was nervous. Dualta made soothing noises with his mouth and his lips and the horse calmed. Then he turned and made his way back to the mare. He rested his back against the bole of a tree and chewed another blade of grass while he waited for her.

She came. He thought she looked pale. But it may have been the odd light in the sky.

'Enjoyed yourself, Dualta?' she asked automatically.

'Yes,' said Dualta, 'the grass tastes of pine.' She looked at him. She laughed. 'How good to be free of care,' she said. 'Let us go.'

84

He led the mare out of the wood onto the road. He helped her up into the seat, mounted himself and set off down the road. They cleared the wood. The river on their left was gleaming dully as it wound its way from the valley. The leaves of the trees were turning. It made the whole place around them look lush, and heavy with wealth. It had been a good autumn. The harvest would be good.

She said, 'Have you got to like this valley?'

He said, 'Yes. It grows on you.'

'But you wouldn't exchange it for your own place?' she asked.

'No, Miss,' he said. 'I don't think so.'

'It's my place, this,' she said. 'My valley. I know parts of it you will never see. When I climb the hills and look down at it on a clear day, my heart is bright. It's where I was born. It means a lot to me.'

'I know it does,' he said.

'It would be very hard to lose it,' she said.

'Are you going to get married?' he asked.

'Married?' she enquired. 'Oh! You think that? No. Not at the moment. You don't lose things if you get married, you gain them.'

He stayed silent.

'Times I was away,' she said, 'in all those wonderful cities I thought of the valley. It is like your religion. You find that the valley is rooted in your heart. I thought how later, when it was mine, I would do things to improve it.'

'No more evictions?' said Dualta, trying to keep feeling out of his voice.

It silenced her. She looked at him.

'Your English has improved since you came to us, Dualta. Lots of the Irish intonations are gone out of it. Do evictions hurt you?'

'I only remarked,' he said.

'I thought of lots of things,' she said. 'Many things. It is not good to plan too far ahead. You never know how your plans will be changed or diverted.'

'Are all your plans changed then?' he asked.

She thought.

'Yes,' she said. 'I am afraid so. You will know soon enough. I'm afraid everybody will know soon enough.'

She sighed.

11

SHE HESITATED at the door of the living-room where she knew he was. She leaned her head against it, and put her arm to her breast to ease the thumping of her heart. For she knew her father.

He was a just man, if you were just with him. You knew where you stood with him. If you were his enemy, that was that. He was built on kindness and fairness, but also built-in prejudices that were as strong as the faith of a saint. She loved him, but his own love was inarticulate. He regarded softness of expression as a concession to Irish romanticism. One must be a realist. A few soft romantic words were for the bedchamber, if gruffly enunciated. When he had been a Major of the Yeomanry, he had been at his happiest. He was built that way, or at least that was the way he had made himself. His one concession to romanticism had been falling in love with Una's mother, and he had fought all opposition as if he was conducting a war until he had got his way. But on many things his mind was closed and this saddened her. She thought her interview could have only one result. Anything else, knowing her father, would amount to a miracle, and in this case there could be no miracle. She knew what she was up against, and also she knew herself.

She opened the door and went in.

He was sitting in the leather-covered chair reading a book and smoking a pipe. There was a whisky decanter and a glass on the small table by his elbow. It was getting dark in the room. The two big windows let in light, but the sky was not light-giving. The oak logs resting on the iron in the fireplace were flaming well. She looked at all those things because she didn't know how she would begin.

86

He looked up.

'You are back, Una,' he said. 'I was afraid you would be caught in the weather. The break is coming.'

'I got back,' she said. 'The break is coming.'

She sat on the arm of the chair on the other side of him. He looked at her. She looked at him. He thought that he had a very pretty daughter, but a sad one.

'Did somebody take your toy?' he asked smiling. It was a sentence taken from memories of her childhood.

She considered this. 'Yes, I think so,' she said. 'Somebody took my toy and presented me with a sword.'

'That sound serious,' he said, chuckling.

'Father,' she said. 'Talk to me about my mother.'

He was surprised. His eyebrows rose. He took up a glass, sipped at the whisky. 'Why?' he said. 'You know everything about her already.'

'All I really know,' she said, 'is that she died when I was thirteen. That is nearly seven years ago. Her memory is fading from me. I remember she was dark and she had a soft laugh.'

'Yes,' he said, clearing his throat. 'She had a soft laugh. She was a gay attractive person, your mother Kathleen. Not as serious as you, you know. You've got a bit too much of me in you, I'm afraid. You could have done with more of her lightness of heart.'

'Why did she die, then?' she asked.

He thought. She could see that the thinking hurt him.

'She got this damn fever that was going then,' he said. 'She used to bring food to some of the tenants, the poorer ones. And medicines. She brought them laughter too. All that is forgotten now, the scoundrels, even forgotten her name and the things she did for them. They killed her, you might say, by accepting her kindness.'

'How did you persuade her to marry you?' she asked.

'What a question!' he said. 'Dammit, I was well set up then. I could stand in a mirror with any man. I wasn't a gay dog, but I liked life and I knew what I wanted. So I went after her.'

'But she was a Catholic,' said Una.

'Yes,' said he, 'she was filled with that superstition. We were in what people call love. She was necessary to me, and I was to her. One of those things. No helping oneself. Never met a woman before or since like her. It was once for all, you see. Of course her people were against me. So were my own for that matter. But I wanted this girl and I got her. She never saw her people again.'

'Wasn't that hard on her?' Una asked.

'It wasn't my fault,' he said. 'They told her if she married me she was cutting herself off from them. She had a terrible time deciding, but then there was no help for either of us, once this thing had us in its grip. So they cut her away as if she was a rotten branch on the family tree. They are a hidebound and stubborn lot, these Irish Catholics once they take a few steps up in the world.'

She stood up. Her back was to the fire.

'Father,' she said, 'I am afraid that you will have to cast me off too.'

He put down the glass slowly.

'What do you mean?' he asked.

'Father,' she said, 'I am going to become a Catholic.'

She watched the changes appearing in his face. Her legs were trembling. She saw the dawn of the knowledge and the shock, as if he had been kicked, and then his face went pale. Later, she knew that it would go red.

'Do you know what you said?' he asked.

'Only too well, father,' she answered.

'You are not joking,' he said. 'This is not an Irish sense of humour.'

'No, father,' she said.

'What are you doing to me?' he asked. He got up. He walked to the window. He looked out at the lowering sky. Already in the distance there was the low murmur of far-off thunder. Not a leaf was moving on a tree in the calm sticky air. His hands were clenched behind his back. She could see that the knuckles were white. Then he turned back to her.

'You are of mixed blood,' he said. 'My father was right. I didn't think so. Some day you will have to pay. We must be calm. Tell me quietly how this stupid notion came into your head.'

There was a shake in her voice now. She was afraid of his desperate calmness.

'My mother taught me to pray when I was small,' she said.

'If she taught you the Catholic way, she was a traitor,' he said. 'Do you hear that?'

'You cannot drive out a deep-rooted belief, merely by saying that you no longer believe in it,' said Una.

'She swore it on the Book of God,' he said. 'She swore it by her own soul. Are you putting your mother in Hell?'

'No,' she said.

'She had abandoned their superstitions,' he said. 'She never met them again, never mixed with them again. She gained truth and love by doing that. Why would she try and pervert her own daughter? Are you making her out a monster?'

'I only said she taught me to pray,' said Una.

He calmed himself. He turned away from her. 'What then?' he asked.

'In Paris, in London, in Dublin,' she said, 'I studied as you know, and I read and I met many people. They were all only milestones on the road back to the religion of my mother. I didn't want it. I fought fiercely with every notion of it that came into my head. You don't know. You will never know how hard I fought against it. But now the fighting is over. I am going back. I am telling you before I do so.'

There was silence from him. He dropped his head. He rubbed his forehead with his hand.

'How can I help you?' he wondered. 'If a cow wanders into a boghole, I can help her. If a mare is covered with mud, I can wash her. What am I going to do with you? Because I could never believe that you could become involved with your logical mind in a religion of superstition and idolatry. Good God, a daughter of mine!'

He walked away again. Then he turned and came back to her.

'Think of what you are getting into, for God's sake,' he said. 'Look at this O Connell, the leader of the Catholics, vulgar, foul-mouthed and unscrupulous, backed up by those ignorant power-mad priests. He is an apostle, with them, of sedition. They are consumed with hatred for the established social order, the Established Church and the British Constitution, ready to overthrow it with a convulsion of society, at the first opportunity. Are these the people with whom you want to cast your lot?'

'Father,' she said, 'I know only a few priests. I found them good and holy men and more than literate. I am not going into politics. I am merely becoming a Catholic because my soul is telling me to.'

'Oh, no,' he said. 'There is more to it than that. You are abandoning your own class. What do you think has made us what we are? Our faith in the Protestant religion. Our knowledge of its truth. Once you change sides you are in politics. You have gone over to the enemies of your own class. Do you realise how they hate us and our holy religion? Do you realise the terror they have brought again and again on this land in order to eradicate it? Have you thought of the thousands of martyrs who have died for the Protestant faith?'

'There have been many deaths on the other side,' she began. He cut her off.

'See, already you are beginning to think on the other side,' he said. 'I can see that you are perverted already.' She noted now that his face was red. He had passed away from paleness. There was sparking anger in his eyes. It made her calmer. The trembling went out of her limbs. He pulled open the door of the room. He roared out there in the hall. 'Come here, all of you from the kitchen! Come here! Biddy, Nora, Teresa, Duane, Christy! Come here, whoever is in the kitchen!' He came back in. He was glaring at her, as if she were a stranger who had deeply wounded him.

'You haven't thought,' he shouted. 'You haven't the least idea of what you have let yourself in for. I pray to the great God to enlighten you to what is before you if you step into the gutter. Because into the gutter you are going. Has anyone in this life deliberately chosen to go down instead of going up?' He went to the door again. 'Come on,' he shouted. 'Hurry up!

Come when you are called!'

He was like the Major again. He was barking out orders as if he was talking to a troop of soldiers dragged from the bowels of the hulk-ships on the Thames, she thought. She was very sad about it.

They shuffled in uneasily, Biddy and the girls. The girls were nearly wringing their hands. Dualta came after them. He was in his shirt-sleeves. He had been eating. Christy, large and lumbering and barefooted, with brown tree bark clinging to his shirt and his hair, little Mocky, with his boy's dirty face, and his ragged clothes, his feet bare and discoloured with brown dried bog mud.

'Stand along in a line there!' he shouted at them. 'Go on now! Stand in a line there and let her see you.'

They were red-faced, sweating, embarrassed, moving from foot to foot. Una felt their humiliation but could do nothing about it. Dualta wasn't humiliated. He was very interested. She didn't look at Dualta. He saw her standing straight at the fireplace, pale, her hands held in front of her.

'These are a cross-section,' Wilcocks was shouting, 'of your travelling companions. A much better section than what you will meet. These are your brothers and sisters. Look at them! Embrace them! Kiss their feet!'

He was in a towering rage. Dualta thought: He should have let us all dress in our Sunday clothes before this presentation.

'Your mistress wants to join you,' the Major was saying to them in a barrack-square voice. 'She wants to be one of you. You hear that? Aren't you flattered, that she has become perverted? She will partake of your rags, your dirty thatched churches, your diseased confessionals. Aren't you pleased? That she is to become one of you?'

'Father!' said Una.

'Not to me,' he said, turning on her. 'Don't say that word to me. Say that word to one of your greasy priests in a curtained foetid box. Don't say that word to me. Don't say that word to me ever again!'

Dualta felt sorry for him. He could see the hurt behind his anger.

Una spoke firmly.

'You can go now, Biddy,' she said. 'Thank you for coming.' They looked at Wilcocks. He had turned his back on them.

'I am sorry,' said Una. 'I am very sorry.' They didn't know what to do. Dualta decided. He turned to the door and went out. They followed him. They went back bewildered to the big kitchen. They sat in silence, their ears strained. Nothing came to them except the sound of the distant thunder. Outside, big separate drops were falling on the dried earth, tapping it play-fully, building up to the force of the storm that was driving them ahead of it, like silver sentinels.

'That did no good,' said Una. His back was turned to her. He didn't answer her.

'I know how you feel,' she said.

'You do not,' he said.

'I can only do one thing,' she said. 'Leave you.' It was a kind of question with her, not a statement. It remained tense on the air, unanswered. 'I will collect a few of my possessions,' she said. 'And I will take myself out of your sight.' He didn't answer. 'Is it any use telling you how sorry I am?' she asked.

'Sorrow!' he snorted. 'You have ended my life and you are sorry. You have debased me. If you do this thing now to me, there are not enough tears in the whole world to wash it away from me.'

'I cannot turn back,' she said. 'It has been too hard coming this far. I have to go on now wherever it leads.'

'As you wish,' he said coldly. He came back. He sat in the chair. He poured a drink from the decanter. He took up his book. His hands were trembling. She had her hand up to her mouth. She had to press her nostrils to stop from crying. She walked to the door. She turned there.

'I will go to the town,' she said. 'Can I have Dualta to drive me there?'

'As you wish,' he said, indifferently.

She went up the stairs slowly. She rubbed her hand on the polished banisters. She looked at the oil paintings that hung on the walls. In her own room, she got the small trunk from the wardrobe. She had it ready. All these actions had been gone

92

over in her mind, many times. She knew it would have to end like this, so she was prepared. She knew everything belonging to her that she would require. It was all soon packed. They filled the trunk, but she was leaving a lot behind her. She stopped thinking of that in case she should cry.

She went downstairs then. She walked to the kitchen. She walked in on their silence. It was becoming very dark. She could barely see them in the light of the fire.

'Dualta,' she said. 'Would you get the carriage horses harnessed? I want you to drive me to the town. Christy, would you come to my room and bring down my chest?'

Christy looked around him, waving his arms helplessly. Then he shuffled past her. Dualta rose and went out. She looked at Biddy and the girls.

She said, 'I'm sorry my father did that to you. He is upset. You must forgive him. I won't say goodbye,' she said, 'I am sure we will meet again sometime.' Biddy was on the point of crying, so she left hurriedly.

In the hall she got her cloak and two hatboxes. She walked to the front door with them. She left them there. Then she went up the stairs again. Christy was outside her door with the chest on his shoulder as if it was of no weight. 'Leave it below at the door,' she said.

She looked around her room. It was such a nice room. It was unlikely that she would ever see the like of it again. She took a small tin hand-case by its leather handle and she walked out of the door. She closed it softly after her.

She went down the stairs very slowly. She had often thought of the way she would come down those stairs on her father's arm, in her wedding dress. Below waiting would be the mysterious bridegroom, never possessing a face, everything else but that, beautiful hair, body and carriage. Maybe dim eyes filled with love and rapture, the rooms resounding to the sound of chamber music, the tinkle of glasses, raised voices. The door was open. Christy was standing there. The rain was coming down, the skies weeping bitterly.

She said, 'Leave those out too.' She could see the wet carriage waiting in the rain.

She went to the door of the living-room. She hesitated again. Then she went in.

He was where she had left him. The book was held listlessly in his hand. She thought that she had never loved her father more than she did at this minute. He knew she was there.

'Una,' he said, 'don't leave me.' This was what he said. It was not fair. It put the whole guilt on her. It implied surrender. With all heart she wished that she could do so. She imagined the wonderful joy of their reunion. She also knew that on the one point he would be utterly implacable. That was his way of life. He could see no other. He could understand no other.

There was no middle way.

She said, 'Goodbye, my dear father,' and then she closed the door and left him. She ran down the steps. She didn't mind the rain. Dualta had the door open for her. He helped her in.

'That was what it was all about?' he asked.

She looked at him, blindly. He could already see the tears in her eyes, held back by the tightening of her jaws.

'Yes,' she said. 'That's what it was all about.' He closed the door on her, climbed on to the high seat, fastened his coachman's thick cloak against the beating rain, shouted at the horses, slapped their wet hides with the reins, and pulled away from the house.

The whole sky was black. Sky and earth seemed to have become one black wet moaning mass. The sky in the distance was lightened now and again by the reflection of the lightning flashes.

It's just as well, Dualta thought grimly as he bent his head to the blast, that she cannot see a thing. It was just as well she could get no long lingering look at the valley as she passed out of it.

'Hup! Hup! Hup!' he shouted at the reluctant horses.

12

HE WAS planting little trees on a hilly place to the north of the house when the word came to him. It was a word he had been afraid of, and when he heard it his heart sank.

They were planting the young trees on what had been the holding of the Fortune family. There was nothing left of them now. The house had been levelled, the garden walls had been used to make drains, the ditches filled, and in years to come the four acres would be a thickly planted wood, a pleasant place on the side of the hill. He wondered if in time men would praise Wilcocks for his love of tree planting, if they would stumble on the ivy-covered ruins of what was once a cottage; and marvel in the sun-filtered wood at the grass-covered ridges which had once grown enough potatoes to fill the bellies of ten people. Let the future look after the future, he had thought then, angrily.

It was in a cleft where the stream came over a black rock on its way to the river below that he saw Cuan.

There was room here for six young trees, by the bank of the stream.

Cuan was sitting on the other side, smoking a long clay pipe.

Dualta looked around him. None of the other planters were in his vision. He sat down across the stream from Cuan. They looked at one another calmly.

'Well?' said Dualta.

'Tonight,' said Cuan.

'Oh,' said Dualta.

It was springtime. It was beginning to show in the valley.

'Whaley has gone to the big town,' said Cuan. 'He won't be back tonight.'

Whaley was the new bailiff. He was from England, a place called Yorkshire. He was a stocky man, without fear, and very efficient. If he had no fear, he took precautions. It was impossible to frighten him with letters. He never came within reach of a gun. He was impossible. Dualta liked him. He got things done. Dualta could admire men who got things done, because Wilcocks wasn't as efficient as he had been. In the six months or so since his daughter left, he was drinking more and caring less. The evictions mounted. There had been four. Fortune's had been the first of them. Dualta was aware that Wilcocks was striking around him like a wounded animal. He didn't think it fair that the little people should be struck to ease his pain.

'Are you sure this is not too soon?' he asked.

'Are you getting soft on Wilcocks?' Cuan asked sarcastically.

'No,' said Dualta.

'The people are too impatient. If he is not struck now, he won't leave a sinner in the valley,' said Cuan.

'Are you going to hurt him?' Dualta asked.

'We are going to burn him out,' said Cuan.

Dualta thought of the fine house he now lived in going up in flames. He supposed that it was just being sentimental. He didn't like to think of the house going up in flames. This wasn't logical.

'I see,' he said. Cuan blew a puff of tobacco smoke into the air.

'Like that,' he demonstrated. He smiled.

'Wilcocks must not be hurt,' said Dualta.

'Burning will hurt him enough,' said Cuan.

'He mustn't be hurt himself,' said Dualta. 'That will bring terrible things on the valley. They will scour it.'

'We'll try not to hurt him,' said Cuan.

'I mean this, Cuan,' said Dualta.

'Can I account for every man in the heat of the moment?' Cuan asked.

'I don't care,' said Dualta. 'You'll have to account for them. You will have to swear he won't be hurt or I won't go on with it.'

'Are you gone soft on Wilcocks?' Cuan asked.

'No,' said Dualta. 'I'm just wise. Leave him alone in his person.'

Cuan sighed. 'All right,' he said. 'I'll talk sense to them.'

They heard voices behind Dualta. Cuan rose. He tapped the

pipe on his heel. 'You know everything,' he said to Dualta. 'Just as it was planned. You are the Trojan horse. Let your belly open at midnight.' He smiled. His eyes were gleaming. Dualta felt daunted by the look of him. He nodded his head. Cuan sauntered away. He was out of sight by the time the other planters came level with Dualta.

The cheerfulness went out of him for the rest of the day.

The labourers remarked it. Normally he would be joking with them, aping the gruff overseer. There were twenty-four of them. They were paid five pennies a day and their potatoes hot in the evening. Eleven of them were estate labourers who got no money at all but paid for their cottage and the few roods of ground for their potatoes by their labour. They were simple men, hard-working, grumbling, keeping themselves away from conspiracies as long as they had nearly enough to eat, a few shillings per year for tobacco and to buy Sunday clothes for their children. They seemed to demand nothing else of life. This was their lot and until somebody bettered it for them they were going to accept it. They remained unfired by ambition. 'He's sick,' one said. And another said: 'He ate too much from the pickling trough.' 'He's in love,' said another. 'He is hungry for Nora,' said another. 'She would never lie with a foreigner,' one said.

He refused to rise. He remained silent, directing them to the lie of the young trees. He himself had been directed by Whaley, in a thick English accent men found it most difficult to understand, so that he had to be drawing his orders on paper most of the time.

They returned to the house as the dusk set in. They washed their hands at the pump in the yard and sat in the covered shed and ate their potatoes from the great pot. Salt and buttermilk garnished the hot potatoes. It was amazing how soon the great pot was emptied and the mound of skins thrown into the trough for the pigs.

So they sat in the shed faintly lighted by the fires under the pots and some of them smoked their pipes and some of them chewed their tobacco, until the cold nip of the evening came on the air and they started to drift away, some to far-away cottages, some to the estate cottages, and the unmarried ones to the rooms over the carriage houses. He thought of the strength available if called upon. About ten men. Would they fight for Wilcocks? They wouldn't exactly fight for him, but they would fight for their five pennies a day and their potatoes. So they would have to be quietened. That had been arranged for. You couldn't depend on them because they had too many mouths depending on them already.

He said good night. He went into the house. He didn't stay in the kitchen to banter talk with them. He went through. They remarked on this with their eyes. It's very strange behaviour for Dualta, they thought. Then they shrugged it off and went on with their work. Young people are odd when the spring comes. They get queer fluxes.

He went to the library. He worked at the books with the light of a tallow candle mounted on a wrought-iron candlestick. Miss Una had liked those. She had got the blacksmith to make many of them almost in his own fancy. He enjoyed the job. He added many flourishes as he went along.

He was only doing the simple accounts. He tried to concentrate on them. The wages book. Biddy a very good cook, £8 per year, Nora £4, Teresa £3 10s., Christy £6, the turf boy, the pump boy, the cow boy, the carpenter, the blacksmith, the slaughterhouse man, stewards, bailiffs, the estate was a little industry. Wilcocks fed many mouths. Many would be hungry without him. But the payment came from the highly priced acres of the tenants. Here you were up against the sacred rights of property, embodied, they said, in the ten commandments.

He thought, Now is the time that I should go around closing the heavy shutters on the windows. But not tonight. Tonight he was to forget to close the shutters. That made it very easy for them.

He looked around at the books. All would be gone, consumed in fire. He didn't think that was fair. Knowledge should not be destroyed. That was vandalism. What could he do? Nothing. He couldn't hide them now. They were too many. He thought of the pleasure he had got from reading, and the indignation, nearly all indignation, but a lot of pleasure too, a great lot of pleasure once the English words started to come easy to him. A lot that was beautiful and inspired amongst all the others. Paine's *Age of Reason, Common Sense, Crisis Papers*, were there. A few years ago you would have been hanged if you were found with the *Age of Reason*. He wondered what Wilcocks thought as he read it. He could see him getting red in the face and hurling the book at the wall, only to retrieve it when he had cooled off and continue reading it. It was opposed to everything he believed in, but Wilcocks also believed in reading the other side, just to know what they were up to, never for a moment giving a comma of it his consent.

It was a great pity about the books, Dualta thought, sighing.

He was restless. He left the library. He took the candle with him into the hall. He listened. The clink of a glass from the drawing-room where Wilcocks was. Dualta could see him as if he was there. Looking into the fire. He was not the same since Una left. It had hit him very hard. Dualta knew this well. He felt sorry for him. The trouble was, he might as well admit it, that he liked Wilcocks. Principles to him were things that you stood for, and if necessary died for. It didn't matter if the principles were faulty. Principles were what you yourself held to be the rule of life as you saw it. You stuck to those. He genuinely regarded the lower orders as lower orders, if Catholic, superstitious, obstinate and irredeemable, and only a little raised above the animal order. As such he treated them as he would favourite animals. He was kind, thoughtful (except where the sacred rights of private property might be in danger), generous (within the spoken limits set by the order of landlords, so you didn't raise your workers by a penny a day if a more feckless member of the class couldn't afford it). Beyond all this he liked him because he had a sense of humour, and just because he was likeable.

There was the sound of voices and laughter from the kitchen. Dualta went softly up the stairs to his own attic room.

He thought Cuan had chosen his night well. All the defences were down. They could do what they wanted to do, have come and gone again inside twenty minutes. He sat on his bed. He knew he would have to gather his possessions, because he would have to escape in the confusion. It would be very obvious that he was an enemy in the house. This upset him, this thought. He had eaten the man's food, earned his money, laughed and joked and forced most of the people to like him. What would they think of him after this? What would Wilcocks think of him? What would Una think of him? What did it matter? When you engaged on things like this, you didn't expect to be liked. What difference would it make?

He gathered his belongings. He noted wryly that he had got used to sleeping in a bed. He remembered the story told of the poor cottager who decided to raise his bale of straw from the floor and pegged up a bedstead for himself, four inches off the damp ground. He slept in this with great joy. The next day his horse was drowned so he lowered the bed to the ground again, saying, 'God humbles those who exalt themselves'.

He folded his clothes and his cheap books and his papers into a tidy budget and wrapped them with cord, so that he could bear them on his shoulders.

He sat there for some time, trying not to think at all.

He heard Biddy and the girls going to their attic rooms. Later he heard Wilcocks coming to the landing below and going into his own room. The house was wrapped in silence then. To the rest of them it would be a normal silence, but to him it was the silence preceding death.

He blew out the candle, caught up his budget and went softly down the stairs. He paused outside Wilcocks' bedroom door. He listened. He could hear nothing. This landing was bathed in moonlight. The raiders needed the light of the moon. He saw the closed door of Una's room. He went to it. He opened it softly. He went in. He would watch from there through the large window. He wondered how much time was left, one hour or two. He went back and sat on the bed. It was a curtained bed. The curtain rails creaked as he sat, the silk rustled. He thought of Una. Very faintly he was enveloped in the remains of the scent that was hers. That and a tang of dampness. Nobody had been in her room since she had left. It was as it was, just for cleaning.

He thought about her. She was an odd girl. He remembered

saying goodbye to her at the town on that wet night when he left her at the inn. He had left her things and then she had taken off her glove and held out her hand to him. He had taken it in his own wet hand. He still could feel the tingle of her soft flesh in his palm. She looked at him. She expected him to say something. He hadn't. What was she to him or her father? She was disappointed in him. He thought she shouldn't have left her father like that. She should have found some other way. If he had a father he would not leave him.

Now he remembered her more clearly, and his sorrow that she had gone away and he would never know where she was. You got used to her, that was it, he thought, and could imagine how her father had missed her; how much he wanted to give in to her, and how completely incapable he was of doing so. He had never mentioned her name since she left, and probably never would again. He would just suffer her inside him.

He remembered another thing then, the day he came, worming his way in like an eel in a shallow pond, about how he hadn't come, had he, to hurt them. He remembered that. He said no, didn't he, neither you nor yours. Was it a lie, then? If this was patriotism was he permitted to lie? Was it patriotism? How would the burning of this house advance the cause of patriotism? Wouldn't it only retard it? Wouldn't the soldiers and the police and the javelins and the bum-bailiffs exact a terrible price from the whole valley?

Would they spare Wilcocks, despite what Cuan promised? There were so many who had been deeply deprived by him. They bore nothing for him but an abiding hatred. If some of these were armed, would they have the patience to hold their hands and let him live? Dualta stood up. He didn't think so. Let him decide now, here at once before it was too late. Did he want to go through with this thing? If he didn't what was he to do, sneak out of the house and leave it helpless and alone, pound his chest in after years and say, 'I had nothing to do with it. I wasn't there.'

On the other hand if he did not approve he would have to do something about it. He couldn't be negative. And if he wanted to do something about it he would have to do it now and do it fast, before it was too late, too late.

His emotions were mixed but his actions were cold and ordered. He went down the stairs quickly. He left his budget handy in the hall. Then he moved from room to room, lifted the window, pulled the heavy shutters close and barred them. The moonlight was shut out, so he had to stumble his way in the dark. At times he was almost in panic in case the dark figures of the horsemen would appear in front of him and the torches break into light. He was haunted by the thought of Tooley and what had happened to him.

His last job was to shoot the heavy bolts on the kitchen door. Christy was there, sleeping in a corner near the fire. He shook him awake. It took a lot of time to shake him awake. He slept as if he had been hit on the head with a block of wood.

'Christy! Christy! Christy!' Got him conscious. 'Get into the hall,' he shouted. 'Into the hall. We are going to be attacked. You hear!' Got him to his feet, staggering as if he was drunk, guided him through the darkness. Left him in the hall, and went up the stairs again on light feet. He went to the room of Biddy. He wakened her with sibilant whispering. Could only see the vague bulk of her in the moonlight. He didn't want her to wake up in terror. 'Listen,' he said, 'there is going to be an attack on the house. Stay where you are and don't move.' He closed the door. The two girls sleeping in the attic room. Fear in the whites of their eyes. 'Stay where you are. Don't move out of the room.' Just in case. If the attack succeeded there would be time to get them out.

He went to a window then on the landing and looked out. He thought he could see the forms of them, converging, terrifyingly ghostlike in the moonlight. His heart was beating fast. One last trip now.

He went to the door of Wilcocks. He knocked. Called 'Mister Wilcocks! Mister Wilcocks!' Again and again, his knocking and voice insistent. He heard a reaction. He waited. He heard the strike of the sulphur match and under the door he saw the light of the candles. 'Put out the light!' he shouted at once. It went out immediately. So Wilcocks was well awake. He waited. The door opened.

'Well?' he said crisply.

'We are going to be attacked,' said Dualta.

'Are the shutters closed?'

'Yes.'

'Rouse the men in the yard,' he said.

'No good,' said Dualta. It was a good plan. As they came one by one the houses would be guarded by silent men, the doors blocked with timber, oak pegs slipped into latches. The house would be completely isolated.

'Go down,' said Wilcocks. 'Light candles in the gun-room.' Dualta left him. Who am I betraying? he wondered as he went. I couldn't see it happen here. What will they think of me? He didn't care. At this moment he didn't care.

He went down. He collected Christy. They lighted two three-branched candlesticks in the gun-room. The light flickered off the oiled barrels of the muskets and the shotguns and the pistols.

'Dualta! Dualta! What's abroad?' Christy was asking. He was hardly awake yet.

Wilcocks wasn't long. His nightshirt was shoved into his breeches and he wore light pumps on his feet.

He was decisive now anyhow, Dualta thought.

'We will load the guns,' he said. 'You, Duane, have we much time?'

'We have very little time,' said Dualta.

'Here, take these,' he said. He gave him three long sulphur matches with a striker. 'Go out on the roof,' he said. 'In the gulley between the two roofs you will find a covered iron pot. Set fire to it. It is a signal light. When they see it help will come. We will load the guns. Take a top window each. Go now.'

Dualta left. Climbed the stairs and the attic stairs and forced the skylight window. The iron bar that held it was strong. He had trouble forcing it. It gave to his strength and he pulled himself out. He walked between the valley of the two roofs until he came to the awkward bulk of the pot. He lifted the lid of it. It was stacked with pitch and wood. He paused a moment. Then he pulled himself up the sloping slates until his head appeared over the top. He looked down. There were horsemen on the front lawn now, and their torches were coming alight one after the other, springing up, smoking.

He returned to the pot. One after another he struck the lights and applied them to the stuff in the pot. It was bone dry. Suddenly it went up in flames with a loud whoosh, almost blinding him. A tall dark-red flame rose from it and clouds of smoke. He went back to the skylight, dropped through, closed it after him, wondering at the perspicacity of Wilcocks. Who would have thought of a signal fire but he? He was sure now that the barricaded houses were better prepared than they had thought. This was the first attack on a big house. But for himself it would have been already successful despite all the precautions. He thought that the Trojan horse had turned into a goat, or an ass, or a sheep, or a snake, he didn't know what. But no name would be nice, not even the first one.

Wilcocks was on the landing.

He handed him a gun. 'Take the room on the right,' he said. 'Break the glass if you have to.'

There was no need. At that moment they heard the glass of the windows breaking, some from stones, some from shots. He went to the room. It happened to be Una's. As he arrived a flaming torch came through the broken window. He caught it and threw it out again, scuffled the smouldering rug with his foot. Then he went to the window, shoved out the barrel of the shot-gun, and pulled the trigger. He took care to aim in the air. From another window he heard the sound of another shot, and the scream of a horse. He peered over the edge of the window. There was a confused milling of horsemen below and shouting. One or two shots from guns. The tops of the trees around about were eerily lighted by the fire on the roof, the tops of them rosy.

Go away now, men! Go away now, men, for the love of God! he urged them in his mind, before the others come up behind and catch you. He didn't want that either, you see. He didn't know what he wanted.

He heard the strong voice calling them. That would be Cuan ordering over the shouts and the shots, and in another moment the men outside seemed to be obliterated as they threw the torches away from them towards the house, and then there was the sound of thundering hooves on the turf. They were going away, flying in all directions. He sighed. Glad that Cuan had seen sense, cut his losses, escaped before it was too late. This violence was too ambitious. It was too big for small men, bloated with success against such lesser opponents, like Tooley. He raised himself, peering, trying to see as the scattering horsemen ran for the river and the woods, and already from the poplar drive there was shouting and the sounds of horsemen. How much better organised they were than Cuan knew, Dualta thought, as he sat on the floor with his back to the window. He felt exhausted. They had not succeeded. What was success? They had not succeeded on account of him. On the other hand Wilcocks had succeeded on account of him. To whom was the victory then? He couldn't say.

Wilcocks was at the door.

'Are you all right, Duane? I think they are running away.'

'Yes, sir,' said Dualta. 'I think they are running away.'

'Let's get down to the hall then,' said Wilcocks. 'Get the door open. Help is on its way. We might be able to catch some of the blackguards.'

Dualta followed after him. He paused for a moment before leaving Una's room. He thought it odd that it should be Una's room. He smelled once more, widening his nostrils for the faint scene of her, but it was completely obscured by the foul-smelling rush-tallow torch that had been a brief lodger.

He went down the stairs listlessly.

Wilcocks was standing in the open door. He held a gun. Christy was lighting the wall candlesticks in the hallway. The place was being filled with light and shadow. Smoke from the dying torches outside was drifting into the hallway like wraiths. He put down the gun, and took up his budget. He knew that now was the time for him to go quietly out the back way and disappear in the woods. But a strange inertia held him. He leaned against the stairs. He couldn't make himself go. He wanted nothing from them, from any of them. He had come to a part in his life when he had taken sides, for no clear reason that he could see, and in this case he couldn't see that taking sides would be of the slightest avail.

So he stood there and watched listlessly, as they came: gentlemen hurriedly dressed, or half dressed, with unshaven faces. Guns and red faces and loud talk. Coming and going, coming and going, and squat men with sticks shouting and going. Horses, voices, that never came into perspective, gentlemen and burly followers reminding him of long ago when they had hunted him like a hare on the side of the Mount. Just these type of people. They were everywhere. How could you escape from them?

They came into focus when he saw that he was suddenly surrounded by angry faces, with the face of Wilcocks in the middle of them. Not angry, but pale and stern.

'Duane! Duane! Wake up!' he was saying. 'You knew they were coming. How did you know they were coming? Speak up, man. How did you know they were coming?'

Dualta looked at them. There were five of them. Three young men and two older grey-haired men, all very dishevelled. And they were angry.

'I just knew,' said Dualta. 'Isn't that enough?'

'No, Duane,' said Wilcocks, 'it is not enough. If you knew they were coming, you must know who they are.'

Dualta shook his head.

'I do not know,' he said.

'You are lying,' said one of the young men.

'That's right,' said Dualta.

'You will have to tell,' said Wilcocks. 'I am grateful to you. You saved the house. But this goes beyond loyalty. These men must be found and hanged. You must name them.'

'No,' said Dualta.

'By God,' said the young man, 'he will be made to tell.'

'Wait a minute,' said Wilcocks. 'You will have to tell, Duane. There is no escape but to tell.'

'No,' said Dualta.

'He'll have to be made to talk,' said the angry young man.

'You hear that, Duane,' said Wilcocks. 'This is too serious. You will have to talk.'

'No,' said Dualta.

Wilcocks looked at him. Dualta met his eyes squarely. Wilcocks held his look for a moment and then his face got red. Like long ago when his daughter faced him. He stepped back. 'All right,' he said.

Dualta saw them coming towards him, with boots and fists and sticks and even the reversed barrel of a pistol.

He thought: Once before I was hit and I hit back. I will not hit back. If I had not hit back then, I would not be here now. Perhaps, he thought, this will purge me of the distaste I have for myself. Perhaps this will make me one of the people again. How subtle is the temptation of the big house, he thought. You get used to it. Regular food, salt mutton and beef at frequent intervals, a soft bed to lie on, like living in a well stocked fort, while outside the natives scratched for a living in the poor ground. Dimly he could understand how the lost Gaelic poets cried for the departed chieftains, long gone and their boards groaning. Were they bemoaning the lost power of the chieftains or the good living conditions that sapped them and separated them from their own and refined their poetry until it was beyond the understanding of common men?

He thought of this as the first blow rocked all the teeth in his head. If he had betrayed his own people he would accept the pain he had to pay for it. If this was the way it had to be he would accept it. This was his thought as the kick of the riding-boot in his groin brought him to the ground.

13

CUAN WAS pleased with his plan, and with the excellent way it unrolled itself smoothly. Once they broke into the estate and fanned out, blinding the houses of the bailiffs, into the back portions to lock the sleeping men in the quarters over the carriage houses, and the house was ringed with determined if nervous men, he felt pleased. In a small way it represented his large dream. This he had thought of many times at night, stirring restlessly in his straw. The world was made up of community cells. This valley was a small one, but only one of many. All were complementary. So what he was doing here in a small way could be built up and spread so that it would take in a whole nation, like a fire in a forest jumping from tree to tree. This was why it drove him to fury to see men content with their lot. He was always angry at the shabby people in the shack towns springing up around the large centres of population, ragged men with large ragged families erecting frail shacks made of wood and mud, begging, half starving, drinking raw whiskey at times to drive away misery, but laughing, lolling in the sun in their rags, cuddling children with rickety limbs. Why did they submit to this? They didn't have to submit like this.

So his plan pleased him. It was organised. It was drilled. It would be swift, and Wilcocks' house would soon be just a blackened pile. If they took revenge afterwards on the people, so much the better. Out of persecution would come bitterness, a lust for revenge, and Wilcocks' house could be a torch that lighted freedom in the south.

He knew at once that it was lost when the signal fire flared from the roof. He hadn't calculated on this. When the horsemen lighted the torches and he saw the shutters fast closed on the lower windows he knew there was not time. Broken glass in the upper windows, shots, firing, all were no use. It was already too late. He was in a cold rage but his mind worked well.

He galloped among them, shouting: 'Get away! Get away! Scatter! Out of the grounds! Leave the horses! Get home on foot!' For there would be pursuit. It was better for the pursuers to chase riderless horses. It would confuse them.

He could feel their disappointment, and worse still he could feel them disintegrating as panic took over from confidence. They milled around. He set his horse and went around the house. The men there were gazing up at the roof. Light was reflecting off their faces. He shouted at them. He gestured with his arm. They got his message and rode out of the yard. All except one, he noticed as he was about to pull the horse's head round. This was Tom Ryan, a relation of Annie's. He was fumbling under his coat, and took out a package that gleamed whitely and then he threw this on the ground before he turned to move away.

Cuan closed on him.

'What are you doing, Tom?' he asked.

'Annie told me to leave this,' he said. 'It'll mislead them, she said.'

'All right,' said Cuan. 'Get out of here. When you cross the river get home to bed fast. Let the horse free. Chase him up the hills. Give them something to follow.'

Tom dug his heels into the horse's flanks. Cuan bent down from the saddle and swept up the package. It consisted of a bundle of papers tied with twine. He hadn't time, but he moved the pages with his fingers. In the glaring mixture of light, fire and moonlight he could see that the writing was that of Dualta. In one of the sentences he read his own name. They were letters that Dualta had written and discarded, carefully saved by Annie. There was one note from Dualta to himself, their names clear in both of them. He knew he was going pale with shock. He heard shouting from the front of the house. He turned the head of the horse and rode out of the yard. The sound of the hooves on the stones ceased and was taken up by the dull clop on the grass of the park.

He swallowed his anger in order to think.

Annie! He was not surprised the more he thought. She had decided to end the affair. There were two strangers in the valley. The affair could not be ended without offering victims. They were the victims. Oh, Annie! Should he be surprised? He peered ahead. He thought he saw Ryan heading down for the river, bent low over the horse. From his left he heard the shouts and the sound of horsemen. These would be the ones answering the signal fires. He thought that he might have to face Annie. He wondered, if he did face her, if he would have the patience not to kill her. The spittle was sour in his mouth. When he got close to the horseman he called 'Tom! Tom!' He saw the man's head turning. He slowed the run of the horse. They were not far from the river.

'Tell Annie,' said Cuan, 'I got the package.'

'All right, Cuan, all right,' said Tom. 'We must hurry, man, they will be on top of us.'

'Tell her I said this,' said Cuan. 'Remember it. Tell her I said, Let her head never rest easy again. Some time I will come back to face her. You'll tell her this, Tom?'

'Yes, yes,' said Tom impatiently.

'It may be tomorrow or next week or next year,' he said. 'Tell her that, but that I will come back to her and I will reward her. Tell her that. Tell her to keep her head over her shoulder for the coming of Cuan McCarthy.'

'Can't you tell her yourself, Cuan?' said Tom. 'You will be seeing her.'

'I will,' said Cuan. 'Just tell her that I will be seeing her.'

Tom slapped the horse's flank with his palm. He jumped and set off towards the river.

Cuan dismounted from his horse. He had the blunderbuss in his hand. He smacked the horse, which went off after the other one, going more swiftly when he was released of his load.

Cuan bent low and set off running across the parkland back towards Wilcocks' house. He was glad of the physical action. It served to calm his hot blood. Who was it had said it somewhere, some time? Behind this conspiracy there is somebody who is making something out of it. It wasn't himself. He made nothing out of it, only the satisfaction he got from the planning and the dreams. He thought they all felt the same as himself, imbued with love of an ideal to be wrested, however violently, from life. As he thought, he realised what Annie was getting out of it. From their meagre collections they would buy a lease here to save someone from eviction, or they would lease fallow land and put an evicted person on to it. The respectable part of the valley was ringed with places they had bought or rented or leased, and they were all in Annie's name. He knew that now. She was a respectable person, who could be expected to be charitable to those who respected her. She was doing it for the people. But she had built up a creditable number of acres in her own name, which one by one would revert to her. It was as simple as that. She had no charity. She had no honour. She had no patriotism. But she had what she wanted. It was so simple. And he was the simpleton. He and Dualta.

Dualta.

That was the name that was bringing him back.

He threw himself on the grass as he saw the massing of men in front of the lighted door of the house. There were horsemen coming and going. Orders were being shouted. Some of them dismounted, leaving their horses outside. Most of them, to commands, set off into the surrounding areas chasing the sound of the fleeing horse hooves. Why had Dualta failed to open the shutters or save them from being closed? Cuan wanted to know this. Had he been discovered? If he had he was in trouble. It would be easy for Cuan to get away. It was no problem, over the hills and wash out his mouth and the taste of Annie from the clean water of a mountain stream. But he wasn't going to do it. Not until he knew what was happening to Dualta, and why.

He waited patiently. All the horsemen had come and gone. The men had been freed from their sleeping quarters. He saw them coming from the back places, armed with sticks, and farm implements, whatever was available, and setting out running, like dogs at the heels of the horsemen. And then there was nobody coming from any direction, just the five saddled horses in front of the open door of the house, moving from the gravelled drive to crop grass in the moonlight. He rose and ran swiftly. He leaped the steps and stood beside the open door.

He saw the blood on Dualta's head and saw him as he fell to the heavy kick.

Then he moved in.

'No more,' he said in a loud voice.

The young man who had his boot raised let it drop slowly as he saw the barrel of the gun gazing at him. Cuan saw the five hard faces looking at him.

'Gentlemen,' he said, 'move away from him.' They were not armed, except for whips. Their guns were leaning against the stairs. They had pistols in their belts. He waved the gun. They moved back a little. 'Are you all right, Dualta?' he asked.

Dualta nodded his head. He rose to his knees slowly, then pulled himself to his feet, by grasping the banisters of the stairs.

'Are you coming, Dualta?' Cuan asked, to encourage him.

Dualta nodded his head. He straightened up. Then he went to where his budget was resting on a chair. He raised it to his shoulder and then walked slowly towards Cuan.

'Take a gun with you,' said Cuan.

Dualta shook his head. 'No gun,' he said, and walked painfully on.

'You can follow us,' said Cuan, 'but some of you will die with us.'

'You can go away,' Wilcocks said. 'You will not be followed by us. The police will take care of you.'

He said this to Dualta. Dualta knew this. He stopped. He looked at him. Was this Wilcocks' way of trying to say something? You never knew with him. 'Anything I owe you,' said Dualta, 'I have paid.' Then he walked past Cuan into the moonlight.

Cuan waited a little longer. He didn't trust them. He wanted Dualta to recover and get a little farther away. He looked at the five of them. Wilcocks he knew. He didn't know the others. They were alien to him. They regarded him with hatred. This pleased him.

When he thought enough time had gone, he stepped back and kept walking back until he was free of the light from the door. The signal fire was dead. The moon was getting low in the sky. He saw Dualta and went to him and put his hand under his arm.

'We will have to hurry,' he said.

Dualta tried to break from his shuffle. Into a walk and then into a shuffling run. Cuan kept looking over his shoulder.

He needn't have worried. When he was gone from the doorway Wilcocks moved to it and closed the door.

The others had gone for their weapons. They saw Wilcocks standing in front of the door.

'George! George!' they said.

'No,' said Wilcocks. 'Let them go. The police will take care of them.'

'Do you know what you are doing?' one asked him.

'Yes,' said Wilcocks. 'He didn't have to tell me. But he told me. Now he can go.'

'You are a damn fool, George,' they said.

'Yes,' said Wilcocks. 'Perhaps I am.'

But he stayed with his back to the door. He thought about Duane. He decided that he would miss him. He introduced a note of youth and wit to his house. He was a traitor but he was not all bad. He would miss him as he would a favourite gun-dog? He thought not. He would miss him as a person, he thought. Now, but he had been so devilishly deceitful that if the police ever caught up with him and hanged him, he would not weep.

'We will go and empty the decanter, gentlemen,' he said. 'We have earned it, and confound their politics.' He left the door and went towards the drawing-room. They looked at one another, shrugged, dropped the guns and trooped after him.

Dualta read the last line of the letters and then slowly tore them into small pieces. He stood up. There was a high wind blowing up here on the Galtee mountains. He let the pieces go and the wind took them and scattered them like snowflakes ahead of it. It allowed some of them to rest on the heather and the soft places before it took them up again and scattered them farther and farther away from his sight. Dualta sighed and sat on the rock.

They had spent the night and most of the dawn laboriously climbing the mountain. They wanted their breath for breathing not for talking. But the talking would have to come, he knew. Cuan had gone to a further height to try to spot smoke that might be rising from a chimney or a mountain dwelling or from the bothan of a shepherd, because they were hungry and they had no food.

It was a clear day. He couldn't see all of the valley they had left. But he could see the river and the houses on the other side of it, and where it opened up into the wide fertile plain, the winding river and the great fields and the sprawling towns, and the clustered villages. A bird's-eye view. He felt pain looking down. It had held no permanence for him, but it held memories. He thought what a nice peaceful valley it could have been, only for some of the people in it. Like himself, say. Annie as well then. Sort of pustules on a healthy body. Not Cuan. Cuan was a dedicated animal. A man of violence. Wherever he went he would bring that with him, but he knew what he wanted and he was prepared to do what he thought was right in order to do it. But he could never be like Dualta or Annie.

He heard his voice behind him.

'Well, and what do you think of that, Dualta?' He came to him and sat on a rock opposite him. His eyes were like sharp needles.

'It wasn't unexpected,' said Dualta. 'She was in it for what she could get out of it. There will always be people like that, who will use people like you for their own ends and then betray you.'

'She had me fooled,' said Cuan. 'Oh, she had me fooled. She never once was working for the people. That she should have used me, a man of my intelligence. That I should have been used by an illiterate. It's killing me.'

'You never asked me,' said Dualta, 'why the shutters were closed.'

Cuan dropped his eyes from him. He leaned on his elbow. He turned his head away.

'So we will part here,' said Dualta.

'What will you do?' Cuan asked.

'I will drift home,' said Dualta. 'I will seek my uncle Marcus.'

'How will you go?' Cuan asked.

'I will go to Limerick,' said Dualta.

'And walk into their arms?' said Cuan derisively. 'Don't you know they will be waiting for you, after this?'

'What will you do?' Dualta asked.

Cuan stood up.

'I will go down into Kerry,' he said, 'travelling the hills. You can walk on hills from here to Cinnmhara; the Galtee, the Nagle, the Boggeragh mountains, on to the McGillicuddy Reeks. It will take time, but it will be safe enough. The hunt will slacken down. They will forget. I have a job to do in Clare then and I will work my way into it quietly across the Shannon mouth. You can come with me if you want to. I do not want to press my company on you.'

'You might find me unpleasant to travel with,' said Dualta. 'If I did that to you once I could do it again.'

To his surprise Cuan laughed, a hearty laugh that lightened the sombre lines of his face.

'Oh, no, Dualta, if you were going to betray me, you would tell me all about it long in advance so that your conscience wouldn't trouble you afterwards.'

'I hope so,' said Dualta. 'I sincerely hope so. What kind of a job will you do in Clare?'

'Some time ago,' said Cuan, 'they sent for help. They want two strangers to frighten an agent.'

'To kill him?' asked Dualta.

'No,' said Cuan, 'just to frighten him. Like Hanley. You remember Hanley?'

'You mean the bang and the blow and he scuttling like a hare?' asked Dualta.

'That's it,' said Cuan.

'I'll do that for you, Cuan,' he said, 'to make up to you, but do you know what I want now?'

'What?' Cuan asked.

'I want to be commonplace,' said Dualta. 'I want to be one with the people. I want to dig and sow and harvest, just being one of the people. You see, down there, that was dangerous.'

'How?' Cuan asked.

'Softened you,' said Dualta. 'You get used to living in a big house. I only realised it. They don't try to subvert you. It's just the things that are there. And you say why shouldn't I have them, too? I understand something. I used to wonder, how can they get Irishmen to work for them, to carry out all the dirty things that have to be done, injuring their own people. I know now. You just slide into it, little by little. Living in two worlds. One day you will slide into their world. You won't even know that you have done it. And you will be unhappy. You will be most unhappy, without knowing the reason.'

'You have learned something,' said Cuan.

'I have learned to take blows,' said Dualta. 'And that's a big lesson. I learned that down there. If you want to help, you are not to be outside kneading the dough. You must be the leaven inside it. Living with it. Do you understand me?'

'No,' said Cuan.

'There are two worlds,' said Dualta, 'and you must choose which one you are going to live in. I have chosen mine now, and I will not desert it again. I will live in it with all my heart, and some way while living in it I will add to it, and survive in the middle of it.'

'No good,' said Cuan. 'Sink into torpor like the rest? Have faith in God who hasn't heard the cries of the Irish for hundreds of years? Be reduced to lower than serfs? No. You hit and hit and hit again. Choosing your place. Only by inducing fear will you get alleviation. You're wrong, Dualta. I know what you mean but you are wrong.'

'Then you will let me go with you?' Dualta asked.

'As long as you frighten an agent at the end,' said Cuan.

Dualta laughed.

'I will do that,' he said. 'I will frighten an agent before I become part of the people.'

'Let us go then,' said Cuan. 'I saw the soldiers gathering around the house. Soon they will be scouring the hills. They won't like it, but they'll do it, and we have to be far away before they are up on this one.'

Dualta rose. He shouldered his budget. He regretted that he hadn't thought to put food into it. He tightened the belt around his breeches. Cuan had gone ahead of him.

'Cuan,' he called.

Cuan turned to look at him.

'Do you know,' said Dualta, 'I'm happy for the first time in a long time.' He looked at the prematurely white-haired man standing there outlined against the sky, and he thought, Now I have affection for him.

'It's a queer time to be happy,' said Cuan, 'with months of walking in front of us and policemen and soldiers on our tail.'

'Well, I am,' said Dualta, 'and I'm hungry too.'

'We will find smoke,' said Cuan. 'Forget your hunger and walk. Time is short for now.' He turned and walked away.

Dualta looked down into the valley once again. He could see

the town where they had hanged Paidi. This brought a lurch to his heart. And he thought of Wilcocks' daughter Una. He thought she was a nice girl and it's just as well she is gone out of my life, because it wouldn't do at all. It just wouldn't do.

Then he turned and followed after Cuan, the tall, tough heather scratching at his stockinged legs.

14

IT WAS raining.

This was mountain rain, driven by the wind, millions of minute misty drops that clung and soaked you to the skin. Sometimes when the extra gust of wind whipped the mist away, Dualta could see a shaft of sunlight in the valley.

Ahead of him he could see Cuan plodding away, his head bowed to the wind, his short cloak flapping soggily against his legs. He thought that Cuan's shape was thinner than it had been. He knew he was thin himself. Months of mountain travelling, some days with no food at all except edible roots and watercress, other days gorged with the flesh of sheep, which Cuan always claimed he had just seen slaughtered by an eagle which he had robbed of its prey. Dualta smiled now thinking of this, and he would always afterwards refer to unexpected things as gifts of the eagle. But they were healthy. They had no soft flesh left on them. They could race a mountain pony. He thought of the many places where they had rested their heads in the months past; stone shelters made by men, or arched rocks in heather wildernesses manured by sheep; crudely built shelters where the herders slept. Once or twice real houses where they slept head to feet, packing a kitchen floor like sods of turf in a clamp. These were good, those houses. They worked in the day for their food and they laughed and sang and danced at night on the mud floors. But always they were pursued by rumours, by men who might have seen a patrol of soldiers, or a troop of police, or even a patrol of Revenue men with their bullies who were searching the mountains for stills.

They were always on the move, rarely at rest, until your dreams were filled with a tidy cottage with a new straw thatch and whitewashed walls, with the sun shining on it. Ordered gardens and children laughing; going to Mass with the people on Sunday dressed in their Sunday clothes. Just order, a little peace. He didn't yearn for the fleshpots of Wilcocks' house, soft beds and meat and hot baked bread. He would settle for much less than that now.

He nearly bumped into Cuan, who was bent down staring ahead of him. They were on a sort of post road now which would join two towns. It was a strange place for a road, but there it was, a good road, drained at the sides, with not too many potholes in its heart.

At that moment the mist rolled away, like a curtain being raised, and below them they saw the mountains sloping and flattening to meet the sea. The sea was shimmering, greenly and bluely; shadowed islands were set in it. It seemed to stretch to eternity to meet the white scudding clouds on the horizon. In an inlet below them the new sun made the yellow sands shine. Below on the coast, cliffs and rocks with the sea breaking over them fought for your looking with the belts of forest trees, the green fenced fields.

Dualta set out running down the coarse ground, breathing in the clean salt-laden air.

He ran a long way and wasn't even breathless from the run, when around the shoulder of the hill came a racing hare and baying beagles and behind them the forms of running and shouting men. He was in the middle of the hare-hunt almost before he was aware of it. When the hare saw him, it paused, fatally, because the dogs got to it. It had only time for one despairing cry before it died and then the panting men were there and they were looking curiously at him, and at the figure of Cuan coming down the hill behind him, his cloak on the breeze, like a great flapping black crow.

They were a ragged-looking bunch of men, mostly bare footed, healthy, bright-eyed, and breathing heavily after the chase. All except one who came from behind, a tall burly man, booted to his calves, his neck stockless. As Dualta met his eyes, his heart started to pound slowly, because you couldn't but recognise the face or the figure. It was strange to see the lines drawn in a newspaper or a magazine, the cartooning and caricaturing of the real, suddenly become reality before your eyes. There it was, the thick curly hair with the reddish tint, dusted with grey, intelligent blue eyes and an impudent snub nose. He found himself looking at Daniel O Connell, who came forward to meet him, as curious as a Kerryman, as strange as if a drawn figure had walked out of the pages of a newspaper.

'Well,' said the deep voice, clear on the air, 'and who are you?'

He spoke in English. Why was this? How did he know that Dualta or Cuan, who had now drawn up beside him, would know English?

'We are scholars,' said Dualta, 'travelling for our health.'

He wondered if the man would understand the subtle humour. He did and Dualta was pleased. His eyes almost disappeared in a network of laugh wrinkles. He threw back his head and laughed. His whole body laughed.

'Well, then,' he said, 'let us sit and get the benefit of your scholarship. We ignorant Kerry people are always open to enlightenment from travelling genius. Ho, Party,' he shouted then in Irish to the huge man near him who was holding the hare and fighting off the dogs, 'that is our second kill so we can afford to eat. Call up the rations.' There were many rocks in the place, making comfortable enough seats, like a Druids' circle. He sat on one, and stretched out his legs. 'Where are you from?' he asked Dualta.

'I am from the Corrib country,' said Dualta, sitting on a stone out from him, dropping his bundle on the ground.

'A Galwayman,' said O Connell, 'and a Connachtman. Where will you meet a Connachtman with learning?' he quoted an Irish proverb.

'Or a Munsterman with honesty?' Dualta quoted back at him.

O Connell laughed. He was pleased. He slapped his thigh. 'Your companion is a dumb man then?' he asked, pointing to Cuan. Cuan did not sit. He rested leaning on a stick he had picked up, one foot wound round it. Dualta glanced at him. His face was set in moody lines. He was looking at O Connell with a blank face.

'It's many a time a man's tongue broke his nose,' said Cuan, adding to the quotations. O Connell didn't laugh. He kept looking at Cuan. He is a shrewd one, Dualta thought. He recognises hostility. He did not resent it though. He waved his arm.

'Have you anything like that in Connacht?' he asked. Dualta looked at the view his wave had embraced. It was wonderful. The bare places seemed to be covered with small houses with blue smoke emanating from them. They were built for the most part of dry stone walls, so that they merged into the mountains, becoming part of them. Below them in the great fields were grazing animals, looking like carved wooden toys. A few bigger houses in parklands with a river seen here and there through the trees, sparkling. Near one of the yellow beaches he could see a large two-storey house at the end of an avenue.

'Is that Darrynane?' he asked.

'Yes,' said O Connell with a satisfied sigh, 'that is Darrynane. A refuge for sinners like me,' he added, laughing. 'Can you beat that in Connacht?'

'For every beauty you have,' said Dualta, 'we can show you seven.'

'Why are you away then?' O Connell asked.

'What is love without possession?' Dualta asked.

O Connell thought over this. 'Maybe you have a point,' he said, 'but what is beauty without life? To be alive is the more important. Better to be alive than never to have been called into being. Aye?'

Dualta agreed.

Party came back. He was carrying a basket. He put it on the ground and knelt behind it.

'Let us eat in the name of God,' said O Connell. 'You look like men who could do with food.'

'We ate,' said Cuan, 'a mile or so back in the home of one of your evicted tenants. In a hedge house.'

O Connell looked at him.

'Who is he talking about, Party?' he asked.

'He is talking about Corpán,' said Party. 'Will I hit this black fellow for you, Counsellor? Corpán couldn't live. If the agent hadn't put him out, we would. Let me take one blow at his black countenance.'

'No,' said O Connell. 'It is more important to eat.'

Dualta took the buttered cake and the piece of meat most gratefully. Cuan leaned on his stick and refused. The rest of the men sat down and took potatoes from their pockets, joined with the pieces of wholemeal cake that Party gave out to them.

All the time that his strong jaws were chewing his food, O Connell was examining Cuan and Dualta.

Dualta felt pleasure, from the food and the company.

He thought that the reality of meeting a famous man was very different from the hearing of him. He had read his speeches. They seemed verbose, wordy and longwinded. But that was the style of speechmaking. But men who were there said that the way he said them bore no resemblance to the wordy words of them. He could send the blood pounding in your veins with the sound of his voice, his inflections. His speeches were unprepared. He spoke according as the mood of the people made him. Dualta thought that the real man used these speeches to hide behind them. There was very little that wasn't known about him now, on the surface. Because he was educated in France and had been caught up with the Revolution he hated the idea of the spilling of blood. Men thought at one time that he was an agnostic. Not any more. Some said he was a hypocrite. He had killed a man in a duel. When he went to Mass and Holy Communion he wore a black glove on the hand that had pulled the trigger. Was that hypocrisy? He was a great lawyer. One of the few professions open to Catholics, he had made it his own. He drove a coach and four, he said, through the perverted laws. Now he was getting a thousand pounds a week from the Catholic Rent. Oh-ho, they shouted! He was earning as much as that at the bar and gave it up to free his country from its shackles, he retorted. You couldn't fight without money, considering the great wealth that was interposed between tyranny and liberty. There was no in-between here. You thought he was an honest man and a sincere patriot and a truly pious Catholic, or you thought he was a deceiver, using public pennies for his own ends, a demagogue, battening on the emotions of a volatile and uneducated people, an impious man using God for his own ends.

Dualta just saw a well-built Kerryman with an open neck sitting mightily on a stone and chewing bread and meat, on the side of a Kerry hill.

He suddenly stopped eating and started to laugh.

They all looked at him, chewing postponed.

'Ah?' said O Connell enquiringly.

'Away from here,' said Dualta, 'you are a great man or a monster. Up here you are just another man chasing hares.'

'Is that bad?' O Connell asked. 'Am I not permitted to chase hares?'

'But certainly,' said Dualta. 'I eat your food. I am only getting part of my own back. I have given about one shilling and tenpence to the Catholic Rent. Now I have eaten it all back again.'

O Connell laughed, genuine laughter. 'I hope to get the worth of the food out of you,' he said. 'Where are you going now?'

'We are going into Clare,' said Dualta.

'A good county,' said O Connell. 'Your comrade stands and scowls at me like a crane that is going to eat a fish. How have I hurt you, friend?' he asked Cuan directly then. He stood up for it, shaking the crumbs from his clothes.

'In London,' said Cuan, 'you reneged on the forty-shilling freeholders.'

'The Forties,' said he calmly, 'were invented by the Establishment to send their fools into Parliament. They went in droves like cattle and voted for the men they were told to vote for.'

'They put the Beresfords out of Waterford,' said Cuan. 'They are braver people than you think.'

'They are much braver than I thought they were,' said O Connell. 'That's dead now, that Relief Act. Next time they will be in.'

'You hate the men of 1798,' said Cuan.

'No,' said O Connell patiently. 'I do not. It was a deplorable insurrection. It was instigated by Pitt. They fell for it. He wanted them to. It helped him to carry the Union. Who can forgive them for that?'

'Do the sufferings of the people, then, under the militia, all that slaughter and violation and death, mean nothing to you?' He was leaning forward, his face was pale.

'Yes,' said O Connell, 'and also this, there should never be militia. There should never be ordinary people with arms in their hands. What can come from that except slaughter and rapine? I saw it in two countries. I am never likely to forget it.'

'So we must save our blood?' asked Cuan. 'We must never shed a drop of it for our country?'

'Not while I'm here,' said O Connell. 'There has been too much blood spilled, without need. Listen, I have called a nation into existence, all of them, not a few here and a few there with pikes in the thatch, but a whole people. I will imbue them like yeast in a cake so that they will rise and swell, and become so peacefully big and cohesive, so morally strong, that they will have to be handed what they want.'

'You are a dreamer,' said Cuan. 'Who ever heard of a Kerry dreamer?'

'No,' said O Connell. 'It is violent men who are dreamers. You are a violent man. When I was a student, I saw the result of violence. I was down with typhus over there in Carhen when Lord Edward Fitzgerald was arrested for death, and Wolfe Tone captured. These men should not have died. They were too talented. They should have lived for their country. That's how I felt then and how I feel now. It is the way I see it, a great cohesive mass boiling and stirring like porridge in a pot, until it overflows and becomes irresistible. Some time then, long ago I made a speech. I said: Moderation is the character of genuine patriotism, of that patriotism that seeks for the happiness of mankind. There is a character that is caused by the hatred of oppression. This is passion, the other is principle. There is a great difference. Unreasonable patriotism will always lead to violence. I wish I could make you understand me. I wish I could win you. You seem to be an intelligent man.'

Could Cuan see, Dualta wondered, the oddity of this meeting, of a man like O Connell pleading on a Kerry hillside for understanding from a tall, white-haired man whom he had never met and was unlikely to meet again? Could he see this and not understand that O Connell was sincere. He tried to think of the wealthy landowners he had met. They would not pass five seconds in the company of a man like Cuan or himself. By now they would have set the dogs on them.

'We have never got anything from them,' said Cuan, 'by being kind and accepting. Nothing has ever come from them except from the point of the pike and the barrel of the gun. Nothing ever will.'

O Connell dropped his arms.

'It will always be the same,' he said, 'unless I win. If I win, what then? Will you acknowledge that I was right? Are you big enough to do that?'

'If you win,' said Cuan, 'I will become your bondman. But you won't. You are fighting against history.'

'No,' said O Connell, 'I am trying to interpret history. You watch.'

'I will watch,' said Cuan.

O Connell turned then to Dualta. He smiled. 'How about you?' he asked. 'Have I sounded a chord in you?'

Dualta thought.

'Oh, yes,' he said. 'You have played a tune on me. I am your man. Haven't I given you one shilling and tenpence?'

O Connell bowed to him in mock thanks.

'Did you tell me your name?' he asked.

'No,' said Dualta. 'I am Dualta Duane. He is Cuan McCarthy.'

'McCarthy is a fighting name,' said O Connell.

'So was O Connell,' said Cuan.

'And still is,' said O Connell. 'I must go. I see my poor secretary struggling up the hill with a basket of letters on his arm. If you are staying here come down and see me at home. We will talk more.'

'We are bound far away,' said Dualta.

'I hope we meet again,' said O Connell. 'Party, free the dogs and let us try to rise another hare before I am caught with the letters. Goodbye, friend Dualta, and you, McCarthy. I am glad we met. I hope we meet again.'

The dogs started howling. The men started shouting. Then they freed them and they scuttled around snuffing and baying and the men followed them. O Connell set off with his long stride, looking at least ten years younger than his fifty years. Once he paused and turned back to regard them and wave his hand, and then he was out of their sight. They stood for some time looking after him, until the whole assembly was hidden by the shoulder of the hill.

Then Dualta turned to Cuan and said:

'Well, Cuan, let us be on our way to Clare.'

'And a bit of beautiful violence,' said Cuan. He kicked at the crumb-littered ground. 'To get the taste of false peace out of our mouths.'

15

THEY STOOD on the hill and looked down at the valley. The sun was shining from a cloudless blue sky. Wearing only shirts and trousers, they had the rest of their clothes and their shoes bundled in the budgets.

'There it is,' said Cuan, and he sat on the flat limestone rock. There were plenty of rocks. The hill on which they were was part of a ring that ran around the valley enclosing it in a rocky embrace. The hills were all stones. Dualta had never seen so many stones in one place in his whole life. The arms of the stony hills ran down to the sea. The valley was about twenty miles across and about ten from the sea beach to where they were. It was a lush enough valley. The pattern was the same. Right in the middle were tall trees through which you could glimpse the grey walls of a big house. On the left nearer the sea there was another smaller one. On the right, high up, there was a third, and down beside the sea was another house standing in the middle of green fields and surrounded by a wall. The cottages were seeming to be climbing the hills, all around the rim of the valley, clustered closely, and beside them small patches of potato and oat fields which seemed to have been wrung from the rocks with great agony. They were all dry stone-built houses with straw-thatched roofs. All you had to do was to pick any field you liked and the stones were there ready for you. Some of them were big and might have to be split with a wedge, but even if you possessed little stone-skill, he thought, you should be able to build a passable house.

Down at the sea the houses were built on top of one another as tightly packed together as a turf clamp. The smoke from their chimneys was lost in the blue of the sky. He raised his eyes a little across the sea to the other side of the Bay of Galway and he could see his own mountains rising mistily out of the earth, like a blue dream.

'I am not far from home now,' he said, 'if I was a good swimmer.'

'You like it?' Cuan asked.

'I like it,' said Dualta.

'Like all pretty things,' said Cuan, 'it conceals ugly things. It is not all smiles. There are slimy things under the stones. The people call it the Valley of the Flowers.'

Dualta could see why. The rocks were not entirely without colour. They had their own different blue-grey colour, and in between them patches of earth that were carpeted with gentians and wild orchids and some sort of yellow flower he didn't know, trying to remember the plant and flower lessons of Uncle Marcus, who knew all of them and what diseases their roots and leaves were good for.

'Some flowers can be poisonous,' Cuan went on. 'They call the town below the Town of the Sea. When the wind is north, a bitter wind comes from the bay and scours the whole valley. The house in the middle is the house of Tewson. That is where his man Clarke holds court.'

'Is he the one?' Dualta asked.

'Clarke is the one,' said Cuan grimly. 'Tewson is rarely here. He is what they call an absentee. If money runs low he pays a visit to spur Clarke to greater effort. Clarke rarely fails him.

Clarke is a just man, you see. He is a good Catholic who works hard for his master as is enjoined in the Gospels. How can he be faulted for doing his duty according to the will of God? Over on the right is the house attached to the glebe lands of the Protestant Bishop. His affairs are very ably conducted by a man called Cringe. He is a good man, to the last farthing. He is a devoted Protestant, as is right, but he cannot see why all those stupid dirty people who are his tenants won't turn and cling to the true faith. The house on the left and its fields are owned by a man named Bradish and his family. He is a Catholic. He bought part of Tewson's place when Sir Vincent was in some scrape with a woman in London and wanted money fast. Bradish is so pleased and grateful for being a landlord of sorts that he can never cease thanking God for the benefits conferred upon him and licking all the hands of the gentlemen who permit such a strange thing to happen. The house near the sea is the house of an honest man named Dogherty. He was one of the people. He opened a shop. He runs in the mail. Bit by bit he bought an acre here and an acre there. He is sound. He is a man of business. He is building acre on acre. In a hundred years it is possible that his descendants will own the whole valley. He has a son who is as dogged as himself. For the rest, they are just people, good and bad, kind and cruel, cheerful enough, happy enough.'

'Are you glad to be back here then?' Dualta asked.

Cuan lay down on the rocks, his hands under his head. He thought.

'I think I am,' he said. 'I will know better when I see my brother. I was quite young when I left after all. You cannot erase the memories of your youth. Besides I'm feeling old. We have travelled a long tiring way. I am not as young as you. Maybe I would try to settle down.'

'Why do we see no people?' Dualta asked.

Cuan sat up abruptly.

'I have been wondering that,' he said. 'They should be everywhere. We shouldn't have been able to poke our nose into the valley without hundreds of eyes watching us. Down there beyond the big house, say halfway between us and the sea, behind the shoulder of the field of the hazel bushes, I think I see a concourse of people. What are they up to then?'

'It must be important,' said Dualta, 'if they are all there.'

'The people of the valley,' said Cuan, 'are very curious. It need not be important to take them away from home.' He shaded his eyes with his hand, peering. He suddenly stood up. He put his fingers in his mouth and whistled shrilly. Then he waved his arm in an inviting gesture. He sat down again. 'I saw a boy minding sheep,' he said. 'Perhaps we will hear from him, if he wants to tell us.'

They waited.

They heard the bark of a dog. The dog arrived before the boy. He sniffed in their direction. He was a black and white collie. He bared his teeth at the same time that he was wagging his tail. The boy appeared from below them. He came towards them. He stood a little way from them. He had a long hazel stick in his hand. He was a tall thin boy with very big eyes, tangled hair. His clothes were not good. They could see his legs and his breast through his torn garments. He pulled flowers from their stalks with his toes.

'Who are you?' Cuan asked. He kept his mouth shut. 'Are you dumb?'

'Who are you then?' he asked.

'I am called McCarthy,' said Cuan. At this intelligence the boy's eyes widened.

'Are you a relation of the File McCarthy then?' he asked.

'He is my brother,' said Cuan.

The boy came closer.

'I have heard of you then,' he said. 'I have heard talk about you.'

'Where are all the people?' Cuan asked.

A look of disgust came over the boy's face. He turned his head. 'Down there, they are,' he said. 'They built a house for a new teacher. There will be school now in the valley.'

'What!' exclaimed Cuan. 'And where is Napoleon then, who had his school in the town?'

'He's not young,' said the boy. 'He drinks too much, they say. Father Finucane got this new one. He got the people to build a house. Now, even the girls have to go to school.'

'Who is this priest Finucane?' Cuan asked.

'He is a young one, a man in place of the parish priest.'

'The parish priest is dead then, Father Melican, is that so?'

'No, then. He was hit by lightning one day on the Carn. The horse he was riding was killed. He is not well. He cannot walk but with crutches. So this young man came. He is our misfortune. This house for the teacher and she a woman!'

'Is that bad then?' Dualta asked.

'Who wishes to be taught by a woman?' the boy asked indignantly. 'Who wishes to be taught at all? Doesn't my father say that there is more education in the sky and the breeze than in the walls of a house?'

'Who is your father?' Cuan asked.

'He is Bottle Daxon,' said the boy. 'I am Colman.'

'Can you read?' Dualta asked.

'Who needs to read?' he asked.

'Can you add two and two?' Dualta asked.

'Of what need is two and two?' the boy asked.

'Do you forever wish to be as ignorant and stupid as you are now?' Dualta asked.

'Who are you?' the boy asked. 'You have the cut of a stranger. I will not be stupid and ignorant. I know more than many people. I can make songs and sing them. You see. I am going now back to my sheep. They are wandering, like you in the head,' he added to Dualta and ran down the hill. Dualta laughed and watched him go.

'His father makes whiskey in the hills,' said Cuan. 'Well, we will push on. We will go to the house of my brother. Let us see if he will welcome us. My goodness, things are changing in the valley if they are bringing in a female teacher. What is the place coming to? No wonder young Colman is filled with resentment.' He walked along the hill in the direction that the boy had gone, and Dualta, taking another look at the placid-looking valley and the glittering sea, hefted his budget and followed after him.

The priest had called for Miss MacMahon at the home of the

Bradish family where she had been staying for nearly four weeks. She was not sorry to see him. The house was an undistinguished plain two-storey house with a portico held up by greater-looking pillars. They were plaster pillars and weathering badly. The house was well furnished but too full of bric-à-brac imported by Mrs Bradish, who on her rare trips to Dublin could never resist the blandishments of the fakers. So thought Miss MacMahon. Mrs Bradish was a rotund apple-cheeked woman who talked incessantly. She had been a Miss O Brien and in some vague way had tacked herself on to the famous O Briens who, since the time of Brian of the Tributes, the King, had ruled large parts of Clare, fighting, killing, changing their shirts, apostatising to hold their lands, persecuting, tormenting or rewarding the inhabitants, turning out bishops, priests, soldiers, cowards, traitors, duellists, a proud gang of saints and sinners, just like all the other clans who had held on to their possessions since the coming of the Norman invaders. Her husband was a second son from a Roscommon family, less distinguished than in Mrs Bradish's saga. He was a bluff hearty man who trod the safe road of neutrality in all issues, like the Catholics of England, keeping his head down when the arguments flowed. He didn't like O Connell. Too radical, ruining quiet progress. His wife knew every family in Ireland, who they married, when they were married, the issue of the marriages, their scandalous or heroic deeds, in war and peace. She kept a book on them, all these items clipped from the newspapers. It went back many years. She was delighted when they were invited to balls in the bigger houses. Miss MacMahon imagined she would be too cloying, too sweet, too agreeable on occasions like that. Miss MacMahon regretted that Mrs Bradish had this effect on her, because she was a kindly and hospitable woman. The two girls, Helen and Margaret, were silent girls in their early twenties. Their mother was pushing them so hard at second and third sons of families that Miss MacMahon thought they would end up unmarried, if they didn't break away from her mismanagement of the mart.

They were in the hall, sitting, waiting. All Miss MacMahon's truck was waiting on the steps of the portico. Mrs

Bradish was fussing.

'But are you sure, Miss MacMahon, that you won't take the carriage? All that truck. What will people think?'

'They would think less of me,' said Miss MacMahon firmly, 'if I arrive in a carriage. My lot is set among the people. It is what I want. There is little use starting off on the wrong foot.'

'But how can you be so brave?' said Helen. 'You will be living in that house, on your own.'

'You will have to do your own cooking,' said Margaret.

'On an open fire,' said Helen.

'Really, Miss MacMahon, it is ridiculous,' said Mrs Bradish. 'We would be most happy if you stayed here with us, and went down to the wretched school every day. What they want with an education, anyhow, I don't know. What will they do with it?'

'Like the rest of us,' said Miss MacMahon firmly, 'they will be better people for it.'

Bradish grunted.

'It's debatable,' he said. 'All the same, a young woman living alone. There are some bad characters in the valley.'

'I have yet to find a really bad one,' said Miss MacMahon.

'But that was Tipperary, not Clare, dear,' said Mrs Bradish. 'They are wilder here, you know. Very temperamental, Terry Alts and Lady Clare. All those secret societies. So frightening.'

'O Connell and the Catholic Association stirring everyone up,' said Bradish. 'Be quiet, I say, and everything will come to us. Nothing will come from agitation.'

'I know very little about politics,' said Miss MacMahon. 'All I want to do is to teach children, to make them better people. That's all.'

So she was overjoyed watching through the open door when she saw the cart, a common cart with block wheels, coming up the short drive from the road. There was a big fair-haired man clicking his tongue at the horse and beside him the young priest was sitting, his black clothes looking heavy in the sunlight.

'He has come,' she said, rising. 'I cannot tell you how grateful I am for your hospitality. If I had ten tongues, I couldn't thank you enough.'

131

'Say no more about it,' said Mrs Bradish. 'I only wish we could hold on to you. We will all pray for your safety.'

Miss MacMahon laughed.

'Really,' she said, 'I am only going a few miles, you know. I am not going into the heart of Africa.'

'There are worse places than Africa,' said Mrs Bradish, darkly.

How little they know about their own people, Miss Mac-Mahon thought. Because they don't really try to know them. They shut themselves up in a cocoon of safety. In their own way they too possessed closed faces like the country people.

She walked out to the steps. The priest waved his arm at her and jumped lightly from the cart. He came towards her. He was a young man with a freckled face and reddish hair.

'You haven't changed your mind, have you?' he asked as he came towards her. He was serious about it, she saw.

'Why would I do that?' she asked. He heaved a sigh, took her hand.

'Thank God for that,' he said. 'It seems too good to be true, that was why I called up bogies. Good day, Ma'am. Goo'day, Mr Bradish, and ladies,' he said, waving his hat at them. 'I am sorry to rob you of such an attractive guest.'

'No sorrier than we are, Father Finucane,' said Mrs Bradish. 'Really the whole thing is ridiculous, you know.'

'Not to us,' said the priest, 'not to all the future geniuses that Miss MacMahon is going to turn out of the new school.'

'You can return to us at any time if you are disillusioned, Miss MacMahon,' said Mrs Bradish.

'Thank you kindly,' said Miss MacMahon, walking down the steps.

'All this, Miss?' the fair-haired countryman asked.

'All this,' she said, smiling.

'This is Moran McCleary,' said the priest.

'I'm pleased to meet you,' said Miss MacMahon, holding out her hand. He looked at it and looked at her and then took it in his own hand, a hard hand, as hard as seasoned bog-deal. He smiled at her then. The heart of Miss MacMahon warmed.

They said goodbye again as Moran piled the stuff on the

cart. It only left enough room for the seat in front. Father Finucane helped Miss MacMahon up to the seat. Not much help indeed. She clambered easily. She could nearly hear Mrs Bradish tut-tutting.

'You drive, Father,' said Moran. 'I'll walk and pick up any that drop.'

The priest took up the reins. He clicked at the horse with his tongue, remembered to turn and wave at the doubtful people on the steps, and then the cart pulled away. Miss Mac-Mahon took a peep to see if they were out of view, and then she relaxed, sighed, took off the hat, held it in her lap, shook her dark hair in the gentle warm breeze, and said, 'Thank God!'

'Oh-ho,' said the priest. 'G'wan up, Liz,' slapping the reins against the back of the horse. The horse ignored him, setting a pace and keeping it. 'They are good people. They mean well,' he added then.

'They are like Job's comforters,' she said.

'Do you really and truly understand what you are doing?' he asked.

'I thought your friend Father Joe explained it all,' she said.

'So he did,' said the priest. 'My God, those days in May-nooth, we didn't know how happy we were. We were not like doctors. It was all theory. Imagine a doctor who never saw the inside of a body until after he was qualified. But you are different. You were brought up well. You have travelled. Do you know what the job you have taken on will be like? Do you know how you will have to live? Such a vast change for you, it will be. The things you have to put up with. Good God!' He rubbed his hair with his hand distractedly.

'Father, do you want a schoolteacher?' she asked.

'You'll know how badly,' he said. 'There is such a terrible hunger for education among the people. What had they? They had Napoleon. He was a soldier with Wellington. He lost a leg at Waterloo, hence the name. Fourpence a day pension. Just enough to keep him in drink. ABC, two and two make four, the towns of Spain and France and southern rivers. That's his limit, that and a bunch of hazel rods to beat their backs, and only boys. What a godsend you would be! But it's so hard.'

'You do not trust me, then?' she asked.

'Oh, yes,' he said. 'But I am afraid you will not be able to stay with us. That frightens me. To give a cup of hope and take it away as soon as their lips are about to touch it.'

'You'll have to have faith in me,' she said.

'Your pupils will pay you a penny a week,' he said. 'I will try to scrape maybe ten, twenty pounds a year from the parish funds. You have no funds of your own?'

'Very little now,' she said.

'So you will be as poor as anyone else in the valley,' he said.

'That's all right,' she said. 'I don't eat much.'

'But it's not right,' he said.

'What is right?' she asked. 'I want to do it. That's all. I cannot explain it. This is what I want to do. I talked it over with Father Joe. What can I do that is really necessary? What is the greatest need? Education is. I am trained. I have knowledge. I can teach. I will be helping. I will feel that I am helping. It is as easy as that.'

He looked at her, the straight nose, the firm chin.

'It won't be easy,' he said. 'It will be terribly hard.'

'That is for me to worry about,' she said. 'I hope I am not as weak as you expect me to be.'

'I do not think that,' he said. 'But I want you to know this. I have to say it to you. The first moment you feel that it is becoming an unbearable burden, I want you to come and tell me. Don't fight it. Just come and tell me.'

'I'll do that,' she said.

'You are so young and pretty, damn it,' he said exasperatedly. 'You don't belong to all the things you will have to live amongst. Tell me, if you feel you have to dedicate your life to educating the children, why this way, why not a convent of nuns? They are doing such great work, slowly but surely. How they would have welcomed you!'

She laughed.

'I don't want to be a nun,' she said. 'I am a woman. I want to get married some day and have children. I do not want to remain a virgin. Now, are you satisfied?'

He threw back his head and laughed.

'Oh, rich,' he said. 'You will have wonderful opportunities in this valley of finding a rich husband. Maximum income ten pounds a year and a pig to pay the rent. Don't you know that all the gentry will frown on you for what you are doing? Don't you know you have no more chance of being invited to their dinners and balls and parties now? You throw in your lot with the people and you have thrown the rich men's board out of the window. You have become a servant. Do you realise that?'

'Yes,' she said firmly.

'What am I?' the priest asked wonderingly. 'The devil's advocate? I have said all on his side. Now on the other, let me rejoice. I will pray for you every day. I will thank God for you in the Mass. You will find your rewards much greater than you imagine. You are on the side of the angels. We have a real teacher in the Valley of the Flowers for the first time in seven hundred years. Praise be to God!' And then he did a strange thing, he stood up in the cart, and he waved his beaver hat three times around his head and he shouted in a loud voice, 'Yoo! Yoo! Hu!'

He startled the horse. He startled the birds. Moran behind laughed heartily at the sight of him. Miss MacMahon laughed too, clapping her hands. He sat down again, grinning.

'Did they not teach you decorum in Maynooth then?' she asked.

'They did, in faith,' he said, 'but sometimes it is as well to forget it. Now we are coming to the cross, so we will have to behave ourselves like decent people. Miss MacMahon, put on your hat. Moran, come to the horse and lead him with sedateness. The people will expect gentility from us, and the behaviour of gentlemen.' He settled his heavy hat on his own head, a bit rakishly because his red hair was thick and it was a hot day. Miss MacMahon, still laughing, put on her own hat and tied the ribbons under her chin, and smoothed the folds of her satin dress. Moran licked his hand with his tongue as he went to the horse's head and smoothed down his hair with the lick. Then they turned into the road that led from the town into the valley, turned away from the town, and from here on the people were waiting for them, thin at first, and then thickening at the approach to the new school which was built in the field of the hazels on a site generously provided by the Bradishes.

They were dressed in their best clothes, she could see; the men had shining shaved faces. Some wore hats, and if they hadn't hats they had their hair flattened to their skulls with mountain water. All the best-dressed people were in front showing off their new clothes with the tailor's crease still in them, corduroy or broadcloth of wool with ducktailed coats, and the girls were colourful in greens and reds, their hair gleaming, and all the children were waving branches of trees, and everyone was taking the fill of their eyes of the new teacher. They shouted 'Fáilte don Gleann, Miss', 'Welcome, welcome to the valley' as she passed, and with her limited Irish she could hear a few things like Man, she is a fine piece. She is as young as a girl. Where did Father Finucane find a lady like that? She'll never stick it. She was conscious as the cart passed of them falling in behind, and it was a big concourse of cheerful talking people that debouched into the yard in front of the school, where the cart stopped and Father Finucane jumped down.

The school was gleaming newly. It was built of dry stone. The split limestone was newly blue. There were two windows and a sound door, all new, and the thatch was last year's oat straw and still retained a little of its golden glow.

The priest helped her from the cart. She was a bit bewildered now. So many faces. So many people. Young girls looking at her very frankly. Young boys looking at her out of the sides of their eyes. Out of the anonymous crowd then emerged a face under a thatch of curly grey black hair. A big face, fat, pitted with smallpox marks, with a huge bulbous nose and side-whiskers, a vast face with missing teeth already rolling out sonorous praises from a thick-lipped mouth.

'This is Mister Shields, Miss MacMahon,' Father Finucane was saying, 'our former teacher now retired after a lifetime of endeavour.'

'Forcibly retired, Ma'am,' he was saying, 'under force of circumstances after the labour of years during the course of

136

which I fought for King and country under the eye of my friend Wellington, giving the man sound advice on several occasions, doomed thereafter to thwack the backsides, if you will excuse the phrase, of the thickest-headed louts that ever God put into a valley. I am most pleased to meet you, and if at any time, as one confrère to another, you wish to be advised by an older mind of the things necessary to the educational elevation of as rude and ignorant a people as God ever put on the face of the earth, all you have to do is send for me, and I will come at speed, waving my most precious possession, a thing of which I am proud and gratified.'

At which he lifted his peg-leg, in case she would miss seeing it, and the people laughed. Apparently they liked to be insulted by Napoleon.

She met other people. She shook their hands. But there were too many of them.

Her things were taken from the cart and carried into the house. There was a bit of ceremony. There was no key, but a hasp and staple that was closed by a wooden peg tied to the doorpost. The peg had been made a bit thick and it took a lot of dramatics and a little mild cursing before it was plucked from the hasp and she was ushered into the house.

It was very bare. But there was a fire burning in the open fireplace. Long benches of new timber were against the walls. In some triumph she was shown the other room, a small room behind the fireplace where there was a peg bed raised four inches from the ground, a sort of mattress made from intertwined rods, woven like the reeds in a basket. A new small table and a new chair. She met the carpenter. She thanked him for his labours. He beamed on her and rubbed the wood softly with his hands.

They said goodbye to her, and she said how wonderful they were to have done all this for her, how she was looking forward to meeting the children in the new school. Many people thought there should be a dance and a bit of drinking to celebrate the event properly, but didn't like to suggest it because she looked like a lady, and they went away one by one commenting on her appearance and wagering on her chances, praising her or shak-

ing their heads, and eventually she was left with Father Finucane.

She looked at him helplessly.

He said, 'I told you!' He indicated the place with his hand.
'It was a triumph for them,' he said. 'They put a lot into it.
They built it in a week of hard work. It looks very bare. You
will put the shape of a home on it. There is no window glass
or they would tax us.'

She nodded her head.

'I will go,' he said. 'Tomorrow I will come back and we can
arrange when the classes will begin.'

She nodded.

'All right,' he said. 'God bless you.'

She nodded.

'I told you it would be hard,' he said.

She nodded again.

'Well, I'll leave you,' he said.

She nodded.

He felt helpless, so did the only thing he could do. He went
out of the place and closed the door softly after him.

Miss MacMahon looked at her piled truck in the middle of
the earthen floor, and the bareness of her new domain, and the
shafts of sunlight through the small windows, and then she sat
down on one of the new benches, and she started to cry.

16

DUALTA FOLLOWED Cuan. It was a stony way; even if their
bare feet were hardened, the soles covered with a quarter-
inch of calloused flesh like the finest of impervious leather, it
was still painful to stub a toe against a sharp stone.

Then Cuan stopped and Dualta came close to him. They
were looking down on a narrow valley sheltered only by the
hills. It was only a few hundred yards across and the same
long. Down its centre ran a stream that disappeared into a gap-
ing cave before it could tumble down the hillside. He noticed

all over the Burren that streams were being gulped like that, as if a giant was lying beneath the hills with an insatiable thirst and ever open pores. This side of the stream there was a house. It was hard to see it in the welter of rock, since it was rock itself, and the thatch was aged and its colour blended with the surroundings, the green parts of it being like lichen. But there was a slow smoke coming from the stone chimney. On the other side of the stream a few roods of earth had been cleared, walls built around the patch, and the potato stalks were green and healthy. Apart from that healthy patch the floor of the small valley was covered with boulders that had been deposited when the stream was in flood.

'It is a hard place for a poet,' said Dualta.

Cuan grunted and started down.

The door of the house was unpainted and sagged. The windows had no frames. Cuan had to lift the door from the earthen floor to get into the place. Dualta followed him.

'Are you within?' Cuan called. The place was most untidy. There was a bench and a stool, and a makeshift cupboard on the wall. There seemed to be pieces of paper everywhere, written upon with blackberry ink, parts of which had faded. They were on the floor, on the bench, on the window-sill. Dualta bent and picked one from the floor. They were words in Irish, a succession of adjectives. They described brightness. The writing was firm and clear and beautifully proportioned. Cuan had gone to the room behind the fireplace. He came down.

'He is not here,' he said. 'He lives like a pig.' He went out of the door again, dropping his budget in the middle of the confusion. Dualta took up another page from the bench. It was a part of a completed poem. It was a lament for Uaithne Mór.

Cuan was calling, 'McCarthy! McCarthy! McCarthy!' The hills threw off his voice and repeated the name three times. Dualta put down the paper. He felt guilty, like reading the private letters of another person. He followed Cuan into the sunlight. There was a movement at the far end of the valley and a man came into view, stopped to look towards them and then came on. There was a collie dog at his heels. He was a tall man, as tall as Cuan. His hair was wild and he wore a beard which was turning white although his hair was still fairly dark. His clothes were not good. They were badly patched, and his pockets sagged with books, and from all of him pieces of manuscript seemed to be peering in a hopeless jumble. His stockings were falling down on his thin legs, and his shoes could do with being repaired. All this Dualta saw as he came towards them, still peering to discover their identity. He had a big nose and deep blue eyes with a piercing look, perhaps because he was short-sighted, or perhaps because he was used to being alone and looking into the middle distance.

'And that's my brother Flan,' said Cuan grimly, as he came towards them. 'God be with you, Flan,' he said then loudly.

Flan came closer. He looked at his brother.

'It's you,' he said. 'You are ageing. What brings you back to us? I thought never to see your face again.'

'You have a soft welcome,' said Cuan.

'I did not urge you to go away,' said Flan. 'What have you been doing? Wild deeds no doubt. You must tell me and I will sing of them. Who is he? Is he one of the bodachs?'

'Since he is a member of the human race, I suppose he is a bodach,' said Cuan. 'He is Dualta, from the other side of the Bay.'

'The Galway men never sang,' said Flan.

'They sang for their own,' said Dualta. 'They didn't sing for posterity.'

Flan snorted.

'Poor rhymes,' he said, 'that died on the air as soon as they were composed, faded from the brain with the fumes of the drink that inspired them. What are you here for?'

'I will stay with you awhile,' said Cuan. This didn't seem to please his brother, but he shrugged his shoulders and moved into the house.

'If you must you must,' he said.

They went in after him. Almost immediately, Cuan started to tidy things here and there. 'Be careful,' Flan called.

'You live like a pig,' said Cuan, continuing to tidy. 'Is there something to eat?'

140

'There are potatoes in the pot,' said Flan. He cleared the bench of its papers by putting them all together and stuffing them into his already stuffed pockets. He got a small packet of salt from the cupboard and put it on the bench. Cuan turned out the potatoes from the pot. They weren't very good potatoes. Dualta thought they must have come from the end of the clamp. He knelt at the bench and reached for one. He was hungry. The other two ate as well. The three pairs of eyes looked at one another and took stock as the jaws chewed. Dualta thought that Cuan had a very peculiar brother.

Suddenly Flan took a bundle of manuscripts from his pocket. He selected one of two pages and handed it to Dualta. 'Read that!' he commanded. Dualta wiped his fingers on his trousers and took the script. He was conscious of the eyes of Flan on his as he read.

> Grim and dark the plight of the Gael (cried Flan's song) in his own land.
> Blame then be on his own head and heart, that has all forgot the beginnings –
> The Thomond chieftains that lost sweet blood on the fair south of the Eiscir Riada,
> Of Conaill, Cutra, great Aengus of Aranmore and Fiacra of the Flowing hair;
> Of Conall dying under the geasa sword of Cuchulan and covered with his carn;
> Of Finn Mac Chumail great in battle and slaughter at Uinche's reddened ford;
> Of Dathi, the great pagan, dying for his gods at the foot of the white-tipped Alps;
> Of the great warriors who died defending hearth and board against Turgesius, the foul Dane.
>
> There were men then who sang them and stout people who cried them sore –
> From the bardic schools of kings and chiefs poured forth their tender songs.
> Like Litanies of the saints they called their generations back to their beginnings
> De Danann, and Firbolg and Formorian, they were the children of Kings, the sons of Milesius;

A race of songsters, among them not the least the O Dalys of
    O'Loughlin;
Donagh Mor, the Ovid sweet of Ireland, grandson of O Daly
    of the schools
And silver-songed Geoffrey, chief ollav of poetry, in wide
    Munster,
Carroll, the ollav of Corcomroe, Donagh, Aengus, Farrell and
    tender-mouthed Teigue.

He came to the end of it. He looked up.

'You see what I mean?' Flan asked.

'No,' said Dualta.

'What's wrong with them?' said Flan. 'A nation of thick-headed louts? How many of them can go back three genera-tions? They have lost their beginnings so they are sunken in poverty and meanness of mind. It happened the day they abandoned the bards.'

'Times change,' said Dualta. 'The bards brought their fate on their own heads, because they sang above the heads of the people. Now instead of dead dreams you should sing of the flowers on the stalks of the potatoes, the suffering of the evicted, the dreams in the hearts of children.'

'Gutter ballads,' said Flan. 'Not poetry.'

'I read you,' said Dualta. 'Brilliant, intellectual, interior rhyming vowels, that stir the beauty hidden in the heart, but for nobody but yourself and the few who can understand you, when you should be singing songs that will raise the people from their knees, fill their hearts with hope and beauty, instead of songs of dead heroes, whose dry bones are rustling.'

'Commonplace clodhopper, earth-grubber, Galway ignora-mus,' said Flan.

'You asked me what I thought,' said Dualta. 'I tell you.'

'Cabbage-head, turnip-top, bog-heart, muck-souled bar-barian,' said Flan. He hardly raised his voice, but the sound was vicious.

Dualta stood up.

'It seems to me,' he said with dignity to Cuan, 'that I am not welcome here.'

He and Cuan looked at one another, and the ridiculous statement suddenly seemed very funny, and they both laughed, and they couldn't stop. Flan was not at a loss for words. He kept using words, poetic and colourful in the Irish tongue, but painfully descriptive of Dualta and his failings and his probable ancestors.

They were like this, two laughing and one upbraiding, when the light was darkened at the door and a voice said over the noise: 'God bless all here, and may I come in?'

They turned then and saw a priest with red hair looking at them with his eyebrows raised.

Flan stood up.

'Come in, priest, and take a seat,' he said. 'I am sad that I cannot offer you better company than what we have at this time.'

'I thank you, File McCarthy,' said the priest gravely. He sat on a makeshift stool as if it was a throne, or, as Dualta thought with a grin, as if it would collapse under him. He had given Flan his title of Poet, and it pleased him.

The priest established good relations further.

'Carroll O Connor recited to me your verses, "The Lament of the Three Princes", and I thought them very fine and very moving,' said the priest.

'Now,' said Flan, 'doesn't it take a man of the Church and a man of education to feel the beautiful? If we had not the present company, we could talk about things of the spirit and beyond, but with an ignorant Galway man in our midst and a hater of the bards we can only talk about dung and dirt and ignorant people.'

'I am Father Finucane,' said the priest. 'I am administering the parish for Father Melican who is disabled.'

'I am Dualta Duane,' said Dualta. 'My birthplace you now know.'

The priest looked at Cuan. Cuan looked at him too, but did not speak.

'You are the File's brother,' he said then. 'I have heard of you.' If he expected talk from Cuan he didn't get it. Cuan skinned another potato.

'Were you wanting me, then, Father?' the File asked.

'Not altogether,' the priest said. 'It is a pleasure to come and see you, even if the road is hard to where you live. And I would enjoy an hour in your company and to hear your songs, but I have something else on my mind.'

Dualta looked closely at him. He saw Cuan's shoulder stiffening. There was a slight feeling of tension in the air. The jaw of the priest was strong, but his eyes were calm.

'Birds sing,' said the priest. 'All communities are composed of individuals essentially. Some are good, some are bad, some are unfortunate, some are peace-loving, but some are not. Some people become part of oath-bound societies. It is an evil of the times. It is hard to stamp out. The way of the authorities is violent. That just breeds violence. My way is to try and nip it in the bud.'

Cuan spoke to him then.

'Talk clearly,' he said. 'You are not a poet.'

'It is the custom,' said the priest, 'if you want something violent done, to send to another district for unknown men who will come and go faster than the swallows, perform a deed of violence, leaving everyone else blameless. It is a good notion, but basically it is evil. I have discovered that two men are expected to come into this valley and that a certain man will suffer. Many people will applaud his suffering. I will not. Because I am a Christian and he is a Christian, and I do not think that this is the way. Also I know this man and his master, and afterwards the condition of this valley would be much worse than it is now. So whenever strangers come I think it well to go and say the things I have now said, out loud, in the hope that if the strangers are the right ones, they will hear and understand.'

'How many strangers have come into the valley in the past few months?' Cuan asked.

'Many,' said the priest. 'Packmen, travelling tinkers, chapmen, many strangers.'

'And you said this to all of them?' Cuan asked.

'I have done so,' said the priest.

'I am not a stranger,' said Cuan. 'I am one of the people.'

'I accuse you of nothing,' said the priest. 'Perhaps I am

awkward, like a blindfolded child playing a game. I am not practised in subtle designing. I thought this was the way, and I have done what I thought was right. If I have offended you, I hope you will say so, and I will apologise to you as humbly as you wish.'

Oh, the clever one, Dualta thought. It was beautifully done, and suddenly he saw that it left Cuan no alternative. Cuan would have to quit. Because he was like that. The night that they assaulted the house of Wilcocks he had been like that. As soon as he saw that plans were going wrong, he called it all off. Dualta watched him closely now. The fierce, piercing eyes were looking at the priest. The priest didn't wilt under them, and Dualta's heart started a slow satisfied pound. I didn't want to do it, he thought. I didn't want to do it. I am finished with all that, all that. He knew he was really free from his promise when he saw the twisted smile that came on Cuan's mouth as he said, 'Well, there's nothing left for you to do, but to apologise then, humbly.'

The priest stood up. He bowed to Cuan.

'If I have offended you with my talk,' he said, 'I state that I am truly sorry and beg for your forgiveness. It is the larger wish of helping the whole community that made me hurt one of its members.'

'That's right,' said Cuan, a little grandly.

'I do not understand all these subterfuges,' cried Flan. 'What is going on? Like a stream going underground. Explain to me.'

'There is nothing to explain,' said the priest. 'It would be as well for all of us if you stay in the land of poetry. I thank you for your hospitality. I have much to do. The parish is large and the legs of my horse are thin.'

'You are nearly talking poetry,' said Dualta.

'That is the effect of being in the presence of a poet,' said the priest, laughing. 'I had no intention of undermining your position, File McCarthy.'

'Would you mind if I travel a little way with you, then?' Dualta asked.

The eyebrows of the priest were raised.

'I don't want to press myself on the bard,' said Dualta. 'I

would like to get lodgings in the village. Maybe you would advise me?'

'I will do that,' said the priest, looking closely at him.

Dualta took up his budget. He looked at Cuan. Cuan's face was flint-like. Dualta thought of the time they had been together. For a few years now they had rarely been out of one another's company. In a way he had been moulded by Cuan, but at many points he had resisted the moulding. But you cannot be with an intelligent person and not get a liking for him. He liked Cuan. But the time had come to part from him.

He knew that now. He had known it for some time. One of them would have to bend to the will of the other, and he was still afraid of himself.

'I will not be far away,' he said in a kind of apology. 'We will meet and talk again.'

'Yes,' said Cuan.

'I thank you for your limited hospitality,' said Dualta to Flan.

To his surprise Flan smiled.

'Come again, ignorant fellow,' said Flan. 'Somewhere you have a brain. If you drink at the well more often, it might awaken.'

'Thank you,' said Dualta, pleased. 'I will come again.' Then he went out and didn't turn back. He walked the floor of the valley and turned left at the sort of sheep-track. He mounted this and stopped where the priest's horse was cropping at the sparse grass. He waited here. The sky was still cloudless. He could see the Galway coast across the shimmering water of the bay, and the mountains rising blue-tipped from the land, looking tiny from here, like ones painted by children on a sheet of paper. He suddenly felt a longing for them. Would he go there? He would like to talk to his Uncle Marcus. Would it be safe to do so? The vicious ones of the Ascendancy had long memories and long arms.

The priest watched him for a moment, the good-looking, clean-cut face with the heavy hair of his head waving in the mountain breeze, a well set-up young man with intelligent eyes, and a good clean body, lithe and healthy.

He said, 'Do you want to go home there then?'

Dualta didn't turn his head.

'What drove you out in the first place?' the priest asked.

To his own surprise, Dualta told him, a tale stale with repetition but almost meaningless as you aged away from it. Somehow only the pain of Paidi remained in the whole of it; Paidi laughing and the house in the glen with the family and the waving children and their feet bare on the dust of the road and the spades on their shoulders as they journeyed into the strange lands.

He told him all this. Sorting it out for himself in a way more than for the telling of it. But he said nothing about the Wilcockses and his period of behaviour in that place. Somehow he felt that the priest might surmise it. They were walking down the hill, the horse between them.

'Are you like a wisp in the wind then?' the priest asked. 'Have you no idea for the future?'

'Only vague,' said Dualta. 'I want to be one of the people. Isn't that a strange ambition?'

'No,' said the priest, 'it is a brave one. Stay here awhile. There are good people in this valley. If you become part of the people then, you must wish to add to them, not take away from.'

'I do not understand you,' said Dualta.

'It is necessary that you give, not take away,' said the priest. 'You are educated. I can see that. Your Uncle Marcus did a sound job on you. You have experience, so there your education is grounded. Now you must use it by giving back to the people what you have got.'

'I'm not sure of your meaning,' said Dualta.

'Think over it,' said the priest. 'I'm sure it will come to you. When the old chieftains were being inaugurated in this place there was always a block of stone in which were imprinted the footsteps of the first chieftain. They set their feet in these footprints and with a white wand in their hand they swore to uphold the Brehon laws and the laws of the people and to give rather than to take away. Sometimes the oaths were empty, but sometimes not.'

'I see what you mean, I think,' said Dualta.

The priest mounted the horse.

'I will go ahead of you,' he said. 'When you get below you must ask for the house of the Scealaidhe, the Storyteller. They will point it out to you. It is the home of Carrol O Connor. They will find room for you. I will see you again. If you have troubles, I would be honoured to look at them for you. Goodbye, and may God bless you, and perhaps undo some of the curses that Flan unloaded on your poor head.'

He laughed, and Dualta laughed, and then he waved and the horse picked its way down towards the rough road that ran into the valley.

Dualta looked after him for some time, and then, shouldering his budget, he set off into the valley, whistling a song and jumping from stone to stone.

17

IN THE DARK of the moon the Revenue cutter had sailed silently into the bay, dropped anchor off the shore, and the Lieutenant and two men had been rowed to the beach. They had walked left through the silent town, scarcely disturbing the dogs. Then they had headed up into the valley on the shoulders of the hills. Halfway they had paused, until before dawn they were joined by seven men from the other side. The Lieutenant was curt with those men. He knew their kind. Hired for a shilling a day, they were the out-of-works, the misfits, the drunkards, whose assets were physical strength and a certain savage courage. In time they would be hired as bum-bailiffs, or tithe proctor's men, or sheriff's assistants. They were available for any unpleasant job that was going.

These were his guides now.

He followed them up the hill and over the hill on the far side. They hugged this, moving by instinct on the barely walkable places in the midst of the millions of rocks. The Lieutenant followed easily. He was used to walking in awkward places in the dark. His object always was tobacco or silks or brandies, imported by daring men in small boats from the foreign ships that they met with, far out in the bay. If they had not powerful customers, he knew they could not exist. If they did not exist, the Lieutenant would not have his job. So it was a profitable circle. Now he was on a job he did not like, smoking out illicit stills. It always involved cold and wet, and boring, probing, intensive searching. The Lieutenant wasn't interested in the morals of the thing, the thousands of people who had become hopeless alcoholics through the easy availability and cheapness of the raw whiskey; in the thousands existing on the bare fringes of poverty who sought ease for their hopelessly worried minds in a few hours of easily attained oblivion. All that was for the clergymen. He acted on information, and when it was clear and patent as now, he had to act on it, plan neatly and swiftly, and get the whole thing over before people were properly awake.

The leader of the rough men came back to him.

'We should be opposite the place now,' he said. 'Let us go over the hill and go down with the dawn. He should be there.'

'Right,' said the Lieutenant. 'Let there be ten yards between each man. Move down in a half circle. When we come near the place, close the circle. Don't let anyone get through.'

The men nodded and went away. The Lieutenant watched them spreading out in a long line on each side of him. Then he walked and they walked with him until they came to the top of the hill. Here he waited.

The sun would rise at his back, very shortly now. It was July and it rose early. There was an eerie light everywhere now that always came before the sun. The Lieutenant had seen many of these mornings. He was grateful that it wasn't raining. Standing here, watching this strange light creeping over the rocks, you could imagine yourself dead and walking a strange place in a strange unknown country. It was a bleak, hard, uninhabited place. No birds sang, and the fitful wind from the sea was stirring the coarse grass against the stones, making a sort of sibilant sound, like the scraping on the soles of innumerable bare feet. The Lieutenant shivered, wished for a mug of strong tea with sugar, and feeling, rather than seeing, the great arc of the sun rising behind him he gave a low whistle, waved his arm and the line of men advanced. He could see a red light creeping across the land, reaching out towards the ship in the bay which had appeared magically as if someone had waved a wand. Then, more practically, he could see the wisp of blue smoke rising almost from the ground, it seemed, some hundred yards ahead of him, and knew that this time he was going to be successful. Most times he got the still and the makings and maybe the filled jars, but rarely was there a human being within miles. It was like *Hamlet* without the Prince.

He stopped and waited, making a circle with his arms. They saw him and moved on, until they ringed the place from which the smoke was rising. He walked then to the smoke. As he came nearer he noticed that there was a sharp fall. He skirted it, walked gently down and was looking into a cave with a narrow opening. Other times the opening would have been closed with the bushes and stones that lay nearby. But now it was open. There was a squatting man in there, looking out at him, with his mouth open in astonishment. The Lieutenant wanted to smile. The man's face was red from the light of the fire that was under the boiler of the still. He could see every emotion on it, surprise and dismay and then savage anger as he came to his feet and made for the opening. The Lieutenant, who was a small neat man and opposed to violence, took the pistol from his belt and held it in his hand. That stopped the man's mad rush. He slowed, bent down and came erect outside the cave. He was a big gaunt man, with a black beard, black hair. His clothes were soiled, his eyes were flaming and red from the smoke. He rubbed them now with his hands.

Jeering voices came from behind them.

'Ho, Bottle, you come like a cork from a jar.'

'Now, Daxon, let us taste your beer. Who will take a jug of the first run?'

He looked around him. He was like a trapped animal. He peered at the faces in the gathering light.

'I will remember you,' he said.

'You will have time,' a man answered him, and they laughed.

'Tie his hands,' the Lieutenant said to his own two men who were behind him with guns in their hands. One of them did so. Daxon did not resist him. He kept looking at the other seven as if he wanted to memorise their faces forever. The big man who was the leader of them came closer to him.

'You know me, Bottle,' he said.

'Yes, Jack Gately,' said Daxon. 'I know you. You were a bad customer.'

'Now I'm a good customer,' said Jack. He laughed.

'I will remember what you owe me,' said Daxon.

'I will be living for that when you come out,' said Jack, 'in ten years or so.'

Daxon said nothing more. He stood impassively as they broke up all they had to break up, and took what they had to take for the evidence the Lieutenant needed, and then they headed without subterfuge straight down the valley. That was part of the exercise, to display the uselessness of opposing the Revenue, that eventually you would be caught, so they set off towards the road across the very rough ground, walking carefully, the seven men from over the hill laughing and jeering, and waving the thick sticks they held in their hands. The Lieutenant walked behind Daxon, and his two men one on each side of him. He didn't expect trouble, but he was a bit anxious. All he knew was that no matter what happened Daxon would end up on the cutter, and then in a court. He would present his evidence, and that was that. It was another job done.

As they came near to the road, all the same, he took precautions. He called to the rough men and they walked three on one side and four on the other. They were big men and formidable. They made the Lieutenant and his two sailors look small. Only the towering figure of the man with the tied hands equalled them, and they walked on the road like that until from the lane that led from Daxon's house the small figure of a boy came running, with the sleep barely out of his eyes, a dog at his heels, and he was calling, 'Father! Father!'

Dualta and Carrol O Connor had come early to the hayfields. Carrol had a good place. He was one of the very few in the valley who held his farm on a lease of two lives, the life of himself and his son. As long as he paid his rent he was safe from eviction or rack-renting until the death of his eldest son, who was now fourteen and likely to live to be a hundred. So he could afford to keep his house and lands looking well. The house was a long house, neatly thatched, with two big bedrooms apart from the kitchen and an offshoot that was used as the priest's parlour. He had four children, a very hard-working earnest wife and a golden tongue. He wasn't yet forty. He was brown-haired, broadly built, and had a very even temper. He had memorised from his own father an enormous number of stories and songs with which, after persuasion, he regaled the people at wakes and weddings and celebrations. He wasn't a creator, as he told Dualta, he was just a storage vessel used to pass on the beautiful native culture by word of mouth in an unbroken line that stretched back to the mists of time. Dualta liked him. He liked living with him, and paid for his board by working in the fields for him. His eldest was a girl and the next to her a girl, and the two youngest were sons who now that a teacher had appeared like a rainbow in the valley were reluctantly going to school. So, since he owned about thirty acres, and hired out his horse and plough, had many cattle and sheep, he needed help.

They were in on the hayfield, sharpening the scythes, when Carrol straightened himself at the sight of the cutter below in the bay. 'Oh, but there will be fluttering in the bird-houses now,' he said, laughing. He was right about that. When the town woke up and saw the cutter in the bay and the armed sailor guarding the small boat on the shore, as soon as the people had rubbed away the sleep, they scurried about like disturbed rabbits. The owners of the tippling-houses hid their unlicensed whiskey and tobacco in stables and thatches. All smuggled goods went underground, the loot from the shipwreck of last winter found new hiding-places. It was like a cleaning of consciences.

Dualta laughed. They talked about the reason for the cutter. They couldn't make out why.

The hayfield was near the road, so when they heard the sound of feet, coming down from the hills, they leaned on their scythes to look.

The men were a long way off when Carrol understood.

'It's Daxon, by God,' he said. 'They have taken Daxon at last. Well, now, who would have ever thought that they would take Daxon?'

'He is the father of the boy Colman?' asked Dualta.

'Yes, the poor little fellow,' said Carrol. Everyone was sorry then for the boy, but few liked his father, even if they drank his raw whiskey. He was a dour man. Just plain stupid, Carrol said. He had kidnapped a girl from the other side of the hills. Her name was Rafteri. He was a big strong good-looking fellow then. Many brides were kidnapped like that. If a father objected, the suitor took her away with help and hid her a night, and since the father didn't know if she was impaired or not, he either made the best of it or cut her off like a limb from a family tree. Daxon's bride had been cut off. She was only two years married when they found her face down in a stream. She was a person with God anyhow, people said, not quite all in the world. Others said Daxon drove her to it. He was unkind, they said. He brought up the boy like a hare.

'So that was why they came,' said Carrol.

Dualta heard the voice of the boy then, as the men came closer to the field. He walked down to the stone wall bordering the road. He looked. The procession was approaching. Daxon walked in the middle, his face blank, his hands tied. The seven rough men were looking behind them as they walked. They were laughing. The tallest of them was holding off the boy, who was trying to break through them to his father. He couldn't get through the ring. His plaintive voice came over the sound of them. 'Father! O, Father!' Once Daxon spoke. He half turned his head. 'Home, boy, go home! I tell you to go home!' he called. It could be like you would talk to a sheepdog, or it could be that he was moved. Dualta couldn't make out.

'Drive him off,' the Lieutenant called. 'He might lead to a riot.'

The big man caught him by the long hair, raised him and hit his backside with the stick. Dualta had often seen a dog thrashed this way. The sight of the boy like that drained the blood from his head. He jumped the wall and ran to the big man and as the stick rose again he unbalanced him with a poke on the head with the handle of the scythe. The dog was barking furiously. The boy fell in the dust. The big man roared and turned, waving his stick. His six companions joyfully moved towards them. Dualta held the gleaming blade of the scythe high in the air. 'Come on now,' he said.

They paused. His face was white. He was straddling the boy. The Lieutenant turned.

'You can be arrested,' he said, 'for resisting the Revenue.'

'Since when have you started to make war on children?' Dualta asked. 'Are you so weak that a boy may frighten you?'

The Lieutenant looked at him.

'Close up,' he said to the men. 'Keep that boy away,' he said to Dualta.

Then he turned and walked on. The rest of them followed him, reluctantly, the big man rubbing the side of his head. Dualta watched until they were around a bend in the road. Then he felt movement under him. He dropped the scythe and reached for the boy, but he was too late. He was up and off down the road. Dualta followed him. The boy dodged, calling. Dualta grabbed for him, caught his shirt. The shirt tore. 'Colman! Colman! Colman!' he was shouting, pleading. Colman dodged again. Dualta reached a hand and caught his leg. He held on to it. It was like holding a year-old calf. He had to fall on him, to lie on top of him, to quieten him. The dog kept barking at Dualta's heels. Dualta kept saying, 'Colman! Colman! Listen to me.' The boy was wriggling and calling and crying. His whole face was dirty with dusty tears. Finally he lay still. He turned on his front and lay with his forehead on his arms. Dualta stood looking down at him, helplessly. Then he went on a knee beside him. 'You can do no good, Colman,' he said. 'These criminals will injure you.' The clothes of the boy were very ragged, but his flesh was very clean apart from the dust. Dualta thought, I was like that at his age, even if my father was dead. I was alone and I felt desolate, and Uncle Marcus found me. It would be worse to have your father go like that.

The boy was very thin. He could do with feeding. He stood up. Carrol was beside him.

'What will we do?' he asked.

'The priest is away,' said Carrol. 'He will be a hard one to manage. You will have to try the schoolteacher. I hear great accounts of her sense. Maybe she could talk to him. I will see what we can all do otherwise.'

'We are all running away,' Dualta thought. He felt helpless. He didn't know the boy well enough to be in his confidence. Nobody in the valley knew him really. He was like a hare, they said, peering at you from a covert with his ears up.

'I'll do that,' said Dualta.

The boy had stopped sobbing. He was just lying supine. The dog was sitting beside him, now and again licking his ear.

'Colman,' said Dualta, 'get up and come with me.' The boy didn't move. He bent down and raised him to his feet. He stood there, his head down.

'It's all I can think of,' said Carrol.

'Come on, Colman,' said Dualta, taking his hand. It was a thin hand. The boy moved with him as he walked. That was all. 'I'll be back soon,' Dualta said.

Carrol watched them for a while, and then, shaking his head and collecting Dualta's scythe, climbed the wall and went back to the field.

It was a strange sight for the birds, the stick-waving men ahead with their prisoner. People came from the fields to look at them. Now and again a clod of turf came sailing over a fence to spatter the road and once or twice to hit one of the stick-carriers. They did no more than that. It was only half-hearted. The people of the town stood and watched and only jeered. They threw some dirty remarks, but that was all. The Lieutenant could sense that there would be no actual opposition, so he relaxed as they walked towards the shore. After all there was nothing political about it. It was a civil crime, and Daxon was not particularly liked and there were many more in the valley just as adept as he at firing still.

Dualta sighed as he turned at the road that led to the school and walked towards it with his most silent partner.

18

MISS MacMAHON was absolutely distracted.

It is always very easy to dream of an ideal. She thought back to the days when she was discussing with Father Joe what she would do with her life, how she had made up her mind inflexibly to devote it to the welfare of the people, and when she thought of teaching it seemed like an inspired pink dream, like a completed woven tapestry, like a work of art, hanging on a wall. She never really gave thought to what it would be in reality. Words like difficult, hard, grinding, out of environment, sacrifice, loneliness, are simply words until in practice they acquire meaning. They were meaningful now. She could have taught in a town where conditions would have been better, where there would have been people of her own kind within reach, where she could lean on somebody who would understand. Here she was like an odd bird blown in by a storm, among birds with strange feathers, native birds who were foreign to everything she had been brought up with. The life of a convert is hard anyhow, abandoned by those you have left and ignored by the ones you have joined. It was of little use to say that it was bound to involve sacrifice, that pearls of price must be paid for. All these were words, and most times words contain little comfort.

She looked at her class now and her eyes were a little wild, and she was not aware that strands of her hair had come loose and were waving around her face.

She thought it would be all right if she had only girls to deal with. It was the boys that were defeating her. Just their names alone. She was in a more difficult position than the postmaster in the town. You have to know who John Pat Éamon is, or Tom Bán, or Seoirse the Son of the Shoemaker, or Tomás the Son of the Cooper, Jack Kitty Tomás. Mostly they were not the sons of tradesmen at all, but the sons of cottagers or labourers. The eldest boy was sixteen. He was a tall rough youth with a heavy fuzz on his face. It did not make him look attractive. He was Móra the Son of the Tinker. His father was not a tinker. He was a labourer for the Bradishes, but he was handy with pots and sometimes fashioned tin lanterns to hold candles. This Móra was a scourge. He was the most illiterate of the lot, stupid and unsettling. If she was capable of giving him a box in the ear, she would be saved, but she was afraid to do this. For a simple reason, he might hit her back, as his father was well known to do to Móra's mother. He made the other boys unruly.

There was that. The girls she could manage. They were willing. The class was divided into three, readers, spellers and writers. It made itself that way. They were readers if they could afford the books. These were what they called the Reddy May Daisy, *Reading Made Easy*, and the Universal, *The Universal Spelling Book*. They were expensive. They cost three shillings and three shillings and sixpence, from the chapmen or the pedlars and hawkers at the fairs. In fact some of the parents had gone as far as Ennis to buy them when the school was started. They sold a firkin of butter or a bag of potatoes, or turf, or pawned a treasured blanket in order to acquire a copy of these, or Gough's *Arithmetic*. The books were then carefully covered in strong canvas or lambskin with the woolly side out, and a dangling thumbshield. The scholars carefully carried them in their breasts to save them from the disasters of their playtimes.

If they could not afford the books they were writers. They used quills plucked from a goose for this, with the small earthenware jar of ink made from the juice of boiled briar roots or the juice of the blackberry mixed with indigo. That and precious writing paper, also costly, sometimes consisting of the blank pages torn from old books. At this time there was great stealing also of the lead from leaded windows. This lead could be melted and when hot poured on to the tip of a gander's quill to make a fine lead pencil.

For sums they used a slate, smoothed by a sea-stone, on which they could put the figures with shaped limestone. Most of the slates were brought to the carpenter, who framed them like a picture, and they could be cleaned with a spit and the rub of a sleeve.

When she saw all this she knew she was right. There was a terrible thirst among the people for learning. If they themselves hadn't it, they would do anything so that their children would acquire it. She knew the joy in the house the first day that a scholar could go home and be able to read aloud the American, the letter that had come from an emigrant with the precious Ticket in it that could be cashed in the bank in Ennis. All this she heard from the first girl who had done so. How embarrassed they had been before, having a letter that meant everything to them and having to have a scholar come in and read it for them, a neighbour but a stranger, very embarrassing, and here now was cause for rejoicing, one of their own reading aloud to the manner born: 'I take this favourable opportunity of writing these few lines to let you know that I am well and doing well. I work in the day and I get a dollar for this. It is hard but it is not slavery and I am my own man. How I abided it at home I do not know. We eat meat nearly every day but on Fridays, and sugar and tea every day with white bread. I look every man in the eye. I am my own man. I do long for home all the same. Sometimes I do cry and I thinking of it. But what use with the great hardship and the hunger there and men no better than slaves to the landlords? Julia O Brien is well. I do see her now and again. She sends you her best wishes as I do now, with these few dollars which will help to meet the wind for you on Gale Day. If Séan will come out I will save up for the fare for him. He will be well off here even if he will be lonely. There are no Gentlemen here. All are one. There is no lords or gentry in this country that you have to put your hand to your hat for. Indeed I do be thinking of ye when ye don't least suspect it. I finish now, hoping this finds ye as it leaves me in good health and happiness your loving son Joe.'

Miss MacMahon had read this letter and little Margaret's carefully composed reply, dictated by her mother, admonished to cover every bit of paper, as what use was it to send white paper to her son?

Rewarding, thought Miss MacMahon, the fact that she had

to work so hard to improve her Irish, so that she could translate English into Irish in order to make them understand the English. Because they all longed to learn English, feeling that it would put them on a better footing, or at the back of their minds the knowledge that some day if things were really bad they would have to emigrate and join the growing band of their race who were scattering all over the world.

That and cleanliness. Most of them were spotlessly clean even if their clothes were very poor. But some of them came from dirty homes and lice walked on them. How did you get them clean then? Did you put them away from the school on that account? How could you do this?

It was very lonely. She saw little of the Bradishes. How she longed now for their goose-feather beds and their fine food. She had no time. She had to cook and clean and make out lessons, and try to improve her house, this barren-looking place that was merely a shelter from the weather, gaunt and bleak with its unplastered walls.

Móra, the son of the tinker, was droning at the back. He was standing. There were three benches. She let them sit in turns. He was droning an arithmetic table. He was making foolish mistakes. He was thickening his tongue to say the unfamiliar English words. There were twelve other boys. They were all being infected by him. The four that were reciting tables were giggling and aping the way he was saying it. She was at the fireplace. She walked to him. Her voice was quite desperate.

'Móra,' she said, 'if you don't behave I will put you out of the school.'

'What am I doing wrong then, noble lady?' he asked, his thick-lipped mouth open. 'I am only doing what you told me.'

'You are not,' she said angrily. 'You are behaving like an animal.'

'I am not an animal, noble lady,' he said. 'I am only trying to do what you tell me.'

'Don't answer me back like that,' she said, wishing she could hit him so that he became unconscious.

'My father says I must always answer up for meself, noble lady,' he said.

'It isn't your father that's at school. It's you,' she said. 'You are very thick. You should be trying harder than anyone to learn.'

'If you were good you could learn me,' said Móra. 'Isn't it easy to blame me for your own weakness, noble lady?'

'Go out!' she said. 'Go outside at once!'

'I will not, then,' he said. 'Haven't I paid my penny like everyone else? Haven't I brought my sod of turf?'

Now what do I do? she wondered. Should she try physically to get him out? She glared at him, completely helpless, and then this man came in the door, and he said, 'You heard what the teacher said then, Móra, so out you go!' Miss MacMahon was looking at him in amazement.

Móra looked at him. He said a rude thing to him. The next minute he was set back on his heels by a blow from an open hand. Then the young man caught him by the seat of his patched trousers and the scruff of the neck and propelled him out of the door like a bullet. He threw him out there, and he fell in the yard. Móra looked up at him amazed. 'Oh, what my father will do to you!' he said. 'Oh, what I will do to you,' said Dualta, 'if you are not on your feet and running in two seconds.' He made for him, and Móra, frightened now, got to his feet and stumbled and then ran as Dualta made for him. He ran fast. Dualta called after him, 'When you come back, come back like a dog on your knees, tinker's son!'

Then he turned back to the schoolhouse door.

Miss MacMahon was at the door, looking for him with her mouth a little open. There was dawning delight in her face as he went to her. He had never before seen her at such a loss.

'Dualta!' she said. 'Dualta! Where in the name of God did you come from?'

'Why, I came from the field behind, Miss MacMahon,' he said, his pulse racing. 'I brought you . . .' He looked around for his charge. There was no sign of him. 'Oh, God,' Dualta groaned. 'He's gone again. I will have to chase him. Come after us, Miss MacMahon. I will explain.' Then Dualta was gone as swiftly as he had appeared. She went quickly back into the house. The children were disturbed. 'Read and write and use your slates,' she said. 'I will examine you when I return. If one of you moves from his place I will murder you when I come back or I will get the young man to murder you.'

Then she left them. She went around the house. She saw Dualta toiling up the hill behind, chasing the figure of a boy, but in good heart she hoisted her skirts a little and set off after them.

The real effort was gone out of Colman. His flight was only token. When he came to the wall he stopped. The dog jumped it, and then jumped back again and looked at him, his tongue lolling, his tail wagging. Dualta stopped in front of the boy.

'Anyone would think you were a child instead of a nine-year-old boy,' said Dualta.

'I'm ten years,' said Colman.

'Isn't that worse?' Dualta asked. 'Why are you afraid of me? Would I beat you?'

'You took me to school,' said the boy accusingly.

'I did not,' said Dualta. 'I took you to the schoolmistress.'

'Is that different?' Colman asked.

'If it is your desire to remain ignorant,' said Dualta, 'you may do so. Even wild hares have manners among themselves, and foxes are polite. They do not act like you. You are like a wild cat spurning friendship. Will you listen to wisdom?'

'I do not need help from anyone,' Colman said. 'I am able to stand on my feet.'

His tear-stained face, his bright eyes, belied his statement. Dualta felt sorry for him, but kept his face stern.

'It is good to be independent,' he said, 'but even the Pope listens to advice from other men. Even a king has counsellors. Are you greater than those?' He looked down the hill. Miss MacMahon was coming close to them. She looked very well, he thought. Her hair was shining, her cheeks were flushed. Miss MacMahon was pretty, even if she was severely dressed.

'She is young,' said Colman in a surprised voice. Dualta thought she would be the same age as himself, turned twenty. What was she doing here in the name of God, in this valley, with that schoolhouse of children? Was she altogether mad?

They waited for her. She slowed her pace, lowered her dress

and stood in front of them.

'Miss MacMahon,' said Dualta formally, 'this is Colman Daxon. His father has to go away for a time.' His eyes drifted down the valley. Miss MacMahon looked too. She saw the knot of men below, small now with distance. But you couldn't mistake the Revenue men, nor the unusual sight of the cutter in the bay. 'His mother died some years ago. He just wanted to talk to you.'

'I'm pleased to meet you, Colman,' she said. She spoke in English. This seemed to surprise him. She had a soft voice. He looked at her hand and then stretched out his own. He nodded at her. She sat on a stone.

'You don't come to the school?' she asked.

He shook his head. He couldn't confess this, but he had wanted to go to the school, that was why he avoided it so much. But where would he get a penny a week? And he would be ashamed to be seen in his clothes which were so bad. Most Sundays he avoided Catechism classes after Mass, in case the others should laugh at him.

'No,' he said. He looked down. He shuffled his bare feet. The dog was sniffing at Miss MacMahon. He liked what he scented. Suddenly he put his head on her knee. She stroked it. 'Why, he likes you,' said Colman, as if this was a wonder.

'Why wouldn't he, indeed?' she said. 'Amn't I harmless?' She said this in Irish. Her eyes crinkled with laughter. Colman laughed too. He went on his knees beside her.

'I didn't know school people were like you,' he said.

'Did you expect me to be like Napoleon?' she asked. 'With a wooden leg too?'

This amused him. He shook all over with silent laughter.

'Do you beat the children with a bunch of sally rods?' he asked.

'No,' she said. 'I am afraid to beat them in case they beat me back.'

'Oh, you should hit them,' he said. 'Some of them are thick.'

'I'll try,' she said solemnly. 'Tell me, Colman, would you ever be able to help me?'

He looked at her in wonder.

'Me help you!' It was almost a snort.

'Yes,' she said. 'I need help in the worst way. I am on my own. I can't do everything. I wish you would consider this. While your father is away, if you would come to me and do little jobs, like the fire and cleaning and many things, I will try to pay you a little. You can sleep by the fire and eat with me. Only if you wish.'

'Would I have to be at school?' he asked.

'Not necessarily,' she said, 'unless you want to listen in.'

'Sometimes I mind Moran McCleary's sheep,' he said.

'I'm sure you could do that too,' she said.

He dropped his head. He was thinking.

'I will go with you for a while,' he said then, 'to see if I like it. Will that be all right?'

'That's fair,' she said.

He stood up. 'I will go and get my things now, so,' he said. 'I will close my father's house. It would be lonely anyhow for a while until I get used to it.'

'That's true,' she said.

He clicked his fingers at the dog. 'Come, Flan' he said.

'What!' exclaimed Dualta. 'Do you name a dog after the poet?'

Colman laughed. 'He knows that,' he said. 'It is because I admire him.'

'Oh, I see,' said Dualta. 'Some time then I hope you name a dog after me.'

The boy looked at him. 'We'll see,' he said, doubtfully. Dualta laughed.

'I will be with you, then,' Colman said to Miss MacMahon and set off running. He kept his head averted from the road on the right where his father was being taken.

They looked after him for a little, then Dualta turned and looked at her. Her eyes met his firmly.

'You have a way with boys,' he said, 'and men, Miss Una.'

She didn't answer him. She looked steadily at him. Then she spoke. 'You will never know how pleased I was to see you come in that door,' she said.

He sat beside her.

163

'Why?' he said. 'Tell me why you have changed your name. Why you are here. What caused it?'

She plucked a blade of grass. She chewed it with her even teeth, small teeth in a determined chin.

'MacMahon was my mother's name,' she said.

'It is strange,' said Dualta. 'One time, long ago, there was a MacMahon among us. My Uncle Marcus told me of him. He kept a journal. Part of it survived. This amazes me, that it should be your name. But your father? How is he? What does he think?'

'You saw my father last,' she said. She left it in the air. Dualta felt his face flaming.

'Yes,' he said. 'I saw him last.'

'I heard all about it,' she said. 'So you didn't come to our house for a good purpose, did you?'

'I never did anything bad,' he said. 'I liked your father. He wasn't injured through me.'

'I know that too,' she said. 'Is it all a closed book? Why are you here? Are you still mixed up with violent men?'

He thought over it.

'No,' he said. 'Some time I will tell you. No more. That's gone. In a way, it was your father that decided it for me.'

'What brought you to the valley?' she asked.

'What brought you?' he riposted. 'It's inconceivable, a person like you, with all that you have, to be here. What about your own mother's people? Did you not go to them? Why?'

'You can never understand what happens when you cut yourself off,' she said. 'But you must have a purpose. The only thing to do was to teach. I was well educated. I wanted to pass this on, if I could, somewhere that it was really needed. That is why I am here. My friend Father Joe was at Maynooth with Father Finucane. He knew he wanted to set up a school. That is why I am here.'

'But it is not right,' he said. 'A girl like you.' He took her hand, turned up the palm. A small hand, it was cracked from toil. It used to be as smooth as finely ground flour. He remembered the touch of it when he would help her on or off the

164

carriage. The nails were short and some of them broken. 'See,' he said.

'It's hard,' she said. 'Just today, it seemed impossible. I thought, It is no use. I am defeated. I cannot go on with this. It is beyond me. There is no hope of my being able to hold out under it. And then, at the very worst moment, you walked in. I was so happy to see you.'

'You would have been happy to see a tinker,' he said, 'as long as he came from your own valley.'

'That's probably true,' she said. 'But now I am so pleased there is somebody I can talk to here. You won't be running off again, will you?'

He laughed.

'No,' he said. 'This is my last refuge. But there are gentry in the valley, how about them? Can't they be helpful to you?'

'You must always go up in this world,' she said. 'You must never go down, even if you know that in going down you may be going up. It is all very hard to explain. All I can say is that it is lonely to be lost in the middle, and that is why I am so happy to see you.'

'I was talking to Father Finucane too,' he said. 'He has an odd way of challenging you without saying anything. I am going to settle here. I am going to build up a small place. I am going to be part of the people. That's what you must do too. You only know them through their children. Bad. Politicians judge people in the mass. Bad. You have to know themselves, individually, the poet and the storyteller and the singer and the carpenter, the drunken ones and the sober ones and the hypocritical ones and the pious ones. You must get a hint of the culture they carry that goes back thousands of years. You see!' He was excited now, on his knees. 'You must go to wakes and weddings and funerals. You must shout God Save Ireland, and grumble about the landlords. You must shout Up Daniel O Connell, and Freedom, and watch the boys hurling in the fields and the girls dancing at the cross-roads. You must get behind the curtain they draw between the stranger and the one like themselves. You see! That way you will be able to survive and become part of them, since you seem to have thrown in your lot now so completely with them.'

'See,' she said. 'I have set a river flowing.'

'And I myself,' he wondered, 'what can I do? I have knowledge. I had the best teacher in Ireland. I didn't appreciate him then. Well, the best teacher apart from the one in the Valley of the Flowers. So I know a lot of things. I too will pass them on. You see. I will take the boys off your hands. Isn't that an idea? I will teach the boys! I'm not afraid of them hitting me back. I will pound knowledge into them! See! Isn't that an idea? Was that what Finucane meant then? Did he see me like thistledown on the wind, aimless, although thistledown is not aimless since it carries the seed that it will sow. How do you think? Would this please you?'

'Oh, how much, how much!' she said. 'If Father Finucane will pass you.'

His face went blank.

'Pass me?' he asked.

'Yes,' she said. 'He is a wise young priest. He will say, How was it humanly possible to preserve the faith in the land when the people had no priest, no altars, when their heads were worth five pounds to an approver? They established the teachers in the hedge schools. They picked highly moral young people who held Catechism classes in the woods and on the bleak shores. They made use of the fibre of their teachers. That way the faith was held like a pure stream that always flows sweetly to the sea, no matter what obstacles it meets. You see I'm telling you all this. He will test you.'

'I will pass his tests,' he said. 'Now that I know I can do something that I want to do. If necessary I will take the three vows for him, I swear.'

She laughed.

'Don't do that,' she said. 'You might be sorry,' She got to her feet. 'I must go back to my crosses,' she said. 'They will have torn the place apart. I'm so glad you came here, Dualta. I'm so glad we met like this.'

'Not as glad as I am,' he said. 'Things will move now. When I have a little place, I will take Colman off your hands. I will look after him.'

`They walked together towards the school.

There she held out her hand. He took it. 'Come again and talk to me,' she said. 'When your plans are laid.'

'I will,' he said. 'I will bring you on a journey into the hearts of the people. You will never be lonely again in the valley.'

'I'm so glad, so glad, to see you,' she said.

He watched her into the school. He was under no illusions, he thought, as he went back towards Carrol and the scythe. She was pleased to see him on account of her loneliness. What a wonderful girl, to do this thing she was doing! But she always had it in her to do something great. Only who would have thought her greatness would have turned in this direction?

She was a lady, he thought, and the flowers of the valley were the more beautiful for her presence.

19

ON THIS 25th of September, three events coincided to make it remarkable. It was a Thursday, and it was fair day, gale day, and mail day. Naturally people remarked on it, and determined weeks in advance to make it more memorable. Nobody was going to work anyhow and everybody was going into the street town, where from two o'clock in the morning the animals were being driven from many miles away, converging on the town. The roads were built in a great Y, west and east and the south coming down through the valley, while the town itself was huddled in the fork of the Y stretching along the rough sea coast. So from early morning, as far as your eye could see their winding lengths, the roads were packed with people and animals and carts.

Una looked at herself in the small mirror that was set in the window-stool of her room. It was hard to see her face. Dualta had scraped a lambskin, dried it and inserted it in the wooden frame. The light through it was not as clear as glass. All the same she thought her complexion was ruined. She looked healthy enough, but her skin was sunburned and had lost its creamy whiteness except under the neckband of her dress, where it had been protected. She contrasted the two, shrugged, and rubbed the last of the buttermilk into her hands. It didn't do them much good, but they felt softer. She was afraid Mrs Bradish would see them and be scandalised, so she went to the rough chest of drawers and pulled out her last pair of long gloves. She smoothed the front of her dress with her hands, lifted her skirt to look at her buckled shoes. They were still respectable. Then, taking her reticule in one hand and her hat in the other, she went down to the big room. It was tidy. Colman had swept it, put the benches against the wall, banked the fire, rolled his bag of straw, all this before he departed for the town. She sighed, went out of the door, shut it after her on the latch. There was nothing for anyone to steal even if the people were thieves, which they weren't.

It was a nice morning. There had been rain during the night. The ageing world looked washed and temporarily revived. Mrs Bradish had sent her a note, lavender-scented, asking her if she would like to accompany the girls to the town. If she wouldn't mind calling. It was a gentle reminder of her fall from high estate. Una didn't mind. She liked to walk. The rain had settled the dust, so her shoes would not be destroyed. All the same she dodged the many puddles in the potholes of the road. The sun was quite hot, but there was a cool east wind that spoke of more rain. She supposed Dualta would be going to the town. She hoped she would see him there. She didn't see much of him. He came for four hours, and his effect was magical. Before he came and after he went away she could always threaten the boys with him.

She opened the gate to the avenue of the Bradishes, and she told herself as she walked towards the house, I am going to enjoy myself. I am not going to let the woman upset me. I have few holidays. I am going to savour this one. I will be like I was at sixteen, a maiden going to a fair, looking for a ribbon favour.

The open car was standing outside the house. She patted the nose of the quiet horse and went up the steps.

All was confusion in the hall. Maids were running in and out carrying things in their hands. One of them screamed up the stairs, 'The schoolmistress is here, Ma'am!' dropped Una a quick curtsey and departed. Mrs Bradish came rolling down the stairs, like a sailor, Una thought, on a rocking ship.

'Dear Miss MacMahon, how good of you to come! You look very smart,' turning her around, feeling the stuff of her dress with her fingers. 'But your face, dear, you have let the sun get at it. You'll be like one of those horsewomen.' Turning to the stairs: 'Girls! Girls! What's keeping you? Miss MacMahon is here!' They answered, 'Coming, Mother! Coming, Mother!' 'How you can do it, dear, those awful children! How can you stand it? Are you not tired of it?'

'No, Mrs Bradish, I love it. I love the children.'

'But most of them are so dirty, dear. I haven't anything against the poor, but they can make soap.'

'Most of them are very clean, Mrs Bradish. It's only the few and they will benefit from the good example of the others. That's what education is for. To elevate the mind. Everything else follows.'

'But elevate them for what, dear? Why above their station? Will they need arithmetic to feed the pigs, grammar to fork the hay; spelling to manure the potato ridges?'

I must be patient, Una said to herself.

'And now I hear you have a young man down there, teaching the boys as well. An ordinary young man, dear. From the wilds of Galway, I hear. Can that be true?'

'Yes,' said Helen, coming down the stairs, pulling on gloves, 'and a very handsome young man too, even if he is from the wilds.'

'But where would he get the education, Miss MacMahon? Was it the priest put him in on you?'

'No, Mrs Bradish,' said Una. 'He came of his own accord. He is very well educated. Better read than myself. In fact I doubt if there is anyone in this valley, high or low, who could equal him, and nobody who could impart knowledge as he can. I knew him in my father's house.'

'Oh,' said Mrs Bradish, relieved, 'that's different.'

'No, Mrs Bradish, it's not different,' said Una. 'He drove

my father's carriage. He worked in the fields. He helped to make up the accounts.'

'You mean he was just like Tom Keane, our handyman?' she asked, with very raised eyebrows.

'Oh, no,' said Helen. 'Tom Keane is about fifty years old and couldn't spell his own name. This is different. Margaret! Margaret! Please hurry! Margaret is always last. Always last. You look well, Una. Sunburn suits you. If I let the sun at me I'd look like a peeled onion.'

'Ah, Miss MacMahon, so pleased to see you,' said Bradish, coming down the stairs, his arm around Margaret's shoulders. Margaret was his favourite daughter. You could see that. Perhaps because she was the prettiest. She was slender too, where Helen was becoming plump and would be a walking edition of her mother in time to come. 'The girls will take good care of you. I have arranged for lunch to be served to you in Glasby's office. He is my agent, you know. I want the girls to keep an eye on him. You can trust nobody. Just because he knows they are there will make him cautious. So I hope you will have a good day.'

'Thank you,' said Una.

'Let us be off so,' said Helen, going out of the door.

'Be careful, dear,' her mother called after her, 'and watch your sister. Don't be late. A lot of drinking goes on. It's disgraceful.'

Una was down the steps by now. Placid Tom Keane helped her in. He was a greying man, with a moon face, wearing his best clothes. He smiled at her all the same. She taught his daughter, Margaret, who was very bright and had been the first child to go home and read a letter for her mother. Margaret joined them, and they listened for a few moments more to advice and admonitions from Mrs Bradish before they went on their way.

Mrs Bradish said, 'That girl has changed a lot. The first time I saw her I said, there's a lady if ever I saw one. Now she's beginning to look like a dairymaid.'

'Shush, shush, dear,' said her husband, and kept waving his hand until they were out of sight.

'Well, she does,' said Mrs Bradish. 'She must have had common blood in her all the time.'

'Please, dear,' said Mr Bradish, urging her towards the house.

'Thank God! Thank God! Thank God!' said Margaret. 'A whole day to spend on our own, and without Mother. You have saved our lives, Una. If you hadn't come we would have been in a stew-pot. Now watch how I am going to make smoke, like a hot fire.'

'Margaret, control yourself,' said Helen, but her heart wasn't in the rebuke.

Una looked at them. Their eyes were shining. What a dull life they must have, she thought, when this means so much to them!

The main square of the town was jam-packed. Tom had to roar and beg and beseech and threaten with the whip to get a way cleared for the horse. The confusion and sound were too great to distinguish anything. Finally he got the horse to the gateway of the yard of Donoghue's. He was sweating and grateful when he managed to get the carriage in there, and helped the ladies to alight.

'We will be a few hours, Tom,' Helen said. 'Don't get too merry.'

'I will only grease my throat, Miss,' Tom said. 'You can be sure of my behaviour.'

'Drink as much as you like, Tom,' Margaret said. 'You can sing croppy songs for us on the way home.'

'Margaret!' said Helen.

'Pish!' said Margaret. 'Una and I will collect the mail, Helen. We will meet you in Glasby's rooms then.'

'All right,' said Helen. 'Don't get into mischief.'

They parted at the door of the shop. It was a low-built place. They had to go down steps to get into it. It was a long place, as if the end wall had been taken out of two adjoining houses, to make this place smelling of meal and spices and leather, and whiskey.

Their entry had been noticed all the same. A bald-headed man with rolled sleeves, bright eyes and an energetic manner waved to them. 'Ho, Miss Bradish, you are here. Come over that we may open the mails,' he said. Margaret was standing on her tip-toes trying to see over the heads of the people to the counter below. 'Oh,' she said, 'all right, Mister Donoghue!' She went over to him. People made way politely for them. He pulled a heavy leather satchel from under the counter. It was sealed and had a big brass plate in the centre stamped with the insignia HM mails. He opened this ceremoniously and took out the tied bundles of letters. Una could feel the people behind them stretching their necks. She noticed some of the yellow envelopes peculiar to American letters. She heard the 'O-o-oh' of people, and a voice said. 'Caffar, son, is one of the yellows for MacInerney?' Caffer Donoghue looked up. He was severe. 'Have manners now, let you,' he said. 'Let all be done with order.' Outside Una could hear shouts that travelled from one to another for miles. 'The mails is open now.' But they had to wait. She knew it was as severe a protocol as being presented at Court. Personal gentry first, then in order of precedence, gentleman's butler, minister's man, priest's servant, policeman, down the line before the ordinary people were serviced. It was amusing to watch. Margaret took her letters and looked at the envelopes, then she came over and took Una's arm and said, 'Come down here.' Una went with her. This was the serious part of the shop, for the buying and selling. There was a young man here inside a counter, with his sleeves rolled. He could have been Caffar Donoghue except that he had a heavy head of curly hair. They made their way to the counter and when he looked up Una saw that he had a pleasant face. Margaret said, 'I want to do some shopping. Éamon, I have a long list.' He looked and swallowed and a glaze seemed to come over his eyes. Una was astonished. She looked at Margaret. The girl was looking at him smilingly and her eyes were bright. Good heavens! thought Una.

'Yes, Miss Margaret,' he managed to get out. 'Just give me one second, one second, and I'll be with you.' He went back to a door and called, 'Murty! Murty! Come to me! Here, Murty!' Margaret said, 'Isn't he a pet?' Then he came back to them. He could see nobody but Margaret. 'What can I do for you, Miss Margaret?' he asked.

'I'll be back, Margaret,' Una said. She went away. They hardly noticed her going. Oh, what will Mrs Bradish make of that? she thought with great joy. She had to push her way out of the place. A call was coming from inside. 'An American for O Halloran!' she heard someone say. 'Hold it up to the light, Caffar. See if there's a ticket in it.' All the way the call preceded her, hurled from place to place. 'There's an American for O Halloran.' All the way the call until it reached the end of the town and travelled the roads and was lost in the hills.

She walked from one end of the town to the other. Sometimes she didn't walk, but was carried in the press. She did not think there were so many people in Ireland. She had never been in the middle of them like this before. She had sat gracefully in a carriage and waited, or was driven around the outside roads so that she would not be involved. Now she was involved, in noise above all. Everybody was talking, shouting, singing. She thought that at least one quarter of those present were drunk. This was not pleasant. But the majority were not. They bargained their pigs for the rent money, and their cattle and their firkins of butter and eggs and fowl, and they bought from the chapmen and hucksters and tinkers, from the stalls of all descriptions. And they listened to singers and fiddle players and soft flute players, and gob singers, and watched jugglers, and flame-swallowers and fortune-tellers. It was a press of people the like of which she had never experienced. She was caught up in them, in the smell of them, of drink and new wool and polished boots, the smell of foetid breaths and milk and little bits of roasting meat, and fresh-baked cakes. She was nearly squeezed to death.

At this time Dualta was fighting for his future.

Carrol had left the house early. He was selling an in-calf heifer, a collop, a pig, and some sheep. The young people were helping him. Dualta drove the horse and cart with Mrs O Connor and Sheila. Mrs O Connor was selling a firkin of butter, which was four churnings packed into the firkin after being kept cool on a slate in her little dairy. She also had eggs and chickens. She was a tidy woman, well fleshed, fresh-faced, with bright eyes and a silent tongue. There are enough talking tongues in the house, she would say. It was true for her. Sheila, her daughter, made up for her. She was a restless type of girl, moving all the time. Even now in the cart, she was shifting in her seat, moving her feet, grabbing Dualta by the arm. She was dark-haired and one of the prettiest girls in the valley, but she didn't seem to be too aware of it. She waved at people she knew, shouted at some girls that she would meet them at the ribbon stall, and kept up a running advice to Dualta of how he was to handle Clarke.

Clarke was the sort of nemesis hanging over the valley. He was Tewson's agent and he was all-powerful. Dualta had just seen the back of him at Mass. His head looked like one that had been carved out of hard wood placed on thick shoulders. That's all he knew of him, but every tenant of Sir Vincent's was due to meet him today, gale day, in order to pay up their six months' rent, or explain why they weren't able to pay, or to give something to stave off eviction.

Dualta knew what he wanted. He wanted something that nobody else did. He knew it would be regarded as an odd thing if a stranger hardly in the valley set himself up for a place that another local man wanted or was due to be evicted from. After advice and some searching he had hit on the Bacach's place. Nobody wanted this. He wondered why. It was a ruined house. The roof had fallen in. The walls were almost hidden with clumps of briars and winding woodbine. He traced the outlines of the land. They were covered in gorse, the walls fallen, but he saw that five acres of it at least could be made sweet and the other three could be grazed if they were cleared. But it was in a terrible state of neglect. Who would want it? Nobody but a fool. It was that way since Bacach died. He died swinging at the end of a rope from a thorn tree. His own act. He had been a lame man with one short leg. He had been an only child. He was slightly hunchbacked as well. So there was nothing but a life of loneliness ahead of him when his mother died. What girl would look at him with all the sound-legged fellows in the place hotly looking for wives? So Bacach died, and his place was a ruin, said to be haunted. Children were frightened away from it. Only the goats grazed it. When Dualta talked about it, men blessed themselves, then they joked, said that it was a hilly place, and only suited to a bacach, one leg up and one leg down. But would he get it from Clarke? He was freshly shaved. His hair was washed and neatly tied. He wore his best white shirt, short coat, breeches and buckled shoes. He wanted to look respectable.

'Don't be spiky, then,' Sheila was saying, 'like you can be. Don't talk over his head like you do over mine when you want to annoy me.'

'Good, good,' Dualta was saying.

'And I'll meet you afterward,' she said, 'and you can be my escort at the fair and all the other girls will be as jealous as old spinsters.' She caught his arm again, pressed her face against his shoulder. 'Can I tell them all that you are in a fever about me?'

Dualta laughed. Her mother grunted.

'You can if you like,' said Dualta, 'only that I'm in a fever of annoyance about you. How can you expect to get a husband when you go chasing one?'

'I can get as many as I like,' she said, tossing her dark ring-leted hair. 'I think I'm deciding to pick on you, and if you do get the Bacach's place and make it successful, my father will approve of you. Besides you are handsome, and you know a lot, and you set about educating me.'

'What? In the art of love?' he asked.

'Oh, no,' she said. 'I can train you in that.'

'Sheila!' said her mother.

'Innocent love, Mother,' Sheila said.

Dualta noted with amusement the looks some of the young men cast at him. Sitting beside this beauty, sleeping in the same house as her, and he a stranger too!

He dropped them and their goods in the market-place. He had to get down and lead the horse through the throng. He parked the cart in Donoghue's yard, tied the horse to the cart and unloosed a bag of hay for him. Then he shouldered and elbowed his way to Clarke's house. There was a small crowd of people lining up patiently waiting their turn. Further up the road there were people waiting to get into Glasby, who was the

Bradish collector, and up the street Cringe held his rent court personally as agent for the glebe lands on the far side of the valley. He was a bitter one. Small, wizened, he was a pint-sized tyrant. Nobody had a good word for him. His latest venture was to set up a small very neatly built school, the other side of the valley, backed by the sinister Kildare Street Society, where he had installed what he called a Catholic teacher, and commanded the children of his tenants to attend his school, under pain of all sorts of penalties. His teacher was a thin-faced young man with skin eruptions on his face who asked the children if they really believed the Blessed Virgin had only one child. Cringe was building a lot of tension over that side.

The people were silent going into Clarke's. They were clutching purses, turning their backs and counting money. Dualta finally got into the first room, and finding a vacant stool sat in the corner and watched. He didn't want to see Clarke until the regular tenants had been with him. He watched the procedure. It made him burn with anger, but he swallowed it. There was this room. It was occupied by Clarke's brother-in-law, a thin man with a stringy neck. He was George Shields. Men said he was the long shadow of Clarke, like the way a butty powerful man can throw a long shadow when the sun is descending. He sat at a table and smiled and checked off their names. Ah, yes, Tim Mahon and Dave Lynch. He hummed and hawed, and affected to be so surprised when they slipped him a 'compliment' of two shillings and sixpence, or five shillings. It all depended on the amount of your land. So nice of you to remember my work. Aren't the people very friendly? I am complimented. Sometimes a poorer worried man slipped a little more on the table and bent down and talked into his ear. He would h'm and ho and hum and say 'I'll see now', and go through the room at the back and return saying, 'You'll have to see him yourself. It might be all right. Maybe it will be all right. He's in a good mood today.'

After George came Julia. She was Clarke's wife. She was in the next room. She was a fat jolly woman with a broad smile. She too was nearly overwhelmed with the compliments. A chicken or a goose or two pats of butter wrapped in cabbage leaves, or eggs, all adding up to sizeable sums. So apart from rent of land, rent of house, tithe tax, cess tax, turbary rent, you had also to worry about the 'compliments' to the agent's relations. It's part of life, he told himself. There is nothing dishonest about it. People are normally generous. They like out of pure generosity to compliment people.

'I can hear your teeth grinding,' said a voice beside him. He turned in surprise. Cuan was standing there. He looked well, but grim. Dualta got to his feet. He took the other's hand, pumped it. 'I'm so glad to see you, so glad to see you,' he said. Cuan said with raised eyebrows, 'We don't live a mile apart.'

'I haven't had much time,' said Dualta.

'Speak truth,' said Cuan.

'Pilate wasn't the only one to ask what is truth,' said Dualta.

'You cut me out of your life,' said Cuan. 'You want to become respectable, forget the past?'

'No,' said Dualta. 'I want to find myself alone. Then when I am what I am, you and I will meet again.'

'You will not be tempted then, later?' said Cuan. 'When you are responsible? When you have picked a girl and raised a family on her? I hear you are with Carrol O Connor's daughter.'

'You are more human,' said Dualta. 'You listen to gossip now.'

Cuan laughed. 'I feel better,' he said. 'I am rested. Whatever stimulation I need I get from my brother Flan, arguing with him. He asked for you. You should see him. Don't become too much of a bogtrotter or a teacher of children. You could decay.'

'No,' said Dualta. 'Children keep your mind alert. They want to know.'

'Why are you here?' Cuan asked.

'I am looking to rent a place,' said Dualta.

'Oh-ho,' said Cuan, 'you must have the child-bearer picked already. Why are you waiting? Come now. I am here to pay my brother's rent. Come with me!' Orders again. Dualta shrugged, followed him.

'I am McCarthy,' said Cuan to George Shields. 'I am the brother of Flan. I don't believe in bribery. There's nothing

177.

you can do for me.' They left George with his mouth open and went into the next room. Here was Mrs Clarke. She was alone. She was looking around at her compliments. No wonder. They were piled high and a joy to behold.

'Are you Clarke's wife?' Cuan asked her. At this gruffness the joy went out of her face. She was like a child deprived of sugar.

'Yes,' she said, 'I am Mistress Clarke.' She always called herself that. She was unaware of the jokes it gave rise to. She had no children. They said, perhaps if Clarke had a wife instead of a mistress he would have a family.

'I am the brother of Flan McCarthy,' said Cuan. 'We have no chickens, butter, eggs, geese. All we can give you is our good wishes and hope for a happy death.' He walked past her to the sanctum and walked in. Dualta thought he was rude. He felt like stopping and consoling the woman whose soft face was becoming blubbery. But the action had started. He followed Cuan.

Clarke was ushering out a tenant by a door that led onto the street. Cuan stood inside the door, Dualta beside him. Clarke turned. Like all butty men he was deceptively tall. He had a strong square face with thick eyebrows. A hard man to daunt, Dualta thought. A man completely assured of his own power. He stood like a tower on the sacred rights of private property. He was always within his rights.

'I am McCarthy,' said Cuan. Clarke looked at him. 'Ah,' he said. 'I have heard that name before. Many years ago a bailiff had it beaten into him. Are you the same man?' He went and sat down behind a table. The table was weighted with money-bags.

'Past events have nothing to do with the present,' said Cuan. 'I have come to pay my brother's rent. Here it is! I wanted to have a look at you.'

Clarke emptied the little canvas sack and counted the coins, slowly, meticulously. 'It seems all right, for this year,' he added. 'I wondered if he would be able to scrape it together. I'm not sure I like you living with your brother. You are a trouble-maker. Don't make trouble in this valley, or you and your brother will go out of it on the back of your necks.'

Cuan didn't speak. He leaned both his hands on the table. He bent down in silence until Clarke raised his head and looked at him. Dualta could imagine the look in Cuan's eyes.

'You want to live?' Cuan asked. Clarke didn't blench, but all the same Dualta thought his composure wasn't quite as certain. He was looking into the blazing eyes that meant what they spoke. Dualta knew the look.

He didn't answer Cuan's question.

Cuan said, 'I am dangerous, Clarke. I am indifferent to death. I am indifferent to you, or the powers behind you.' He walked to the door. Dualta knew from the way he walked that his whole body stiffened with rage. So did Clarke. He turned at the door.

'I will see you outside, Dualta,' he said. He closed the door softly after him. Clarke watched the closed door. Then he turned his eyes to Dualta. Dualta thought, Cuan has really put me in the briars now.

'You are a friend of his?' Clarke asked.

Dualta debated. 'Yes,' he said.

'You are teaching in the school?' he asked.

'Yes,' said Dualta.

'Do you teach the boys treason?' Clarke asked.

'No,' said Dualta, 'just reading and writing and arithmetic.'

'They can be as dangerous as gunpowder,' Clarke said. 'What do you want from me?'

'I want to rent the Bacach's place,' said Dualta. Clarke's eyes opened wide. Then he threw his head back and laughed.

'By God,' he said, 'that's a good one. What do you want it for?'

'I want to bring it back to life,' said Dualta, 'so that I can make a living on it.'

'You know what it's like?' Clarke asked.

'Yes,' said Dualta.

'Do you expect to get it cheap?' Clarke asked.

'Yes,' said Dualta.

'You won't,' said Clarke. 'You will get it at one pound seven shillings an acre.' Dualta felt as if he had been kicked in the stomach. How to find rent like that and make enough to eat

179

would be a terrible challenge. Clarke was looking at him. He expected him to refuse.

'If I get a ten-year lease,' said Dualta, 'I will take it.'

'Tenant at will,' said Clarke.

'No,' said Dualta. 'You know it will take at least five years to bring it to anything. After another five it will be something. I don't want to be kicked out of it as soon as I have made it into a decent place. It's that or nothing.'

He didn't think he would get away with it. But Clarke thought. He was constantly being pressed from the agent in Dublin who was pressed by Tewson in London. He was being squeezed. This which was earning nothing would now earn something.

'All right,' he said. 'I'll have the papers drawn. You will have no leeway. Rent will be paid every six months. Miss one gale day and you are out. You understand that?'

'Only too well,' said Dualta.

'Right,' said Clarke. Then he called, 'Send in the next one, Julia.' Dualta was dismissed. He walked to the door. He knew Clarke's eyes were on his back. He didn't care. He had got what he wanted.

He stood outside the door in the sun, and while he felt pleased he also felt that a great burden was now placed on his shoulders. He thought that now he was at the beginning of being a common man.

Una had come up to the town on the opposite side. Having failed to find Dualta, she was going to the inn where Glasby had his rooms. For a few moments, like a calm stretch in the middle of ruffled lake waters, the crowds between her and the other side of the road faded away and she saw Dualta on the street, standing in contemplation, his head bent to one side, his hands on his hips and a furrow between his brows. She watched him. She raised her arm and was just about to shout his name when a girl came running from the right and stood in front of him, one hand on his arm. She saw his face coming from meditation to awareness. She thought he had a mobile and expressive face. The girl was asking him something. She was a most pretty girl. Dualta smiled and answered her, and there in the middle of the street, throwing decorum to the winds, the girl flung her arms around his neck and hugged him. Dualta seemed to enjoy it. He laughed and didn't avoid her lips. Una lowered her arm. She thought it only right that Dualta should have a girl, particularly a pretty girl like that. She had heard about her, Sheila O Connor. Their names were being linked. Well, it was time for Dualta to settle down. It would make a man of him, and she was one of his own kind, though hardly very bright, she imagined from the look of her, but then what countryman, even a countryman like Dualta, above the average intelligence and education, wanted a girl to be a genius? As long as she was pretty and knew how to milk and rear hens and feed pigs, what more did they want? Una was surprised at the leaden feeling. It was just that she had known him for a long time, it seemed, and he was such a help with the school and she wondered if he would continue to help her if he became a family man. She saw an elderly woman, an old edition of the girl, come up and rap her on the back, and almost pull her away, expostulating, and Dualta begging for forgiveness. The woman was looking around, hoping nobody had seen the shameless behaviour of her daughter. But many had and were grinning broadly.

Then Una saw Colman. He was running into the cleared space. His face was red, his thin fists were clenched. There was a man and his companions there in the middle of the street. Talking and laughing. They carried sticks in their hands or under their arms. Colman bent to the ground. He took up a handful of the madder of the street. He shouted 'Gately! Gately!' The big man turned and as he did so he got the fistful of dirt straight in the face. Colman didn't stop here. He kept running and he beat at the near-blinded man with his fists, and kicked at him with his bare feet. Then one of his companions reached out and hit the boy on the head with his hand and he fell back on the ground.

Una was already running towards him shouting 'Dualta! Dualta!' but by the time she reached him and bent over him she was involved in a welter of legs and shouts and clashing sticks. It was as if Colman's cry of 'Gately' had been the awaited signal for battle. There were great cries and shouts and hurroos as the factions of near-drunken men ran from each side with swinging sticks, and Una, kneeling on the ground over Colman, was suddenly the centre of a circle of bloody violence.

Dualta was startled as he heard her calling his name. He looked up. He was in time to see Colman on the ground and Una running towards him. Then he saw the men running from his left and Gately's men lining up, pushing Gately behind them, as both sides met and swung their heavy sticks. He was furious. A faction fight. They were looking for it of course. They were waiting for it. The curse of God on them, he thought, disgracing the country, shaming their own people. This illiterate desire for senseless violence. Would it ever be rooted out of them? Thinking this as he shoved and pushed his way through them, bending, dodging, holding an arm over his head, receiving a blow on his arm that nearly paralysed it. He could see their faces, squinting eyes, open mouths. Hear the cursing, the great shouts, the blows of sticks falling on skulls. Spatters of blood fell on the back of his hand. With disgust he rubbed it on his coat. He hit out and used his feet. He could hear the screaming of women; young girls screaming as they ran from the fight in fear, and older women screaming at their husbands, as well they might, 'Come back! Come back!' thinking of the split scalps that would have to be tended, the wounds and the embarrassed shame when the hot blood cooled and the drink-fumes left the head.

He bent over her, who was bent over Colman. 'God!' he shouted at her. 'What were you thinking coming into the middle of this? Come on!' He raised her. He held her in front of him with one hand around her and walked her away. He shouted at Colman, 'Hold my coat!' He felt him grasping it and made his way through them. Una couldn't believe what she was seeing. She would never forget the looks on the faces of the men, these men she had been feeling so good about, kindly people, respectful. Faces squinting in hatred, low atavistic growls coming from their throats, the bright blood on the sunburned faces.

He pressed them against a clear space when he reached Clarke's house. He sheltered them at the wall, holding off the violence behind with his hands held over them, pressed against the white-washed mortar.

'Colman,' he said, 'I could murder you. You see what you started.' The boy's eyes were wide. 'Look at the shirt I got for you,' he went on. It was torn and dirty. His face was close to Una's. He saw the bewilderment and fear on it and complete distaste. 'You see what you are living with?' he asked. 'Now, won't you go home to your father? What use is it? What use when at the turn of a wrist things like this can arise in all of us?'

'Their children will not be like this,' she said. She had to shout. 'If we educate them.'

'Can you hold back the sea?' he shouted angrily. 'Can you bring the hills low?'

'Somebody can,' said Una, noting the change in the shouting.

Still protecting them with his arms, Dualta turned his head.

The red-headed priest was fighting his way right into the middle of them. He was shouting. His red hair was flaming, part of his stock had been torn away. His fists were rising and falling like flails. He seemed to be swimming to the centre of the disturbance. Shouting 'Animals! Creatures! Oh, animals, stop it! I tell you to stop it!' Where was the policeman? Dualta wondered. Everyone knew where he was. He would be in his house with the door bolted. There was only himself. He would have to send for help to the next town, and if things got very bad to Ennis or Galway. Now he was in a safe place. Dualta watched.

By sheer force the priest got to the centre of them. He held his arms out from him with the knotted fists at the end of each arm and swung around, shouting 'Enough! Enough! Enough!' When he had cleared a space they fell back from him. But they were not finished. They were ready to clash again, priest or no priest. He turned his back on the town faction. He faced Gately. He pointed his finger. He walked towards them. 'Go back!' he said. 'Start going back, or I'll curse you to the seven generations. Are you men? Look at you! Like the slaughtered blood-stained beasts in the shop of a butcher.'

Dualta admired him. His anger seemed to give him height.

There were lights flashing from his eyes.

'Go home, Gately,' he said, 'and bring your gang with you. You hear. Don't come near this town again or I'll have you arrested. You hear!' He turned back to the others. 'You!' he said, walking towards them. 'Are you brutes or respectable married men? Are you Christians or are you pagans? What has become of your faith and your holy religion, or your families and all you are suppose to hold dear?'

He had won. He had created a space. He had created a pause. Dualta saw the madness dying from their faces. Sheepishly some of them wiped away the blood with the palms of their hands. One of them turned and went away. Then another and another. Of the townsmen there were wives waiting for them with arms akimbo. Then the priest turned back to the Gately contingent. He said nothing to them. He just stood there, silently, an angry man with a torn stock, a little colour coming back into his face. They shuffled and looked down and then half turned and walked away from him. They shouted threats. 'We'll get you, men! Don't come over.' But when the shouting was started the fighting was over. They pulled away in a body.

The priest turned and came over to them. He looked closely at Una.

He said: 'I saw what you did. It was a reckless thing, but you were a brave girl. You, Colman, I will talk to you again.' Colman hung his head, shuffled his bare feet. His mouth was a thin line. 'You will have to forgive us,' the priest said to Una. 'There are reasons, reasons, so many reasons. Soon these faction fights will be no more. Don't judge us on them. I am afraid you will go away.'

'I will not go away, indeed,' she said.

'You must take the bad with the good,' he said. He sighed. 'There is such a lot of bad.'

'And such a lot of good,' she said, but she was watching the pretty girl who had come back and was holding Dualta's arm and looking into his face and saying, 'Oh, Dualta, Dualta, are you all right? Did nobody hit you? I hope nobody hit you.'

20

IT IS a little trickle in a high place that makes a great river flowing to the sea. In the same way, but almost as fast as the journey of the sun across the arm of the sky, men heard before nightfall in this remote place that Daniel O Connell was going to stand in the election for Clare. The sitting member, Vesey-Fitzgerald, was invited into his Cabinet by the Duke of Wellington, known derisively by O Connell as The Great Captain, and so he would have to stand for re-election. Vesey-Fitzgerald, they said, was no more corrupt than any of the others, but he had used the cover name for corruption, patronage, with great skill, so that there was no second or third son in the Army or in places of patronage in the whole of the county, with all their families, who wasn't under geasa, as they say, to his favour. Whom would they get to stand against him? There was nobody in the Catholic Association, and no presentable Protestant, who would dream of doing it. So O Connell put himself up and wrote out his address, and it was like a fire burning in a dry field of corn.

Father Melican sent for his administrator. Since his accident with the lightning he lived mostly in his book-lined study sunk in a leather-covered chair with a pair of crutches handy. He had been a big athletic man and sitting so much had made him weighty. He was surrounded by books, magazines and papers, which were his only source of extravagance. He was always looking for his papers and never able to find them, because as soon as he had finished with one the housekeeper Bridie always removed it, and passed it on so that it went the rounds of the place. Newspapers were too expensive for most people, so everyone was grateful to Father Melican for being a subscriber. When the paper had passed through many hands it ended up with the dressmaker, who used it for cutting out patterns, so it was cheap at the price.

Father Finucane, who lived in a small house near the church, left his account-books, put on his coat and hat (Father Melican insisted that his young priest be properly dressed) and went over to the neat two-storey stone house of the parish priest. He paused outside the study door and tidied himself and tried to put a look of gravity on his countenance before he knocked and entered. He saw Father Melican's eyes checking over him.

'You wanted to see me, Father?' he asked.

'Have you heard about O Connell?' Father Melican asked.

'I have indeed,' said Father Finucane. 'Isn't it wonderful? Isn't it the best thing that has happened in history? I hardly slept last night thinking of the excitement and the wonder of it.'

'Your attitude is wrong, Father,' said the old priest. His lips were tight. The spontaneous joy went out of the young priest's face.

'In what way, Father?' he asked.

'It's nothing to do with us,' said Father Melican. 'It can do nothing but bring trouble and confusion on the whole county. It will excite men to foolish dreams, and turn tenants against their landlords, dangerously. You see this. We must stay out of it.'

Father Finucane looked at him. He sat carefully down on a chair, his hat in his hands.

'Father,' he said gently, 'we cannot stay out of it.'

'We are here to care for men's souls,' the priest said. 'Do you think we should be like the Wexford priests, leading men with pikes in their hands to death and destruction? I have thought over this, Father Finucane. We must stay out of it.'

If O Connell wins this election,' said Father Finucane slowly and carefully, 'we will get Catholic Emancipation.'

'We will get that without the demagogue,' said the priest. 'It will evolve. Time we couldn't put a steeple on a church. Now we can. Time we lived in the hedges and the woods. Now look at us. It will improve. It must not be forced.'

Father Finucane looked at him. Father Melican had been ordained on the Continent. There he had been indoctrinated with the terrible lessons of the French Revolution. He was for passive peace, quiet advance, slow evolution. Father Finucane could understand him, but he found it hard to sympathise with him.

'Father,' he said, 'I do not agree with you. Ninety per cent of the people want to live quiet and peaceful lives. It is always a small minority that can excite them to blood. It has happened before. They are wary of violent men. Of seven million people at least two-thirds are living in wretched conditions of poverty and hopelessness. This man has arisen. He doesn't want their blood. All he wants from them is courage and resolution. If he can get seven million people to say Yes, all together, just peacefully saying together, We want change, then change will have to come. This is his testing time. He is the first Catholic to stand up and talk back. He is the first one to test their laws and find loopholes in them. This is a chance for the seven million to find their voice. We must not stop them. We must be with them.'

'No,' said Father Melican vigorously, 'you will leave this alone.'

'There is scarcely a priest in the whole country who will not urge them to do the brave thing,' said Father Finucane.

'What the rest of them do is nothing to do with us,' said the old priest. He bent down. He got a poker and banged the smouldering turf in the hearth. 'I absolutely forbid you to encourage revolt against the landlords,' he said.

Father Finucane put his hand into his pocket and took out a letter. It had been written by himself.

'Here, Father,' he said, 'is my resignation as administrator. It is addressed to you. I am also sending one to the Bishop.'

The old man craned his neck to look at him. His heavy face got red under his head of white hair.

'You wouldn't do that?' he asked.

'I would,' said the young priest. 'Also when I have resigned, I will consider it my duty as an Irishman to encourage them, in my private capacity.'

The old priest looked at his resolute face and the letter in his hand. He shook his head. He put his hand up to his forehead.

'This is sad,' he said. 'We are generations apart. How can we

187

communicate? Tell me, your contemporaries from Maynooth, do they feel like you too?'

'Most of them feel like I do,' said Father Finucane. 'O Connell is the man, and this is the acceptable time.'

'I don't understand,' the priest said. 'When he was young O Connell was a rationalist. Hume, Godwin, Voltaire, Rousseau, and Paine were better known to him than the Book of Genesis. He has killed a man in a duel. He is a man who plays on people's emotions with the power of words. He has insulted institutions and men of high station with farmyard invective. And you say this is the man for the acceptable time.'

'Have you met him, heard him speak, Father?' the young priest asked.

'No! No! No!' said the old priest vigorously.

'Then don't judge him,' said Father Finucane. 'You want to see him. He is the yeast in a mass of dough. You can see the cake baking. People know. They cannot tell you why, but they know. He is the man who is making them a nation and he wants nobody to die for him. They have never seen his like before and probably they never will again.'

'I cannot accept your resignation,' the old priest shouted.

'You will have to, Father,' he said. 'I am determined.'

'Not because of that,' the old man said. 'It's because I like you. You are a good young man How could I get better than you? Go away! Do what you like! I am not to be responsible! People must know that. I have nothing to do with it. I didn't approved of it. We are not here to build temporal kingdoms.' He took up a book. He was agitated. The book was wrong side up, Father Finucane saw. 'But don't blame me afterwards. You know where I stand. I want to hear nothing. Know nothing. Now! You have heard me! Go away. And don't neglect your duties. Get that woman Bridie to bring me my tea. She spends more time gossiping than working. Tell her the fire is going out, like my own. I am old. I cannot remember when the blood was hot in my veins. Do what you like! Disobey your parish priest. That's right. Off with you. That's the kind of man Maynooth is turning out. No culture, if you ask me. None of the finer things of life.'

When he looked up, Father Finucane was gone. The old priest let the book drop in his lap. He looked at the smouldering turf, and sighed, and then called, 'Bridie! Bridie!'

Looking for Dualta, Father Finucane tied his horse under the famous thorn-tree. It was the first time for many years that anyone could get that close to it, not to mind tying a horse off it, he thought with a grin. The jungle of briars and hazel had been cleared all around the approaches to the house, opening up a wide yard. He could see the round black spots where the great piles had been burned. The collapsed roof had been cleared away, some of the black beams salvaged and erected, with bright new ones. These had been branched and scrawed ready for the pointed sticks of the thatcher. He was curious. He went into the house. There was a new frame but no door as yet. It had been a good house. It was completely bare. Light was still coming through the scraws. But it was wide and roomy. There was a room behind the open fireplace, a big comfortable room, and another smaller one off the kitchen at the other side. He came out of the door again. He was looking across the valley. It was at his feet and the rocky hills on the other side were level with his eyes. The sea was on his left. There was a heavy rain-cloud scudding across it like a rippling cloth. He went around the back of the house. The yard was cleared. There were three small houses, for a pig and a cow and a small dairy. They had been cleaned out, roofed afresh with scraws, and white-washed. He went through the yard and looked up the hill. He could see the figure of Dualta in a small field way up. He could see the fields that he had already passed through, with great labour, he judged, all cleared of scrub, stone walls rebuilt. It seemed impossible that one man could have rescued so much from wildness and decay.

He started to walk up the hill through the fields. The sun was blotted out. The squall of rain caught him, but it was June and the rain was warm. He got within a few yards of Dualta. Watched him. He was uprooting young hazels with a matlock. He was wet from the rain but he was intent on his job. Three tools he had, a matlock, a spade, and a crowbar. The exposed parts of him were browned by the sun.

'You'll kill yourself, Dualta,' said Father Finucane.

Dualta straightened himself and turned.

'I will not,' he said. 'You have only to do this once, and then you keep it clean with little labour. In two weeks Carrol will give me his horse and plough and I will turn it to the sun for the first time in twelve years. A little more labour and it will be as fruitful as a tinker woman. Then I will rest and just look at it.'

'You have done great work,' said Father Finucane. 'I hope you don't lose it all again.'

'I won't lose it,' said Dualta.

'Daniel O Connell is standing for Clare,' said the priest.

Dualta's eyes widened. 'He is! Is this true? Where did you hear it? This is of great account! Is it true?'

'It is true,' said Father Finucane, 'and you are a forty-shilling freeholder. You have a vote.'

Dualta looked at him closely. 'Now I see what you meant,' he said.

'It will be a terrible fight,' said the priest. 'How do you feel?'

Dualta dropped his head. He put the handle of the implement under his arm. He leaned on it. After a while he looked up.

'My heart went cold,' he said.

'Many men's hearts will go the same,' said the priest. 'Tell me why? What will they do?'

'It meant little to me before,' said Dualta. 'Now, with all this!' He waved his hand at the reclaimed land. 'It's easy to be free when you have nothing to lose.'

'But you are safe, you have a lease,' said the priest.

'I have a lease,' said Dualta, 'with a lot of small writing in it. Don't forget the landlords interpret the law. They are the judge and jury. They can read the writing whatever way suits them. I think of this and I am afraid. Most men will be. O Connell is asking a lot from them!'

'I am glad to see you have changed to a cautious man,' said Father Finucane.

Dualta laughed. 'Only a part of me. I remember. I saw forty-shilling freeholders being driven to the vote like cattle to a fair.

190

We jeered at them. We baaed at them like sheep. Now I know how they felt. I will not feel this way. But will I be on my own? How many will come with me? Can you say?'

'No,' said Father Finucane. 'There are eighty-seven voters in the valley. They will have to fight their fear. We must help them. There is not a lot of time. This is Monday. Next Monday will be nomination day and the polling will start on Tuesday. It leaves us little time. It is the opportunity of a lifetime. We must grasp it.'

'Then let us start now, in the name of God,' said Dualta. He picked up the spade and the crowbar. The rain-squall passed and the sun burst on the valley, for a moment reflecting from millions of raindrops, almost blindingly.

'The sun has come out,' said Dualta. 'That's a good sign. What will we do? Will we talk to everyone? Do all men know?'

'They will know by now,' said Father Finucane. 'They will be bursting with talk. They must get a lead. You are a good talker. You have won your way into their affections with your teaching of their children. You see! They will trust your word. They have seen what you are doing with this property.'

'Carrol O Connor and Moran McCleary will be with us,' said Dualta. 'They have a lease of two lives.'

'It is the men that have everything to lose that we must persuade,' said the priest.

Dualta put his tools in the empty house. He took his coat from there and pulled it on.

'You have done great work,' the priest said. 'Nobody but you knew what a grand place this was. You will live on a high hill. You must not be like the poor Bacach. You must marry and make the place bright with the laughter of children.

Dualta laughed.

'Nobody will have me,' he said. 'I am too literate for some, and too foreign for others. I will be like the poor Bacach, biting my nails waiting for a princess to come in the door.'

'I know many girls would be glad of you,' the priest said as he untied the horse.

'When they get to know me better,' said Dualta, 'they shy away like colts. I have no magic attraction.'

191

The priest mounted. 'Get up behind me,' he said. 'You won't be a bachelor.' Dualta leaped up behind him. The horse was gentle. He ambled off with his double load. 'Do you remember our first conversation?'

'I remember,' said Dualta. 'I feel good.'

'I see the children's games,' said the priest. 'Now they play at school. The teacher and the children. The man teacher, the master, always speaks with a Galway accent, and the mistress speaks in parody the beautiful precise English of Miss MacMahon. You like Miss MacMahon?'

'I like Miss MacMahon very much,' said Dualta.

'You had met her before then?' the priest asked. Now, how did he figure that out? Dualta wondered.

'Yes,' he said, 'I had met her before.'

'And yet you are not too friendly?' said the priest.

'Oh, yes we are,' said Dualta. 'I work a lot. Running for a few hours to the school and running back to the fields and the house, it is little time I have.'

'And Sheila O Connor is a nice pretty girl,' said the priest. Dualta laughed at him.

'Are you a matchmaker then?' he asked.

'I want to keep you in the valley,' he said. 'You are good for it, like Miss MacMahon. She is worth harvests. She does not know her value. Life is hard on her away from people of her own kind. She would be a great loss.'

'Let us think about the election,' said Dualta.

'We'll divide the valley,' said the priest. 'You take the west and I'll take the east. Parcel the place. We must be victorious, here, anyhow, whatever happens in other places. Sunday after Mass will be the testing time. We will see the fruit of our work. I'll drop you here at O Connor's. God guide you. Be eloquent. You have a good cause. Use it. On to victory!' He waved his hand and galloped away. Dualta watched him for a time and then he started to run into O Connor's yard and he was shouting: Wake up! Wake up, the O Connor clan! O Connell is standing for Clare!' He frightened the chickens and the grubbing pig and brought a bark from the dog and the astonished face of Mrs O Connor from the dairy.

It was a small chapel. Two pointed windows in each side wall, a pointed window behind the altar, and a square doorway. It was built of rubble and mortar. Inside it was peeling. It was damp. Patching could never save it. There would have to be a new one. Each family in the parish was paying a halfpenny a week into the fund for one. It would take a long time before it would reach the stage where they might begin. It didn't hold half the people. The rest were outside at the door, around the windows, which were open to let the voice of the priest and the sound of the little bell bring solemnity into the air. Father Finucane knew it was too small. Every year there were more and more children being born. That was part of the trouble. If a family had half an acre they could grow enough potatoes to feed them for a year. So when sons and daughters were marriageable, they got married. Their fathers cut off another bit of their holding, they built a small house and they were away. It was rare in the parish for anyone not to be married before they were twenty-one. It was good for morals, he knew, but bad for congestion. Half the holdings in the valley were sub-let and sub-sub-let. No wonder a third of the people couldn't fit into the chapel.

He was trying to divert his mind from his worries thinking about these things when he had finished Mass and was about to turn and address them. He debated if he would take off his vestments first or not and decided not to. Vested he might appear to have more authority.

He turned to them abruptly. The coughing shushed. They shished the people outside. Young men clambered up on the windows. The first people his eyes found were the Bradishes, sitting in the front seat. The face of Mr Bradish was grim. Over in the other front seat, Clarke sat with his family. His hands were folded across his chest. One thick leg was crossed over the other. It wasn't a good attitude, but it was typical of him.

'You have searched your hearts,' he said. 'You know the cause. There is a Catholic standing for Clare. You are Catholics. If he was a bad Catholic, you would know. He is not. He is a good man. He is the first one for many years who is capable of bringing you freedom for the practice of your religion. You have a measure of freedom now, but not in law. He will make your freedom lawful. You must pay for all good things. Nothing good can be gained without sacrifice. You are afraid. You must conquer your fear and do what is right. Many elections there have been no contests. Powerful men have come together and said: Such a one will be the member for Clare. And so it has been. Now there is a contest. You have the privilege of exercising your vote, eighty-seven of you. You can be eighty-seven heroes, honest men, able to live with yourselves whatever the consequences, or you can be eighty-seven weak men who will have to live with the knowledge that you have voted against history. We will start the march for Ennis tomorrow morning. It is a long way to go. It is a sacrifice. I will be at the cross-roads. I will lead whoever is going to vote for the Catholic candidate. The others can follow their landlord's representative. For my part I will never by word or deed or look or act condemn any man whose conscience or fear makes him vote at the dictates of his landlord.'

He was interrupted. 'No, then, but we will!' a voice shouted from outside. Dualta had been listening. He was at the door-way. The voice came from behind him. He knew it. The voice of Cuan. He turned to look. Cuan was with Moran McCleary and his wife. She spoke then: 'Hurrah for O Connell!' she shouted. She was a dark-haired woman, with heavy hair pulled back on her head. She had a strong handsome face. 'O Connell and Freedom!' her husband Moran shouted. People were surprised. Moran was known as a quiet man.

'Deeds speak louder than words,' said the priest. 'You have until tomorrow morning to think over it. Think over it prayerfully. I will be waiting at the cross-roads.' He had spoken very quietly. That was against his nature because with the red hair he was impulsive and quick enough to anger. Dualta thought his words had been telling. There were only a few seats in the church. People were rising to go. There was shuffling at the back. It was customary for the ordinary people to make a lane and let the gentry out first before they followed.

'You will wait a minute!' said the voice of Clarke. He was

194

standing up facing them. His voice brought tension into the chapel. Father Finucane went on disrobing at the altar.

'I didn't think a priest would use the altar for politics,' said Clarke. 'Since he has and I am a member of this church, I think I have the same right. A priest may be a good guide to heaven but he can't claim to be a good guide to the House of Commons. Priests should stick to their prayer-books. That is my opinion. I'm not afraid to state it. I have here a letter from your benefactor, the man who has provided you with fields and land and food for over a hundred years. You will listen to it.' He cleared his throat. He rustled the paper of the letter.

'My dear tenants,' he read. 'Here in London I have heard with dismay that that good man Vesey-Fitzgerald is being opposed by Counsellor O Connell. I wish you to understand that Vesey-Fitzgerald is a good friend and a powerful politician. With a seat in the Cabinet, he will be in an extraordinary position for bringing benefits to the whole of the county. Therefore it is my wish that you go en masse and vote for him. I know you will listen to my counsel as you have always done. ['Like sheep!' said a voice from outside. Clarke stopped for a moment. His hands trembled with anger.] O Connells come and go but the families of Vesey-Fitzgerald go on for ever. ['Until they are shot,' said the voice.] I have always been a benevolent landlord. ['That's a damn lie!' said the voice.] I have treated you well, cared for you like my father and grandfather before me. I may say I have loved you all. ['Like his strumpets,' said the voice.] I have never been a stern father to you ['He fathered half London,' said the voice], but if you proceed on a course of electing this powerless demagogue I will have no option but — ['Ah, close your gob, Clarke,' said the voice, 'you are catching flies'].'

Clarke couldn't go on. People started tittering. There were a few hurroos and laughter. He stood there, the letter clenched in his fist, his face red.

'By God, if you won't listen to him, you will listen to me,' he said. 'You will do what you are told. Let any man listening to me who is on a hanging gale tremble in his shoes. I tell you that. People have been hanging on to land that they owe for seven times over. If they want to keep it they will do what they are told. I will be at the cross-roads on Monday too. If you want to live without fear you will follow me. If you don't you can look out for the results.'

He walked out. If they didn't get out of his way quickly enough he pushed them aside with his hands. Outside he stood. He was hemmed in. It didn't frighten him. Dualta thought he was without fear.

'Who was that voice?' he asked.

'It was a bird,' he was answered. 'It was a sheep,' said another. 'It was the landlord's get,' said a third. 'It was the fairies,' said another. 'Hurrah for O Connell!' 'Hurrah for Tewson's fair ladies.' From all sides they came, remarks loud and clear or whispered. It had never happened before. Clarke stood there, his jaws tight. 'Come into the open,' he said. 'I will bet that no voice with a vote spoke. You'll regret it! I promise you!'

He went through them. He walked out the gate and turned down towards the town. His back was tight with anger and menace.

Mr Bradish was at the door. He was talking. They listened to him.

'I want my tenants not to vote for O Connell,' he said. 'You already see the sinister design. These men want to come between the landlords and the tenants. Don't let them do it. It will lead to strife and violence. That is their object. Don't let them do it. Do what you have always done. You have more to gain. I am a Catholic too. Now I tell you to vote for a Protestant gentleman, a literate civilised man who has always been on the side of Catholic Emancipation, and who is in a better position to gain it than a man like O Connell.'

They said nothing. He ushered his wife and the two girls out to the gate. The girls were pale. Mrs Bradish was silent. ('That's the first miracle,' someone remarked.) The carriage drew up at the gate. They went in. It moved off and the people started to go home. They were talking in groups. The young men were laughing. Some of the people who knew no English were saying, 'What did he say? What was the letter about?'

196

Dualta was leaning against the wall of the church. He was looking at Cuan. Cuan caught his eye. He winked sardonically. Cuan was a leaven too, working in the valley. Dualta ought to have known that he wouldn't be quiet. He was going away. He waved an arm. 'See, Dualta,' he called, 'how I am working for O Connell. He has won me over. Are you pleased?'

Dualta said nothing. Just kept looking at him. I feel that I am his enemy, he was thinking in wonder. Cuan was at the source of the voices. He had been working hard.

They were gone. Father Finucane stood beside him.

'Have we won, Dualta?' he asked.

'I don't know,' said Dualta. 'Only tomorrow morning will tell.'

'Then let it come quickly,' said the priest.

21

THE PRIEST sat his horse at the cross-roads. The rain was dripping in streams from his hat. The cloak he wore was sodden from the rain. The mane of the horse was sodden, his appearance woebegone. The sun was risen. It was completely obscured by the grey pregnant clouds that lay helpless on the hills. He was at the town side of the cross-roads. On the other side there was Clarke's carriage. It contained Clarke and his wife and his brother-in-law. Buach, Clarke's strong field bailiff, was mounted on a horse beside them. Buach was very big. He had a mashed face that appeared as if it had been crushed between two rocks. Another bailiff, Páid, barefooted, ragged, but muscular, held the reins of the carriage horses, moving impatiently in his wet clothes. He was called Páid Monuar, because every time he had to carry out an unpleasant chore for Clarke, he would say 'Mo nuar! Mo nuar!' but carry it out he would all the same.

Now and again Clarke poked his head out of the carriage window, looked down the empty road, and withdrew again impatiently.

It was some time before the silence was broken by anything except the splash of the big raindrops in the puddles of the potholes, then from far away there came the thin sound of a boy's voice singing. It was a strange sound to hear on the leaden air. Even the priest's horse cocked his ears for a little at the strangeness of it. You could make out no words, just the sound. It had an odd refrain like the quick lilting notes of a dance tune. It brought pleasure into the grey day, the priest thought, as he turned his head to look. He saw the man and the boy coming to the cross-roads through the fields. His heart lifted. He recognised Dualta and Colman. When Dualta saw his turned head, he waved an arm. They were barefooted, the collars of their coats turned up against the rain. Dualta wore his shoes around his neck and on his shoulder carried a small budget tied to a stick.

As they came nearer Father Finucane found his fingers tapping the pommel of the saddle in rhythm to the boy's clear tune. He was singing in Irish. Father Finucane had never heard it before. As they came nearer he could translate the words, which were repeated over and over, the boy jigging in the heavy grass to the sound of his own mouth. He sang:

'Down near the fall by the willow tree
On a stone by the well, did he wait for me,
With shoes of gold and a shining light
Which he stole from the stars in the dark of night.

Then he danced and he sang like the good people can,
Over the trees and the streams of the glann,
Fol-dil-di-diddle, fol-dil-di-diddle,
This was the song of the small little man.'

Dualta jumped the wall with Colman behind him.

'It's a right good morning, Father,' he said. 'Are we the first to join you? Colman hasn't the vote but he comes to prepare himself for the day.'

'Where did you get the song, then, Colman?' the priest asked.

'He made it himself to an old tune,' said Dualta. 'Isn't he a one for you?'

'It's a very good song,' said the priest. 'My love to you. I didn't know you had it in you.'

'I'll make better than that,' said Colman casually. Dualta and the priest laughed loudly at him, the way he said it. It brought Clarke's head out of the carriage. He looked over at them. Then he pulled back again.

'Is there much movement in the town?' the priest asked.

'We came by the fields,' said Dualta. 'To tell you the truth I was afraid to go the other way in case.' The rain was streaming off his hair and his face. 'Don't worry,' said the priest. 'You have done all you can. Here is the first of them now and it is a poor omen.'

The procession had come from the other side. They were Cringe and his people. The priest knew he had lost them. There was no joy in them. Cringe rode at their head, a small cock of a man on a black horse. His bailiff McInerney rode a rough pony behind him, and then came the schoolmaster, the pimply-faced one, riding an ass. Very suitable, the priest thought, and chided himself. After them came ten male tenants. They walked heavy-footed, dourly, with secret faces. They were dressed in their best clothes. They weren't talking. They avoided the eyes of the priest. He could understand. Cringe was a really ruthless man, like most small men. None of the ten had leases. They were all tenants at will. He could see them at home in their houses, looking at their few possessions, their small fields for which they had given so much of their sweat and toil, the tears of their wives, the stomachs of their children. He felt no anger.

Cringe stopped at the carriage.

'Your people come yet, Clarke?' he asked.

'Not yet,' Clarke told him.

'If they don't come, go in and round them up,' said Cringe. 'That's what I did with my lot. We'll go on, then. You can catch us up. On, men, to the hustings.' He waved his arm. The wet procession straggled after him. As he passed the priest, he raised his black hat politely. There was no sneer in it, just politeness. Father Finucane nodded his head at him and kept his eyes from the tenants. They were sad enough without making them sadder. The last of them had hardly passed before the strains of distant music came from the town road. The horse again cocked his ears. The priest and Dualta held their breaths as they listened. The band was ragged. It seemed like a band. It was playing an Irish marching tune. The sounds didn't seem to blend. The priest turned the horse's head to face the sound. From where it was coming there was a break in the overcast. It seemed as if the ill-assorted sounds had broken through the clouds and dispersed them, bringing brightness with the noise. He could distinguish the sounds of what they called the soft flute, that would pierce the ears of a flying bat, and fiddles, and tin whistles and the loud bang on a skin drum. As he watched they came around the bend of the road. The band was up on Carrol O Connor's cart, sawing and blowing and banging, and behind them came people on carts, and donkeys and horses, women behind men, and children danced and laughed beside them, and most of them had fresh tree branches in their hands which they waved, and two men carried a green banner on two ash poles and written on the banner in words of gold was O CONNELL FOR CLARE, and another one had the words THE MAN OF THE PEOPLE. They were all dressed in their best, the girls in gay fresh cotton skirts, skipping barefooted on the road. There were seventy-seven voters there, walking or riding or holding the reins of the carts, and with them were their wives, and their daughters and their sons, and every single person in the townland he would say and from every house in the valley. They even brought the dogs and the infants with them, he noticed, for one woman in a cart was suckling a child.

He just stood there petrified, shivers running up and down his back, whether from the awful martial music or just from joy, he did not know. He looked at Dualta. Dualta's eyes were shining. He reached up and pressed the priest's arm. The procession swung on to the road to Ennis.

Carrol O Connor shouted:

'Well, then, Father, are you ready to lead us or must we go alone? It's a long road and you should be ahead to bless it.'

Father Finucane laughed and swung the horse out in front

of the cart, raised his arm like a general going into battle, shouted 'Forward for freedom, then!' There were loud cheers, and calls and boys' voices breaking as they sang the words of the band's song. It was a brave colourful sight and it was only right that the sun should shine on it, Dualta thought, as he took Colman's hand and joined in the procession, and soon Clarke, standing on the road, was looking at the tail of the procession and his wife was frightened at the look on his face. It availed him nothing. Not one of the people had given him even a second glance.

Una sat in the body of the courthouse and wondered. She had come to Ennis the day before with the Bradishes. They were staying in a house a few miles outside the town with a distant relative of Mrs Bradish. Margaret said her mother brought them to Ennis because the town was ringed with three thousand soldiers and stiff with policemen and all the aristocracy of Clare, and if her mother couldn't find husbands for them at all the routs there would be for the election, then they were doomed to be old maids. Her mother heard her. She claimed it was their duty to be there to give backing to Vesey-Fitzgerald. Una had been taken along to act as unpaid maid to the woman and the girls. She didn't mind. She wanted to see. She thought the price she had to pay was high but it was worth it. They had difficulty coming through the streets this morning. Nobody would have recognised it. Banners hung from every window. About thirty thousand people were already crushed into the narrow streets. People said in the big houses, Where will it all end? O Connell had come like a king. He had been passed from county to county, from town to town, by bands, bonfires and hundreds of horsemen carrying torches to light up the night.

And no disorder. That was why the aristocrats were perturbed. They didn't know the order that had gone out. Every man coming into Ennis was under a pledge to drink no whisky, to raise no hand against a fellow. They were pledged under the direst threats. The first man found drunk was to be thrown into the Fergus. In all, sixty thousand people were expected to crowd into the place. There will be riots, they said, drink, and faction fights. So throw in the army, one soldier to twenty men, and all the policemen in the county. When they start, break them up, swiftly, ruthlessly. Clear the town. Get as many voters in jail or thrown out of the town quite legitimately, and there is no doubt about the election.

But there were no riots. People bowed respectfully, got out of your way elaborately if you were well dressed, touched their hats to you, maybe they licked their lips at the sight of the whisky houses, but there was no disorder. So people said, Where will it all end? and a little doubt about the result may have bent their complacency.

The cause of it all stood up there beside the Sheriff. He was alone. He held his hands in front of him. He was dressed in a blue coat with a black velvet collar, yellow waistcoat, white breeches, and he wore a gilt button on his shoulder as a sign of his leadership. He had a powerful face, its strength leavened by the snub nose, the curly hair touched with grey. Vesey-Fitzgerald, surrounded by all the gentry of the county, clean, very well dressed, pomaded, a small man with a round face, hazel eyes and gentle almost effeminate gestures. O Connell in his stillness and calm looked equal to the lot of them, she thought, even if she disliked the notion. 'Look at him! Look at him!' Mrs Bradish kept saying in a whisper as if she was telling you to look at the Devil. The gallery was crowded with the people and priests.

For Vesey-Fitzgerald, Sir Edmond O Brien spoke. He was one of the most powerful landlords in the county. He looked powerful. His speech was taken up more with the ingratitude of his tenants who had deserted him, stolen by the priests in this grave hour, than with Fitzgerald. He wanted to know if the country was any longer fit for a gentleman to live in when property lost all its influence and things were brought to such a pass. He produced tears but they affected very few, Una saw, since he was well known to be able to cry at the drop of a hat. But he dropped a few words of menace for his tenants after the tears. He was applauded by his own side. Other men spoke whom she didn't know, and the strange O Gorman Mahon for

O Connell and a 'villain called Steele', said Mrs Bradish.

The gentle Vesey then spoke. He spoke more powerfully than his appearance would lead you to believe. But he was a practised politician. He spoke of his dying father's fight against the Union, of his own efforts to establish Maynooth. He spoke of his father. How they were afraid to tell him that his son was actually being opposed in an election lest the blow would prove fatal. He turned away to wipe tears from his eyes. Una was amazed to see how he had affected everyone about her. His speech seemed to leave behind him a wave of genuine sympathy, even among the people in the gallery.

She was impatient. Do they realise, she wondered, who they are up against? The big silent figure of O Connell with an immovable countenance. Do they think a man like that is to be defeated by tears? He wasn't.

He annihilated them, she thought. It wasn't his actual words. The very moment he opened his mouth, power seemed to emanate from him. The words themselves were nothing, they were like the instruments that play the notes. She could feel it herself, this attention he drew from you. Even if from her and all about her, it was a sort of distaste, a sort of fear that a man who was opposed to your beliefs should have such power in him. The actual things he was saying were not more insulting than the usual political insults, but it was the way he said them that made them deadly, like a blunt instrument hitting you on the top of the head. It was small wonder that he was hated, she thought.

One of Fitzgerald's supporters, a Mr Gore, had acquired his property at the time of Cromwell. It was said this ancestor had been a nailor in the Puritan massacre squads. So O Connell spoke about Gore 'striking a nail on the head' or putting a 'nail in a coffin', and each time he drew a shout of pure glee from the balcony, while poor Mr Gore shrank in his clothes. He tackled Fitzgerald's other supporters and then turned on Fitzgerald himself. He had a deep voice. You couldn't miss a word of it. It was musical. It was like being insulted with thick rich wine instead of water. Now and again Fitzgerald stood up and said, 'Is this fair?'

He heard the words repeated that he was a friend of the people. What? A man that had enrolled under the banner of bloody Perceval a friend of the people? This friend of the people is also a friend of Peel – the bloody Perceval and the candid and manly Peel – he is our friend! He is everybody's friend. The friend of the Catholic was the friend of the bloody Perceval and the friend of the candid and manly Peel.

'Monstrous,' Mrs Bradish was muttering, 'monstrous. Why doesn't somebody do something?' There wasn't a landlord who wouldn't like to murder him, Una thought. She thought she could understand some of the pattern of his insulting language. It was as if he was saying: Look, all your life you have to touch your hat and bow your head when one of the Ascendancy pass by. Open your mouth and you get a whiplash across the face. Now look at me. See how easy it is. Talk up to them. Show them what you feel. Assert your independence of speech. They have reduced you by cartoon and ridicule in everything they write about you. (She remembered suddenly Dualta's anger as he looked at the drawing in a magazine long ago.) From the highest to the lowest they had felt the lash of his speaking, his lack of respect for their pride and their wealth, their position and power, and being a lawyer who knew their laws and could drive a coach and four through them, he remained immune, like a flying bull dropping dung on them, someone said.

He had the place in a frenzy. They were shouting and cheering and calling. 'Where will it all end?' she even heard Fitzgerald say as they made their way out of the courthouse. It was impossible. Gentlemen had their fists clenched on their walking-canes. But what could they do? It was an election. There had to be freedom of expression. But not this, O God, not this! Wouldn't you think God would strike him dumb? There was no malice in his eyes, she saw. It was the words, the love of words and the way he could play on the emotions of people, like a great musician. He was looking for effects and getting them in the best way possible, reducing men to helpless fury or to wild adulation.

By the time they got to their carriage the square outside was jammed with people cheering him. Good-looking handsome women leaned out of the top windows of the tall houses in the narrow streets and waved handkerchiefs with the figure of O Connell stamped on them.

He was staying in a house across the square from the court-house, and from this house a platform had been run out and decorated with fresh tree branches and ribbons and banners and favours. When they were coming back, slowly making their way in the carriage through the densely packed cheering crowds, Una thought that O Connell might have known that Mr Bradish was passing by. He was on the platform. Unfortunately he was talking about Catholic landlords. They had all gone over to Vesey-Fitzgerald in a body. He hoped their tenants would not be so foolish as to follow their example.

'What are they??' he asked in his glorious voice. 'Orange Papists, they are!'

'Drive on, Tom! Drive on!' said Mr Bradish, leaning out of the carriage window.

'I'm trying, sir, but it's hard,' said Tom. 'Make way! Make way!'

And they got out of his way, hardly giving a look at the people in the carriage, their eyes glued to the big man on the platform, but it was slow and as they went they heard a lot of what he was saying. Mr Bradish was gripping a strap, his knuckles white, his breathing heavy.

'Byron had a word for them,' said O Connell. 'Let them hear it now.' You would think he was talking especially to Bradish, that he knew he was there.

> 'And thus they plod in sluggish misery,
> Rotting from sire to son, and age to age,
> Proud of their trampled nature, and so die,
> Bequeathing their hereditary rage
> To the new race of inborn slaves, who wage
> War for their chains. . . .'

'Oh no, it's insufferable!' said Mrs Bradish. 'It's insufferable! What are the police doing? What are the army doing?'

'It's a good job you have no sons, Father,' said Margaret,

205

'or they would be inborn slaves too.' She giggled.

'Silence,' said Mrs Bradish. 'Silence!'

They left his voice and the laughter behind them.

Dualta savoured it. There could never be a time like it
again, he felt. It was the joy of people who threw off their
chains for however short a time, said 'Tomorrow the consequences, but we do not care'. Everyone seemed to be uplifted.
The long tramp to Ennis, taking many hours, the rain falling
on the whole of them for an hour at a time and then hot sun
for another hour steaming them. He got second-hand joy
through Colman's naïve wonder. Colman had never been
abroad from the valley before. From many villages they were
joined by others, or had to wait until the road was clear. There
were bands and banners and waving branches. There was
laughter and song and wild shouting that should only have
come from a drunken people. But they were not drunk.

They heard of the gaunt priest of Corofin, Father Murphy,
who had faced the great landlord Sir Edmond O Brien and
stolen his tenants from him, with deep-sunk blazing eyes and
awesome eloquence. They were cheered by the few people
remaining in Corofin as they passed through. The road to the
far-away town was lined by the staybehinds who cheered and
encouraged them. It was a great feast day.

As they got near the town, they could almost hear it heaving. All the roads into it were black with people, who shouted
and cheered and made a way for them, and armed them with
fresh laurel branches, smooth dark green and shiny with
rain.

Around they went and into the long narrow Gaol Street, that
led into the square of the courthouse. Cheering people leaning
from windows, waving and calling. They stood in front of the
green-bowered platform in the square, with Father Finucane
at their head, and all the people around called 'O Connell!
O Connell!' and when they saw him emerge from the house
and walk onto the platform, and raise his arm in greeting, even
Dualta couldn't help the roar that burst from his throat as he
held Colman on his shoulder to see him. It was the same man

he had last seen on the hillside of the hares, but he wasn't carelessly dressed. His eyes twinkled at them. He was smiling.

'We are for you, O Connell!' they shouted all around, and 'Talk to us! Talk to us!' they called.

He said, 'I need lungs of brass, and a tongue of iron. There are no words left to me. We have freedom in our grasp. You can provide it. I see your priest at your head. I know you are for me. Tomorrow the vote. That will be your voice. We will lay them low.' That was all he said to them. You would think he had been dropping jewels in their path. They cheered and roared, and he went in and they passed on through more streets and around again until they came to the great fields by the winding Fergus. Here they set up their tents, like the tabernacles of the Israelites, Father Finucane said, before he left them.

Dualta helped Carrol O Connor to drape sacks around the cart so that underneath it provided a shelter for them. He saw the McClearys doing the same thing with their cart. Other people copied the tinkers and piled stuff around bent branches stuck into the ground. Many big fires were lighted, and people dried their clothes around them, and danced around them and ate around them, while pipers and fiddlers played themselves into a state of exhaustion. He would long remember the packed fields with the makeshift tents, and the great blazing fires almost throwing shadows on the clouds.

He danced with Sheila. She was as light as a feather and as gay as if she had taken of a herbal drug. Later he roved the town with her and Colman. Colman was wide-eyed, looking in at the windows of the candle-lighted shops, book shops and cook shops and clothes shops. Only the whisky shops were empty, some despondent owners standing and saying, 'Won't you come in and take just a small one. Sure it won't break the pledge!'

The sight of a big man in the square standing tall and straight and a little man hammering on his chest with small fists, and the big man praying aloud to God in the moon-lighted sky. 'Temper me, God,' he was asking. 'Don't let me hit him. Hold my temper on me until the voting is finished. I made a promise. After that I will squash him into the earth like I would a beetle with my big toe. Only let me hold my temper until then!' Everyone laughing, the little man leaving his futile chest-beating, throwing his hat on the ground and stamping around calling, 'Come to me! Come to me until I pulverise you! Come to me until I half-sole your eye!'

It was good. Sleeping under the stars.

The voting was slow and wearisome, but nobody faltered. To delay it the authorities decided that all voters must take the oath singly. A ridiculous oath, going back to something about the Pretender. But there were protests and loud calls and finally they were lined up twenty-five at a time against four walls and they took the silly oath and then they went in a great body to one or other of the fifteen polling booths and in a loud voice they declared, 'Daniel O Connell for Clare.' There were many who didn't. Poor men under the spell of fear and free men who were doing what they thought was the best thing to do and did it fearlessly and were willing to argue their vote and willing to fight for it if the oath of restraint was not on the others and kept them from boiling over into battle.

Dualta wandered. He feasted his eyes on the colour and movement. He lost Colman, who went to look at the soldiers, gaudily attired. Dualta remembered a few things.

The priest and the man talking to O Connell. O Connell walked around from booth to booth, from place to place. Anyone could talk to him. He had a word for everyone, but sometimes the press of adulators made him withdraw from sight.

This man was saying to the priest: 'Father John, I think I rounded up everyone to the vote. All except one, that fellow called O Connell. What else could you expect from a man with that name? The bastard comes from Kerry too, and I never knew a man from there that was worth a pinch of dust.'

Dualta was watching O Connell's face. It broke up into creases as he laughed. The man then suddenly thought of what he had been saying and put his hand in front of his mouth and looked over it with wild eyes. This made O Connell and the priest laugh even more.

At night he worked his way into Carmody's hotel where they were eating after the long day. Father Finucane was in the lower place. He had sent a message to Dualta that he wanted him. There were many freeholders with priests there. The talk was loud. Father Finucane saw him. He made his way to him, 'Are the people hungry?' he asked. 'Did they bring enough food?' 'Yes, they are,' said Dualta, 'and no, they didn't bring enough food. Some of them will only be able to vote tomorrow. The swearing took too long.'

'I'm trying to get something done about it,' said the priest. 'Father Murphy!' he called. 'Father Murphy! Will we be able to get something to eat for them?'

The tall priest turned. He had a long face like a Tipperary man. He said, 'We will, Father! We will indeed, and we will do it now.' He went out of the door calling in a loud voice that hushed the great noise into silence: 'The wolf is on the walk! The wolf is on the walk! Shepherds of the people, what are you doing here? Should you stuff yourself while the freeholders are unprovided for and temptation in the shape of famine among them? Rise up! Rise up! The wolf, the wolf is on the walk!' They heard him going up the stairs where the eating was, and the call of the wolf brought a burst of officials with tickets and orders to the priests to provide meat and beer, but no whisky, to the freeholders who were far from home and food.

The people of the valley ate then in a great warehouse where huge pots steamed. Bread and meat and beer. They needed it because the poll of the first day was O Connell 850, Vesey-Fitzgerald 538. Eat and vote! Eat and vote, for tomorrow is the day. Tomorrow we will let them see. Today is too close, too close for comfort.

Tomorrow would be the day indeed and it was to mean a lot to Dualta, as well as to Daniel O Connell.

22

THE DISILLUSION of Una set in slowly. You cannot go back,
the small voice said in her ear at odd moments. When she
discovered that her one really good dress that she had been
saving had moth-holes which she carefully patched and
darned. They were scarcely noticeable, but she knew they
were there. She wore long gloves to cover the coarseness of
her hands. She had no scent, nor powder to whiten her sun-
tanned face. She was a friend of the Bradishes, which was the
only cachet she possessed; the schoolteacher (this with a lifted
eyebrow), which negatived the cachet. She had lost the offhand
way of dealing with people. She had become too interested in
people as people.

There was a ball this evening of the first polling. It was held
in the big living-room, from which most of the furniture had
been removed with the rugs, and the floor polished. In the
dining-room there was a long table groaning under the weight
of food and claret cups. Liveried men and neatly dressed servants moved about with trays.

She danced once or twice with a young lieutenant. He had
fair hair and fair whiskers, combed out. He liked those. He
fondled them often. He had blue eyes and a young face. He
smelled nicely of wine and tobacco. She would never know his
name, but she would remember him. Small talk. Yes, she was a
schoolteacher. Yes, she taught the natives, not genteel ladies.
She liked it! Oh yes she did. If the country was to advance it
could only begin to advance by climbing the ladder of the
alphabet and mathematics. Books and science. No, indeed,
she found them brighter than children who were better off
than they. They had a need. They had a desire. The others
had neither, except for a few. She agreed that O Connell was
crude, but powerful. She was not sorry there had been no
violence. She did not agree that the people were incapable of
continence. She was glad the army had no chance to intervene

in the election.

She walked with him down the steps into the garden. It was so hot in the crowded dancing-place. And she knew her status when he immediately reached for her with his hands. No preliminaries at all, you see, no fending off, bright eyes over the top of a fan. It was a crude attack. It showed her her position with great exactitude, so she was glad of her hard work when she hit him in the nose with her clenched fist. She was proud of that, that she drew claret. It gave her satisfaction to see his look of outrage over the hand holding his bleeding nose. She walked away from him, pulling on her glove. Perhaps it was the glove, because she had taken it off to cool her warm hand and he had felt, not the powdered smoothness of delicate skin, but the hardness of a working hand. Perhaps he had thought she was a milk-girl in disguise or a hearty horsewoman with the morals of an animal.

She went in the back way, her face white under the tan, ignoring the looks of the kitchen scullions. She went up the back stairs to her room and sat on the bed, thinking. If it was different my father would shoot him, or he would horsewhip him. If it was different it would not have happened. I would be treated with deference. She thought of the many decent young men who had once danced attendance on her, for her own sake and for the sake of her father. Now she saw the change in herself, that she had chosen a life that left her open to this just because she was wandering in the twilight between two worlds. For several painful minutes she longed for her father, and all that he had meant to her, for the magic wand of his presence that would change her status in the twinkling of an eye like the story of the Princess of Ireland that Carrol O Connor told.

She tried to get rid of her misery by saying her prayers and climbing into the soft bed, but she was very depressed. There was no one on whom she could release the torrent of her depression. She wondered if she was altogether mad to be doing what she was doing. If she went back to her father, if she pleaded with him, would he not welcome her and embrace her and cry over her bent head? Deeply she knew he wouldn't unless she would say: Father, I have sinned against your religion. Take me back into it and you.

In the morning she had a headache. She knew she couldn't face Mrs Bradish with her eyes and her unconscious air of superiority. She wore her other dress, the second-best one. If only people knew, it was also neatly patched and darned. She was darned all the way in, she thought lightly. She walked the mile to the town. On all sides there were people and talk. They were camping at the side of the road, in the fields, under trees, everywhere. They seemed happy. They did not seem to have lost their lust for life. They greeted her politely, got out of her road when they had blocked her way. She came into the streets of the town. They were packed with people. The banners were limp and discoloured after a night's rain, but the crowd still shouted and called, and in the square they were packed in front of the platform calling, 'O Connell! O Connell! Come forth!' They smelled of wet wool and sleeping in close quarters, and sweaty excitement. There was no sense of anti-climax about them. The musicians were even playing. Stalls were abounding, selling their wares and calling them loudly. The shops were packed, mostly with people looking, and now and again a woman was coming into the light gazing deeply into the crevices of her water-wheel purse.

She was past the square and walking down another less crowded street when she came face to face with her father. They were both shocked. She knew the two gentlemen with him. They were walking from a house to a carriage that was down a side street. She felt as if she had been kicked in the heart. He had aged. He was using a walking-cane. His hair under his hat was much whiter. He had a port-wine flush on his face. She saw his shock, his face paling. She saw his eyes devouring her and then a look of coldness come into them as he looked from her face to her shoes, all the way up and down, assessing her as she was. He looked in her eyes again. Was he looking for a lowered flag? for a glint of encouragement? She didn't know. But he didn't find it. He remained a gentleman. He raised his hat and turned towards the side street. The two gentlemen with him paused, found their hands awkward, went to speak, could find nothing to say, looking painfully embarrassed, and then followed after him.

She stood there, listening to the sound of the closing carriage door and the sound of the turning wheels on the cobblestones, and then, as a blinding flood of tears came into her eyes, she lowered her head, quickened her pace and walked without direction. She ought to have known he would come, like all the many gentlemen of Tipperary. She ought to have known and remained where she was. Now he would know. He would enquire until he found out, and he would know what she was doing.

She didn't know where she went, nor did she notice the looks of people who stood aside to let her pass, watching her tear-stained face. Who ever saw a lady crying in the streets and on foot? Over the humped bridge and right by the river and a little way along there was a ring of boys and girls, dancing and laughing to the sounds of a soft flute. She brushed by them, her head lowered, seeming to find it the crowning blow of all that one of the dancers was Dualta and that he saw her and caught the look on her face before she averted it, and that he cried out and called. A lot he cared, lecturing about the hidden people and the secret people that you must find, working slowly to discover a new land that was so much more lively and dramatic than the other, even if it was hidden under a veil of poverty and dirt and lice. They were there all right, she thought viciously, there was no mistake about that. But where were the great songs and the laughter and the poetry and the music and the heartwarming neighbourliness, the people who would die for you to save you from a heart-ache, the people who would take your burdens on their back and carry them for pure love, because there was nothing to gain?

'Miss MacMahon!' she heard him call behind her. 'Miss MacMahon!'

'Leave me alone! Leave me alone!' she called back over her shoulder. She jumped over a stone wall of low size and headed across the cropped field towards the rushes that grew at the wind of the river. There were no camps here, just the water and the green grass and a curious cow that looked at her

213

with enormous eyes. She went on her knees there and she sat on her heels and covered her face with her hands.

She heard his feet on the grass behind her. She heard his heavy breathing. He had run fast.

'Let me help you, Miss MacMahon,' said his voice to the side of her. 'Please let me help you!'

'Don't call me Miss MacMahon!' she said. 'I am not Miss MacMahon!'

This nonplussed Dualta. He scratched his head.

'All right, Miss Wilcocks,' he said.

'Don't use that name!' she said. 'Don't dare use that name!'

'All right, Miss,' said Dualta, sighing patiently.

'How dare you be patient with me!' she said. She turned on him then. He was on one knee looking at her. It was so strange to see tears in her eyes, mixed with a flaming anger that seemed to be directed at himself. 'I have met my father,' she said. 'Do you hear that? And he passed me by! Do you hear that? My own father!' Her head went down again.

'Lord, I'm sorry,' he said.

'I don't want your sympathy,' she told him. 'Go back to the bridge and dance with the pretty girls.'

'I would dance with you, if you would dance,' he said.

'It's your fault,' she said. 'You and that O Connell man. What do I care about him? What do I care about you? I wouldn't have come at all but for that. I wouldn't have been insulted. What do you think my father would have done to that lieutenant in decent times, when I was decent and normal?'

'What lieutenant?' Dualta asked.

'What he did to me!' she said. 'Oh, if only my father was there!'

'What lieutenant?' asked Dualta. 'Who was he? What did he do to you? I'll cripple him if you will point him out to me!'

'What does it matter to you?' she asked, facing him, her eyes blazing. 'What do you care about me, or what happens to me? Your life is cleaning scruffy fields and dancing and flirting with pretty girls.'

'I wasn't flirting with anyone,' said Dualta. 'I'll leave that to your fine-feathered friends.'

'You see,' she said. 'You are making a distinction of me! You will never accept me. I am set apart from one side and the other. I have nowhere to go.'

'You can come to me if you like,' Dualta shouted. 'I'll be a better father than your own father, if that's what you want.'

'I don't want you to be my father,' she shouted.

'Well, dammit, I'll be your grandmother so,' said Dualta.

'Now you are making a joke of me,' she said, tearful again.

'Oh, God!' said Dualta. 'I love you. I want to marry you. I wanted to marry you from the first minute I set eyes on you, but what chance was there for me?'

'What are you saying?' she asked.

'See,' he said, 'you are sneering at me. You become the lady of the big house when I say this.'

'What did you say?' she asked. 'Just say it again.'

'I love you,' Dualta shouted loud enough to startle the cow. 'I have always loved you. From the beginning I have loved you. The last time I was in your house, I sat in your vacant room and smelled your presence and my heart nearly broke.'

'Dualta,' she said, 'you are joking. You are only being kind to me because I am sad.'

'What do I have to do?' he asked the sky. 'Do I have to eat grass? Do I have to strip myself bare? What chance was there for me to say it until you were reduced to what you are feeling now? What would you have said to me at other times? Just answer me that!'

'Why,' she said, 'I would have said, What took you so long to say it? That's what I would have said.'

'You're joking me,' said Dualta.

'I am not,' she said.

'You mean you felt the way I felt? You couldn't.'

'Oh yes, I could.'

'You mean this?'

'Would I be saying it if I didn't mean it?'

'You mean back in your father's house you knew?'

'Not altogether then. I thought I just had a sick stomach.'

They both laughed now. Great God, this is madness!

'You were as high as the sky from me,' he said. 'See how you have been brought to my level.'

'It was you that was high,' she said. 'I have come up, and I haven't gone down.'

'Do you believe this?' he asked.

'What do you want me to believe?' she asked. She was close to him. He could feel the warmth from her body.

'Believe me,' he said.

'I believe you,' she said.

He wiped the tears from her face with his rough fingers, and the cow, no longer curious, went back to the grass.

For them the day passed like a bright dream. There was heavy rain but they sheltered in shops and arched doorways. They bought halfpenny rolls of bread, and little pieces of cooked meat on sticks, and they ate them on the tombstones in the ruins of the old monastery, the great window of the church bereft of glass rising to the sky as sublime as their feelings.

She waited while he bought her a favour. Normally it would be a ribbon for her hair, but he came from a dark shop and gave her a small bottle of scent. The apothecary thought he was mad. No wonder the country was going to hell, with countrymen buying scent! Great God, where would it all end with upstarts like O Connell outfacing the gentry? Back to your sty, boy, back to your sty and shake it on the pigs!

Una was so pleased. 'How thoughtful!' 'It will probably have to last you a lifetime,' Dualta told her, and they laughed. 'We will make our own scent,' he told her, 'from the flowers and the herbs.' 'But it was such a thought,' she said. 'Who else would have thought of such a foolish thing but a person like Dualta?'

They met O Connell near the square. 'Watch,' said Dualta. 'Just watch.' And he stood there with Una, holding her arm, and he waited patiently until the eyes of O Connell swivelled around in his direction. He saw the eyes rest on him and pass on. He waited. They came back again. They focussed on him, a frown between them, and then they brightened and he left his companions and came across to them, his hand out. 'The hares,' he said, 'the hares on the hill. I remember. Odd name. Odd name. Don't tell me! Dualta. See! Am I right?'

'You are right,' said Dualta proudly.

'You are still paying your halfpenny to my welfare, then?' he asked, laughing.

'Oh, yes! Oh, yes!' said Dualta.

'See where they have led, all the halfpennies,' he said. 'I am pleased to see you. You didn't come back to talk to me.'

'I will,' said Dualta. 'I will. This is Miss MacMahon.'

He took off his hat. He bowed over her hand. She felt his magnetism, his shrewdness as he assessed her. He was smiling. 'Are you a convert to the cause?' he asked.

'No,' said Una. 'I am on the other side. It is in my blood. I don't like invective.'

'Even when it is dramatic?' he asked. 'You do not desire my victory then?'

'I don't know,' she said.

'Are you afraid of change?' he asked. She thought over this. She and Dualta. That was change enough for anyone. 'No,' she said, 'I embrace change.'

He saw their eyes meeting. 'I envy you,' he said. 'What happened to your dark violent friend, then, the brooding man? Has he changed?'

'No,' said Dualta, 'he has not changed.'

'He never will,' the man said. 'He is like the other side of a penny. He and I will always be at odds.' He was fingering his lower lip. He seemed to have left them. 'We are the conflict of the Irish character, he and I. I have not forgotten him. In ways he is a greater enemy to me than the ones I oppose. He will be eternal, unforgiving. War or peace. You see?'

'Yes,' said Dualta. 'Will you win this one then?'

A wave of his hand. 'Oh yes, Vesey-Fitzgerald is done. It

won't be long until the bells ring out for Emancipation. You watch. You have done it. Don't forget that. You and your halfpenny. Don't forget that. It could not have been done without.'

'Mister O Connell! Mister O Connell!' they were calling him urgently. He looked at them again, his eyes bright, and then he went away.

'See,' said Dualta. 'He remembered after one meeting. That's what power means. That's what leadership means, who remembers the faces of the little people.'

'You are not little,' said Una.

He laughed and they searched for Colman. They found him in a state of wonder. Soldiers, uniforms, shops. 'A policeman knuckled me on the head,' he said. 'I was doing nothing. May he roast in hell.' They fed him. He didn't notice anything different about them. He was too busy absorbing sights and sounds. Dualta bought an ass from a tinker. There was tremendous bargaining over the ass. He needed one for carting seaweed from the shore, and many things about the house. He got him in the end for three shillings and ninepence. He was a young sturdy ass. Una wrote a note to Mrs Bradish: 'Dear Mrs Bradish, I am going home by another method of conveyance. Please bring my few belongings home with you and oblige your servant.' They laughed a lot over that. Mrs Bradish would think she had met a gentleman who was returning her in a carriage, perhaps after disgraceful interludes. She wouldn't know that Miss MacMahon was going home sitting on the back of an ass with a sack of straw under her.

They left the town while the place was bursting with the result of the day's poll: O Connell 1,820; Vesey-Fitzgerald 842. For good or ill, it proclaimed the reign of the Liberator, a demagogue, a thief, a scoundrel, a saint, a hypocrite, according to your impressions. But here and now he was a never-ending shout of joy and release that followed them far from the town into the fresh air of the evening, over a long trip on muddy and potholed roads that seemed to them as soft as cotton, as short as a happy dream, as promising as if paved with gold.

And Colman sang and skipped and made up odd songs about the wonders of Ennis, and none of them was afraid of the future.

23

FLAN McCarthy came to their wedding feast. He sang. This was his song, in a quavering off-key voice:

Let me sing of the sons of the King,
Of Murcha and Conchobar and Flan
So dear to the heart of Brian.
Let the strings break with
the wet of my tears
when I recall them.

Young and fair with shield and sword
they fought the sea-borne men.
(In northern lands the hearths were cold
and widows of beauty ashed
their long fair hair.)

O, well might Brian cry
as he prayed in a shaded tent
foreknowledged of the loss of his lions;
well welcome death with
his three brave sons.

In the Kingdom of God they reign,
the three fair princes of Brian,
Murcha and Conchobar and Flan
riding the winds of the world,
sons of the New King.

They cheered him. Now you talk to us, Flan the Poet, they called. Now we understand you. You are the last of the Bards. He was ridiculously pleased, shedding bits of paper from many pockets, smoking a pipe. He sang another song for them. It was obscure, but they pretended it was even better than the other one. He basked in their praise. Moran McCleary danced on his own. He was a big man, but he was as light on his feet as the feather of a duck. His wife Sabina, the regal-looking woman, danced with him then. It was song and dance and story for many hours. It was not unruly. Outside, when it became too crowded, young people made their own dance in the yard with young men playing the rhythm of the dance blowing with their mouths on green leaves.

Una met the eyes of her husband on several occasions. See, they seemed to say, will you get entertainment like this in the ballrooms of great houses? She smiled her pleasure at him.

It was a great night. People said it was one of the best nights they could ever remember, and it would be long until they saw another like it.

It was really too good to last. It was abruptly ended by Cuan McCarthy.

Una had missed his sardonic presence from the kitchen. Suddenly he was there dominating it.

'Stop the dancing! Stop the music!' he called. He stood in front of the fire, a tall thin man with fire in his eyes.

'Tewson is here,' he said. 'The house is a blaze of lights. Tomorrow they are going to call in the hanging gales.'

He had succeeded in sobering them. There was none didn't get a cold feeling in his spine. There were three months to go to gale day. That meant there was three months' rent owing, since all of them were in arrears. It meant that before the harvest was in, before the potatoes were up or the corn, or pigs ready for the market or turf or eggs or butter, they would have to find three months' rent on demand.

'How do you know, Cuan?' Dualta asked.

'I know,' said Cuan. 'I have sources of information. We will have to stop them. And stop them now. He waited a long time. Now he is going to leap for the votes for O Connell.'

'Have you a notion what we can do, Cuan?' Moran McCleary asked him.

'I have,' said Cuan. 'I want a hundred men with me who will get their spades and in the light of the moon we will turn up ten acres of their grassland. That will give them pause. That will set them back.'

'It's a brave notion,' said Moran McCleary.

'It is not,' said Dualta. 'It's a bad notion. If you are being made to pay for this voting, what do you think will happen after this?'

Una noted with a beating heart that a coldness had descended in the joyful atmosphere, and a lot of it was being directed at Dualta.

'Nobody asks you to dig on your wedding night,' said Cuan.

'That has nothing to do with it,' said Dualta. 'Many men will not be able to afford the hanging gales. Let us go in a deputation to Tewson and plead for them. If that fails let those of us who have a few shillings pledge ourselves to find the rent for those who haven't. Let us sell what we possess to help our neighbour.'

Una looked around at them. They dropped their eyes from Dualta's challenge.

Sabina McCleary said, 'Turn up the land. We have been too long lying down under them. Let us awaken the valley. If ye are men let ye go and turn up the grasslands.'

'You are wrong,' said Dualta.

'You weren't long changing from a man to a woman, Dualta,' said Cuan. 'Has a patch of land made you a coward then?'

'Experience has made me see that what you want is wrong,' said Dualta. 'Patience and sacrifice are more important than violence.'

'The priest has trained you well,' said Cuan.

'Life has trained me,' said Dualta. 'Has O Connell taught you nothing?'

'No,' said Cuan. 'Forty-shilling freeholders were to be pro-tected. Where are their votes? Dead. Where are the ones that were to be saved from eviction? They are evicted. Now here. They threaten us. We strike back. That is the way. Who is coming with us? The young men are gathering their spades. This is a testing time. We can stop them. Let us stop them now and not wait until caution clears our heads.'

'Don't do it,' said Dualta. 'Let us have time. Let us educate your sons. Let us be patient, for the love of God. We are too many. We will force them eventually by opinion, by being educated. You see your children, what different people they are. Let us train them to win for you while we hold on with patience and perseverance. I appeal to you. Don't listen to Cuan. He is my friend and I tell you that.'

'I am no longer your friend,' said Cuan. 'Come, men, any of you that have the courage to come with me.'

He walked to the door.

The people felt hurt. There was hurt in their eyes as they silently left. Because they were outraging hospitality, breaking a thread of happiness. Very soon they were all gone, except the fiddler, who was staying for the night, and Napoleon in a drunken sleep in a corner and Carrol O Connor and his wife Sheila and Flan McCarthy.

Una thought, what a thin thread there is between complete happiness and gloomy dismay.

'You cannot talk to the wind, Dualta,' said Carrol O Connor.

'My talk is true,' said Dualta. 'They are wrong.'

'Time will tell,' said Mrs O Connor.

Flan rose to his feet. He walked towards the door. He talked to the sky.

> 'We are the silent people.
> How long must we be still,
> to nurse in secret at our breast
> an ancient culture?
>
> Let us arise and cry then;
> call from the sleeping ashes
> of destiny a chieftain who
> will be our voice.
>
> He will strike the brass
> and we will erupt
> from our hidden caves
> into the golden light of new-born day.'

Dualta went to him. 'Flan,' he said, 'isn't he here if they will listen to him?'

'Tainted,' said Flan. 'Will he stand at the ford with a bronze shield and a warlike spear? Will he call the bards from their poverty?'

'You can teach wisdom,' said Dualta. 'They will listen to you!'

'No,' said Flan, 'tillers of the soil! War with spades! It becomes the men of turf to make war with spades. Let me go home. I am sick of men. Come and see me, Dualta. I am not unaware of life. I grieve that your wedding night has been put in upon. You have won yourself a fair bride. Enjoy her before the tears. Come and see me. I wish you well. I have no power. I am impatient of men.' He went across the yard. He started again to sing his song of the three sons of Brian, his voice quavering on the night air. Dualta felt Una beside him. She put her hand on his arm. Below in the valley through the trees, they could see lights in the windows of the big house. The unusual lights seemed very menacing.

'No good will come of it,' said Dualta. 'They are wrong.'

'You are no longer alone to argue it with yourself, Dualta,' she said. 'Remember I am here now. For ever.'

He looked at her.

'I am sorry I forgot,' he said. 'You are worth everything.'

The O Connors came into the night. Dualta helped him to tackle the horse to the cart.

They were silent. When they were going Carrol said: 'I am your friend, Dualta. I am not the only one. You must not forget this.'

'Don't let them altogether spoil your wedding night,' said Mrs O Connor. 'Tomorrow I will come and give you a hand to clean up.'

They went away.

Una and Dualta stood there. It was a soft night. He had been on the point of winning the friendship of the whole valley.

'It is like Cuan to wreck this day of our life,' he said.

'You mustn't let him,' she said.

'It is difficult to think of hard-earned acres of grass being turned up to the light of the moon,' he said. 'Now that I know how hard it is to make a single field, I grieve at the loss of made

223

ones. It will stop Clarke for a time, but time is on their side. They can afford to wait.'

'You will have to weigh my love against the loss of the green fields,' said Una.

'The scales are weighted,' said Dualta. 'You have no competition. But my heart is sore.'

'I will balm it for you,' said Una. 'Remember me, I am a stranger. I am far from home. I feel sad. You will have to comfort me. You will have to console me. Don't let them win you. I want you.'

'You have me,' said Dualta, turning her determinedly towards the house. 'Let them dig their own folly. We will bed Napoleon and the Fiddler and then we will blot out the night.'

'Now you are saying something worth while,' said Una. 'You must remember that you are no longer alone.'

24

DUALTA WAS moulding his lumpers and felt depressed. The stalks were thick, the plants were healthy, soon they would be in flower. He had planted two kinds of potatoes, lumpers and Irish Apple. The lumpers were big and fruitful, the Irish Apple small and much tastier, but they grew those only for sale. He thought of the immense amount of labour that had gone into the saving of this potato-field, cleaning and burning, and the first year setting it out in lazy beds, ridges about six foot wide. Then the field in the following year had to be manured with bog, or mould, lime clay and, when he had it, dung and seaweed. All costly. Lime had to be burned with turf and one barrel of it went to a perch of land. He found that when God threw seaweed from the deep it would be taken away laboriously with the donkey and baskets at the cost of 4/2 per ton, and if you wanted sea sand to liven the soil you had to pay from 5/– to 10/–. If seaweed and sand weren't free in the world weren't all men slaves?

But the soil was improving, he told himself as he took some

of it in his hand. It was becoming more powdery, even if it was very stony, but that allowed air to travel in it, so perhaps stones were good too.

He straightened his back and leaned on the spade and was suddenly pleased to see the figure of Una, far below, coming out of the house with the basket in her hand and starting to walk through the fields. Almost he could hear her humming.

He kept his worries from her; the cold wind of fear that blew on the back of his neck when gale day began to loom up. Only now after all those years he could feel genuine sympathy with the forty-shilling freeholders going in like sheep to vote in Galway. The loss of a cow or the failure of one crop was all that stood between you and beggary. In the three years since he had the place the only thing that saved them was the few pounds that Una got for teaching school. At a penny per pupil per week this amounted to about six pounds per year. Many children could not afford to pay the penny at all. It was a poor parish. It had to support two priests. Father Finucane himself seemed to live on very little, and his supplement to the school fund would be about five pounds per year.

There was a fair wind. It was ruffling the green shoots of the oats.

He dropped the spade and went down to meet her. He jumped the wall of the potato-field, walked the headland of the oat-field feeling the texture of the green shoots with his palm. He came to rest in the next field, sitting with his back to a sweet-smelling cock of first-crop hay. Here he waited for her. He knew where she would come. First he would see the top of her head and then her eyes and then her smiling mouth and then the rest of her. She would be happy. She seemed to be always happy since the day they were married, as if she had said: Here now, you are my husband. You will bear all the burdens. I will be happy. He looked forward to seeing her every time they were separated, even for short periods, as if he was seeing her again after a long absence.

He saw her head, the sun shining on her hair, uncovered. She always wore it that way, and then her eyes, deep-sunken and crinkling as soon as they alighted on him, and her smiling mouth. She was humming Tra-la-la. She always hummed in English even if she was becoming very expert with the speaking of Irish. He thought: What does all the rest matter when I have her? The basket was swinging in her hand. She was thinner, finer, than when he had known her long ago. Her body was lithe and the fine bones of her face more obvious, but a healthy fineness she had. She wore shoes. She couldn't use her bare feet. She had tried. Anything but that, she said, so the cobbler had to come for a week with all his paraphernalia, and measure her feet and make her shoes on his lap-stone. In all the shoes cost seven shillings and fourpence. They were made of harder leather than she was used to, but he could mend them himself and with care they would last a year.

She got on her knees between his legs and she put the basket aside and bent forward and kissed him.

'God be with you, O man,' she said.

He held on to her hands.

'You will never learn to be of the people,' he said.

'In what am I lacking?' she asked.

'You must never show you love your husband in public,' he said.

'Who can see but the birds?' she asked.

'It is the spirit of the thing,' he said. 'When you are of the people you are not expected to have finer emotions. You must be like an animal, a little higher-class animal. You eat, you sleep, you love when hunger arises in you.'

'I am hungry,' she said, leaning forward and kissing him again, 'and you are bitter. Don't be bitter.'

Her hands were very small. They were very roughened too. He looked at them.

'Why wouldn't I be bitter?' he asked. 'No matter how hard we work, your hands will never be smooth again. They are right to regard us as animals, except that animals have a certain measure of freedom. We have none at all.'

'You'd better eat,' she said. 'Your stomach is upset.' She took her hands from him, and lifted the cloth from the basket. It was simple fare: potatoes freed from their skins, a bottle of buttermilk and a coolin, a halfpenny salted herring. The smell

226

of them made him hungry, but the sight of her picking at a potato with her even white teeth and taking up a fingerful of the boiled herring daintily, made his heart sink as he saw her in a picnic setting as he had once seen her. All those delicacies.

'It's not right!' he said. She laughed at him over the potato. 'How long will it be,' she asked, 'before you lose your pride? I am happy, Dualta. How can I make you see this? Totally happy. I am married to a man I love, and I am doing things that I feel are fruitful. There is nothing that can cause me dismay, only sadness in you. So please don't be sad. Are you grieving because I haven't given you a son?'

'You mustn't say that!' he exploded. 'Down there in the school you have many sons and daughters. They are important. It may be that God does not want us to have any of our own until we have dealt with those. You must not worry over this.'

'I won't, she said, 'if you will stop worrying over my lost white hands. What were they anyhow?'

'They were beautiful,' he said, 'even if they are just as beautiful now.'

She bent forward. She rubbed the finger of her left hand between his brows.

'You have a growing furrow there,' she said. 'What causes it?'

He sighed.

'Do you understand about tithes?' he said.

She thought over it.

'Mr Glasby is the tithe valuator,' she said. 'Clarke is the tithe proctor. Glasby comes and looks at everything we own. He sets one-tenth value on everything we might sell.'

Dualta saw the list:

Hearth tax	4/– (2 hearths)
Potatoes	5/9
Corn	3/6
Turf	1/7½
Hay	4/10
Poultry	8
Pig	5/–
Small dues	5/5

It all amounted to a sizeable sum. It took gathering. It was the price of one good pig or a year's supply of tobacco. That was the joke. They said a man smoked a pig a year if he used tobacco.

'You know why they make us pay tithes?' he asked.

'Yes,' she said. 'Tithes are for the support of the Church of Ireland, for the upkeep of Protestant bishops and ministers, and cess tax is for the erection and repair of Protestant edifices and the expense of its services. I know that.'

'Most people in this valley have never even seen a Protestant minister,' he said. 'Is it fair that Catholics should have to pay for the upkeep of a religion that is contrary to all they believe?'

'It is an unjust law,' she said. 'That is obvious.'

'There is trouble in the land,' he said. 'Last month thirteen people were shot dead in Newtownmountbarry and twenty were wounded at tithe sales. In Carrickshock a process-server and twelve police were slaughtered with scythes, spades and pitchforks. Now there is trouble in our valley. Police have been brought into the town. There have been letters flying round, warnings, notices signed by Lady Clare and the Terry Alts and Captain Moonlight. I am afraid.'

'Why, Dualta?' she asked.

'I do not want to pay tithes,' he said. 'Even O Connell said don't pay tithes. He was not going to pay them himself. It is all right for him. What happens to us?'

'What happens?' she asked.

'The process-server comes,' he said, 'and he will take away our cow. She will be brought to the town, and she will be auctioned. Most of the violence has arisen from these forced tithe sales. I do not want to pay these tithes, but I do not want to lose my cow. I do not know for sure but I feel that I am a coward. Now that I have something, I do not want to lose it. When I had nothing to lose I was not a coward. You know what they say: Use the whip on another man's horse.'

She thought.

'Will everyone in the valley refuse to pay?' she asked.

'That's the point,' he said. 'They won't. If they did there would be no problem. They couldn't take a cow from everyone in the valley. The weak will pay. Will I be among the weak?'

'Maybe they are strong, not weak,' she said. 'Why will you seek violence?'

'There comes a time when oppression becomes too hard to bear,' he said, 'and men must assert themselves.'

'Don't Father Finucane's sermons against violence mean anything to you?'

'Yes, unfortunately,' he said, 'but in this case I am in doubt.'

'If the law is unjust,' she said, 'it will be changed, but violence only breeds violence.'

'Who will change the law?' he asked.

'Why, those boys and girls down in the schoolhouse,' she said. 'We will make them change the law. We will educate them to justice by perseverance and the force of their literate opinions. It's a long-term plan but it is the most important.'

'You think I should pay then?' he asked.

'Whose head is on the coin?' she asked.

'The image and inscription of Caesar,' he said. He got to his feet. He reached for her hand. He pulled her to her feet. He put his arms around her. 'You are the most valuable possession in the world,' he said. 'If I had to pay tithes on you there would not be enough gold and silver in the world to meet the tax.'

She laughed at him, and then, as his eyes were caught by a movement in the valley, she felt him stiffening. 'What is it, Dualta?' she asked.

'Look,' he said, pointing down. 'The police are moving in on Moran McCleary. See, that's what they do. Take one person and make an example of him. I hope to God Moran pays, but I am in doubt. Cuan has been working on him.'

He left her. He started to run.

'Dualta! Dualta!' she called.

'I'm going down,' he called. 'Stay at home. It doesn't feel right. You see the sun glinting on the bayonets. Who do they think we are!'

Then he turned and was gone. She called after him again: 'Dualta! Dualta!' then, unrewarded, she gathered the fragments and put them in the basket and, lifting the skirt of the cotton dress, she ran down after him.

As a small swallow-hole in the water attracts to its core all the flotsam that floats on the surface, so the band of men who set out from the town towards the farm of Moran McCleary attracted the young people of the town and the lazy ones and the wretched ones from the cottages, and the farmers from the fields, a silent crowd that followed on the rough dusty road behind them, or moved through the hedgerows and over the walls like a scattering of mice leaving a depleted cornstack.

Clarke was mounted. Buach, who was the process-server, walked at his stirrup armed with a heavy stick. Páid Monuar with the soft pleading eyes walked at the other stirrup. There were six policemen with the constable from the town. They carried guns and the bayonets were fixed to them and glinted in the sun. Only one man was a Peeler. The others were baronial policemen, rough-and-ready boys without the proper policeman's neatness of dress and carriage. They were burly men and they were apprehensive. They were slightly dismayed by the gathering of people all around them, and the man at the end would turn now and again and say to them, 'Back there! Keep back there, now!'

Clarke looked neither to the left nor the right. It was left to him to choose the man who would be an example for the valley and he had chosen McCleary. It was a daring thing to do, because McCleary was one of the few with a two-life lease on his farm and therefore independent. But Clarke didn't like him. He told himself this was legitimate. He was sure McCleary was behind the revolt in the valley, that would have to be ended. McCleary had made a very good farm out of his acres. Clarke would have liked to give this farm to a more honourable man, but he was baulked by the lease. But as a tithe proctor he could harass him and this he was determined to do. His duty compelled him to it, he told himself.

So they turned off the road into the track that led to McCleary's house. It lay on a plateau, a smiling property. He could afford to keep it well, as improvements couldn't mean extra rent for him, like some of the other people. It shone in the sun, gleaming white with a new gold-coloured thatch, a long house with flower-beds under the windows, and on each side of the yard stables and dairy and pig-house, all clean and gleaming with wash. Behind the house there was a fruitful kitchen garden and an orchard.

Clarke admired the place as he came into it. It was well kept. A lot of labour had gone into the making of it. He thought it was too good for the rent that the estate was getting out of it.

He stopped out from the door.

Moran came from the kitchen. He was in his bare feet, breeches and shirt with his big chest straining the cloth of it. He was a fair-haired man with blue eyes and his mouth was grim over a square chin.

'Stop there now, Clarke,' he said. 'Come no farther. Speak what you have to say and then go away.'

'Hand him the process, Buach,' said Clarke.

Buach went up to Moran with the paper in his hand. His stick was across his shoulder, a smile on his mashed face.

'I serve this on you,' he said, 'in the name of the Sheriff of the County. Take heed of it and obey.'

Moran took it from him. He crushed it, unopened, and threw it on the ground.

'I will not pay tithes,' he said. 'That is all.'

'Then we have no option,' said Clarke, 'but to take possession of a cow of our choosing. It will be auctioned in the town on a day to be stated in payment of the tithes owing. Do we have to take possession of the animal peacefully or do we take it forcibly? You can decide.'

'You will get away from here,' said Moran, 'as fast as you are able. The first man to lay a hand on a beast of mine, policeman, proctor or bullyboy, will be stretched on the yard.'

'What's come over you, Moran?' Buach pleaded. 'Will you fight the whole world?' He put his hand on his shoulder. Moran threw it away so forcibly that Buach staggered.

'Weary of taxes, rack rent, tithes, cess, or the whole lot,' shouted Moran. 'This is the last of it. I will not pay! You hear that, Clarke? And I will defend my possessions until I am dead. You hear that, Clarke?'

Clarke signalled to the police.

'Restrain him then,' he said to the Peeler. This man signalled and two of the rough-and-ready boys moved on Moran, their guns held across their chests.

'Now, come easy, man,' one of them said. 'We have no wish to hurt you.'

The action was probably instigated by Buach. He was behind Moran. He reached a hand for his shoulder. The big man sensed this, swung around and hit him on the neck with his fist. Buach roared and fell. The two policemen moved in quickly, but Moran caught one of them, and in a flaming rage threw him at the other. The gun fell from the man's hand and Moran reached for it, as Dualta came running panting into the yard.

'Now go! Now go, by God!' Moran shouted, taking the gun into his hands. Someone shouted. It was like a command. The Peeler shouted, 'No! No! Don't shoot! Don't shoot!' But two of them had levelled their guns and had shot, probably in a panic. They were not disciplined men and all the people in the yard saw the bullets hitting Moran's chest, heard the shout strangled in his throat, saw the two blood-roses appearing on the cloth of his shirt, just before he fell, heard the scream from his wife Sabina who was standing behind at the door. For a few seconds everyone stood there, almost petrified, and then shouting, the people all around reached to the ground for whatever was handy, clods or dung or stones, and hurled them at the officers bunched in the yard. Under the hail of missiles, Clarke turned the horse's head and, with his free arm over his head, galloped from the yard.

The Peeler rallied his men, got them moving, shouting, 'Don't shoot! Don't shoot!' One of them did shoot but he hit the barrel of the gun and deflected the shot into the air. Dualta himself was bending and groping and firing, inarticulate sounds coming out of him. The band of men got out of the yard, their arms over their heads. Stones hit them, clods dirtied them. Clarke came back and put the horse between the people and the policeman while the Peeler got some order into them. Clarke was shouting, 'Enough now! Enough now! Hold off or the men will shoot! This is the law! This is the law!'

Gradually they got on to the main road.

As suddenly as it had started, the noise ceased. The people stopped still, suddenly aware of a tragedy. You could hear a bird singing in the quiet, Dualta thought. It seemed to him an indecent sound.

'Pull away quietly now,' the Peeler said. 'Just walk along the road slowly, under the hedge.'

They did so. He could hear their heavy breathing, smell the sweat off them. He was an ex-soldier. He hated them.

'That pair of bloody fools didn't have to fire,' he said. 'I told you warning shots would serve. You didn't have to shoot the man!'

'They did right,' said Clarke loudly. 'He would have used the gun.'

'That's right, that's right,' the fat sweaty one of them said. 'He would have used the gun. I saw his finger on the trigger.'

'It was his own fault,' said Clarke. 'The men did no wrong. They shot in defence of the rest of us.'

The Peeler looked up at him. 'There was no need to shoot,' he said.

'If that is your opinion, it's not mine,' said Clarke.

'Will you get a medal for them then?' the Peeler asked.

'Be careful with your tongue,' said Clarke. 'I am the Sheriff's representative. They did no wrong. They probably saved all our lives. You saw how we were attacked. See the blood they drew from some of the men.'

'They'll live,' said the Peeler, looking at the bleeding scratches. 'But the shot man won't.'

'That's enough,' said Clarke. He pulled the head of the horse around and set off on the road. The others followed him. He found his hands were shaking. It is a pity, he thought, about Moran. He should have had sense. Wasn't it better to pay a few pounds than to lose your life? An odd thing. A two-life lease and here was one of the lease lives gone. It was a pity. Why should a man have to die over a few pounds of money?

They heard the clattering of a horse's hooves coming around

233

the bend of the road. Clarke stopped. He waited. Then the horse and the young priest came into view. He had no hat, such was his hurry. His stock was untied. Clarke thought primly that priests shouldn't be seen abroad like that. The priest pulled up his horse.

'What happened?' he asked. 'I heard shooting.'

'Moran resisted,' said Clarke. 'He grabbed a gun. Some of the men fired in defence. He was hit.'

'You are very calm,' said the priest.

'I have nothing on my conscience,' Clarke shouted. 'He seemed to go mad. There was nothing else to do.'

'I hope God takes as easy a view of it,' said Father Finucane. He urged his horse past them and set him galloping again. Clarke looked after him. I'll complain to the Bishop, he decided. He is too cocky to be an administrator. He will have to be taught manners.

When Dualta turned back into the yard again, it seemed to him that all of the people had become statues. They just stood where they were looking at the man lying in the yard. His wife was still outside the door, her hand up to her mouth. But the man on the ground was not alone. Una was kneeling beside him. She had raised his head and shoulders on to her knees. She was trying to stem the flow of blood from his chest. Dualta walked to her. She looked at him. Her face was pale, her eyes were desperate. He got on his knees beside them.

'Is he alive?' he asked.

'Only just,' she said. There was sound coming from the wounds as if he was breathing through the holes. 'Oh, Dualta, what will we do?'

'We'll have to get him in,' said Dualta. He stood up. He looked around at the people ringing them helplessly. 'Get a board,' he called. 'Someone get a board, we'll take him in.'

It broke the spell that held them. They moved then, paused when they heard the sound of the horse coming back, tensed and waited until they saw it was the priest. Dualta was relieved. He went to him. 'It's bad, bad,' he said.

'All right,' said the priest. He went to Moran. He was sur-

234

prised to see that it was Una who held him. 'How is he?' he asked.

'Not good,' said Una. 'He is dying.' He wondered at her knowledge. She had seen two men dying of wounds from guns, young men who fought in duels for an intangible and stupid thing called honour. She knew Moran was shot in the lungs.

'Go to Sabina,' said the priest. 'Look after her. Get the children away from here. We will take care of Moran.' He took off his coat. He put it under the big fair head as Una withdrew her knees. Her dress was stained with the blood that flowed from his back. It had soaked into her. She could feel its moistness on her knees. She walked to the woman as Dualta and the men came with a door they had pulled from the stable.

Una said, 'Sabina, get the children out of the house. We will send them to a neighbour. Sabina! You hear me!' She took the hand that was covering her mouth and held it. She shook it a little as she called her name. 'Sabina!' She saw then the shock dying out of Sabina's face and a little of the strength but none of the colour coming back into it. She turned her. They went into the house. There were six children in the kitchen. The eldest boy and the girl she knew well from teaching. The boy Fiacra was twelve. He was bright and intelligent. She spoke to him.

'Fiacra,' she said, 'take the children, go out the back way and bring them to O Connor's. You hear me?'

'Yes,' he said. 'I'll do that. But I must come back myself.'

'All right,' she said. 'You come back then.'

Fiacra collected them. The youngest, a flaxen-haired boy wearing a petticoat, didn't want to go. The girl Julia took him in her arms. He protested. He cried. The girl put her hand over his mouth, but he kept crying. They went out the back way. They could hear his crying for a long time. Sabina sat on a stool in the corner. She rubbed her forehead with the back of her hand.

'Soon I will be all right,' she said. 'So quick. I do not understand. What happened?'

'Where is the bedroom?' Una asked. Sabina pointed. Una went up there. It was a neat room with a five-shilling bedstead covered with white quilt. It was ready for Moran. There was nothing she could do. She went down again and stood in front of Sabina as they brought him into the kitchen and worked him into the bedroom. Then the three men and Dualta came down and left the priest with him. They stood awkwardly in the kitchen. All of them seemed incapable of movement. Outside she could see the people standing in the yard close to the house. They were not talking. There was a terrible shocked silence which you felt you ought to break by screaming. The priest came down. He was taking the stole from around his neck.

'Moran is dead,' he said. His face was stricken. His words reached to the outside. There was a loud wail from a woman. It seemed to bring Sabina to life.

'Mrs Duane,' she said to Una, 'you must change that dress. Come with me. You will have my Sunday dress.' She walked up to the room on the other side. Una followed her.

Father Finucane stood looking at them. They were watching for him. What could he do? The only thing he knew about. He said: 'We will pray,' and he took out his rosary beads and got to his knees and faced towards the door of the dead man, and the men in the kitchen and the people in the yard got to their knees and the only rival sound to the music of their voices was the song of the birds.

And they got ready for a wake and a funeral. He was washed and dressed in a cotton nightshirt and he looked very handsome, and the people came and the provisions came, but he had a quiet wake and he would be buried with the wailing of pipes and the flying of flags and it was so sudden and so shocking that it would take time for them to believe that it had happened.

It was two in the morning when Dualta and Una were walking home. They had no words. What could they say? A decent man was shot to death over a few shillings. He wouldn't get the benefit of a Coroner's Court. There was a Coercion Act in force. He was legitimately dead. He didn't matter. He wasn't even a footnote in history.

A voice called from the shadow of the hedge.

'Dualta! Dualta!' Una felt his arm stiffening. She knew the way the wrinkles of determination would form at the right side of his mouth. He was striding on. He wasn't going to wait. She held him.

'It's Cuan,' said Una. He stopped.

'Are you happy, Cuan?' Dualta asked. 'Now you are right! Here is Moran dead. Good God, Cuan! Now you can really go to work.'

'No, Dualta,' said the voice. 'I would give my own life for him. This is wrong, Dualta. Listen to me.'

Dualta went close to the hedge. He couldn't see his face. It was just a blur.

'I have listened to you too long, Cuan,' he said. 'You will always bring death. Only death to other people. That is what the great patriots do. They are like the generals. They are always safe behind the battles while they incite the innocent to die.'

'Dualta,' said Cuan, 'I didn't mean Moran to die. He was too fine to die. He was a big man. He makes a protest and others follow him.'

'They have a bloody way to follow him now,' said Dualta.

'You must tell me what I can do,' said Cuan.

'Go to hell,' said Dualta.

'Dualta! Dualta!' said Una.

'I cannot tell you how I feel,' said the voice of Cuan, 'because I have never felt this before. I am truly desolate, Dualta.'

Una heard the pain in his voice. She went forward a little and caught his arm. She pressed it.

'I don't know what to do,' said Cuan. 'What would you do, Dualta, tell me! Just tell me.'

'Replace him,' said Dualta. 'That's what I would do. I would take on the burden of his life, that's what I would do. But all the great patriots do is to write a penny pamphlet and a song.'

'How can I take on his burdens, tell me?' Cuan persisted.

'Go to his wife and children,' said Dualta. 'Say to them: I am responsible for the death of your father.'

'That's not true,' said Cuan.

'It's the way I see it,' shouted Dualta.

'Please, Dualta,' said Una.

'Say: I will be your father, to the children, and I will be your husband to the mother. Take all the burdens of a great broad-shouldered man on your thin back. Plant and sow and reap and mow, day after day, week after week, and pay the rent and sell the crops. You think you are able for that! It's so much easier to talk and incite rapparees and burn thatches.'

'You think I should do this then? Would they receive me?'

Dualta laughed. 'You, is it? They would prefer Buach or Páid Monuar or Clarke himself or one of the policemen that shot him. They would be of more use than you.'

'Don't mind him, Cuan,' said Una. 'Go and talk to them.'

'I do not know what to say to them; how to express myself; what they will say to me.'

'They will be kinder to you than Dualta,' said Una. 'They might even understand your pain.'

'I will do that so,' said Cuan. 'I didn't want this to happen. I didn't think it would happen like this. Thank you, Una. You are a person of the people. I am very sad.'

They stood and watched him walk away from the shadows of the hedge into the light of the moon. His shoulders were bowed and his head bent as he made his way towards the house of Moran.

'A lot of good he'll be,' said Dualta. Una walked away from him. He went after her. 'You are displeased with me?' he asked.

She didn't answer him.

'If you knew all the pain he is responsible for,' said Dualta. 'I only know it now.'

'Kindness costs nothing,' she said. 'He feels it deeply.'

'Late has it come to him then,' he said.

'It's harder for him to be humble than you to be kind,' she said.

'You take his side against me?' he asked.

'Dualta,' she said, 'don't be righteous. It does not become you.'

'Now you are aristocratic,' he said.

'Must I suffer because you are mixed up?' she asked.

He was silent. Until they got to the house and found that the candles were lighted in the window and the door opened and in the kitchen Colman was waiting for them, and sitting on a stool in the corner was his father, Bottle, unshaven, with prison pallor still on him, his clothes very ragged, and grinning at them over a mug of buttermilk. Colman was exalted.

'See,' he shouted, 'my father is home again. I said that one day he would come home. He is let out. Isn't it a great day?'

Dualta's heart sank as he saw the boy with the lank hair falling into his eyes. He was tall. His eyes were shining as if he had found a crock of gold. Did we mean so little to him? he wondered, thinking of the training, the coaxing to give his bright brain a disciplined education. Did he really prefer this dirty illiterate maker of illicit whiskey to them?

'You are welcome, man,' he said to Colman's father.

'This is your wife?' said Bottle. 'It was decent of you to care for Colman. He turned into a fine young fellow. He will be a great help to me now.'

'You are going back home, then?' Una asked.

'Yes,' said Colman. 'I have been keeping the house above warm. One day, my father will come home, I said. Now he is home. Isn't this great news? What greater news could happen in the valley?' He knelt by the stool. He put his thin arm around the old man's shoulders.

Una was looking at Dualta's face.

'You will stay with us tonight at least,' she said to Bottle.

'No trouble,' said Bottle. 'I'll doss in the ashes.'

'I knew one day it would happen,' said Colman. 'I was watching the road. I saw him way below coming over the hill. I said: That is my father coming over the hill. I travelled the rocks like a goat until I came to him.'

'I'm glad you are so glad, Colman,' said Dualta.

'You got him to read and write too, and make up sums,'

239

Bottle said. 'Imagine that! It was a brave task.'

'He's not finished being educated,' said Dualta. 'He still has a lot to learn.'

'He knows enough now,' said Bottle. 'Isn't he a scholar? He will have little time for the books now. We have to build up the place again. It will be more important for him now to learn how to fire a still. I must have been sorely missed in the valley.'

Colman laughed. 'You hear that? I will have a place of my own again. Won't that be a great thing? We will be living near to Flan too. I will blind him with my songs.'

Una said, 'You ought to get more schooling, Colman.'

'I will. I will,' said Colman. 'Now you have seen him, I will spread a bed for him near the fire. Tomorrow we will move on. It will be a great adventure.'

Dualta and Una wished them well and went to their room. They didn't take a candle. They undressed in the dark. They lay silently untouching in the bed. She could almost feel the depth of Dualta's suffering.

'He is his father,' she said.

'All we did and we mean so little to him,' said Dualta. 'He casts us off like a worn-out kerchief.'

'He is his father,' she said.

'But what a father,' said Dualta.

'You see now, maybe,' she said, 'that Cuan was really in sorrow.'

He didn't reply.

'Oh, Dualta,' she said. 'I will give you a son. I swear I will give you a son.'

He pressed her hand. Lying on his back. All he could hear was the sad wailing of the pipes that would follow a shouldered coffin.

'I will! I will! I will!' she said.

25

YOU SAY to a person: You have ten years. When you are twenty, ten years seems as long as eternity. When you are thirty, ten years past seem as short as a pleasant dream.

In this September Dualta shaved himself in the piece of broken mirror and discovered two grey hairs. He had to search for them but he found them. Why, he thought, I am getting old, I am a man. He looked more closely at his face. It was lined, he saw in some amazement. Wrinkles on his forehead and between his eyes and by his mouth could be pressed out with his finger, but they returned.

He was dressed in his best clothes. A new body-coat of frieze costing sixteen shillings and elevenpence. It would have to last three years. A new cotton shirt 2/–, breeches 7/4, stockings 1/–, a waistcoat 1/8, and stout shoes 6/–. He had come to the stage that everything had a price. It had to. You had to know if you could afford it, and if you couldn't afford it now that maybe you could afford it next year.

He gathered the money on the table and put it in the canvas sack. It was exact. For here was another gale day, and he thought grimly as he tied the mouth of the sack, it might be his last gale day. His ten-year lease was up. Next week, if Clarke so wished, he could be thrown out on his head.

That would be a pity, he thought, as he looked around. It was a pleasant house now. There were curtained windows and painted furniture that he had made himself, many cupboards, a collection of delf, harness for a pony hanging on wooden pegs.

He threw ashes on the turf fire to rake it. Then he went out and closed the door after him. He walked out of the yard and turned to look back at his property. It was pretty. Men had said to him: Don't make it look pretty on the outside. You will suffer. Put your dung-heap outside the front door. Don't whitewash. Don't paint. Let it look as poor as possible. You will pay for your cleanliness. You will attract covetous eyes. It doesn't pay to be clean. He didn't listen. It was a neat place, it was clean. There was a flower patch under the windows, and wild roses were trained to climb the thatch. Even the fearsome thorn tree had a seat built around it and neighbours had lost their fear of it, and gathered there some evenings smoking and telling tales and spreading news. Behind the house his clean fields climbed the hills, seeming with their neatness to be holding back the wild lands. All right. He had worked for it. He had earned it. It would be a strong man who would take it from him. Even if he died now they could say: The Galwayman achieved something.

He whistled to raise his heart. Then he discovered that it was one of Colman's songs, so he stopped whistling it. His heart dropped always when he thought of Colman. He had never come back to school. He was a young man now, a tattered lanky young man who sang songs and sold whisky for his father. Clever too. Bottle had never been caught since. He provided a need and so he was protected. Publicans who held a licence were pleased to mix his with their legitimate brew. He was the mainstay of the whisky cabins, who needed him like the land needed water. But Colman could have been so different.

He liked going to the school. The few hours he spent there seemed to refresh him. It was a great thing to see children becoming literate. There were always the stupid ones. So difficult to put anything into their heads. But there were the bright ones who soaked up knowledge. They had effected a visible change in the valley. Mainly due to Una. He himself forced knowledge into the children, but she inculcated culture. Cleanliness and manners, and faith, and they went home to the poor houses and they spread this like gospellers. Una was the most popular person in the valley.

Before he went into the school he tried to cast the worry out of his face. He had cause for worry but it was for himself.

There were voices droning from inside. He could hear the spellers chorusing over and over again the English word 'procras-tin-ation'. He went in. He expected Una to be there. She wasn't. There was a smell of home-made ink, confined young bodies. They twisted the whites of their eyes on him. Those who were sitting on the forms stood and chorused: 'God be with you, Master.' The spellers chanted their word louder than ever. He said: 'With you, too. Sit down.' The door of the other room was closed. He walked towards it. He thought that the place looked like a school now. The stones were mortared and whitewashed. Cupboards held books. There was a map of Ireland and a map of Europe on the wall. There was a bright fire burning in the open fireplace. It needed a fire. It was a cold September. It had been a wet summer.

He opened the door and went in. Una was standing there with her back to him. She was talking to little Finola Mogue. She turned her head when she heard him come in and he was shocked at her face. It was drawn and white and as sad as the face of a painted Madonna.

Finola was a small girl dressed in a poor frock that was well patched. Her feet were bare. She was about twelve. She was Una's favourite scholar. She had stopped her in the town last year, plucked her dress and said: 'I want to go to school, I have no penny.' She was a small one. She was not pretty. Her dark hair was straight. She had a small nose, small eyes, and thin lips, but when she smiled her face lighted up like a candle in darkness. She lived with her father and family in one of the cottages.

Una, of course, got her to school. She was bright, she said. A quick little brain. She answered to affection as if she was starved of it. Before Dualta could say anything, Una caught the little girl by the hand and led her to the door.

'Just go to your place, Finola,' she said. 'I will be with you. You are all right now.'

She watched her down, closed the door after her, leaned against it and said: 'Little Finola is pregnant.'

'In the name of God what are you saying?' he exclaimed.

'I didn't want to believe it,' she said, 'but it's true. How low, how beastlike can people become?'

Dualta had to sit on a stool. He put his head in his hands,

243

tried to think. Of people like Mogues. By May or June their potatoes would be finished. They would have their turf cut. So they would put the latch on the door and take to the roads, during what men called the hungry meal months. They would wander and beg and work where they could get it, the mother for fourpence a day, the children for their food. From June to September the whole land seemed to be swarming with beggars, living in the open or in squalid suburbs near the towns where they erected makeshift shelters, nearly a million people living on the verge of starvation until the tubers grew and swelled in the ground and they could tramp home again and dig their potatoes.

'It cannot be,' he said. 'You are mistaken. There are ugly ways they seek to live, but not this. It is not so.'

'It is,' she said. 'We have to face it. They went away in June. She spoke of her father. He is fond of drink. She spoke of money passing. Of grass under trees. Of funny men smelling who did things to her. She doesn't even understand. She cried out. Her father said it was all right, all right. You hear that! Her father. He should be killed. He should be killed slowly. If I was a man I would kill him. I would flay him to death! Oh, Dualta, I cannot stand this. This is too much. That child!'

He rose to her. He held her. 'Easy, easy,' he said, patting her, but he had a cold feeling in his stomach. This child. Great God! 'I'll do something, Una,' he said, at last. 'Leave it to me. I'll do something.'

'What can you do, Dualta?' she asked. She was furiously rubbing her wet eyes. 'This is something for which there is no cure. This is final. How do you tell Finola what's wrong with her? How do you explain?'

'Leave it,' he said, 'for a time. I have to go to the town. I will see her father. I will be calm. I will bring no weapon. You cannot take the whole world on your back. This is terrible. But it will resolve itself. We'll find a way. It does something for me. It makes Clarke seem less important.'

'This is the day then,' she said. 'I forgot. I should be with you. I cannot think. Let God go with you. Don't lose your temper with Clarke. That's all. We can't afford it. But now it seems to me that the whole valley is smudged. What is the use of trying? A thing like this. Is the world filled with monsters?'

'No,' he said. 'Most people are good. You have to think of the good people. If it wasn't for them God would have the world wiped out long ago. Stay here for a while. I will go. You see, you are doing good. Think of all the fine young people you have turned out from the valley school. Finola's father was not a pupil of yours.'

'I will go down,' she said. She wiped her eyes with her palms and the sleeve of her gown (6/–). Here was his mind turning again on costs. Cloak 9/6, three shifts 3/9. Aprons and hand-kerchiefs she made herself like all the other things. Just the price of the stuff. In dress she was no longer a lady, just a lady in her face, that was maturing like his own, settling into the groove of life, being carved benevolently by the years. He put his hand on her cheek.

'You are a wonder,' he said. 'Don't suffer too much over it.'

She went ahead of him. There was a scurrying as some of them ran back to their places. A louder hum from the spellers. Dualta walked out. He patted Finola on the shoulder as he passed. A thin shoulder, a child just coming into bud. He felt his jaws tightening with rage as she smiled up at him. An un-affected smile. Her small teeth were sharp-pointed. They gave her smile a peculiar charm.

'Be good scholars,' he said, and he went out of the door. He went for the pony. He mounted him, sitting on a sack, behind the panniers that held the baskets for provisions.

He saw what Una felt, the smudge on the valley. Although the sun was shining on it, on the harvested fields, on the wet rock mountains, on the sea, it seemed that it had been smudged with a dirty thumb. Yet it was nothing, one little girl among millions. Who would care? They would say high up: Well? Is this the kind of people you want to be free, selling their own daughters for the price of a drink in a tavern? Ignorant, illiterate, dirty, unscrupulous, wallowing in enjoyable wretchedness. He thought of Flan's picture of benevolent chieftains, ruling a clan, every member of which belonged, important. This was a dream of nostalgia. It probably wasn't like that at all. It was why people believed or pretended to believe in fairies, or listened to stories of giants who could do impossible things. All you wanted was to find a crock of gold at the end of a rainbow, or from the hidden store of a small green cobbler. Then your troubles would be over. All afflicted people would turn to a dream world to get away from the harsh reality of bleak oppression, of helpless wretchedness.

In the town he felt he hated them. They roared and shouted and sang, chapmen and bakers and buyers and sellers, a deafening noise arising from them. This was in the mass. You had to look closely at each separate face then to see that they were not like the sound of them. Friendly, kind, cruel, brutal faces, and the brutal faces would probably belong to kind people and the kind faces to brutal people. Flan's silent people indeed. And yet he knew what he meant, that the louder they were, the more silent they were. They would shout to hide themselves.

He paid his compliments to Clarke's brother-in-law and to his fat frightened wife. Frightened because by a strange chance Cuan was there at Clarke's house was him, Cuan and Fiacra McCleary, a stocky youth with very fair hair and blue eyes. Cuan was thin. The ferocity had never left his face, but he could smile. Dualta didn't see him often. He was running Moran's place better than the dead man had done it. This won the wonder of everyone in the valley. But then he had married Sabina. People said they didn't sleep together. There were no fresh children. Dualta could believe this. If Cuan had decided to do a thing he would do it with dedication. If he married Sabina it would be to protect her name, he thought. Since Moran died there had been no upheavals in the valley.

'We do not see you, Dualta,' Cuan said.

'Who sees anyone?' Dualta asked. 'Life is too hard. Unless we bury the dead or bed the wed, we do not meet. Will we have time to meet then when we are old?'

'If we have life,' said Cuan. 'Fiacra, pay the little gentle-

246

man five shillings. That's necessary. It's a sort of bribe, but it is as well to go with the customs of the people.'

'Now, McCarthy,' said little George Shields.

'He has his eye on your place, Fiacra,' said Cuan. 'There is nothing between his getting of it except your life. You must remember that. You must stay alive for his funeral.'

'Now, now, McCarthy,' said George. Dualta laughed.

He went and handed his box of eggs to Mrs Clarke. 'I do appreciate it, Mister Duane,' she said. She was the only one in the valley to call people Misters.

'Here's a hen, ma'am,' said Fiacra. 'It is a young hen. My mother sends it with her compliments.'

'See how polite the boy is, ma'am,' said Cuan, fixing her with a cold eye that made her shudder.

'Well, well,' said Clarke, leaning back in his chair when he saw Dualta.

'I know you have been waiting for this for ten years,' said Dualta. 'Another day it would have mattered to me. It doesn't matter now, Clarke. Here is your money. You can play with me. I haven't time. I have something to do.'

'You know that I could put you out of the place tomorrow?' Clarke asked.

'I do,' said Dualta. 'I also know that there would be trouble in doing so. I don't want trouble. I know that I am a hard worker, that I have brought something from nothing. But I am at the greatest strain to make it pay. If I cannot make it pay, nobody else will. You know that. Your money is safe from me. But don't stretch me too far or there will be no money.'

'I like straight talking,' said Clarke. 'You people don't understand my position. Private property is sacred. It must earn. It cannot lie fallow. The estate must pay, or Sir Vincent will get an agent who will make it pay. Probably a meaner man than I am. You will be a tenant at will.'

'No lease?' asked Dualta.

'No lease,' said Clarke. 'You have had your lease. You made a nice house out of the Bacach's place. There was no rent on it in the lease. Now we will settle for three pounds rent on the house. I won't increase the rent on the land. I think I am being decent. Now that the tithes have been put on the land-lords we will put a rent of two pounds ten shillings spread over the eight acres. This will take care of the tithes you used to pay. So you will have to find five pounds ten shillings extra. This is not a great burden.'

'So we lost the battle for the tithes,' said Dualta.

'No, you won,' said Clarke. 'Didn't you know? Parliament have abolished the tithes. They have put the burden on the landlords.'

'Who put the burden on us,' said Dualta.

'But you won the battle,' said Clarke. 'The people will always prevail. O Connell won the tithes battle, didn't he?'

'I have to accept your terms,' said Dualta. 'I can't do any-thing else. It will take finding, all this. It represents the earnings of one hundred and forty days extra. Do you know that?'

'Hard work never killed anyone,' said Clarke. 'You have no family to support. It's not like as if you had.'

Another time, Dualta might have hit him and destroyed everything. Now Clarke sardonically watched the white on the knuckles of his fists. He knew tenants at will could not afford displays of temper. He felt that he had won a measure of respect from the disrespect of this independent stranger.

'That's all, Duane,' he said. 'I'll see you next gale day.' He called. His face clouded when he saw Cuan and young Fiacra coming into the room.

Dualta left. He breathed hard outside, and then, recov-ered, he went into Donoghue's shop. No change. Mail-day crowds, smells of spirits and spices. The only change was young Mrs Éamon Donoghue sitting on a high chair at the far counter. Once Margaret Bradish. They knew she was go-ing to marry Éamon when Mrs Bradish came in her carriage to the school and in front of the scholars, and much to their delight, told the schoolmistress what she thought of her. She had lowered herself to marry a common spade man from Gal-way. Was it any wonder that the valley was infected? Her own daughter Margaret announcing that she was marrying the son of a merchant. Margaret had told her mother if she didn't get her permission she would live with him in the open (more to Éamon's dismay than his mother's, Una thought). So they were married and the only one who really suffered was Tom Keane who had to drive many weary miles to the next town for provisions, since Mrs Bradish wouldn't deal with the commoner who had captured a queen. Maybe old man Donoghue suffered too. Margaret reigned in the business like a queen. She was improving everything, including old Donoghue. Sometimes he was proud of his son's bride, but other times he wished he had married the daughter of a tinker.

Dualta thought of all this as Margaret treated him distantly. Oddly enough she seemed to be more of a snob now than when she had cause to be one.

So he left there and loaded the pony, tied him in Donoghue's yard, and grimly set off down the town towards the cottages to seek out Mogue, the father of Finola.

He answered greetings mechanically. He made his way through the mobs of people almost unconsciously. Where the houses of the town gave way to the clustered cottages near the sea, he paused. The cottages were built like flies in summer swarming around the eyes of cattle. But between the town houses and the cottages there were four better-type houses near the road roughly walled off with slab rocks. He paused, then went into the second of these. At the door he called, 'Sheila! Sheila! my darling, are you within?' There was a pause and then a shout of glee and Sheila O Connor erupted from the house, threw wet hands about his neck and kissed him.

'Dualta! Dualta!' she said, holding him back to look at him and then kissing him vigorously again.

'Hi, hi, hi!' Dualta exclaimed.

'Are you finished fondling my wife, Duane?' said the man who came to the door behind her.

'Come in! Come in! Come in!' said Sheila, 'we'll boil an egg.'

'Is it a cuckoo's egg we'll give him then?' her husband asked.

Dualta laughed. He went in. Three children swarmed around him calling 'Dualta! Dualta! Dualta!' Dualta raised them and kissed them, and said, 'You might find things in my pocket,' so they screeched and put their small hands in his pockets and pulled out the few boiled sweets that always rested there. It was the mark of a childless man, they said, always to carry boiled sweets in his pocket for children.

'We are so pleased to see you, Dualta,' said Sheila. 'So pleased. How are they all in the valley?'

He thought: What a relief to see happiness! He looked at her husband, a tall very dark man, dark hair, dark eyebrows, always looking unshaven, with a thin handsome face and a lithe body. He was the son of the cobbler, Mac an tSiuneara, just that. His name was Tom Walsh but people rarely used his name. He had kidnapped Sheila a few years ago. Farmers did not like tradesmen. They did not like their children to mate with them. So one night poor Carrol O Connor came home to find his daughter gone and a letter from the cobbler's son saying he had taken her away as he loved her, and if Carrol gave his consent to their nuptials she would be returned to him intact. Usually the farmers consented. Even if she had not lost her virginity, how would you ever be sure? But not Carrol. She was his favourite child. The loss of her like that was a terrible blow to him. But he did nothing. He did not give his consent. So they were wed without it, and they settled in this small place in the town. Cobblers could earn about one shilling and sixpence a day if they were good cobblers, and Tom was, but the better you made the shoes the less call there was for your services, and in summer most people used their bare feet anyhow, so they found it hard to live, but as he looked at them, he realised that hardship was as you made it. The house was neat and clean; the children, two girls and a boy, had only playing dirt on them. The few years had matured Sheila, but had not hurt her gaiety. Tom was kind. He was an athlete, a great runner and jumper. She fell in love with his long legs, and his face like a black donkey, she said, when she saw him running at the parish sports meetings or playing mighty hurling in the fields.

'My father? My father?' she asked. 'How is he?'

'He has not come to see you then?'

'No. No.' She was sad for a second. 'God is good. What brings you? You will eat with us? How is Una?'

'I'll not stay with you,' he said. 'I have a mission. I am seeking a man called Mogue. Can you tell me where to go?'

'Oh,' said Tom, 'he is a bad one. What business have you with him? You better seal your pockets.'

He wouldn't tell them. It should be told from the tops of houses so that people would beat him and drive him away. But what about Finola herself? No. People must not know.

'We like his daughter Finola,' he said. 'We want to know if he will let her stay with us for a while.'

'That would be good for her,' said Tom. 'Do not despair. You can buy her from him for sixpence. He is a drinking man.' He spat in the ashes of the fire.

'Let me go so,' said Dualta, standing. 'I will come back again.'

'No, no, no!' said Sheila.

'No, no, no!' said the children, holding his legs.

'I am jealous of their affection for you,' said Tom. 'Leave him be, children. He has a mission.'

'But you will come back,' said Sheila, holding his arm.

'Don't I always come back to you, Sheila?' he asked.

'Such talk,' said Tom.

'I saw her before you,' said Dualta. 'Let me go. I swear I will come back. Not today, but another day. Visiting you is like clover fields in the summer time or the warm wash of the cleansing sea.'

'You must, you must come back,' Sheila said, as they went to the door with him, holding on to him, the small jaws of the children bulging with the hard sweets.

'I will be back,' he said, 'as sure as God.'

He got away from them. Tom walked a piece of the road with him.

'There is something moving you, Dualta?' he asked.

'Yes,' said Dualta. 'It will pass. You are happy, man. Hold your happiness. You have something precious.'

'Sheila aches for her father,' said Tom.

'One day he will come,' said Dualta. 'Just men are very severe on themselves.'

'I want nothing from him,' said Tom. 'He must know that.'

'If he searched the world,' said Dualta, 'he could not have found a better son-in-law. One day he will know.'

'You turn into the second lane,' said Tom, pointing, 'and go first right and first left and the dirtiest and most smelling house is the one of Mogue. Come to us again.'

'I will,' said Dualta. 'Your happiness refreshes me.'

'God bless you,' said Tom, and watched him go into the lane. The houses were thrown at one another. The dirt ways between were muddy and smelled vilely of pigs and the dirt of dogs and the leavings of humans. Most of the houses wanted re-thatching. They were green with moss and decay, and the walls were stained green. Few of them had chimneys. The smoke came out of the open doors, along with screeching chickens chased from the houses, so that the women could come and look at the stranger, their heather brooms in their hands. Many children sucked thumbs as he passed. Very poorly dressed, almost naked, extremely dirty. How had a flower like Finola come from such a place? One or two of the houses were well kept in the midst of the general poverty. Whose fault? They lived on a few roods of potatoes, a few days' work during the year. Made enough to pay an exorbitant rent on the patch of land and the terrible houses. Sometimes they rarely saw an actual penny. They used their labour to pay their rent, and when that ran out they took to the roads, like migrating sparrows. Whose fault? They rarely blamed God.

He found Mogue's. He recognised two children sitting on a dung-heap. They had the odd sharp features of Finola, the big hungry eyes.

'Is your father within?' he asked them. They just looked at him. They didn't answer. He went to the door. He was standing in a puddle of mud. The place was wreathed in blue smoke that made his eyes ache. It was dark. The two openings in the walls were deep and narrow, without glass or stuffed rags. 'God bless all here,' he said. He waited for a word. He didn't hear any. A sort of grunt perhaps. He bent his head and went in. There was a man sitting at a badly made table which was merely a potato-cish standing on a three-legged pot. His eyes were the part of him most easily visible. The rest was a mat of tangled hair, tangled beard. He was a big-bodied man covered in places with old oddly patched clothes. He was eating potatoes.

'You are Mogue?' Dualta asked. He had to rub his aching eyes with the back of his hand. They started to stream.

'Sit down,' said the man. He had a deep voice. Dualta felt wood behind him. He turned. A woman was holding a stool at his knees. 'Thank you, ma'am,' he said. She was a thin-faced woman. Her face was grimed from the smoke. 'You are welcome, sir,' she said in a small voice. Dualta had never been called 'sir' before.

'Eat,' said the man Mogue, waving a dirty hand at the cish of peeling-littered potatoes.

'I thank you, I have eaten,' said Dualta.

'You don't like our salt,' the man said.

'I will eat a potato,' said Dualta, taking one and starting to peel it with his nails. 'You have good potatoes.'

'New,' said the man. 'What do you want? You are the man of the Mistress?'

'Yes,' said Dualta. 'It's about Finola!'

'She is bold, hammer her,' said Mogue. Dualta saw that his eyes were red-rimmed, from smoke, and the whites bloodshot from drink. He was a most unprepossessing man. How could he be the father of Finola?

'She is good,' he said. 'Will you let her stay with us?'

'Keep her. She is yours,' he said.

This reply maddened Dualta. He had been holding on to his temper. He knew the people. The poorer they were, then the more precious were their children to them. It was always the way. When you could create nothing else, to create a child of your own was as precious as discovering a jewel in a turnip field.

253

'She means so little to you! Would you sell her then? If I offer you sixpence for her will that be enough? Is it so little she means to you?'

'Don't insult me,' said the man. 'What is under you?'

'You!' shouted Dualta. He was standing. 'Have you no feeling? Are you an animal? What have you done to her? You took her away? What did you do to her? Are you human? You take her away and sell her body to a tinker for the price of a glass of whisky. How many? May the great God rot you! May the worms eat you! May the pigs feed on you!'

The man Mogue kicked the pot and rose to his feet. He was very big. He was nearly touching the roof. He hit Dualta in the face with his two fists held in front of him. Dualta went down in the dirt and the man fell on top of him. His breath was foetid. His clothes smelled. Dualta was smothered. He heard a cry from the woman. He wriggled from under the great weight of him, grabbed the stool he had been sitting on, and raised it up to bash the man on the head. The woman's voice stopped him. 'No! No!' she said. Dualta lowered the stool. The man lay on the floor. He turned over on his back. 'He is drunk,' she said. 'He does not know what he is doing.'

She bent to him. Dualta put down the stool and helped her. They put him sitting on a stool. He leaned back against the wall, his big head lolling.

'You will come outside,' she said. He went with her. He breathed the outside air into his lungs. She was rubbing a sack apron on her eyes. He couldn't make out if she was crying or if it was the smoke. The two children kept looking at them.

'You will look after Finola,' she said. 'God reward you. Here is no place for her.'

'You know what way she is?' he asked.

'No, no, no, please God, not that, not what you said,' she said. 'It cannot be. Just to look after her. She is a good girl. She will work hard for you.'

He looked at her. She was very thin. She was a young woman but very old beyond her years. What was the use?

'All right, ma'am,' he said.

'He was a good man,' she said. 'You must believe. We were put off three years ago by Cringe. He wouldn't send the children to that school. So we were put off. We had to come down here. He was a good man. His place was fine. He lost his heart. He was a good man, a good man.'

Who is good? wondered Dualta. Who is good? But he still wanted to kill him. He wanted to tear him to pieces. He took two half-crowns from his purse. 'These are for you,' he said, 'for you. Not for him. You hear?'

'God reward you,' she said. 'God reward you.' He felt in his pockets. There were four boiled sweets remaining. He gave two each to the children. They looked at them a long time before they shyly took them. They sucked them then, and their faces lighted up with pleasure.

He turned and left. Mogue would probably get the money anyhow, he thought. But what did it matter. The day was still smudged. The palms of his hands were almost cut from the way he clenched his nails into them. But it was good to feel the clean air from the sea blowing on his face.

When he got home Father Finucane was sitting on the seat under the thorn tree. Dualta went over towards him. The priest's head was in his hands, and it was only when he got near to him that Dualta knew the priest was crying. He looked up then and saw Dualta. He turned his face away as he reached for a handkerchief. Dualta sat beside him.

'It is good that you have tears,' he said. 'I saw her father.'

'Did you kill him?' Father Finucane asked.

'No,' said Dualta.

'I would,' said the priest.

'No, you wouldn't,' said Dualta. 'He has stopped being human.'

'You work and you work and you work,' said the priest. 'So much goodness. So much humour. Hardships borne smilingly. A thing like this is beyond comprehension. It wounds the world.'

'Una! Una! Una!' Dualta called. They watched. She came to the door. The girl was with her. 'Come over here with you both,' he said.

They came; he took Finola's hands and pulled her between his knees.

'Your father wants you to stay with us, Finola,' he said.

He saw her breast rising and falling fast. He felt the clasp of her small hands tightening on his own. 'He does?' she asked. 'To stay with you? Always or for now?'

'It will be for always,' he said. 'If God is good. Your mother wishes you to stay with us. Will you be able to abide us, do you think?'

'Oh, yes, yes, yes,' she said.

'This is a gift,' he said, taking the satin-dressed doll from under his coat. 'It is for you. I got it at a stall.' It cost three shillings and ninepence out of his tight stores. It was worth eight times that sum to see the light in her face. A girl expecting a baby, overjoyed by the possession of a rag doll! This is the world. He looked at Una over the top of her head.

'We have a daughter,' he said. 'Not a son.'

'He will come,' said Una.

Father Finucane stood up.

'You are blessed,' he said. 'I will not go near the cottages for a year. I have not your patience. You are a better man than I am, Dualta.'

'That is a plain lie,' said Dualta.

'God bless you,' said the priest, and walked away.

God was good. She didn't carry the embryo, so she didn't know, and Dualta had a daughter, and a spoiled daughter she became, but Una longed for a son, and she got him at a peculiar time.

26

FATHER FINUCANE spent the Friday night at Maynooth. He had been several days on the road, feeling guilty at leaving his parish even though he was a sort of official Repeal Association emissary from the Valley. He hadn't had a holiday since he was ordained. He felt like a schoolboy released from school jogging on his horse to Dublin. It was October and the harvest had been good and nobody talked about anything but O Connell and the monster rally that had been called at Clontarf on Sunday next. Men said it would be the greatest meeting until the Last Judgment. O Connell had called thirty-one great meetings between March and August. Each of them was bigger than the last. The one at Tara in August was still spoken of with awe. From thirty miles away on the western road he had passed thousands of people who were on their way by foot to Clontarf, their silken banners rolled, camping cheerfully in fields and ditches, singing and dancing at night by the camp fires. He had thought the hosts at the Clare Election were big, but they would be nothing to the crowds that would be gathered at Clontarf.

He stayed with his friend Father Pat in the College. He greeted him joyfully. They had been in the same ordination class together. They could talk over many things, past times and what had happened to all the men who had been ordained with them.

It was a bit of painful nostalgia, to see the old corridors, the old lecture rooms, to think of the fire of fervour, the heated dialogues; wanting to convert the world overnight; the sad awakening, growing old. He saw his age in the features of Father Pat who was a lecturer. They smoked pipes sitting on leather-covered chairs in the book-lined room.

Father Pat was filled with O Connell.

'Yes, I was at Tara,' he said. 'And it is true about the crowds. If you said a million people you would be near the mark. There wasn't a coach or carriage or four-footed beast left in Dublin. If you could stand on the mound at Tara you couldn't see a blade of grass with the bodies of men, women and children. I have never seen anything like it. Never will again. There were people stretching from Tara to the Hill of Slane, I declare. Bands without number, banners, bunting. It was a riot of colour.'

'How did he take it?' Father Finucane asked.

'He is a master of mobs,' said Father Pat. 'There isn't

another man living in the world who could handle a million people. It's just amazing. He is sixty-eight and he looks young. Standing up there his voice reaches out to the horizon. He plays tunes on the spines of people, like a great fiddler. He tells them this is the year of Repeal. We will get Repeal. We will get our own Parliament back where it belongs, the one that Pitt stole from us forty-three years ago. They believe him.'

'Will he get it?' Father Finucane asked.

'No one else will,' said Father Pat. 'He is ruling Ireland. Such a master of symbols. Tara of the Kings. It belonged to the High Kings. They feasted there, called the great fairs there for hundreds of years. Here was O Connell standing on Tara. As far as the people were concerned he was their descendant, crowned and all. And Clontarf! You see. That was where Brian Boru won his great victory over the Northmen. This is where Daniel O Connell is going to win his great victory over Peel and the Englishmen. How can any Government ignore the moral pressure of a million people gathered on one place saying: We want Repeal! Before they said: We want Emancipation. They had to get it. Since the beginning of history there has never been peaceful pressure like this brought to bear on a single subject. I tell you, I am a fairly cold analytical man, and there at Tara I felt myself burning, and all without bloodshed. That will be his great triumph if he succeeds, that he succeeded without bloodshed.'

Later some of the young students came and sat on the floor. They reminded Father Finucane of his lost youth.

'O Connell is a bluffer,' one young red-head said. 'If I was Peel I would call his bluff.'

'Man, listen to the politician,' one jeered at him.

It heated the red-headed one.

'Who wants a Parliament back as it was before?' he asked. 'What good was it to the people only to pass laws repressing them, and feathering their own nests? A bunch of unprincipled scoundrels is all they were, social criminals.'

'Oh, oh, oh!' they called him.

'It is true,' he said. 'You get nowhere with soft words and bluff.'

'He has been reading *The Nation*,' another one said.

'Why not?' he asked. 'Davis is a better man than O Connell. O Connell is gone soft in the head. He won't be contradicted. The Young Irelanders are the ones for me, building a national ideal with power instead of blather.'

'Listen to him! Listen to him!' they said and piled on top of him smothering him, laughing and tumbling until Father Pat put them all out.

It was a nice interlude. Father Finucane was sorry in the morning when he had to leave. Yes, he would come back again, sometime. When would sometime be? Pity, he thought, as he looked back once, that you cannot always remain behind those sheltering walls, loving the theory, not knowing the reality. Talking your head off, settling all the affairs of your country in an evening's passioned oratory.

The people were piling into Dublin. I must remember all that I see, he thought. I will be questioned so closely sitting under the thorn tree. He crossed a bridge and went his way by the Liberties near St Patrick's. The thoroughfares were filthy here, the tall dilapidated houses jampacked with people. They lived, he saw, in the most appalling poverty. Thousands of children were playing in the gutters, dogs barking, draymen cursing. Was there a difference, he wondered, between the poverty of the small towns and the poverty of the great towns? It was only in towns of any size that you saw why the country was called a nation of beggars and O Connell was their king.

He went up the good shopping street. Here were carriages and coaches and liveried footmen, sellers calling wares, and beggars, little children pulling at his gaiters. He had nothing for them. His pouch was empty. He was getting by on charity himself. So all he could give them was his blessing. Into the Green with its foetid stench, where the people discarded rubbish and dead dogs in the trench surrounding it. Coming to the house of his friend near the church. Thinking of them all: Father Pat, Father Joe who had sent him Una,

259

Father Pete, Father Mike. And here was Father Phil.

Wide-eyed. 'Fin! Fin! Where did you come from? I thought you were dead.'

'Not dead,' he said laughing. 'I'm in Clare.'

'Same thing,' said the Dublin man. 'The culchies will be the death of you. Come in. I'm so happy to see you. And why are you here?'

'I am here for Clontarf,' said Father Finucane, going in with him. He had tied the horse to the railings outside.

'Oh, man, this will be it,' said Father Phil. 'It will be the greatest day in history. Have you been at any of the great meetings at all?'

'I was at Ballycoree,' said Father Finucane. 'Repeal Police, white staves in their hands, ribbons on their hats. Great order. People in parishes and counties. And no drinking. That's what makes you think the people are so serious. Whoever heard of ten thousand Irishmen together and not a drop of whisky between them?'

'It's a wonder, man,' said Father Phil. 'Father Matthew came at the right time, but even if he hadn't, they wouldn't. They listen to O Connell's voice. If he said: Take the country with your bare hands, they would do it.'

'You are all for him, then?' Father Finucane asked.

'He is the greatest Irishman that ever lived,' said Father Phil.

'Now I got my answer,' said Father Finucane, laughing.

They were not properly in the house, when the great knocking came on the door. It was very urgent knocking.

'At this time!' said Father Phil. 'Sit down and wait. I will be back.'

He went out of the room. Father Finucane sat on the arm of a chair. He had hardly seated himself when he heard the calling: 'Come down! Come down!' He went. Father Phil was taking off his soutane. There was a big man with a ribbon in his hat standing at the door. Father Phil's face was strained.

'Peel has proclaimed the Clontarf meeting,' he said.

'It's not true!' said Father Finucane.

260

'As true as day,' said the man. 'They are calling it out with the handbells. The posters are going up.'

'I will have to go over to the Hall,' said Father Phil. 'Will you come? This is so serious. What will O Connell do?' he asked.

'He will let the meeting go on,' said the man. His jaw was hard. 'Will they massacre a million men?'

Father Phil gave orders for the horse to be brought around to the yard and then they hurried away through the streets. It was not far. There was a tremendous babel of noise arising. They saw one of the notices going up. So that was true. And they heard the bell-ringer calling it, so that was true as well.

Father Finucane was glad of Father Phil. The Repeal Police at the Hall knew him. They let him through. Thousands of people were milling around outside now. They were calling for O Connell. Inside, the stairs and passages were jammed with sweating men. Their faces were red. They were angry. They were bewildered. The man pushed a way through for them. The police at the door to the room opened it for them and they were inside. There were not many there. O Connell was facing them. He was pale. Father Finucane was shocked by his appearance. He had his hands behind his back. Why, he thought, the man looks his age. He was ringed by men. They were hitting the table with their hands.

'He cannot get away with it,' they were saying. 'They daren't fire. We can match them!'

'How?' O Connell suddenly shouted. That silenced them. He spoke in a lower key. 'They have brought in thirty-five thousand troops. The Martello Towers are fortified. There are three men-of-war in the Bay with their guns cleared. On Clontarf they have the 60th Rifles and the 5th Dragoons; the 54th Foot and the 11th Hussars are on Conquer Hill. They have the Royal Horse Artillery with four six-pounder guns unlimbered and ready for action.'

'It's bluff,' a tall thin man with a fierce moustache shouted at him. 'There are Irishmen among those soldiers. They will never fire their guns on other Irishmen. They will not kill their own.'

'They have killed their own before this,' said O Connell. 'They will do it again.'

'You must not call off the meeting,' the man said.

'I am an old man,' said O Connell. He stopped as if he was listening to what he had just said. His body sagged. He sat into a chair. 'I am an old man,' he repeated. 'In a terrifyingly short time to come I am to meet God. It would be easy to be a hero!' He shouted this at their faces. 'I could say: Come! and they would come. They would walk into the mouths of the cannon. I could die with them. It is a wonderful picture. I would live forever. It is a great temptation. Can't you see that? It is a great moment. But I won't face God with the blood of innocent people on my hands. Make what you will of it! That is all. Call off the meeting. Send men out on horseback to every road. Turn them back. Just turn them back.'

'So Peel has won the victory over you,' said the tall one with a terrible taunting.

Father Finucane watched him fascinated. Peel and he. The one he had called Orange Peel — 'his smile is like the glint of the plate on the lid of a coffin,' he had said. The patient Peel who had been willing to wait long years for his revenge.

"He may have won a battle,' said O Connell, 'but he has lost the war. What is the alternative to me? Did he think of that? Leave me alone for a while now. Just leave me alone. Later I will talk to the people before I am arrested. He will have to do that. He can't have one without the other.'

Father Finucane thought he would never forget O Connell's face as it looked at that time.

He told them all these things sitting under the thorn tree.

'He had the greatest opportunity of any man in history,' said Cuan, 'and he rubbed his name out of the books talking like a pious old woman. Even if a thousand had been killed wouldn't it have been worth the sacrifice?'

'He wouldn't think so,' said Dualta.

'I don't think you understand, Cuan,' said the priest. 'Many mistook his attitude for fear. It will be long debated. I don't think he was ever greater than at that moment. His decision was worthy of a great poem. Do you think so, Flan?'

'No,' said Flan. 'He was not the voice. How can you raise a million people to the stars and then dash them down? He was not worthy.'

Flan rose from the seat. He spat on the ground and walked away from them softly humming the song of the sons of the King. They listened to him until they could hear him no longer. Their mood was as depressed as the fog in the valley.

'He has a point,' said the priest. 'How can you raise the hopes of the people so high, and then dash them? There has to be something to fill a vacuum. There are angry voices writing in *The Nation*. They say they are Young Ireland.'

'Their voice has a truer appeal,' said Cuan.

He rose too and walked away.

'O Connell had nearly won him,' said Dualta.

'O Connell is in jail,' said the priest. 'When he comes out he will die. He has left too much undone, unravelled. Explosive.'

'Only God knows what will happen,' said Dualta.

'It's His mystery,' said the priest, rising.

Shortly now, the mystery was to be revealed.

27

YOU CAN purchase satisfaction in a field. Why do men till if there is no satisfaction? It cannot be expressed. It would be foolish and a cause of laughter to say: I love the flowers on the potato stalks. Who would not laugh if you said that a healthy potato field is like a poem, a song, a painting, a cathedral? There is creative satisfaction and a sense of frustration attached to all of those things. But the potato field has an added quality – you can eat it. You cannot eat a poem or a song or a cathedral. Life would be empty without these beautiful things, but you could survive without them. If your belly is empty, then you will die, so in a way a potato field is of higher cultural value than a poem or a song or a cathedral.

Dualta was laughing at these fancies as he jogged home from the town on the pony. His head was slightly light. He had been drinking whisky, for Páidi the Smith had pulled a back tooth out of his head. Dualta thought it had not been too bad. Thinking about it had been worse than the actual thing. It had been an admirable strong tooth with a root like an oak tree, said Páidi, as he waved it in the pincers. Dualta had to drink whisky in order to stop the bleeding and to restore feeling to his legs which had been shaky. He kept putting the tip of his tongue back to feel the empty space in his jaw, tenderly. Getting a tooth pulled like that made you feel you were really getting old, he thought. Part of you was gone from you for ever. As you got older and older, he supposed, more and more of you was pulled out or fell out.

The men had laughed at him, but it was the sort of protective laughter that paled when he reminded them that, one day, they too would have to pay a visit to the forge, not to get shoes on their horse, or to get an iron band on their wheel, but to have a strong tooth pulled from their jaw with an iron pincers, the Lord save us. Drink up there, for God's sake, and we'll have another one.

For it was a beautiful July day. This was remarkable. This year had been one of the strangest any of them could remember. They were used to rain, but not the kind of rain they had, that sent the grass growing hip-high. One week it would be clammy weather with the clouds down on your head. It was like living in a baker's oven. Then next week there would be hailstones and you would be shivering with cold. This happened in June. It was remarkable that there was not much wind. In the valley they were used to wind. You cursed it but you missed it when it was not sweeping up the valley so that you could taste salt on your lips. And now here was a day that was scalding hot, almost burning. The heat in the forge from the charcoal had been unbearable, so that the operation took place in the street outside to the awe, sympathy, and laughter of the people. People didn't mind the hot sun. They were sick and tired of the awesome rain-clouds that seemed to depress the spirit and portend evil.

Going to the Town he had remarked on the potato fields. He had said it to the men, what a great crop there would be this year. Since most of their food depended on the crop, everyone was pleased with this and said even if the weather was depressing it was great for the crops, all the warm humidity. You could hear the tubers growing below the ground, they said, and it was as well. By Garlick Sunday, the first of August, last year's crop of lumpers would be uneatable, and the meal months would begin.

He was pleased with his own fields. He thought how you cursed the back-breaking labour. A week to bring seaweed and sand from the shore, and burnt lime from the kiln, digging, manuring sparsely from the dunghill at the stable, the careful cutting of the seed and the way the planting of them with the stibhín or the dipple-stick made the muscles of your back ache. All that hard labour, that seemed it would never end, but you knew that one day the fields would be like they were now, that your labour was not in vain.

He was near Carrol O Connor's when he was disturbed by the smell. First he thought it might be from his mouth. The smith had held the tooth under his nose when he pulled it and said, 'Smell that now. Smell the decay of it. You are well without it.' Dualta could have murdered him.

What he smelled now was like that. But it couldn't be. Mists always rise at evening from wet land after a hot day. It was happening now. It was bright, only eight of the clock, but this smell seemed to be rising from the ground with the mist. He sniffed around him. It was the smell of decay, like an unburied animal, say? Some people were careless with dead dogs, but then that couldn't be either. You would smell a dead animal just passing it by. You would close your nostrils for a few minutes and when you opened them again the smell would be gone. Now he tried this, but the smell remained. He was suddenly very disturbed. He looked at the road all around him. The road was clear. There was nothing dead under the hedges of fuchsia and blackberry all coming heavy with fruit. He went to an opening in the hedge where a field was barred to the road by withered thorn bushes.

He looked in here. He wondered what strange crop could have been grown in the field. He smelled. The stench came from the field. He left the reins of the horse tangled in the thorn bush and went into the field. It was a sloping field overlooking the valley.

He examined the crop. He didn't want to believe it. He had passed this way in the morning after all. It was a potato field then with blooming flowers. Now it was nothing. It was a brown soggy mass of corruption. The whole field. He wouldn't have believed it was potatoes, but here and there a green stalk still stood, but the green leaves were being devoured with brown spots, like animals, like locusts eating into the green, fouling it with the touch of their breath. He looked down then. Everywhere there were potato fields the brown corruption was resting, only emphasised by the odd few stalks that stood green and pitiful in the welter of decay.

He felt his stomach go cold. He shook his head. Maybe it was the whisky. He bent then. He scooped under the rotten stalk, and scrabbled with his hands, feeling for the tubers. His hands were wetted and sticky with a glaucous substance that couldn't be potatoes. He was on his knees then. He scraped at the rich ground. He tore up a yard of it. The potatoes were rotten. There were one or two muddy white little balls, looking forlorn, in the middle of the wet stickiness. He stood up. This was the field of Carrol O Connor. He went out to the road again. He untangled the reins from the bushes. He mounted the pony. The pony felt his disturbance. He danced on the road before Dualta could control him, then he galloped up the hilly road until they reached the turn off to O Connor's. On all sides of him was the smell. The fields were brown. The oats stood tall and green in a terrible comparison, the hay was cocked in the fields. He raced into O Connor's yard.

He didn't go any further. Carrol was there in his shirt-sleeves and Mrs O Connor and Carrol's son, Bercan, a good young man of solid build like his father.

Dualta pulled up. They looked at one another.

It was Carrol who said the word. 'You see it?' he asked. 'It is the blight. It is over the world.'

Dualta looked at them with his eyes wide. What could he say? All over the valley by now men would be out looking, staring, at the fields. He turned the head of the pony and he went away. For he was thinking of his own fields climbing the hill. They were high up. They might not have been hit. They were up in the clear air. He cut across the fields before he reached the house. He kept his eyes half closed. He thought, surely, surely they are green. The pony was labouring. He was kicking him with his heels, leaping the stone walls.

His fields of potatoes were a brown mass.

He had to sit on the wall, his hands between his legs, saying, 'No! No! Oh, no! This is not so. This cannot be so.' The pony cropped the after-grass of the meadow with joy.

Hearing distant calling, he raised his heavy head. Tiny figures on the top of the rocky hill, waving, calling. That was Colman and Finola. Another time he might have worried about Finola seeing so much of Colman, a ragged young man; you could use him as a scarecrow, the hair on his face never shaved since it started to grow, a wispy fair beard. 'He has songs,' said Finola. 'Such songs. He dances like a goat on the stones. He makes me laugh so.'

He saw Una near the house. She waved to him. She started towards him. He couldn't bear that. He mounted the pony, having to drag his muzzle from the soft green grass, and he went down to the house. Gaining time, he took the reins and bit from the pony and turned him into the field behind the house. He heard her calling then, 'Dualta! Dualta!' He thought how funny it was that he still got pleasure from hearing the sound of his name on her lips.

He ran from the back of the house by the gable. She was running the other way. He stopped her. 'Una!' he said. 'Una!'

He thought she must have seen, that she was as coldly fearful as himself. But to his surprise there was joy in her face. Her eyes were alight. She came running to him, with her arms wide. He had to spread his own arms to hold her.

'Dualta!' she said. 'Oh, Dualta! Now you can know! Now you can know! I knew. We are going to have a child. You are going to have a son.' She put her head on his chest, squeezed his body with her arms. He tightened his arms around her, looking over her head at the blasted fields which had not got her attention. He turned her towards the house. Let it wait a time, he thought. Let there be joy in my heart instead of fear.

'Oh, my woman,' he said, 'you have picked a wonderful time for a noble deed.'

'You are pleased, Dualta?' she asked. 'Say you are pleased? Say the long waiting has not made you sad?'

'Oh, I am pleased,' he said. 'Only God knows my pleasure. You have left me without words. I love you with all my heart. You are the most wonderful person who was ever created.' Lighten my heart, he prayed. Please lighten my heart, for now your long-awaited child will be born in the middle of a famine.

It takes only three weeks to starve. This is for the poor. Dualta knew this. That was why he was on his way to the house of Finola's people. You have a little oats growing as well as the potatoes. Fine, but you can only harvest one quarter of that, or draw one quarter of your turf from the bog. You are forbidden to move the rest until you have your rent paid in September. The landlord requires a mortgage on your ability to pay. Clarke hired extra stewards to see that only a quarter of either was harvested before September. The oats and the pig paid your rent. What did you feed the pig on if you had no potatoes or offal? If you weren't wise enough to kill the pig and eat him, he would die. They were very susceptible to cholera. Then you could eat a diseased pig before you were evicted. It was the law. It was legal. You may have thought it unjust, but you understood it was the law. How could the world function otherwise if things weren't paid for? You grew cabbage. That was good. So you ate boiled cabbage. Or turnip boxty called champ. This was mashed turnips mixed with the roots of fern or dandelion. This and also boiled crushed roasted leaves of dock sorrel. Put in nettles and you had an exotic-tasting dish. You could go at night and steal a pint of milk from the udder of a richer man's cow, or you could nick a vein in an animal's neck and extract a quart of blood. You could cook this with mushrooms and cabbage and you had a dish called relish cake. This did not last long because men with cows or cattle took to housing them at night or setting a guard on them, or selling them off altogether before they were bled to death.

Then you could turn to the sea for the fruit of the shore, seaweed and shellfish, and later on, as other sources dried up, you could cook snails, frogs, hedgehogs baked in clay, and after that crows or blackbirds which you picked from the hedges at night with a light to blind them. But even the birds became wily. Later you found that your strength was not as good as it was, and that a journey to the shore to search for bairneachs or cockles or even seaweed was wearing on your strength. So you took to eating what they called laughingly the scadan caoc, or blind herring – that is, one that wasn't there but existed in your imagination. And all the time, in the poor cottages by the sea, their determination was to survive until the spring, find some seed for the planting of the new crop of potatoes, hang on somehow and next year would be all right. Eat anything, anything at all. Some of them took to the road, as they had always done in the meal months. Some of them weren't strong enough. They had to stay. Some of them went into the poorhouse in Ennis, hoping their strength would stay with them until they reached it.

For you can survive on nettles and dandelions and seaweed, grass, roots, as long as you have the strength to look for them. If you are not struck by the fever. No famine, no fever, they said. Dualta found the fever.

He had Carrol O Connor's horse and cart. He had been many miles to the mill for the last three days. Three-quarters of his oat crop he had sold raw. From this money and what he had got from the calf, he had enough to pay his rent. For himself he had four sacks of oatmeal. They were hidden in the cart.

There was turf loaded on top of them. Besides his own four he had one belonging to Carrol O Connor that was to be delivered to Carrol's daughter. He didn't like any of this. He kept his eyes fixed on the fat rump of the horse. He had to force himself to think of his own needs and his dependants. He didn't let his mind think of next March, another gale day, where they would find the rent, the money for new seed. That was tomorrow. Let us survive until then.

In the town he noticed the emptiness of the streets, the closed doors. He wondered at this. Many of them had locks on the doors. The people were gone.

Not Sheila. Not yet. But she was going. He stood and looked at it. It was bare. Tom was on his knees tying the neck of a sack. Sheila was tying a ribbon in the hair of her eldest daughter.

He said, 'God bless all here!'

They turned and looked at him. His heart sank. The eyes of the children were big with hunger. Sheila wasn't plump. The face of Tom was cavernous.

'You are welcome,' said Sheila in a subdued voice. She was not exuberant. She did not run to kiss him.

'Your father sent me with some meal for you,' he said.

They looked at one another.

'Tell him,' said Sheila, 'to give it to somebody who really needs it. We are going away.'

'Where are you going?' he asked, his heart falling.

'We are going to America,' she said. 'Tom sold all his tools. We sold the furniture we had. Most of the clothes on our back. We are walking to Galway to get a ship. We have our oatcake. We are beholden to nobody. We are taking the emigration.

'Your father doesn't know,' he said.

'It won't worry him,' she said. 'He didn't know we were here. We could have died. All he cares about is his two-life lease and his eldest son. He will be happy to know we are away from his conscience.'

'Don't say that,' said Dualta.

'Take the meal to the cottages, Dualta,' said Tom. 'I hear

there is fever down there. They need it. See, we are happy to be leaving it all behind us. It is death to remain. Who wants new shoes or mended shoes? It is better to go. This is a miserable land.'

'You won't win it by leaving it,' said Dualta.

'Who wants to?' said Tom. 'It belongs to them. You cannot snare a rabbit, cut a tree. You cannot even own the fresh air.'

'Things will change. They won't change if everybody goes away,' said Dualta.

'Don't be mad, Dualta,' said Sheila. 'Everybody will die. I don't want my children to die.'

'People have died on the America ships,' he said.

'We won't,' said Sheila. 'We won't.'

'Won't you go and say goodbye to your mother even, Sheila?' he asked.

'I tried,' said Sheila. 'They are afraid of the fever. She had to talk to me from behind the closed door.'

There was nothing more for him to say. The change in them was a symptom of the change in the land. People were hungry. They were afraid. You had to look after yourself. Who would do it for you if you didn't? Wait until next year. Just hold out until next year. He felt like crying. That was weakness induced by hunger, because he was on low rations himself, counting every bit that went into his mouth, watching Una, her growing body, making sure that she got more than she knew.

He left the cart near the cottages. They were all silent. Smoke was coming from some of the chimneys but all the doors were closed. There was a terrible smell about the place.

He stopped outside the door of the house of Finola's father. It was closed. He tried the door. It was bolted from the inside. He called. There was no reply. He turned and went to a house where smoke was coming from the chimney. He banged on the door. 'Where are the Mogues?' he called. 'Tell me where are the Mogues?' There was a call from the house. Then a woman's voice spoke. 'Go away, amac,' she said. 'We have the fever. Go away!' He pulled back from the house.

Then he went back again to the Mogue place. He looked at the door. Suddenly he put his shoulder against it and pressed. It was frail. The door opened. He was in the kitchen.

They were all dead. All four of them. The turf fire was out. There had been a pot on the fire. Its contents had been burned black. The two children and the father were on the straw. The children were heads and points. Their limbs and faces were black, their lips drawn back from teeth which were white. The father was naked from the waist, his body a mass of purple marks. The woman was lying on her face near the cold fire. She had her hand stretched out to the pot. He turned her. Her face was yellow and purple. He was back again in his terrified youth with fever and dysentry and scurvy; Irish ague, bloody flux, with all its symptoms and its smells and its appalling terror. He was tempted to light a fire and burn the whole place, bodies and all. He didn't. He lifted the woman. She was as light as a feather. He placed her by the side of the children. Then he left the place and ran out. He didn't take the cart. He ran.

Outside Father Finucane's house the people, women and children, rested their backs against the wall, or sat on the ground, listlessly; the row of them went from the road to the open door.

He was there.

He was measuring meal. To each person three pounds of meal.

Dualta stood away from him and called. He looked up.

'Come,' said Dualta. He left the measuring to the blacksmith who was there. 'No more, no less,' he said. 'I'll watch it,' said the smith.

'The Mogues are dead, the four of them,' said Dualta.

'Oh, no,' said the priest.

'It's the fever,' said Dualta.

'God spare us,' said the priest. 'They are the first.'

'There are more of them in the cottages,' said Dualta.

'What can we do? What can we do?' the priest asked. 'I have sold all I possessed. The only thing left to me are the sacred vessels.'

272

'We will have to bury them,' said Dualta. 'If we leave them over the ground more and more will get it.'

'Leave it until night then,' said the priest. 'I will get a grave dug. We will be wanting graves. Nobody is doing anything. Don't they know what's happening? Don't they know its a disaster? What's going to become of us, Dualta?'

'I don't know,' said Dualta. 'I will go to the carpenter. I will get some coffins made.'

He did this. The coffins weren't dear. The carpenter was making cheap ones out of inferior timber. He had the wit to know what was coming.

Nobody came near them. The priest and Dualta put them in the coffins with their own hands. They carried them to the cart. Dualta drove the cart and the priest walked in front saying prayers from his book. It wasn't an Irish funeral. Where were the banners and the slow march of the wailing pipes, the jammed mourners? The people watched them from behind closed doors.

The smith and the carpenter filled in the grave while Father Finucane prayed. It was moonlight, so they could see. Afterwards, Dualta went to the sea, and he washed himself in the cold water. He was afraid. Was he to bring home the breath of fever? Was he foolish to have done the things he had done? He scrubbed his hands with sea sand.

They were waiting up for him.

'You are safe then,' said Una. 'You were so late. We were afraid.'

'I am all right,' said Dualta.

'Did you see them?' Finola asked. 'Did they get the meal? How is my mother?'

'They did not get the meal,' he said. 'Many people have gone away. They have gone away.' He put his arm around her thin shoulders. 'They are well away,' he said. She would know soon enough. They had the distinction of being the first to die.

273

28

H E WAS digging the last blighted area in the potato field. Behind him Una and Finola worked. It was early December and it was very cold. The ground was hard. It was slow digging for him. He felt that if the ground was turned up to the frost, and not left until the spring, the blight in the earth would be turned away. If blight came from the ground. No man knew where it came from. Over the few months in half an acre they had gathered a basket of not altogether blighted potatoes. They were not good, but if they were grated, soaked in water and the bad matter skimmed off it could be made into a sort of boxty bread – if a handful of oatmeal was added to it. It didn't taste good but it might ward off scurvy. Men knew that potatoes kept scurvy away for some reason. Many people were suffering from scurvy. If they got scurvy and the fever they couldn't live. They called it black-leg because when you were dead your legs were completely black up to the middle of the thigh, your teeth would have fallen out and your body would be covered with blood blotches.

He rested on the spade and looked at the two in his care. They didn't look too bad. Finola was very thin and her eyes were bigger, but Una looked less drawn. That was the cow and the milk. Now the cow was dry and would not be giving milk for a few months. The cow would have to be giving milk when his son was born. He was aiming at that, varying her diet of hay, which was all they had, with a few turnips which they wanted themselves, some roots and herbs from the hill. She was a spoiled cow, but she was necessary for their life.

He told himself: They will live. Una will have my son.

From the hill behind they heard the thin sound of the singing. It was like the call of a bird from a great distance. Finola's head came up at once, a pleased light in her eyes, her pointed teeth showing in a smile. Then she saw Dualta looking at her and she dropped her head in confusion.

'Why don't you take a walk up the hill, Finola?' said Una.

'Will I do that?' Finola asked.

'Do that,' said Una. Finola looked at Dualta. He smiled. Then she rose and brushed off the front of her heavy skirt and she set off up the hill walking slowly, pausing to let the breath settle in her breast. It would take a long time to climb the hill, but there he would be huddled in the sheep shelter, waiting for her, wondering if she would come.

'Don't worry,' said Una, looking at Dualta. 'He treats her like a precious china-cup, or a song-bird with a wounded wing. There is so little light left in the world.'

'It's just that you become attached to her,' said Dualta. 'You don't want anything more to happen to her. She is frail.'

'Nothing will happen to her from Colman,' she said. 'Listen!' The thin sound seemed to be part of the frost air. Una hummed. She sang the Irish words to the lilt of the old melody.

'I found a bird in the hazel tree,
    O sing, sweet bird, so sing for me.
    I will shelter you round with ribbon and string
    From the blight of the night and the hawk on the wing,
    In my breast you will rest like the child of a king,
    So sing, little bird, O, sing, sing, sing!'

'They are too young to know what is on top of us,' said Dualta.

'They are as well off,' said Una. 'Soon enough they will know.'

He spat on his hands. He finished digging the ridge. They looked at the basket with its light load. If you didn't know better you would think you were looking at a dozen lumps of earth.

'We'll go down,' said Dualta. He helped her to her feet. 'You feel well?' he asked. 'You don't feel tired? Is your head clear?'

She laughed. 'Don't worry, Dualta,' she said. 'I will not die. Everything is going to be all right. You must believe this.'

'I believe,' he said. He put the spade on his shoulder. He carried the basket in his other hand. She held on to his arm. They walked down slowly. He could feel the warmth coming from her. Her face was flushed. He wished with all his heart that suddenly, as quick as a thought, he could transport her to a safe valley of lush land where there was no blight, no famine, no death. Was there a place like this anywhere in the world?

'Oh,' he said, 'if only you knew what you were letting yourself in for! If only you had sense at the right time!'

She laughed at him.

'If only you had remained single,' she said, 'you could be far away. With nobody to care for. Are you sorry then for your marriage bargain?'

'You know,' he said.

Father Finucane was sitting tiredly on his horse in the yard in front of the house. They stopped when they saw him. Then they walked over towards him.

'Don't come too close,' he said. 'I have been with the dying again today.' As he saw Dualta's face hardening, he turned the horse away from his approach. 'If you don't think of yourself, think of Una,' he said. That stopped Dualta.

'I had the fever when I was a child,' said Dualta. 'They say it does not hit you again.'

'Did anybody come back from the dead to prove this?' the priest asked.

Una thought back to the day she had first met the red-haired priest. He was so different. He had gone speckled white the way red-haired people do. He was very thin. His stock was loose on his neck, the hands that held the reins were all bone.

'You want me?' Dualta said.

'Yes,' said the priest. He dismounted from the horse. He stood away from them. 'Something will have to be done, Dualta. Things are very bad.'

'I would give my life,' said Dualta, 'to stop it all.'

'As of today,' said the priest, 'there are ninety-seven dead in the parish. They don't seem to care. Governments move slow, I know. There is a Relief Committee founded. No priests are allowed on this committee, so how is the true tale to be told? There is American meal being sent on American ships. Depots are being set up. There is not one in our town. Soon, they say, soon. You hear? They cannot sell this meal until all local supplies are used up. Then it must be sold at the price prevailing in the district. Where will the people get three shillings for a stone of meal? If you own any land at all, you are not supposed to be poor. The poorhouses are crowded. They are dying like flies there. You cannot get into the poorhouse if you are a tenant of land. The Board of Works are setting up task jobs. When will they be here? Soon, soon, they say.'

He took a newspaper clipping from his pocket.

'In the Government, they speak of us. One fellow says that the famine is not as bad as the Irish members make it out to be, that they are shamelessly exaggerating for low political purposes. Here is what a Royal Duke says: "I understand that rotten potatoes and seaweed and even grass, properly mixed, afford a very wholesome food. We all know Irishmen can live on anything, and there is plenty of grass in the fields even if the potato crop should fail." You hear. Many people in England are pouring their pennies into a Famine Fund. None of this has reached us. Dualta, we have no voice.'

'What can I do? Who would listen to me?' Dualta was shouting.

'O Connell would listen to you,' said the priest. 'You must go to him.'

'But he knows, he must know,' said Dualta.

'He knows,' said the priest. 'But you must go to him. You must tell him to talk louder. It's no use talking from Kerry. He must go to the place where his voice will reverberate. Why isn't he going there?'

'They say he is sick,' said Dualta.

'He must drag himself on one leg,' said the priest. 'We will be wiped out, Dualta. Before the new crop of potatoes comes in next July at the earliest the most of us will be dead. There is no help for us. The Bradishes have locked up and fled. Clarke

277

has pulled into the big house. You cannot approach them. You must do this, Dualta.'

'You think too big of me,' said Dualta.

'Once a week a carriage comes in from outside,' said the priest. 'They set up a soup-kitchen in Cringe's school. This is Friday, so they make meat soup. You see? So none of the people go. Because it is Friday and it is meat soup. The Quakers are coming, they say. They are good people. But not yet. They haven't come yet. We have to have a voice, Dualta. You must go. Let him write a letter, anything. But you must go.'

'I will go,' said Dualta.

The priest relaxed. 'I knew you would,' he said. 'You will want sustenance on the way. Here is two shillings. This will buy your food. It is a long way.' He saw the face in front of him. 'You are a rich man, then? You have stores of money hidden away? You do not need this humble subsidy? You are proud?'

Dualta dumbly held out his hand. The two-shilling piece landed in it.

'You are just part of something, Dualta,' said the priest. 'I am writing letters to the papers, to the Grand Jury, to the magistrates, to the landlords. We are at the end of our own resources. If we do not get help then we will all die.' He was back on the horse.

'If you don't take it easy, you'll be dead for sure,' said Dualta. 'Will you be of use dead, Father Finucane?'

'I won't die,' said the priest. 'There is too much to be done.'

He turned away from them. He waved a hand, then he slumped down in the saddle. He was like an old man.

Dualta was looking at the ground. His hand was clenched on the two-shilling piece. Una was watching him.

He said, 'There are cracks in your shoes. Tonight I will have to mend them before I go.' She looked at her shoes.

'I will bake oaten cakes for you,' she said.

'Only one,' said Dualta. 'One will do. You must be careful. Don't let people in. Keep the door closed. You have to shut your heart. They might bring the fever. You will promise this?'

'I will be careful,' she said.

They walked towards the house.

The pony was strong. He had hay to eat. There was plenty of hay along the road. There were few animals left to eat it. The people who moved on the road were like walking skeletons. He had to stop his eyes sending messages of intelligence to his brain. They were all on their way to the towns or the poorhouses, unencumbered by anything except their tattered clothes. They had already sold their best clothes to buy food, their blankets, shoes, furniture, anything at all. Pedlars with their four-wheeled carts were gobbling all the raiment in the land. The warehouses of the pawnbrokers were bulging. He couldn't stop remembering the time he had travelled this road to the Clare Election. Think of the bands and the banners and the songs and the great jollity and the cooking fires. It was a terrible contrast. He had to let himself think of that much. Now there was only the silence of shuffling bare feet on the frost-bitten road. Feet raw and thin, dirty and red with the burn of the frost, and they were without greeting. This was a terrible thing. They didn't look up at him. Their eyes never came farther than the likely body of the pony. Were they thinking then how nice a chunk of the pony would be, boiled in a pot? Some men were carrying old women on their backs, walking a few paces, stopping, going on again. Some men were wheeling their thin children in turf barrows.

He galloped the pony, and then he stopped galloping him, because it seemed to him that he was disturbing this silence. He longed with his whole heart for this thin stream of shuffling people to be ended. But it was never-ending. A free mile and then there would be more.

He was near the town when he saw the man and the woman and the three children. The woman was supporting the man. The children were holding on to her tattered skirt. In front and behind there were no others. It was coming towards evening. The sky was a pitiless steel-blue and there were white banked snow-clouds on the horizon, being tinted with a fiery, heavy red colour.

He got off the pony. He didn't greet them. They looked at him from their enormous eyes. He took the man from the woman. He was no weight. His breath on Dualta's cheek smelt of the smell he knew so well, the smell of the shrinking stomach. The man would have been big at one time. He had big bones. Dualta got him on to the horse. He put two of the children in front of him and the other behind him. The pony was restless. Dualta went to his head and led him. The woman was by his side. She had no words. This is the worst thing about it, he thought. It has brought silence down on us.

When they could see spires ahead of them they passed a turnip field. In the fading light he saw movement in it. Then he saw it was covered with people. They were standing or sitting or squatting. They were eating the raw turnips. The field had been full. They were eating what had been left, some soft with frost, some half eaten by birds or rats. All you could see in the sunset was their eyes. Some of them were nearly naked, as they stopped to look at the people on the road. Dualta hurriedly moved on.

It was that way to the town. Every turnip field had squads of people gleaning it.

He knew why when he got to the poorhouse. There was no admittance. The man there held the gates shut. There were hundreds of people lying and sitting and standing along the walls outside the gates. Their faces were lighted by the yellow glow from the light at the gate.

The gate-man was loud and he was fat. Dualta would always remember that about him. He was so fat. No! No! No! In the morning. Not now. In the morning when they counted the number of the dead. Could you put a gallon into a pint? It can't be done.

Dualta heard a voice say. 'They have a coffin with a bottom on a hinge. They drop you into the pit and they can use the coffin again.' Tomorrow! Tomorrow! Tomorrow!

He left his people by the wall. Into the woman's hand he placed the two-shilling piece. She looked at it listlessly. What could you buy with it? How long would it stave off the inevitable?

He went away. It was dark, but he had to get away from the town, as far as he could, as far away, wishing that the pony could grow wings and take to the air, so that you could see nothing, nothing, nothing at all on the ground.

By the light of the moon, he found an empty house, with a sagging door, black within. He didn't go in there. He found the garden hay-cock. He pulled hay for the pony, and he pulled some for a bed for himself. He took out his oaten bread, but he couldn't eat it. In the morning I will eat, he thought. In the morning. He pulled his coat about him. He was thankful to sleep.

He went in the long avenue, the back way. He had shaved himself at an icy mountain stream. He was so cold that he had dismounted and walked. He had had a feeling that by the time he reached Darrynane the cloak of the Liberator would have thrown an invisible and magical protection around his own land. It was not so. He had seen unburied bodies. In one deserted village he had found a man who had died crawling towards the graveyard. In another house he had found a dead woman who had succeeded in burying her husband and two children in the dirt floor of the place before she died. His inclination had been to stop and bury the people, but if he did that he might spend his whole life at it. His brain was numb. He felt that he was empty of all emotion. He wondered what he was doing this for, or why, or what difference it made.

He tied the pony and walked towards the kitchen door. It reminded him long ago of the house of Una's father. There was not a great difference. The yard and the out-offices and the servants' quarters and the carriage-houses and the cooking quarters. And around the front the carriage drive. There would be a pleasant library looking on the sea and the mountains.

He knocked at the door and nearly fainted when it opened and the smell of cooking came to his nostrils and made his stomach ache. He had to bend forward to stop it.

281

A woman stood there, a plump woman with a soup-ladle in her hand. 'Well?' says she. 'I want to see O Connell,' he said. 'I have come from far away.'

She snorted. 'Have you indeed? Well, you can go back the way you came. He is not seeing anybody. He is not a well man.'

'I am staying here until I see him,' said Dualta. He said it politely.

'Are you now?' she asked. 'We'll see about that then!' She went back and called: 'Party! Party!' She turned to Dualta again. 'Now we'll see how long you will last,' she said.

Dualta waited patiently. A man came into the kitchen. He was the very big man they had met on the mountain with O Connell long ago. But he had been dusted with years. He stood in front of Dualta, towering over him. He said nothing. Just looked at him, bent forward. 'I have seen you before.' He spoke in Irish. 'Yes,' said Dualta. 'You were chasing hares.' The man shook his head. 'I cannot remember. But your face I do. What do you want of himself?'

'I was sent from Clare by the priest to talk to him,' said Dualta. 'He is not a well man,' said Party. 'Come in!' Dualta went into the kitchen. 'You,' said Party to the woman. 'Pour the man a bowl of soup while he waits. I will see. I begin to remember you now. It is long ago.' He went out by another door.

There was a long scrubbed table.

'Sit down,' the woman said. He sat at the table. She ladled out soup from the sweet-smelling copper pot. She placed it in front of him. He kept his hands under the table in case she would see them shaking. The smell rising from the bowl was almost overpowering. She cut off a chunk from a wheaten loaf and put it there too. Slowly he brought his hands from under the table. In one he took the big pewter spoon and in the other the bread, and he forced himself to eat slowly, slowly.

She was watching him, a thin-faced man with fine eyes, and his tied hair growing grey at the sides. A handsome fellow if you liked them lithe, she thought. Maybe dangerous. She hadn't liked the firm way he looked at her. He thought it

282

might be a dream that this rich meat and vegetable soup was going into his stomach. He thought of them at home, how they would appreciate this. He thought of the many thousands who would literally give an arm or an eye for it. If he kept thinking that way he wouldn't finish it. So he finished it, slowly, carefully.

Party came back with a woman. She was a low-sized woman with brown hair. She was plump. He wondered at how you noticed plump people now.

'Have you had fever?' she asked.

He paused.

'No,' he said. 'I am free of fever.' She blushed under his gaze then.

'We have to take precautions,' she said. 'What was your name?'

'Dualta,' he said. 'He might remember that.'

'I'll see,' she said. She went out. Party sat at the table.

'Things are bad with you?' he asked.

'Things are bad with everybody,' said Dualta.

'That is true,' said Party. 'Wait until the O Connell is his own man again. He'll make things well. We must have patience.'

'We have nothing else,' said Dualta.

'Is it bad abroad?' Party asked.

'It is death abroad,' said Dualta.

'Aye, aye,' said Party, rubbing his thick thatch with a large hand. 'Wait until the O Connell is well. He will wipe it all out.'

They sat there thinking until the woman came back.

'All right,' she said. 'Not for long. He is expecting people. You must not tire him.'

He didn't answer her. She was uneasy with him. She turned and walked. He followed her. He walked carefully on the polished floors. He had rubbed his shoes with the bottom of his coat. He smelled of damp wool, and of good soup, he thought with pleasure.

They went into the room on the left. There were many windows. On the right the estuary and the islands in the sea.

Ahead of him the looming mountains. There would be less smoke from the thatched cottages.

He was sitting in a big chair in front of the turf fire. He had a woollen thing around his shoulders. Dualta was shocked, as the pale, almost yellow face turned to him. He had been in jail. He was sixty-nine. Now he would be seventy. Before he went to jail he hadn't looked like this. He had looked eternal, Dualta thought, to those who saw him before Clontarf. Being in jail and being freed by the Lords on appeal, the ones he had called the soaped pigs of society. Now he looked older than his years. 'Come down!' he ordered. Dualta went towards him. O Connell closed one eye to look at him. He smiled. The flesh was loose on his face. That was the thing about him that was lost. He had filled himself. Now his jowls were loose. There was a slight shake in the hand that rested on the chair.

'I'm glad to see you, sir,' said Dualta.

He pointed a finger at him. It was the hand of an old man. The flesh was loose at his wrist.

'Dualta,' he said. 'You see. Not forget.' He turned to the woman. 'All right. He will not shoot me.' Showing his yellowed teeth. 'Go!' She was going to protest. She didn't. She left. They heard the door closing after her. The walls were lined with books.

'You have trouble?' asked O Connell. 'The world has trouble. There is no end of it. You come from where?'

Dualta told him. About Father Finucane. About what was happening to them.

'All for Repeal,' he answered. 'If we had a parliament in Dublin, they would not let an ounce of food leave the country. You see. All for Repeal. I will get Repeal. I will get it. Without it we are dead. Like now. If we had Repeal would the oats be leaving the country while the Indian meal was coming from America? Socialism. You must not give something for nothing. I will make them see.'

'You are going to talk to them?' Dualta asked.

'After the Christmas,' said O Connell. 'You'll see. I feel. In here. How can I abide it? Along the coast they die. I do what I can. I am emptying my granaries. What I have. Like a spoonful of sea-water to the sea.'

'You will rouse them, sir,' said Dualta. 'You will rouse them, but soon, sir, soon.'

'In 1800, I said it to them, at the Royal Exchange,' he said. 'Have I changed since? Have I said any different? I told them what would happen. Did they listen? They listened. Now that this happens, am I a prophet? No Repeal, famine, pestilence. It had to be. They should stop the ships. Feed the people. Forget famine. Forget rights. Forget finance. Anarchy, they say.' He put his head back. His eyes were still blue, Dualta saw, but they were as if they had been misted over. The brilliance had been scraped away. To Dualta's eyes, this great man, this O Connell had what the people called the smell of the earth from him. He was due for death. The very vague hope in Dualta's heart withered away.

Weak tears forced their way from O Connell's eyes.

'There is only one for each person. I talk of a friend, of a companion of the soul, for a soul. Gone. She was Mary, the name of the Mother of God. Where do you find balance, love, silence, restraint? I could have been Robespierre. Bloody! Agnostic! Filled with Paine.' He chuckled now. Raised his head again. Dualta wasn't sure if he saw him at all, even if he was looking at him. 'That is a pun. Rousseau, Voltaire, Hume, Paine, Godwin. Like racehorses in your veins. When you are young. Mountain torrents. Uncontrolled. Head in the clouds. Heart red with anger. But she saw. You take an idea from one and the other. The good ones. The moral ones. They do not understand God. All good ideas come from God. Like a good stew, these are mixed. You see, and the evil parts skimmed away. She could see. So she goes and there is a deep hole at your feet. You will be buried. Is there use in going on? Only for Repeal. Hauled back from the sea of sorrow. For that. Noble.'

He leaned forward. He was looking at the blaze in the turf fire, unseeingly.

'I am in a grave. Before they close this grave, they will come and spit into it. The others and my own too. These rash young men. They are wanting in guile. They are wanting in

285

wisdom. They will not learn. Let them listen to me. I held back the tide. With my arms. I held back the red tide. I am building barricades of peace. You have to see this. Repeal is the last gap. If this is filled, then there is peace. It is the damming of the tide. Will they break my arms? If they do, who will be there? I have stood like the Skelligs. Can they see this? I have baked a cake. Where is the leaven now? Who will savour salt?'

He put his head back in the chair again. His eyes were closed. There was sweat on his forehead.

Dualta rose to his feet.

'I will go now, sir,' he said.

O Connell nodded. He did not open his eyes. Dualta thought that he was nodding to a speech in his own mind. He took one last look at him and then he walked out of the door, turned right and went down the long corridor and into the kitchen. He didn't look at the people there. He walked into the yard. He took his pony and he mounted him. And he was crying. For what else could he do?'

See this man towering on a platform, the strong planes of his face lighted by torches, alive, vibrant, the golden voice propelling words that sent shivers up your spine.

He was sorry he had come. There was no hope. Now the people were really on their own. The voice was silent. It was weak and dying, it was ten, twenty, years too old, and the black horseman could ride unreined.

29

WHILE DUALTA rode the long road home, he was impressed by the great silence. No dogs barked. People did not eat their dogs. They drowned them. They had to do this, because in their hunger the dogs became vicious, or they started to eat unburied corpses. The two sounds you would always associate with the land, the bark of the dog and the crow of the cock, were no longer to be heard. He would always remember the silence. It was so profound that he could not have heard anyhow the sound of the other horseman who rode ahead of him.

For ten days, Finola had left her chores to go into the yard at the back and look up at the hill. Sometimes she brought knitting with her and faced up the hill while her bone needles clicked. She could not stay too long. Her limbs would become stiff with the cold, even cutting through the blanket she wore around her. No tall figure was seen on the hill. She heard no shrill song.

Una would say, 'Do not worry. He is all right. He is doing things for his father.'

'I suppose so,' said Finola. 'He would not be sick, you think?'

'You would know,' said Una.

They had not much to do. The school was closed. Who could study on an empty stomach? Some of the children were dead. Una didn't want to think about this. So all they had to do was look after the cow and cook their measure of meal, keep a bright fire burning in the hearth, spin a little wool saved from the sheep they once owned, six of them, that had been sold. So they had time on their hands to watch the roads. Una watched one and Finola watched the other while they knitted grey-white woollen garments for the small body of the son of Dualta, ready for him when he came. Una was sure that he would come, that he would be a son, and that he would need the woollen garments.

Finola saw the column of black smoke rising in the frosty air one morning. There was no wind, so it was like a black finger poking into the merciless hazy blue of the cold December sky. Her heart started beating fast for some reason. The smoke was rising from the direction of Colman's house. It needn't be his. There were many poor houses in the folds of the rocky fields up there. It could be from the house of Flan McCarthy, but she thought that would have been a little higher and to the south.

She went into the house. She caught Una's hand. Una came

with her. 'Look!' she said, pointing. 'What is that?'

Una looked at it. Who would be burning in December? What would they be burning? Later on the bog lands were burned so that the green sedge would grow better for the sheep. Or men burned land if they were carving a new potato field from the heather. The hand Una held was trembling. 'I am afraid,' said Finola. By now, Una thought, we should be saturated with fear. There should be no more fear left in us.

'Go and see,' she said. 'You will not be satisfied. Go and see.'

Finola left her. She kept the column of smoke in her eye like a beckoning beacon. She crossed the fields of Dualta's land and got into the wild reaches of rock. She paused often as she climbed. They were nearly always hungry. She realised this. They were living on oatmeal and that alone. Two times a day. One potato would be better. It would put strength in you. There were no potatoes. There was cold sweat on her forehead. She had to pause and lean on a rock, panting. Little by little she made her way to the top of the hill. Then she looked down. She had to hold her arm against her breast to ease the racing of her heart. Because it was Colman's house and it was burning.

She got her strength back and she ran down into the valley. She had to climb another hill then, a shorter one, and go into another valley and climb another hill. Each valley held a mountain stream. They were not spated. They were partly frozen.

She came on the last hill, and the burning house was at her feet. There was a man sitting on a stone looking down at the house. She closed her eyes, and opened them again. A ragged man. Ragged hair, ragged clothes, the breeches torn, the feet bare and cracked with the frost. His head was hanging, and his long thin hands were listless.

She got on her knees beside him.

'Colman,' she said, 'Oh, Colman!' He turned his face to her. Her hand was on his arm. His eyes were red from weeping.

He looked at her as if she were his enemy.

288

'He is there,' he said. 'I piled straw around him and I lighted it from the coals of the fire.'

'It is your father?' she asked. 'Oh, Colman.'

'It is my father,' he said. 'Eight days he took to die. He withered in my eyes. I brought him roots and little birds. I stole two chickens from the big house, and eggs. I milked a cow. It was no good to him. My father died.'

'You should have brought him the priest,' she said.

'Did they care for him?' he asked. 'They did not care for him. They made him live alone. They took from him what they wanted and they did not like him in return. They will not come near him when he is dead. He has a fit grave in the flames. He will belong to the earth.'

'Colman, please, Colman!' she said.

'They do not know,' he said. 'He was a good man. He was abrupt. My mother died on me when I was born. He brought me from that, like a baby rabbit. Sometimes he hit me, like you would for good. He had silent laughter. He knew the sky and the birds. You think he had no love in him. He loved my mother. Life went out of him when she died. He looked a dark man without feeling or wit. He was not. To me he revealed himself. My father is gone and the world is empty for me!'

He buried his head in his arms.

She put her two hands on his arm. Tears were easy in her eyes.

'The world is not empty while somebody loves you,' she said. 'It is when nobody loves you that the world is empty and you are better dead.' It took a little while for this to reach his mind. He turned his head and looked at her, a girl with straight dark hair and a thin face. You would say a face without beauty.

He said: 'You are like a bird. Sometimes you have a face like a hare. You know that, or a little creature, or a likeness made from hazel twigs, or a reflection of a cloud in a bog pool.'

'I am a girl,' she said. 'I have a soul and a heart. I would give all I possess, which is only my life, to save you from suffering. I am sad I did not know your father.'

'I will tell you of him,' he said.

'Come home with me,' she said, rising to her feet.

'You have no home,' he said. 'Now I have no home either.'

'I have a home,' she said. She said it with a little anger.

'Is charity a home?' he asked.

'No,' she said. 'A heart is a home. Has Dualta no heart then or Una? Are they monsters? Do they gain riches by loving me and loving you? But for them would I ever have met you? Would you have sung songs to me?'

He rose to his feet abruptly.

'I will go with you,' he said. He looked down at the house. The flames were coming out of the window and curling up to the burning thatch. She caught his hand. She tugged at him. He gradually came with her. 'I will sing no more,' he said. 'My song is dead.'

She said nothing. She thought: You will sing again, Colman. I will cause you to sing.

'I want to see the priest,' said Dualta to Father Finucane's girl. She was a virgin of about sixty and notoriously cantankerous.

'Then you'll have to go to the graveyard,' she said. She saw the shock in his face. 'No, no,' she said, 'he's not dead, yet, but he will be if ye keep after him, mark me. He's gone to the Carrol O Connor funeral.'

'Carrol O Connor is not dead!' said Dualta.

'His son is,' she said. 'Big funeral. Biggest since the deaths started. Rattle his bones over the stones, he's only a pauper that nobody owns. Not for the O Connors. Everyone else goes down in the famine pit.'

He was not listening to her. He turned away. Which son, he wondered. Carrol O Connor had shut himself and his family away from contagion. As if he was besieged. It had made no difference then. The fever had crept into his fortress. Dualta knew now that there was no keeping it out. He had seen big funerals on his way, of wealthy people. All the trappings had been there, black coaches and widow's weeds, white handkerchiefs. At least they could afford dignified death. It was strange, like an anachronism, to see a real funeral.

He was horseback-sore, so he left the pony and walked to the church.

They were coming out with the coffin when he got there, four men carrying it on two white sheets. There were not many people. The smith was carrying the coffin, sharing a sheet with Cuan and Fiacra and Carrol's son Seán. That meant that Bercan was the dead one. Bercan was Carrol's eldest son. Bercan was the half of a two-life lease, he thought. Now there was only the life of Carrol himself to hold the lease.

He held himself straight, but his face was ravaged, he saw, as he came out of the church putting on his hat. Mrs O Connor and the youngest girl Fiona. Their state was predictable. He couldn't help thinking how well nourished they were in comparison to the thin haggard people who waited outside the walls to pay their respects.

They walked to the graveyard. It was not far. He was surprised at the amount of disturbed earth that was in it now. They were going to bury Bercan at a big stone that marked the resting-place of Carrol's people. He helped them to let down the coffin into the ground. He could see the few rotted remains of the coffins that had gone in there many years ago. Mostly they were dust.

Father Finucane said the prayers. They knelt and said a decade of the Rosary. They covered him in. Nobody was talking. They were all avoiding each other's eyes.

Dualta went to Carrol. He took his hand. Empty eyes that focussed and then settled on him.

'There was no need for him to die,' said Carrol. His voice carried on the quiet air. 'He should have stayed at home. He was going down to the town after a girl. You hear. He should have stayed at home. He was protected. He bought the fever himself then.'

'Father,' said his son Seán, 'come on home.'

'He was my eldest son,' said Carrol. 'He should have protected himself.'

'Come home father,' said Seán. 'He is not himself,' he said to Dualta.

Seán caught his arm, and walked him away. They watched him out of the place and then Father Finucane came and took Dualta's arm.

'You are back, Dualta,' he said. 'Tell us, did you see him?'

'I saw him,' said Dualta.

'Did he send a thousand pounds for relief?' Cuan asked.

'No,' said Dualta. 'But he will talk. He is going over there to talk.'

'One talk from him in the right place will be worth more than a thousand pounds,' said Father Finucane.

'Can you eat talk?' asked Cuan. 'Did you tell him how bad things are with us, Dualta?'

'I told him,' said Dualta. 'But things are bad everywhere. We are even a little better off than most.'

'There are less of us to die,' said Cuan.

'As long as he talks,' said the priest. 'As long as we got to him and he will talk.'

'He will talk,' said Dualta.

'Can the dead hear?' asked Cuan.

'I did what I could,' said Dualta suddenly angry. 'It is a long way. I went that way. It was like a journey into hell. I can absorb no more sights. No more talk. I am sick of it, Cuan. Words.'

'Let us do deeds then,' said Cuan. 'Let us band together and attack the grain carts. Will any of you do that with me?'

'You cannot cure a fever with the prick of a pin,' said Dualta.

'You are tired, Dualta,' said Father Finucane. 'Go on home. It is Christmas Eve. Maybe in the new year they will move.'

'Is it Christmas Eve?' Dualta asked.

'Yes,' said the priest. They walked to the gate. They stood there. 'I must go now and see Mary Greevy,' said the priest. 'She was Bercan's choice. His father did not approve of her. That was why Bercan had to sneak away to see her. Carrol didn't learn the lesson from Sheila after all. I do not know about people. Is Carrol grieved for the loss of his son or the loss of half his lease? I'm sorry. I shouldn't have said that. But the girl's heart is broken. Bercan would have got the fever if he was shut up in a glass cage. Go home, Dualta. You have our gratitude. You have tried. The day he speaks, the whole world will come awake to our plight.'

Oh, no, Dualta thought, it will not, as he walked to the town. They will see this old man speaking in a cracked voice. He will have no command. They will greet him with a great silence. His thoughts will not be incisive. His magic will be gone. His enemies will gloat and the hearts of his friends will quail. But how could he say any of this?

'You have not much hope, Dualta,' said Cuan beside him. Dualta looked at him.

'You look well, Cuan,' he said. 'You are eating well?'

'You reproach me?' asked Cuan angrily.

'You know I do not,' said Dualta. 'All your care is well?'

'They are all well,' said Cuan. 'They will stay well.'

'The sorrow is gone out of death,' said Dualta. 'That is a terrible thing, that even death can become commonplace and you cannot share in the sadness of your friends. I look at Carrol and my heart is cold. I think of Bercan, and I do not cry. Isn't that a terrible thing to happen to us?'

'You were always soft, Dualta,' said Cuan. 'You spent more time thinking of other people than your own plight. Are you hungry? Have you enough food at home?'

'We are not hungry,' said Dualta. 'We have enough food. We can live until the next harvest.'

'If you need,' said Cuan, 'I will give you what we can spare. It is even becoming tight with us and our forty acres. Don't be hungry, Dualta.'

'No,' said Dualta. 'I must go into the shop. I didn't know it was Christmas Eve.' They looked at the deserted street. 'What this would be like on another Christmas Eve!' he said.

'It will be again,' said Cuan.

'Never again,' said Dualta.

'We can make it,' said Cuan. 'If we were on our own we could make it.'

293

'Is Flan well?' Dualta asked.

'We keep him fed,' said Cuan.

'That is good,' said Dualta. 'For he would be a greater loss than any of the rest of us.'

'Sometimes I don't know what to make of you,' said Cuan.

'It is the lightness you get in the head in times of hunger,' said Dualta. 'I wish you a happy Christmas, Cuan, and all belonging to you. Next Christmas we will meet and we will talk over this one. We will rejoice.'

'Let us live until then,' said Cuan.

Dualta went into the shop.

It was changed. He knew that Caffer was dead. People said his funeral was the most notable of the famine. His son put him down well.

Éamon was taking no chances of the fever now. The counters were almost barricaded. Éamon peered at you through slotted timber. There was no contact. It was almost empty. His turn came.

'I want —' he began, but Éamon looked away. He was looking down below where Margaret was, Dualta knew. She must have shaken her head.

'Sorry, Dualta,' he said. 'Things are very bad with us. How can people buy when they have nothing to buy with? I cannot give you more credit. You have three pounds on the books.'

'I wanted to pay,' said Dualta, feeling his slim purse.

'You understand how it is,' said Éamon. 'And if they start giving out free Indian meal, where will we be? Don't we have to live too as well as the poor?'

'You do,' said Dualta. 'I want four ounces of Twankey tea. I want one pound of priest's sugar. I want six salt herrings. That is one shilling and elevenpence. Here is the money.'

He pushed it under the barricade. He took his little parcel through the square hole. He wasn't even angry. He didn't care. He was thinking: Tomorrow, Christmas Day. They said: Two days in the year are good for the belly, Easter Sunday and Christmas Day. Because people eat meat on these days and they had tea and sugar.

'You understand how it is,' Éamon was saying. "We are up

294

to our ears in debt. Everyone wants credit. We have to pay for the things we buy.' He was still looking for sympathy when Dualta left.

He forgot Éamon and Margaret as he started on the road out of the town. He was weary, but his heart lightened a little as he thought of Una and Finola. There would be a bright fire. The kitchen would be clean. He would have a real bed to rest on. His heart was bitter as he weighed the little purchases. But some people couldn't even have a salt herring for Christmas Day, he knew, so really if you thought of tea and sugar and salt herring with an oatmeal cake, in comparison to some they would be eating like kings.

They met him out in the lane. Una's arms were wide. She didn't care if the whole valley was looking at her as she embraced him. Una embracing him in front and Finola with her arms around his waist.

It was a great pleasure. It was nearly worth going away. Her skin was as soft as rose petals. Her face was a little fatter from the baby she was carrying. He could get lost in her eyes and forget all he had seen. He could lose his sense of hopelessness in her courage.

They walked to the house. The pony trailed after them, nuzzling at Una's back, he feeling neglected, so they walked one side of him and he felt better.

'You must know,' said Finola, going ahead of him, turning and walking backwards as she spoke, anxiously looking at his face, 'that Colman's father died and we brought him into the house with us.'

Her head was on one side, like a sparrow, waiting for a crumb.

'I am sorry,' he said. 'Colman must be fierce sad.'

'Oh yes, he is,' said Finola. 'His heart is broken. You do not mind because we took him into the house?'

'I do not mind,' said Dualta. 'I told him when he was a little boy that what we had belonged to him. I do not go back on my words.'

'You are wonderful,' said Finola. 'You are a saint. You are a hero. I am pleased that Una married you. I will run and get him. He was inclined to fear when we saw you on the road.'

She turned and ran away, skipping. Dualta had to laugh. He was amazed at himself. I am laughing.

'She is like a fairy,' he said.

'It is good to hear you laugh,' said Una.

He stopped. 'I laugh because I am home again, and you are here and nothing happened to you,' he said. 'All the things I saw, I feared for what I might find at home. I am sad because I have nothing to give you. And it is Christmas. I did not even know this until I was told.'

'You give me yourself,' she said. 'You are home. Now I am happy.'

They were in the kitchen when Finola came back. Her eyes were bright.

'Here he is,' she said.

Colman came in. He looked at Dualta. Dualta thought, Why, this boy has become a man. Seemingly in the same ragged clothes in which he had first seen him. He was looking at Dualta as if he expected to see unwelcome in his face.

'I am sad about your father, Colman, I truly am,' said Dualta. 'I would be pleased if you would spend some time with us, until things are right again.'

'Look what he has! Show them what you have, Colman,' said Finola.

She held up his hands. There was a dead rabbit in each one of them.

'See,' said Finola. 'Now we have Christmas. Who will be eating rabbits for Christmas except us? Isn't Colman clever?'

Dualta laughed.

'Man, you are rich, Colman,' he said. 'We will eat like princes. You could get six months in jail for the two rabbits. You are a criminal. We will eat your sins.'

Colman looked down at the rabbits.

'It was sad to kill them,' he said. 'I didn't really like to kill them. But it is Christmas.'

'That's right,' said Dualta. 'It is Christmas, so we will boil the kettle and we will make tea.'

'You have tea!' exclaimed Una.

'Yes,' said Dualta.

'This will be a wonderful Christmas,' she said. 'I will boil the kettle.'

They laughed. Why, they didn't know. But they laughed. There is great hope in laughter. Even Colman's sad face broke into a smile.

30

DUALTA LEANED against the lintel of the doorway and looked down the valley. Sometimes he moved his eyes from the valley to the figure of Una, sitting on the seat under the tree, knitting the grey wool. She was heavy with the child now. There was a shine from her hair. The March sun was unusually warm. He thought: Love is not what you imagine. It is like a seed planted in good soil, cared for and attended to. It will grow slowly like a hardwood tree. Each day that passes I love her more. Without her there would be no point in my life. He sighed. His breeches nearly fell down his hips. He laughed, thinking, I will have to put another notch in my belt or I will lose my breeches. He had given up thinking of the succulent things you could eat. That only occurred in the early hunger stages. Finola was standing out from him looking down into the valley. She was standing on one leg like a crane, the free foot wound around the standing one. She was chewing a blade of grass.

'You think Colman will find the Pedlar?' he called.

She looked over at him. She nodded her head.

Dualta laughed. 'You are so sure,' he said.

'Colman will bring him,' she said.

'Come here to me,' said Dualta. She walked towards him, her arms behind her back. She was thin. The bones on her face were too defined. She came close to him.

'You think Colman is wonderful?' he asked.

Her face flamed but she did not drop her eyes. She nodded her head.

Dualta laughed. 'You must be married,' he said. 'One evening I saw you walking the hill. You walked close together. You know what people say: They walked so close together that if the priest was at hand, all was lost.'

She laughed then, her thin hands up to her mouth.

'Does Colman wish to wed you?' he asked.

'Colman says: If I had a blanket to cover her I would marry the girl I love.' She said this, looking at him from the corner of her eyes. She made him laugh. Then she went on. 'It is a dream. We have nothing.'

'When the new harvest comes, things will be different,' said Dualta. 'You'll see. There are many holdings vacant now. We will get you one. I will loan Colman a blanket.' They laughed again. Then he sobered. He put his hands on her shoulders. 'You will be married. I tell you this. You will be like a little candle of hope lighted in the valley.'

'I think I hear wheels,' she said. She walked away from him out to the rough road. She stood there.

Dualta thought of seed. What it would be like to see real potato seed. If he had enough to bargain for them, he saw the four of them carefully cutting them, putting the verdant eyes on one side and the unrewarding remains another. What was left could be eaten. Put in a pot and boiled, and drained and mashed with a little of the precious butter from the cow.

You could buy Indian meal. It was three shillings a stone. The Poor Relief Act was in force, but not for people like Dualta. Owing to a fellow called Gregory, may his name be blessed, there was what men called an exterminating clause in the Act by which if you held a quarter-acre of land you were not eligible for relief. Men wanted their little plot of land. It would grow enough potatoes to feed them in the future when the famine was over. But Gregory and his kind thought there were too many smallholdings and they wanted them eradicated. So if you wanted relief you had to forfeit your holdings. Relief was 2 lbs of mixed meal, $\frac{1}{4}$ lb oatmeal and $\frac{3}{4}$ lb Indian meal per person, per week. It was little but it would sustain life if you were not fever-ridden. If you wanted this you had to abandon your little holding. It was hard for men seeing their family starving to death. If you could hold out with remittances from America, you would leave them their poor relief. If you had nothing else, you had to abandon, so many thousands dragged themselves to the meal depots or to the poorhouses, where if they were healthy they were liable to get the fever. But their homes were lost.

First the Indian meal came raw. There were no mills to grind it in penny packets, so people who knew nothing about this strange corn didn't know how to cook it, and ate it half raw, and many of them died from gripe, wondering how it was that food could kill you. This strange stuff spat as it was boiled so men called it Peel's brimstone. Men like Dualta with their few acres were supposed to be able to look after themselves. He could manage, half-starved, until the harvest. Everyone had his hopes pinned on the harvest. Early seed potatoes planted in April should come in six weeks later if the weather was suitable. So by July they should be eating well again, God grant.

He moved out to the road as the heavy four-wheeled cart came towards the yard. It was pulled by two jennets. Colman was sitting in front with the Pedlar. 'I got him! I got him!' he called as the heavy cart turned into the yard. Colman jumped down.

'Whoa! Whoa!' said the Pedlar. 'He got me all right. Do you think it pays me to climb the mountains?'

He was a tall thin man. He wore a three-cornered hat from a past age, and a sort of military coat with a few pieces of blackened braid still sticking to it. 'Oh, the things that Jack does for the people,' he said as he let himself down to the ground. He always called himself Jack. Who knew his real name? Did he know it himself? He was an alternative to the pawnbroker. If you went to the pawnbroker you generally went surreptitiously. You had to go a long way. To Ennis. The pawnbroker charged you 25 per cent interest on every pound. You paid a penny for every pound ticket. You had twelve months to redeem. But pawnbrokers didn't travel and people were ashamed to be seen dealing with them.

His cart was piled with clothes and blankets and pieces of furniture. It made Dualta's heart sink to see these things. It meant that people were stripping themselves of all their best possessions to get seed. Girls' Sunday dresses and women's cloaks that had been in the family for generations, improving with age, and shoes and boots and men's good Sunday clothes.

'You are welcome, Jack,' he said automatically.

'So well Jack should,' said the Pedlar. 'Amn't I a benefactor? Wouldn't half the people of the land be dead next year if it wasn't for me? I greet you, ma'am,' he said then, taking off his hat with a flourish as Una come over towards them.

'Won't you come into the house?' said Una as if she was welcoming a lord.

'I thank you, ma'am,' said Jack. 'Jack will be pleasured. Ye don't look so bad,' he went on, walking behind her. 'Ye look far from death, God bless ye. Not like others. They have a soldiers' tent below in the town for the fevers, with a real doctor. Times are hard. Time a man would be asked to throw his straw hat in the corner and eat his sup. Now they have you to get rid of you. People are afraid now. What has happened to hospitality then? Isn't it the greatest victim of the famine?' Dualta took the hint. He took the bottle from the cupboard and poured a half mug of it.

'It is Bottle's make,' he said, looking apologetically at Colman who stood inside the door.

'God rest him,' said Jack, 'he had the best right hand of any man in Ireland. I wish ye health.' He drained the mug. 'Good! Now what have ye for Jack that ye try to rob him? What seed do you need, then?'

'We need half a sack for an early crop,' said Dualta, 'and four for the main crop.'

'Oh, you are riding high,' said Jack. 'Have you a notion of the price of seed? It has to be imported, no less. Look what they do with the Indian meal. They buy it at £13 a ton and sell it at £19. Where does the difference go? Aren't there people that'd rob their own mothers! The land is desolate.

300

The seed is three pounds a sack.'

Dualta drew in his breath.

'It is high,' he said.

'Is it Jack that makes it high?' the other asked. He hit his breast. 'I am favouring you. I am giving it to the people at what it cost me. Won't they erect a monument to me in every village in the land when this is over?'

'As well as seed,' said Dualta, 'I have to find the rent for the end of this month.'

'Will you sell the whole house then?' Jack asked. 'I am a poor man. I will help you all I can.'

'Here are two best blankets,' said Dualta. They were made from 16 lbs of clean wool, woven in Ennis, making two blankets five yards long and two yards wide. They cost ten shillings and tenpence. Jack felt them. 'They are worth five shillings,' he said. Dualta's heart sank. How are we going to do business at this rate? he wondered.

'They are worth more,' he said.

'To you they are. Not to me,' said Jack. 'I would not bargain with you. Jack does not bargain. Fair is fair.'

'All right,' said Dualta. He put them aside. 'Here is my great-coat,' he said. 'It is one year old, and my trusty. This is two years old.' New they had both cost together five pounds ten shillings. Jack felt them. 'They are worth half a sack of seed,' he said.

Dualta felt like saying, Get up from there and get out of my house! Of course he didn't say it. Jack knew that he couldn't say it.

Una was looking at Dualta, at the sweat on his face, forcing himself to keep his temper. She went up to the room. She brought down her two best dresses. She had been looking forward to wearing them again when she would be slender.

'No,' said Dualta.

'Yes,' said Una.

'Fifteen shillings,' said Jack.

'Each,' she said.

'For the two,' said Jack.

At this point Colman left. Finola followed him. Colman

was ashamed he had brought Jack.

So they bargained. There was no bargain. Dualta's best shoes, and his Sunday clothes, small-coat and vest and breeches. Two solid stools he had made himself, the table. They were still short. They shouldn't have been. But Jack was doing them a favour. Where would they get a better bargain? He walked out with the clothes.

'I should kill him, you know,' said Dualta. 'I should leave my mark on him.'

Una put her hand on his taut arm.

'Clothes and furniture we can get again, Dualta,' she said. 'We cannot buy a harvest. Let these things go. He is the small man.'

'I have not enough,' he said. 'We cannot pay Clarke yet.'

'Maybe he will let it hang,' she said.

'You do not know him,' said Dualta. 'He will not let it hang.' He went out. They took down the sacks of potatoes from the back of the cart. Dualta let Jack load the stuff himself. He would not put a hand on them.

'Colman,' he said then, 'go and get the pony.'

'No,' said Una.

'It has to be,' said Dualta. Colman looked at him and walked away around the back of the house. It doesn't matter, Dualta told himself. I have worked him. The seaweed and the sea-sand and the lime were drawn to the fields, and the manure. It meant he would have to spread it now with a basket, but that could be done.

'This is a good pony,' Dualta said. 'If you do not give me a fair price for him, I will not let him go. I will sell him in the town, or in Corofin, or I will even go to Ballinasloe. So make your price fair if you want him.'

'My price is fair, always fair,' said Jack. 'You farmers do not understand figures. What it costs to go from place to place. What it costs to sell the things I buy. When will they be sold? Is there a crossed halfpenny in the country to buy these things from Jack? Isn't seed potatoes worth your life?'

They looked at the pony. The pony looked at them. He was in good condition. He was beginning to lose his winter coat. Where he had lost it, he was shining brown. Una went back into the house. Finola followed her. The pony was sold for £6 10s 0d. Dualta knew that feeling about animals was only sentiment. He kept telling himself this. Jack paid out the money over and above the value, his value, of the seed potatoes. Mostly greasy notes and well-worn coins. Dualta didn't put a hand on the pony. Colman tied him with a rope to the back of the cart. Then he stood beside Dualta as the Pedlar got up and turned the heads of the jennets in the yard and out on the road. The pony kept turning his head towards Dualta. He was wondering. Wouldn't any pony? What have I done? Where am I going? Dualta kept his face hard, and kept telling himself that people like themselves had no sentiment for animals. They just did what had to be done. They were only animals. It would be a sin to think of them as having intelligence.

And then they were gone and there was only the sound of the heavy cart-wheels on the rough road. Colman broke away from him and went to the seat under the tree. Colman is a singer, thought Dualta. He has the heart of a singer. He can see this far more clearly than I can. That is why he can cry for a sold pony. But I am not a singer. I am a man who needs seed to feed my people, to pay my rent, to live until the harvest.

So, a strong unfeeling man, he went back into the house, but when he saw Una and Finola he had to defend himself.

'I had to do it!' he said. 'I had to do it! It was us or the pony. You understand that? It was us or the pony!'

Dualta was paying his rent on the twenty-seventh when Colman caught up with him.

Clarke had barricaded himself from contagion. You had to kneel in front of a window and talk to him through a small opening. This meant the end of the compliments, but he was lucky to get anything at all. Dualta was reluctant to hand over the money. It would mean absolute security until the harvest. He thought in terms of the food it would buy and his heart was sore.

'No,' said Clarke. 'I cannot let it hang. Do you know the state we are in? How many have not paid their rents? Where do we find money to keep going ourselves? Free meal! Who pays for it? We do. The Poor Relief is only loans. For us it is poor rates and cess and tax. Where are we to find it? Aren't half the people of Ireland eating off the Poor Rates? Where are they coming from? Who is paying for the poorhouses and the infirmaries and the extra doctors?'

'I do not wish to be lectured on social things,' said Dualta. 'All I want is a little time. Will you take half now and the rest with the September gales?'

'No,' said Clarke. 'No! No! I can find a tenant for your place easy enough.'

Dualta handed over the money. He took his receipt. There was no great rush to kneel in front of Clarke's window. Dualta sat there with his back against the wall. Everywhere there were posted notices. If the rents on the estate were not paid, drastic action would be taken. He hadn't talked to a soul. Undernourished, the passers-by just looked at one another. To talk was too much of an effort. What was there to talk about? Most people, in their old patched clothes, looked like beggars. That's all we are, Dualta thought, a nation of beggars. So low we have come. He thought of the planted seed. They would be sprouting in the ground. Next month the green shoots would be over the soil. That was all you could hope for. That was the vision you longed for.

Then he saw Colman walking towards him. Colman had been running. Now he had stopped running. His face was expressive. Dualta's heart started a slow pound. 'Sit beside me, Colman,' said Dualta. Colman sat beside him on the cold ground. He was panting. It took time for his breathing to become normal. He didn't speak.

'Something is wrong,' said Dualta. 'Something bad.'

Colman didn't speak. Oh God, thought Dualta, so you cannot ward it off just by saying: It won't happen to us! It won't happen to us! Three people, Una, Finola or the baby that was not born, or was it born and was it now dead? 'Tell me, Colman,' he said savagely.

'Una has the fever,' said Colman.

Dualta's head dropped on his arms that were resting on his knees. He didn't want to do anything. He thought it would be nice to go to sleep for two weeks and when you woke up somebody would say: It's all right, Una did not have the fever. He knew it was the hunger that sapped the energy in him. He wanted to weep, helplessly.

'When?' he asked. 'She didn't have it this morning.'

'She didn't say to you,' said Colman. 'She has been having the headache for a few days. She didn't say. She hoped. And the mist.'

'She is clever, clever,' said Dualta. 'I didn't see.' How could he see? Colman and himself in the fields all day, planting. The effort it required to walk up the hill to the fields alone weakening, so that when they came home in the near dark all they wanted to do was sleep.

He rose to his feet, after he thought.

'Come,' he said, 'we will try this doctor.'

He knew there was little chance of him. When they came to the field where the dirty brown bivouac was set up, he made Colman stay outside. 'No,' said Colman. 'Stay,' said Dualta. 'If I was to get it I would have got it from my father,' said Colman. 'Stay here!' Dualta commanded him.

There was a terrible smell in the tent. The people were lying on straw covered by blankets. The brown canvas did not let in much light. Over the other side of the town they were building makeshift places where they put the sick and they gave them their food with long-handled ladles through an opening in the earth walls. Clarke's people were burning many of the cottages down by the shore. Dualta thought he would prefer to die in the open air than in this tent.

'The doctor! The doctor!' he called. He pulled back from the place. He seemed to be enveloped in a tangible mist emanating from it, groans and cries and moaning and the terrible smell of the dysentery and the famine dropsy.

This man came out. His face was sweating. He was a big grey-haired man, like a soldier. He had a grey moustache. His eyes were bloodshot.

'My wife,' said Dualta. 'She is expecting. She has the fever. Will you come?'

'Man, you are mad,' said the doctor. 'I am serving three towns. I sleep in the carriage between the towns. Bring your wife here.'

'No,' said Dualta. 'No! No!'

The doctor shrugged.

'I will pay,' said Dualta, who had no money. He would get it.

'No,' said the doctor. "It's no good. It's time. No time. No time to live. Doctors die too, young man. One in every fourteen is dying.'

'Next month she is expecting the baby.'

'She will not carry it,' said the doctor.

'For God's sake,' said Dualta.

'I can't help you,' the doctor shouted. 'Keep her warm. Give her the cure of the Irish nurses, milk heated and whey and whiskey. I know. I have seen. What you need is a miracle. Seventy out of a hundred the baby is born with the disease if the mother has it. Fifty out of a hundred get it from the milk of the mother. What can I do for you? I am not God. Get your priest, you will need him.'

'Oh, doctor,' said Dualta.

'She is only one in many millions,' said the doctor. 'I cannot help you. You must see. I will send the priest to you.'

He was gone. Dualta stood there. For the first time in his life, he was without an idea, without a plan.

'Dualta,' said Father Finucane. He came from the tent. He looked like an old man. There was sweat on his face.

'She is going to die,' said Dualta. 'She has the fever.'

'She does not have to die, Dualta,' said the priest.

'If she does not die on me the baby will,' said Dualta. 'It is too much. I have lived to here. I have seen many things. I have brought great suffering on her. She would be safe if I had not seen her. This is too much. I cannot abide it.'

'Who says she will die, that the baby will die?' the priest

asked. 'Have you spoken to God about this that you are so sure?'

'I know this is the end of the road,' said Dualta.

'Come on, Dualta,' said the priest. He caught him by the arm. He walked out of the field. 'Is it the slow or the fast fever?' he asked Colman.

'It came slow,' said Colman.

'It could be worse. The yellow fever is worse, I see,' said the priest. He turned into the church.

'Where are you going?' Dualta asked.

'We are going to pray,' said the priest.

Dualta laughed. 'You look around you and you still say this? How many have you dead now? How many people are without graves? They have been eaten by the dogs. How many more are due? They prayed. Who heard them? We were faithful. We didn't turn. We didn't jump. We didn't take soup. And we are stricken. We are being wiped out. Is this our reward? I will not pray.'

'Come with me, Colman,' said the priest. Colman looked at Dualta and he followed the priest. Dualta just stood there, and watched them go into the door of the church. He thought dully: What ráiméis! It was like throwing buttons down a holy well.

Colman felt awkward in the church kneeling down behind the priest. There was only one coloured window. The priest's head was sunk in his hands. He was as thin as the handle of a hayfork. Colman thought: Dualta has been good to us. He has been good to Finola. If it wasn't for him would we be here? He thought: Would I be willing to sacrifice Finola so that Una would live or that Dualta could have his long-awaited baby? This was a very hard thought. Have I enough gratitude to be able to say this? Is this carrying gratitude too far? When my father was dying and I waited on him, I cried and said, 'I would give my life for you, father.' Nobody heard me then. Well, can I do the same now? Who will see Finola through the world if I am gone? Why, Dualta will. That would be sure. So if it will balance the earth that Una stays and I go, then I want to go to repay a great friendship.

307

Amen. I mean that. I hope with all my heart I mean that.

The priest thought: This woman sacrificed many things. She came to the valley at a time when she was needed. She had put into many heads ideas and thoughts that would one day be fruitful. It seems now that this is all gone, wiped out, but it is not so. Some remain. They will be fruit. There are many millions. If it is not necessary, do not let her go. Let there be one gleam of light in the midst of all this death and decay and hunger and pestilence. She sent many children into the world. Let her have one of her own. Life and death must balance. Who knows why?

'I will not die, Dualta,' she said, every time she was aware of him, bending over her, sitting beside her, making her take two-milk whey. This was new milk, with boiled skim milk added to it. He made her drink this and eat the whey with a spoon he held to her mouth. She kept it from him, the frightful sickness of the head that seemed as if your skull was being sawed, the shivering fits, the aching in every joint. Until the day he went to pay the rent and she could hold it no more. She knew she had the typhus mist, seeing all through a dreamy white cloud. She had seen his face when he came back. She had heard him shouting at Finola and Colman. 'You must go and live in the school, the pair of you. You must stay away. You hear? You must stay away. You must not get it too.' She wondered what happened about them. They didn't seem to go. Sometimes Dualta was her father and she would explain to him why she had done all these things, why she had abandoned so much for the seeming sake of so little. Not so. There is the hidden life of the people. A real race. Not made up by words distorted on white pages. You hear new songs and poetry that in a line here and there can be sublime. Sometimes she taught the children. Dirty. Lousy. Only some. You saw the difference. Bright brains. Needle-like intelligence. One or two had written from America. They said: Oh, so much you did for us. What it meant to count and add and write. She was walking in the woods with fair-haired young men who smelled of pomade. All the clean things of life. But they didn't know the other. The secret joy of being handi-capped. The secret pleasure of abandoning. The tinkle of the harpsichord. The smell of wine. Her father's face looming over her. Not understanding. Why? Why? Why? Sometimes she felt as if she was drunk. She was aware of the red rash that broke out all over her. In lucid moments she touched herself to feel the child. She would cry then. Was the child moving? He would wipe off her tears. She could see him do this. I will not die. He bathed her forehead with cold water. She never became lucid and found him absent. Oh, my poor Dualta. So bewildered. So seeing. All the things he saw. She knew she was delirious. She knew she was sinking into stupor. She knew the day that she was like as if her body rested in a river of moisture, floating on a stream of flower-strewn water like a painting of the drowned Ophelia. She knew all this.

And she knew when she awoke, and she could see. There was morning light coming through the window. It was clear morning. She saw Dualta. He was squatting beside her, his legs crossed, his head bowed, asleep like the statue of Buddha. She reached her arm. She saw it was white. It was free of rash. She remembered the cool touch of the bathing that Dualta had used on it. She rested her hand on his hand. My hand is so much thinner, she thought. She thought she said: It is all right, Dualta. It is all right. She didn't. But he awoke.

She saw the intelligence coming into his face. He unwound himself. He caught her hand. He pressed it. 'You see me, Una?' he asked. 'You see me?' 'I see you, my beloved,' she said. He put his hand on her face. She could feel its coarse-ness. He called, 'Colman! Colman! Finola! She sees me! She sees me!' She saw them come in the door. She would greet them but for the pain. This was not the same. It was the other. So she said: 'Dualta, Mrs O Connor! You must get Mrs O Connor.' And he looked at her and he was gone and Finola was beside her holding her hand. 'We prayed and we prayed and we prayed,' said Finola.

'Keep away! Keep away! Keep away!' Carrol O Connor

309

was shouting at him from inside the locked door.

'She wants her! The fever is over! For God's sake, Carrol, let her come. There is no more danger of the fever.'

'No. No!' he shouted. 'I have lost too much. I will not lose any more.'

'For the love of Christ, Carrol, I pray you!'

'No,' said Carrol. 'No! No! Go away, Dualta. I ask you, do not bring us the fever. I have had enough now. I am the last life. I will not be killed. I am the last life!'

Helpless, he stood. How far are we driven from all the good things of our race?

But Finola knew. She had been with her mother at a tender age. She knew. And it was a son. Was it any wonder the sun shone? And they had a cow giving milk, to take the place of the absent milk of the mother. And they could scrape sixpence to buy a pound of sugar to give strength to the milk. They could fight for the life of the child and they could win. Now that they had got this far, they would not be beaten.

This was good. And the green shoots were sprouting in the potato fields.

31

NO PLANT in the world was watched with greater care or got more attention than the potato plant of this year. Each separate plant was moulded and re-moulded with devotion, its colour commented on. They were all of a good colour. The summer came with great heat, hotter than men had remembered for a long time. But the dew was heavy in the night and the plants seemed to thrive. And the sturdier the stalks grew and the greener was their colour, the lighter the hearts of the people became. Soon now, they saw, the plants would be in flower and their troubles would be at an end, for once they could eat with abandon, they could work with ease. When bellies were full the fever would lose its force and die away.

Dualta and Colman were at task-work for a few weeks when the weather broke.

They had to take it up. They were almost at the end of their own resources. It meant going to the town and lining up to get a work ticket. This came from an Inspector of Works and the Engineer in charge. He was expected to ask how much land they owned, what was their rateable valuation; were they in receipt of meal under the Poor Relief Act? Many questions. The Engineer just asked their names and gave them tickets.

So they moved to the mountain behind Tewson's and helped to build a road. They got tenpence a day if they could supply their own implements. They could, a spade and a shovel. People who could not supply an implement got fourpence-halfpenny a day. It wasn't hard work. Climbing the hill on a half-empty stomach was the hardest part of it. The road seemed to be starting nowhere and going nowhere. Its eventual end would be the bog. They dug a ditch on each side and they threw the dirt in the middle. This was covered with broken stones delivered by the horse carts of Fiacra McCleary and Seán O Connor from a roadside quarry where men beat the stones between their legs with hammers and tried to keep the chips from blinding them. A lot of them were successful in this. Over the stones would go a thin layer of clay and over that would go a heavy layer of gravel.

Dualta and Colman were at the gravel pit, digging and chopping, making a cliff that would fall on them if they didn't keep an eye on it. They loaded this gravel into the carts. There were many people working. There were women, whose husbands and sons had been killed off by the fever. They wheeled barrows of earth, with determined faces, their bare feet slipping and sliding. There were young girls. There were young boys. These were the children of people who were not entitled to poorhouse porridge.

There were many men in charge of the work, gaffers and gaugers and clerks. These were ex-policemen or men appointed by the bailiffs or the javelin men who were assistants to the High Sheriff and whom he was rewarding. Dualta thought the staff was top-heavy, but this was to be understood in all Government work. It was patronage. It was all right. It was part of life. They were well paid, these men. They drove pegs and watched. They kept you up to the mark. If a man was too weak to work, they made him rest for an hour and knocked a penny-farthing off his pay. The worst thing Dualta had against them was that they were strong and well fed and looked it. At midday, the dinner time, they took and ate from fat hampers, bread and butter and meat. They were not consciously cruel in this. It is understandable that the satisfied never understand the emaciated. For few people on the work could eat. They ate in the morning before they came and they ate when they got home after the long day. In a week each man could earn the price of a stone of meal. With caution, it would last his family for a week, but it left little over for himself. So no matter how hard he tried, his work was slow, and capable of being reproved.

He hated the pay clerk. He was a small white-faced man with a pinched mouth who came with the money tied on his horse. Sometimes he didn't come with the money. There was a shortage of coins, or the order hadn't come through. This happened two or three times. One time they waited three weeks for their wages. But he was kind, this pay clerk. He loaned people money out of his own pocket and then when the wages came it was understandable that he should charge twenty-five per cent interest. Without his kindness they wouldn't have had any meal at all.

Dualta liked the Engineer. He was interested in his work. He would work himself. He was as kind as he could be. You couldn't be too kind. Dualta would help a woman with a barrow, or he would carry a large stone for a girl, or shovel a hard part in the ditch for a thin panting man. You couldn't keep this up, because each time you did it, the lost time was deducted from your pay. This was understandable. If everybody did somebody else's work, no work would ever be done.

What work?

'You must be proud of your work,' said Dualta to the

Engineer. He was inspecting the gravel pit.

The man looked at him under his eyes.

'Well, you are building a good road,' said Dualta, 'even if it is going nowhere.'

'It is going to a bog,' said the Engineer. 'Some day it can be used to draw turf from the bog.'

'In five years,' said Dualta, 'the soft spots will be buried as deep as hell. There will be no road.'

'Why should you complain?' the Engineer asked. 'You are getting meal for your belly out of it!'

'I was just wondering if you were happy driving roads to nowhere,' said Dualta. It was dinner-time. The Engineer got the saddlebags from his horse. He took out bread and meat wrapped in a linen cloth and a bottle of porter. He sat on a flat stone.

'Would you join me in my meal?' he asked.

Dualta could smell it, even if he was ten feet away.

'Thank you,' he said. 'I am not hungry.'

The Engineer shrugged. He was about thirty years old. He had a thick body and black hair on the backs of his hands. But he had clear eyes. He ate his meal.

'Task work is under the direction of Poor Relief Committees,' he said. 'They pay the piper. They call the tune. We know this. So a landlord wants a road to a bog. He gets it. A man wants a high wall built around his demesne. This is task-work too. He gets it. There are more high walls being built around demesnes at the present day that contain enough stone to build the pyramids of Egypt. But' – he paused to take a drink from the bottle of porter – 'here and there,' he went on as he wiped his mouth, 'there is a harbour wall going up, or there is a useful road going where no road ever went. So you see, by stealth we in the Board of Works are getting some things done that would never have been done.'

'That is true,' said Dualta. 'There are so many beautiful roads being built to carry the bare feet of beggars.'

The Engineer stopped eating to look at him.

'Also for coaches and carts,' he said. 'The price of transport will be cut. Whatever you feel, a road is a good thing. It is there, it must be kept. The quicker a thing is brought from the farm to the port, the cheaper it will be. Everybody will benefit.' Dualta laughed heartily. The Engineer didn't lose his temper.

'You'll see,' he said. He got to his feet. 'Meanwhile it is time to continue this road to nowhere.'

He looked closely at Dualta. Dualta's eyes didn't shift.

'People like you are dangerous,' said the Engineer. 'Don't let others hear your thinking. They might not agree with you like I do.'

Then he mounted his horse and left. Dualta heard Colman sighing.

'You should have taken one lump of bread from him,' he said. 'Even if you are not hungry, I am.'

'There is little left to us except pride,' said Dualta.

'I would exchange that for four ounces of mutton,' said Colman.

They laughed then and spat on their hands and dug gravel.

So in July the hot weather broke. The cloudless misty skies became like cauldrons of black clouds shot through with the red-tinged ones of thunder, and the rain was driven on the land from the southwest, roaring in swathes across the valley, bending the strong shoots of the potatoes, bowing them to the soil. And in a morning when Dualta and Colman came from the house, unprotected from the rain (for who had protection when it was sold long ago for seed?), and set off across the hills to work on the road going to nowhere, even above the whistling of the wind they heard a cry on the side opposite them. They looked, wiping the rain from their faces, and there was a man standing in a field with his arms to the sky looking like a figure dressed to scare the crows. And he was crying, 'They are gone! They are gone!' The replies to him were like an echo in the valley. They saw other men in the fields. It was five o'clock in the morning. It took them time to get to the task work. The sun was somewhere behind the clouds. And they paused and heard and turned away and ran to their own fields behind the house, and could not believe their eyes. For the green fields were blasted to death. The strong stalks and the broad leaves were lying like brown muck on the ground, and the same smell was with them that had been there last year. They were blighted to death. Every single stalk. It was no use going digging with your fingers. You didn't have to look under the stalks to know. You knew what was there. It couldn't be true. Not now! After all the sacrifice! After all the pain! After all the beggary! Not again!

There was a silent wail went up from the valley that would have drowned the highest wind, if men had the strength to shout it. He thought of the baby in the house, the feel of the soles of his fat feet under his finger.

'We will not go back to the house,' he said to Colman. 'It is too painful. We will go to the road.'

They set off. They joined the straggle of tattered thin people who were climbing the hill, looking back, standing, shaking their heads. It cannot be so. Where was God, they asked? What is He doing to us? What have we done to deserve this? Wasn't one year enough? Were there not enough of us eliminated from the face of the earth like muck scraped off with a shovel?

They would not forget this day.

Nor the news at the top of the hill.

The pay clerk was waiting for them. They were to be paid off. The task-work was over. The harvest was in. It was ready to be garnered. That was the law.

They laughed, those of them who had strength. Are they mad? Don't they know? What will we do? Where will we get food? See our fields! Smell them from here!

It is not our fault. That is the law. There was a date set for the end of the task-work. It is here. It is the law.

The Engineer was white-faced.

'I will do my best. I knew it was too early. There was always the chance. Who could predict a second blight? The wheels will move again. But it will take time. I will move heaven and earth. I will do all that I can. In a few weeks. Just a few weeks.' He was genuinely disturbed.

'In a few weeks we will all be dead!'

'No, no, hold on! You'll see. I will ride tonight to the county town. I will explain. They will do something. You'll see. Just hold on. Hold on.'

They walked down from the road. They trailed shovels and spades and wheelbarrows. It was like a silent group of the damned. There were no words from them. Only silence, beyond tears. Beyond hope, it seemed. How could you live until another harvest a year away when you had expended everything you possessed for this one? Dualta thought of the work put into the fields, of what they had paid for the seed.

He stopped at Moran's whisky cabin on the hill outside the town. 'Go home,' he said to Colman, 'I am going in here.'

'It is a foolish solution,' said Colman.

'Go home,' said Dualta.

'Have you lost your wits?' asked Colman.

'Do not advise me,' said Dualta. 'Just go home. Leave me alone! I am on my own. Go away!' He went in. Many of the men were there too. They were counting their coins. Their wet clothes dripped with the rain. They smelled. The atmosphere was foetid. Colman did not go home. He pulled himself under the overshoot of the thatch where the rain would not reach him and he squatted on the ground.

It was nearly dark when he was rewarded. Dualta came out. He was not as bad as Colman expected him to be. Dualta was no man for whisky, he knew. So he let him walk the road. Then he padded after him.

Dualta heard him. He stopped. He turned.

'I told you to go home, Colman,' he said. 'You should have bought meal and gone home. Have you no respect for me?'

'I will go home now with you,' said Colman, 'if you are satisfied.'

'I will not go home,' said Dualta. 'I must wear out my wits. I will not go home.'

'You are like that ship out there,' said Colman. 'Even a big ship has to run for shelter. Where will you get shelter but in your own home?'

Dualta looked at the bay. There was a three-masted ship anchored in the bay below them. It was laden, you could see, riding, and it would have been one that set out from Galway across the way, and, unable to beat out against the south-west wind, turned in here for shelter.

'A ship,' said Dualta. He looked at it. He shook the rain out of his eyes. He shaded them with his hands. 'A ship,' he said. 'God sent it.' He started to run. 'Come on, Colman, we will not starve. We will hold off the day.' He started to run carefully, finding holes under his feet that were not really there.

'Where are you going?' Colman asked. 'What are you going to do?'

'Come with me and find out,' said Dualta. 'You'll see. By God, you'll see.'

Cuan came to them from one of the outhouses which was lighted by a couple of tin lanterns. If Dualta had been normal he might have remarked on this. It was raining very hard. Cuan peered at them from the dim light. Somewhere behind the dark weeping clouds there was a moon.

'Cuan,' said Dualta, 'now is your time. You must come with us.'

'What's up?' Cuan asked. 'Where are you going?' His eyes adjusted to the darkness, he could see Páidi the Smith and McGreavy the Carpenter and even the thin pale face of Slowey the Weaver, and Colman. They were all very wet.

'There is a ship in the bay,' said Dualta. 'We are going to get food from it.'

'You are in drink,' said Cuan. 'A night like this!'

'Do you fear then?' Dualta asked. 'You have always urged us to action. You have sneered at me for timidity.'

'This is not true,' said Cuan. 'How will you take a ship? Are you strong enough? Can you overcome a well-fed crew? Have you given thought to a deed like this? Will you walk into disaster because you do not plan?'

'You will not talk me out of it,' said Dualta. 'We are the men in the middle. Nothing for us, except take what we want.

317

It is under our hands. We will go and take it. We will need your horse and cart and we will need you, if you have the heart to come. If you have not the heart say so and give us the cart.'

'It's not that I am afraid, Dualta. It is something else altogether,' said Cuan.

'What is more important?' Dualta asked. 'Tomorrow the ship will be gone. We cannot wait. You must say. Will you come? Will you not come?'

'Do you know what you are doing?' Cuan asked. He was surprised that Dualta had talked these men into such an adventure.

'What have we to lose?' the smith asked. 'With the second blight we are in poor shape. If we succeed we will have staved off the hunger.'

Cuan thought.

'All right,' he said, 'I will go. The horse is in the stable. Harness him to the cart. I will be with you.'

He turned to go to the lighted shed again.

'Bring a weapon,' said Dualta.

Cuan turned to him. 'You are like a man with the rup-rap, Dualta,' he said. 'All right. I will bring a weapon.' Dualta seemed to be in a fever. He got the horse and they harnessed him to the heavy cart and they waited impatiently for Cuan, who came to them carrying a sickle. Cuan drove the horse. Colman sat in the cart with him and the weaver. The others walked. They were silent, drenched by the rain.

Dualta felt his head as clear as spring water. He knew exactly what he would do.

They left the cart at the shore. The wind outside the harbour was strong. The harbour was free of the wind but there was a back-lash from the stormy sea outside. Moghan and his son were waiting at the shore with the four-oared heavy boat. They had a job launching it into the water. Dualta was the last to haul himself aboard. He had been in the water up to his neck. It was a change to feel the salt on his lips. They kept themselves from the oars. Dualta stood in the bow. Cuan was behind him.

'Will we kill, Dualta?' he asked.

'What are you saying?' said Dualta.

'Have you decided?' Cuan asked. 'If they oppose us, if we can get on board in the first place, will we kill them to get the food?'

'We'll face that when it comes,' said Dualta shouting.

'You better face it now,' said Cuan. 'You have to know. If you will not fight you cannot win.'

'We will fight,' said Dualta. He was clutching a makeshift pike belonging to the smith.

'As long as I know,' said Cuan. 'I will wait for you to strike the first blow.'

'If I have to, I will strike the first blow,' said Dualta. 'You go with Colman and the weaver to the hatch of the seamen. The rest of us will go to the Captain's cabin.'

'All right,' said Cuan.

The ship was anchored quite near the shore, about a quarter of a mile. They could hardly see it until they were almost on top of it. Then they saw it looming, looking much bigger when it was viewed from here. It was a three-masted ship. The sails were tied. The wind was whistling in the riggings. It was creaking and groaning, smelling of fresh tar. The rope-ladder was hanging. Even if it wasn't it was well loaded and low in the water. They would have no trouble getting aboard. Dualta gripped the side and climbed until his head was free of the boat. He looked closely. He could see no figure of a man against the dark sky. He could see a light coming up from the hatch in the centre and near the middle mast there was a light from the superstructure, through round portholes. He climbed over. He whispered to the Moghans, 'You hold the boat. The rest of you come.' Then he sat crouched until they joined him. The big ship was rocking gently, waving away from its anchor. For a moment Dualta wondered: What in the name of God am I doing here? There was no sign of a watchman. They should have had one. Maybe he had gone below for something. He pointed at the hatch leading below, the stairs covered from the weather by a half-circle. 'Go now,' he said to Cuan. He walked himself towards the cabin under the wheelhouse. He paused a moment until he felt the others about him, the smith with an old blunderbuss, the carpenter with a pitchfork. Oh, he thought, oh, and then he opened the door and went in with the pike held in front of him.

There were two men at a bolted-down table. They turned to look. He saw the utter surprise coming into their eyes as they saw three wet scarecrows facing them, dripping water on to the white-scrubbed floor. One was a big man. He wore a beard. The other wore oil clothes that were gleaming in the light of the tin lantern.

The big man coughed.

'Are you the Revenue men?' he asked. They saw his teeth as he smiled.

'No,' said Dualta. 'We want food. We intend to have it. You have plenty of it. There will be enough left over for your destination.'

The Captain considered this. He wondered if he and the mate would be able to overpower them if they rushed at them. It was possible. The three men didn't look well fed. The one who spoke was a small man, with a lithe body. But the Captain didn't like the glitter in his eyes. He didn't like the blunderbuss in the hands of the muscular one with the black-and-grey bristles on his face.

'Is that gun loaded?' he asked the smith.

'There's nails in it,' the smith said.

'You could get seven years' transportation,' said the Captain, 'if you were caught with that.'

'You could get death,' the smith said, 'if you try to take it from me.'

The Captain looked at the mate. The mate was tensed. The Captain shook his head. He thought. If this had happened in a port he would not have been surprised. He often wondered why the starving men who loaded his cargo didn't do something like this. Of course they filched from the cargo. That was understood.

'This is a sort of piracy,' he said then. 'If you are caught you could be hanged.'

'First we will eat,' said Dualta. 'And then we will hang.

At least we will hang on full bellies.'

'It's better that way,' said the Captain. 'The blight is with you too then?'

'It is,' said Dualta.

The Captain didn't think deeply about economics. He was a simple man with a hard fist who brought manufactured goods to an Irish port and brought back food. A simple exchange. He thought it odd that he should be going out with Irish grain and meet American ships coming in with grain and holds filled with clothes gathered by famine committees. But then, if grain did not go to England the poor people who made the goods in the factories would starve, and you would have two famines instead of one. The men who sold the grain for transportation said that if they did not sell their produce, where would they get the money to pay the taxes and rates for the Poor Laws? It was all very complicated. But he wasn't a hard man. He had seen terrible destitution and death. He wondered for a moment: If I was starving and had a family, would I risk an adventure like this for food? He thought he would.

'I'll tell you,' he said. 'You can take as much as you can carry. Each man.'

Dualta looked closely at him.

'You are trying to trick us,' he said.

'No,' said the Captain. 'I am not. We could fight you. We might defeat you, even with our bare hands, but then we might have to spill our blood trying. So it is easier to let each man carry what he can, and let the police recover it afterwards, if they can. Is this a fair bargain?'

'We do not want pity,' said Dualta, feeling deflated.

'Who pities you?' the Captain asked. 'We are giving in to force. Would you use that weapon in your hand?'

Dualta tried to look fierce.

'I think I would,' he said then, beginning to feel desolate, thinking that the effects of the whisky were wearing away from him, wondering what Una would say if she could see him now, what Father Finucane would say if he was standing at his shoulder.

'We won't test you,' said the Captain. 'This is what we will do. Mister Pendrive, my mate, will go down in the hold and tie a rope around as many bags of grain as you can carry. Is this fair? How many of you are there?'

Dualta felt everything was being taken out of his hands. He counted, 'Three and two five, and two seven,' he said. 'Seven.'

'You can have seven sacks of grain,' said the Captain. 'Let us set about it.' He walked towards the door. Dualta barred his way and then stepped aside. 'You are not trying to trick us?' he asked again.

'No,' said the Captain. Dualta let him by. Pendrive came after him. Pendrive looked scornfully at them as he passed. They followed him. The Captain stopped at the steps leading to the crew's quarters. He saw the three men standing there.

'You better stay there,' he said to them. 'Don't let them up. They might get wet. They should have been standing watch.' He walked on.

'What is it?' asked Cuan surprised.

'I don't know,' said Dualta. 'He is either a Christian or a deceiver. Stay there.'

The Captain and Pendrive unlashed the tarpaulin covering the hatch. They loosened some of the heavy timber. Pendrive got a coiled rope, threw it over his shoulder and prepared to go down. Dualta stopped him.

'Are you deceiving us?' he asked. 'Can he get to the men's quarters from below?'

The Captain sighed.

'You are like all pirates,' he said. 'You wouldn't trust your own mother. There is no way out of that hold. Down you go, Mister.'

He took an end of the rope. 'Now,' he said, as he took the weight of it. Dualta used one hand to help him and the smith, bewildered, did the same and they hauled up a sack. They did this seven times. Then they moved the sacks over to the side and they lowered them to the Moghans waiting below. The Captain took charge of the whole operation. He advised the

Moghans where to stow, the sacks in the tossing boat below. Then one by one the others went down into the boat while the Captain watched them. He was smiling broadly. Dualta could see his face in the rain and the clouded moonlight, his teeth gleaming.

Before he went over, he said, 'Why?'

'I told you,' said the Captain. 'You forced me. Go away. I will send a boat after you to report to the police. I must do this. I hope you eat well.'

'Have you a name?' Dualta asked.

'Have you?' the Captain asked. When Dualta was silent, he went on, 'Ships pass in the night. You look decent men. I think you must be badly off to do a thing like this.'

'You will go to heaven,' said Dualta.

The Captain jeered. 'Won't the Devil be disappointed!' he shouted.

They pushed off. The Moghans rowed away. Dualta kept looking back at the ship. It was an adventure, he thought. What happened to it?

'We could get the dory out,' said Pendrive, 'and be there before them.'

'We could,' said the Captain, 'but we won't.'

'Are you going soft in the head?' asked Pendrive. 'Will you let them get away with this?'

'Our people are not going to miss the grain,' said the Captain. 'The rats eat more than that on a voyage. Leave them be. The wind is dying outside. Get those lazy bastards up from below. They could have stolen the sails and they wouldn't notice. We will get under way.'

'I do not understand you, man,' Pendrive shouted.

'My wife always says that too,' said the Captain. 'She is Irish. She came from around those parts somewhere. I met her in Bristol.'

'Oh,' said Pendrive.

'Rouse out, ye lazy devils,' the Captain was shouting down the hatch. 'Rouse out! Hoist sail! We are on our way.'

Dualta and the others heard his voice over the waters. The Moghans bent to the oars. They listened for sounds of pursuit. When the boat grounded they very quickly unloaded it, and piled the sacks on the cart.

'Put the boat away,' said Dualta to the Moghans. 'Deny you were ever out. We will drop your share at the house. Your family can hide it.'

They nodded. They were quiet men.

They separated as they went, dropping off the grain at the houses on the way. They left Cuan's sack at his house.

'Take the cart,' he said to Dualta.

'You did not tell me I was a fool,' said Dualta. He had been waiting all the time, his stomach tight, for Cuan's sneers. I am not a leader, he had thought, I am not even a man to do things out of the common mould. What madness brought me to this? He knew it was the whisky.

'Why would I say you were a fool?' Cuan asked. 'By their fruits you shall know them. You were successful.'

'But not for the right reasons,' said Dualta. 'You heard that man out there. He made me feel like a child. I am a mature man.'

'Do not worry, Dualta,' said Cuan. 'I did not want to go with you, because Fiacra has the fever. He is in the shed. He is not good. I am afraid he will not live. He has the yellow fever.'

'Oh, Cuan!' said Dualta.

'You must not be sad,' said Cuan. 'That is the way things happen. I am beginning to think we cannot help our fate. We are moved around like twigs in a rushing river. God speed you. You can bring back the cart.' He left them.

Colman had to drive the horse.

'Do not grieve,' he said, 'you did not know, Dualta.'

'I should not have been a fool,' said Dualta.

'A man is entitled to be a fool sometimes in his life,' said Colman. 'They will be pleased with the grain, you'll see.'

'I wish it was at the bottom of that ship,' said Dualta. 'I am a mature man with the heart of a boy. I wish with all my heart that Fiacra doesn't die. If Fiacra dies I will never feel the same.'

'God is good,' said Colman. He clicked at the horse with

his tongue and slapped her on the flanks with the reins. The rain was ended. There were clouds rushing across the face of the moon, and Dualta felt sad.

32

IT WAS different this time. Last time there had been clods and stones flying. The policemen were cowering. Lines of people were running from the far fields.

Now there was just Clarke, sitting on his horse, ordering from the saddle, terrified of infection. He kept putting a handkerchief soaked in mint juice to his face. The only force was the constable and the new sub-constable. Even those weren't needed. They were just used as a gesture to show that the McClearys were leaving by law.

Father Finucane helped Dualta to carry Cuan to the cart. It was Cuan himself, fighting the typhus mist, who had ordered this. They carried him from the shed where Fiacra had died, with his life terminating a lease which Clarke would not renew. The two blond McCleary boys were herding the cattle and the sheep, and had driven them ahead. They had spent two days emptying the house of its effects, and the out-offices of the implements.

They placed Cuan on the straw-strewn bottom of the cart and put two blankets over him.

Then Father Finucane got on his horse and led the way. Dualta sat on the seat and started the horse. The cart rumbled out of the yard. Father Finucane paused as he passed Clarke. Their eyes met. Then the priest went past him. He knew it was no use. The only concession he would make was that when the fields of oats and rye were ripe the McClearys could come back and harvest them. They could also take the saved hay. He pointed out what a concession this was. Most landlords would have claimed the growing crops on the expiration of a lease.

It would have been different, Dualta thought, if Cuan had

been well. Or would it? They all remembered too clearly how Moran had died. Would they have been able to resist this?

He pulled up the cart while Sabina came out of the door. She stood and looked at the house. It had been a great credit to her. It was always cleanly thatched and whitewashed. She had been proud of it, the small kitchen garden, and the little orchard. She remembered the time she had come to wed into it. She remembered Moran. She remembered the children coming and growing. She remembered great evenings of songs and house dances and merriment. But all that went with Moran. She thought that that had really, for her, been the end of the place. She wasn't sorry to leave it now. She was broken-hearted for her sons who were being deprived of it, but when Fiacra died the last of her attachment went with it.

She went to mount the cart. She threw the last of the things she carried in a blanket in beside Cuan. She met his gaze.

'You are comfortable now, McCarthy?' she asked. He nodded. He wetted his yellow lips with a white tongue. 'Drive on, Dualta,' she said. 'Stop now for a minute,' she said as they came close to Clarke.

'You will have no luck with it, Clarke,' she said. 'I don't know who you want it for, probably one of your own, but you will have no luck with it.'

'That's no way for a Christian woman to talk,' said Clarke.

Cuan thought: Oh, if only I were well. He had imagined this day coming, as we all anticipate disaster. It would have been different. He would have killed Clarke. He knew this. He would have spitted him on a hayfork, before he himself was killed. It was the last debt he owed the McClearys and he would have paid it. He groaned. Now he could not even lift his head to blaze hatred from his eyes.

'Are you all right, Cuan?' Dualta asked.

'There was blood spilled in the yard,' Sabina said to Clarke. 'Your horse is standing on the spot. From now you will not pass it without a shake in your soul. You will get no benefit from the place. It will wither, Clarke, like potato stalks under the blight.'

He moved his horse from the spot. He couldn't help his eyes flicking down to the ground.

'Be on your way, now,' he said.

'Go now, Dualta,' said Sabina.

When they were gone, Clarke got down from the horse. He walked to the house. He looked in the windows. Like all empty houses it looked bleak, but it was clean and spacious. He was pleased with its condition. He walked around the back. He looked into the stables. He lifted the latch on the door of the small cool dairy under the sycamore tree. He admired it. It was a good sound place. It was worth four times what the McClearys had been paying for it. It was too good for them, he thought. It was above their station. It would be very lucrative. Everything comes to those who are patient, he thought. Normally Moran McCleary and his sons would have lived for a hundred years and more between them. So it is an ill wind that blows nobody good.

He walked around to the front. He saw the cart turning out on to the road. It would be a change for them, he thought, to be trying to live in Flan McCarthy's cabin. Where would they find grazing for the cattle? They would have to ask him for grazing rights on the commonage. The old lady shouldn't have said things like that to him. She would still have to beg for favours.

He looked and saw where he was standing, and he couldn't help himself. The hair rose on the back of his neck and he felt a chill in his spine. The warm July day seemed suddenly cold. It is pishreoges, he said, just pishreoges. I am a good Catholic. I do not believe in superstitions.

'You will have to keep watch for a few days,' he said to the constable. 'You never know. These people might be bad enough to come down and set fire to the place. From meanness. You never can tell with people like those.'

Then he jogged away. He doubted if they would do that. After all he had left them the standing harvest. That had been tactical. It was a clever move. Like buying off destruction.

Well, anyhow, Sir Vincent will be pleased with me, he

thought. Bit by bit I am improving his property, making it successful. He thought of the uneconomic holdings that had been taken over, the filthy cabins destroyed. The famine had been a help. You had to admit that. It was a calamity, but most of them who hadn't died were taking the roads to the ports. It was the best thing that ever happened to the country to get them off the bits and pieces of land, to divide it into economic holdings. Most people admitted this. There was a certain hardship involved admittedly, but it was all for the eventual good, and why would the good God have permitted it all to happen like this, if it wasn't meant to be? You had to be practical. That was good Christianity. You couldn't be sentimental. There was too much sentiment. Not enough commonsense about all this. The fittest would have to survive. When it was all over, it would be a tranquil country. It would have been cleansed of the parasites. Things would be ordered, like a good estate. He was redrawing the holdings in his head, adding here, amalgamating, drawing a blueprint of a smiling healthy valley. This kept him happy. He did not wish anyone bad luck who had interfered with him. Where was O Connell now, the man who had stolen the voters? He was dead, dying in a foreign place called Genoa, saying: I have it here in a box. I have Repeal here in a box. He had it in a box all right, Clarke thought, a wooden one, and there it would be. He knew Cuan McCarthy had turned up the beautiful fields, the green fields. He would never forget the sense of desecration he had felt as he saw those fields, like somebody spitting in the face of Christ. Where was Cuan McCarthy now and the men who went out with their spades? Cuan was in a cart with the yellow fever. So it was that all men who used violence would perish. If only they would see this! If only they would understand this!

He thought of his dinner. He felt hunger. He set the horse galloping.

The McClearys had built a shelter for Cuan away from the house into the steep side of the hill in the rock-strewn valley where Flan lived. They had done this at Cuan's command. He ordered that none of the young people were to come near him.

He ordered Sabina to send in his needs on a long shovel. Nobody knew how you got the fever from another person, just to keep away from them. Sabina paid no attention to this command. It was a good shelter, covered and bound with scraws, and drained around outside. He was lying on thick straw.

Dualta thought that Cuan looked older than his brother Flan. He had always been thin. Now his face was yellow. His eyes were very big and burning with the fever. They were bloodshot. The bristles on his face were almost white. He was sitting beside him. Through the square opening he could see the sun shining, and the well-fed cattle on the hill moving impatiently from place to place searching for sparse grass. Now and again, as the great beads of sweat formed on Cuan's forehead, he would wipe them away with the wet cloth. His white hair was soaked with sweat. He moved restlessly, his tongue trying to dampen his dry lips. Dualta would put another wet cloth to his lips. Cuan would suck at it.

'I have never been sick,' said Cuan. 'People like me are only sick once.'

'It is a chance to make you lie on your back,' said Dualta.

'Too much thought,' said Cuan. 'Time to remember. You were wrong, Dualta.'

'How?' Dualta asked.

'About him, O Connell,' said Cuan. 'Spoke the wrong things. He should have called them out. Clontarf. Before. Millions to fight with bare hands. They would have done so. He held them. He had the power. Now you see. They could not have killed millions. Clean death and victory. Not like this, the way. By the roadside. In the ditches. Smelly stinking death. What came of peace? This. All this came of peace. Turning away wrath.' The opening was darkened. He sensed it even with his eyes closed. 'Who is that?' he asked.

'It is Flan,' said Dualta.

'Go away, Flan,' said Cuan. 'Keep away. You must not catch it.'

'Talk,' said Flan, coming. He sat the other side of Dualta. 'Not far away from it, I am not, already. It doesn't matter.'

'Remember down in Tipperary,' said Cuan. 'Good times, Dualta. Planning. Action. You see. That is the way. Not oratory. One doer better than forty talkers.'

'Too late,' said Flan. 'By long. The pattern was set from long ago. Not now. The longer you wait, the harder it is. The people bring this on their own heads. They betrayed their beginnings.'

'No,' said Cuan. 'They were betrayed. No leaders.'

'They forgot,' said Flan. 'They turned their backs on their precious possessions.'

'I am tired,' said Cuan. 'I will sleep. You will come again, Dualta. You are immune to death.'

'No,' said Dualta, 'I am not. I will come again.'

'What will you do now, Dualta? What will become of you?'

'I don't know,' said Dualta. 'Just that I will survive. Me and my wife and my son, Dominick. We will survive.'

'Not here,' said Cuan. 'It is too late. It will never rise.'

'You are in fever, Cuan,' said Dualta. 'You do not mean this.'

'You have seen,' said Cuan. 'What nation could survive? Who will bring hope? Who cares? You are right. I am in fever. Tell the priest to come to me later. Eh?'

'Yes,' said Dualta.

'I am so tired,' said Cuan. 'I got tired the day they killed Moran. You remember.'

'You have paid well for that,' said Dualta.

'No,' said Cuan. 'Wrong effect. That was wrong. Blundering. Not necessary. Think of me, Dualta. I meant well. First time I saw you in the market-place. Young eyes. So bold. Bring up your son that way. Don't let them tramp on you. Go away. Leave me alone now.'

Dualta wiped the sweat from his forehead again. Then he rose and went out of the shelter. Flan stayed looking closely at the face of his brother. Then he got up and came into the sunshine.

'I didn't know him,' he said. 'I do not know him now. It is like looking at the face of a stranger. He had violence in him.

I, in words. Just words on paper. Visions and dreams, beyond the understanding of men.'

'You must keep them and put them on the paper,' said Dualta. 'Some day they will be understood.'

'No,' said Flan. 'Too late now. I am bewildered. So many people in my house. They make it clean. They make it like a house. I do not know what to do. I am like a dry well.'

'You must give me some of the papers,' said Dualta. 'I will learn them. I will teach them to young ones who will carry them in their heads, and mingle them with their own dreams.'

'You might as well have them as others,' said Flan. 'It will be no good. You too will forget. You will put them in a box, and some day they will be used to light bonfires. Come.'

He went to the house. Dualta followed him. It was a small house. The furniture the McClearys had put into it made it smaller. One of the girls was sweeping vigorously with a heather broom. One was hanging curtains at the window. Another girl was wielding a whitewash brush. They stopped and looked curiously at Flan. He scratched his head. 'My box! My box!' he said, tumbling his thin white hair with his hands.

'Here,' said one of the girls. 'We put it in the loft out of the way.' She stood on a chair. She reached for the box. She brought it down. She put it in his hands. He held it, looking at it. Weak tears came into his eyes. He went out into the air again.

'You see,' he said. 'I am dead.' He sat on the long stone outside, the box on his knees. He jumbled the papers. 'Here and here and here,' he said. He put manuscripts into Dualta's hands. Dualta glanced at the neat script, then put them inside his shirt. Flan himself was reading now, caught up, showing his few teeth in a smile, saying 'Hum', and 'Ah, now'. He became completely absorbed.

Dualta left him and walked towards Sabina who was coming from the river with a bucket of water.

'I am going now,' he said. 'I will come back again.'

'You have been kind to McCarthy,' she said. She looked

at Flan. 'I am sorry for Flan,' she said. 'We have ruined his way of life.'

'What will you do now?' asked Dualta.

'Later we will look for another place to rent, out of this valley,' she said. 'We can live until the harvest. You do not think McCarthy will recover?'

Dualta looked at her. He thought of Cuan. Was there ever anything of tenderness between them? he wondered. Had she just married a need in a time of need? Had she never grown soft towards him?

'I am not a doctor,' he said. 'I do not know.'

'He was a good man,' she said. 'He came in our hour of need. God will reward him.'

Dualta wondered: Why shouldn't people reward him? Was Cuan so constructed that he could not be truly loved by people?

'I hope he does not die,' said Dualta. 'With all my heart I hope he does not die.'

'God's will be done,' she said. He looked at her. A tall woman with big bones and a face that was ageing well. There seemed to be no softness in her. Was it because she couldn't disclose it or because she did not feel it? He did not know. Suddenly he wanted to be at home.

'I will come back,' he said. 'I will send the priest. Cuan is sleeping.'

'Sleep is a good cure,' she said.

He walked away. He stopped at the opening of the shelter. He looked in. Cuan's mouth was open. He was getting his breathing hard.

He walked over the hills, remembering when he and Cuan had come into the valley. That day they had met Colman, a young, bold boy, with a dog. Cuan had been different then. I had been different then. We were younger. Too many things happen. You grow away from people. You grow old. That was it, you grow old.

Una saw him sitting on the seat under the tree. His head was in his hands. She left him for a while, and then she came out to him. She sat down beside him. She knew he was crying. She could understand this. He turned away from her and angrily rubbed his eyes on the sleeve of his shirt.

'It is the hunger that makes you weak,' he said. 'Cuan will die.'

'Here,' she said then, and put the baby into his hands.

He was surprised at the weight of the boy. He was a healthy-looking baby. His eyes were opening. He was looking up at his father. He was dribbling at his small fists with a red-lipped wet mouth. Dualta rubbed a finger on his cheek. It felt like velvet.

'It is he that matters,' said Una.

'That's right,' said Dualta. 'It is he that matters. All like him who are born and survive. It is they that matter. You must get Finola and you must start baking oatcakes. You will bake them three times until they are hard. You must bake enough of them from what meal we have to last for four weeks.'

'We are going away then?' she asked.

'We can do nothing else,' he said. 'We cannot pay the rent next September. We have nothing more to sell for seed. We are at the end of the road. We will walk to Galway. We will sell our books and our last possessions. We will buy passage on a ship to America.'

'This is what you want?' she asked.

'There is no other way,' he said. 'You have read the letters. There is work. There is land that you can own outside the cities. It is good virgin land. Where else will we find freedom? It must be so.'

She did not sigh. She rose. She put her hand on his head. Her son was smiling up at him. People said it was not a smile, but wind in his stomach. Dualta did not believe this. He believed his baby was smiling at him.

'We will bake the oatcakes,' she said. She went towards the house.

Dualta raised the baby, so that he could see the waters of the ocean below.

'Out there,' he said. 'On a ship. It will have tall black sails. It will sail across the world. You will never know the things

333

we knew and you will be the better for not knowing them.'

The baby clapped its small hands, and Dualta put his lips against the silky hair.

33

THEY WERE married by Father Finucane on this August morning. He might have been marrying a prince and his bride. He wore his best vestments. There were bunches of wild flowers decorating the altar. Dualta and Una stood for them, best man, bridesmaid, father and mother. Before the Mass he married them. They knelt at the altar then while he said Mass, a small town-boy serving him.

Behind in a seat Dualta sat beside Una. She was holding the baby. The baby was saying 'Ah-ah-ah' and varying that by making sounds with his small fingers pulling at his mouth. The sounds of the baby's mouth and the intonation of the Latin of Father Finucane did not seem incongruous.

It was not a too tattered wedding. Colman looked almost leanly handsome, with his lank hair cut and tied back. He was shaved. He wore a blue coat that almost fitted him. It was good cloth, breeches of white, stockings and shoes. Finola was wearing a cotton dress with flowers printed on it, blue stockings and shoes and a hat that had once graced Una's head.

They got the second-hand clothes from the Quakers. They were afraid of Dualta, what he would say because they had gone to the Quakers for the clothes. They said, 'Just while we are wed, and then we will give them back.' He had to turn away from their eyes, and then say, 'You must think of me as a beast.' They said, 'No! No! The Quakers are good. They do not want anyone to spit on the Blessed Virgin.' He said, 'Not that! Why wouldn't you go to them for clothes? I am pleased that you went to them for clothes when I have no clothes for you. They are good people to give you the clothes.'

He glanced out of the side of his eyes at Una. She was very intent on the Mass. Her lips were moving. There was a rosary beads in her hands. She looked well. The fever had left its effect only in her hair which was turning. Her clothes were not good, but her dress was neatly patched. She wore a kerchief on her head.

They were alone in the church except for a few old ladies who knelt at the back, and sighed loudly and prayed audibly. Dualta didn't want it to end. It was peaceful here. It was full of comfort. He felt shut in from the outside and what lay ahead of them. He did not want to part from Father Finucane. He felt as if he was abandoning him when he needed him. Not that he could do anything, and Father Finucane could not come with them.

Too fast it ended, and the priest took off his vestments and they went into the tiny sacristy to sign the book. Marriage, Birth, and Death. The Death Register was open. It was the most used book. Dualta looked at it while the others signed the Marriage Register. He could make out the names in Father Finucane's uneasy script. Each name he read was like a kick in the heart. It made the erasing of people so final to see their names recorded in a book. At the end of the year he had written in a line in a despairing hand: One hundred and nineteen people died in this parish last year. What would be put down next year, with the Poor Relief Laws suspended because the harvest would be in and none to come? He shut the book quickly. It was no reading for now.

They were all silent. He could imagine the feelings in the heart of Colman, could envy the light in his eyes, the flush on the thin face of Finola. It made no difference to them that there were no gifts, no wedding spree, with food and drink freely flowing, and dancing, and songs and story-telling, and the fiddler and the piper, and young people courting in the haggard.

Una hadn't the heart to say Goodbye now to the priest. She walked out of the church and stood waiting by the slide-car.

Father Finucane looked after her wistfully. He said to

Colman and Finola: 'You will never forget me, because I was the one who joined you. You are in my keeping. I will not forget you while I live. You must have faith. Everything will go well for you. I look at you and I know this. You are like a shaft of sunlight breaking through dark clouds.' They shook his hand and walked away, past Una on the road out of the town, holding hands.

'If you did nothing else in your life, Dualta,' said the priest, 'these two should be your reward.'

'I gave them little,' said Dualta. 'They even had to get wedding clothes at second hand from the Quakers.'

'They look well in them,' said Father Finucane.

They were silent then.

'You do not approve of me leaving,' said Dualta. 'You know I could not stay. We have nothing left to pay. I have to go.'

'Go where your head leads you,' said the priest.

'Can you tell me why it happened, all this terrible thing?' Dualta asked. 'Why He permitted it all? Can you tell me?'

'No,' said Father Finucane, 'only that it is meant. I do not know. O Connell had raised the expectations of the millions to a great height. There would have been an eruption, I think, a violent one after the dashing of the hopes. I think it was just anticipated by the famine. Was that the purpose? I do not know. Was it to wake people to the contempt in which they are held in the eyes of the wealthy? I do not know. The crowded emigrant ships have a reason. There is purpose, somewhere, there is purpose, but I do not know what it is. Each time I anoint a dying man, I say, Why? Why? Why? Such good people. What have they done? They wanted so little from life. They were content with so little. I do not know.'

'I will write to you,' said Dualta.

'I will watch for your hand,' said the priest.

'You must take care of yourself,' said Dualta.

'One day at the other end of the parish,' said the priest, 'I was very tired. I was in despair. So much death. So much starvation. I stopped the horse near a wood and I went in to pray. I prayed out loud. Why? And spare us! And give me the strength. Give me the means! And it seemed to me that a voice echoed my prayer. I listened. There was a voice. I rose and walked through the woods. There I saw another priest from the next parish. He was kneeling on the pine needles. He saw me. We clasped hands. We sat on a fallen tree trunk and we smoked a pipe. He had the pipe. I had none. And then we parted. We were stronger. I don't know why this is.'

Dualta held out his hand.

'May God be with you,' said the priest. 'I will miss you, that is understood. One day we may meet again, who knows?'

Dualta said nothing. He turned away. He went to the slide-car. It held their remaining possessions, not very much, spade and fork and scythe and implements, what few rags of clothes they had and books and the food for the journey. This slide-car he had used behind the pony to bring turf over the soft bog, or manure or seaweed up to the high hills. It was a wooden sleigh with iron runners. He took the rope and tightened it against his chest.

'We will go,' he said softly to Una, who was facing away from him. The road was soft. There had been much rain. Now the sun was shining. There were many white clouds in the blue sky.

He pulled and the slide-car came with him. It was not a great weight. He was glad of having something to do.

When they were out of the place a bit he said, 'Look back and see if he is still there.'

She looked and turned back quickly.

'He is still there,' she said.

Later he said, 'Look again.' She looked. 'He is gone,' she said. So Dualta stopped to look back at the Valley of the Flowers. He could see the many broken houses of the town with their roofs knocked in, and many houses on the Bradish place and Tewson's place, where no smoke rose from the chimneys. The brown blighted fields, and the green fields of growing oats and barley, soon to ripen. And on the far hill he could see his own fields where he had ploughed the high hills, the ridges

337

distinct. Soon, he thought, the heather will come back and the gorse and the scrub. But the ridges and the shape of them grassed over will remain, so that in a hundred years men will look and wonder why people ploughed so high in such poor land; so much labour for so little gain. He turned and walked on, taking the weight of the car.

Colman and Finola were sitting on the grass by the road. They had taken off their shoes and stockings.

'We must preserve these,' said Colman. 'They are our dowry. They will have to be well walked before they can be replaced.'

'You show great wisdom,' said Dualta.

'Besides,' said Colman, 'the damn things are hurting my feet.'

They laughed as if he had made a witty remark. It was a relief to laugh.

'Have we lost our cow, then?' Dualta asked, suddenly remembering her. 'She is Dominick's dairy.' This made them laugh again. They looked and found the cow. She was ahead of them, cropping the grass.

'She has found food on the long meadow,' said Dualta. 'Let us go.'

They slept one night in a deserted holding, at the gable end of a house. Dualta and Una slept here on heaped hay. They were in sight of the sea at this place. Colman and Finola did not sleep until late. They sat with their backs against a haycock, in this field. They chewed on the hard oatmeal cake, and they drank milk, warm from the cow, and they could look down on the moon-lighted waters of the bay below them. They slept, and the strangest thing of all, they were awakened by the song of a girl.

This is so. She was in a field below them. She was collecting charlock and dandelion and dock leaves and nettles. They saw this and she was singing .It was the song of a Munster poet. He met a maid by the wide flowing river, strange and beautiful was she, her braided hair a river of silver kissing the ground at the feet of him. A golden robe and a belt of diamonds around her waist and her eyes so sad. She looked at him with pity and he called out, lying he was wounded there, the blood from his breast flowing free, and he said, You have the power with your tears so bright to give me back my green fields. My green fields, oh, my green fields.

They stood there holding hands, wondering if they were hearing or imagining her in the early morning mist. She stopped then, and she was only a girl gathering charlock, and they went back to the house. Una and Dualta were standing there too, as if they had been listening.

'Did you hear?' Colman asked. 'We heard a girl singing.'

'We heard that,' said Dualta. 'It was more beautiful than the birds.'

'It is a great thing that somebody can sing,' said Colman.

'Some day we will sing too,' said Finola.

Their elation did not last long. They came on more people as they came to the town. They were all silent people. They carried baskets and babies. They were like the snails carrying their possessions on their backs.

Some of them carried fever-ridden in carts.

They knew the reason for this when they came in the Bohermore and saw the crowds lying on the road, sitting against the walls, crowding around the County Infirmary. It was a big tall bleak building ugly enough to inspire terror in the beholder and the people were packed around it like flies around a wound.

At the Fair Green Dualta left them.

'I will not be long,' he said. 'Do not move away. I will come back for you.'

The town had a smell of sickness, even if they were keeping the famished outside the crumbling walls. The streets were potholed and the potholes filled with water from the recent rains. Dualta was glad he was in his bare feet. He carried on his back a sack with books and some of his implements. He could sell the cow. He wanted this to be the last thing on account of Dominick. He remembered the town the last time he had seen it, with the election and the markets, the fine-fed people and the beasts. This was no more. The principal thing now was rags and dirt, and all-pervading misery. Only when he broke out on the ship quay from the Fish Market and walked the Long Walk through the Spanish Parade, and he smelled the river and the rising tide, could he unclamp his nostrils. The walk was crowded with people making for the dock, carrying baskets and sacks, women and children. They were not people of the Town but country people, most of them with pinched hungry faces. Now he could even pick out the people who had the fever and had recovered.

He had to push his way. He marvelled again at the silence of them. Never before could you have been in an Irish crowd like this and not be greeted and shouted at. There would be jokes and obscenities flying. Calling and shouting.

He stopped a man with a sailor's jersey.

'Can you tell me of a ship to America?' he asked. This was a middle-aged man. He was smoking a clay pipe. His skin was dark from sea exposure. He looked well fed.

'Be careful,' he said. 'Careful, man. If you go, go with Pat Maloney. He runs a good ship. She is a three-masted ship in the Eyre's Dock. Tell him Lynch sent you. He will know.'

Dualta went on. There was a confusion of ships. Across the way on the Rintinane beach he could see many fishing boats and coracles drawn up, and brown nets drying in the sun. On his left at the Dock the ships were bigger.

Here there was a gaunt man, badly dressed, standing on a barrel. He was saying: 'Don't go! Turn back! I have been. You can walk on drowned corpses from the Aran Islands to Grosse Island in Quebec. I left my wife and child dead in the lazaretto in Quebec. You will die, I say. Turn back. Do not go on the coffin ships. There is a road of skeletons, shifting with the tide from here to Ellis Island. Go back! Do not go! You are sailing with death.'

There were many people here sitting and lying. There were many gathered around a tall sailor man who was giving out yellow tickets. He was saying: 'Pat Maloney runs a good ship. You will have sweet water and space. The ship is sound. She will run as sweetly as a bird. In three weeks you will be in the land of freedom.'

'One and a half pounds,' a man was bargaining. 'For me and

my wife and my son. It is all we have for each head. You will take us for that, man.'

'No, I will not,' he said. 'It would not pay for the water. Go to Dublin. Go to Liverpool. Five pounds a skull you will pay, with rancid water and people packed like salt herrings in a barrel. Two pounds ten shillings is the price of freedom and bursting granaries, where you can eat enough to burst for twopence.'

'Do not go! Go back!' said the man on the barrel. 'It is death to go.'

Dualta pushed his way to Maloney. 'Have you room for four, then?' he asked.

'I carry one hundred and fifty,' Maloney said. 'Head to toe, there will be room for all, you'll find. Bring your own food. There will be no food in the locker, just sweet water and a good sailor to bring you safe over the sea.'

'Give me four tickets,' said Dualta. 'I will be back then and pay.'

'High tide in two hours,' said Maloney. 'Money before you board. Here are the tickets. Go and look at the ship. She is well found. She is a better ship than Columbus had when he sailed.'

He laughed at this sally. Then he called out again. 'Sweet water and space and a sound bottom to sail to freedom.'

Dualta looked at the yellow tickets. They were numbered 146, 147, 148, 149. He went to the wall. The ship was almost level with it on the rising tide. He stepped on board of her. The hatches were open. The decks were clean. He went and looked down into the hatches. Already there were people down there, some of them eating oatcake, others of them just lying wearily, their dirty bare feet turned up to the sky. There was a smell rising from the hold already. He could imagine what it would be like after a few weeks.

He went on the quay again.

'Only the sound,' the man was saying. 'Only the sound can sail. If you have the fever go to the Infirmary. Only the sound can sail.'

Dualta went past him, hefting his sack. As he passed, the

man on the barrel jumped down and walked beside him.

'You look a wise man,' he said. 'Don't use the tickets. It's a plot. They want us all to die. I have seen the corpses. No man since the history of the world began has seen so many corpses. It is pure death. The yellow tickets are the tickets to death. Don't use them, friend. Listen to one who knows. Grosse Island, Partridge Island, Ellis Island, they are the Islands of the Damned and the Dead. Listen to me.'

'There is a choice of death here or death abroad,' said Dualta, trying to shake off the grip on his arm. The man's eyes were wild. He was dribbling. He was hoarse. 'It is case equal.'

'Not so,' said the man. 'To die on the green fields with the Irish sky over you, that is bliss. Listen. I know.'

'Leave me be! Leave me be!' said Dualta and shook him off.

'Poor man! Poor man! Poor blind man!' he called after him.

Up from the docks he found a pawnbroker. He was a thin yellow-faced man. He bargained with him. His books and his implements, also the spade and the fork and the slide-car he described, on all these things after hard bargaining he would get five pounds five shillings, when they were all delivered. He gave him a piece of paper making this bargain which would be sealed on the delivery of all the goods.

Then he walked slowly towards the Fair Green. He was thinking. He could appreciate the eagerness of the people to seek the ships. It was as if all of them were in the grip of a frenzy. Once they had said: Let us go. There is no hope here. As if the whole land was imbued with this idea and had to carry it out at any cost. Some landlords were giving five pounds to families to help them towards the ships. It would pay to get rid of them this way since they were now uneconomic. In the papers they were praised for their generosity. What would happen if every single person in the country would seek the ships? How many of them would survive into freedom? He thought of some men in the Valley, holding to their land, like Carrol O Connor, battening down a house besieged, determined to hold on and survive with his own lease-life. Others too. Grim-faced, scouring the blighted fields for the scrapings of the bad potatoes that would keep them alive, even going to the soup-kitchens to take soup and turn their backs on their fathers' faith. To survive, to hold on. Not to be driven.

At the Fair Green there was a black-dressed man talking from a mound. 'Repent! Repent!' he called. 'For now you see. The Famine and the Pestilence are God's vengeance for Catholic Emancipation. Now you must see this. Turn your eyes away from the Roman Whore and fix them on the Bible of Christ. Repent! Repent!' Nobody cursed him.

His family looked at him anxiously.

He sat beside them on the grass.

'I will not go,' he said. He watched their faces. Colman's eyes widening in surprise. Finola not minding. Come or go, she was happy he saw. She was still holding Colman's hand.

And Una. No change in her features. Just smiling at him. Wait for him. You don't know what in the name of God Dualta will do.

'I have four tickets for the ship,' said Dualta. 'I have a ticket from a pawnshop man who will give us five pounds five shillings. This will pay for the fare of two people with a little money over. I tell you this, Colman, because you are now a man. You can go on the ship or you can come with me.'

'Where are you going?' Colman asked.

'I am going back to my own hills,' said Dualta. 'I am going back to seek my Uncle Marcus. We will go there. We will survive there. We will resist death.'

'If your Uncle Marcus is not alive?' Una asked gently.

'I would know if he was dead,' said Dualta. 'Somehow I would know. Even if he was, there are some of us there. We cannot all be gone. So you see, Colman, you are your own man. You have taken a wife. You can make your choice.'

'I will take the ship,' said Colman.

They looked at him in surprise.

'There is nothing here for me,' he said. 'I see stone walls and blighted fields. I want to be where the birds will sing over

343

fat meadows. I want to be free. You have educated me to this. I want to be on my own. My own man. I have leaned on you too long. Not any more. I will be my own man. I was like a hare on the hills. I was happy with this. Now it is not enough for me. I think Finola and I will be well out of this land. I think now that I hate it. It has lost my song. You see? Do you understand?'

'You have about an hour and a half,' said Dualta. 'The ship sails on the tide. It is a clean ship. We will divide the food. You will take the slide-car to this selling man whose name is on the docket. He will give you the money. You will pay for two of the tickets at the dock. You will ask for Pat Maloney. Tell him the other two are not going. You understand this?'

'This is clear,' said Colman, rising from the grass.

From the car Dualta took only a spade and clothes and some of the hard cakes. He put those in a sack for himself. Then he handed the rope of the slide-car to Colman.

'Go now,' he said. 'Let us part at speed. We know what is in our hearts. There have been too many tears. When you are settled you will write to us from wherever you are in care of the Post Office at Clifden. It will reach to us. When your first child is born, you must warn us.'

He caught Finola by the shoulders and pressed her to him. He felt her trembling, so he released her fast. Then he heard her crying with Una and the baby.

He said to Colman, 'Take the car for God's sake and be on your way. We will all be broken if you do not go.'

Colman said, 'Come on, Finola.' He took her arm and started to haul on the rope. She held on to him. Dualta could hear her crying as they went across the Green. He gritted his teeth. He started to stuff things into the sack. Think of something, of the body of O Connell coming home on this day. Muffled drums. Black drapes. He died when too many were dying. But his dying was exceptional. It was the end of hope. The death of an era. Now there would have to be a new one rising from the pus of death and famine and emigrant ships, with enemies and his own too, spitting into his grave, small-minded men making

344

crimes of his failings, mortal sins of his faults, and burying his greatness under a stone monument. Let me cry for that rather than Colman and Finola.

When he looked now, the opening of the street had swallowed them. 'I will take the baby,' he said to Una. 'You drive the cow.' He didn't look at her. He knew what way she would look. So he took the baby in one arm, swung the sack and the spade on his shoulder and set off. He saw the road clearly before him, winding towards the strong mountains. The intense man was still shouting 'Repent! Repent!' to a tired and hopeless and indifferent mass of ragged people, as they moved to walk through the town.

L'Envoi

THEY WERE clear of the town. They were sitting at the side of the road.

They were breasting a current of people who were walking wearily towards where they had come from. They were almost the only people on the road who were going west.

They could see down into the Bay.

They watched the three-masted ship tacking out towards the Aran Islands. They could see white water at the prow.

The passing people looked at them indifferently, a woman and a man and a baby sitting by the side of the road.

A carriage passed them. It was loaded with trunks and cases and it was pulled by four horses. There were two well-dressed ladies in it and a man with a grey beaver hat. Their glances rested on them, then passed on.

'We will go now,' said Dualta.

Una rose. She carried the baby.

'On now,' said Dualta to the cow. The cow stopped grazing the free grass and walked ahead of them, her udder swinging.

'Long ago I came this road,' said Dualta. 'I had a spade and some shillings. Now I am going back this road and, do you

345

know, I am a wealthy man.'

'Is that so?' she asked.

'Yes,' he said. 'I have a wife and a son and a cow and a spade. My people will see us and they will welcome us and they will say: Why, Dualta, you left us a poor man and here you are. coming back with great wealth. You are happy I did not take the ship?'

'Oh yes,' she said. 'I am very happy you did not take the ship.'

'Would you be happy then if I had taken the ship?'

'I would be happy if you had taken the ship.'

'Why is this?' he asked.

'Because where you want to go, I want to go,' she said.

'Then there is no fear of us, or of my son,' said Dualta. 'We will survive.'

Walter Macken
The Scorching Wind £4.50

From 1915 to the end of the Civil War the indomitable Irish fought a
continuing struggle for freedom . . . this was the time of the Sinn Fein, the
dreaded Tans, dark deeds and loyalties strained to the breaking point. This
bitter struggle is seen through the eyes of two young brothers from
Galway, and the lovely Finola Brady who came to know Ireland's agony for
her own . . .

'A really great novel' BOOKS AND BOOKMEN

Seek the Fair Land £3.99

Ireland, 1649 – Cromwell's armies ravage the land in an orgy of death and
destruction. As the English soldiers trample the homesteads, a few brave
men set out to seek a 'fair land' over the brow of the hill. Among them is
Dominick MacMahon, whose wife has been killed in the bloody massacre
of Drogheda. Snatching from the flames his daughter, his boy and a
wounded priest, Sebastian, he journeys in search of peace and freedom.

'Both exciting and moving' THE TIMES

E. V. Thompson
Chase the Wind £4.50

The prizewinning story of love and bitter destiny in Cornwall more than a century ago . . .

For the men who dug the Cornish earth of Bodmin Moor, the flourishing copper trade brought little but poverty and exploitation. Josh Retallick, son of a respected local family, and the wild Miriam, daughter of a drink-sodden miner, explored together the wild moorland until fate swept them apart . . .

'A keen eye for detail . . . astonishing energy' SUNDAY TIMES

The Music Makers £3.99

In the troubled countryside of Ireland, the 1840s were the bad years, when the potato crops failed and the spectre of hunger stalked the landscape. Against this backdrop, prizewinning novelist E. V. Thompson spins the tale of Liam McCabe, one-time fisherman of Kilmar, who turned his hand to politics and offered his hungry fellows a gleam of hope. Never far away, the women in his life, Kathie the winsome fiddler's daughter and Caroline, dazzling lady of the aristocracy, whom he would heed as he faced a host of enemies and a web of corruption – the source of a nation's torment . . .

Harvest of the Sun £4.50

A magnificent saga of passion and conflict in Africa a century ago   The ship was bound for Australia. Aboard Josh Retallick and Miriam Thackeray, prisoners destined for the convict settlements – until their vessel was wrecked on the Skeleton Coast of South West Africa. Far from their Cornwall origins, the two strangers in the hostile land meet Bushmen and Hereros, foraging Boers and greedy traders in an alien world of ivory tusks and smuggled guns.

'A host of characters and adventures' MANCHESTER EVENING NEWS

Daphne du Maurier
My Cousin Rachel £4.99

Ambrose married Rachel, Countess Sangaletti, in Italy and never returned home. His letters to his cousin Philip hinted that he was being poisoned, and when Philip arrived in Italy, Ambrose was dead . . .

Rachel comes to England, and soon Philip too is torn between love and suspicion. Is she the angel she seems? Or is she a scheming murderess?

'The tension is admirably built up and maintained. The ending is dramatic, surprising and masterly' QUEEN

Piers Paul Read
The Free Frenchman £4.50

The Free Frenchman is the story of Bertrand de Roujay – first-born son of a land-owning dynasty – from the years that led up to the war and occupation, through the betrayal of the Vichy, to the Liberation and the long healing that came after.

It is also the story of de Roujay's women – Madeleine, his first wife and final ally; Lucia, the refugee from Franco's Spain who was his passionate mistress; and Jenny, the faithless wife of his second disastrous marriage.

Above all, it is the story of the cause de Roujay made his own – the fierce resistance of freeborn Frenchmen to Nazi oppression as they rallied round the Cross of Lorraine.

Here is an epic canvas of triumphs and disasters, bitter conflict and ultimate reconciliation, through four turbulent decades in the history of the French nation and its people.

'*The Free Frenchman* does for France what *Dr Zhivago* did for the Russian Revolution' COMPANY

'People, ideas and issues jostle the pages as the narrative unfolds at a vigorous, racy pace. Read weaves a tale of moral complexity and richness' SUNDAY TIMES

'A marvellous novel of great scope and understanding' ANITA BROOKNER, SPECTATOR

'Read has produced the intelligent person's blockbuster' TIMES LITERARY SUPPLEMENT

All Pan books are available at your local bookshop or newsagent, or can be ordered direct from the publisher. Indicate the number of copies required and fill in the form below.

Send to: **CS Department, Pan Books Ltd., P.O. Box 40,**
             Basingstoke, Hants. RG21 2YT.

or phone: 0256 469551 (Ansaphone), quoting title, author
             and Credit Card number.

Please enclose a remittance* to the value of the cover price plus: 60p for the first book plus 30p per copy for each additional book ordered to a maximum charge of £2.40 to cover postage and packing.

*Payment may be made in sterling by UK personal cheque, postal order, sterling draft or international money order, made payable to Pan Books Ltd.

Alternatively by Barclaycard/Access:

Card No. | | | | | | | | | | | | | | | | | |

                              Signature:

Applicable only in the UK and Republic of Ireland.

While every effort is made to keep prices low, it is sometimes necessary to increase prices at short notice. Pan Books reserve the right to show on covers and charge new retail prices which may differ from those advertised in the text or elsewhere.

NAME AND ADDRESS IN BLOCK LETTERS PLEASE:

....

Name ——————————————————————————————————

Address ————————————————————————————————

——

——

——

                                                        3/87